HISTORY + FOR EDEXCEL A LEVEL



# COMMUNIST STATES
## in the twentieth century

ROBIN BUNCE
PETER CLEMENTS
ANDREW FLINT

DYNAMIC LEARNING
HODDER EDUCATION
AN HACHETTE UK COMPANY

In order to ensure that this resource offers high-quality support for the associated Pearson qualification, it has been through a review process by the awarding body. This process confirms that this resource fully covers the teaching and learning content of the specification or part of a specification at which it is aimed. It also confirms that it demonstrates an appropriate balance between the development of subject skills, knowledge and understanding, in addition to preparation for assessment. Endorsement does not cover any guidance on assessment activities or processes (e.g. practice questions or advice on how to answer assessment questions), included in the resource nor does it prescribe any particular approach to the teaching or delivery of a related course.

While the publishers have made every attempt to ensure that advice on the qualification and its assessment is accurate, the official specification and associated assessment guidance materials are the only authoritative source of information and should always be referred to for definitive guidance.

Pearson examiners have not contributed to any sections in this resource relevant to examination papers for which they have responsibility. Examiners will not use endorsed resources as a source of material for any assessment set by Pearson.

Endorsement of a resource does not mean that the resource is required to achieve this Pearson qualification, nor does it mean that it is the only suitable material available to support the qualification, and any resource lists produced by the awarding body shall include this and other appropriate resources.

The Publishers would like to thank the following for permission to reproduce copyright material:

Every effort has been made to trace all copyright holders, but if any have been inadvertently overlooked the Publishers will be pleased to make the necessary arrangements at the first opportunity.

Although every effort has been made to ensure that website addresses are correct at time of going to press, Hodder Education cannot be held responsible for the content of any website mentioned in this book. It is sometimes possible to find a relocated web page by typing in the address of the home page for a website in the URL window of your browser.

Hachette UK's policy is to use papers that are natural, renewable and recyclable products and made from wood grown in sustainable forests. The logging and manufacturing processes are expected to conform to the environmental regulations of the country of origin.

Orders: please contact Bookpoint Ltd, 130 Milton Park, Abingdon, Oxon OX14 4SE. Telephone: +44 (0)1235 827720. Fax: +44 (0)1235 400454. Lines are open 9.00a.m.–5.00p.m., Monday to Saturday, with a 24-hour message answering service. Visit our website at www.hoddereducation.co.uk



First published in 2015 by

Hodder Education

An Hachette UK Company

Carmelite House

50 Victoria Embankment

London EC4Y 0DZ

www.hoddereducation.co.uk

Impression number 10 9 8 7 6

Year 2022 2021 2020 2019



Cover photo © Alamy BEDMGJ

Illustrations by Integra Software Services

Typeset in 10/12.5pt Bembo Std Regular by Integra Software Services Pvt. Ltd., Pondicherry, India

Printed in Dubai

A catalogue record for this title is available from the British Library

**ISBN 978 1471837913**

# CONTENTS

# INTRODUCTION

*History+ for Edexcel A Level: Communist states in the twentieth century* supports Edexcel's Route E. Specifically, it supports the following papers:

- Paper 1E: Russia, 1917–91: from Lenin to Yeltsin
- Paper 2E.1: Mao's China, 1949–76
- Paper 2E.2: The German Democratic Republic, 1949–90

## About the course

Your overall A level History course for the Edexcel specification includes three externally examined papers and coursework. If you are studying AS History, there are two externally examined papers. The papers are:

- Paper 1: Breadth study with interpretations (AS and A level)
- Paper 2: Depth study (AS and A level)
- Paper 3: Themes in breadth with aspects in depth (A level only).

This book covers the breadth study with interpretations 'Russia, 1917–91: from Lenin to Yeltsin' and two depth studies of which you must study one: 'Mao's China, 1949–76' or 'The German Democratic Republic, 1949–90'.

## How to use this book

This book had been designed to help you develop the knowledge and skills necessary to succeed in Paper 1 and Paper 2.

The book divides into three main parts, dealing with Paper 1, Paper 2.1 and Paper 2.2 respectively. The structure of each part parallels the structure of the specification. Therefore:

- Paper 1 has four themes, each divided into three chapters, and a final section dealing with the historical interpretation, again divided into four chapters. Each theme and historical interpretation begins with a Big Picture, setting the scene for the material which follows.
- Paper 2 starts with a Big Picture overview of the whole period and then is divided into four chapters dealing with the four key topics of the specification.

Each chapter begins with an overview of the theme, topic or interpretation discussed to set it in context, and ends with a chapter summary to help with revision of the key points included in the chapter. Summary diagrams at the end of chapters should also help with revision.

There are a series of other features throughout the book to aid your understanding of the period and develop your essay writing skills.

## Essay writing skills

There are features throughout the book to help develop your essay writing skills. The skills developed by the book will directly relate to the skills necessary to do well in the AS and A level exams.

Essay technique sections at the end of chapters develop essay skills. These include how to:

- focus on the question
- structure your answer
- deploy detail
- analyse
- create and sustain a balanced argument

and, where necessary, how to approach the sources and extracts that accompany some exam questions.

Practice questions provide exam-style questions so that you can practise answering questions related to the different topics and themes that you study.

## Help with note making

On page ix there is a series of note-making styles, which you can use as you work through the book. These are designed to ensure that your note making is clear, and sets you up to revise for the exam.

Note it down activities appear throughout the book to guide your note taking. They sometimes refer back to the note-making styles outlined at the beginning of the book.

## Work together

The book also contains work together activities. These consist of activities designed to help you work together to check your understanding of the topics as you go along.

## Extended reading

In addition to the traditional textbook narrative, this book contains four specially commissioned essays from practising academic historians. These address the historical interpretation and are designed to introduce you to the historical debate in a way that is directly related to the exam.

## Recommended reading

You can find recommended reading sections throughout the book. These are designed to point you in the direction of both classic works on the subject and examples of more recent historical writing.

# About the exam

## The A level exam

The A level comprises three papers and coursework. Papers 1 and 2 are examined at the same time as part of the same route. Paper 1 is worth 30 per cent of the total A level and Paper 2 is worth 20 per cent. Paper 3 is examined separately and is worth 30 per cent, with the coursework making up the final 20 per cent of marks. This section looks at Paper 1 and Paper 2, as these are the papers this book supports.

### Paper 1

The Paper 1 exam paper is divided into three parts: Section A, Section B and Section C. The different sections will test different skills and aspects of the history you have studied.

Sections A and B test your knowledge of the period 1917–85. The questions test your breadth of knowledge of four key themes:

- Communist government in the USSR, 1917–85
- Industrial and agricultural change, 1917–85
- Control of the people, 1917–85
- Social developments, 1917–85.

Section C tests your depth of knowledge regarding a historical interpretation.

#### Sections A and B

Sections A and B test the breadth of your knowledge, and each section requires you to write an essay. In both Sections A and B you have to answer one question from a choice of two.

Section A of the exam paper contains two questions, of which you are required to complete one. Questions in Section A will test the breadth of your knowledge by focusing on at least ten years.

Section B of the exam paper also contains two questions, of which you are required to complete one. Questions in Section B will test the breadth of your knowledge by focusing on at least one-third of the period you have studied: *c.*23 years.

Neither Section A nor Section B requires you to read or analyse either sources or extracts from the work of historians.

Section A and B questions require you to deploy a variety of skills. The most important are focus on the question, selection and deployment of relevant detail, analysis and, at the highest level, prioritisation.

Questions in Sections A and B will focus on one of the following concepts:

- cause
- consequence
- change/continuity
- similarity/difference
- significance.

Therefore the questions will typically begin with one of the following stems:

- How far …
- How accurate is it to say …
- To what extent …
- How significant …
- How successful …

#### Section C

Section C of the exam paper is different to Sections A and B. While Sections A and B test your own knowledge, Section C tests your own knowledge and your ability to analyse and evaluate interpretations of the past in the work of historians. Therefore Section C contains two extracts from the work of historians. Section C of the exam contains one compulsory question.

Section C focuses on an interpretation related to the following controversy:

What explains the fall of the USSR, c.1985–91?

It looks at the following aspects of the potential crisis:

- The significance of the economic weaknesses of the USSR and the failure of reform
- The effects of Gorbachev's failure to reform the Communist Party and the Soviet Government
- The impact of the national resurgence in the late 1980s in the Soviet republics and in the communist states of Eastern Europe
- How far Gorbachev and Yeltsin can be seen as responsible for the collapse of the USSR in 1991.

Section C tests your ability to analyse and evaluate different historical interpretations in the light of your own knowledge. Therefore it tests a variety of skills including:

- identifying the interpretation
- writing a well-structured essay
- integrating own extracts with own knowledge
- reaching an overall judgement.

## Paper 2

Paper 2 is a depth paper. This means that the questions will test your knowledge of short periods of history.

The key topics of Mao's China, 1949–76 are:

- Establishing communist rule, 1949–57
- Agriculture and industry, 1949–65
- The Cultural Revolution and its aftermath, 1966–76
- Social and cultural changes, 1949–76.

The key topics of The German Democratic Republic, 1949–90 are:

- Establishing and consolidating communist rule in the GDR, 1949–61
- The development of the East German state, 1961–85
- Life in East Germany, 1949–85
- Growing crises and the collapse of communist rule in the GDR, 1985–90.

The Paper 2 exam is divided into two sections. Section A is a source question while Section B requires you to write an essay from your own knowledge.

### Section A

In the A level paper questions in Section A require you to analyse two primary sources. They will typically be phrased in the following way:

How far could the historian make use of Sources 1 and 2 to investigate [x]?

You are required to use the sources, your own knowledge and the information given about the sources. You might consider the following:

- what the sources would tell the historian about the topic
- how nature, origin and purpose of the sources could give the historian more information about the critical stance of the author, as well as some evidence about usefulness
- how you can use your knowledge of the historical context to support or develop inferences made from the sources, and to either confirm the accuracy or limitations of information within them or to note limitations and challenge the accuracy of the source
- what you could say about the two sources in combination.

### Section B

You should answer questions in Section B in the form of an essay. The questions can focus on the following concepts:

- cause
- consequence
- change/continuity
- similarity/difference
- significance.

The questions can begin with the following question stems:

- How far …
- How accurate is it to say …
- To what extent …

# The AS level exam

The AS level exam comprises two papers. Paper 1 is worth 60 per cent of the total A level and Paper 2 is worth 40 per cent.

## Paper 1

The AS level exam tests all of the same content as the A level exam and is structured in exactly the same way. However, there are differences between the two exams:

### Sections A and B

There are three key differences between A level and AS level in Sections A and B:

- **Wording**: The wording of AS level questions will be less complex than the wording of A level questions. Specifically, there are likely to be fewer adjectives or qualifying phrases in the question. For example:

| A level-style question | AS level-style question |
|---|---|
| How accurate is it to say that in the years 1928–1980, the government of the USSR relied wholly on repression? | Was repression the main reason for the survival of the Communist government in the USSR in the years 1928–1980? Explain your answer. |

- **Focus**: Section A questions can focus on a more limited range of concepts at AS than at A level. Specifically, at AS level Section A questions can only focus on cause and consequences (including success and failure), whereas A level questions can focus on a wider variety of concepts.
- **Mark scheme**: The A level mark scheme has five levels, whereas the AS level mark scheme only has four. This means that full marks are available at AS for an analytical essay, whereas sustained analysis is necessary for full marks at A level.

### Section C

Section C of the AS level exam focuses on the same aspects of the same debate:

What explains the fall of the USSR, *c*.1985–91?

As in the A level exam you have to answer one compulsory question based on two extracts. The AS level exam is different from the A level exam in the following ways:

- **The question**: The AS level question is worded in a less complex way than the A level question. For example:

| A level-style question | AS level-style question |
|---|---|
| In the light of differing interpretations, how convincing do you find the view that the USSR collapsed because 'rather than strengthen the Soviet state, glasnost eventually suggested that the Soviet Government was no longer sustainable'. To explain your answer, analyse and evaluate the material in both extracts, using your own knowledge of the issues. | Historians have different views about the reasons for the fall of the Soviet Union. Analyse and evaluate the extracts and use your knowledge of the issues to explain your answer to the following question. How far do you agree with the view that the collapse of the Soviet Union came about because of Gorbachev's political reforms? |

- **The extracts**: At AS level the extracts will be slightly shorter and you may get extracts taken from textbooks as well as the work of historians. In this sense the extracts at AS should be slightly easier to read and understand.
- **The mark scheme**: The A level mark scheme has five levels, whereas the AS level mark scheme only has four. This means that full marks are available at AS for an analytical essay, whereas sustained analysis is necessary for full marks at A level.

## Paper 2

The AS level exam tests all of the same content as the A level exam and is structured in a similar way. However, there are differences between the two exams:

### Section A

Section A of the AS level exam is structured in a different way to the A level exam. In essence, Section A at AS tests the same skills as Section A at A level, but over two questions rather than one.

The AS level Section A is divided into Part (a) and Part (b).

Part (a) contains one compulsory question related to a single source. Part (a) asks you to consider how the source is of value to a historian who is engaged in a specified enquiry.

The question requires you to reach a judgement about the ways in which Source 1 is valuable. In that sense the question is not primarily about looking for the ways in which the source is unreliable. Examiners are looking for the following skills:

- detailed contextual knowledge that explains the meaning of relevant points made by the source
- valid inferences
- an overall judgement about the value of the source related to valid criteria.

Part (b) contains one compulsory question related to a single source. Part (b) asks you to consider how much weight to a source for a specified enquiry. Therefore Part (b) requires you to consider the value and the limits of the source.

Part (b) tests your ability to:

- comprehend and analyse source material
- use historical knowledge to weigh the value of the source
- reach a judgement, based on valid criteria, about the value of the source.

### Section B

Section B of the AS level exam tests the same content knowledge as Section B of the A level exam. Section B comprises three questions, of which you must complete one.

Paper 2 Section B questions are very similar to Paper 1 Section B questions (see page vii). The key difference relates to the period on which the question focuses. Paper 2 examines your knowledge of depth. Therefore Section B questions can focus on a single event or a single year. Alternatively they might focus on the whole chronology of the course.

# Note taking

Good note taking is really important. Your notes are an essential revision resource. What is more, the process of making notes will help you understand and remember what you are reading.

## How books work

Most books are written as clearly as possible. Therefore writers use a variety of techniques to help you learn.

Authors often break up their work into key points (the most important ideas and themes) and supporting evidence (the details that support the key points). Key points are usually general statements. For example, a key point might be 'During the Civil War the government increasingly became a party-state based on the Communist Party.' The supporting evidence might be a list of detailed examples that indicate the key point is correct.

## How to make notes

Most note-making styles reflect the distinction between key points and supporting evidence. Below is advice on a variety of different note-making styles. Throughout each section in the book are note-making activities for you to carry out.

### Hints and tips

The important thing is that you understand your notes. Therefore you don't have to write *everything* down, and you don't have to write in full sentences.

While making notes you can use abbreviations:

| Full text | Abbreviation |
|---|---|
| Communist Party | CP |
| New Economic Policy | NEP |
| Civil War | CW |
| Lenin | L̲ |
| First World War | WW1 |

You can use arrows instead of words:

| Full text | Arrow |
|---|---|
| Increased | ↑ |
| Decreased | ↓ |

You can use mathematical notation:

| Full text | Mathematical notation |
|---|---|
| Equals | = |
| Plus, and | + |
| Because | ∵ |
| Therefore | ∴ |

Here is an example:

| Text | Notes |
|---|---|
| The Crisis of 1921, which included rebellion among the peasants, workers' strikes and military mutiny, showed the extent of opposition to Lenin's government and therefore forced Lenin to reform. | Crisis 1921 = ↑ opposition ∴ L̲ made reforms |

## Note-making styles

There are a large number of note-making styles. You can find examples of four popular styles below. All of them have their strengths. It is a good idea to try them all and work out which style suits you.

The examples below are of notes taken from Chapter 1 on page 4.

### Style 1: Bullet points

Bullet points can be a useful method of making notes because:

- they encourage you to write in note form, rather than in full sentences
- they help you to organise your ideas in a systematic fashion
- they are easy to skim read later
- you can show relative importance visually by indenting less important, or supporting points.

1 Scan the section before you read it in depth. Identify headings (points of explanation). Significantly, you should try looking for the key points in the first sentence of each paragraph. On your page of notes, set the key points out in sections.

2 Now read carefully through the section. Write supporting points or points of evidence under the relevant headings.

The end result should look like this:

Key features of Russia before 1917
- Empire ruled by all-powerful Tsars
- Repression widespread
- Weak rural economy: poverty + little industry
- Underground opposition (RSDLP) (SRs)
- Impact of WW1 – economic chaos =

1 Feb Rev. = Prov. gov
2 Oct. Rev = L + Bolsheviks take power

## Style 2: The 1:2 method

The 1:2 method is a variation on bullet points. The method is based on dividing your page into two columns: the first for the main point, the second for supporting detail. This allows you to see the structure of the information clearly.

1 Divide your page like in the example below:

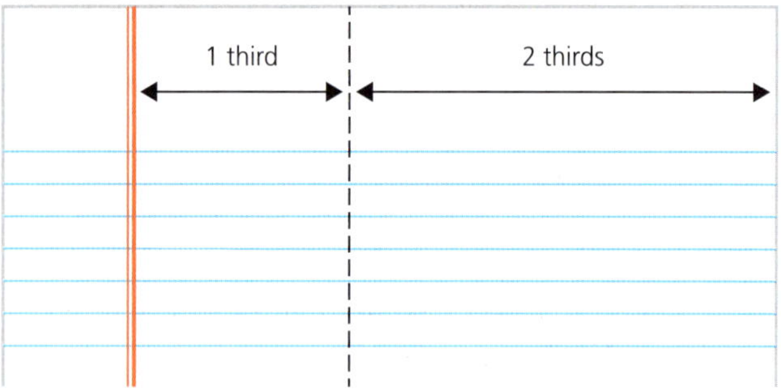


2 Write the key points in the left-hand section.
3 Write the supporting detail in the right-hand section.

The end result should look like this:

| Key points | Supporting detail |
|---|---|
| Russia before 1914 | • Powerful Tsars ruled; 1884–1917 = Nicholas II<br>• Empire – Russia, Ukraine, Georgia, Finland, Estonia<br>• Repression widespread – e.g. Lena Goldmine massacre 1912<br>• Little modern industry: 2.4m/140m industrial workers<br>• Opposition – underground; aim to overthrow Tsar + end poverty, e.g. RSDLP and SRs |

## Style 3: Spider diagrams

Spider diagrams or mind maps can be a useful method of making notes because:

- they will help you to categorise factors; each of the main branches coming from the centre should be a new category
- they can help you see what is most important; often the most important factors will be close to the centre of the diagram
- they can help you see connections between different aspects of what you are studying; it is useful to draw lines between different parts of your diagram to show links
- they can also help you with essay planning; you can use them to quickly get down the main points and develop a clear structure in response to an essay question.

1 Draw a circle in the middle of your piece of paper. It should be large enough to contain the section title.
2 Scan the section and identify headings. Draw lines out from your central circle – remember to leave plenty of room between them so that you can fit in all of your notes.
3 Read through the section carefully. Write supporting points or points of evidence under the relevant headings.

The end result should look like this:

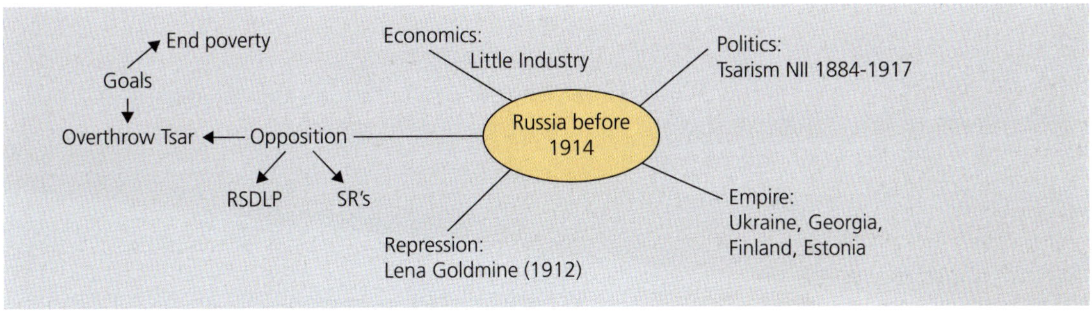


## Style 4: Index cards

Index cards are particularly useful when you are revising for your exam, or when you are planning your essays.

**Revision**

Index cards are small and therefore they encourage you to prioritise by forcing you to note down only the most important information.

**Essay planning**

You can use index cards to help plan essays in the following way. First, select all of the cards that are relevant to your essay. Arrange the cards in order to develop a structure for your essay. Rearranging the cards can also help work out the best structure for your essay.

1 Scan through the section. Identify either themes or important sub-sections. Use a different index card for each sub-section. On one side of each index card write:
   - the title of the main section in the top left corner in one colour
   - the title of the sub-section that you are currently reading about in the middle of the index card in another colour.

2 Now read the section carefully. On the back of each index card bullet point the relevant notes.

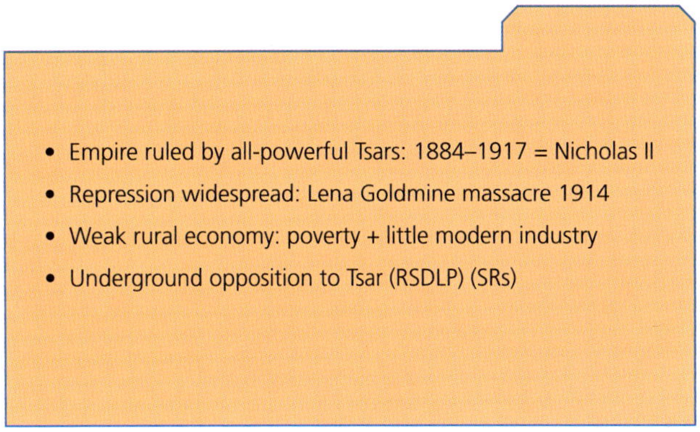


3 You can punch a hole in the corner of the cards and tag-tie the cards for each section together.

## Paper 1 Russia, 1917–91: from Lenin to Yeltsin

# Theme 1 Communist government in the USSR, 1917–85

## The Big Picture

The story of communist government in Russia is one of rise, transformation and decline.

At first, under Lenin, the new government was radical, uncompromising and revolutionary. Lenin overthrew the existing government, fought a bitter civil war, and created a wholly new type of government. Lenin claimed he was establishing a government of the workers. However, Lenin's Russia was a mix of a utopian vision and skilful political compromise. Therefore, in order to ensure the survival of the new government at all costs, Lenin's government was based much more on administrators and bureaucrats than it was on working people. Fundamentally, Lenin's government was based on the Communist Party. In fact Lenin established a one-party state which guaranteed the supremacy of the Communist Party within Russian Government.

Stalin started a revolution of his own. His 'revolution from above' was designed to build on Lenin's achievement. Lenin had ended capitalism, but Stalin would begin the world's first serious attempt to create a socialist society. Stalin's revolution made Russia an economic giant. But it also created a totalitarian state: a government based on terror, propaganda and a cult of personality.

After Stalin's death Khrushchev attempted to reform the Russian Government. Communism in Russia became more humane – people were no longer sent to labour camps or executed in such large numbers. After the horrors of Stalinism, Khrushchev wanted to revive popular faith in Communism. But Khrushchev's reforms had the potential to destabilise communist rule in Russia. Consequently, in order to protect the power of the Party, Khrushchev was replaced by Brezhnev, a leader that the Communist Party could rely on to protect its position. Under Brezhnev, Communism in Russia lost its revolutionary energy and finally completed its journey from revolutionary movement to party of government. Brezhnev's greatest strength was also his greatest weakness: his ability to guarantee stability meant that he was unable to reform. Between 1982 and 1985, Russia's final leaders struggled with the same problems that had faced Khrushchev and Brezhnev: how could the Communist Party reform without abandoning the one-party state created by Lenin?

In this theme you will consider the following.

- ➜ How Lenin and the Communist Party won and consolidated power, 1917–24:
  The changing nature of Lenin's government from the October Revolution, through the Civil War to Lenin's death.
- ➜ Russia under Stalin, 1928–53:
  The elimination of Stalin's opponents, the Great Terror and the creation of a personal dictatorship.
- ➜ Communist government, 1953–85:
  Khrushchev's attempts to reform the Communist Government, Brezhnev's attempts to stabilise communist rule, and the growing political difficulties of the Communist Government under Andropov and Chernenko.

## TIMELINE

| | |
|---|---|
| 1914 | Russia enters the First World War |
| 1917 February | The February Revolution overthrows the Tsar |
| 1917 March | a Provisional Government is established |
| 1917 October | The October Revolution overthrows the Provisional Government. Lenin establishes *Sovnarkom*. |
| 1918–1921 | Increasing political centralisation during the Russian Civil War. Lenin disbands Constituent Assembly |
| 1921 | Opposition political parties banned. The Communists triumph in the Civil War. Russia becomes a one-party state |
| 1921 March | Party Congress bans factions. |
| 1924 January | Lenin dies |
| 1928 | Stalin emerges as leader of Russia |
| 1934 January | Private criticism of Stalin expressed at the Congress of Victors |
| 1934 December | Kirov is murdered in Leningrad |
| 1935 | The Great Terror begins with a purge of the Leningrad Communist Party |
| 1936 August | Stalin removes high profile opponents in the first of Moscow show- trials |
| 1936 September | Yezhov becomes head of the secret police. The Great Terror intensifies |
| 1953 March | Stalin dies |
| 1956 February | Khrushchev's secret speech – beginning of widespread de-Stalinisation |
| 1957 July | Greater freedom of expression is permitted following the World Festival of Youth and Students |
| 1964 October | Khrushchev removed from office. Brezhnev begins to reverse Khrushchev's reforms |
| 1966 December | New criminal code tightens laws on political dissent |
| 1975 | Brezhnev becomes increasingly ill and unable to govern effectively |
| 1976 February | Brezhnev fails to introduce reforms at the Twenty-Fifth Party Congress, in spite of growing economic, social and political problems |
| 1982 November | Andropov initiates reforms to tackle corruption |
| 1984 February | Andropov dies and is replaced by Chernenko before his reforms had taken effect |

# 1a: Establishing Communist Party control, 1917–24

## Overview

Russia experienced two revolutions in 1917. The first led to the downfall of the Tsar – the head of the royal family. The second led to the creation of a radical new form of government which promised freedom and equality for Russia's working people. In order to achieve this, revolutionary leader Lenin constructed a new government. At first, Lenin promised a democratic government, which would be based on the support of all working people. Lenin's first actions were truly popular, reflecting long-standing desires of Russia's workers, peasants and soldiers. However, Lenin's new government was also ruthless, and from the very start it terrorised its opponents. Moreover, for Lenin, democracy was less important than his desire to maintain control. Therefore, when his party lost elections Lenin disregarded the results.

Lenin abandoned democracy altogether during Russia's Civil War, and the new government became increasingly centralised and authoritarian. Lenin's victory in the Civil War did not lead to the restoration of democracy. Rather, Lenin outlawed rival political parties and by 1921 had created a radically new kind of government: a one-party state. However, it was highly centralised and authoritarian, and therefore nothing like the free and democratic society that he had promised in 1917.

This chapter examines the creation of the communist one-party state through the following sections:

1 Background to the Bolshevik Revolution
2 Lenin's state, 1917–18
3 The impact of the Civil War, 1918–21
4 1921: Crisis and reform
5 Conclusion: Lenin's legacy.

## 1 Background to the Bolshevik Revolution

Before the revolutions of 1917 Russia was ruled by a series of all-powerful emperors. **Tsar** Nicholas II, Russian Emperor from 1894 until 1917, was widely regarded as more repressive than other European rulers. Repression was widespread and the vast majority of the Tsar's subjects were impoverished and had no political rights. For example, hundreds of miners who protested for higher wages at the Lena goldmine in 1912 were brutally massacred by the Tsar's troops. The Tsar's empire extended beyond Russia and included the Ukraine, Georgia, Finland and Estonia.

While the government was strong, the economy was weak compared to that of Britain, Germany, the USA and other major powers. Russia had very little modern industry. Indeed, by 1913 only 2.4 million of Russia's 140 million people worked in large factories. Nicholas II's government tried to encourage economic growth, but it was only partly successful. What is more, even in periods of economic growth, the population as a whole remained extremely poor.

Political repression and massive economic inequality led to the growth of underground opposition to the Tsar. Around 1900 the two largest opposition parties were the Russian Social-Democratic Labour Party (**RSDLP**) and the Socialist Revolutionaries (**SRs**), both of which were committed to overthrowing the Tsar, liberating the people of the Russian Empire and ending poverty. However, neither group were able to organise effectively due to the Tsar's political police, who routinely spied on these groups and arrested and exiled their leaders. Inspite of repression, Tsarism was rocked by the **1905 Revolution**, a series of revolts that almost led to the overthrow of the Tsar. Political compromise and renewed repression ensured the survival of the regime until the **First World War**.

### The First World War

Russia entered the First World War in 1914. Russia's economy was incapable of providing the food and equipment necessary to fight the war. Additionally, the Tsar was an incompetent wartime leader. By early 1917 economic chaos, military defeat and political mismanagement led to the February Revolution: a popular uprising in Petrograd, Russia's capital city that overthrew the Tsar and set up a **Provisional Government**.

### The Provisional Government

Following the February Revolution, the Provisional Government introduced a series of reforms. The Tsar's **despotism** was replaced by a liberal system, which included **freedom of expression**, **freedom of assembly** and **freedom of religion**. Additionally, the Provisional Government promised democratic elections to form a new government. However, the Provisional Government continued to fight the First World War.

Lenin, a radical member of the RSDLP, argued for a second revolution. Following his return from exile in April 1917, he demanded an immediate end to the First World War and the **redistribution** of land to the peasants. These demands were summarised in the slogan 'Peace, Land and Bread'. As the Provisional Government continued to fight in the war and Russia's economic problems grew worse, Lenin's message became increasingly popular.

By October 1917 Lenin and his followers the **Bolsheviks** had enough support to overthrow the Provisional Government. Lenin and Trotsky (see page 7) seized the moment and organised a ***coup d'état***, which allowed the Bolsheviks to take power.

### Note it down

Using bullet points (see page ix), make notes on the key features of Russia prior to 1917. As this is background you do not need a great deal of detail. Rather write a single bullet point on the key political, economic and social features of the period. Additionally, summarise the impact of the First World War on the Russian Government in a single bullet point.

## Lenin's ideology

Lenin seized power because he believed that a global revolution was necessary to replace **capitalism** and **imperialism** with **socialism**: a new social system that would allow all people to be genuinely free and equal. This view was based on a Marxist view of history.

### The Marxist view of history

Karl Marx was a German philosopher and revolutionary, who lived in the nineteenth century. He became famous

### Vladimir Ilyich Lenin, 1870–1924

Vladimir Ilyich Lenin is one of the most famous revolutionaries of all time. Born in the late nineteenth century, he is remembered as the man who led the first successful communist revolution. Lenin's early life was troubled by radical politics. Aleksandr, his older brother, was executed in 1887 for the attempted assassination of Tsar **Alexander III**. Following this, Lenin's family were shunned by their community. As a student Lenin joined a radical socialist movement; this led to his expulsion from university for protesting in favour of student rights. In spite of this he continued to be involved in revolutionary politics. Even as a young man, Lenin was a natural leader and therefore tended to play a leading role in the underground radical groups he joined. As a result he was targeted by the police and in 1897, like many Russian revolutionaries, he was arrested and exiled.

Between 1899 and 1903, Lenin played a leading role in the foundation of the RSDLP - which became Russia's most influential Marxist party. Lenin became leader of the Bolshevik **faction** of the RSDLP. Lenin, like many Russian radicals, wanted to transform Russia. He wanted to destroy the royal family, end the power of the Russian Church and create a modern nation, which embraced cutting-edge science and industry. In so doing, Lenin hoped to improve the lives of millions of working Russians who lived in poverty. Between 1903 and 1917 Lenin spent a great deal of time in exile. He was a brilliant writer and organiser, but he also had a reputation for being manipulative and for getting his way by scheming within the RSDLP.

Lenin's personality affected his approach to politics. He could be extremely **pragmatic** and therefore willing to sacrifice important principles in order to safeguard his power. He enjoyed arguing with his colleagues and getting his own way. He also had a reputation for experiencing fits of rage - in fact his outbursts were so frequent towards the end of his life that his colleagues suspected he was mentally unstable. Finally, Lenin despised 'sentimentality'; therefore he felt little sympathy for the suffering of others and was prepared to use violence and terror to achieve his goals.

for arguing that the workers should rise up and destroy capitalism in a revolution. Marx's view of revolution was based on his theory of history. Marx argued that history had progressed through a series of stages, as Table 1 shows.

**Table 1: Marx's four stages of history.**

| | |
|---|---|
| **Primitive Communism** | Humans lived in a simple society where they hunted and gathered. There was no government and all people were essentially equal. |
| **Classical slavery** | In ancient Greece and Rome society was divided into masters and slaves. Society became more sophisticated, but was deeply unequal. |
| **Feudalism** | During the Middle Ages, society was controlled by noble families who owned the land and controlled the lives of the peasants who worked for them. |
| **Capitalism** | Following the Industrial Revolution, power passed to people who owned the new factories. Workers, the **proletariat**, were essentially powerless due to their extreme poverty. |

Marx argued that progress from one stage to another occurred due to **class** conflict. For example, at the end of feudalism the new capitalist class overthrew the old feudal lords and established a new kind of society based on industry rather than on the control of land. Marx argued that the English, American and French Revolutions were examples of the victory of capitalism over feudalism.

Marx believed that capitalism would also come to an end. He argued that, following a workers' revolution, capitalism would be replaced by socialism in Europe's most advanced economies. Lenin believed that the chaos produced by the First World War provided an opportunity to overthrow capitalism across Europe.

### The state and revolution

Marx's writings did not contain a clear indication of how a revolution would be carried out, or what socialism would look like. Indeed, Marx's writings were contradictory. In some places, Marx argued that a revolutionary government would be more democratic than a capitalist government; however, he also famously wrote about the 'dictatorship of the proletariat', which would use its power ruthlessly to destroy the power of capitalists. Lenin seems to have taken both of these ideas seriously.

## 2 Lenin's state, 1917–18

Lenin's new **state** changed over time. Initially, he embraced a radically democratic state. However, by the summer of 1918, the revolutionary state was much more **authoritarian**.

### Note it down

Using the 1:2 method (see page x) make notes on the following topics:

- How did Lenin justify his new state?
- How was Lenin's new state structured?
- How powerful was Lenin's state between 1917 and 1918?
- How democratic was Lenin's state between 1917 and 1918?

### Creating a 'soviet-state'

In October 1917, Lenin seized power on behalf of the **soviets** – small democratic councils that had emerged spontaneously in every town and village across Russia after the February Revolution. Between February and October 1917, the soviets played a key role in governing Russia. Additionally, the local soviets sent representatives to the **All-Russian Congress of Soviets**, which met in June 1917 to discuss Russia's future. Lenin and other senior Bolsheviks argued that the All-Russian Congress of Soviets, which met for a second time in October, should become the basis of the new Russian Government. Indeed, the October Revolution formally handed power to the All-Russian Congress. However, as the All-Russian Congress was too big to meet regularly they elected the Council of People's Commissars (*Sovnarkom*) to govern Russia on a day-to-day basis.

#### *Sovnarkom*

*Sovnarkom* was essentially the new Russian **cabinet**. The first *Sovnarkom* was made up of 13 People's Commissars. Lenin was elected Chairman of *Sovnarkom*, and other Commissars included Leon Trotsky (see page 7), who was head of the **People's Commissariat of Foreign Affairs**, and Joseph Stalin (see page 8), who was head of the **People's Commissariat of Nationality Affairs**. All of the new Commissars were revolutionaries. The vast majority had supported Lenin since 1903. Many had worked with him in exile, and all had supported the Bolshevik seizure of power.

## Leon Trotsky, 1879–1940

Before 1917 Trotsky was already a revolutionary hero due to his role in the failed 1905 Revolution. Trotsky and Lenin disagreed violently about politics before 1917. However, following the February Revolution they worked closely together until Lenin's death. Trotsky played a leading role in the October Revolution and in the first years of Russia's Communist Government. He also led the Communist's Red Army to victory in the Civil War (see page 9). In spite of his brilliance, he was not universally popular among Lenin's followers. He was viewed as arrogant and unreliable. Additionally, he was viewed as a threat, and therefore other senior members of the Party plotted successfully to expel him from the Party and from Russia.

Lenin's first government passed a series of **decrees** that were genuinely popular. Immediately following the October Revolution, Lenin gave a speech to the All-Russian Congress of Soviets. He proposed a series of decrees which the Congress of Soviets voted to approve:

- the Decree on Land (October 1917), which gave peasants the right to seize land from the nobility and the Church
- the Decree of Peace (October 1917), which committed the new government to withdrawing from the First World War and seeking peace.

Lenin continued to publish popular decrees for the first few months of the government, including:

- Workers' Decrees (November 1917), which established an eight-hour maximum working day and a minimum wage
- the Decree of **Workers' Control** (April 1918), which allowed workers to elect committees to run factories.

These early measures allowed Lenin to establish control over Russia in two main ways. First, the decrees won popular support for the regime from workers, peasants and soldiers. Second, ending the First World War gave the revolution what Lenin called 'breathing space' in which to begin to rebuild the economy and to start constructing a new government.

For the first few months, *Sovnarkom* had little real power. The October Revolution had occurred in Russia's capital city, Petrograd. At first, it did not give Lenin control of Russia's other major cities or the vast rural areas that made up the majority of Russia's territory. Senior figures from the former government still had a great deal of power and refused to recognise Bolshevik authority. For example, in late November General Dukhonin, Chief of Staff of the Russian army, refused a direct order from Lenin to stop fighting and begin peace negotiations. Equally, the Russian State Bank and State Treasury went on strike immediately after the revolution, denying Lenin's new government the funds that it needed to operate.

Initially, *Sovnarkom* was also extremely disorganised. This is evident from Lenin's early appointments of People's Commissars. For example, in the first few days of the new government, Stalin's Commissariat for Nationalities was, in reality, just a desk in the corner of a room at the Smolny Institute, the building where *Sovnarkom* was originally based.

Equally, Vyacheslav Menzhinsky's Commissariat of Finance was initially nothing more than a sofa with a large piece of paper pinned to it bearing the words 'Commissariat of Finance'. Lenin's government would need to fight a civil war before it had genuine control of the whole of Russia.

## How democratic was Russia in 1918?

Lenin and the Bolsheviks claimed that the new government was truly democratic. Lenin argued that the new state was based on committees of working people who participated in government on a day-to-day basis. He claimed the soviet-state was more democratic than the systems in Britain, the USA and France where people merely voted once every four or five years. This commitment to people power was also reflected in the title of the new leaders, who were known as People's Commissars. Trotsky suggested this title in order to demonstrate the revolutionary nature of the new government. In so doing, he deliberately used the terms that were associated with the government that took power after the French Revolution.

### Broad-based support

There is clear evidence that the new government was genuinely democratic. For example, the first decrees were genuinely popular and reflected what the majority of the workers, peasants and soldiers wanted. Equally, in 1918 Russia was not yet a one-party state. According to the **Constitution of 1918**, *Sovnarkom* was responsible to the Congress of Soviets – which contained representatives

## Joseph Stalin, 1878–1953

Prior to the October Revolution Stalin was one of a number of dedicated revolutionaries who spent long periods in exile due to their political beliefs. Born in Gori, Georgia, then part of the Russian Empire, the young Stalin trained as a Christian priest. However, after reading the work of Marx, he abandoned the Church in favour of revolution.

Stalin was one of the first members of the revolutionary RSDLP in Georgia and from 1906 was a regular at RSDLP Party Congresses, becoming known to Lenin. Stalin was not regarded as an outstanding speaker or as a gifted intellectual, but was respected as a capable administrator. Lenin valued his loyalty. Consequently, he became part of Lenin's inner circle and played small but important roles in the October Revolution and the Civil War (see page 9). Stalin was highly ambitious and once in power his desire to dominate the Party and punish his opponents became evident.

of many political parties including the Bolshevik's main rivals, the **Mensheviks**, and the Socialist Revolutionaries (SRs). What is more, a faction of the SRs supported the new government and some SRs initially had junior roles in the new government.

One of the reasons that there was broad-based support for the new government in Petrograd and Moscow was the belief that it would become a **coalition government** representing all of Russia's main socialist parties. Indeed, moderates within the Bolshevik Party, such as **Zinoviev** and **Kamenev**, argued that Lenin should form a coalition government and work with other political parties. However, when Bolshevik moderates were unable to persuade Lenin to compromise they resigned in protest. As a result, by November, Lenin's new government was dominated by people who wanted the Bolshevik Party to govern alone.

Additionally, there was genuine support for a Bolshevik-dominated government among the workers of Petrograd in the early days of the revolution. For example, the Petrograd Trades Union Council, which met on 31 October, and the First Conference of Female Factory Workers, which met on 5 November 1917, both gave their full support to the new Bolshevik Government. They supported Lenin's early decrees and the courage the Bolsheviks had shown by overthrowing the Provisional Government in the October Revolution.

### The Constituent Assembly

In January 1918, there was a clear indication that Lenin was turning against democracy. Specifically, Lenin refused to recognise the results of a nationwide election held in November 1917. The election created a **Constituent Assembly** with a Bolshevik minority, which met for the first time in January 1918. Lenin closed the Constituent Assembly by force after only one day, claiming that it posed a threat to the power of the soviets.

However, Lenin was also willing to disregard the soviets. In March 1918, Lenin approved the Treaty of Brest-Litovsk, which gave away a significant proportion of Russian territory to the **Central Powers** in order to end Russia's involvement in the First World War. The treaty was extremely unpopular and therefore the Bolsheviks lost the soviet elections across Russia in April and May 1918. In order to retain power, Lenin refused to recognise the results, arguing that the elections had not been fair. Moreover, Mensheviks and the Socialist Revolutionaries were expelled from the soviets. Lenin demanded new elections, but quickly postponed them due to the outbreak of the Civil War. **Nikolai Bukharin**, the official Bolshevik **Party theorist,** argued that 'formal democracy', by which he meant elections to the soviets, had to be abandoned in order to win the Civil War. As a result of the abolition of the Constituent Assembly and Lenin's refusal to recognise the results of new soviet elections, Lenin was able to consolidate Bolshevik power. However, it became more difficult to argue that the new government was democratic.

### How democratic were the early decrees?

Many of Lenin's early decrees were extremely popular. However, it could be argued that Lenin was forced to be democratic, because, in the early days, the new government had very limited power. Therefore Lenin was forced to allow the peasants to seize land, and the workers to take control of their factories. In this sense, rather than extending the rights of Russian people, the early decrees merely authorised what was already taking place.

# 3 The impact of the Civil War, 1918–21

The Russian Civil War (1918–21) allowed Lenin to establish communist control over the whole of Russia. Moreover, it radically changed the nature of the Bolshevik Party (renamed the Communist Party in 1918), and the new government. The Civil War led to the creation of a 'party-state' and, as a result of the Civil War, the state became increasingly authoritarian and **centralised**.

> **Note it down**
>
> This section focuses on the transformation of Lenin's government during the Civil War. Using a mind map (see page x), make notes on the following topics:
>
> - Changes to the government
> - Reasons for government changes
> - Nature of the government by 1921.

## The Russian Civil War

From the start, Lenin's revolutionary government faced serious opposition. Lenin described the war as a battle between the Communist Reds and the **reactionary** Whites, but in reality the war was more complex. The Bolsheviks had opponents on all sides. Senior members of the Russian army wanted to re-establish Tsarist rule, while others wanted a military dictatorship or a democratic system like France or America. The new government had radical opponents too. The SRs and Mensheviks wanted a more democratic type of socialist government, and **anarchists** wanted to abolish government altogether. Britain, France, the USA and Japan also sent troops to fight the new government. Some countries feared that a successful revolution might spread, while others wanted to gain territory.

The first signs of military conflict emerged in January 1918 as General Kornilov organised an anti-Bolshevik army in the Don region. SRs and liberals set up a rival government in Omsk, Siberia, while other SRs based in the city of Ufa tried to revive the Constituent Assembly. A full-scale civil war broke out in the summer of 1918, with the enemies of the Bolsheviks gaining significant ground in the first six months of 1919. Following the failure of anti-Bolshevik forces to capture Petrograd and Moscow, Russia's new capital city, in the summer of 1919, the **Red Army** began to win the war.

The Red Army extended communist power by winning victories against Nestor Makhno's anarchist army in the Ukraine, against Alexander Kolchak's authoritarian government in Siberia, and against Anton Denikin's army in the Crimea (see Figure 1).

## Government during the Civil War

Lenin's primary objective during the Civil War was to ensure the survival of the new government. Lenin was willing to do whatever was necessary in order to win. As a result of the Civil War, government changed in two ways:

- Lenin's government became increasingly centralised.
- The Communist Party became increasingly powerful.

▲ **Figure 1: The Civil War, 1918–21.**

Lenin's prime method of ensuring victory was to centralise power.

- He centralised control of the economy with the policy of War Communism (see page 43).
- He also relied on political centralisation, working through the loyal Party ***nomenklatura*** rather than the more democratic soviets, and using terror to suppress opposition.
- Trotsky, leader of the Red Army, made the Red Army more authoritarian. He introduced conscription, harsh punishments and relied on former Tsarist generals to lead the army.

Centralisation ensured that the government, the economy and the army were able to win the war. However, it also took power away from the workers, peasants and soldiers who the communists claimed to represent.

## The emergence of a 'party-state'

At first, the new regime described itself as a 'soviet-state' (see page 6); however, during the Civil War the government increasingly became a party-state, based on the Communist Party.

Civil war meant that the new government often had to act quickly to achieve victory. Consequently, Lenin tended to rely on the **Politburo**. Lenin preferred working with the Politburo to *Sovnarkom* as it was smaller – between five and seven members – and therefore could reach decisions more quickly. Additionally, he preferred working with the Politburo because it contained his most loyal supporters, people such as Stalin, Trotsky, Zinoviev and Kamenev.

Lenin did not abolish *Sovnarkom*. Rather, it simply ceased to function as the main centre of government. From 1920, the Politburo effectively became the government of Russia. *Sovnarkom* played a much smaller role, merely approving the decisions that had already been made by the Politburo. The Politburo clearly provided clear and effective leadership during the Civil War. However, the rise of the Politburo indicated that the new government was based on the Communist Party rather than the soviets.

This pattern of Communist Party dominance also emerged at a local level. Senior Communists preferred to work through the Communist Party, which had branches all over the country. They did not trust the local soviets, as SRs and Mensheviks were still present on many of them. Therefore the soviets were often bypassed in favour of the communist *nomenklatura*: Party members who senior officials trusted to implement government policy without question.

By 1921, the new government was based on two parallel structures: the Communist Party and the soviet-state. As the Civil War continued and other political parties were increasingly excluded from the government, the soviet-state lost power to the Communist Party. Due to increasing Party dominance the new form of government became known as the 'party-state'.

## Red Terror

In December 1917 Lenin created the All-Russian Emergency Commission for Combating Counter-Revolution and Sabotage (**Cheka**), a political police force tasked with defending the revolution. During the Civil War **Chekists** were responsible for raiding anarchist organisations, closing down opposition newspapers and expelling Mensheviks and Socialist Revolutionaries from the soviets. The Cheka was willing to imprison, torture or kill anyone who the communists viewed as a threat. For example, in Kremenchuk in the Ukraine, Church leaders were impaled on spikes, while in the city of Oryol victims were frozen and put on display as ice statues. Women captured by the Cheka were routinely raped. Lenin argued that during a revolution, civil war and terror were necessary to protect the new government from its enemies.

## Building the Red Army

In order to fight and win the Civil War, Lenin reformed the army. Following the February Revolution, the Russian army had been democratised: soldiers' committees were empowered to elect senior officers. Lenin abolished this system and Trotsky put Tsarist generals back in charge of the army. This created outrage among **idealists** in the Party, who accused Lenin and Trotsky of betraying the principles of the revolution. Nonetheless, abolishing democracy and putting highly trained experts in charge of the army paid off, and the Red Army became a disciplined and successful fighting force.

# The changing nature of the Communist Party

By 1921, the Communist Government was no longer a government of the workers, peasants and soldiers. While the soviets had been made up of working people, the communist *nomenklatura*, who administered the policies of War Communism, were largely educated members of the former middle class – economists, statisticians and engineers – who had worked for the pre-revolutionary government. The communists needed their administrative and technical expertise to help run industries and supply the army during the war.

## 4 1921: Crisis and reform

The communists had won the Civil War due to their ability to control the whole Russian economy and their willingness to dominate the government. However, this had made the new government extremely unpopular. The Crisis of 1921, which included rebellion among the peasants, workers' strikes and military mutiny, showed the extent of opposition to Lenin's government and therefore forced Lenin to reform.

> **Note it down**
>
> This section focuses on the impact of the Crisis of 1921 on Lenin's government. Using a spider diagram (see page x), make notes on the impact of the Crisis.

### Popular unrest

By early 1921, the communists had won the Civil War. However, the Civil War had ruined Russia's economy. Droughts in 1920 and 1921 made the situation worse, threatening famine. Peasants in Tambov, led by Aleksandr Antonov, began a rebellion against communist **grain requisitioning** and Cheka brutality. By January 1921 Antonov had a force of 50,000 anti-communist fighters. Antonov's revolt was not the only challenge to the Bolsheviks in the countryside. In March 1921 there were peasant attacks on government grain stores all along the Volga River.

In the major cities there were strikes against communist policies in early 1921. In Petrograd the Red Army responded by opening fire on unarmed workers. Sailors at the Kronstadt naval base, horrified by the communists' suppression of the Petrograd strikes, rebelled. The Kronstadt sailors demanded a series of reforms, including:

- the immediate free and fair election of new soviets
- release of all anarchist, Menshevik and SR political prisoners
- a restoration of freedom of speech and the press
- the abolition of the Cheka
- an end to War Communism (see page 43).

In essence, the Kronstadt sailors wanted a return to soviet democracy. This demand was summed up in their slogan 'Soviets without Communists'.

Even some communists felt that Lenin had gone too far and that the time was right to revive soviet democracy. Lenin responded swiftly to these challenges. By mid-March the Red Army had crushed the Kronstadt uprising. The Red Army was equally ruthless in Tambov. In May they suppressed the rebellion by deporting 100,000 people to labour camps and attacking peasant villages with poisoned gas.

### One-party state

Lenin responded to the unrest by suppressing opposition political parties. In so doing he created a one-party state. During the Civil War, opposition political parties were often persecuted by the Cheka. In spite of this they had survived the Civil War and therefore were able to play a key role in the strikes of early 1921.

From February 1921 Lenin authorised the Cheka to destroy opposition political parties. At the end of February 1921, all Mensheviks in Petrograd and Moscow, including one of the Mensheviks' leaders, Fyodor Dan, were arrested and sent to the Butyrka Prison. Similar steps were taken against the SRs. Twenty-two leading SRs were put on trial in early 1922 and sentenced to prison or exile. Consequently, between 1921 and 1922, the communists' dominance of Russia was consolidated by crushing opposition political parties.

### The 1921 Party Congress

Lenin recognised that the unrest in Tambov, Petrograd and Kronstadt reflected the fact that Russian workers and peasants were deeply dissatisfied with the regime. As a result, Lenin pushed through a series of reforms in the 1921 Party Congress. The New Economic Policy (see page 45) liberalised the economy, while the ban on factions tightened Lenin's political control.

Lenin faced opposition from several factions within the Bolshevik Party, including:

- the Workers' Opposition: a group who wanted to reintroduce workers' control of industry
- the Democratic Centralists: a group who wanted to make the Communist Party more democratic.

Lenin introduced a **resolution**, entitled 'On Party Unity', which banned factions inside the Party. Party members found guilty of forming factions could be expelled from the Party as punishment. The ban on factions helped strengthen Lenin's position within the Party by making opposition to his policies more difficult to organise.

> **The Soviet Union**
>
> The Soviet Union was created in 1922. In theory the Union was made up of independent republics. By 1940 there were fifteen Soviet republics including the Ukraine, Georgia, Estonia, and the Uzbek, Kazakh and Tajik Republics. Each republic had its own Soviet system, and each republic, apart from Russia, had its own Communist Party.

## 5 Conclusion: Lenin's legacy

Between 1917 and the time of Lenin's death in 1924, Russia was transformed. Lenin succeeded in creating a Dictatorship of the Proletariat to defend the revolution. However, he destroyed soviet democracy and replaced it with a one-party state. The original **institutions** that had been created after the October Revolution had lost their power to Party institutions that had emerged during the Civil War. For example, *Sovnarkom* ceased to play an important role in government, while the Politburo made all of the important decisions that affected Russia.

During the Civil War Russia became extremely centralised. The creation of a one-party state and the ban on factions meant that political centralisation increased after the Civil War.

Lenin argued that the ban on factions, the ban on other parties and the decreased role of the soviets were temporary. However, there was no sign before Lenin's death that the government had plans to make Russia more democratic.

Lenin also created a system in which the political police played a significant role. Again, the Cheka were introduced in 1917 as a temporary measure. But after the Civil War they still played a significant role, persecuting opposition political parties. In this sense, Lenin created a system in which individuals had no rights as the Cheka were free to persecute anyone that the government perceived as a threat. Indeed, Lenin established the principle that violence was justified in order to protect the revolution.

Finally, Lenin replaced a workers' government with a highly bureaucratic one. Soviets full of workers, peasants and soldiers were replaced by specialists and administrators, few of whom were from the working class.

### Work together

Having made notes on this chapter, swap them with a partner. Consider the following questions:

1 Has your partner taken all of the key points down?
2 Has your partner got enough supporting detail points to support the key points?
3 Has your partner missed anything?
4 Have you missed anything that your partner has noted down?
5 Could you revise from your partner's notes?
6 How could you both improve your note-making style?

Use these questions to feed back to each other and improve your note making.

### Chapter summary

- Lenin seized power in Russia in the October Revolution of 1917, proclaiming 'All power to the Soviets'.
- Initially, Lenin's government was based on the soviets.
- Bolshevik popularity declined between October 1917 and April 1918.
- Lenin refused to recognise the results of new elections to the soviets in mid-1918.
- During the Russian Civil War, 1918–21, the Russian Government became increasingly centralised and dominated by the communists.
- During the Civil War the Politburo replaced *Sovnarkom* as the effective government of Russia.
- The communists won the Civil War using a combination of political and economic centralisation, military discipline and terror.
- Following the Civil War Lenin banned opposition political parties and created a one-party state.
- Following the Civil War Lenin banned factions within the Communist Party, further centralising the Party.
- The Communist Government continued to use political centralisation and terror to govern Russia after the Civil War.

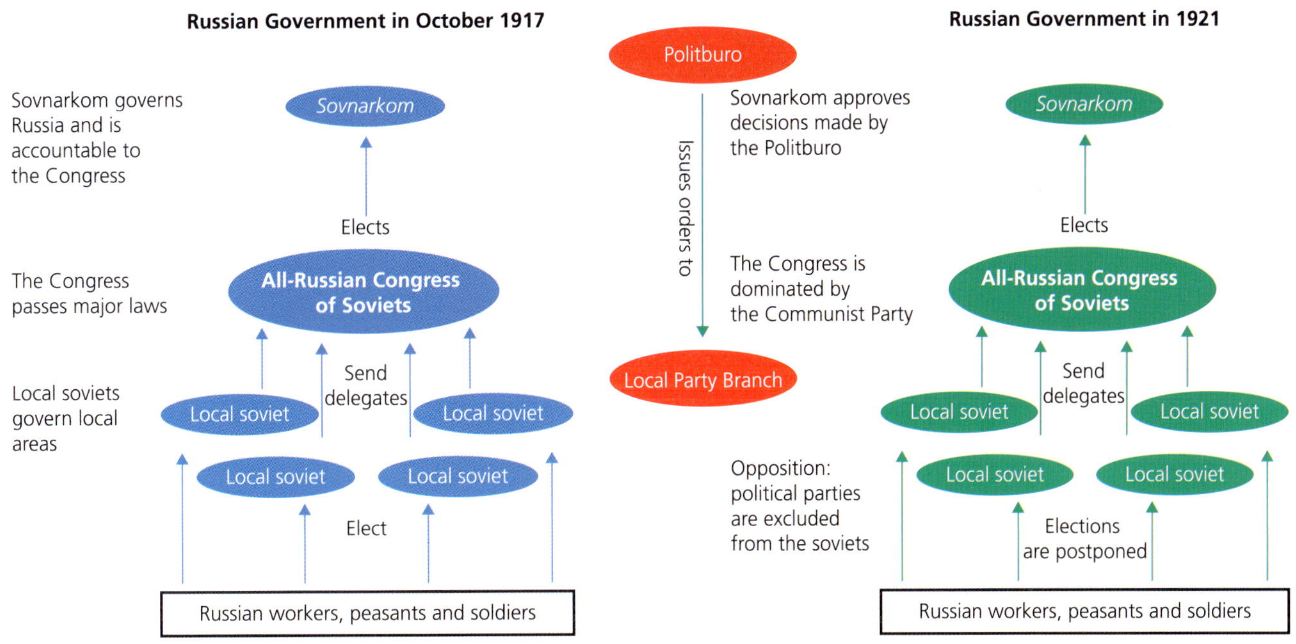


▲ **Summary diagram: Establishing Communist Party control, 1917–24.**

## Recommended reading

G.L. Freeze (ed.), *Russia: A History* (Oxford University Press, 2002), especially pages 253–262 on the political consequences of the Russian Civil War.

R. Service, *Lenin: A Biography* (Pan Macmillan, 2010), especially the Introduction which provides an overview of Lenin's life, ideas and legacy.

R. Service, *The Penguin History of Modern Russia: From Tsarism to the Twenty-first Century* (Penguin, 2009), especially Chapter 1 which deals with Russia prior to the First World War.

R.G. Suny (ed.), *The Cambridge History of Russia, Volume III* (Cambridge University Press, 2006), especially Chapter 4 which deals with the revolutionary period of 1917–18.

# Essay technique: Understanding the question

Section A and B questions require you to deploy a variety of skills. The most important are focus on the question, selection and deployment of relevant detail, analysis and, at the highest level, prioritisation. The introduction to this book gives more detail about Section A and B questions (see pages vi-vii). Section A and B questions for AS level are different from those for A level, and some guidance about this is given on pages vii–viii. However, you will need to develop very similar skills for the AS exam, therefore the activities will help with the AS exams as well. There are also some AS-style questions to practise at the end of chapters.

In order to answer the question successfully you must understand how the question works. The question below is written precisely in order to make sure that you understand the task. Each part of the question has a specific meaning.

'How accurate', like other stems such as 'How far', indicates that you are required to evaluate the extent of something, rather than giving a yes or no answer.

**How accurate is it to say that Russia was a totalitarian state in the years 1928–41?**

This sets out the subject that you must address.

The dates define the period that you should consider.

Overall, **all** Section A and B questions ask you to make a judgement about the extent of something, in a specific period. In order to focus on the question you must address all three elements. The most common mistakes come from misunderstanding or ignoring one of these three elements.

## Activity: What should a good answer look like?

Having read the advice on essay questions on this page and in the introduction (page v), complete the following activity:

1. Make a bullet-point list of the skills that you need to do well in this type of essay.
2. Number the skills in order of their difficulty, so the easiest skill to demonstrate is 1, and the hardest 4.
3. Try to work out what a good essay would look like. Specifically, note down your thoughts about:
   - roughly how many paragraphs the essay should have
   - which skills you should deploy in which sections of the essay
   - how you should structure the different types of paragraph.

**TIP:** Don't just guess; use the advice in this section and in the introduction to try to figure out what a good essay should look like.

## Work together

Having completed these activities, swap them with a partner. Consider the following questions:

1. Did you agree on which skills were easiest to demonstrate and which skills were hardest? How did each of you make this judgement?
2. Did you agree on the number of paragraphs in the essay?
3. How did you and your partner make the judgement about the number of paragraphs you should write?
4. If you had different reasons for the judgement, whose reasons were better and why?
5. Did you agree on where the different skills should be used?
6. Were your reasons for locating skills in different parts or throughout the essay as good as your partner's reasons?
7. Did you agree on how to structure each paragraph?
8. Can your partner justify their thoughts on how to structure a paragraph?

Use this discussion as a basis for further notes on how to approach the question. For advice on the structure of the essay see page 26.

# 1b: Stalin in power, 1928–53

## Overview

**Between 1928 and 1953 the Soviet Union was transformed from a Party dictatorship to a personal dictatorship. This process went through a series of stages. By 1928, Stalin had changed the nature of the Party in a way that allowed him to emerge as the Soviet Union's undisputed leader. This process went further in the 1930s. Through a series of violent purges, known as the Great Terror, Stalin destroyed the generation of Communist leaders who had known Lenin, fought in the revolution and therefore had authority that was independent of Stalin.**

**In this sense, during the 1930s Stalin reduced the power of the Party and made himself supreme. By 1938, the essential features of Stalin's Communist Government were in place. In his final years he made small changes to the Party and the state in order to safeguard his power. His efforts were successful. He died in 1953 the master of a totalitarian superpower.**

**This chapter considers:**

1. **The elimination of Stalin's opponents**
2. **The purges of the 1930s**
3. **Stalin's power over party and state.**

## 1 The elimination of Stalin's opponents

Between 1923 and 1928 the leadership struggle transformed the nature of the Communist Party. Between 1917 and 1922 Lenin's government had been quite **pluralistic**. There were a number of powerful people in the government and various different views about the future of communist society. The 1921 Ban on Factions (see page 11) had reduced the scope of party pluralism, but it had not destroyed it. However, by 1928 Stalin had transformed the Party in four ways:

- He had established an ideological orthodoxy.
- He had destroyed the authority of the other main contenders.
- He changed the nature of Party membership.
- He had created the patronage system.

In so doing he ensured his victory and destroyed the political authority of his key rivals.

### Note it down

Make an index card (see page xi) for each of the main contenders for power. On each, note:

- their relationship with Lenin
- Lenin's comments on them in his Testament
- their key strengths
- their key weaknesses.

### Leadership in the Soviet Union

Lenin's leadership was based on his personality and his authority. He was able to lead because he had the respect of all his senior colleagues. They knew that he had masterminded the revolution, and that the government that emerged reflected his vision. In that sense, he was leader of the Soviet Union because he was Lenin, not because he held official positions.

This created problems on Lenin's death. Specifically, replacing Lenin was not a matter of winning a post in the government. Rather, each of the contenders had to persuade the Communist Party that they were a true Leninist.

Nonetheless, the Politburo had emerged as the most powerful part of the government. Therefore gaining a majority in the Politburo was the key to power in the Soviet Union. Winning a majority in the Politburo meant winning votes at the Party Congress as the Party Congress elected the Central Committee, which in turn elected the Politburo. The battle for leadership was a battle for support within the Party, not a battle for support within the Soviet Union, which was not a democracy.

### Stalin's rivals for power in 1923

The leadership struggle was prompted by Lenin's declining health. Lenin had become unwell towards the end of 1921, and in May 1922 he had the first of a series of strokes that left him unable to work. By mid-1923 it was obvious that Lenin would never return to government. Therefore a struggle began at the top of the Party which had a profound impact on the government of the Soviet Union. From 1923 there were four key contenders who had a realistic chance of emerging as leader of Russia: Zinoviev, Bukharin, Trotsky and Stalin. None of them rivalled Lenin, but all of them had a significant degree of authority in the Party.

#### Gregory Zinoviev

Zinoviev emerged as the front-runner to lead the Soviet Union in 1923. Zinoviev could claim to be a true Leninist as he was Lenin's closest friend. The two spent so much time together that Zinoviev's handwriting became like that of Lenin. Additionally, Zinoviev had supported Lenin since the beginning of the Bolshevik movement in 1903. Between 1903 and 1917 Zinoviev had been Lenin's right-hand man.

Between 1923 and 1925 Zinoviev led the Triumvirate, an alliance of himself, his friend Lev Kamenev and Stalin, which formed a majority in the Politburo. The alliance kept Trotsky out of power and laid the foundation for Stalin's emergence as leader. Specifically, Zinoviev and Kamenev persuaded the Central Committee to ignore Lenin's Testament, which contained an instruction to sack Stalin. Consequently, Stalin retained his position at the top of government.

Zinoviev also created an extremely effective political strategy which denied Trotsky power. He made a series of speeches about the differences between Leninism and Trotskyism. The purpose of these speeches and these two new categories was to demonstrate that Trotsky was not a Leninist and therefore should not lead the government.

## Nikolai Bukharin

From 1925 to early 1928 Bukharin was the most prominent figure in the Soviet Government. In 1925 he formed an alliance with Stalin, known as the Duumvirate. The alliance gave Bukharin and Stalin a majority in the Politburo due to the support of more junior members who were allies of Bukharin.

Bukharin could claim to be a true Leninist for a number of reasons:

- He joined the Bolshevik faction in 1906 and supported Lenin consistently until Lenin's death in 1924.
- Lenin and Bukharin were close and had a father-and-son relationship.
- Lenin entrusted Bukharin with a series of important jobs, including the editorship of the Soviet newspaper *Pravda*.

However, it was widely known that Bukharin and Lenin had disagreed over a series of issues. For example, in 1918 they disagreed over ending the First World War, and in 1921 over the introduction of the NEP. Moreover, as he was the youngest of the contenders for power, some in the Party thought he was too young and inexperienced to be the new leader.

## Trotsky

Trotsky was the most famous member of the government other than Lenin. He was well known as a revolutionary hero due to the role he played in the October Revolution and the Civil War. Moreover, from 1917 he had been Lenin's right-hand man and closest political collaborator. However, he was not popular within the Communist Party. Many communists remembered that between 1903 and 1917 he had opposed Lenin. Trotsky had joined the Bolsheviks in mid-1917, and therefore many Bolsheviks believed that he joined the Party to gain power rather than because he was a true Leninist. Moreover, Trotsky had disagreements with Lenin in 1917 over the timing of the October Revolution and in 1922 over the NEP (see page 45). There was a great deal of evidence that Zinoviev was right and Trotsky was not a true Leninist and therefore did not deserve to lead the Party.

Trotsky retained his position in the Politburo until 1927, but he was unable to influence the direction of policy. He was continually in opposition to the ruling alliances.

## Stalin

Stalin was continually part of the Politburo majority between 1923 and 1928. However, he played a supporting role, letting Zinoviev and then Bukharin play the leading roles in the Triumvirate and then the Duumvirate.

### Lenin's Testament

In late 1922 and early 1923 Lenin was too ill to play an active part in government. Nonetheless, he was able to dictate essays and notes which set out his ideas for the future of the Soviet Union.

Lenin's Testament refers to a series of notes that he dictated about leading members of the Party. The notes were addressed to the Central Committee and were highly critical of the main contenders for power. The Testament:

- accused Trotsky of arrogance and in coded language of being too willing to use violence
- accused Stalin of impatience and rudeness
- reminded the Central Committee that Zinoviev and Kamenev had been disloyal to the Party immediately before the October Revolution
- argued that Bukharin did not fully understand Lenin's ideology.

The first part of the Testament advocated a collective leadership based on an alliance between Trotsky and Stalin. However, following an angry phone call between Stalin and Lenin's wife, the second part of the note instructed the Central Committee to sack Stalin.

All of the five contenders voted to keep the Testament secret at a 1923 meeting of the Central Committee, as it was damaging to all of them.

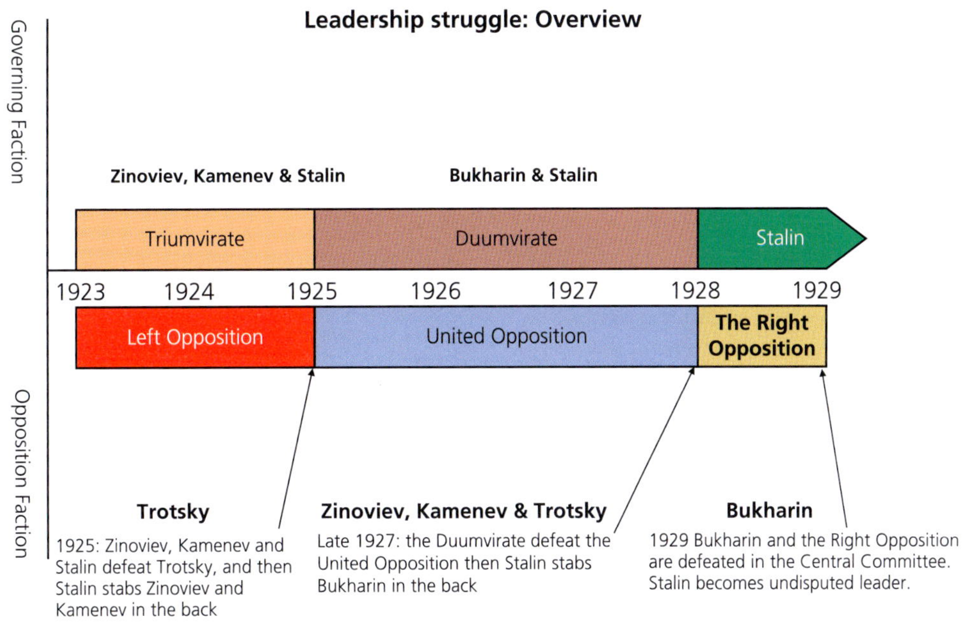


Stalin could claim to be a true Leninist for a variety of reasons. He had joined the Bolsheviks at the very beginning in 1903 and had been loyal to Lenin throughout the whole period from 1903 to 1921. Stalin began being disloyal to Lenin in 1922 when Lenin was too ill to fight back. Moreover, this disloyalty was kept secret from the majority of the Party.

Lenin held Stalin in high regard, referring to him as 'that wonderful Georgian'. Lenin trusted Stalin with important administrative tasks and supported his promotion to the position of General Secretary in 1921.

## The Communist Party in 1928

The leadership struggle led to a series of important changes in the Communist Party. In general terms the Party became more centralised and disciplined as a result of the leadership struggle as the contenders tried to gain greater control of the Party.

### Ideological orthodoxy

First, in order to win the leadership struggle, Stalin had to establish that he, rather than the other contenders, was a true Leninist. This changed the nature of the Party by establishing a new ideological orthodoxy.

Between 1917 and 1928 the Communist Party included members who believed a variety of different things. During the leadership struggle Stalin and his allies discredited a number of ideas, which became known as Trotskyite.

By 1928 the Communist Party was committed to two ideas which Stalin advocated:

- Socialism in one country: From 1924 Stalin and Bukharin had advocated the idea that the Soviet Union could construct socialism. Traditionally, Marxists had assumed that socialism could only be achieved following a global revolution. In that sense, constructing socialism was believed to be a global project, not something that could be done in one country. However, from 1924 Bukharin and Stalin argued that the Soviet Union could build socialism without waiting for a global revolution. They argued that socialism in one country was the correct Leninist idea, and that Trotsky, Zinoviev and Kamenev were Trotskyites, rather than Leninists, because they wanted to wait for a global revolution before constructing socialism.
- Collectivisation and industrialisation: In 1928, Stalin argued that the time was right to abandon the NEP and transform the Soviet economy. Lenin had argued that the NEP would 'last a long time but not forever'. While this statement was vague, Stalin argued that Lenin's commitment to the NEP was pragmatic. When the economy under the NEP stopped growing in the late 1920s, Stalin argued that the correct Leninist policy was to abandon the NEP and introduce a more radical policy. From 1928 Stalin argued that peasants should be forced to work on state-owned farms, and that the profit they produced should be used to industrialise the Soviet Union at a rapid pace. He argued that Bukharin's desire to continue the NEP indicated that Bukharin was no longer a true Leninist.

This new ideological orthodoxy was a significant change in the nature of the Party. Lenin had tolerated differences of view at the top of the government and was prepared to work with people he disagreed with. Stalin, by contrast, argued that Trotskyites and Bukharin's followers posed a real threat to the Party. Therefore he had Zinoviev, Kamenev and Trotsky arrested and Trotsky expelled from the Party and the Soviet Union.

## Authority at the top of the Party

Under Lenin there were many people who had authority within the Party. Stalin, Trotsky, Bukharin, Zinoviev and Kamenev all enjoyed the respect of significant parts of the Party, and therefore all had power bases within the Party. Stalin's strategy for emerging as undisputed leader was to destroy the authority of his opponents. He undermined the authority of his opponents by:

- establishing a new ideological orthodoxy and branding his opponents enemies of Leninism
- demanding that Trotsky, Zinoviev and Kamenev apologise to the Party for the errors when they lost votes at the Party Congress
- accusing Bukharin, Zinoviev and Kamenev of plotting against the Party and forming a faction; these were serious crimes, as Lenin had banned factions in 1921.

By 1928, the Party had been transformed from an organisation in which there were a large number of people who had a degree of authority to an organisation in which Stalin had a near monopoly of authority. Significantly, Stalin did not succeed in completely destroying Bukharin's authority by 1928. Bukharin was still highly regarded by most of the Party, even though his policies were rejected.

## Party membership

Another change in the Party introduced by Stalin to help win the leadership struggle was an increase in Party membership. In 1924, Stalin initiated the Lenin Enrolment. From May 1924, the Lenin Enrolment allowed 128,000 people to join the Communist Party. Stalin justified this by arguing that the Party needed new working-class members.

However, in practice the new members were poorly educated people who wanted well-paid jobs within the Party. Due to their lack of education, the new members were suspicious of Trotsky and Bukharin, the Party's leading intellectuals. Moreover, because they were interested in getting well-paid Party jobs they tended to support Stalin, who was able to promote them within the Party.

Therefore by 1928 the Party was quite different to the Party of 1921. The new recruits were less interested in ideas or the goals of the revolution and more interested in their careers.

## Stalin's patronage system

Party democracy also weakened between 1921 and 1928. In 1921, the Party was based on Democratic Centralism. All Party members voted for delegates who attended the Party Congress, which elected the Central Committee. However, from 1923 Stalin began to issue an 'approved list'. Rather than having a free choice, local parties were encouraged to send delegates to the Party Congress from the approved list. In 1923 approximately one-third of the delegates at the Party Congress were selected from Stalin's list. As the 1920s went on this figure grew, giving Stalin a greater degree of control over the Congress.

Additionally, Stalin had a number of positions in the Party which allowed him to win support by acting as patron. As General Secretary, he could give well-paid and powerful jobs to lower-ranking Party members. Equally as head of the **Central Control Commission** and the **Rabkrin** he had the power to investigate and, if necessary, sack Party members and government officials. Stalin's power to promote and sack Party members meant that he could count on the loyalty of Party members who wanted to retain their positions or get a promotion.

Changes in the Party increased Stalin's power. They also led to a change in the nature of the Party. First, from the mid-1920s the Party increasingly had the role of administering and implementing the decisions of the Politburo and the leader. Party members became known as 'apparatchiks', people who worked in the Party 'apparatus', implementing orders rather than thinking creatively about politics. Secondly, the Party became increasingly privileged. People with full-time positions in the Party were known as the '*nomenklatura*', people who enjoyed power and status due to their Party position, and ultimately to patronage. In this sense, under Stalin the Party ceased to be full of dedicated revolutionary radicals and became full of professional administrators dedicated to their own careers.

## Conclusion

The struggle for leadership in the 1920s transformed the Party by 1928. Stalin emerged as leader of the Party by creating an ideological orthodoxy, by destroying the authority of his opponents, by transforming the Communist Party and by the extensive use of patronage. In so doing, he changed the Communist Party from a relatively pluralistic organisation to a party in which Stalin alone was dominant.

▲ 'Long live the Stalinist Order of Heroes and Stakhanovites' by Gustav Klutsis (1935). In what ways does this poster from 1935 emphasise Stalin's authority?

## 2 The purges of the 1930s

By 1928, Stalin was undisputed leader of the Communist Party and the Soviet Union. However, in some ways his power was insecure. In essence, Stalin feared that he would lose power, just as Trotsky, Zinoviev and Bukharin had in the 1920s. He was concerned that:

- his own supporters were prepared to challenge his authority
- his old rivals could conspire against him and overthrow him.

Stalin responded to these perceived threats by launching the Great Terror, or Great Purge, a campaign of arrests, torture, mass imprisonments and executions that finally removed his opponents. The Great Terror was at its height from 1935 to 1938. It was responsible for the deaths of around 10 million Soviet citizens, approximately ten per cent of the population.

### Note it down

Using a spider diagram (see page x), make notes on the causes of the Great Terror. Use the sub-headings as your main topics and make sure you get down the key details, including dates and names. Under every heading, highlight the reason why each of these factors led Stalin to launch the Great Terror. Finally, make a judgement about whether the factors were long- or short-term causes – and note these judgements down on the diagram.

### Causes of the purges

The Great Terror had several causes. However, they were all related to Stalin's desire to safeguard his own position.

#### Opposition

Opposition from the Politburo was one of the causes of the Great Terror. By 1932 there was a group of moderates in the Politburo associated with Sergei Kirov, head of the

### Sergei Kirov, 1886–1934

Born in 1886 into a poor family, Kirov became a leading member of the Communist Party in the 1920s. In 1925 he was appointed leader of the Communist Party in Leningrad. He was a Stalinist, who supported collectivisation, the Five-Year Plans and the use of political terror. Although he was a Stalinist, he had a reputation for being more pragmatic than Stalin. Indeed, he used his influence to ensure that the Second Five-Year Plan was more realistic and more focused on consumer goods than the First. Additionally, he was a good orator, he was considered handsome and he was a Russian – whereas Stalin was a Georgian – and therefore popular within the Party. In 1933 he was nominated Stalin's deputy, and therefore Stalin saw him as a potential rival. There is considerable debate surrounding the extent of Stalin's involvement in his murder.

Communist Party in Leningrad. Kirov and the moderates were able to force some changes in policy in the early 1930s:

- In 1932, Kirov defended Martemyan Ryutin. Ryutin had circulated a document that was highly critical of Stalin's policies. He also formed the Union of Marxist Leninists, an opposition group, which included supporters of Bukharin, Zinoviev and Trotsky. Stalin demanded his execution. However, Kirov, with the support of Politburo moderates, argued successfully that he should be sent to prison.
- In 1933 Kirov and the moderates argued for more realistic targets in the Second Five-Year Plan and for a greater emphasis on the production of consumer goods (see page 53).

Kirov's growing authority within the Party was clearly a challenge to Stalin.

### Economic problems

Economic problems were also a cause of the Great Terror. First, senior figures within government were aware of the problems with Stalin's industrial and agricultural policies, which undermined Stalin's authority in government 53–54. Secondly, by accusing workers and managers of being 'wreckers' and 'saboteurs' Stalin could blame them for the problems, rather than accepting responsibility for the failure of his policies. Finally, Stalin sent 'wreckers' and 'saboteurs' to **Gulags**, huge labour camps. In this sense, the terror created an army of slave labour, which he could use to build factories or mine resources.

### The Congress of Victors

Events during the Congress of Victors, held in February 1934, also indicated that Stalin's position was under threat. Stalin came second to Kirov in the vote at the end of the Congress which elected the new Central Committee; Kirov received 1225 votes compared to Stalin's 927. Senior members of the Party approached Kirov, urging him to stand against Stalin as General Secretary. Kirov refused, and the vote was kept secret. Nonetheless, the Congress demonstrated that Stalin had a rival in the Communist Party.

### Kirov's murder

Finally, Kirov's murder was a useful **pretext** for launching the terror. Kirov was murdered in December 1934. Some historians have speculated that Stalin ordered the attack, but conclusive proof has never been found. Certainly, the murder removed Stalin's main rival. Additionally, the murder allowed Stalin to claim that there was a dangerous conspiracy that aimed to overthrow the Communist Government. In that sense, it gave Stalin a reason to arrest his rivals and launch a mass campaign to hunt down his enemies.

## The Great Terror, 1934–38

The Great Terror started in Leningrad in December 1934. Immediately after Kirov's murder, Stalin arrested Zinoviev and Kamenev and organised an investigation into the Communist Party in Leningrad. The Great Terror spread throughout the Soviet Union in 1936 and reached its height in 1937.

### Show trials

The most public aspect of the terror were three **show trials** that took place in 1936, 1937 and 1938. These finally removed Stalin's rivals from the 1920s:

- The Trial of the 16, 1936, led to the execution of Zinoviev, Kamenev and 14 of their supporters.
- The Trial of the 17, 1937, led to the execution and imprisonment of 17 of Trotsky's former supporters.
- The Trial of the 21, 1938, led to the execution of Bukharin and many of his closest supporters.

Not only did the trials lead to the deaths of Stalin's former rivals, they also destroyed the reputations of the key defendants. All of the defendants confessed to plotting to murder Kirov and working with capitalist nations to overthrow the Soviet Union.

The show trials were only a tiny fraction of the Great Terror. The terror affected all aspects of the Party and the government. Indeed, 95 per cent of those affected by the terror were men between the ages of 30 and 45 who held senior positions in the Party or played an important role in the economy.

### Secret trials

In addition to the public trials, Stalin organised a trial of the Red Army's leaders. In 1937 eight senior generals were tried

Table 2: The victims of the purges.

| Date | Victims | Accused of | Punishment |
|---|---|---|---|
| 1928 | Engineers at Shakhty | Treason and sabotage | Shot or sent to labour camps |
| 1934 | Supporters of Ryutin | Treason and plotting against Stalin | Expelled from the Party |
| 1936 | Zinoviev and Kamenev | Being Trotskyists and being involved in the murder of Kirov | Shot |
| 1937 | Pyatakov and Serebryakov | Espionage and being German agents | Shot |
| | Yagoda, head of the NKVD | Treason and murder | Shot |
| | Marshal Tukhachevsky and the majority of the army's senior officers | Treason | Shot |
| | The junior army officers – an estimated 35,000 | Treason | Shot or sent to labour camps |
| | All the admirals of the Soviet navy | Treason | Shot |
| | Radek and Sokolnikov | Espionage and being German agents | Shot |
| 1938 | Bukharin, Rykov, numerous other Party leaders and members of the soviets of other republics | Various crimes including treason | Shot or sent to labour camps |
| 1939 | Yezhov, head of the NKVD | Treason – being a British agent | Shot |
| 1929–39 | An estimated 24 million people | Treason, being kulaks, having bourgeois views and many other crimes | Sent to labour camps where some 13 million died |
| 1940 | Trotsky | Long time critic of Stalin | Killed at his home in Mexico City |

for plotting to overthrow the government. The eight leaders had worked with Trotsky when he was head of the Red Army, and therefore Stalin did not trust them. All were executed.

Following the trial more than 37,000 officers were purged from the army (see Table 2).

## Consequences of the Great Terror

The Great Terror led to significant change in government:

- It finally eliminated Stalin's rivals from the 1920s.
- It also led to the death or imprisonment of a whole generation of communists who had known and worked with Lenin. In this sense, it removed all Party members who could claim authority that was independent from Stalin.
- It led to the emergence of a new generation of Communist Party leaders who owed their positions to Stalin, and who were therefore loyal.
- It established the principle that Stalin had the right to use terror against anyone who was disloyal.
- Stalin's political police, the NKVD, became a powerful organisation within the regime. Consequently, Lavrentiy Beria, Stalin's NKVD chief from 1938, also became a powerful figure within the government.

In sum, the Great Terror established that Stalin was the only source of authority in the Soviet Union. Other politicians and the Party itself could not be trusted. Only Stalin could be trusted to defend the Soviet Union.

### Totalitarianism

Stalin's form of government has often been described as totalitarian. In essence, many historians and political scientists argue that Stalin constructed a new kind of dictatorship. Unlike previous dictators, Stalin:

- had complete control of the economy (see pages 50-51)
- used widespread political terror to eliminate his opponents
- had complete control of the media
- used extensive propaganda to win the hearts and minds of his people (see page 75-76).

Stalin's dictatorship also had different aims from previous dictatorships. Whereas dictators such as the Tsar had been content with the absence of opposition, Stalin demanded heartfelt enthusiasm from his people. In that sense, Stalin did not simply want obedience; he wanted the full commitment of his people.

# 3 Stalin's power over party and state

Stalin dominated both party and state. The relationship between the Party and the state in the Soviet Union was complicated and changed over time. Crucially, Stalin used the changing relationship between the two organisations to his advantage.

### Note it down

Between 1928 and 1953 Stalin established his dominance of the Party and the Soviet state. Using a large piece of paper draw a timeline beginning in January 1928 and ending in March 1953. Add the different strategies that Stalin used during these years to the timeline. In each case, make a note of the methods that Stalin used and his goals. Also, make sure you add events to the timeline, such as the Great Terror and the Second World War.

## The party and state's relationship

Stalin inherited the Communist Party and the Soviet state from Lenin. Lenin had created both, but had failed to define the relationship between the two organisations. In 1917, Lenin established a state based on the soviets. However, as non-Communist political parties were outlawed, the Communist Party, rather than the state, became the most powerful organisation in the Soviet Union.

However, the exact relationship between the Party and the state was never defined. Moreover, the relationship changed in the period 1928 to 1953. Stalin used the vagueness of the relationship between the Party and the state to his advantage throughout the 1940s and the early 1950s.

## The Second World War

The Second World War began in western Europe in 1939 between nations including Germany, Britain and France. Initially, the Soviet Union was neutral, but supplied materials to the Nazis. However, Hitler invaded the Soviet Union in 1941. Subsequently, the Soviet Union allied with Britain and the USA forming the Grand Alliance against Nazi Germany and Fascist Italy. The war in Europe ended with an Allied victory in May 1945.

The Second World War led to a change in the relationship between party and state, a change that emphasised Stalin's power. From 1928, Stalin had been the most powerful man in the Communist Party. However, it was only in 1941 that Stalin became Chair of *Sovnarkom* – the most senior committee in the state.

This change reflected the need for an efficient government during wartime. Stalin's government in the 1930s had been grossly inefficient. Indeed, by purging the senior levels of the state, the Party and the military he had sabotaged the effectiveness of all aspects of the government. Nonetheless, the government needed to run effectively in order to win the war. Therefore from 1941 Stalin took the leading position in the state, as well as the Party, in order to ensure better co-ordination of government. In addition to becoming Chair of the Council of Ministers, Stalin promoted effective government during the war in the following ways:

- He ended mass terror. During the Great Terror thousands of effective administrators had been purged. During the war, Stalin allowed state and Party officials to continue working in order to ensure that government could run more smoothly. Stalin believed that administrators should be allowed to work without the threat of violence during the war, as they could always be shot once the war was won.
- He allowed state power to grow. During the war there was a shift in power within the government from the Party to the state. State Ministers, rather than Party bosses, made important decisions.
- He changed the composition of the Politburo. As the power of the state grew, Ministers joined the Politburo, and members of the Politburo were given important ministerial jobs. This meant that the Politburo increasingly co-ordinated state activity as well as Party activity.
- He created the State Defence Committee (GKO). The GKO was responsible for economic co-ordination and military production and defence during the war.

### Titles in the Soviet Union

Between 1928 and 1966 there were regular changes in the titles of senior posts in government. Under Lenin senior government officials were known as Commissars. However, Stalin changed this to Ministers. Similarly, under Lenin the most senior committee in government was called *Sovnarkom* (the Council of People's Commissars). Under Stalin this became the Council of Ministers and later the Presidium. Brezhnev, Soviet leader from around 1964 to 1982, reverted to the names used in the 1920s.

## The Soviet Constitution of 1936

The Soviet Constitution of 1936, sometimes called the 'Stalin Constitution', set out the structure of the Soviet Government and the rights of citizens (see Figure 2). Western socialists who studied the constitution described it as the most democratic in the world. Indeed, the government was based on the election of local soviets, which elected higher bodies such as the Supreme Soviets, which, in turn, elected the Council of Ministers. In addition, the constitution guaranteed rights to freedom of speech, freedom of movement and freedom of religion.

In reality, the constitution had little to do with the government of the Soviet Union. The soviets, the Supreme Soviet and the Council of Ministers were dominated by the Communist Party. The Party held power, rather than the constitutional bodies. Additionally, there was no rule of law in the Soviet Union. Therefore legal rights were meaningless, as the government did not have to obey the law.

In the 1980s, Gorbachev, the last leader of the Soviet Union, tried to revive the power of the soviets and other aspects of the constitution (see pages 157–164). However, between 1936 and 1988 they were largely irrelevant.

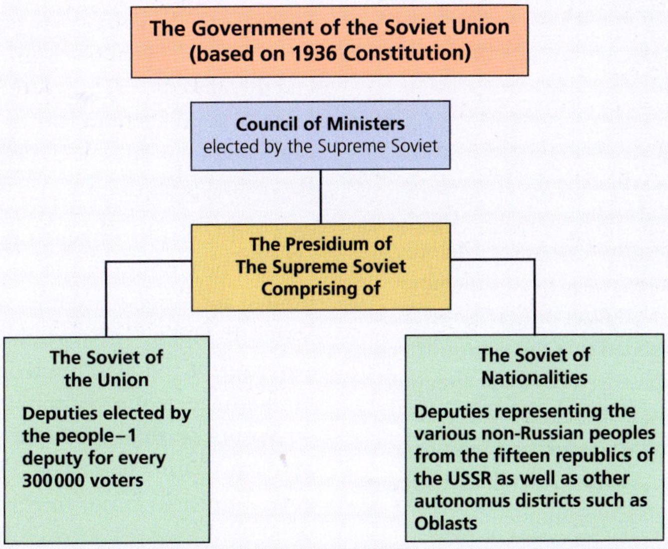


▲ Figure 2: The Government of the Soviet Union (based on the 1936 Constitution).

## Competition between party and state

Following the war Stalin used the party–state relationship to his advantage by encouraging competition between the two organisations. First, he did this by appointing rival personnel to key positions in the Party and state. For example, he placed Andrei Zhdanov, Beria's key rival, in charge of Party supervision of Beria's political police. Encouraging competition between Party and state officials meant that senior officials in the Soviet Government competed with each other and not with Stalin.

Secondly, Stalin shifted power from the Party to the state and back again. In 1938 the Politburo was the most senior committee in government. By 1942, the GKO was the most powerful committee, and after the war the Council of Ministers became more powerful. By shifting the centre of power within the government, Stalin was able to ensure that none of these senior committees grew to rival him.

## Post-war terror

A final way in which Stalin held on to power was the continued use of terror. Stalin did not use terror to the same extent after the war as he had in the 1930s. Nonetheless, by purging hundreds of Party and state officials in his last years he inspired fear in thousands more.

## The Leningrad Affair, 1949

During 1949 Stalin launched a purge against the Leningrad Party. Stalin was concerned that Leningrad, Russia's second city, was developing a degree of independence from his powerbase in Moscow. Around 100 officials were shot and around 2000 arrested and dismissed.

Significantly, the Leningrad Affair may also have been part of the struggle to replace Stalin that emerged in the late 1940s. In 1948, Stalin celebrated his 70th birthday. Clearly, his life was coming to an end. Two of the main rivals for his position were Beria and Zhdanov. Beria's powerbase was in the MVD (the Soviet political police – see page 30), whereas Zhdanov was the chief of the Leningrad Party. The Leningrad Affair followed Zhdanov's death in 1949, and one explanation was that Beria encouraged Stalin to purge Leningrad because it contained a group of senior officials who had been his rivals.

## Testing loyalty

A final technique that Stalin used was to test the loyalty of his closest allies. One way in which he did this was to imprison or sack the wives and daughters of senior figures in government. One example concerns Vyacheslav Molotov, one of Stalin's closest allies. Molotov had been a member of the Politburo since 1926 and Minister of Foreign Affairs since 1939. In 1948 Stalin demanded that the Politburo vote to expel Molotov's wife from the Party. Molotov abstained from the vote and later apologised to Stalin for this disloyalty. In 1949, Stalin had Molotov's wife arrested and imprisoned. Having learned from his previous mistake, Molotov made no effort to stop the arrest or end the imprisonment.

### Vyacheslav Molotov, 1890–1986

Molotov was born into a relatively poor family in 1890. He was a committed Bolshevik, dedicated to overthrowing the Tsar and liberating the working class. In the 1920s he became close to Stalin. He supported Stalin's key policies in the late 1920s and early 1930s. He was incredibly hard working. Winston Churchill, who met Molotov during the Second World War, claimed he had 'never seen a human being who more perfectly represented the modern conception of a *robot*'.

## Conclusion

The struggle for power and the Great Terror transformed the Soviet Government. Under Lenin various politicians, and the Communist Party itself, had an authority that was independent of Lenin. Moreover, Lenin established the convention that political terror should never be used against Communist Party members. Therefore under Lenin and for much of the 1920s there was room for debate and discussion within the Communist Party.

By 1938 this had changed. During the 1920s Stalin established a single ideological orthodoxy and a party which rewarded loyalty rather than free discussion. The 1920s also saw the authority of Lenin's closest allies destroyed. By 1928 Stalin and his allies were in control of the Party. The Great Terror took this process further. Many of Stalin's allies were purged; he believed that people were more likely to obey him out of fear than loyalty and therefore he even attacked his supporters. Moreover, Stalin was prepared to rule through terror, and therefore organised opposition and widespread public debate in the Party disappeared.

As a result, Stalin, rather than the Communist Party, ruled. The Communist Party and the state had very limited authority. Certainly, they could not oppose Stalin. In Stalin's last years, he fostered competition in government and used limited political terror to ensure that his dominance of party and state continued. Therefore on Stalin's death in 1953, the Soviet Union faced a new problem. Stalin's heirs would have to revive the Party and state in order to create an effective Soviet government.

### Work together

Having read this chapter, write a list of the ways in which Stalin transformed Soviet politics. Make sure the list has at least four statements. Each statement should include:

- a specific aspect of government that changed
- the reason it changed
- the impact of the change.

For example, you could write: 'Stalin centralised the Party to ensure his dominance and this increased his control of the Party.'

Having completed the list swap lists with a partner. Compare the lists and ensure that you note down any statements that you missed.

Discuss which of the changes was the most significant, and then write a sentence together explaining which change was most significant and why.

## Chapter summary

Between 1928 and 1953 Stalin's control of the government went through a series of phases:

- Phase 1: 1928–34: Stalin dominated the government, but key rivals remained in the Party.
- Phase 2: 1934–38: Stalin's Great Terror removed his rivals, consolidating his dominance of party and state.
- Phase 3: 1938–53: Stalin used the relationship between the Party and the state to his advantage, in order to stop new rivals emerging.

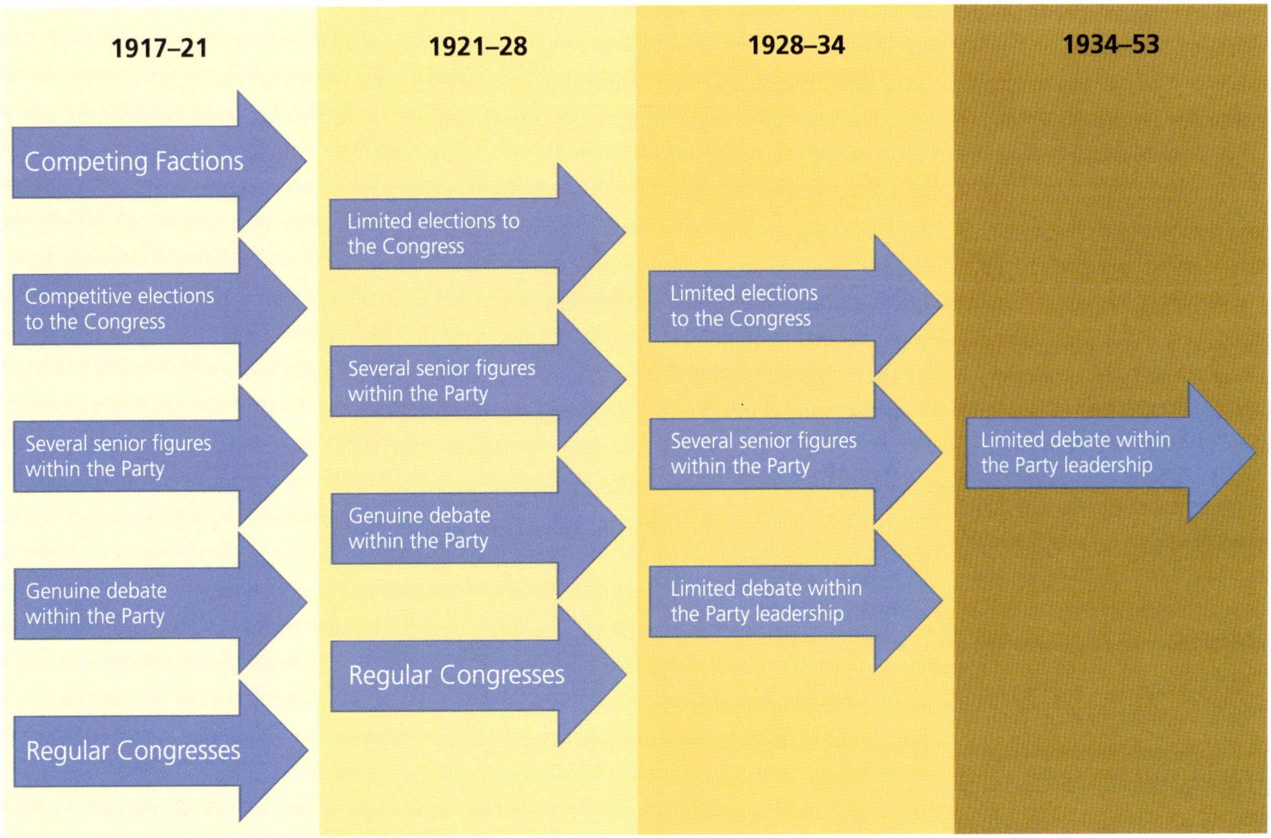


▲ **Summary diagram: Creating a monolithic party – changes to the Communist Party 1917–53.**

## Recommended reading

A. Brown, *The Rise and Fall of Communism* (Random House, 2010), pages 71–72. Brown considers the extent to which Stalin established a personal dictatorship.

P. Kenez, *A History of the Soviet Union from the Beginning to the End* (Cambridge, 2006), pages 75–79. Kenez discusses the events of the power struggle.

R. Sakwa, *Soviet Politics in Perspective* (Routledge, 1998), pages 45–48. Sakwa provides an overview of the key features and important dynamics of the Stalin era.

# Essay technique: Focus and structure

All of your examined essays will be judged on how far they focus on the question and on the quality of their structure; the better your focus and the clearer your structure, the better your chance of exam success.

## Focus of the question

First, you must identify the focus of the question. Imagine you are answering the following question:

**How far do the policy changes of 1921 explain Stalin's increasing domination of the Communist Party in the period 1928–53?**

The question has two parts:

- the policy changes of 1921
- Stalin's increasing domination of the Communist Party in the period 1928–53.

Essentially, the question asks you to explain Stalin's increasing domination of the Communist Party; therefore that is the primary focus of the question. However, you must evaluate the role played by the policy changes of 1921; this is the secondary focus of your essay.

## Structuring your essay

Your essay should be made up of three or four paragraphs, each addressing a different factor which helps to explain Stalin's increasing domination of the Communist Party. One of these paragraphs has to explain the factor stated in the question: the policy changes of 1921. Therefore your essay plan should look something like this:

- Paragraph 1: (Stated factor) The policy changes of 1921
- Paragraph 2: Stalin's personality
- Paragraph 3: Communist ideology
- Paragraph 4: Stalin's successes

It is a good idea to deal with the stated factor first, otherwise you may run out of time and then miss the opportunity to deal with this important part of the question. Once you have dealt with the stated factor, deal with the other factors in order of their importance. Write about the most important factor first.

In addition to your three or four main points, you should begin your essay with a clear introduction and end with a conclusion (see page 68–69) that contains a focused summary of your essay.

The example above is a causation question, which asks you to consider how far a stated factor caused a specific process. Significantly, not all questions deal with cause, and not all questions have an obvious stated factor. Nonetheless, you will need to consider a range of themes in any essay you write. Therefore you should always begin by thinking of the three or four main topics you want to discuss, and these should be the basis of your essay.

## Writing a focused introduction

Having made your plan, it is important you write a focused essay. One way of doing this is to use the wording of the question to help write your answer. For example, the first sentence of your essay could look like this

This sentence begins with a clear focus on the question by addressing 'how far' the policy changes of 1921 explain Stalin's increasing domination of the Communist Party. In this sense, the first sentence provides a focused answer to the whole question.

Clear focus.

> The policy changes of 1921 clearly explain Stalin's increasing domination of the Communist Party in the period 1928–53 to a small extent.

Answers 'How far'.

## Focus throughout the essay

A second way of maintaining focus is to begin each paragraph with a clear point, which both refers to the primary focus of the question and links it to a factor.

For example, you could begin your third paragraph with the following point:

Introduces a new factor.

> Communist ideology was another reason for Stalin's increasing domination of the Communist Party.

Maintains focus on the question.

This sentence clearly introduces a new factor: communist ideology, while maintaining focus on the question.

## Summary

- Work out the primary and secondary focus of the question.
- Plan your essay with a series of factors that focus on the question.
- Use the words in the question to formulate your answer.
- Return to the primary focus of the question at the beginning of every paragraph.

### Activity: Question practice

Having read the advice on how to write a structured and focused essay, using your notes, plan and write the first sentence of the following questions:

1 How far was Stalinism a continuation of Leninism? AS

2 Were Stalin's purges of the 1930s the main reason for his power in the USSR in the years 1928–53? Explain your answer.

# 1c: Reform, stability and stagnation, 1953–85

## Overview

From 1953 to 1985 Khrushchev, and then Brezhnev attempted to deal with the legacy of Lenin and Stalin. Lenin had created a revolutionary government dedicated to transforming Russia. Stalin had turned the Soviet Union into a superpower.

Both of these legacies posed problems. Russia's new leaders struggled to keep Lenin's revolution alive, while also attempting to create a stable and successful government. Equally, Stalin's superpower was in fact a weak state. Stalin's dominance meant that the government itself had little power independent of Stalin.

Khrushchev attempted to reform the system. He wanted to build on what he viewed as the positive aspects of Lenin and Stalin's system, while ending the use of terror and improving the lives of Soviet citizens. Moreover, he wanted to keep the revolutionary vision alive. However, reform destabilised communist rule – threatening to end the Party's hold on power. Khrushchev was continually caught between the desire to reform and the need to ensure the Party's power. Khrushchev's personality was also problematic. He was often overconfident, he was prepared to take big risks, and his impulsive leadership style caused a series of crises during his time in power. Khrushchev's attempts to reform and his rashness led to his fall from power in 1964. Senior Communists replaced Khrushchev with new leaders who were more cautious and wanted stability rather than reform.

Brezhnev's great success was the establishment of a stable government. However, Brezhnev's government abandoned Lenin's goal of revolutionary transformation in favour of maintaining the status quo. This created problems of its own as an increasingly old, ill and corrupt government attempted to run a struggling superpower. His immediate successors Yuri Andropov and Konstantin Chernenko were unwilling and unable to deal with the problems that Brezhnev left behind.

This chapter considers:

1 Khrushchev's reforms and de-Stalinisation
2 Brezhnev and stability, 1964–82
3 Political stagnation, 1970–85.

## 1 Khrushchev's reforms and de-Stalinisation

From 1955 to 1964 Soviet leaders tried to reform the government. The reforms were radical, but did not alter the fundamental politics or economics of the Soviet Union. Specifically, while Soviet leaders recognised there were problems with the system, they accepted the foundations of a single-party state and central economic planning laid by Lenin and Stalin. Within this framework, Khrushchev wanted to regenerate the Soviet Union. He believed in the revolutionary goals of Lenin and wanted to create a society of plenty, in which there was no poverty and no inequality. Moreover, he believed that mass commitment to the revolution was central to the future of Communism. Therefore he wanted to encourage greater public participation in politics and greater dynamism within the Party. He also wanted to create a humane form of socialism in which people were free from the threat of arbitrary terror. In this sense he rejected Stalin's belief that terror was central to revolutionary transformation.

While Khrushchev had clear aims, he lacked a coherent plan. He was naturally impulsive and therefore had a habit of announcing bold plans without thinking them through and making unrealistic promises. Consequently, he often announced major changes and then backtracked. Khrushchev's repeated retreats also reflected the fact that his authority was never as complete as that of Lenin or Stalin. Other Soviet leaders were willing to challenge his authority and force him, on occasion, to back down.

His impulsiveness, inconsistency and his relative weakness within government were all factors that contributed to his fall in 1964.

### Note it down

Using the 1:2 method, make notes on the stages by which reforms were introduced in the years from 1953 to 1964. You can use different coloured pens to distinguish the goals of reform, the methods used and the outcomes of reform.

## Leadership struggle

Stalin's death led to a struggle for power. The power struggle from 1953 to 1955 was the context in which the first reforms and the first steps to de-Stalinisation took place.

Stalin dominated the Soviet Government. His authority was unique. Although he had many positions in the Party and government, his power was based on his reputation and his willingness to use terror. In that sense, his power was personal; it was not based on his positions either in the Party or in the government. Although new people filled his positions in the Party and the government, none of them could claim to be the undisputed leader of the Soviet Union. Unlike Lenin, Stalin left no 'Testament': no indication of who he wanted to replace him as leader.

### Contenders for power

Immediately following Stalin's death there were three main contenders for power, each with their own powerbase.

- Georgy Malenkov was rumoured to be Stalin's choice for successor. Following Stalin's death Malenkov replaced Stalin as Premier of the Soviet Union, the head of the Soviet Government. Malenkov's powerbase was the Soviet state, which he assumed was superior to the Communist Party.
- Lavrentiy Beria (see page 86) was the head of Stalin's political police. He was responsible for implementing Stalin's terror and was deputy Premier in Stalin's last years. His powerbase was the MVD: the Soviet political police.
- Nikita Khrushchev became Secretary of the Central Committee on Stalin's death. He had no state role. The Party was his powerbase; he was a popular member of the Politburo with a reputation for being the 'apparatchik's apparatchik'.

## Early government reforms

Stalin's heirs were faced with a series of problems, which prompted discussion of reform. Stalin had successfully turned the Soviet Union into a military and industrial superpower. However, he left a major political problem: Stalin's power was personal; it was independent of the

### Nikita Khrushchev, 1894–1971

Khrushchev was born in the Ukraine in 1894. He worked as a miner in the Ukraine, joining the Bolsheviks in 1918, and served as a Political Commissar in the Red Army during the Russian Civil War. In the early 1920s there is evidence that he supported Trotsky in debates over economic policy. Nonetheless, in the early 1930s he developed a good relationship with Stalin. He was elected to the Central Committee in 1934 and became the leader of the Communist Party in the Ukraine in 1935. In the mid-1930s he publicly supported the terror.

He had little formal education, but had great faith in the communist system. In fact, he believed that his rise from poverty to the leadership of a global superpower was evidence of the superiority of the Soviet system. His poor background made him popular with ordinary Russians. While working for Stalin he came to believe that reform was essential to ensure a good standard of living and freedom from terror. He remained committed to Soviet socialism, believing it to be a superior system to capitalism and democracy until his death in 1971.

### Georgy Malenkov, 1902–1988

Born in 1902 into a relatively wealthy farming family, Malenkov joined the Bolsheviks during the Russian Civil War. He served in the Red Army and became an ally of Stalin in the 1920s. He played an important role in the fall of Yezhov in 1938 (see page 85) and was promoted to the Politburo in 1941.

After Stalin's death he and Khrushchev were the leading contenders to succeed Stalin. Malenkov was eclipsed by Khrushchev by the end of 1955. He was expelled from the Party and forced into internal exile for his role in the Great Terror in 1961.

Party or the state. Therefore on his death there was a **power vacuum**, which threatened to cause chaos within the government. Malenkov and Khrushchev attempted to address this by shifting the balance of power away from the leader, and in so doing ensuring that the state and the Party had independent power.

### Beria's reforms: the MVD

One way in which the new generation of leaders attempted to empower the Party and state was to reduce and restrict the power of the MVD, Stalin's weapon against the power of the Party and the state.

Initially, Beria led the reform of the MVD. This was partly to calm the fears of his rivals who assumed that he would use the MVD against them, as Stalin had used the MVD against his rivals.

Beria informed the Presidium that the Gulag system had become inefficient and difficult to manage. Indeed, from the late 1940s there were an increasing number of uprisings in the Gulag, including the camps at Steplag, Kolyma and Ozerlag. Beria reformed the system in the following ways:

- In March 1953 he introduced an amnesty for non-political prisoners who were serving short sentences.
- The amnesty was extended in April to some '**counter-revolutionaries**'.
- A Party commission was set up in May to investigate past executions. The Commission **rehabilitated** 4620 communists who had been executed on the basis of **forced confessions**.
- Finally, the MVD lost a great deal of its economic power. The MVD had used Gulag labour to construct factories and power stations, as well as to mine precious metals including gold. These projects were terminated. Prison labour was no longer used in this way and responsibility for mining and construction was passed from the MVD to Soviet economic ministries.

As a result of the reforms introduced by Beria the Gulag population dropped from 2.4 million in 1953 to 1.6 million in 1956. Together these measures significantly undermined the power and authority of the MVD.

### Beria's reforms: the republics

Under Stalin the republics had been dominated by central Soviet institutions. In June 1953 Beria introduced two measures that were designed to make republican governments more representative:

- He introduced a measure that required all senior Party officials to speak the language of the republic that they worked in.
- He ordered that all official publications should be available in the languages of the republics as well as in Russian.

### Beria's fall

Beria's reforms had significantly weakened the MVD. However, his rivals still feared that he would use the secret police to terrorise and eventually execute them. Therefore Khrushchev and Malenkov organised a plot to arrest and execute Beria. At a meeting of the Presidium in June 1953, Khrushchev accused Beria of handing Soviet secrets to the British government and of crimes against the Soviet people.

Beria was arrested, tried and executed. At his trial Malenkov accused Beria of using the MVD against the Party. In this sense the trial and execution of Beria was another way of restricting the power of the MVD and restoring the power of the Party.

Beria's arrest removed one of the main contenders for power. From mid-1953 to the end of 1954 Khrushchev and Malenkov effectively ruled as a duumvirate.

## Khrushchev's early government reforms

Although Khrushchev and Malenkov worked together after Beria's arrest, they were still engaged in a competition for power. Therefore Khrushchev's reforms were designed to achieve two related goals: he wanted to enhance his own power and also the power of the Party at the expense of Malenkov and the state.

### Personnel changes

One of Khrushchev's first attempts at reform involved replacing Stalin's supporters with his own. Khrushchev used his position as Secretary of the Central Committee to replace senior officials throughout the Party. Between 1953 and 1956 Khrushchev replaced around half of the regional Party secretaries and 44 per cent of the Central Committee.

In so doing, he secured his position within the Party by filling the top levels of the Party with people who were loyal to him and people who were prepared to back reform.

### Khrushchev's anti-bureaucracy campaign

Having secured his position within the Party, Khrushchev's second initiative was designed to weaken the state.

Khrushchev proposed cutting bureaucracy by devolving power from the Soviet Government to republican governments. This was a direct attack on Malenkov's powerbase.

In mid-1954 Khrushchev restructured government, cutting the number of central Soviet ministries from 55 to 25. The amount of economic power exercised by the republics increased. The reforms meant that the proportion of Soviet industry controlled by central government dropped from 68 per cent to just 44 per cent.

Khrushchev's reforms, and the apparent success of his agricultural Virgin Lands Scheme (see page 61), meant that Malenkov lost the Premiership in February 1955. Nikolai Bulganin, the new Premier, was one of Khrushchev's key allies.

## De-Stalinisation

Khrushchev and Malenkov were united in the desire to end important aspects of Stalin's rule. Both men wanted to 'humanise' Communism. They wanted to end Stalin's use of terror and enhance the lives of Soviet citizens by improving their standard of living, ending widespread terror and enriching Soviet culture with new novels, plays and other art forms.

Equally, both men were Leninists. Therefore they rejected the 'cult of personality' that had grown up around Stalin. Both men wanted to shift the focus from Stalin as a heroic leader to the achievements of the Communist Party and the Soviet people.

The process of ending the 'cult of personality' and the widespread use of terror started immediately after Stalin's death. The first steps towards ending the cult of Stalin were small. Plans to turn Stalin's **dacha** into a museum celebrating his life were scrapped. Additionally, the annual Stalin prizes were cancelled and, for the first time since the 1930s, there were no official celebrations of Stalin's birthday. Newspapers, which had traditionally been full of quotes from Stalin's works, started quoting from Marx and Lenin.

### The cult of Stalin – cult of personality

The cult of Stalin refers to the use of art, photography, books, newspaper articles and speeches to stress Stalin's genius. According to the culture of the 1930s, Stalin was responsible for every major Soviet victory since Lenin's death. The cult of Stalin was an attempt to win the loyalty of the Soviet people. It was also one of Stalin's methods for ensuring his authority was independent of the Party and state.

The cult of personality was a different concept. Khrushchev used the phrase to criticise Stalin's style of government: the abandonment of collective leadership and the introduction of personal rule.

### The Secret Speech

The first wave of de-Stalinisation focused on ending the cult of Stalin. Khrushchev wanted to go further and formally criticise Stalin. However, criticising Stalin was a huge risk. Stalin was widely respected as a founder of the Soviet system – criticising Stalin risked undermining the authority of the Soviet Union and Communism. It also risked outraging the Party, since many senior Communists still respected Stalin. Equally, many feared that criticisms of Stalin would reflect badly on them as they had helped implement Stalin's policies.

Khrushchev negotiated with the Presidium to present his criticisms of Stalin at a secret session of the Twentieth Party Congress of 1956 – the first Congress since Stalin's death.

The Congress started on 14 February. On the night of 25 February, a day after the Congress officially finished, delegates were summoned to an unscheduled late night meeting. Khrushchev spoke for four hours, setting out a profound **critique** of Stalin's rule.

Khrushchev focused on the cult of personality. He argued that Stalin had abandoned collective leadership and set himself up as dictator. In so doing, Khrushchev argued, Stalin had placed himself above the Party and robbed the Party of its leading role. Without the wisdom of the Party, Stalin made serious mistakes, such as purging the Red Army immediately prior to the Second World War (see page 19). Moreover, he claimed that Stalin committed enormous crimes, particularly during the terror when he ordered the deaths of hundreds of thousands of innocent people. Khrushchev revealed the scale of the terror, which Stalin had concealed from the Party, and quoted the criticism of Stalin in Lenin's Testament, which had also been kept secret.

Significantly, Khrushchev did not criticise Stalin's policy of industrialisation or collectivisation (see page 17), or any aspect of communist ideology. Indeed, Khrushchev consistently argued that the foundations of the Soviet system were sound.

Stalin was widely loved and respected in the Party and therefore many of the delegates were profoundly shocked. Some accounts indicate that some delegates were so horrified that they suffered heart attacks during Khrushchev's speech. Others apparently took their own lives after learning the true scale of Stalin's crimes.

The speech was kept secret. However, printed copies were sent to senior Communists across the Soviet Union and Eastern Europe. One of these was leaked to the West, and with the help of the **CIA** it was printed in the *New York*

*Times*. Nonetheless, while the content of the Secret Speech became well known in the West, it was not fully published in the Soviet Union until 1989.

### Ending terror

Another important aspect of de-Stalinisation was further steps to deal with the legacy of the terror.

In May 1954 Khrushchev and Malenkov set up a special commission to review the cases of political prisoners who had been sent to the Gulags. In the first year, progress was slow and only 4620 of the 113,739 political prisoners were released.

However, following the Secret Speech the process escalated. In June 1956, 51,439 prisoners, including 26,155 political prisoners, were released. The cases of political prisoners who had been executed were also reviewed. By 1961 half of those who had been executed by Stalin had been rehabilitated.

## The problems of de-Stalinisation

Khrushchev's criticisms of Stalin caused a series of problems. Communist Parties in Hungary and Poland began their own process of de-Stalinisation. In Hungary students and artists seized the opportunity, initiated a revolution and elected a new prime minister. After the new government ended its military alliance with the Soviet Union, Khrushchev ordered Soviet troops to crush the revolution.

There was also unrest in the Soviet Union. Leaked information about Stalin's crimes was shocking and caused some to question the legitimacy of communist rule. Indeed, there were student demonstrations in favour of multi-party democracy at Moscow State University in 1957. Again, they were supressed by the communist authorities.

### Khrushchev's retreat

Stalinists in the Party argued that de-Stalinisation had destabilised the government. Some moderates also accused Khrushchev of reforming too fast.

Khrushchev responded by backtracking, agreeing with his critics that the Soviet people were 'not ready' to know the truth about Stalin. In June the Central Committee issued a statement to the Party revising Khrushchev's speech. In October the editors of the Soviet magazine *Questions of History* were disciplined for publishing revelations about Stalin's terror. In mid-December Khrushchev secretly authorised the establishment of a Special Commission, headed by Leonid Brezhnev, to supress anti-communist activities. Finally, Khrushchev's New Year's Eve speech acknowledged that all communists were 'Stalinists'.

Clearly, by the end of 1957 radical de-Stalinisation had come to a halt.

## Democratisation and decentralisation

Khrushchev continued with political reform in 1957 introducing measures to reduce the size and power of the central party.

Democratisation was designed to increase the participation of workers in the government. It did not, however, involve new elections. Rather, Khrushchev introduced two measures:

- He allowed an expansion of Party membership. Membership grew from 6.9 million in 1954 to 11 million in 1964. This made it more democratic as a greater proportion of its members, 60 per cent by 1964, were workers of peasants.
- He introduced fixed terms for senior Communists to ensure that they were replaced regularly. As a result, two-thirds of regional Secretaries and the Presidium were replaced between 1957 and 1961.

In order to decentralise the Party he abolished some of the central ministries that oversaw the economy and devolved power to 105 newly created economic councils (see page 64). He moved the Ministry of Agriculture away from Moscow to make it 'closer to the fields'.

Khrushchev's reforms meant that many Communist officials were demoted, lost their jobs, or were forced to move away from Moscow. Consequently, there was renewed criticism of Khrushchev within the Party.

## The Anti-Party Group

Discontent over Khrushchev's reforms and the problems created by de-Stalinisation led to an attempt to overthrow Khrushchev. In June 1957 a majority of the Presidium, led by Malenkov, voted to replace Khrushchev.

Khrushchev argued that the decision to replace him could only be taken by the Central Committee – where Khrushchev had a majority of support. As a result, Khrushchev survived the attempt to oust him and sacked his opponents. Khrushchev consolidated his position in March 1958 by taking over the position of Prime Minister in addition to his existing offices.

The attempted coup of 1957 was significant for the evolution of Soviet government for two main reasons:

- It demonstrated that senior Communists would no longer use political terror against each other.
- It recognised that the power of the Party leader depended on the support of the Central Committee.

## Khrushchev's final reforms

The Twenty-Second Party Congress of October 1961 introduced Khrushchev's final major political reforms.

The main focus of the Congress was economic. However, Khrushchev also used the Congress to restart the process of de-Stalinisation. He accused Stalin of being involved in Kirov's murder (see page 20). Additionally, the Congress voted to remove Stalin's body from public display.

Khrushchev also introduced a radical Party reform. He built on his earlier democratisation measures by introducing fixed terms for all jobs within the Party, including a fixed 16-year term for Central Committee members.

Khrushchev's 1962 Party reforms effectively split the Party in two. According to the new structure, one half of the Party was put in charge of agriculture and the other of industry. This new division went right to the top of the Party: the Central Committee was divided into industrial and agricultural bureaus. Khrushchev hoped that this reform would boost economic growth.

## Khrushchev's fall

Khrushchev's political reforms created discontent in the Party, and his economic reforms failed to boost economic growth (see page 64). From the late 1950s, the economy slowed. Consequently, there was no possibility of fulfilling Khrushchev's rash promises. Finally, there were concerns that Khrushchev's foreign policy was rash and dangerous. As a result, in June 1964 senior figures in the Presidium began plotting Khrushchev's overthrow. In October Khrushchev was summoned to a special meeting. He was criticised for mishandling the economy, foreign policy and creating his own cult of personality. On this occasion the plotters had the backing of the majority of the Central Committee. Consequently, Khrushchev retired, and the Soviet media put out the story that he had stepped down due to ill health. Khrushchev was given a pension and lived under guard for the remaining seven years of his life.

### Khrushchev's foreign policy

Khrushchev was leader of the Soviet Union during a crucial phase in the Cold War. Many of his decisions and policies were designed to try to win an advantage over the USA. One of the key areas of conflict during the Cold War was Germany, which was divided between the communist East and capitalist West. Khrushchev gave President Kennedy an ultimatum to withdraw his forces from West Berlin and give control of the whole city to the communists. Kennedy refused and forced Khrushchev to back down – humiliating the Soviet Union. Khrushchev also sent nuclear weapons to Cuba, around 100 miles from the USA. This created an international crisis that almost ended in nuclear war. Again, Khrushchev was forced to back down. The repeated policy failures leading to the Soviet Union's humiliation were crucial to Khrushchev's fall because senior Communists wanted a foreign policy that emphasised Soviet strength.

## The extent of de-Stalinisation

Khrushchev's biggest political achievement was ending the use of political terror against party officials. Khrushchev's enemies were sacked, but not tortured or killed. Similarly, Khrushchev himself was allowed to retire, with a pension, a car and various luxuries, rather than being shot or publicly humiliated. In this sense he achieved a significant degree of de-Stalinisation.

He also ended Stalin's system of personal rule. Under Khrushchev the Party gained a new authority. Unlike Stalin, Khrushchev was forced to work with other senior figures in the Party. The Secret Speech, for example, had to gain the approval of the Presidium, and the Central Committee forced Khrushchev to accept revisions to the Speech several months after it was given. Unlike Stalin, Khrushchev's power depended on retaining a majority of support on the Central Committee. Indeed, Khrushchev's overthrow in 1964 demonstrated the extent to which the Party's power was independent of the leader by 1964.

However, some aspects of Stalinism lived on. The government never publicly rejected his legacy or admitted the extent of Stalin's crimes. Therefore, under Brezhnev, the government was able to revive the cult of Stalin. The adoration of Stalin was never as widespread as it had been between 1930 and 1953, but Brezhnev authorised articles celebrating Stalin on important anniversaries between 1964 and 1982.

Clearly, Khrushchev was able to achieve a significant degree of de-Stalinisation in the sense that political terror was never used on a mass scale again. However, de-Stalinisation was never completed as he refused to publicly denounce the former leader and therefore left his reputation intact.

## 2 Brezhnev and stability, 1964–82

Khrushchev's government was associated with 'reform'. Leonid Brezhnev's government, by contrast, focused on 'stability' and 'restoration'. Brezhnev's first acts were to reverse Khrushchev's most unpopular Party reforms. He also reversed aspects of de-Stalinisation and ended economic change. Nonetheless, the restoration was not complete. Brezhnev, like Khrushchev, rejected the use of mass terror.

The emphasis on stability created new problems. Brezhnev's policies led to stagnation, and the last years of Brezhnev's rule were characterised by ever growing problems and corruption which Brezhnev failed to address.

Under Brezhnev the revolutionary aspects of Soviet society became less obvious. He believed that the revolutionary transformation of society had been achieved between 1917 and 1930. Therefore the Communist Party merely needed to keep going on the course set out by Lenin and Stalin. In this sense, under Brezhnev the Party became the defenders of the **status quo** rather than a revolutionary force for change.

### Note it down

Using bullet points, or the 1:2 method, make notes on Brezhnev's goals, his methods and the outcomes of his reforms in the period 1964–82. Make sure to note down specific phrases such as 'stability of cadres' with their meanings.

### Restoration

The post-Khrushchev leadership was keen to undo Khrushchev's governmental reforms. During 1964 and 1965, the new leadership was based on an informal pact between Brezhnev and Alexei Kosygin, who together had a great deal of support in the Politburo and Central Committee. The pact was designed to ensure government stability. In general terms, Brezhnev and Kosygin committed themselves as follows:

### Leonid Brezhnev, 1906–81

Brezhnev was born in the Ukraine to a Russian family. From 1923 he worked as a metal worker. He studied at a technical school in 1927 and 1928, joining the Party in 1929. From 1929 to 1937 he had a succession of minor roles in the Party. His big break came during the Great Terror, when he received a series of promotions as his superiors were purged. He was also promoted during the Second World War. By 1950 he was First Secretary of the Communist Party of Moldova, and in 1952 Stalin promoted him to the Politburo. He backed Khrushchev against the Anti-Party Group in 1957, but he was no reformer. His notes from the period show that he was critical of Khrushchev's de-Stalinisation. Following 1962 he became increasingly critical of Khrushchev, and was central to the plot to remove him from mid-1964.

Brezhnev was known for his vanity. He encouraged journalists to praise his genius and regularly awarded himself medals. Indeed, during the 1970s he encouraged the creation of his own cult of personality. Brezhnev, a lifelong smoker, suffered his first heart attack in 1975 and was in poor health for the rest of his life.

### Alexei Kosygin, 1904–1980

Kosygin was born in 1904 into a working-class family. He fought for the Red Army during the Russian Civil War before becoming an industrial manager. He joined the Party around 1930 and gained important economic posts during the Second World War. He played a prominent international role under Khrushchev and continued to play an important role in government after his fall.

Kosygin was an advocate of economic reform in the 1960s (see page 65), but his reforms were short lived. He was eclipsed by Brezhnev in the early 1970s. Kosygin remained a senior member of the government until he resigned due to ill health in 1980.

- They ensured that the two top jobs in government were not occupied by the same person – in order to stop the emergence of an all-powerful leader. Brezhnev led the Party as General Secretary; Kosygin was Premier and therefore had the most important job in the Soviet state.
- They divided key posts in government roughly equally between supporters of Brezhnev and Kosygin.
- They ensured that Party and state officials kept their jobs for long periods to limit the opportunities for patronage.

This pact held from 1964 to 1970 when Kosygin lost his job as Premier and Brezhnev emerged as the most powerful person within the Soviet leadership.

## 'Stability of cadres'

Brezhnev's government was based on the policy of 'stability of **cadres**', or 'trust in cadres'. In essence the policy discouraged promotions or demotions within government. This was part of the Brezhnev–Kosygin pact and ensured that there would be few battles over patronage.

'Stability of cadres' replaced Khrushchev's 1961 policy of limited terms, which had been very unpopular with the Party. In this sense the policy ensured support for the new leaders from government officials because it gave them job security.

## Restoration of the Party

Brezhnev reformed the Party, reversing Khrushchev's key reforms:

- Centralisation: Khrushchev had repeatedly tried to break up central ministries and decentralise government by giving more power to the republics. Brezhnev reversed this, re-establishing the all-union ministries that Khrushchev had abolished.
- Brezhnev ended the split between industrial and agricultural wings of the Party.
- Article 6 of the new 1977 Soviet Constitution, known as the 'Brezhnev Constitution', officially recognised the Party's leading role in Soviet society. In this sense, it established the superiority of the Party over the state.

▲ Leonid Brezhnev at the podium. Why has Brezhnev chosen to be photographed in front of a picture of Lenin rather than any of the other Soviet leaders?

# 3 Political stagnation, 1970–85

Brezhnev's government reforms led to a period of stagnation at the top of government. His policies meant that change in government was slow, or in many cases non-existent.

## Gerontocracy

Brezhnev's 'stability of cadres' policy led to an increasingly static government, in which there was little change:

- Between 1964 and 1971, only two people were promoted to the Politburo.
- Between 1966 and 1971, between 80 and 90 per cent of Central Committee members retained their jobs following Party Congresses.

Consequently, the government aged. Brezhnev's style of government was nicknamed a gerontocracy: rule of old people. During the late 1960s and 1970s the average age of senior officials kept rising (see Tables 3 and 4).

**Table 3: Average age of members of the Politburo.**

| Politburo | |
|---|---|
| **Date** | **Average Age** |
| 1966 | 58 |
| 1972 | 62 |
| 1982 | 75 |

**Table 4: Average age of members of the Central Committee.**

| Central Committee | |
|---|---|
| **Date** | **Average Age** |
| 1961 | 52 |
| 1981 | 62 |

As the government aged it became less effective:

- Brezhnev's critics argued that his style of government created a generation gap between the government and society. In this sense, Brezhnev's government no longer understood the society they governed.
- Senior officials became increasingly ill and therefore unable to perform their jobs.
- 'Stability of cadres' meant that there were extremely limited opportunities for promotion. As a result, middle-ranking officials were effectively stuck in dead-end jobs with no prospect of promotion.
- The system provided no incentives to work hard because there were so few opportunities for promotion.

## Corruption

Under Brezhnev sackings were rare. Opportunities for advancement were also extremely limited. This created the context for huge corruption. Soviet officials, who could not grow rich through hard work and promotion, used their positions to grow rich, knowing they were unlikely to be disciplined.

One form of corruption was to sell goods on the **black market**. For example, Yury Sokolov, the director of a major Moscow food store, took bribes from rich customers for passing on luxury food.

Brezhnev was implicated in the corruption. His daughter Galina Brezhneva was able to get access to diamonds. One of her lovers smuggled millions of pounds worth of diamonds out of the USSR. He was eventually prosecuted after Brezhnev's death.

## Andropov and Chernenko

Between Brezhnev's death in 1982 and Gorbachev's appointment as General Secretary in 1985, Russia was led by Yuri Andropov and Konstantin Chernenko. Both men were old and part of the gerontocracy that had emerged under Brezhnev. Andropov recognised that there were problems with the system, and both men attempted cautious reforms. However, neither was prepared to introduce fundamental reforms.

> **Note it down**
>
> Using bullet points or the 1:2 method, (see page x) make notes on Andropov and Chernenko. Note down the extent to which they wanted reform, the extent to which they changed the Soviet system and the obstacles to their rule.

### Andropov, November 1982–February 1984

Andropov became Soviet leader at the age of 68. He believed that the Soviet system was fundamentally stable but that minor reforms were necessary. Specifically, he believed that the Soviet Union needed to become a more disciplined nation. In order to achieve this he introduced three main reforms:

- He abandoned the 'stability of cadres' policy, replacing a quarter of senior officials.
- He introduced small-scale economic reforms focusing on labour discipline (see pages 66).
- His most important initiative was an anti-corruption campaign. The campaign:
  - attacked senior figures, for example he prosecuted Red Army General and **Minister of the Interior** Nikolai Shchelokov and investigated Galina Brezhneva's lover 'Boris the Gypsy'
  - included media exposés of corrupt officials.

He died just over a year after his appointment as Soviet leader. His biggest achievement was removing old and corrupt officials and allowing a younger generation to rise within the Soviet Government.

## Chernenko, February 1984–March 1985

Chernenko was also unwilling to consider major reform. Indeed, he was 72 years old and already extremely ill at the time he became leader. Poor health meant that he could not play much of a role in the government for much of his 13-month period as leader. Due to Chernenko's ill health Gorbachev routinely led meetings on his behalf. The brevity of his rule and his ill health meant that he achieved very little as Soviet leader.

### Konstantin Chernenko, 1911–1985

Born in 1911 into a working-class family, Chernenko joined *Komsomol* (Communist Youth League) in 1929 and the Party in 1931. He completed military training and later worked for a Party propaganda department. He became friends with Brezhnev in the late 1940s. He gained high office following Khrushchev's fall, and due to his continued friendship with Brezhnev became a senior figure in the Party during the 1970s. He was one of the front-runners to replace Brezhnev on his death in 1982. Despite being extremely ill, he became leader of the Soviet Union in 1984, and was the first Soviet leader to use a stairlift to get to the top of Lenin's tomb.

## Conclusion

The period 1953–85 was dominated by two attempts to create a stable revolutionary government. Khrushchev wanted to maintain revolutionary dynamism by introducing decentralisation, a degree of democratisation and keeping the leadership of the Party constantly changing. This was part of his broader vision to keep the focus of the Communist Party on building socialism, fulfilling the goal that Lenin had set out in 1917. Khrushchev was also determined to end the Stalinist terror and create a humane form of socialism. Khrushchev's style of government led to a series of problems, most obviously instability, which played a part in his downfall.

Brezhnev stressed stability. From 1964 to Brezhnev's death in 1982 revolutionary transformation was largely forgotten. Brezhnev believed that the fundamental transformation had already taken place under Lenin and Stalin and that the Party merely had to administer their legacy. This approach created problems of its own. Reform stopped, the leadership became increasingly old and out of touch, and the revolutionary goals of Lenin were largely forgotten. Brezhnev died in 1982 leaving his successor huge economic and political problems. Andropov and Chernenko continued to govern in a way that reflected Brezhnev's essential style. Both initiated small-scale economic reforms (see pages 65–66), but neither was prepared to address the Soviet Union's fundamental problems or reform the foundations of the regime.

### Work together

Working with a partner, write a list of the problems facing the Soviet Government in 1953. On separate pieces of paper list the solutions to these problems – one of you should list the solutions tried by Khrushchev, the other the solutions tried by Brezhnev.

Check each other's lists. Is it clear which solution relates to which problem? Has your partner missed anything? Add additional items to the list where necessary.

Discuss which approach to the problems of the Soviet Union was more successful. Having done so, you should both write two paragraphs explaining the strengths and weaknesses of the different approaches and evaluating which approach was better.

### Chapter summary

- With the death of Stalin in 1953 the Soviet Union lost a strong leader.
- Stalin's heirs tried to deal with the problems that they had inherited.
- They succeeded in ending the use of political terror against the government.
- Khrushchev's reforms threatened to destabilise the Soviet system.
- Brezhnev's more stable approach to government led to stagnation.
- Between 1982 and 1985 Andropov and Chernenko proved unable to revive the system.

▲ **Summary diagram: Reform, stability and stagnation.**

## Recommended reading

E. Bacon and M.A. Sandle (eds.), *Brezhnev Reconsidered* (Macmillan, 2002), pages 25–32. Bacon and Sandle consider Brezhnev's style as Soviet leader.

G.L. Freeze (ed.), *Russia: a History* (Oxford, 2002), pages 347–53. Freeze provides an overview of the Khruschev years.

R.G. Suny, *The Soviet Experiment*, (Oxford, 1998), pages 449–50. Suny discusses the problems facing Soviet leaders after Stalin's death.

# Essay technique: Deploying detail

So far we have looked at how to structure your answers with a clear line of argument (see page 93–4). This is essential, but you also need to ensure that your paragraphs are sufficiently detailed. Vague or imprecise statements will weaken your essay.

## What is detail?

Essentially, correct dates, proper names and statistics are all examples of detail. You can also increase the level of detail in your essays by using correct technical vocabulary: words or phrases like 'Marxism' or 'Politburo' that you have learned while studying this unit.

## How to use detail

You should use detail to support the points that you are making. The main points provide the overall structure for the essay; the details help prove the points that you are making.

Imagine you are answering the following question:

**How far did the Russian economy improve in the years 1921–64?**

You might want to make the point that heavy industry improved. You could support this by referring to the achievement of the Five-Year Plans. Specifically, you could quote statistics for the production of iron, steel, coal and oil showing how they improved from 1921 to 1964.

### Activity: Adding detail

Here is a plan in answer to the question above:

- Paragraph 1: Agriculture improved from 1921 to 1964.
- Paragraph 2: Industry production increased from 1921 to 1964.
- Paragraph 3: Collectivisation created significant problems for agriculture, 1928–64.
- Paragraph 4: The Five-Year Plans led to significant problems in industry, 1928–64.

Using your notes, find at least three pieces of detail to support each of these points.

Try to use a variety of types of detail. If possible make sure you use statistics, dates, the names of people and organisations and technical vocabulary.

### Activity: Question practice

1 Was political stagnation the main consequence of Brezhnev's rejection of reform? Explain your answer. AS
2 To what extent were Khrushchev's reforms successful in the years 1953–64? AS
3 How far did de-Stalinisation change the nature of Soviet politics in the years 1955–85?
4 How far do you agree that Soviet politics were transformed in the years 1953–85?

Paper 1 Russia, 1917–91: from Lenin to Yeltsin

# Theme 2 Industrial and agricultural change, 1917–85

## The Big Picture

The Soviet economy changed radically from 1917 to 1985. Initially, Soviet leaders faced a fundamental problem: how would a socialist economy work? Socialists had produced extensive criticisms of capitalism, but there were no blueprints or detailed plans for a socialist economy.

Between 1917 and 1921 Lenin improvised, coming up with a series of economic alternatives to traditional capitalism. All of his policies created political and economic problems. Stalin was also forced to improvise in order to solve the problem of a socialist economy. He introduced 'the Great Turn', massive industrial and agricultural change, ending capitalism in agriculture and industry. Stalin's model of state-run farms and state-planned industry was the foundation on which successive Soviet leaders built, at least until 1985. All accepted the essential system that Stalin had created. Nonetheless, Stalin's system was problematic. It was inefficient, wasteful and economic growth did not lead to higher standards of living. Moreover, Stalin's 'Revolution from Above' ruined agriculture. Therefore Soviet farms were never able to provide the food that the nation needed.

However, Stalin's industrial policies did lead to some successes; they helped the Soviet Union fight and win the Second World War. Moreover, his economic methods helped rebuild the Soviet Union after the war.

After Stalin, economic priorities changed. Khrushchev and Brezhnev both accepted the need for a socialist economy to provide a comfortable standard of living for the Soviet people. Khrushchev introduced economic reforms to try to ensure that the Soviet economy outperformed the West and that Soviet citizens enjoyed a higher standard of living than people in capitalist nations. This required a massive expansion of agriculture, including the cultivation of large areas of land known as the Virgin Lands. His vision also required investment in light industry. After initial success Khrushchev's policies failed. Khrushchev's failures discouraged future leaders from initiating significant reforms. As a result, the essential problems of the system remained unsolved. Under Brezhnev economic growth declined. Nonetheless, due to international trade and international loans living standards improved. In this sense the growing crisis was hidden from Soviet citizens and even many in the government.

Ultimately, the Soviet economy was an attempt to do away with the problems of capitalism and produce a fairer and more efficient system. By 1985 it was clear that the Soviet economic experiment had failed.

In this theme you will consider the following:

- Lenin's economic policies including War Communism and the New Economic Policy
- Stalin's economic revolution: the Five-Year Plans in industry and the collectivisation of agriculture
- Economic change 1953–85, reform, modernisation and decline.

## TIMELINE

| | |
|---|---|
| 1917 October | Decree on Land |
| 1918 March to June | Lenin introduces state capitalism |
| 1918 July–December | Lenin introduces War Communism |
| 1921 March | Lenin introduces the New Economic Policy |
| 1923 | The Soviet Economy experiences the 'scissors crisis' |
| 1928 July | Stalin introduces emergency economic measures ending the NEP |
| 1928 October | Stalin introduces the First Five-Year Plan |
| 1929 December | Stalin orders compulsory collectivisation of Soviet farms |
| 1932 | Beginning of the Great Famine |
| 1941 June | German invasion leads to Soviet entry into the Second World War |
| 1945 December | Introduction of the Fourth Five-Year Plan |
| 1953 September | Khrushchev launches the Virgin Lands Scheme |
| 1957 February | Khrushchev launches the *sovnarkhoz* reforms |
| 1958 September | Khrushchev launches the Corn Campaign |
| 1959 January | Khrushchev launches the Seven-Year Plan |
| 1962 February | Khrushchev divides the Party between agriculture and industry |
| 1968 January–August | 'Kosygin reforms' are introduced and scrapped |
| 1982 November | Andropov initiates anti-corruption campaign |

# 2a: Towards a command economy, 1917–28

## Overview

Lenin knew that a political revolution alone would never destroy capitalism. Socialism and Communism entailed profound economic changes, changes that would end the economic exploitation that was essential to capitalism. Additionally, socialism and Communism required the construction of a highly advanced economy.

However, Lenin also had other objectives. In the early stages of his regime he needed to win the Civil War, and after 1921 he needed to rebuild and stabilise the regime. Lenin's economic policies reflected all of these concerns: his desire to destroy capitalism, his need to supply his troops and his need to compromise to retain power. As a result, Lenin's policies changed, as he replaced one policy with another, often in ways that reflected radically different values.

This chapter considers:

1. The nationalisation of industry
2. War Communism
3. New Economic Policy
4. State control of industry and agriculture.

## 1 The nationalisation of industry

Lenin's economic policy in the period 1917–21 went through a series of radically different phases. These reflected the problems that Russia faced, Lenin's hopes about the future and his fundamental beliefs about economics and politics. In short, the **nationalisation** of industry was a revolutionary response to an unprecedented set of problems.

### Note it down

As you read this section make two spider diagrams (see page x) on the same large sheet. The first should deal with the problems facing Lenin in the early months of the revolution. The second should focus on the economic measures that Lenin introduced in the first phase of the revolution. Having completed both, draw links between the two spider diagrams to show how the problems of 1917–18 and Lenin's ideas led to the creation of Lenin's first economic policy.

### Capitalism and Communism

One of the key problems facing Lenin was uncertainty about what a communist economy would entail. Marx had produced a detailed analysis of the strengths and weaknesses of **capitalism**. However, he had been deliberately vague about the nature of a future communist society. He argued that once capitalism was abolished, the economy would be organised according to 'a common plan', but he refused to speculate about the future, arguing that it was impossible to describe the future in detail.

Marx was clear, however, that a communist society would have an extremely advanced economy. Indeed, most communists in the early twentieth century believed that a revolution would take place in Britain, the USA, Germany or France, as these were the most advanced economies in the world at the time.

### Problems facing Russia

Russia had serious economic problems in the early twentieth century. Specifically, compared to Western European nations and the USA, Russia's economy was unsophisticated and backward. Russia had begun to industrialise and between 1890 and 1914 the economy grew significantly. Even so, Russia was still far behind more developed nations in terms of industrialisation. Therefore the majority of Marxists and socialists in Russia at the time of the February Revolution expected the revolution to lead to capitalism, and that a socialist revolution was many years away.

Not only was the Russian economy generally less developed than that of the West in 1917, it was also shattered during the **First World War**. Any new government would need a policy to help reconstruct the economy and promote economic growth.

### Lenin's early ideas

Unlike many Marxists, Lenin believed that **socialism** was possible in Russia in 1917. He argued that as the revolution spread across Europe, advanced countries would send aid to developing countries and therefore the Russian economy would develop rapidly without the need for capitalism.

However, while Lenin was waiting for the revolution to spread, he needed to begin rebuilding the Russian economy to ensure that people had food and that the economy was strong enough to provide the materials necessary to defend the revolution.

Lenin initially argued that the October Revolution had created a society between capitalism and socialism. The revolution, he argued, had destroyed capitalism, but the economy was not strong enough to start building socialism. Lenin called the new phase '**state capitalism**'.

## Lenin's vision of a socialist economy

Lenin believed that a socialist economy would be highly efficient. He believed that it required modern technology, expert management and well-educated and highly disciplined workers. Workers would be free, in the sense that they would no longer be working for capitalists. This would mean that workers were better paid and better treated, and therefore they would no longer resent the work that they did. However, Lenin's vision of socialism had little time for leisure, and Lenin had no sympathy for laziness. Rather, he assumed that after the revolution people would find their work extremely fulfilling and therefore large amounts of leisure time would be unnecessary. Lenin's various economic policies reflected his faith in expertise, his desire for efficiency and discipline, and his disregard for leisure.

## State capitalism

In essence, Lenin's state capitalist economy was based on the nationalisation of industry. Nationalisation ended capitalism by taking industry away from middle-class owners. All nationalised industries were run by the Supreme Soviet of the National Economy, or Vesenkha – a group of economic experts. The Vesenkha was designed to:

- ensure factories were properly managed by placing them under the control of well-paid specialists
- co-ordinate economic production to meet the needs of new society.

Only large industries were nationalised. Small factories and workshops were either controlled by workers or handed back to capitalists.

State capitalism was extremely unpopular. In many ways, there was very little difference between state capitalism and life before the revolution. Therefore many workers and radicals like Bukharin (see page 16) rejected state capitalism in favour of **workers' control**. Nonetheless, Lenin ignored this opposition and state capitalism was the official policy of the new government from March to June 1918, when policy had to change due to the outbreak of civil war.

## Land reform

Nationalisation of industry was only one part of Lenin's initial policy.

In order to win support and stimulate agriculture, Lenin introduced land reform. Following Lenin's 1917 Decree on Land, large estates belonging to the Church or to aristocratic landowners were broken up and peasants were allowed to own the land they worked. Land reform was extremely popular with the peasants.

# 2 War Communism

War Communism was created as a series of emergency economic measures to ensure communist victory in the Civil War. However, at the same time it embodied some aspects of communist ideology and therefore some radicals believed that War Communism was a step towards a truly communist economic policy.

War Communism was designed to ensure:

- high levels of industrial production of war goods
- an efficient allocation of workers
- food production to feed soldiers, workers and the civilian population.

### Note it down

Using a spider diagram, make notes on the key measures that made up War Communism. Make sure you make notes on the specific nature of the measures. Pay particular attention to technical terms and the detail.

## Measures

War Communism evolved over time as Lenin introduced new economic measures.

### 'Food dictatorship'

Lenin introduced a series of measures to ensure food was available to soldiers and workers. Lenin's 'food dictatorship' consisted of the following:

- **Grain requisitioning**: **Cheka** squads were authorised to seize grain and other forms of food from peasants without payment.
- Rationing: The Supply Commissariat rationed the seized foods. The largest rations went to workers and soldiers, the smallest rations were given to members of the **bourgeoisie**.

## Labour discipline

War Communism also entailed intense labour discipline:

- In 1918 the working day was extended to eleven hours.
- In 1919 work was made compulsory for all able-bodied people between 16 and 50 years of age.
- Harsh punishments were given to workers who were late or were caught slacking.

## The abolition of the market

The chaotic conditions of the Civil War led to a breakdown of the existing market. The following measures were introduced to try to abolish the market:

- The abolition of money: In the short term, the government simply printed more money, which led to **hyperinflation**. Money became worthless, workers were paid through their rations and many public services, such as tram services, were provided freely.
- The abolition of trade: Private trade was made illegal.
- Complete nationalisation: All businesses were taken over by the state.
- Conscription: Workers were assigned either to work in factories or fight in the army.

Lenin argued that the abolition of money was also a step away from capitalism towards a socialist economy in which economic production and distribution were centrally planned. Bukharin too argued that the abolition of the capitalist market was a major revolutionary achievement. Both agreed that these measures destroyed the power of the capitalist **class**.

# Consequences

War Communism succeeded in keeping the **Red Army** supplied and allowing them to win the Civil War. However, it led to economic collapse, and failed to abolish the market.

## Economic collapse

Firstly, grain requisitioning led to lower rates of agricultural production. The peasants were not paid for their grain or their labour and therefore the policy provided no incentive to work.

Secondly, industrial production declined significantly. Again, there were few incentives to work hard. Hunger also led many workers to leave the cities and seek work on farms where there was more chance of being fed. In total, the industrial workforce declined from 3 million workers in 1917 to 1.2 million in 1922 (see Figure 1), partly due to the war and partly due to workers escaping the cities.

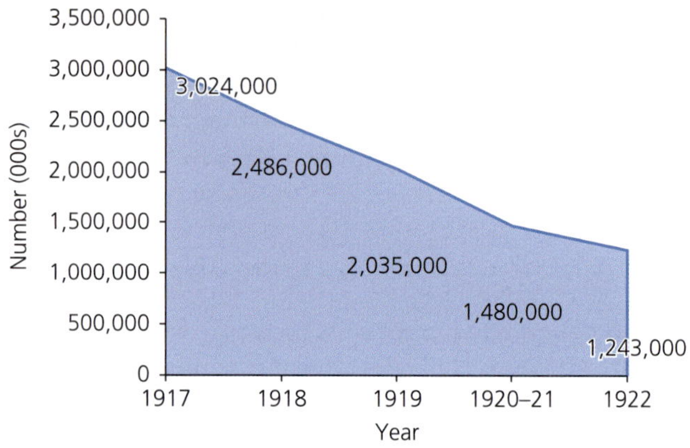


▲ **Figure 1: Numbers in the industrial workforce, 1917–22.**

The extent of economic collapse is clear from Table 1.

**Table 1: Economic decline in Russia, 1913–20.**

| Commodity | 1913 index | Production 1920 |
|---|---|---|
| Gross output of all industry | 100 | 31 |
| Large-scale industry | 100 | 21 |
| Agricultural production | 100 | 60 |

## Growth of the black market

Lenin's extensive economic controls failed to abolish the market. Historians estimate that only 40 per cent of the food consumed in Russia's cities came through rationing during the Civil War. Around 60 per cent of the food came from the **black market**. Moreover, workers were forced to steal government resources in order to make goods that could be bartered for food. For example, metal workers would steal scrap metal and fuel to make cigarette lighters.

## Mass poverty

By 1921 the Russian economy was near collapse. There were shortages of all kinds of commodities. By late 1920 workshops in the major cities were closing due to a lack of fuel. Indeed, fuel was in such short supply that the government ordered the destruction of wooden buildings in Petrograd in order to use the wood for fuel. Unemployment rose and harvests declined further. The 1921 harvest was only 46 per cent of the 1913 harvest, and in rural areas a famine began, which led to the deaths of around 6 million people.

## Political crisis

Mass starvation and the deepening economic crisis led to a political crisis. Between August 1920 and June

1921 peasants in the Tambov region rebelled against the Communist Government (see page 11). In Kronstadt, too, sailors who had supported the communists unquestioningly in 1917 turned against the government, demanding a return to free trade and new multiparty elections to the **soviets**. In March 1921 the sailors mutinied (see page 11). The communists responded with extreme force, defending their government with military action. Although both rebellions were crushed, Lenin realised that the political crisis meant the end of War Communism.

### Conclusion

War Communism led to military victory but economic ruin. It was also an ideological victory. The abolition of money and of the capitalist market led many communists, including Lenin himself, to believe that War Communism was the foundation on which the new society would be built. Bukharin even welcomed the economic crisis, arguing that the destruction of capitalism needed to be complete before building socialism could start. In that sense, senior Communists did not see the economic crisis as a reason to stop the policy. However, the political crisis was more worrying. Further rebellions risked the end of the Communist Government. In order to save the revolution Lenin was forced to accept an economic compromise.

## 3 New Economic Policy

Lenin introduced the New Economic Policy (NEP) for a series of reasons:

- To retain political power: Lenin described the NEP as an economic retreat, which was designed to stop a political defeat. In that sense, Lenin made economic compromises in order to retain political power.
- To revive the economy: Lenin needed a policy that would stimulate grain production and end the famine.
- To build socialism: By 1921 it was clear that a European revolution would not happen. Therefore Lenin needed an economic policy that would allow Russia to build socialism without foreign aid.

As 1921 went on, Lenin began to argue that the NEP, rather than War Communism, was the correct economic foundation on which to build socialism. He argued that the Communist Party must learn to trade and use capitalist methods to achieve communist goals. He also emphasised that the NEP would create peace with the peasants, and allow peasants and workers to build socialism together.

### Note it down

Using bullet points, make notes on:

- the reasons why the NEP was introduced
- the measures that made up the NEP
- the successes and failures of the NEP.

When dealing with the extent to which the NEP succeeded you might organise your notes in two lists, one for the ways in which it succeeded, the other for the ways in which it failed.

### Measures

The NEP ended War Communism. It created a mixed economy, which had capitalist and socialist elements:

- Agricultural production was left to the free market. Peasants could buy, sell and produce freely. Grain requisitioning ended and was replaced by a **tax in kind**.
- Small factories and workshops employing fewer than 20 people were denationalised. Small factories were allowed to trade freely. Many were returned to their former capitalist owners.
- Large factories and major industries remained nationalised.
- Money was reintroduced.

The NEP was a major economic compromise. Lenin emphasised the need for a stable currency and for all factories and workshops to make a profit. Even government-run industries were expected to make money, and therefore people were expected to pay for services, such as transport, which had been available free of charge during the Civil War.

### Consequences

The NEP led to political and economic stability. However, it did not lead to rapid industrial growth; nor was it wholly popular within the Party.

#### Political and economic stability

Ending grain requisitioning was extremely popular among the peasants. Free trade also encouraged peasants to grow more food. Therefore the famine ended, and food of all kinds became widely available in country and city markets. The growth in grain production is evident from Table 2 (see page 46).

The end of grain requisitioning led to a return of political and economic stability by ending the famine and ending a policy that was extremely unpopular with the peasants, who made up 80 per cent of Russia's population.

**Table 2: Grain production 1913–26.**

| Grain harvest | Million tons |
|---|---|
| 1913 | 80.11 |
| 1920 | 46.10 |
| 1921 | 37.61 |
| 1922 | 50.30 |
| 1923 | 56.60 |
| 1924 | 51.40 |
| 1925 | 72.50 |
| 1926 | 76.80 |

## Industrial growth

The NEP also led to industrial growth. The market stimulated production, and the government invested the money gained from taxing the peasants in reopening factories that had been closed during the Civil War. Lenin authorised a major electrification campaign which revived an industry that had effectively been destroyed by the Civil War.

By the end of 1921, Lenin argued that the NEP was not merely the right policy for creating economic growth. He claimed that the NEP was the best way to industrialise the Soviet Union and therefore lay the foundation for socialism. Lenin argued that the NEP was a form of state capitalism, the policy that the government had adopted in early 1918. In essence, Lenin argued that the NEP would allow the communists to 'build socialism with capitalist hands'. By 1926, industrial production, with the exception of pig iron and steel, had recovered to 1913 levels (see Figure 2).

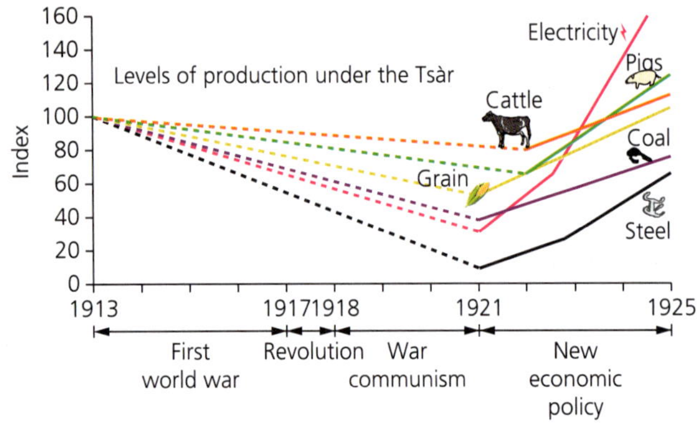


▲ **Figure 2: Production under the New Economic Policy, 1921–25.**

Crucially, while taxing the peasants provided sufficient funds to reopen and modernise existing factories, it failed to provide the money necessary to build new large-scale factories. Therefore from 1926 to 1928, the industrial economy **plateaued**.

## Scissors crisis

The NEP led to uneven economic growth. Agriculture recovered quickly. Greater food supplies led to a drop in agricultural prices. Industry recovered much more slowly, therefore industrial prices, which had been low during the famine, grew steadily. A gap opened up between farmers' incomes and industrial prices. Trotsky nicknamed the crisis the 'scissors crisis', as the lines on the graph illustrating the problem looked like the blades of a pair of scissors (see Figure 3).

By 1923 the gap between farmers' incomes and industrial prices had reached crisis point. The rise in industrial prices meant that farmers could not afford to buy industrial goods and therefore there was no incentive for farmers to keep producing large quantities of grain. The government intervened and subsidised the prices of industrial products, making them affordable to the peasants. However, this meant that there was less money available to improve the economy. In this sense the scissors crisis indicated to radicals like Trotsky that the NEP was not capable of industrialising the economy.

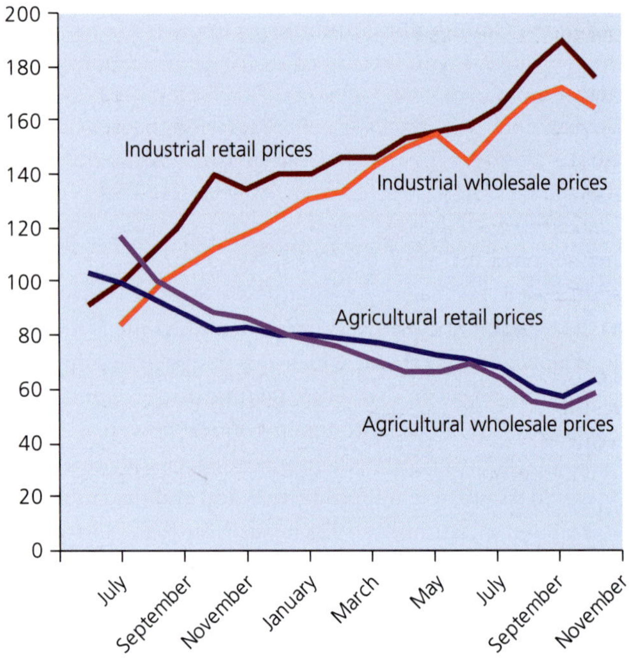


▲ **Figure 3: The 'scissors crisis' – industrial and agricultural prices in the Soviet Union, July 1922 to November 1923.**

## Inequality and corruption

The NEP led to the re-emergence of inequality and widespread corruption. First the NEP led to the emergence of 'Nepmen' traders who made money by spotting gaps in the market. Nepmen would travel the country, transporting highly desirable goods from

▲ Nepmen in Smolensk market, 1921. What would right-wing communists approve of in this scene? What would left-wing communists disapprove of in this scene?

factories or farms to the markets. The Communist Government regarded Nepmen as parasites, because they produced nothing, and made money from selling luxury goods. From time to time Nepmen were arrested by the Cheka for **profiteering**. However, they continued to operate until the end of the NEP. Nepmen grew rich by trading, while ordinary peasants and industrial workers stayed relatively poor in spite of their hard work.

Corruption also grew. Gambling, prostitution and drug dealing all took place under the NEP. Prostitution was the result of wider social and economic problems, which led to widespread poverty among women in the 1920s (see pages 126–127).

## Conclusion

The NEP stabilised the economy, replaced an extremely unpopular policy and therefore ended widespread rebellion. In that sense, the NEP achieved Lenin's key goal of ensuring the Communists' hold on power.

However, the NEP led to various problems, including slow industrial growth, an unbalanced economy, a return of inequality and the growth of various kinds of crime.

Finally, the NEP was deeply unpopular with some sections of the Communist Party. Indeed, the NEP led to a bitter debate over state control of industry and agriculture which raged during the 1920s.

## 4 State control of industry and agriculture

The NEP led to great debate within the Communist Party. All communists agreed that the Soviet Union must industrialise. However, there was dispute over the correct policy. Broadly, there were three positions within the Party:

- On the left Trotsky and his followers wanted to adopt a radical socialist policy: the Dictatorship of Industry.
- On the right Bukharin and his supporters advocated continuing with the NEP in order to ensure social peace.
- In the centre Stalin and his followers were prepared to back which ever policy worked.

### Note it down

Divide your page into three and make notes on:

- what the different parts of the Party advocated
- their reasons for advocating these policies.

Bullet points would work well for this kind of activity. You could use different coloured pens for the two parts of the note-making task.

## The Left: the Dictatorship of Industry

Left-wingers, like Trotsky, favoured a policy of forced agricultural collectivisation. Merging farms together and placing them under state control would, Trotsky argued, allow the state to take all of the profit generated by farming and use the money to industrialise quickly.

Trotsky argued that this scheme would end all private property, end the capitalist market and therefore end inequality. However, he acknowledged that it would lead to massive discontent among the peasants.

## The Right: building socialism with capitalist hands

Right-wingers, such as Bukharin, argued that the NEP was the best way of industrialising the Soviet Union. He argued that the NEP was slowly allowing the economy to grow and therefore industrialisation would happen eventually. Importantly, Bukharin argued that the NEP allowed the Soviet Union to remain a harmonious society. The NEP allowed peasants to own and work their own farms, which kept them satisfied. Bukharin argued that the slow pace of economic growth was necessary in order to keep the peasants happy.

The Left, however, argued that this policy of 'riding the peasant nag' to socialism, was highly dangerous. They argued that it could lead to the re-emergence of a capitalist class determined to overthrow Communism.

## The Centre: whatever works

Centrists or **pragmatists**, like Stalin, argued that the correct policy was the one that worked. In that sense, Stalin argued that economic policy was not an ideological issue, but a practical issue. Until 1927 Stalin supported the NEP as it was clearly leading to economic growth. However, when growth rates declined, Stalin shifted position.

## The legacy of War Communism

In a sense, the Left wanted to return to policies similar to War Communism. For Trotsky and the Left, War Communism was a heroic period in which the government implemented a truly socialist policy, whereas the NEP was a period of compromise which lost sight of true socialism. The Right, however, argued that War Communism had proved that extreme measures caused chaos and rebellion.

## Economic debate and the leadership struggle

The 'Great Industrialisation Debate' was a central part of the leadership struggle. Contenders presented their rival economic plans to the Party Congress. During the 1920s, again and again, the Right won the debates at Congress. Consequently, the leaders associated with the NEP held on to power, while the leaders who advocated radical left-wing solutions were unable to win power. Nonetheless, most communists were centrists and supported the NEP for **pragmatic** reasons. Therefore when the NEP started to fail, Stalin started to advocate a new more left-wing policy which attracted a great deal of support from the Left and the Centre of the Party.

## Conclusion

Lenin's economic policy went through a series of phases. The radical changes in policy reflected the fact that Lenin did not have a detailed plan, that the revolution did not proceed as he expected and that he was prepared to compromise.

Lenin adopted War Communism due to the crisis of the Civil War, a crisis that required state control of the whole industrial economy. Nonetheless, he quickly saw War Communism's potential for destroying capitalism and creating an economy built on socialist foundations.

By 1921 War Communism had created a political and economic crisis. It was clear by 1921 that the European revolution that Lenin had expected would not happen. The Soviet Union would have to build socialism without outside help. Once again, Lenin was forced to improvise, instituting the NEP, a compromise with the peasants and a compromise with capitalism. Again, Lenin saw the potential of the new system and by the end of his life he argued that the NEP was a form of state capitalism that would allow the Communist Party to build socialism in the Soviet Union.

However, the NEP was controversial within the Party. The Left wanted radical change, a return to a policy much closer to War Communism. The Right wanted to maintain the peace between the government and the peasants and move to socialism slowly. The majority backed the NEP while it worked. However, even in the good years the NEP was unable to create significant industrial growth. As the NEP plateaued at the end of the 1920s Stalin abandoned the policy and initiated a new economic revolution.

## Chapter summary

- Between 1917 and 1928 Lenin and his successors experimented with a series of economic policies:
  - State capitalism, 1918
  - War Communism, 1918–21
  - The New Economic Policy, 1921–28
- These policies reflected the needs of the country, the political circumstances and the long-term goals of the regime.
- However, none of these policies delivered the economic results that the communists wanted.

## Recommended reading

S. Malle, *The Economic Organization of War Communism, 1918–1921* (Cambridge, 2002), pages 495–515. Malle considers the successes failures and impact of War Communism.

R. Service, *Comrades! A history of world Communism* (Harvard, 2010), pages 70–81. Service gives an account of the early years of the Communism in Russia including Lenin's economic policy.

L. H. Siegelbaum, *Soviet state and society between revolutions, 1918–1929* (Cambridge, 1992), pages 63–6. Siegelbaum analyses the nature and consequences of War Communism.

## Work together

Having read this chapter, look over your notes from Chapter 1a, and write a paragraph answering the question:

**What was Leninism?**

Your paragraph should deal with the political and economic aspects of Lenin's government.

Having written the paragraph, swap it with a partner and consider the following questions:

- Did your partner miss anything obvious?
- Did your partner consider both the political and economic aspects of Leninism?
- Did your partner consider the ways in which Lenin's policies changed over time?

Discuss both paragraphs and work out which paragraph is best and why.

Note down three things that you could do to improve your written style.

## Activity: Question practice

1 How accurate is it to say that Lenin's economic policies failed to improve Soviet industry groups in the period 1918–28? AS

2 To what extent were there changes in Soviet government in the years 1928–64? AS

3 How far do you agree that the Communist Government faced severe economic and political challenges in the years 1917–28?

4 How significant was the creation of a one-party state in the establishment of communist power in the years 1921–53?

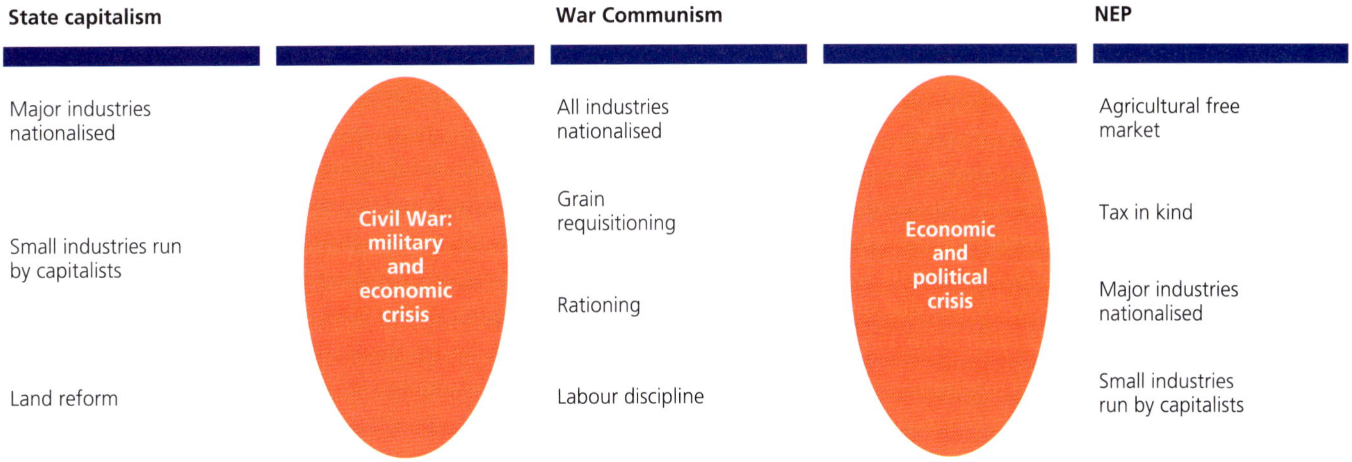


▲ Summary diagram: Towards a command economy, 1917–28.

# 2b: Industry and agriculture in the Stalin era

## Overview

Between 1928 and 1929, Stalin initiated the 'Revolution from Above' or 'Great Turn', a series of radical policies which transformed the Soviet economy. State planning of industry and the collectivisation of agriculture were designed to end the NEP's semi-capitalist market economy and transform the Soviet Union from a backward agricultural economy into a modern industrial state. In short the 'Revolution from Above' was Stalin's plan for building socialism in the Soviet Union.

Stalin's policies succeeded in turning the Soviet Union into an industrial giant. Moreover, they laid the foundation for Stalin's war economy, which was crucial to the Soviet victory over Germany in the Second World War. Nonetheless, Stalin's economic model created profound problems, particularly in agriculture, which were proved impossible to solve within the context of state planning that Stalin had established. Even so, the 'Revolution from Above' created a new type of economy, which became essential to the Soviet system. Collectivisation and the industrial planning endured from the late 1920s through to the 1980s as an essential feature of the Soviet economy.

This chapter considers:

1. The Five-Year Plans and industrial change, 1928–41
2. Agricultural collectivisation and its impact
3. Recovery from war after 1945.

## 1 The Five-Year Plans and industrial change, 1928–41

Centralised economic planning of industry was one of the key features of Stalin's industrial policy. Under the NEP state-owned industries had a considerable amount of **autonomy**. NEP managers could organise production levels and choose which goods they produced. However, in 1928, Stalin introduced the First Five-Year Plan, the first of a series of plans that were designed to replace the market with a more efficient and truly socialist economic system.

### Note it down

On a large sheet of paper draw a spider diagram and make notes on the aims of Stalin's industrial policy. Make sure you put his aims into appropriate categories, such as ideological aims, economic aims and political aims.

### The aims of the Five-Year Plans

Stalin introduced the Five-Year Plans for a series of reasons. His primary objective was to industrialise Russia by combining centralised planning with large-scale investment. His industrialisation goals were extremely ambitious. He claimed that the Soviet Union was 100 years behind Britain and the USA, but that through planning the Soviet Union could catch up in 15 years.

Soviet economists hoped to eliminate the inefficacies of the NEP. Specifically, they wanted to eliminate Nepmen, who made money through trade rather than production.

### Socialist economics

During the nineteenth century, socialists and communists were largely critical of capitalism. Karl Marx, for example, recognised that capitalism created large amounts of wealth and huge technological innovations. However, he was critical of the inequality and exploitation that capitalism created. Socialists argued that the key problem with capitalism was private property, because property was the key to growing rich. People who owned property, including factories and shops, could grow rich. People who owned little or no property by contrast would remain poor.

A second problem that socialists identified with private property was that it led to competition. Companies competed with each other in the market. They argued that this competition was inefficient, because it led to a duplication of production. Consequently, socialists argued that abolishing private property was the key to equality and efficiency. Socialists disagreed over how private property could be abolished, but by the early twentieth century many socialists argued that the state should own all property and plan production for the good of all people.

Finally, although socialists spent a great deal of time in the nineteenth and early twentieth centuries speculating about how a socialist economy might work, prior to 1917 there had been no large-scale attempt to create a socialist economy. Therefore neither Lenin nor Stalin had a model for their economic policy. Both were forced to improvise.

They believed that government-controlled production and distribution would be much more efficient than small-scale disorganised NEP-style trading.

Stalin argued that the Plans were necessary because of the failings of the NEP. The NEP had helped to revive existing Soviet industry, but had not led to the development of new factories.

The Plans also reflected Soviet military concerns. Stalin, and many in the government, feared that Germany would invade the Soviet Union. Defending Soviet territory would require modern industry which could produce the weapons necessary to fight a modern war.

Finally, Stalin wanted to assert his own authority. The Five-Year Plans were more ambitious than any of Lenin's schemes for transforming the Soviet Union. In this sense, they would demonstrate that Stalin was initiating a new phase of building socialism.

## Five-Year Plans 1928–41

Between 1928 and 1941, there were three Five-Year Plans:

- First Five-Year Plan (October 1928–December 1932)
- Second Five-Year Plan (January 1933–December 1937)
- Third Five-Year Plan (January 1938–June 1941).

The first was cut short due to problems with the Plan, and the third ended prematurely due to the German invasion of the Soviet Union.

### The nature of the Plans

The Five-Year Plans were a government initiative designed to increase production. Gosplan, the Soviet Union's central economic agency, formulated production targets for every factory, mine and workshop in the Soviet Union, and Soviet workers and managers were responsible for meeting these targets.

At the same time, there was a massive propaganda campaign designed to inspire workers to fulfil the Plans. These campaigns:

- focused on the heroic objectives of the Plans
- celebrated the successes of the Plans
- claimed that the Plans had led to the destruction of capitalism
- described the modern, industrial future that the Plans would create.

However, the Five-Year Plans were not plans in the strict sense. They were merely a list of targets backed by a propaganda campaign.

There was no attempt to ensure that factories had the resources they needed to reach their targets, nor were there any clear ideas about what the goods would be used for once they were produced. Therefore Stalin's economy is better understood as a **command economy** rather than a planned economy.

## Achievements 1928–41

Overall, Stalin's first three Five-Year Plans succeeded in industrialising the Soviet Union. Broadly, Stalin's economic policy was successful in terms of heavy industry, transport, labour productivity and rearmament.

### Heavy industry

Heavy industry was the biggest success of the first three Five-Year Plans. Production of iron, steel, coal, oil and electricity all increased massively (see Table 3).

▲ **A propaganda poster showing Stalin marching alongside miners, made during the first Five-Year Plan. What does this poster suggest about Stalin's economic and political priorities?**

Table 3: Industrial production, 1927–40.

| | 1927 | 1940 |
|---|---|---|
| Electricity (milliard kWhs) | 5.05 | 48.30 |
| Coal (million tons) | 35.40 | 165.90 |
| Oil (million tons) | 11.70 | 31.10 |
| Pig iron (million tons) | 3.30 | 14.90 |
| Steel (million tons) | 4.00 | 18.30 |

This was achieved, in part, by building new factories to exploit the Soviet Union's natural resources (see Figure 4). Magnitogorsk, Kuznetsk, Zaporozhye, Tula and Lipetsk metallurgical works were all built between 1929 and 1936, and contributed to the huge increase in the amount of iron and steel produced.

## Transport

Transport was another success of the Plans. The Moscow Metro's first train lines opened in 1935. Additionally, the Moscow–Volga Canal was constructed between 1932 and 1937. The Metro allowed people to travel around Moscow more easily, and the Moscow–Volga Canal made the transportation of goods more efficient.

## Labour productivity

Labour productivity in the Soviet Union was extremely low. Indeed, Soviet workers were significantly less productive than workers in Britain, the USA or Western Europe. Low productivity can be explained by the long hours, low pay and lack of incentives in the system, at least during the first Five-Year Plan. Low productivity was addressed through a nationwide initiative introduced in 1935. Stalin authorised higher payments and a system of rewards for the most productive workers. Additionally, Stakhanovites, workers who had proved themselves to be exceptionally productive, were able to reorganise their workplaces to ensure that they were efficient. The campaign took off in 1936 and in the late 1930s productivity rose significantly across industry as Stakhanovites educated other workers in the most effective ways of working (see Table 4).

Table 4: Productivity gains, 1936–40.

| Industry | Estimated productivity gains |
|---|---|
| Chemicals | 34 per cent |
| Electricity production | 51 per cent |
| Coal mining | 26 per cent |
| Oil production | 25 per cent |

Nonetheless, the Stakhanovite movement created problems of its own. Stakhanovite workers were often resented by their colleagues or their management because they got higher pay.

## Rearmament

The Five-Year Plans were very successful in terms of rearmament. As war approached, economic planners increasingly prioritised arms production. By 1940 one-third of government spending was devoted to rearmament. Moreover, the Plans led to the successful construction of nine military aircraft factories between 1939 and 1941. However, shortages of quality materials such as steel held up arms production.

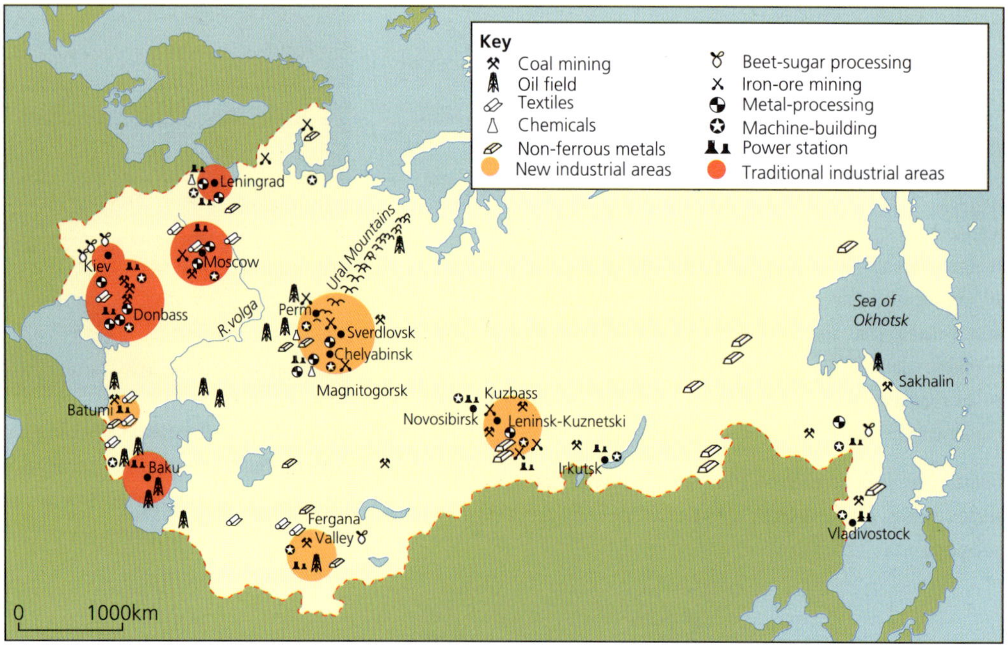


Figure 4: The new industrial centres.

## Alexei Stakhanov, 1906–1977

Alexei Stakhanov was the first of a new movement. According to the Soviet media, in August 1935 he mined 102 tons of coal in six hours - 14 times the output of an average miner. In September he mined 227 tons of coal in a single shift. As a result he was rewarded with one month's wages, a new apartment, a telephone and holiday tickets. He was held up as an example to all Soviet workers of the kind of superhuman effort that they should aspire to. Stakhanov also became a celebrity, even featuring on the cover of *Time Magazine*.

Notably, Stakhanov's amazing records were achieved with the help of assistants and the latest technology. Even so, the publicity value of his achievement was huge.

## Problems with the Plans

While Stalin's Plans did lead to the industrialisation of the economy, they proved to be a very inefficient way of industrialising. In addition to problems in specific areas of the economy there were also systemic problems with the Stalinist model of economic planning.

## Production problems

The command economy was plagued by problems. First, production quality was often low. The Plans set targets for production, not for quality. Therefore factory managers were rewarded for producing large quantities of material, regardless of the quality of what was produced.

Secondly, the Plans did not specify what materials should be used for, and there was little co-ordination between different factories. Materials that were produced were often stored at the factory and allowed to decay rather than being used. This problem was made worse due to the lack of transport in the first years of the Plan. Indeed, in some industries as much as 40 per cent of what was produced was wasted.

Finally, the Plans themselves were disorganised and undermined by Stalin's other policies. In terms of disorganisation, the First Five-Year Plan was launched in October 1928, and yet the Plan itself was only published in April 1929. Equally, Stalin's terror led to the purge of industrial managers and economic planners – the very people necessary to making the Plan work. Stalin's terror attacked officials at Gosplan to such an extent that the third Five-Year Plan was never finished. Therefore, for periods during the First and Third Five-Year Plans, the Soviet Union had a planned economy, but no Plan.

The effectiveness of the Plans was also undermined by unrealistic targets set by Gosplan. Industrial managers were under enormous pressure to ensure high levels of production and they would therefore lie about their production levels and falsify figures. Falsified data made economic management even harder, as effective planning relies in accurate data.

Historian Donald Filtzer argues that these problems meant that Soviet economic growth was 'self-consuming': the process of economic growth was so inefficient that it consumed extremely high levels of resources that could otherwise have been used to improve the quality of life of Soviet citizens.

## Consumer goods

Between 1928 and 1941 there were continual shortages of consumer goods, such as clothes, shoes and furniture. Shortages were the result of the following:

- Stalin's priorities: He prioritised heavy industry and defence rather than consumer production.
- Poor planning: Planners underestimated the needs of consumers.
- Production techniques: By the mid-1930s the Soviet economy was good at producing large quantities of **raw materials** such as iron, steel and coal. However, producing more complex consumer goods required more sophisticated techniques, which the economy still lacked.

The scarcity of consumer goods was managed by rationing. Between 1928 and 1941, most consumer goods were rationed. However, in the early and late 1930s there were often such severe shortages that the government could not even supply the minimum level of rations. For example, shoe queues in Moscow in the early 1930s often exceeded 1000 people. Some reports suggest queues for clothes and shoes in Leningrad numbered over 6000 during 1938.

## Housing and living conditions

Housing was a significant problem between 1928 and 1941. The Plans required a huge increase in the urban workforce. However, the necessary housing was never built. Most houses built during the Plans did not have running water. Moreover, bathhouses were scarce. For example, there was not a single bathhouse available for the 650,000 people living in the Liubertsy district of Moscow.

The industrial centre of Magnitogorsk was planned with state-of-the-art housing for the workers who would build the factory. A small village was built to house the American specialists who were employed to supervise the construction of the factories. Once the American specialists had returned to the USA, Magnitogorsk's managers moved into these houses. However, the majority of the workers lived in wooden shacks, tents and mud huts.

Living conditions between 1928 and 1941 were poorer than they had been under the best years of the NEP. A better standard of living was never one of Stalin's key objectives and this was a genuine failure of the Plan. Food rationing continued for most of the Plan, except for a period known as the 'three good years' in the middle of the 1930s. Working conditions were harsh. Workers were forced to work seven days a week, and long hours were common. Lateness and **absenteeism** was criminalised. Towards the end of the period, **internal passports** were introduced to stop workers moving from town to town in search of better-paid jobs.

## Black market

The Five-Year Plans also failed to end the free market. Shortages of materials led to the growth of a thriving black market. The black market was possible due to the inefficiencies of the Plan. Workers would steal goods and material from their workplaces and sell them to the highest bidders. The thefts would be covered up by falsifying paperwork.

## Conclusion

In spite of the problems, Stalin's Five-Year Plans transformed the Soviet economy. In 1928, the Soviet Union was a largely capitalist agricultural economy with a small working class. By 1941 the Soviet Union was a powerful, urban industrial economy that was able to produce the resources necessary to defeat the German army. However, the Soviet economy was profoundly unbalanced. Arms production was only possible at the expense of consumer goods. Moreover, the wastefulness of the Soviet economy was another reason why economic growth did not lead to higher standards of living.

# 2 Agricultural collectivisation and its impact

Between 1928 and 1941 Soviet agriculture was collectivised. Collectivisation was a process by which small farms were merged into large farms of anything between 20 and 150 families. At the same time ownership of the farmland and all of the farm's resources was taken over by the state.

### Note it down

On a large sheet of paper draw a spider diagram, and make notes on the aims of Stalin's agricultural policy. Make sure you put his aims into appropriate categories, such as ideological aims, economic aims and political aims.

## The causes of collectivisation

Collectivisation had a series of causes. Communist ideology set the general direction. However, the specific failings of the NEP and the nature of the leadership struggle also shaped the way that the policy developed.

## Communist ideology

Communists believed that private property was one of the foundations of capitalism and one of the causes of inequality (see page 50). During the period of the NEP, peasants with large farms had been able to grow rich, while peasants with small farms had done much less well. Therefore all communists wanted to abolish private property and replace private farming with state-run farming to end capitalism and inequality.

Communists were also suspicious of peasant farming. Historically, Russian peasants had wanted to own the land they worked. This implied an individualistic desire to make money which was closer to capitalism than socialism. By collectivising farms, communists hoped that peasants would see the superiority of socialist methods and embrace Communism wholeheartedly.

Communists also wanted to create an efficient economy. They believed that large farms were likely to be more efficient than small farms, as expertise and equipment could be shared to increase production.

In sum, communists believed that collectivisation would create a fairer and more efficient society and would win over the peasants by abolishing private property and sharing resources.

## The failure of the NEP

By 1928 there were clear signs that the NEP was failing. Until 1926 the NEP led to rising agricultural production. However, in 1927 and 1928 agricultural production was lower than it had been in 1926.

Agricultural production fell because there was no market for additional farmed goods. In essence there was a limit to the amount of food that Soviet consumers wanted. Increased production in 1926 led to a fall in prices as farmers produced more than consumers wanted. Therefore in 1927 farmers decreased production to push up grain prices. This led to what the right wing described as 'the grain procurement crisis': food supplies decreased, leading to shortages in the cities and higher profits for farmers.

Left-wing communists described this reduction of production as the 'Kulak grain strike'. They claimed that kulaks, rich farmers, were putting their own profits ahead of the Soviet Union's need to industrialise. In essence, radical communists viewed this as the re-emergence of class war: rich, capitalist peasants deliberately holding back the construction of socialism.

The NEP's economic problems and the threat of Kulak capitalists holding the government to ransom led many communists to believe that the NEP had run its course and needed to be replaced by a more radical policy that dealt with the kulaks and restored economic growth.

## The leadership struggle

Stalin also had political reasons for wanting to end the NEP and collectivise agriculture. At the end of 1927, Stalin and Bukharin had defeated **Zinoviev**, **Kamenev** and Trotsky, expelling them from the Party. Zinoviev, Kamenev and Trotsky, the **United Opposition**, had advocated a radical left-wing policy of collectivisation and rapid industrialisation. Their defeat and expulsion meant that the left wing of the Party, a significant minority, had no leader. By moving to the left, Stalin hoped to retain his supporters, pick up supporters of the United Opposition and in so doing gain more support than Bukharin. Stalin's strategy worked. As he moved to the left he gained a majority of support in the Central Committee and was therefore able to become the undisputed leader of the Communist Party.

# Introducing collectivisation

Collectivisation was introduced in a series of phases. In 1928, Stalin did not propose the full-scale collectivisation of agriculture. However, as his new policies won support within the Communist Party he became bolder. In late 1929 Stalin ordered full-scale collectivisation (see Figure 5). By 1930 he claimed 100 per cent success.

## Emergency measures, 1928

In July 1928, Stalin effectively ended the NEP. To end the 'Kulak grain strike', Stalin ordered the Red Army and the Cheka to requisition grain from the peasants. The requisitioned grain would then be used to feed workers and to sell overseas in order to raise money for industrialisation.

Introducing requisitioning effectively ended the NEP. The NEP had been based on free trade and taxation. In the cities, Stalin reintroduced rationing – another aspect of War Communism. Rationing and requisitioning did not necessarily indicate that collectivisation was beginning, but they did signal the end of the NEP.

# Dekulakisation

Peasants responded to the introduction of requisitioning with violence. Requisitioning was the most hated aspect of War Communism. Peasants resisted requisitioning by hiding or even destroying grain. Stalin claimed that this resistance was an attack on socialism by the capitalist kulaks. Therefore he initiated the 'liquidation of the kulaks as a class', or dekulakisation. In theory this was meant to take farms and equipment from the richest peasants. However, in practice it meant mass deportations and killings of all peasants who resisted government policies. Around 1.5 million peasants were sent to labour camps as a result of the dekulakisation campaign.

# Collectivisation

Collectivisation was introduced in late 1929. Farms were forcibly merged, and equipment was taken from richer peasants and given to the poorer peasants. Peasants who worked on collective farms were allowed to keep a small amount of grain to live on. The rest was used to feed workers in the cities or sold abroad to provide money to fund industrialisation.

# The consequences of collectivisation, 1929–34

Collectivisation devastated Soviet agriculture, but released much more money to fund industrialisation.

Between 1929 and 1930 there was a drive to ensure that all farms were collectivised. However, this led to chaos, and therefore Stalin halted the collectivisation drive temporarily in 1930. Collectivisation was reinstated in 1931. By 1941 almost all Soviet farms were collectivised (see Figure 6).

## Destruction of Soviet farming

The peasants responded to requisitioning and collectivisation by destroying their crops, animals and machinery. Many peasants would rather destroy their farms than hand them over to the government. Therefore, between 1928 and 1934, Stalin's policies led to the destruction of:

- 17 million horses
- 26 million cattle
- 11 million pigs
- 60 million sheep and goats.

At the same time, grain production also decreased (see Table 5).

**Table 5: Grain production, 1928–34.**

| Grain harvest | Million tons |
|---|---|
| 1928 | 73.3 |
| 1929 | 71.7 |
| 1930 | 83.5 |
| 1931 | 69.5 |
| 1932 | 69.6* |
| 1933 | 68.4 |
| 1934 | 67.6 |

The reduction of agricultural production was due to:

- the execution or deportation of kulaks who were often the most experienced and successful farmers
- the absence of incentives as farmers were no longer able to make a profit.

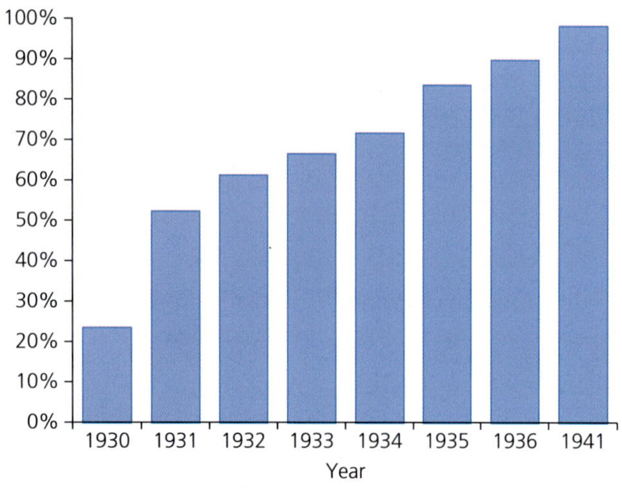


▲ **Figure 6: Cumulative percentage of peasant holdings collectivised in the USSR, 1930–41.**

## Famine

Collectivisation also led to famine in the Ukraine. Ukrainian farmers were unable to meet government targets for farm production. Moreover, resistance to collectivisation had been at it fiercest in the Ukraine. Therefore Stalin punished them by seizing their grain and livestock. The result was a government-created famine between 1932 and 1933 which resulted in 5 million deaths. Stalin refused to accept international offers of aid to help the starving farmers. He wanted to use the famine to destroy the resistance of the Ukrainian farmers.

## Mechanisation

Collectivisation was accompanied by mechanisation. The government allowed farms to hire tractors from machine tractor stations, which were set up across the country. The 75,000 tractors that they provided had a limited impact on Soviet farming. At best, they made up for all of the horses that were lost due to collectivisation.

## Grain procurement

Collectivisation allowed the government to procure much more grain than the NEP. In 1928, the government procured 10.8 million tons of grain from the peasants. This had risen to 22.6 million tons in 1933. Grain exports also rose from less than 1 million tons in 1928 to 4.7 million tons in 1930 and 5 million tons in 1931.

# The long-term consequences of collectivisation

Collectivisation caused long term-problems that Stalin and his successors were never able to fully solve.

## Agriculture, 1934–41

Soviet agriculture recovered slowly from the disruption of collectivisation. Grain harvests were regularly smaller than they had been in the best years of the NEP. Although there was a record harvest in 1937, grain production declined again from 1938 to 1940. Low grain harvests were, in part, a result of the fact that collective farms were less productive than private farms. On average private farms produced around 410 kilos of grain per hectare, whereas collective farms produced about 320 kilos per hectare. In short, prior to the Second World War collective farms were less productive than farms under the NEP.

Private farming continued on a small scale until 1941. Around seven per cent of farmers stayed independent of the collective system. However, they made a major contribution to Soviet agriculture. Indeed, the private farms produced double the amount of meat and milk produced by the state farms.

## Agriculture during the Second World War

The failings of the collective system were obvious during the Second World War. Farming was consistently unable to meet the needs of the citizens and the army. During the war:

- the Soviet Government relied on US imports to provide almost a fifth of the calories consumed by the Red Army
- harvests declined from a pre-war high of 95.5 million tonnes to 46.8 million tonnes in 1945
- bread rations fell by 40 per cent
- potato rations fell by 80 per cent.

# 3 Recovery from war after 1945

The Second World War led to widespread devastation. In general terms, the war destroyed almost all of the economic progress that had been made during the first three Five-Year Plans. In 1945, 25 million people were homeless; Soviet industry was producing two-thirds less than it had in 1940.

Stalin planned full-scale reconstruction over the course of three more Five-Year Plans.

### Note it down

Using the 1:2 method (see page x), make notes on the success of economic reconstruction following the Second World War. Make sure you distinguish between different aspects of the economy, for example you should have headings on the success of agricultural reconstruction, industrial reconstruction as well as recovery of living standards.

## The Fourth Five-Year Plan, 1945–50

The Fourth Five-Year Plan led to extremely high levels of industrial growth. Around 88 per cent of investment during the Fourth Five-Year Plan went into heavy industry. As a result, industrial output increased by 80 per cent from 1945 to 1950. Indeed, some factories and mines, particularly the metal producing regions of the Ukraine and Siberia, were able to achieve or exceed pre-war production rates by 1950 (see Table 6).

**Table 6: Industrial output 1940–50.**

| | 1940 | 1945 | 1950 |
|---|---|---|---|
| Coal (million tons) | 165.9 | 119.3 | 261.1 |
| Electricity (milliard kWhs) | 48.3 | 43.2 | 91.2 |
| Oil (million tons) | 30.1 | 19.4 | 37.9 |
| Pig iron (million tons) | 14.9 | 8.8 | 19.2 |
| Steel (million tons) | 18.3 | 12.3 | 27.30 |
| Cement (million tons) | 5.7 | 1.8 | 10.2 |

Soviet post-war Plans continued to focus on military spending. The emergence of the Cold War in 1946 led to the expansion of the Soviet military and an increase in military spending. By 1952, total military expenditure was almost a quarter of the government's budget. Military spending meant that there was less money available for other sectors of the economy (see Table 7).

**Table 7: Military expenditure, 1950–52.**

| | 1950 | 1951 | 1952 |
|---|---|---|---|
| Total expenditure (milliard roubles) | 427.9 | 451.5 | 476.9 |
| Military expenditure (milliard roubles) | 79.4 | 96.4 | 113.8 |

Production of consumer goods increased too, doubling during the course of the Pan. However, like the pre-war Plans, the Fourth Five-Year Plan focused primarily on heavy industry. Only 12 per cent of investment went into food production and consumer goods. Therefore although the production of consumer goods doubled, they continued to be scarce.

Reconstruction focused on factories rather than homes. Equally, reconstruction of historic cities was given priority over more remote towns. Therefore, while Kiev was reconstructed quickly, towns in Dnieper were neglected until the late 1950s.

Wages were kept low. This had two benefits. First, it meant that there was more money available for reconstruction. Secondly, it meant that women were forced to go out to work because families needed their income. Stalin recognised that women had a vital role to play in rebuilding Soviet industry.

Like previous Plans, the Fourth Five-Year Plan was plagued with inefficiencies and problems. Nonetheless, between 1945 and 1950 the Soviet economy was the fastest growing economy in the world. By the time of Stalin's death in 1953 economic recovery was well underway, even if there were still major shortages of consumer goods and housing.

## Post-war agriculture

Soviet agriculture recovered slowly from the devastation of war. Stalin's top economic priority after the war was industrial reconstruction. As a result, agriculture suffered severe shortages of resources and workers from 1946 to 1949.

Additionally, as soon as the war was over Stalin re-imposed strict discipline over Soviet farms. During the war there had been a small increase in private farming. Stalin ordered an end to private farming and therefore production dropped.

Nonetheless, production grew between 1947 and 1953. By 1952 grain production had reached its pre-war levels (see Table 8).

**Table 8: Grain harvest, millions of tonnes.**

| | |
|---|---|
| 1940 | 95.6 |
| 1941 | 56.3 |
| 1942 | 30.0 |
| 1943 | 30.0 |
| 1944 | 48.7 |
| 1945 | 46.8 |
| 1946 | 39.6 |
| 1947 | 65.9 |
| 1948 | 67.2 |
| 1949 | 70.2 |
| 1950 | 81.2 |
| 1951 | 78.7 |
| 1952 | 92.2 |

## Work together

Having read this chapter write a paragraph in answer to the following question:

**In what ways were Stalin's economic policies socialist?**

Try to think of at least three ways.

Swap your paragraph with a partner, and discuss:

- Which paragraph demonstrates the clearest focus on the meaning of socialism?
- Which paragraph links its three points to socialism most clearly?
- Which paragraph provides a better answer to the question, and why?

Make a note of at least two ways in which you could improve your writing.

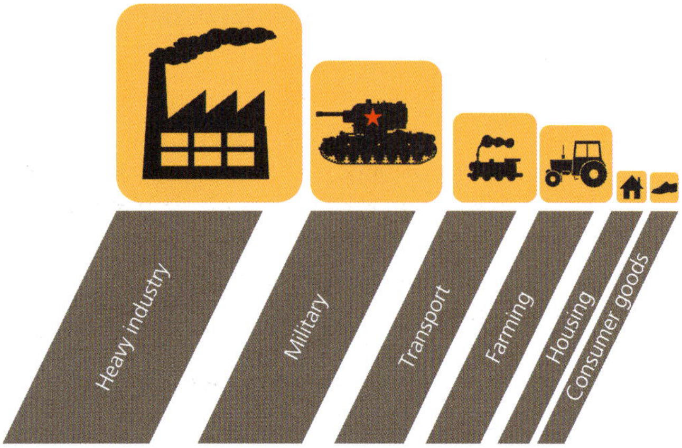


▲ **Summary diagram: Stalin's economic priorities.**

## Conclusion

Stalin's 'Great-Turn' transformed the Soviet economy and the Soviet Union. While his policies were harsh, inefficient and wasteful, the Five-Year Plans transformed the Soviet Union into an industrial giant. Equally, collectivisation placed farming firmly under state control.

Stalin's 'Revolution from Above' had long-lasting consequences. It established the basic nature of the Soviet economy from 1928/29 to the 1980s. Indeed, between 1928 and 1990 there would be 11 Five-Year Plans. Crucially, Stalin's legacy also determined the basic problems that later Soviet leaders would have to face. Low labour productivity, an unproductive agricultural sector, inefficient industry, scarce consumer goods and a massive military budget would continue to trouble Soviet leaders until the fall of the Soviet Union in 1991.

## Chapter summary

- From 1928 to 1953 Stalin established the economic model that the Soviet Union would follow until the 1980s.
- The key features of the economic model included:
  - collectivised farming
  - 'planned' economic production and development.
- This model led to the industrialisation of the Soviet Union
- It also led to a series of persistent economic problems:
  - low levels of agricultural production
  - poor-quality production
  - inefficient production.

## Recommended reading

D. Filtzer, *Soviet Workers and Late Stalinism: Labour and the Restoration of the Stalinist System after World War II* (Cambridge, 2004), pages 1–12. Filtzer's book deals with Stalin's economy in the last years of his reign.

S. Fitzpatrick, *Everyday Stalinism – Ordinary Life in Extraordinary Times: Soviet Russia in the 1930s* (Cambridge, 2000), pages 40–66. Fitzpatrick analyses the way in which the Soviet people lived during the first Five Year Plans.

R. Sakwa, *Soviet Politics in Perspective*, 2nd edition (Routledge, 1998), pages 38–40. Sakwa considers the impact of Stalin's command economy on Soviet society.

# Essay technique: Analysis

In Sections A and B of the exam your essays are judged on their focus and structure (see pages 26–27), the extent to which they include relevant detail (see page 39) and the extent to which they are analytical. Therefore having made a relevant point, and supported it with accurate detail, you should conclude each paragraph with analysis.

Analysis is a term that covers a variety of high-level skills including explanation and evaluation. In essence, analysis means breaking down something complex into smaller parts. Therefore a clear structure, which breaks down a complex question into a series of paragraphs, is the first step towards writing an analytical essay.

The purpose of explanation is to account for why something happened or why something is true or false. Therefore an explanatory statement requires two parts: a **claim** and a **justification**. For example, imagine you are answering the following question:

> **How far do you agree that the Soviet economy was transformed in the years 1928–53?**

You might want to argue that the Soviet economy was transformed radically due to the introduction of the Five-Year Plans. Having made this point, and supported it with relevant detail, you can then explain how this answers the question. For example, you could conclude your paragraph like this:

Claim — Therefore the Soviet economy was transformed radically following 1928 due to the introduction of the Five-Year Plans

Relationship — because

Justification — the planned economy abolished the free market in industry.

> Therefore the Soviet economy was transformed radically following 1928 due to the introduction of the Five-Year Plans because the planned economy abolished the free market in industry.

The first part of this sentence is the claim, the second part justifies the claim. 'Because' is a very important word to use when writing an explanation, as it shows the relationship between the claim and the justification.

## Activity: Claim and justification

Here is a plan in answer to the question above:

- Paragraph 1: Five-Year Plans: radical transformation of industry
- Paragraph 2: Collectivisation– radical transformation of agriculture
- Paragraph 3: Persistence of black market– limited transformation
- Paragraph 4: Limited modernisation– limited transformation

Using your notes from this chapter:

1 Write a paragraph about how far agriculture was transformed by collectivisation. Make sure your paragraph:
- begins with a clear point that focuses on the question
- develops the point with at least three pieces of accurate detail
- concludes with an explanation: a claim and a justification.

2 Write a conclusion to the essay in which you weigh up at least two factors and reach a judgement about how far the Soviet economy was transformed in the years 1928–53.

# 2c: Changing economic priorities, 1953–85

## Overview

From 1953 to 1985 Soviet leaders struggled with a series of economic problems. Khrushchev recognised that collectivisation and central planning under Stalin had failed to improve the standard of living for Soviet citizens. Moreover, he recognised that large military budgets starved other areas of the economy of the resources necessary to grow. Nonetheless, Khrushchev was convinced that the basic model of agricultural collectivisation and industrial planning was the best economic system. What is more, initially Khrushchev's reforms led to an economic golden age in which the economy sustained high rates of growth, the standard of living improved and overtaking the US economy seemed possible. Khrushchev was confident that the Soviet system was essentially sound and that small-scale reforms rather than fundamental change was the solution to Soviet economic difficulties.

More serious economic problems emerged at the end of the 1950s. Growth rates slowed and by the mid-1960s the economy began to stagnate. Even so, Brezhnev was unwilling to authorise reform, let alone wholesale economic change. Therefore problems of stagnation and low growth continued. By 1985 the economy was in crisis. Slow growth through the 1970s had turned into economic decline in the early 1980s, and yet the burden of military expenditure continued to rise.

This chapter considers:

**1** Investment in agriculture, 1953–64
**2** Industrial modernisation, 1953–64
**3** Economic reform and decline after 1964.

## 1 Investment in agriculture, 1953–64

Khrushchev broke with tradition in 1953 by acknowledging that Soviet agriculture was inefficient and less productive than it had been under the NEP. He argued that reforms were necessary to increase productivity and to ensure a better standard of living for agricultural workers. In order to revive the Soviet economy, Stalin's heirs introduced a series of reforms.

### Note it down

Divide a large sheet of paper into three equal columns. Under the headings Goals, Policies and Success/Failure, make notes on Khrushchev's investment in agriculture. Bullet points or the 1:2 method (see page x) would suit this activity well. Remember to note down specific information that will help you demonstrate how far his policies succeeded.

### The politics of agriculture

Khrushchev's rise and fall as Soviet leader was bound up with agriculture. Malenkov's early policies had focused on agriculture. Having promised much higher agricultural production in 1953, and having failed to deliver in 1954, Malenkov was eclipsed by Khrushchev.

Khrushchev too promised great improvements, and his success in delivering larger harvests between 1954 and 1958 was crucial to the consolidation of his power. However, Khrushchev's promises to produce more than the USA by 1960 led to an embarrassing failure. Some of his policies, such as maize cultivation, were extremely ineffective. Indeed, they led to Khrushchev gaining a reputation for introducing 'hare-brained' schemes rather than effective policies. The slow growth of agricultural production between 1960 and 1964 persuaded many in the Party that Khrushchev's reforms were unnecessary and counterproductive, and therefore he should be replaced by a more cautious leader.

## Improved incentives

In 1954, Khrushchev changed the relationship between collective farms and the government in order to incentivise higher production rates. In essence, Khrushchev wanted to invest in farming by offering farmers higher prices for their produce. Under Stalin, each farm had to produce a quota of goods, which was bought directly by the state at extremely low prices. Khrushchev reduced the quota and introduced higher prices for everything that was produced in addition to the quota. This led to a 250 per cent rise in farm incomes between 1952 and 1956.

## Investment in resources

Khrushchev also invested in farm equipment and fertilisers. In 1954 Khrushchev announced the construction of new fertiliser factories and an increase in the production of tractors. By 1955 this resulted in a 30 per cent increase in the number of tractors available and a 40 per cent increase in the amount of fertiliser produced.

## Virgin Lands Scheme

The Virgin Lands Scheme was Khrushchev's most ambitious agricultural policy. Khrushchev hoped to increase Soviet agricultural production by turning unfarmed lands in the northern Caucasus, Kazakhstan, and western Siberia into new farms. Launched in September 1953, it required a significant investment, so agricultural investment grew from under 3 per cent a year to 12.8 per cent of the Soviet budget between 1954 and 1959. Between 1953 and 1964 this led to a significant increase in the amount of farmed land in the Soviet Union (see Table 9).

**Table 9: Expansion of farmland, 1953–64.**

| | 1953 | 1956 | 1964 |
|---|---|---|---|
| Total area sown (million hectares) | 18.2 | 35.3 | 97.4 |
| Total labour employed (million workers) | 2.6 | 2.9 | 8.6 |

### The Corn Campaign

In addition to the Virgin Lands Scheme, Khrushchev introduced the Corn Campaign. From September 1958 Khrushchev encouraged farmers in the Ukraine to grow maize. His plan was to shift wheat production to the newly created Virgin Lands farms while maize would be produced in the traditional farms of the Ukraine. The maize would be used to feed animals and would therefore increase the amount of meat available to Soviet consumers.

The Corn Campaign was a failure. Khrushchev's initiative was based on the success of US farms. However, Soviet farms were only able to produce 50 per cent of the corn per hectare that US farms managed due to differences in climate, lower labour productivity and the inferiority of Soviet tractors and fertilisers. At the same time, growing more corn meant that Soviet farms produced less hay. As a result the amount of animal feed produced by Soviet farms dropped by 30 per cent between 1958 and 1964.

## Agricultural successes, 1954–58

Initially, the Virgin Lands Scheme was extremely successful. Grain harvests, meat and milk production all rose significantly between 1953 and 1958. Overall, agricultural production increased by around 35.3 per cent in this period (see Table 10).

**Table 10: Early impact of the Virgin Lands Scheme.**

| | 1953 | 1958 |
|---|---|---|
| Grain harvest (million tons) | 82.5 | 134.7 |
| Meat (million tons) | 5.8 | 7.7 |
| Milk (million tons) | 36.5 | 58.9 |

The scheme led to greater availability of food in Soviet shops and therefore a better standard of living for Soviet citizens. Greater production also led to a 400 per cent rise in the income of farm workers. Additionally, the success of the scheme allowed Khrushchev to consolidate his position and led him to advocate even more ambitious schemes. In 1956, Khrushchev introduced a new commitment to produce more food than the US by 1960. This required a 300 per cent increase in production in four years.

## Problems in agriculture, 1954–64

Even during the successful period of 1954 to 1958, Soviet agriculture remained extremely inefficient. First, the Virgin Lands Scheme was expensive. Kazakhstan is naturally dry and therefore the farms needed sophisticated irrigation systems, which were expensive to run and maintain. Moreover, Soviet agriculture was labour intensive. During the 1950s and 1960s, between 54 and 44 per cent of the Soviet population worked on farms. By comparison only 5 per cent of the American population worked on farms, which produced more than twice as much food. Clearly, Soviet agriculture was deeply inefficient in comparison with US farms.

After initial success, the Virgin Lands Scheme failed to lead to further growth. Harvests in 1959 and 1960 were slightly below the 1958 levels. Between 1960 and 1964 production slowly increased, so that overall agricultural production was around 15 per cent higher in 1964 than it had been in 1958. These figures were historically high, but they were nothing compared to the targets that Khrushchev had proposed in 1956. Therefore his policy was judged a failure.

There were various problems with Khrushchev's policy which led to the slower growth rates between 1958 and 1964:

- Machine and tractor stations (MTS) were abolished; therefore farm workers were less able to obtain modern farming equipment.
- Centrally directed campaigns were ineffective because they did not reflect local conditions. For example, Khrushchev advocated maize production, which was inappropriate to the climate of many Soviet farms. Therefore labour, fertilisers and farmland was wasted.
- Soviet planners did not always deliver the correct fertiliser to the farms or deliver it when it was needed.
- Khrushchev repeatedly reformed the ministries dealing with agriculture. Contradictory reforms led to administrative confusion.
- Soviet farms often had inadequate storage facilities, and therefore some of the food produced was wasted.
- Pay for agricultural workers increased, but remained inadequate.
- Khrushchev cut investment in agriculture from 12.8 per cent a year from 1954 to 1959 to 2 per cent a year in 1960.
- Khrushchev's investment failed to make Soviet farms more efficient, therefore long-term problems of inefficiency and waste continued.

In sum, Khrushchev's reforms did much to improve Soviet agriculture. However, further improvement was hampered by problems with the system. Specifically, central direction of agriculture meant that local conditions were not taken into account and therefore farming could never be truly effective. Additionally, Khrushchev's reforms did not address the inefficiencies in the system. Finally, reorganisations also created problems, but even without them, Soviet agriculture was too inefficient to meet his ambitious targets.

▲ Khrushchev on a visit to the Institute of Genetics of the Academy of Sciences. Why was Khrushchev so concerned about agriculture?

# 2 Industrial modernisation, 1953–64

The most significant difference between Stalin and the new leadership who took over in 1953 was the emphasis on the need to modernise the Soviet economy. Stalin's Plans created an economy dominated by heavy industry. They were based on the kinds of economy that developed in Britain and Europe in the nineteenth century. However, during the twentieth century, advanced economies had moved away from heavy industry towards **light industry** which produced more high-tech goods and consumer goods.

The Soviet Union's new leadership were aware of this trend and wanted to modernise the Soviet economy in order to make it more consumer oriented and more high-tech. However, the planning methods that had been so successful in creating heavy industry were less effective at creating a modern economy.

### Note it down

Divide a large sheet of paper into three equal columns. Under the headings Goals, Policies and Success/Failure, make notes on Khrushchev's industrial modernisation. Bullet points or the two-thirds one-third method would suit this activity well. Remember to note down specific information that will help you demonstrate how far his policies succeeded.

## Military spending

High levels of military spending were a continual problem for Soviet leaders after 1953. Stalin had deliberately kept living standards at a very basic level in order to ensure that there was enough money available for the military. However, Stalin's heirs were committed to raising the standard of living for the Soviet people. The fundamental problem was that the Soviet economy did not produce enough wealth to continue high levels of military spending and improve living standards.

Khrushchev initiated cuts in military spending in 1955. As a result, military spending fell from 12.1 per cent of GDP in 1955 to 9.1 per cent in 1958. However, between 1958 and 1962 there was a series of nuclear stand-offs between the Soviet Union and the USA, and therefore in 1962 Khrushchev increased military spending. By 1964, military spending was around 11 per cent of GDP. Significantly, the rise in military spending coincided with a fall in economic growth, indicating that increased military spending led to a reduction in economic growth.

## The Seven-Year Plan: Light industry

Khrushchev's economic ambitions were set out in the Seven-Year Plan launched in January 1959. The Plan was designed to boost agricultural production and the production of consumer goods by investing in light industry. Khrushchev hoped that more chemical production would lead to better fertilisers and therefore increased production of crops as well as synthetic fibres, which could be used to make clothes. He believed that chemical production through light industry would encourage growth in the two sections of the economy that needed to be stimulated in order to raise the standard of living in the Soviet Union. The shift in focus also reflected the view that the construction of heavy industry had been largely completed and therefore further investment in heavy industry was unnecessary.

### Khrushchev's vision

For Khrushchev, the purpose of the Soviet economy was to build Communism. Khrushchev and all Communist Party members believed that by the time of Stalin's death the Soviet Union had ended capitalism and entered a new historical stage, the stage of socialism. Khrushchev believed that continued economic growth would lead to the next and final stage of human history: Communism. In 1962, Khrushchev stated that the Soviet Union would achieve Communism by 1980, at which stage housing, transport and food would all be available freely, and consumer goods would be cheap and widely available.

### Years of maximum danger

The Cold War had a major impact on the Soviet economy. Initially, Khrushchev had hoped that the USA and the Soviet Union could compete peacefully. However, between 1958 and 1962 the two superpowers came to the brink of nuclear war on three occasions. The Taiwan Strait Crisis of 1958 led to a stand-off between the USA and the Soviet Union in Asia. The Berlin Crisis of 1961 led to superpower conflict over Germany that was only ended by the erection of the Berlin Wall. Finally, the Cuban Missile Crisis of 1962 led to a raised level of nuclear alert and predictions that the world was days away from nuclear apocalypse.

The period between 1958 and 1962, which historian Gerard J. DeGroot describes as years of maximum danger, led Khrushchev to abandon his hopes of peaceful competition and falling military spending. Indeed, the repeated military stand-offs led to a sharp increase in military spending in the USA and the Soviet Union.

Khrushchev's optimistic plan, which he hoped would lay the foundation for the Soviet Union overtaking the USA by 1970 and building Communism by 1980, was based on a wave of optimism about Soviet economic and technical performance that took place in the late 1950s. This optimism was based on several factors:

- the apparent success of the Virgin Lands Scheme until 1958
- continuing high rates of economic growth
- Soviet technical success in the **space race**: the Soviet Union launched the first artificial satellite in 1957 and the satellite to the moon in 1959.

These achievements suggested to Khrushchev that the Soviet economy was capable of strong rates of growth and technical sophistication.

## Success of the Plan

Production of chemicals and consumer goods certainly increased between 1959 and 1965. However, the increases were not as significant as planners had hoped. There was a 60 per cent increase in the production of consumer goods (see Figure 7), 5 per cent below Khrushchev's target. Fertiliser production increased by 19 million tons, 3.5 million tons short of the target, and synthetic fibre production also increased by 241,000 tons, around 200,000 tons below target.

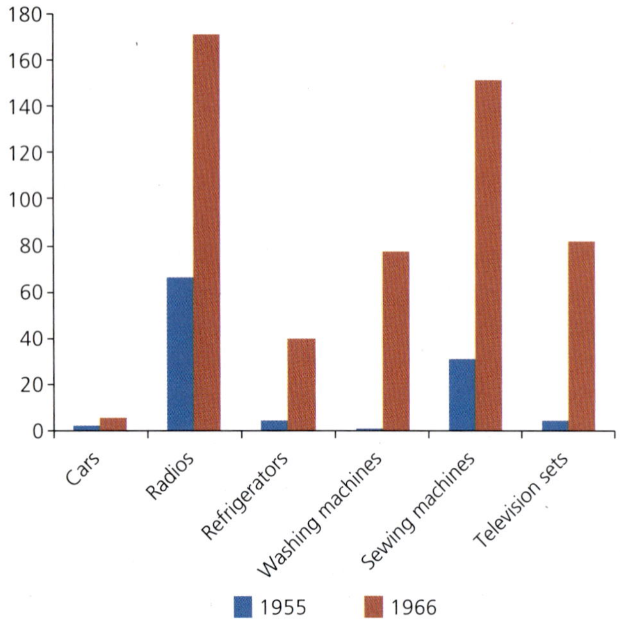


▲ **Figure 7: The increase in the availability of consumer goods in the Soviet Union, 1955–66 (ownership per thousand of the population).**

## Problems with the Plan

The Plan was undermined by Khrushchev's continual economic reforms and by the nature of the Soviet economy.

First, Khrushchev continually introduced economic re-organisation. The reforms were often counterproductive, or at least so short lived that they did not have time to work.

- The February 1957 *sovnarkhoz* reforms decentralised power from Gosplan to 105 *sovnarkhoz:* regional planning agencies. The reforms hampered economic growth by destroying the central co-ordination of the Plan. Moreover, the decentralisation did not solve the problem that planners had too little information about the factories they were directing.
- Between 1958 and 1964 Khrushchev introduced increased centralisation in order to solve the problems created by the *sovnarkhoz* reforms. However, the responsibilities of the *sovnarkhoz* and the new central bodies were not clear, therefore there was confusion in the planning system.
- In February 1962 Khrushchev divided the Party in two: one half of the Party was responsible for agriculture, one half for industry. These reforms were deeply unpopular and took place mid-way through the Seven-Year Plan.
- Khrushchev changed the targets of the Plan in 1962, setting more ambitious goals.

Khrushchev's continual meddling led to a joke that Khrushchev had replaced the Five-Year Plan not with a Seven-Year Plan, but with 'three plans a year'.

Secondly, the Soviet economy itself was not designed to produce consumer goods; the economy was designed to meet targets. Soviet factories produced thick sheet steel, for example, because it made it easier for the factories to meet their production targets: thick sheet steel weighed more than thin sheet steel and production targets were set in weights. However, light industry required thin **sheet steel** to turn into lamps and watches. The lighting industry also set targets in weight. Therefore factories produced light fittings that were too heavy to hang on walls or ceilings.

Similarly, consumer industries were set targets for the value of the goods that they made. Therefore it made sense for factories to produce a small number of expensive goods rather than large quantities of cheap goods. As a result, Soviet furniture factories, for example, produced large expensive sofas that consumers could not afford in order to fulfil the Plan. The fundamental problem with the command economy was that it focused on production rather than consumption. Indeed, planners had to guess at consumer needs. Thus, although the economy did have a greater focus on consumer goods after Stalin's death, the consumer goods that were produced were often useless, undesirable or unaffordable.

# 3 Economic reform and decline after 1964

The failure of Khrushchev's reforms discredited the idea of reform at least until the end of the 1970s. Brezhnev and subsequent Soviet leaders even abandoned the word 'reform'. Nonetheless, there were changes in priorities and small economic changes between Khrushchev's fall in 1964 and Chernenko's death in 1985.

### Note it down

Using bullet points or the 1:2 method (see page x), make notes on the following topics:

- policy change after 1964
- economic success, 1964–85
- economic decline, 1964–85
- causes of Soviet economic decline.

Make sure you note down enough detail to demonstrate both the extent of the success and the extent of the failure during this period.

## Restoration of the economy

Khrushchev's fall led to a rejection of many of his reforms:

- The Party was reunited; the division between the agricultural and industrial sections was ended.
- Seven-Year Plans were abandoned. From 1966, the economy continued to follow Five-Year Plans.

In essence, Brezhnev was content to manage the system that Stalin had set up. Like Khrushchev, he too hoped to be able to provide more consumer goods. However, Brezhnev was far less ambitious than Khrushchev in terms of the quality and quantity of consumer goods he expected from the Soviet economy.

## The 'Kosygin reforms'

Khrushchev's successors continued the attempt to stimulate light industry. Kosygin (see page 34) advocated reforms that were designed to cut investment in the most inefficient collective farms and divert the money to light industry. Additionally, he proposed giving power over production to factory managers and judging their success not by production levels, but by the profit they made. This was designed to force factories to produce goods that consumers wanted.

The 'Kosygin reforms' were introduced in January 1968, but ended in August. Similar reforms in Czechoslovakia had been part of a series of reforms that led to a Czechoslovakian rebellion against the Soviet Union. This rebellion discredited Kosygin's programme, and therefore the reforms were halted in August. Authority was returned to central planners.

## Increased military investment

Brezhnev increased military investment. His goal was to achieve parity with the USA in terms of their nuclear firepower. During the Berlin Crisis of 1961 and the Cuban Missile Crisis of 1962 Khrushchev had been forced to back down because he knew that the USA had much larger nuclear arsenals and therefore could wipe out the Soviet Union in a nuclear war. Brezhnev wanted to achieve parity with the USA so that the Soviet Union would never be forced to back down by the USA again.

Military spending increased from around 11 per cent of GDP in 1964 to 13 per cent in 1970. The policy was a success; nuclear parity was achieved by 1970. However, achieving and maintaining nuclear parity was a significant drain on the Soviet economy, which led to growing economic problems (see page 147).

## 'Developed socialism'

Brezhnev dropped Khrushchev's commitment to building Communism by 1980. Slower economic growth in the 1960s and 1970s and increased military spending meant that there was no possibility of transforming the Soviet Union into a land of plenty. Nonetheless, Brezhnev argued that the Soviet Union should deliver a rising standard of living for the majority, of its citizens. This meant abandoning Khrushchev's promise of Communism by 1980 and replacing it with 'developed socialism': an economy in which there was job security and low prices. Low food prices were achieved by importing large amounts of grain from the West, rather than by expanding the Virgin Lands Scheme or by initiating economic reform.

### Second economy and the black market

From 1928 and the beginning of Stalin's economic transformation of the Soviet Union a black market developed in the Soviet Union. However, the black market remained relatively small due to Stalin's willingness to punish black marketers with death or long-term imprisonment in labour camps. With the death of Stalin and more limited use of terror the black market grew. Consequently, after Stalin's death it became known as a 'second economy' or 'black economy', indicating its scale.

## The second economy

Brezhnev also accepted the second economy, or black economy, as a necessary evil. Rather than trying to stamp out illegal trading Brezhnev allowed it to continue as it increased access to consumer goods and food, and therefore aided his goal of raising living standards.

## Andropov's 'reforms', 1982–84

Andropov, like Brezhnev, refused to talk of reforms. However, his approach to the economy was important because, unlike Brezhnev, he was willing to admit that there were considerable economic problems that needed to be fixed. Nonetheless, Andropov was not willing to change the fundamental nature of the economy. For Andropov, the key issue was labour discipline. To improve productivity he initiated three campaigns:

- Anti-corruption campaign: In November 1982 Andropov investigated senior Party officials and industrial managers who were using Soviet resources to make themselves rich. For example, Brezhnev's **Minister of the Interior** Nikolai Shchelokov was sacked and put on trial for corruption. He took his own life before the end of his trial.
- Anti-alcohol campaign: Workers could be sacked for drunkenness and could be fined for damaging machinery or products if they were drunk at work.
- Operation Trawl, an anti-drunkenness and anti-absenteeism campaign: KGB officers visited parks, restaurants and train stations arresting people who were drunk or who were absent from work.

Andropov's campaigns did lead to a reduction in the consumption of traditional vodka. However, the consumption of 'Andropovka', a lower-quality cheaper vodka, increased. Additionally, Andropov's campaigns were poorly enforced and therefore drunkenness and poor discipline continued. Andropov's reforms did not lead to the end of the Soviet Union, nor did they stop economic decline.

## Soviet economic decline

Soviet economic decline became evident in the 1970s. However, its roots were much deeper. Fundamentally, neither Khrushchev's reforms nor Brezhnev's management were able to address the fundamental issues of the Soviet economy which led to its decline.

### Declining growth

In 1945 the Soviet economy was the fastest growing economy in the world. Between 1950 and 1958 the economy grew at an average rate of 7.1 per cent a year. The USA, by contrast grew by an average of about 2.9 per cent a year during the same period. Therefore the Soviet economy seemed to be outperforming the US economy. However, Soviet growth rates declined to an average of 5.3 per cent between 1958 and 1964 and to around 2 per cent in the 1970s.

This shift reflected some of the fundamental problems in the Soviet economy. In general terms, the command economy was good at producing 'extensive growth': growth that was based on building new factories, workshops or opening new mines. However, it was unable to create 'intensive growth': growth that is based on improving the efficiency of existing factories, workshops or mines. Intensive growth relies on good information about how individual factories work. Central planning agencies, even at a regional level did not have the information to improve the efficiency of individual factories.

The problems with central planning meant that the Soviet system was never able to conquer the inefficiencies that had emerged in the system in the 1930s.

### The impact of oil prices

One of the features of the Soviet economy in the 1970s was declining growth and yet rising standards of living. The general rise in the international price of oil in the early 1970s masked the problems of the Soviet economy. Rising prices ensured the Soviet Union could make more money from selling oil. Oil production increased from 243 million tons in 1965 to 603 million tons in 1980 in order to supply international demand. This allowed the Soviet economy to keep importing grain from the West. Additionally, the Soviet Government was able to borrow money from Western governments based on their income from oil. As a result, standards of living continued to improve in spite of lower growth rates.

## The Soviet economy, 1964–85

Economic reforms after 1964 were minor. In essence, Brezhnev accepted the Soviet economy as it was, and rather than try to improve the economy he attempted to lower expectations.

Andropov's reforms did try to address the problem of Soviet economic decline that had become evident in the 1970s. Nonetheless, he too remained committed to the essential features of the system: central planning of industry and collectivisation of agriculture.

## Conclusion

Between 1953 and 1985 the successive leaders failed to solve the economic problems of the Soviet economy. Khrushchev and Brezhnev both had some success in raising the standard of living. But Soviet citizens still had less to eat and fewer consumer comforts than citizens of the USA or Western Europe. The golden age of the 1950s, with high levels of economic growth, large harvests, declining defence spending and technical successes in the space race, gave way to a period of economic stagnation from 1964 to 1985. During this period growth rates declined, military spending increased and the government was forced to import large amounts of grain to feed its own citizens. Inefficiencies in the economy were never solved. Khrushchev's reforms were largely counterproductive, and Brezhnev's economic management did nothing to stop the decline. However, while oil prices remained high, Brezhnev was able to allow growth rates to fall and still see a gradual rise in the standard of living. In short, the Soviet Union remained a dysfunctional economic giant that was able to produce a massive nuclear arsenal but was unable to grow enough food to feed its own people.

### Work together

Using your notes from this chapter and previous chapters, discuss with a partner which of the Soviet leaders was most successful in the period 1917–82. In order to do this draw four spider diagrams on a sheet of paper – one for each of the major leaders in this period. Make notes on each diagram about the political and economic success of each leader.

Having completed the diagrams, discuss which was the most successful. Remember you will have to consider what 'success' means in this context. Moreover, 'success' may not have meant the same for each leader.

Having done this write a paragraph together evaluating the success of the four leaders. The paragraph should contain the following features:

- an opening sentence that clearly indicates which leader was most successful
- details of the leader's successes
- comparisons to all three other leaders
- a criterion for success
- a concluding sentence that explains why one leader, rather than the others, was the most successful.

### Chapter summary

- Economic policy under Stalin's successors essentially went through two phases:
  - reform, 1954–64
  - restoration, 1964–85.
- The economic policy failed to solve the fundamental problems of the economy.
- As a result growth rates slowed and by the mid-1970s the economy had begun to stagnate.

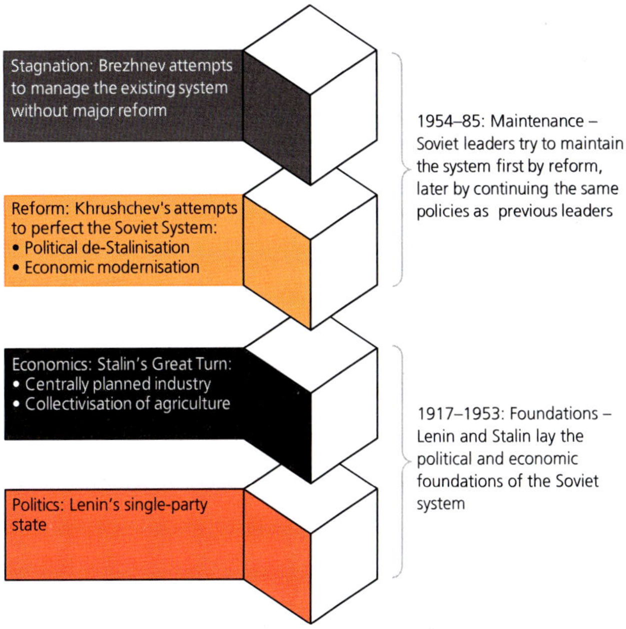


▲ **Summary diagram: Changing economic priorities, 1953–85.**

## Recommended reading

E. Bacon and M. Sandle (eds.), *Brezhnev Reconsidered* (Palgrave McMillan, 2002), pages 38-67. Bacon and Sandle consider the nature of the Soviet economy under Brezhnev.

R.G. Suny (ed.), *The Cambridge History of Russia Volume III* (Cambridge, 2006), pages 278-280. Suny analyses the successes and failures of Khrushchev's economic policy.

W. Taubman, S. Khrushchev, and A. Gleason (eds.), *Nikita Khrushchev* (Yale University Press, 2000), pages 138-159. Taubman, Khrushchev and Gleason consider Khrushchev's economic policy in the context of his wider vision of Soviet society.

# Essay technique: Overall judgement

In addition to focus and structure (see page 26–27), the level of relevant detail (see page 39) and analysis (see page 59), your exam essays will be assessed on how far you reach a supported overall judgement. The clearer and better supported your judgement, the better your mark is likely to be. The mark scheme distinguishes between five levels of judgement. (This is a summary – the full mark scheme can be found on Edexcel's website.)

| | |
|---|---|
| **Level 1** | No overall judgement. |
| **Level 2** | Stated overall judgement, but no support. |
| **Level 3** | Overall judgement is reached, with weak support. |
| **Level 4** | Overall judgement is reached, and supported. |
| **Level 5 (HIGH)** | Overall judgement is reached, and supported by consideration of the relative significance of key factors. |

This section looks at reaching and supporting an overall judgement. Dealing with the relative significance of key factors is discussed at the end of Chapter 4c (see page 142–143).

## Reaching an overall judgement

The conclusion of your essay should reach an overall judgement. This judgement should reflect the overall argument of your essay.

Imagine you are answering the following question:

**How far did the economic priorities of the Russian Government change in the period 1928–64?**

Your essay plan might look like this:

- *Paragraph 1: Key priority: industry*
- *Paragraph 2: Preparation for war*
- *Paragraph 3: Consumer goods*
- *Paragraph 4: Economic innovation*

Your essay might argue that in the period 1928–64 the Russian Government's key priority was always industry. However, the government's focus on other priorities such as war, consumer goods and innovation, changed. This argument should be reflected in your overall judgement. Therefore your conclusion might look like the one below:

> *In conclusion, the main economic priority of the Russian Government changed very little in the period 1928–64. However, other aspects of economic policy changed more significantly.*

Establishes that you are reaching your overall judgement.

The words of the question are used to answer the question – ensuring a clear focus.

The judgement distinguishes between 'the main economic priorities' and 'other aspects' and therefore creates a sophisticated and balanced judgement.

This is a good start, because an overall judgement has been reached that reflects the argument of the essay. But so far the overall judgement only has weak support.

## Supporting your overall judgement

In order to reach the higher levels it is important to support your overall judgement. This can be achieved by backing up your judgement with a summary of the key points of your essay. For example, the overall judgement you have just read could be improved by adding the following summaries of your argument:

> In conclusion, the main economic priority of the Russian Government changed very little in the period 1928–64. Indeed, Stalin and Khrushchev both agreed that industrialisation was an essential part of socialism. Therefore the Five-Year Plans and Seven-Year Plan reflect a continuing commitment to building industry in the USSR. However, other aspects of economic policy changed more significantly. For example, there was little focus on rearmament before 1936, and consumer goods were less important to Stalin than they were under Khrushchev. Therefore, in spite of changing policies, it is clear that economic priorities of the Russian Government were broadly consistent, although the shifting focus on rearmament and consumer goods indicates that there was some change in the period 1928–64.

This summary supports the judgement about the main economic priority.

This summary supports the judgement about other aspects of the economy.

The final sentence provides a summary overall judgement.

This conclusion is an example of high-level work because it reaches an overall judgement and supports it with material that reflects the rest of the essay.

### Activity: Writing an overall judgement

Here is a plan in answer to the question:

**How successfully did Soviet economic policy meet its aims in the years 1928–85?**

- Paragraph 1: Military – very successful
- Paragraph 2: Heavy industry – broadly successful
- Paragraph 3: Consumer goods – moderately successful
- Paragraph 4: Agriculture – partially successful

Using your notes:

- Write two summary sentences that state an overall judgement about how far Soviet economic policy succeeded in meeting its aim.
- Support these with a summary overview of the successes and failures.
- Write a final sentence that summarises your judgement.

# Theme 3 Control of the people, 1917–85

In this theme you will consider the following:

- Soviet control of the media, use of propaganda and suppression of religion
- The secret police: its changing role under Yagoda, Yezhov, Beria and Andropov
- Communism and cultural change: the avant-garde, Socialist Realism, non-conformity and dissident artists.

## The Big Picture

Lenin's one-party state gave the Communists control of the government, and Stalin's policies of collectivisation and central industrial planning gave him control of the economy. However, Communist leaders aspired to even greater levels of control. The Communist project was not simply to remake politics and economics. Communists dreamed of remaking humanity, of replacing Homo sapiens with Homo Sovieticus: Soviet man. This new kind of human being would live for the good of the whole of society having been purged of selfish ambition. The total transformation of humanity required total control – control of the media, control of religion, control of art, and control of human behaviour through the use of a terroristic secret police.

The extent to which the different Soviet leaders achieved total control, or even tried to achieve total control, varied. Lenin's government, for example, worked with radical artists rather than imposing its own artistic vision. Stalin's government, particularly in the late 1930s, was broadly successful at controlling the whole of Soviet life and has therefore been described as totalitarian by some historians. However, even under Stalin there were spontaneous initiatives from below that Stalin did not control. Khrushchev and Brezhnev abandoned the use of widespread terror and were prepared to tolerate some degree of independence on the part of Soviet citizens.

## TIMELINE

| | |
|---|---|
| 1917 October | Decree on Land |
| 1917 November | Decree on the Press |
| 1917 December | Cheka established |
| 1918 January | Decree Concerning Separation of Church and State |
| 1918 January | First photograph of Lenin published |
| 1920 | Department of Agitation Propaganda (*Agitprop*) set up |
| 1920 | Commissar of Enlightenment established *Glavpolitprosvet* |
| 1922 | *Glavlit*, a new organisation which oversaw a more systematic censorship regime, introduced |
| 1932 | Union of Soviet Writers established |
| 1934 | Yagoda appointed head of the NKVD |
| 1938 | Beria became the head of the NKVD |
| 1938 | Two histories of the Communist Party, both edited by Stalin, published |
| 1949 | Leningrad Affair |
| 1953 | Beria arrested and executed |
| 1954 | *Doctor Zhivago* refused publication in the Soviet Union |
| 1966 | Sinyavsky-Daniel trial |
| 1967 | Yuri Andropov promoted to head of the KGB |
| 1968 | Prague Spring |
| 1968 | Sakharov circulated his essay, *Reflections on Progress*, criticising the Soviet Union's stance on human rights |
| 1973 | Solzhenitsyn forced into exile |
| 1975 | Helsinki Agreement on human rights |

# 3a: Media, propaganda and religion

## Overview

In 1917 Lenin seized power in the name of the Russian workers. He wanted to end capitalism and exploitation. However, he had little time for what he considered 'bourgeois freedoms', such as freedom of the press or freedom of religion. Therefore in the extraordinary situation of the revolution and the Civil War he permitted press censorship and the persecution of religion. By 1921 it was clear that the Communists had won the war, but they had not won the hearts of the people. Therefore censorship and religious persecution, which had been introduced as temporary measures, became permanent features of Soviet rule, at least until Stalin's death in 1953. Nonetheless, the government's approach to both issues changed over time. There was more press freedom for ordinary people under Khrushchev and Brezhnev than there had been in earlier years, and the government's policy on religion swayed between repression and toleration as leaders came and went.

Even though Communists rejected religion, they understood its power. Stalin and Felix Dzerzhinsky (see page 83), for example, had considered becoming priests, and many of the leaders had religious upbringings. Therefore senior Communists often used religious language and imagery. On a deeper level, senior Communists believed that ordinary Soviet citizens were not well educated enough to understand the truths of Marxism. Consequently, they developed art, culture, political rituals and even political cults which used religious imagery in order to appeal to ordinary people in a way that the leaders believed would help them embrace the government. Cults of personality, first of Stalin and Lenin, then of Khrushchev and finally of Brezhnev, were designed, in part, to give the Soviet people an alternative to religion. They also helped foster support for the regime.

This chapter considers:

1. State control of mass media and propaganda
2. Personality cults
3. Communism and religion.

## 1 State control of mass media and propaganda

Lenin viewed the press and the media as central to advancing the revolution and ensuring the Communists retained power.

Prior to the revolution Lenin had announced his intention to close down 'bourgeois newspapers'. However, this was only part of the revolutionary strategy. Lenin believed that revolutionary success required control of all communications in Russia. The new government established control of the press and media by:

- announcing the Decree on the Press in November 1917, which gave the government the emergency powers to close any newspapers which supported a counter-revolution
- creating a **state** monopoly of advertising in November 1917, which ensured that only the government could publish adverts
- nationalising the Petrograd Telegraph Agency in November 1917, which gave the new government control of electronic means of communication
- establishing a Revolutionary Tribunal of the Press in January 1918, with the power to censor the press; journalists and editors who committed 'crimes against the people' could be punished by the **Cheka** (see page 10), who were empowered to impose fines or prison sentences, confiscate property or exile offending writers
- establishing the All-Russia Telegraph Agency (ROSTA), which was solely responsible for distributing news.

Initially, Lenin closed down papers that supported the **Tsar** or the **Provisional Government**. However, by mid-1918 he had outlawed opposition socialist papers as well. By 1921 the Communists had closed 2000 newspapers and 575 printing presses. Control of the press was also aided by the economic controls introduced under War Communism, as they allowed the government to control all printing presses and stocks of paper.

As a result of these policies *Pravda*, the newspaper of the Communist Party, gained a much higher circulation, and by the early 1920's it was one of the best selling publications in the Soviet Union. Communist control of Sovnarkum also gave them control over the official newspaper of the Soviets, *Izvestia*.

## Note it down

On a large sheet of paper, draw a timeline of the period 1917–85. Next divide it into periods that correspond to the rule of the different leaders. Make notes on Communist control of the media from 1917 to 1985. Use different coloured pens to distinguish aspects of policy that change and aspects of policy that stay the same.

## Early propaganda

Propaganda was as important to Lenin as censorship. Early propaganda took various forms.

### The initial cult of Lenin

Initially, the Communist regime was quite pluralistic. Equally, before 1928 there was a relatively high degree of debate and disagreement about how Communist principles should be put into practice. This pluralism was reflected in the kind of propaganda that was produced in the first years of the revolution. Significantly, Lenin did not approve of all of the images, or approaches used by those working for the new government.

The cult of Lenin was one example of a type of propaganda that emerged early in the regime that Lenin did not approve of. Pictures of Lenin were a form of propaganda used to promote the government from the beginning of 1918. January 1918 saw the publication of the first photograph of Lenin. The focus on Lenin increased in August. Following an assassination attempt, Lenin was described in essentially religious terms. His survival was described as 'miraculous', and the emphasis on his willingness to suffer and sacrifice his life for his people made Lenin into a modern day Christ.

The cult flourished, in spite of Lenin's disapproval. Many senior Communists believed that ordinary workers and peasants needed a very simple message that they could understand. Others believed that the Communists should use techniques similar to those used by the Orthodox Church and the Tsar to support the new regime. These included a focus on a good and kind leader. In 1919, during the Civil War, even though resources were scarce, busts and statues of Lenin were produced. Lenin's photograph also appeared with various titles, such as 'Leader of the Revolutionary **Proletariat**'. Significantly, the new cult had a socialist edge.

During 1919 and 1920, a new style of writing about Lenin emerged. Increasingly, Lenin was depicted as being humane, a man of the people, a man who refused luxury, a visionary and a man of great power. At the same time, from 1919 Lenin was often photographed wearing a cap, as the cap implied that Lenin was approachable and down to earth.

Lenin was aware of these trends and was uncomfortable with them, but he understood their importance and therefore allowed the cult to grow. The media and propaganda focus on Lenin gave the revolution and the Communist Party a face, someone the Russian people could identify with and support.

▲ A spectre is haunting Europe, 1920. How does the poster reflect the goals and values of Communism?

## Karl Marx and Communist propaganda

Communist propaganda made use of Marx and his works in a variety of ways. For example, Communists took phrases from Marx's work and incorporated them into posters. The phrase 'A spectre is haunting Europe – the spectre of Communism', for example, comes from the Communist Manifesto. Marx's face was also used in posters, often in a line with the faces of Lenin and Stalin, implying that Lenin and Stalin were his revolutionary heirs.

### Cartoons and photomontage

In the first years of the revolution, the government collaborated with avant-garde artists to produce posters promoting the revolution (see page 72). Many of these featured Lenin. 'A Spectre is Haunting Europe – the Spectre of Communism' was one early poster which showed a grim and determined Lenin standing in front of a red banner pointing to the west. Gustav Klutsis used photomontage to create posters advertising Lenin's electrification plan, which was unveiled on his fiftieth birthday.

## Media and the NEP

Lenin's initial press censorship regime continued throughout the Civil War. Military victory did not, however, lead to increased press freedom. Rather, in 1922, Felix Dzerzhinsky, leader of the Soviet political police (see page 83), introduced *Glavlit*, a new organisation which oversaw a more systematic censorship regime.

*Glavlit*'s censorship worked on the following principles:

- The GPU was put in charge of policing every publication available in the Soviet Union.
- New professional censors were employed.
- All books were investigated for anti-Communist bias.
- The GPU compiled a list of banned books.

As a result of *Glavlit*'s work, Soviet libraries were purged of politically dangerous books. New special holding libraries, or 'book **Gulags**', were set up to house the banned books. Access was restricted to senior Party members.

## Stalin's media

Under Stalin, censorship was tightened still further. In the mid-1930s the works of **Zinoviev**, **Kamenev**, Trotsky and other leading revolutionaries from the 1920s had to be purged from Soviet libraries. Lenin's own works were 'edited' to remove complimentary statements about Stalin's opponents. Even Stalin's works were edited to remove any indication that he had once been close to those he purged. Soviet history was rewritten, too, to remove the contributions of Stalin's opponents and to emphasise Stalin's role in the revolution (see page 75).

From 1928, *Glavlit* controlled access to economic data. Additionally, restrictions were placed on all kinds of 'bad news'. The Soviet media were forbidden from publishing stories about natural disasters, suicides, industrial accidents or even bad weather in order to create the impression that the Soviet Union was a place in which good things happened. Those bad news stories that did get reported were attributed to the work of saboteurs. Stalin was given the credit for all the achievements of the regime.

Propaganda in the Stalin period focused on the leader. The cult of Stalin turned him into a semi-divine figure, whose unique vision and unique wisdom would lead the nation to **socialism**. Propaganda also focused on archetypal Soviet workers. Socialist Realist art (see pages 99–100), including sculptures such as 'The Worker and the Collective Farm Woman' (1937), depicted Soviet people as muscular, heroic, dedicated and beautiful, the perfect embodiment of the society that Stalin was trying to build.

## Growing media pluralism

Under Khrushchev and Brezhnev the media changed. As part of their attempts to create a new consumer society magazines proliferated, as did radios and television sets.

### Consumer magazines

Popular magazines changed the Soviet media in the 1950s and 1960s. As part of the drive to create a consumer society, magazines were encouraged to publish readers' letters. However, rather than praising the achievements of socialism, readers' letters often exposed long-term problems with Soviet society. In consumer magazines, readers complained about the quality and scarcity of consumer goods. Letters to women's magazines, like *Rabotnitsa* (the Woman Worker), exposed more profound problems. Readers complained about male alcoholism, inequalities in the home relating to childcare and housework, as well as domestic violence. Rather than suppressing the letters, Khrushchev's media responded with its own campaigns against worthless men. Instead of focusing on the domestic failure of men, they focused on male hypocrisy and lack of devotion to Communism. Cartoons in *Krokodil,* a satirical magazine, poked fun at men who arrived at parades drunk, late or not at all.

## Soviet cinema and television

Soviet cinema also changed under Khrushchev as part of a broader cultural 'thaw', or liberalisation (see page 100). Many of the films of this era focused on traditional themes such as the Soviet victory in the Second World War or the Communist victory in the Civil War. Yet, rather than focusing on the contribution of Stalin, films such as *The Forty-First* (1956), *The Cranes are Flying* (1957) and *Ballad of a Soldier* (1959) focused on the role played by ordinary people.

Television also took off in Khrushchev's last years. Between 1960 and 1964 Soviet television was broadly successful in supporting the regime. First, it played a major role in celebrating the Soviet Union's triumphs in the **space race**. In 1961 millions of viewers watched a five-hour programme celebrating Yuri Gagarin's space flight. Similar shows in 1963 focused on Valentina Tereshkova, the first woman in space. Television coverage stressed her ordinariness: she was born on a collective farm and then became a textile worker in a Soviet factory. Also in 1961, Soviet television broadcast the nation's first television news show, *Estafeta Novosteo* (News and Mail). The programme contained regular features about model workers on farms and in factories as part of Khrushchev's drive to increase labour productivity.

Under Brezhnev film and television culture changed. There were traditional elements such as films celebrating Soviet victory in the Second World War (see page 105). However, during the same period there were more films dealing with working people and their daily lives. Significantly Soviet film makers tended to focus on fashionable citizens living in luxurious apartments. In so doing they stoked public desire for consumer goods and fashion.

Brezhnev attempted to use television to his advantage. In some ways this was successful. For example, the Soviet Government was able to keep tight control of the footage of the war in Afghanistan, and in so doing could keep the truth about the scale and horrors of the war hidden. Soviet officials also ensured that Brezhnev's speeches were transmitted in full, and that he was at the centre of a great deal of domestic media coverage. However, by the late 1970s this tactic backfired. The cameras showed a man who was clearly physically and mentally incapacitated, who struggled to make speeches, became confused mid-sentence and had difficulty walking. Television coverage of Brezhnev continued until the last week of his life; his last television appearance shows him struggling to walk up the steps of the Lenin Mausoleum. Television voice-overs praised Brezhnev, but viewers could see his physical and mental decline for themselves.

### Soviet War in Afghanistan

The Soviet War in Afghanistan lasted from December 1979 to February 1989. The Soviet Union intervened to aid a pro-Soviet government at the outbreak of a civil war. China, Pakistan, Britain and the USA provided support for insurgent forces.

The war dragged on for almost a decade. During that time, mounting losses and the seemingly endless nature of the war led many Soviet citizens to lose faith in the war and in their government. The war is sometimes called the 'Soviet Union's Vietnam War' due to its impact on the prestige of the nation.

Under Brezhnev, Soviet leaders also lost control of the print media. The KGB continued to police political publications, particularly the work of dissidents (see page 104). However, Western magazines became increasingly available in Soviet cities as part of the second economy. These tended to be consumer magazines such as *Vogue*. While not overtly political, these magazines undermined faith in the Soviet system by showing the quality of Western goods and the luxury of Western lifestyles.

## Conclusion

Control of the media was an essential part of Lenin's vision for consolidating power. For many years Soviet media control was extremely effective. The Soviet media turned Lenin into the first hero of the revolution and a man that people could identify with. Under Stalin, propaganda focused on the Soviet Union's god-like leader and his heroic nation of perfect workers. However, with the advent of consumerism and increasing emphasis on consumer choice, the system changed. Consumer choice led to increased magazine circulation, the availability of television sets and even a **black market** in Western magazines. All of these changed the nature of the media. Under Khrushchev there was an increasing emphasis on ordinary people. Television showed ordinary people who had travelled into space, ordinary people who worked well on collective farms, while magazines carried letters about ordinary people's lives, and films focused on ordinary people who fought in the Second World War. Finally, television exposed Brezhnev's frailty and Western magazines revealed the gap between the rich West and the relatively poor Soviet Union, trends which both undermined the Soviet system.

## 2 Personality cults

Between 1918 and 1924 the Soviet media had created a cult of Lenin's personality. It led to public trust in Lenin, and Soviet leaders appealed to Lenin's legacy throughout the 1920s in an attempt to legitimise their actions and keep the Soviet Government stable.

Stalin's emergence as leader led to a new cult of personality, which projected Stalin as a second Lenin, 'the Lenin of today'. The cult served a similar purpose: media techniques turned Stalin into the face of the regime, a person the Soviet people could have complete faith in. Propaganda turned Stalin into an all-powerful, infallible semi-divine figure, the Soviet people's 'leader, teacher and friend'.

De-Stalinisation led to a rejection of Stalin's 'cult of personality'. Even so, Khrushchev and Brezhnev both became the subjects of personality cults. Personality cults after 1953 were much smaller affairs. Khrushchev's was dogged by failure and Brezhnev's inspired cynicism rather than respect.

### The cult of Stalin

The cult of Stalin was much more extensive than the cult of Lenin (see page 72). It also required more elaborate techniques in order to make the past fit with the myth created around Stalin.

#### The purpose of the cult

Stalin's cult, like Lenin's before it, served a specific political purpose. First, it emphasised Stalin's legitimacy to take over leadership of the Party. Stalin was fit to rule because he was carrying on Lenin's work and because he was a heroic genius. Equally, the cult created a figure that Soviet citizens could trust, respect and even worship. Moreover, dissatisfaction with daily life could be blamed on local leaders while citizens could trust Stalin to make a better future.

> **Note it down**
>
> On a large sheet of paper draw three spider diagrams, one for each of the leaders covered in this section. On each make notes about the nature of the personality cult and the ways in which it helped support the regime. The last two personality cults were less effective than the cult of Stalin. Using a different coloured pen, make notes on the ways in which the cult of Khrushchev and the cult of Brezhnev undermined the regime.

#### The Myth of Two Leaders

Stalin's cult was bound up in the 'Myth of Two Leaders'. This myth led Soviet people to believe that the October Revolution, victory in the Civil War and the foundation of the Soviet Union had been masterminded by a duumvirate consisting of Lenin and Stalin.

The myth required Soviet history to be extensively rewritten, to place Stalin at the centre of events and to remove Trotsky and other leaders from the story. This was achieved by:

- the publication in 1938 of two histories of the Communist Party, both edited by Stalin
- Socialist Realist paintings which were created showing Stalin working closely with Lenin
- altering photographs – Trotsky and other former leaders were taken out of pictures with Lenin.

#### Lenin's heir

As well as recreating the past, the cult of Stalin implied that Stalin was continuing on the path created by Lenin. Painters used a variety of techniques to show that Stalin was Lenin's true heir. Grigory Shegal's *Leader, Teacher, Friend* shows Stalin standing immediately in front of a bust of Lenin. Gustav Klutsis' photomontages use a different technique. They show a row of figures running from Marx, through Lenin to Stalin, implying that Stalin is the latest in a tradition of revolutionary leaders.

#### The *vozhd*

The cult of Stalin also turned Stalin into an infallible and celebrated figure. He was routinely known as 'the ***vozhd***', which simply means leader. The term is significant, because unlike words like President or Prime Minister, *vozhd* has no legal significance. Therefore while the powers of a President or a Prime Minister are limited by law, the powers of the *vozhd* have no obvious limit. *Pravda* and other Communist newspapers praised the *vozhd*'s wisdom daily. Stalin's birthday became a national celebration with parades.

#### Generalissimo

The Stalin Cult changed following the Second World War. From 1945, Stalin's role as Generalissimo, or war leader, became the focus of much Soviet propaganda. While Stalin preferred the title Marshal to Generalissimo, both titles reflected an increasing emphasis on Stalin as a military figure. Before the Second World War Stalin was presented as a revolutionary and a thinker. However, as Generalissimo he was presented as a military genius, as the man who

## The Cult of Impersonality

Khrushchev described the Stalin cult as a cult of personality. Stalin's biographer, Robert Service, argues that it is better understood as a Cult of Impersonality. The cult, he argues, gave very little away about Stalin's history and character. Rather, the Stalin Cult centred on the successes of the Soviet regime. Stalin was regularly photographed with heroes of the Soviet air force and Russian explorers who had returned from the North and South Poles. In this sense, the Stalin Cult associated Stalin with the heroic side of the regime, rather than focusing on Stalin as an individual.

defeated Hitler and as the saviour of the nation. This change in presentation was accompanied by a change in the way Stalin was depicted in pictures. Up until 1945 Stalin tended to be pictured wearing blue-grey or green military tops. However, in his last years he tended to be painted wearing a white uniform. Stalin designed the uniform himself and the military rank of Generalissimo was created specifically for Stalin.

## Cults of personality under Khrushchev

After Stalin's death cults of personality were less grand. Khrushchev criticised Stalin's cult, but established two of his own. First, Khrushchev revived the cult of Lenin. However, whereas the cult of Lenin in the 1930s had stressed Lenin's death, the cult of Lenin in the 1950s was based on the slogan 'Lenin lives!' Under Khrushchev, Lenin was depicted as fun, approachable, humane, a person who loved children, family and lived a simple life. In many ways Khrushchev's Lenin resembled Khrushchev himself. The purpose of the cult was to move away from Stalinism. For Khrushchev, this meant rediscovering Leninism. It also reminded Soviet citizens that the government was founded on Lenin's revolution rather than Stalin's terror.

Secondly, by 1958 Khrushchev had a personality cult of his own. According to Soviet propaganda Khrushchev was:

- a disciple of Lenin who was completing the journey that Lenin had started
- responsible for new successes such as the Soviet space programme and rising harvests in the Virgin Lands
- a respected statesman who negotiated with the US President as an equal
- a hero of the Second World War
- an authority on literature, art, science, industry and agriculture
- the great reformer who was perfecting the Soviet system.

The Khrushchev Cult became more problematic in the early 1960s. By associating himself so strongly with the success of the Virgin Lands Scheme, he was seriously damaged by its failure. The claim to expertise became less credible following the disastrous results of his Corn Campaign. His embarrassing foreign policy climb-downs (see page 33) and his failure to deliver on his wildly optimistic promises about out-producing the USA led to a collapse in confidence in Khrushchev's fitness to govern.

## The Cult of Brezhnev

Brezhnev's personality cult was a shadow of Stalin's. Brezhnev adopted a cult of personality for **pragmatic** reasons. By 1964, a cult of the leader was well established as an essential feature of Soviet politics. Brezhnev decided to adopt a leadership cult to consolidate his position and help stabilise the regime.

The Brezhnev Cult had four key aspects. According to Soviet propaganda Brezhnev was ideally suited to rule because he was:

- a great Leninist: Brezhnev had not known Lenin, but he claimed to be continuing the work started by Lenin, particularly working for world peace
- a military hero: Brezhnev attempted to present himself as a military leader and official publications stressed his military prowess in the Second World War; he was promoted to the position of Marshal of the **Red Army** and received 60 medals
- dedicated to ensuring world peace: Brezhnev stressed his foreign policy successes in developing **détente** with the USA
- a true man of the people: Brezhnev biographies told of his humble origins and how he worked as an engineer in the steel industry.

Brezhnev constructed his image through a series of public festivals marking important anniversaries, such as the fiftieth anniversary of the October Revolution in 1967, the twentieth and thirtieth anniversaries of the victory in the Second World War in 1965 and 1975, and Brezhnev's major birthdays. Speeches by Brezhnev dominated these occasions, and photographs of the leader were an important part of the press coverage of the celebrations.

However, the Brezhnev Cult was counterproductive. Brezhnev was mocked for his claims to greatness. Veterans of the Second World War resented the inflation of Brezhnev's role in the war. Young people, aware of the size of the Soviet military, were not taken in by his claims to be an advocate of peace. Also the lavish and luxurious lifestyle of Brezhnev's family undercut the claims that he was a man of the people. Brezhnev's Cult was simply not plausible. Whereas Stalin had been respected and feared, Brezhnev became the butt of numerous jokes that focused on his vanity and his hollow claims. Whereas Stalin's cult inspired loyalty and respect, the Brezhnev Cult inspired cynicism.

## Conclusion

In the early years of the regime the cult of Lenin had been an important factor in winning and retaining power. While the Lenin Cult had helped the Party control the Soviet Union, the Stalin Cult helped Stalin gain control of the Party and the country. In that sense, the cult of Stalin was a method of creating and sustaining personal rule. Later cults were much less impressive. Stalin had ensured that the gap between the myth and reality was never exposed. Khrushchev was caught out by claiming credit for policies that later became public failures. Brezhnev's Cult was implausible from the beginning. Whereas people had believed that Stalin was an all-conquering genius, the Soviet people were not taken in by Brezhnev's military awards.

# 3 Communism and religion

The Communist regime's attitude to religion changed over time. Lenin and Khrushchev, for example, were dedicated to the destruction of religion for ideological reasons. Stalin was more pragmatic, at least from 1941, and Brezhnev was prepared to rethink the relationship between Communism and Islam.

## Marxism and religion

Lenin, and most Marxist revolutionaries of his generation, believed that Marx was an enemy of religion. Marx famously claimed that religion was the 'opium of the masses'. Therefore Lenin and other Marxist radicals believed that their revolution would liberate working people from capitalist exploitation and from the delusions of religion.

### Note it down

On a large sheet of paper draw a timeline of the period 1917 to 1985. Next divide it into periods that correspond to the rule of the different leaders. Make notes on Communist religious policy from 1917 to 1985. Use different coloured pens to distinguish aspects of policy that changed and aspects of policy that stayed the same.

Lenin was also critical of the Russian Orthodox Church, the dominant organised religion in Russia. For Lenin, the Russian Orthodox Church was an essential ally of the Tsar. Moreover, the Church was an extremely rich institution, and some Russian Orthodox priests led lives of immense privilege while working people were poor.

Finally, the new Communist Government was suspicious of organised religion for two reasons:

- Because religions stood for values that were sometimes opposed to Communist values
- Because religious groups were organisations that were independent of the Communist Government and therefore could organise in opposition to the government.

For these reasons, successive Communist governments tended to persecute the Russian Orthodox Church as well as other faiths, including Islam.

## Religious groups in the Soviet Union

The Soviet Union was a multi-ethnic and multi-religious nation with large religious minority groups. There were sizeable Muslim communities in Central Asia, the North Caucasus and Azerbaijan. Lithuania had a large Roman Catholic Community and there was a significant Baptist minority in the Ukraine. Soviet leaders approached different groups in different ways. Moreover, religious policies changed as the leadership changed and as government policies shifted.

## Early campaign

Lenin's early religious policies reflected two different motives. The first Communist laws reflected a commitment to legal equality of all people regardless of their beliefs. However, at the same time there was a terror campaign against the Orthodox Church.

### Legal reforms

In the first months of the revolution, Lenin introduced a series of **decrees** that defined the relationship of the government and religion:

- The October 1917 Decree on Land gave peasants the right to seize land belonging to the Church.
- The January 1918 Decree Concerning Separation of Church and State, and of School and Church meant the Church lost its privileged position in society. Church land, buildings and property were nationalised, state subsidies for the Church were ended, and religious education was banned in schools.
- The 1922 Soviet Constitution guaranteed freedom of conscience for all Soviet people.

In practice, religious freedom, which had been guaranteed after the February Revolution, was seriously compromised by Lenin's measures. Although the right existed in law, Soviet courts lacked the power to force the government to obey the law or respect citizens' legal rights.

## The Church and the terror

Lenin was convinced that the Church was an enemy of the revolution, and therefore he used terror to try to undermine the Church. In the first year of the revolution senior priests in the Orthodox Church were terrorised:

- In November 1917 Archpriest Ivan Kochurov was murdered outside Petrograd.
- In January 1918 **Metropolitan** Vladimir was tortured and shot in Kiev.
- Orthodox priests in Moscow were massacred in January following a Church decree excommunicating the **Bolsheviks**.

More extreme measures were sanctioned in November 1918 when the **Politburo** issued a secret order to the Cheka sanctioning the mass execution of priests. Within two years most of the most popular Orthodox priests had been killed.

Roman Catholic priests were treated differently because they had traditionally been a persecuted minority rather than part of the Church that backed the Tsar. In the first half of 1918 they were deported and executions only started when the Civil War began.

In addition to executions and deportations, the new government also used propaganda against the Church and seized Church property. These two policies operated together during the 1921 famine. Soviet authorities seized Church assets to fund famine relief and blamed priests who resisted for sabotaging relief efforts.

The government's policy regarding Islam was contradictory. Initially Communist forces used the Decree Concerning Separation of Church and State to justify seizing the property of *waqfs* – Islamic foundations and charities. However, this policy was quickly reversed, *waqfs* continued to fund schools in Muslim areas and the Communist leaders encouraged local Muslims to join the Party. Communists were less antagonistic towards Islam than Russian Orthodox Christianity because there had been no official link between Islam and Tsarism.

# Religion in the 1920s

Communist policy regarding religion changed after the Civil War. Mass executions, violence and deportations stopped. They were replaced by more subtle techniques. The new strategy emerged in 1921 and early 1922.

## The Living Church

One strategy used against the Orthodox Church was the establishment of the Living Church. The Living Church claimed to be a reformed version of the old Orthodox Church in which ordinary people had power. The Living Church, aided by the GPU, organised a national congress in April 1923 which deposed Patriarch Tikhon and introduced a new decentralised structure. This was part of a government-backed strategy to split the Church, take away its central leader and weaken its national structure.

However, the leader of the Living Church, Archbishop Vedenskii, was not prepared to support the Communists. In 1923 he publicly debated science and religion with Anatoly Lunacharsky (see page 95–96), gaining widespread support for his argument that science could not disprove the existence of God. Public debates proved counterproductive and therefore in 1925 the Central Committee stopped public debates with the Church. Their policy of splitting the Church by backing the Living Church was more successful, but the Church split did not diminish Church growth, nor faith in saints and miracles which continued through the 1920s.

## Islam

During the 1920s Soviet authorities initiated campaigns against Islamic groups. Communists objected to Islam for two main reasons. First, they claimed that Islam encouraged 'crimes based on custom', particularly those infringing women's rights. Secondly, they recognised that Islamic organisations had the loyalty of many people in the Caucasus and Central Asia, and therefore they wanted to destroy the religion in order to extend their own power.

In order to weaken Islam the Soviet authorities:

- closed mosques, turning them into sports clubs or storage depots
- discouraged pilgrimages
- attacked Islamic shrines
- started campaigns against women wearing the chador, a traditional form of dress which sometimes included a veil
- opened anti-Islamic museums in the midst of recognised holy places.

### Patriarch Tikhon, 1865–1925

Born in 1865, Patriarch Tikhon became head of the Russian Orthodox Church in 1917. He regularly clashed with the Communist Government, criticising their use of violence, their seizure of land and their role in creating the famine of 1921. He was placed under house arrest in 1922 and remained a prisoner of the Communists until his death in 1925.

### Media, religion and totalitarianism

Some historians have described the Soviet Union as a totalitarian regime (see page 21). Totalitarianism has been defined in a variety of ways, but broadly the phrase describes a form of modern dictatorship which attempts to control all areas of life.

Control of the media and suppression of religion are often considered to be important aspects of totalitarianism. Media control allowed the government to control the information that Soviet citizens were exposed to, and the suppression of religion meant that Soviet citizens were less likely to be influenced by alternative views.

## Stalin, religion and terror

Stalin's policies often had religious implications. His religious policies tended to be driven by his other priorities. In that sense, he was often quite pragmatic when dealing with religion.

During the collectivisation drive, Stalin ordered the closure of many churches in the country largely because they were aiding resistance to his policies. Outside of Russia, Stalin set targets for the number of people from different ethnic groups that he wanted purged. In the Central Asian republics, where Islam was the dominant religion, the NKVD attacked local priests and intellectuals. The NKVD also attacked groups that had been set up to defend Islam in the 1920s from Soviet attacks. This included attacking Jadids and Sufi groups who were dedicated to 'saving Islam from Marxist pollution'. By the end of 1936, Sufi groups, even those in former Islamic strongholds of the Ferghana Valley of Turkestan, had been destroyed. Nonetheless, in spite of the claims of Soviet propaganda, Islam survived and Sufi groups, often led by women, kept the traditions alive and growing, particularly in Kazakhstan.

## Religion and war

During the Second World War Stalin made a pragmatic alliance with the Church. One of his strategies for winning the war was to appeal to the patriotism of the Russian people to boost morale and inspire them to fight. This appeal to patriotism was combined with a new understanding between the government and the Church. Stalin reached out to the Church during the war for a number of reasons:

- The Russian Orthodox Church was linked to Russian national identity. Therefore as patriotism re-awoke, it was natural for Russians to look to the Church.
- The war was a time of continual crisis when all families faced losing loved ones. The Church provided comfort for bereaved families.
- Soldiers also found comfort in the thought that God would welcome them into heaven. When facing death in battle, one soldier commented that there was more comfort and inspiration in a few of Jesus's words than there was in the entire works of Marx and Lenin.

Early in the war Stalin reached an understanding with leaders of the Russian Orthodox Church. Metropolitan Sergey, the Russian Orthodox Church's most senior figure, urged Christians to fight for the motherland, proclaiming Stalin 'God's chosen leader'. In return, the government changed its policy towards the Church:

- From the outset of war anti-religious propaganda ceased. Communist publications, such as *Bezbozhnik* ('The Godless'), were officially closed.
- Stalin granted Metropolitan Sergey an official residence in Moscow.
- Stalin promised to end the censorship of religious magazines following the war.
- Stalin promised that churches that had been closed by the government would re-open; 414 churches re-opened during the final year of the war.

The easing of restrictions on the Church led to growth. Indeed, the Orthodox Church grew and the priesthood expanded from 9254 in 1946 to 11,827 in 1948. The Orthodox Church was not the only denomination to benefit. Numbers of Baptists, Pentecostalists, Methodists and Jehovah's Witnesses increased following 1945.

## Khrushchev and religion

Khrushchev's approach to religion was more hard line than that of Stalin. Khrushchev saw it as part of his mission to revive the anti-religious campaign of the 1920s in order to liberate Soviet society from the last vestiges of religion. Moreover, the government realised that church attendance was a form of resistance. This awareness was heightened by the fact that from the mid-1950s certain Protestant Churches began to prophesy that the Soviet regime would end within a generation.

Khrushchev's major anti-religious campaign started in 1958. It included the following measures:

- Churches re-opened during and after the Second World War were closed.
- Anti-religious propaganda was reintroduced.
- Anti-religious magazines were reintroduced, for example *Science and Religion* was published regularly from 1960.
- Roman Catholic monasteries were closed in 1959.

- Orthodox convents were placed under surveillance.
- Patrols refused to let believers have access to holy sites.

Khrushchev also used the Soviet space programme to attack religion. Yuri Gagarin famously commented that having travelled up to the heavens he had found no God. Valentina Tereshkova, the first woman in space, also argued that her trip into space had led to the victory of atheism over 'the mysterious heavens that used to mystify the imagination'.

Khrushchev's campaigns particularly targeted female believers, as government figures showed that two-thirds of Orthodox churchgoers were women and over 80 per cent of Protestant Christians were women. Moreover, he was concerned that women were passing on religious beliefs to their children. Therefore from 1960 a propaganda campaign encouraged men to take the leading role in the education of their children. There were also campaigns against nuns, which accused them of being 'unnatural women' for refusing to do their 'natural duty' by becoming wives and mothers. Churches and Islamic groups were banned from running special events for women, such as women-only prayer meetings. Khrushchev's campaign also targeted Islamic women, reviving the 1920s campaign to 'liberate' women from Islam. School teachers were also expected to deliver an anti-religious message.

Aspects of Khrushchev's campaign succeeded. For example, the KGB successfully closed thousands of churches, reducing the number of Orthodox Church buildings from 8000 in 1958 to 5000 in 1964. However, he failed to win the battle for the 'soul of the Soviet people'. Women organised their own campaigns to protect their religious freedoms. Some marched, others circulated pamphlets defending Christianity or Islam, while others took their children out of schools in order to counter the anti-religious propaganda. In short, Khrushchev's anti-religious campaign led to the birth of a new dissident campaign that flourished in the 1960s and 1970s.

## Religion in the Soviet Union, 1964–85

Brezhnev ended Khrushchev's overt campaign against religion. Church closures stopped and so did the poster campaigns. Brezhnev advocated spreading the philosophy of atheism rather than attacking religious organisations or practices.

In 1968 he opened the Institute for Scientific Atheism, which published articles in newspapers and advised teachers how to spread atheism in the classroom. Brezhnev's foreign policy of seeking allies in the Middle East led to a change in policy towards Islam. Previous leaders had described Islam as a 'backward and barbarian' religion. Under Brezhnev, the government started supporting anti-American Islamic groups. As a result, from the late 1960s the Soviet Government described Islam as a 'progressive, anticolonial and revolutionary creed' that was compatible with socialism. Moreover, Brezhnev established the Spiritual Board of Muslims of Central Asia and Kazakhstan, which allowed Soviet Islamic leaders and scholars to have limited contact with fellow Muslims in other countries.

Brezhnev's attempt to promote atheism did not lead to a reduction in the numbers of people professing religious faith. No more churches or mosques closed. Moreover, the proportion of people professing a religious faith remained stable at 20 per cent from 1960 through to 1985.

## Conclusion

Successive Communist governments attempted to neutralise religion. In some cases this meant direct attacks on religious leaders; in others it meant working with religious groups and leaders to ensure support for the regime. Notably, while the regime could close churches and convert mosques into storage depots, they could not kill the faith of Soviet citizens who looked beyond politics for life's ultimate meaning.

### Work together

Write a paragraph in answer to the following question:

**How far did the Soviet Government control media and religion in the years 1917–85?**

Make sure your answer focuses clearly on the question, considers both sides of the question, considers media and religion, covers the whole time period and concludes with some genuine evaluation.

Having written the paragraph, swap it with a partner. Discuss which paragraph:

- focuses more clearly on the question
- uses the most appropriate evidence to support its points
- most effectively covers both religion and the media
- most effectively covers the whole period
- contains the most effective evaluation.

Having discussed these different aspects of your paragraphs, note down three things you could do to improve or maintain your essay technique.

## Chapter summary

- Between 1917 and 1985 Soviet governments tried different ways of controlling the media and religion.
- Lenin established the pattern of state control that continued throughout the period.
- However, Stalin and Brezhnev were both prepared to co-operate with religious groups when it suited them.
- Under Kruschev and Brezhnev there was greater freedom to contribute to magazines through letters pages. This reflected the fact that personal freedom was more important following Stalin's death than it had been in the early years of the revolution.

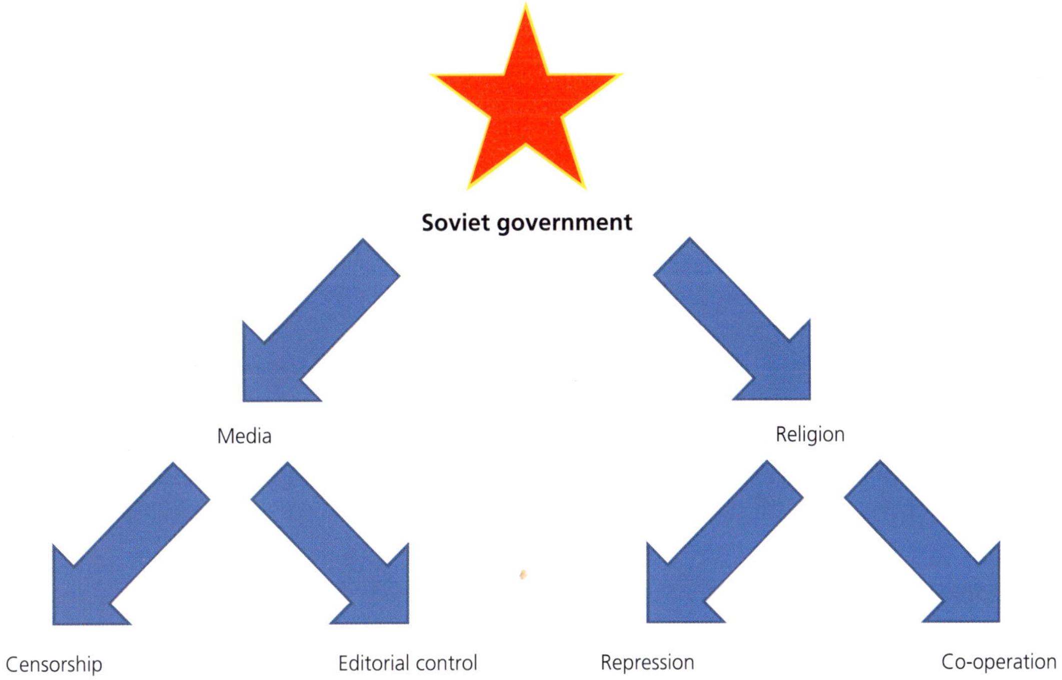


▲ **Summary diagram: Media and religion – methods of control.**

## Activity: Question practice

1. Was economic decline the main consequence of Brezhnev's economic policy in the years 1964–85? **AS**
2. How significant was control of the media in the achievement of Communist political dominance in the years 1917–41? **AS**
3. How accurate is it to say that Soviet Governments were consistently hostile to religious groups in the period 1921–64?
4. How far did the fundamental features of Stalin's government of the USSR remain in place from 1953 to 1985?

## Recommended reading

J. Anderson, *Religion, State and Politics in the Soviet Union and Successor States* (Cambridge, 1994), pages 102–36.

V. Brovkin, *Russia After Lenin: Politics, Culture and Society, 1921–1929* (Routledge, 1998), pages 26–9. Brovkin's work provides a detailed account of life in the Soviet Union in the 1920s, including the government's attitude to religion

K.B. Eaton, *Daily Life in the Soviet Union* (Greenwood Publishing, 2004), pages 270–7.

# 3b: The secret police

## Overview

The secret police were a constant feature of Communist rule. Communist leaders tended to think of the Soviet Union as a regime beset by enemies. Capitalists, imperialists, other socialists, frivolous women and hooligans were all a threat in the view of Soviet leaders. Most of the leaders viewed the regime as extremely fragile – vulnerable to an uprising from the people and therefore in need of defence by a ruthless police force.

Initially, Lenin argued that his terroristic Cheka, who had the power to torture and kill at will, were an emergency measure necessary to protect the revolution in its early stages. However, by 1924 it was clear that they had become a permanent feature of the regime. Their role changed between 1917 and 1928. In the early days they had fought organised political groups who opposed Lenin's government. However, a decade later they were employed to enforce a Communist moral code on people who had become too rich under the NEP, experts who disagreed with the government and young people who enjoyed Western music like Jazz.

Under Stalin the political police attacked the Communist Party, the only organisation left in the Soviet Union that could rival Stalin's power. Terror reached new heights during the mid-1930s, establishing Stalin as the only authoritative figure in the government.

Following Stalin's death, mass terror against the Party was renounced by the new leaders, and for a decade under Khrushchev the secret police became a much less prominent part of the government. Under Brezhnev, the political police became important again. However, there was no return to mass terror. Andropov, Brezhnev's police chief, attempted to use more subtle techniques to achieve maximum repression with minimum violence. Nonetheless, the new techniques did not stop widespread disillusionment with the regime by the early 1980s.

This chapter considers:

1. Attacks on opponents of the government, 1917–28
2. Stalin's terror
3. Andropov's suppression of dissidents, 1967–82
4. Monitoring of popular discontent, 1982–85.

## 1 Attacks on opponents of the government, 1917–28

Terror was an essential part of Lenin's strategy for staying in power. Lenin was willing, from the earliest phase of the revolution, to use terror against his political opponents.

Lenin and other Communist leaders had studied the French Revolution and knew that terror was one of the weapons used by the new rulers against the old rulers. In that sense, Lenin believed that revolutionary terror was a legitimate part of a revolution. Significantly, Lenin repeatedly stated that he hoped the Red Terror would be less severe than the French Revolutionary terror. Moreover, Lenin believed that political terror was a temporary measure, which should be abandoned once the revolution was secure.

### Note it down

Using bullet points, make notes on:

- Lenin's initial vision of the Cheka
- the Cheka's role during the Civil War
- the role of the secret police in the 1920s
- the reasons for the change in the role of the secret police over time.

### The Cheka and the Red Terror

The Cheka, Lenin's first secret police, embodied Lenin's views on revolutionary violence. Established in December 1917, the Cheka, or Extraordinary Commission for Combating Counter-Revolution and Sabotage, were a political police. Their target were the **counter-revolutionaries**: those who tried to overthrow the revolution. Felix Dzerzhinsky served as the head of the Cheka from 1917–26.

### Felix Dzerzhinsky

Dzerzhinsky was born into an aristocratic Polish family. Prior to the revolution he had the right to call himself Prince. He became head of the Cheka shortly after the October Revolution and quickly gained a reputation for efficiency. Dzerzhinsky was ideologically committed to the use of terror against counter-revolutionaries, and was an advocate of swift and harsh revolutionary justice.

During the 1920s Dzerzhinsky continued to head the political police. He sided with the Duumvirate against Trotsky, Zinoviev and Kamenev. He died of heart failure in 1926.

## The secret police

In many ways the phrase 'secret police' is misleading. Under Lenin and Stalin there was little secret about the political police. Indeed, arrests and executions were often carried out publicly in order to intimidate potential opponents and create an atmosphere of fear.

The Soviet secret police had a series of names between 1917 and 1991:

- Cheka 1917–22
- GPU 1922
- OGPU 1922–34
- NKVD 1934–41
- NKGB 1941–46
- MGB 1946–54
- KGB 1954–91.

## The role of the Cheka, 1917–21

During the Civil War, the Cheka's role was to protect Communist rule in areas held by the Communists. The Red Army, by contrast, was responsible for defending and enlarging Communist-held territory.

Significantly, from the early days of the revolution, the Cheka attacked not only the Communists' capitalist enemies, but also other socialists. For example, in January 1918, the Cheka and the Red Army closed down the **Constituent Assembly**, a democratically elected parliament that was dominated by the Communists' rivals, the Socialist Revolutionaries.

Additionally, the Cheka did not enforce laws. Nor were they bound by laws. Rather they dispensed 'revolutionary justice', which allowed them to act arbitrarily.

Between 1917 and 1921 Lenin's secret police used terror in a variety of ways. The Cheka:

- helped the Red Army requisition grain from the peasants as part of War Communism (see page 43)
- closed down opposition newspapers and imprisoned, tortured and executed socialist opponents of the new government
- used extreme violence against the enemies of the Communist Party in recently captured areas; priests were crucified, members of the white army were allowed to freeze to death and turned into ice statues, others were scalped or buried alive
- supported the Red Army's attack on the Kronstadt Naval base; Cheka agents with machine guns were positioned behind Red Army soldiers and instructed to shoot any soldiers who retreated or refused to fight
- ran concentration camps that housed the Communists' enemies
- stopped private trading, which was outlawed under War Communism.

## The secret police and the NEP

The end of the Civil War led to a change in Lenin's policy. The Red Terror was brought to an end. However, as socialism had not been wholly victorious, Lenin still believed that there was a need for a political police. During the period of the New Economic Policy the Cheka, and later the GPU, continued to attack the government's political opponents. Nonetheless, terror was on a much smaller scale than during the Civil War.

## Surveillance and deportations

In 1922 Lenin instructed Dzerzhinsky to set up an agency within the GPU to monitor the press. In addition to this, the GPU kept former Tsarist officers, who now served in the Red Army, under surveillance.

Lenin was also suspicious of intellectuals and experts who did not support the government fully. Again, in 1922 he instructed Dzerzhinsky to supervise the deportation of professors and engineers that he suspected of anti-Communist sympathies.

More generally, the GPU kept public opinion under close scrutiny during the 1920s. The GPU had the power to intercept post and other forms of communication. The GPU kept intellectuals and students under close scrutiny, fearing that these groups were unlikely to support the new government because of their privileged, almost bourgeois position in Soviet society. GPU surveillance reports were sent directly to the Central Committee. The GPU also reported to the Central Committee about moral problems, such as drunkenness, gambling and other signs of inequality that were developing during the period of the NEP.

## Political trials

Lenin was profoundly insecure about the future of the revolution. He feared that the economic compromise of the NEP (see pages 47–48) would lead to political overthrow. Therefore he ordered Dzerzhinsky to set up political trials of his leading socialist opponents.

In 1922 Dzerzhinsky organised the trial of Socialist Revolutionary leaders. They were accused of treason, sabotage and plotting to overthrow the Soviet state. At the end of the trial in August 1922 all of the defendants were sentenced to death. Most were, however, imprisoned and only executed in the Stalinist terror of the mid-1930s.

## Religious, moral and economic crimes

The GPU also policed the semi-capitalist marketplace established by the NEP. This included:

- imprisoning Nepmen who had grown too rich (see page 46–47)
- harassing women who dressed in Western styles (see page 102)
- persecuting young people who danced to jazz (see page 98)
- persecuting priests (see page 78).

There were no laws against these activities, but the GPU defended the interest of the revolution and therefore could act arbitrarily against perceived **class enemies**.

# 2 Stalin's terror

The Soviet secret police was transformed under Stalin. Lenin had used the Cheka, GPU and OGPU to attack the enemies of the Party. Stalin used the secret police against that Party. Moreover, he used terror much more widely, sending millions to his Gulags. In order to justify the radical extension of terror, he developed a new doctrine that led to a change in the culture of the secret police.

### Note it down

Using the 1 : 2 method (see page x), make notes about the role of the secret police under Stalin:

- how Stalin changed the role of the secret police
- how Yezhov changed the workings of the secret police
- how Stalin justified the terror
- the scale of the terror
- the impact of the terror.

## The NKVD under Genrikh Yagoda

Genrikh Yagoda was appointed head of the NKVD in July 1934. Following Kirov's death he was responsible for leading the hunt for enemies of the Party.

However, Yagoda proved to be a disappointment. Although Yagoda organised the arrest, interrogation and trial of Zinoviev and Kamenev, Stalin expected more. He wanted to use the opportunity created by Kirov's murder to move against Bukharin and Trotsky's supporters. Moreover, the scale of the terror in 1935 and 1936 was not unusual by Soviet standards. In that sense, too, Yagoda disappointed Stalin.

Yagoda did, however, play an important role in the Great Terror: he collaborated with Stalin in turning the NKVD against the Communist Party. In that sense, his appointment as NKVD chief was a turning point in Soviet politics.

## Terror under Nikolai Yezhov

Yezhov played an important role radicalising the NKVD. Under Yezhov the Great Terror spread to engulf the whole of the Soviet Government.

### Genrikh Yagoda, 1895–1940

Born in 1891, Yagoda joined the Bolsheviks in 1907. He joined the Cheka soon after its creation, being promoted to deputy chief in 1923. During the 1920s he was close to Bukharin and the Right of the Party. Between 1921 and 1933 he supervised the construction of the Moscow-Volga Canal. The project was completed by labourers from the Gulags. Over 20,000 prisoners died during the project. Yagoda became close to Stalin in the early 1930s. Allegedly, Stalin confided in Yagoda that he preferred people to be loyal through fear rather than conviction as convictions could change whereas fear was constant. Yagoda was also responsible for ensuring the starvation of victims of the Great Famine in the Ukraine.

Stalin was unhappy with Yagoda as NKVD head, blaming him for the slow progress in the first years of the terror. Yagoda was eventually arrested and tried as part of the Trial of the 21 in 1938.

## Sharpening class struggle

In order to justify more extensive terror, Stalin put forward a new theory: the doctrine of sharpening **class** struggle. Stalin argued that as socialism advanced, the class struggle intensified. Capitalists, he argued, fought harder as socialism succeeded. This theory turned Lenin's assumptions on their head and provided the justification for ever increasing terror.

## Yezhov and the new NKVD

Yezhov transformed the NKVD. His reforms reflected the doctrine of sharpening class struggle by turning the secret police into a ruthless organisation capable of enforcing ever growing terror.

Under Yezhov, terror was accelerated through a series of changes:

- Stalin set targets for arrests, executions and deportations.
- In 1937, the NKVD was purged. Many NKVD agents had been Communists since 1918. Therefore they were loyal to the Party and sometimes loyal to Stalin's opponents. They were also opposed to the use of mass terror in a socialist society for ideological reasons. Removing these old agents allowed Stalin to speed up the pace of the terror.
- New NKVD agents were recruited. The new agents had no loyalty to the Party and no ideological opposition to terror. Many simply enjoyed the power and the violence, or wanted a promotion.

Yezhov also introduced the 'conveyor belt system' to speed up the process of getting confessions from the NKVD's victims. The system involved groups of NKVD agents working in shifts around the clock. This meant torture and interrogation could continue relentlessly until prisoners confessed.

The new methods bore fruit, leading to the Trial of the 17 and the Trial of the 21 (see page 20).

## Yezhovshchina

Under Yezhov the terror attacked all aspects of Soviet life: the Party, the army, industry and collective farms. The result, between 1937 and 1938, was what historian Donald Rayfield describes as the 'Yezhov bloodbath'. During this period, around 1.5 million, approximately ten per cent of the male adult population, were arrested by the NKVD. Of these around 635,000 were deported, often to Siberia, and over 680,000 were executed.

This period became known as 'Yezhovshchina', meaning that the whole of Soviet society was engulfed in Yezhov's terror. Yezhovshchina transformed the government districts of Moscow and Leningrad into ghost towns. Mass arrests of government officials left entire apartment blocks empty.

The terror focused on the social group that was most likely to oppose Stalin. Urban educated men between the ages of 30 and 45 holding senior positions in the government were therefore targeted. Manual workers and women were much less likely to be arrested as they were not in a position to threaten Stalin. Indeed, 95 per cent of those targeted were men; only 5 per cent were women.

## Local initiatives

The terror was not solely directed from above. The terror expanded and accelerated in part due to popular participation. For example, NKVD agents demanded higher targets. Additionally, at a local level, workers and peasants organised their own **show trials**. Government employees, Party officials and factory managers were arrested by groups of citizens and tried for their crimes. In Kazan, for example, Communist officials were publicly tried for misusing government funds. They were accused of living luxurious lifestyles and falsifying figures. Having been found guilty, the officials were handed over to the NKVD.

### Nikolai Yezhov, 1895–1940

Nikolai Yezhov was born in 1895 and joined the Communist Party in October 1917. Yezhov was head of Stalin's secret police during the worst phase of the terror. In the mid-1930s he was one of Stalin's most trusted ministers. In addition to being head of the NKVD he was a member of the Politburo and had various senior positions in the Soviet Union's economic ministries. He was a committed Communist and very skilled at manipulating the system to gain promotion. For most of his time in the government he was considered an efficient and hardworking minister. However, when it became clear that Stalin was planning to arrest him he became depressed and turned to drink. Unable to cope with the pressure of his position as head of the NKVD, he resigned in 1938 and was arrested in 1939. His execution was kept secret for a decade as Stalin did not want to draw attention to Yezhov's work at the NKVD.

## The consequences of the terror

Stalin emerged from the terror stronger than ever. The terror removed almost everyone from government who had fought in the Civil War or who had worked with Lenin, and therefore could claim to have authority independent from Stalin. Moreover, Stalin replaced these officials with his own supporters, people who owed loyalty to him alone.

The terror also caused massive economic problems. Deporting and executing factory managers, economic planners and government officials removed the experts needed to run Stalin's **command economy**. Therefore during the first years of the Third Five-Year Plan production rates either declined or stagnated.

Finally, the terror claimed the lives of Yagoda and Yezhov. Yagoda was tried as part of the Trial of the 21. Yezhov and over 300 of his closest associates were shot in 1940. Yezhov claimed that his only crime was not killing enough Russians.

## Lavrentiy Beria's secret police

At the end of 1938 the Great Terror began to wind down. Yezhov resigned as head of the NKVD in November, to be replaced by Lavrentiy Beria. Beria's first major successes as head of the NKVD were Yezhov's arrest in April 1939 and Trotsky's murder in Mexico in 1940.

### The NKVD at war

During the Second World War Beria and the NKVD were responsible for policing ethnic minorities, groups that Stalin feared would side with the Soviet Union's enemies:

- In 1942 Beria organised the mass deportation of the Kalmyks, from Kalmykia which is north-west of the Caspian, to Siberia. Stalin feared that the Kalmyks would welcome a German invasion. By 1953, only 53,000 of the original population of 130,000 survived due to the brutal treatment they received in Siberia.
- In 1944, Beria ordered the deportation to Siberia of all 460,000 Chechens from their homeland in Chechnya within seven days. Chechens who were unwilling to leave their home or unable to leave were locked in stables and barns and burned alive. The deportation resulted in around 170,000 deaths.

### Beria after the war

After the Second World War Beria's NKVD continued to persecute the Soviet people:

- In 1945, the NKVD interrogated the 1.5 million Soviet prisoners of war who had been liberated from Germany. Stalin viewed these men as traitors for allowing themselves to be captured rather than fighting to the death. Most were deported to Siberia.
- 'The Leningrad Affair': In 1949, Stalin launched a purge against officials in the Leningrad Party. Stalin claimed that the Leningrad Party acted independently as if it were 'an island in the Pacific'. Around 200 Party members were arrested and forced to confess to crimes against the Party. Beria may well have been behind the Leningrad Affair, as his rivals were based there (see page 24).
- 'The Doctors' Plot': During 1952 and 1953 many of Stalin's medical staff were arrested for trying to poison Stalin. Notably, anti-Semitism may have been a cause of this purge as many of the doctors were Jewish, or had Jewish names, and Stalin was a well-

### Lavrentiy Beria, 1899–1953

Born in 1899, Beria distinguished himself as an excellent student of maths and science. He joined the Bolsheviks in 1917. His political career began in earnest in the early 1920s when he was involved in the ruthless repression of anti-Communist movements in Georgia. In 1926 he was rewarded for his work by being promoted to head the Georgian OGPU. In this role, he organised Stalin's purges of the Georgian Communist Party in the mid-1930s.

Beria became the head of the NKVD in 1938. He stayed in this role for the rest of his life and became one of Stalin's most trusted allies in government. Beria's ruthlessness was obvious during the Second World War. During this period he organised mass deportations and mass executions.

After the Second World War, Beria was put in charge of Soviet efforts to build a nuclear bomb. He was also one of a number of senior figures in government who had a realistic chance of winning power after Stalin's death. Indeed, for most of 1953, Beria, along with Khrushchev and Malenkov (see page 29), was part of the ruling alliance that replaced Stalin. Beria was arrested and executed in 1953. His death marked the end of the use of mass terror as a political weapon in the Soviet Union.

known anti-Semite. Stalin died before the doctors could be executed, and following his death they were released.

### Beria's death

For Stalin's heirs, Beria was associated with the policy of terror. Stalin's heirs were agreed that after Stalin's death there would be no return to mass terror and no further use of the NKVD against the Party. Therefore, three months after Stalin's death, Beria was arrested by the NKVD and executed for treason and terrorism. Beria's death was the symbolic end of Stalin's policy of terror.

## Conclusion

Stalin's Great Terror took the use of terror to unprecedented heights. Terror became, for a while, a regular part of government, and following 1938 there was the continual threat that Stalin would unleash another wave of terror as large as that of the 1930s.

Khrushchev renounced the use of mass terror and stopped using it as a weapon against the Party. More than that, he organised the rehabilitation of thousands of former Party members (see page 32). Khrushchev's preferred method of social control was to encourage 'popular oversight' in which ordinary citizens disciplined themselves and each other (see page 101). In 1959 Khrushchev proudly proclaimed that there were no longer any political prisoners in the Soviet Union, declaring 'there are no *political prisoners*, only persons of unsound mind'. The statement is indicative of Khrushchev's preferred approach to dissidents, which was to subject them to compulsory psychiatric treatment (see page 88).

## 3 Andropov's suppression of dissidents, 1967–82

In 1967 Brezhnev promoted Yuri Andropov to head the KGB. Andropov made a significant impact on the KGB. In the Khrushchev period, heads of the KGB had been low profile, and the job had become a dead end, no longer leading to positions of power within the government. Under Andropov this changed. This was partly due to a change of emphasis at the top of the Communist Party. Khrushchev had been committed, for at least some of his premiership, to a degree of cultural freedom. Brezhnev and the new leadership who took over in 1964 were suspicious of cultural freedom (see page 34). Andropov was a conservative, suspicious of liberalisation. Additionally, Andropov was an astute politician, capable of getting his own way, and he enjoyed the trust of Brezhnev.

Andropov's role was much smaller than that of previous secret police chiefs. Whereas Dzerzhinsky, Yezhov and Beria had limitless authority to imprison and execute, Andropov's goal was to control dissidents, the tiny minority of citizens who refused to conform to the expectations of the Soviet regime. His strategy was to achieve maximum control through a minimum of violence.

In this sense, although Andropov was a conservative and suspicious of cultural freedom, there was no return to the mass terror of the Civil War or of the Stalin period. Andropov was also keen to expose and prosecute corruption in the Communist Party, but Brezhnev was less sympathetic to this agenda.

### Yuri Andropov, 1914–1984

Andropov was born in 1914, the son of an administrator on the Russian railways. He was orphaned at the age of 13 and was forced to work. As a teenager he had a number of jobs including that of sailor and telegraph clerk. He made the most of the educational opportunities available under Stalin and graduated from college at the age of 19. He was promoted within the Communist Party during the 1930s, partly as a result of the purges. In the mid-1950s he became Soviet ambassador to Hungary. In that position he witnessed the 1956 Hungarian Revolution – which temporarily ended Soviet control of Hungary. The events of the revolution, and the speed with which the Hungarian Communist Party lost control, horrified him. The events of the Hungarian Revolution persuaded him that reform should be undertaken with extreme caution and that dissident movements were potentially extremely dangerous.

In 1967 he was appointed head of the KGB. He used his influence in government to advocate suppression of dissidents and any anti-Soviet activities. Specifically, in 1968 he argued for swift Soviet intervention to crush the reformist government that had taken over Czechoslovakia. Andropov was promoted to the Politburo in 1973 and played an important role in spotting new talent in the Communist Party. Indeed, he was responsible for the promotion of Mikhail Gorbachev.

## Andropov's aims and methods

Andropov's key priority was the suppression of dissidents. In 1968 he issued KGB Order No. 0051, 'On the tasks of state security agencies in combating ideological sabotage by the adversary'. The Order set out the policy of increased surveillance of and action against dissidents.

Andropov adopted a number of strategies for dealing with dissidents. These were informed by a series of trials of well-known artists that took place from 1964 to 1966. These embarrassed the Soviet Government due to outcry from other nations who demanded the preservation of artistic freedom. Based on this experience, Andropov developed a series of strategies that dealt with dissidents in a more subtle way which avoided adverse publicity.

### Discipline in the KGB

Andropov reformed the KGB to ensure that it could effectively identify dissidents. Between 1967 and 1970 he introduced the following measures to ensure that the KGB was highly efficient:

- KGB agents were not allowed to accept gifts and were forced to declare their financial assets.
- KGB agents whose relatives broke the law were sacked.
- He promoted KGB agents from across the whole of the Soviet Union, based on their success in dealing with dissidents.
- In 1967 he established Directorate V, a special branch of the KGB, to deal specifically with dissidents.

### Emigration

Having identified dissidents, Andropov had two ways of dealing with them. High profile dissidents with an international reputation were allowed to emigrate. A number of famous artists who consistently opposed the authorities were allowed to emigrate in the 1970s (see page 104–105). Indeed, the policy was extended and over 100,000 potential 'trouble makers' were allowed to leave the Soviet Union while Andropov was head of the KGB.

The policy was related to Jewish emigration. Since the establishment of Israel in 1948 Soviet Jews had campaigned for the right to move to the new Jewish state. For years Soviet leaders had refused. Andropov, however, changed the policy, ensuring that most Jews who wanted to leave were given **exit visas**. Andropov justified the policy by referring to the demographics of the Soviet Union. Jews, he argued, were around one per cent of the Soviet population. However, they were well represented in creative and intellectual industries. One-fifth of writers and journalists, to take one example, were Jews. In that sense, Jews were more likely to be found in the professions that produced dissidents. Therefore, Andropov argued, allowing Jews to leave the Soviet Union was a pragmatic way of dealing with potential dissidents without resorting to overt oppression.

### Repressive psychiatry

Emigration was Andropov's preferred weapon against well-known dissidents. However, less well-known figures could be sent to psychiatric **institutions** for compulsory psychiatric treatment. The policy had been used by Stalin and Khrushchev, but was expanded dramatically under Brezhnev. Andropov proposed the measure in April 1969, and the policy was endorsed in a secret **resolution** of the Council of Ministers later that year. Officially, the government argued that anti-Soviet behaviour was a sign of a 'paranoid reformist delusion': a mental illness. Andropov did not believe this. However, he recognised that sending someone to hospital was much less likely to attract the attention of the world media than sending someone to prison. Moreover, criminal records were public documents and therefore Western journalists could trace dissidents who were sent to prison. Psychiatric records were private; therefore it was easier for the government to hide its repression. Repressive psychiatry had other advantages too. As psychiatric patients, their 'treatment' could continue indefinitely, whereas prison terms had to come to an end. Finally, psychiatric patients could be prescribed medication to keep them quiet.

The practice was used against Protestant Christians and Jehovah's Witnesses. These groups were small and considered as heretics by Russian Orthodox Christians. Therefore they were vulnerable to official persecution.

Rumours about the practice of repressive psychiatry reached the West in the early 1970s. A delegation of US psychiatrists visited the Soviet Union to inspect hospitals. Andrei Snezhnevsky, President of the Association of Soviet Psychiatrists, persuaded the American visitors that Soviet psychiatry was serving its patients well.

### Prevention and repression

Andropov changed the emphasis of the KGB from repression to prevention. He did this for two main reasons. First he believed that Stalinist repression was ineffective. Second, there was a growing belief in the party that socialism was incompatible with widespread repression.

From November 1972, the KGB adopted a policy of issuing official warnings. The KGB set up a process whereby dissidents were interviewed and warned to stop their unorthodox activities. These people were then kept under surveillance. This strategy was designed to stop dissident activity without resorting to repression and without creating the adverse publicity of a trial. Around 70,000 Soviet citizens received a KGB warning in the 1970s. KGB agents estimated that these warnings stopped the formation of around 2000 subversive groups in the early 1970s alone.

Nonetheless, warnings did not always persuade dissidents to conform. In such cases dissidents could be:

- demoted or sacked from their jobs; indeed many intellectuals ended up working as janitors during the 1970s as a punishment for their anti-Soviet attitudes
- sent to psychiatric institutions for 'treatment'
- exiled
- sent to prison.

The number of dissidents sent to prison increased significantly after Andropov's appointment in 1967 (see Table 1).

**Table 1: Numbers imprisoned for creating anti-Soviet propaganda.**

| Year | Numbers imprisoned |
|---|---|
| 1965–7 | 171 |
| 1968–70 | 528 |

Andropov was also prepared to use show trials, such as the 1972 trial of dissidents Pyotr Yakir and Viktor Krasin, who ran the *samizdat* human rights magazine *Chronicle of Current Events*.

In addition to prison, the KGB would use violence to intimidate dissidents, as in the case of the 'Bulldozer Exhibition' of 1974 (see page 105).

### *Samizdat* publications

Self-published, or *samizdat*, materials began to circulate in the Soviet Union from the late 1950s. Underground publishing was made possible by Khrushchev's policy of increasing the availability of consumer goods. The availability of typewriters and paper allowed dedicated writers and their supporters to publish and circulate their own magazines and books.

## Sakharov and Solzhenitsyn

Andrei Sakharov and Aleksandr Solzhenitsyn were the most high-profile dissidents of the Brezhnev period. The two dissidents represented quite different traditions. Sakharov advocated human rights; Solzhenitsyn was a Russian nationalist and a devoted member of the Russian Orthodox Church. For Andropov they represented the two great threats to the Soviet Union: the doctrine of human rights and Russian nationalism.

Sakharov had come to prominence through the Soviet nuclear programme and was regarded as the 'Father of the Hydrogen Bomb'. From 1962, Sakharov became critical of the damage caused by Soviet nuclear tests. Moreover, in 1964 he led a campaign to expel Trofim Lysenko, Khrushchev's favourite scientist, from the Soviet Academy of Sciences. In 1968 Sakharov made his criticisms public, circulating an essay, *Reflections on Progress,* arguing that the Soviet Union should respect human rights. The essay was a *samizdat* production and therefore not officially authorised. The *samizdat* network was extremely effective, and within a month the essay had been published in the West and broadcast on the BBC. However, Sakharov was well respected in the West and in the Soviet Union. Therefore the KGB were reluctant to persecute him. The KGB restricted his right to travel and the government reduced his salary. He was also warned to stop his dissident activities by the KGB. However, this backfired. Sakharov gave a full report of the intimidation to the *New York Times.*

By the end of 1968 Sakharov's case was so well known that the KGB could not arrest him. Moreover, his disappearance to a psychiatric institution would also have caused outrage. Nonetheless, the KGB orchestrated a press campaign against him. Sakharov, however, kept writing. In 1975 he published *My Country and the World*, which proposed the reform of the Soviet Union on the basis of human rights, for which he won the **Nobel Peace Prize**. Sakharov was refused the right to leave the Soviet Union and was kept under constant surveillance. KGB documents described him as 'Public Enemy Number One'. Eventually, Sakharov was sent into internal exile, forced to remain in the city of Gorky.

Solzhenitsyn was a writer who became famous for his novel *One Day in the Life of Ivan Denisovich* (see page 101). Solzhenitsyn finished his novel *The Gulag Archipelago* in 1968, smuggling the manuscript to the West for publication. The book described the horrors of Stalin's prison camp system and it was therefore not possible to publish it in the Soviet Union. Two years later, he was awarded a Nobel Prize for Literature. Solzhenitsyn's fame in the West meant that the KGB could not imprison him and instead he was forced into exile in America in 1973.

## The Helsinki Agreement

The 1975 **Helsinki Agreement** committed countries across Europe to respect human rights. The Soviet Government was a signatory of the agreement. Consequently, following 1975 dissidents used this to show that the treatment of dissidents was in breach of Soviet obligations under the Helsinki Agreement. Dissidents knew that they could not legally force the government to respect human rights even after the agreement was signed. But they could use the agreement as publicity to embarrass the government and thereby create pressure for change.

## Law and order campaign, 1979

With the exception of one or two high-profile outspoken figures, Andropov's methods were successful in dealing with Soviet dissidents. However, 1979 was a difficult year for the Soviet Government and therefore they introduced stricter policies in anticipation of growing dissent. The problems facing the leadership included:

- economic slow down
- poor harvests
- war in Afghanistan (see page 74)
- the failure of Brezhnev's negotiations with the USA
- growing corruption
- growing non-conformity.

These problems, and the prospect of the 1980 Moscow Olympics, an event that would bring the world media to the Soviet capital, led to a law and order campaign. Backed by a Central Committee decree passed in August, Andropov attacked various forms of anti-social behaviour such as hooliganism, drunkenness and corruption.

# 4 Monitoring of popular discontent, 1982–85

Andropov succeeded Brezhnev as Soviet leader in 1982. Nonetheless, he retained control of the KGB. In the early 1980s the KGB continued to monitor public opinion, an initiative that Andropov had headed up since 1968. KGB agents monitored public opinion in a variety of ways. One technique was for KGB agents to pose as Westerners and initiate anti-government conversations with Soviet citizens. They also used techniques such as phone tapping and intercepting mail.

Andropov was aware of Brezhnev's failings as a leader: the corruption of large parts of the government and popular discontent with the government. Moreover, he was concerned about growing anti-Communist feeling in Eastern Europe, particularly in Poland where rising food prices had led to mass strikes. Andropov used information about popular discontent to justify a series of **authoritarian** policies.

## Popular discontent and social malaise

KGB reports pointed to a growth in popular discontent in the late 1970s and early 1980s. There were several causes of discontent. Soviet citizens:

- were anxious that as the 1970s progressed standards of living were improving more slowly
- were dissatisfied with the quality and availability of food and consumer goods
- felt that there were insufficient opportunities for promotion within Soviet industry and therefore hard work would not lead to improved status or pay
- resented the privileges and corruption of Party members and managers.

These problems were serious, as since 1964, Soviet rule had been based on the 'social contract': the people supported Communist rule in return for regular increases in their standard of living (see page 117). Moreover, according to KGB reports, loss of faith in the system led to **social malaise** which included an increase in:

- alcoholism
- poor labour discipline
- increased black market trade
- avoidance of military service
- demand for Western goods
- sympathy for strikes taking place in Poland
- increased Church attendance
- falling birth rate.

## Dealing with discontent, 1982–85

Andropov introduced a series of policies (see page 36) designed to tackle the malaise by heightening discipline. KGB reports also showed that some Soviet citizens supported a return to Stalinist discipline. In this sense Andropov's policies enjoyed some backing:

- Anti-corruption: Andropov investigated senior party officials and industrial managers who were using Soviet resources to make themselves rich. For example, Brezhnev's **Minister of the Interior**, Nikolai Shchelokov, was sacked and put on trial for corruption. He took his own life before the end of his trial.
- Anti-alcohol campaign: workers could be sacked for drunkenness and could be fined for damaging machinery or products if they were drunk at work.
- Operation Trawl: an anti-drunkenness and anti-**absenteeism** campaign. KGB officers visited parks, restaurants and train stations arresting people who were drunk or who were absent from work.

Operation Trawl led to less absenteeism in the short term. However, Andropov became ill soon after his appointment as leader and was unable to sustain the campaigns. Chernenko, who became leader of the Soviet Union on Andropov's death in 1984, continued the policy of workplace discipline, but scaled back the anti-corruption campaign in order to protect his supporters.

## Conclusion

The Soviet political police were a constant feature of the Communist regime. However, their role and tactics changed over time. Andropov's policies were much more subtle than the policies of Lenin's or Stalin's police chiefs. While Andropov was largely successful in dealing with dissidents, the KGB could not stop the growing social malaise, nor the corruption that had become an essential part of the regime by the 1980s.

### Chapter summary

- Initially, Lenin hoped the Cheka and their use of terror would be a short-lived feature of the new regime.
- However, the failure of the world revolution and the economic retreat of the NEP led Lenin to rely on the violent political police in order to defend the regime.
- Stalin expanded the role of the NKVD under Yagoda and Yezhov, using torture, forced labour and execution against Communist Party members in order to consolidate his own power.
- After Stalin's death, terror was never used on the same scale again.
- However, after the liberalism of Khrushchev, Brezhnev re-emphasised the role of the KGB and under Andropov the KGB effectively destroyed the Soviet Union's dissident movement.

## Recommended reading

J.A. Getty and R.T. Manning (eds.), *Stalinist Terror: New Perspectives* (Cambridge, 1993), pages 40–62. This book focuses on Stalin's terror.

P. Kenez, *A History of the Soviet Union from the Beginning to the End* (Cambridge, 2006), pages 227–9. This section of Kenez's book examines repression under Brezhnev.

W. Taubman, S. Khrushchev and A. Gleason (eds.), *Nikita Khrushchev*, (Yale, 2000), pages 85–112. Taubman, Khrushchev and Gleason's book examines Khrushchev's life. This section of the book considers his use of repression.

### Work together

Write a paragraph in answer to the question:

**What was the most significant turning point in the development of the Soviet police state?**

You could choose one of the following turning points or another of your own:

- the end of the Civil War
- the appointment of Yagoda
- the appointment of Yezhov
- the death of Stalin
- the appointment of Andropov.

1. Work with a partner who is writing a paragraph on a different turning point. Your paragraph should contain a clear focus on the question and detail about how the turning point changed the police state and how things stayed the same. A concluding sentence should explain why the turning point is so important.
2. Swap your paragraph with your partner. Read your partner's paragraph. Now write another paragraph explaining why the turning point you selected is more significant for the development of the Soviet police state than the one your partner selected.
3. Swap again, and read both paragraphs. Discuss whose argument is more persuasive and why.
4. Note down three ways in which you can make your arguments more persuasive.

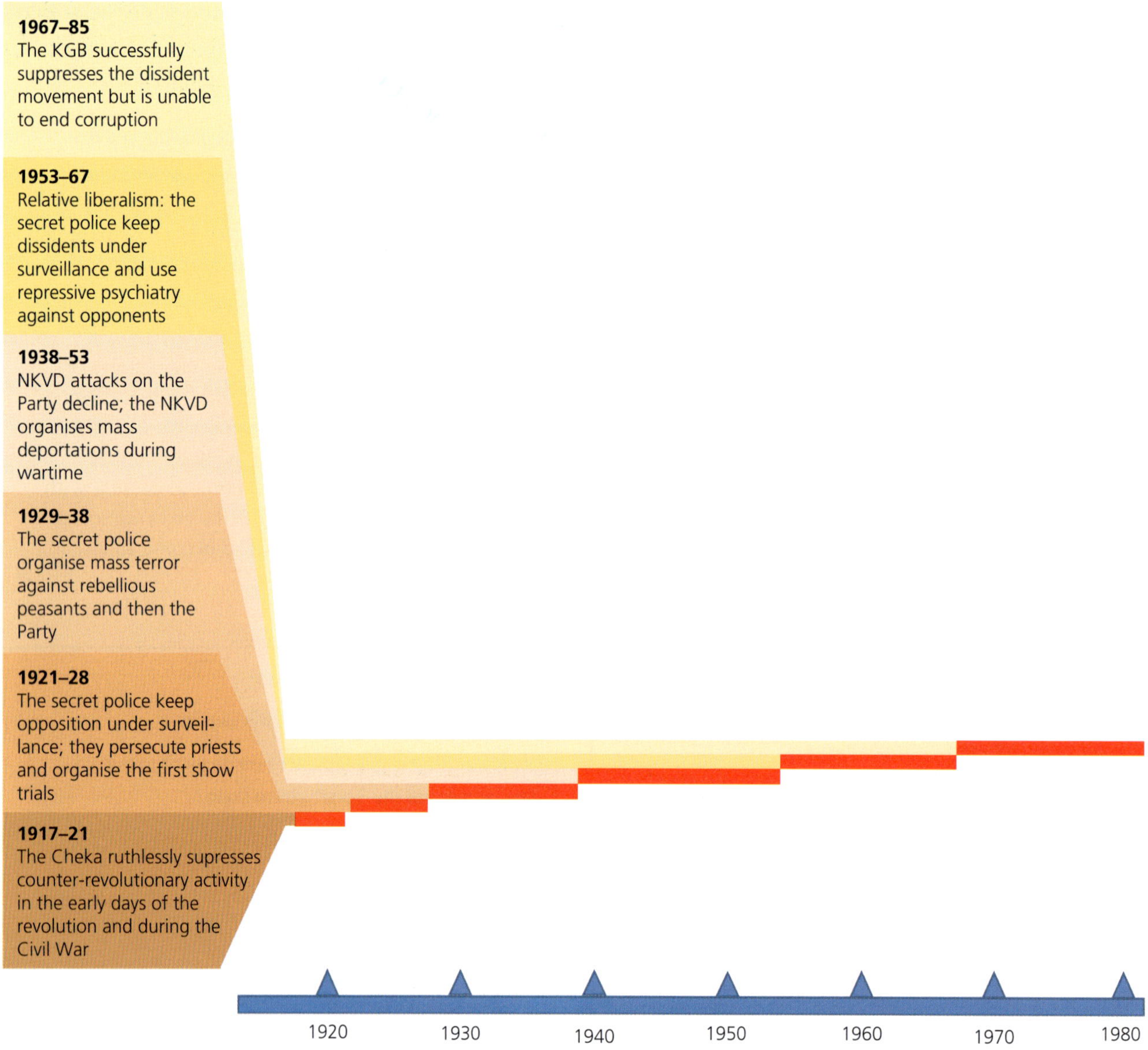


▲ **Summary diagram: The secret police**

# Essay technique: Argument

Essays that develop a good argument are more likely to reach the highest levels. As you know, your essays are judged on the extent to which they analyse (see page 59). The mark scheme distinguishes between five different levels of analysis. (This is a summary – the full mark scheme can be found on Edexcel's website.)

| | |
|---|---|
| **Level 1 (LOW)** | Simplistic or no analysis. |
| **Level 2** | Limited analysis of key issues. |
| **Level 3** | Some analysis of key issues. |
| **Level 4** | Analysis of key issues. |
| **Level 5 (HIGH)** | Sustained analysis of key issues. |

The key feature of the highest level is sustained analysis: analysis that unites the whole of the essay.

## High-level arguments

Typically, essays examine a series of factors. A good way of achieving sustained analysis is to consider which factor is most important.

Consider the following question:

**How accurate is it to say that Widespread political terror was a constant feature of Soviet government in the years 1921–53.?**

The following introduction addresses the question, without developing an argument:

**Introduction 1**

Widespread political terror was an important feature of Soviet government during the period 1921–53. Lenin and Stalin both used political terror against their opponents during the Kronstadt Mutiny, while oppressing religious groups, during the Great Terror and in Stalin's last years. But the terror was more extensive in the 1930s than it was in other periods.

Clear focus on the question.

Considers a wide range of factors.

Considers aspects of change and continuity.

This introduction could be improved by introducing an argument. An argument is a type of explanation. Therefore an argument is a claim supported by a reason. A good way of beginning to develop an argument is to think about the meaning of the words in the question. For example, what is meant by 'widespread', and what is meant by 'a constant feature'?

Here is an example of an introduction that begins an argument:

**Introduction 2**

The argument begins with a claim: terror was consistent, but it was not always widespread.

Political terror was a constant feature of Soviet government in the years 1921–53. However, political terror was only widespread in the late 1930s. Lenin used political terror against specific targets, such as the Kronstadt mutineers in 1921 or against outspoken priests. In this sense, political terror was a feature of Soviet government in the 1920s, but it was not widespread. Political terror became widespread during the late 1930s, particularly the period of Yezhovshchina (1936–38) in which the Great Terror was at its height. However, even under Stalin political terror was not widespread for the whole of his reign. He did use political terror from the mid-1930s until his death in 1953, but the Great Terror was an exceptional period. Therefore, while political terror was a constant feature of Soviet government, it was only truly widespread for a short period of Stalin's reign.

The claim is supported by a reason which is based on the meaning of the word 'widespread'.

The introduction concludes with an argument about the extent to which terror was consistent and widespread.

This introduction focuses on the question and sets out the key issues on which the essay will focus. However, it also sets out an argument that can then be developed throughout each paragraph, and rounds off with an overall judgement in the conclusion. Therefore Introduction 2 is of a higher level than Introduction 1 (see page 93).

## Activity: Developing an argument

Look at the following question:

**How accurate is it to say that the period 1964–85 were years of complete stagnation?**

Using your notes from previous chapters:

1 Write a brief definition of stagnation.

**TIP:** How is stagnation different from stability?

2 List the aspects of Russian life that could have stagnated under Brezhnev.

3 Write an introduction that clearly answers the question.

- Begin with a clear claim about the extent of stagnation.
- Justify this with reasons based on your understanding of stagnation.
- Make an argument about which aspect of Russian life was most stagnant.

**TIP:** Remember, Brezhnev's government changed over time – the extent of stagnation may have changed throughout the period.

# 3c: The state and cultural change

## Overview

Soviet leaders attempted to use art to motivate their people to support the government and build socialism. However, Soviet leaders were also keen to control painters, sculptors, writers and musicians. Stalin described artists as 'engineers of the human soul'. In that sense he recognised the power of art, power that could be used against the regime if it was not correctly directed.

In the early years of the Soviet Union there was a great deal of creativity as avant-garde artists worked to produce a new revolutionary art. However, Party officials did not understand or approve of the new experimental revolutionary style. As the Party extended its control of society it tightened its grip on art and artists. Under Stalin there was an approved style: Socialist Realism created idealised paintings and sculptures of heroic Soviet workers and the utopian future they were building.

Khrushchev tried to encourage a greater freedom in the arts, hoping to create an alliance between the government and artists. However, liberalisation led to literature that was hostile to the Soviet Government and therefore Khrushchev's policy zigzagged from openness to repression. Brezhnev's policy was much more consistent: experimental art was not tolerated. However, the new form of consumer socialism that Khrushchev pioneered and Brezhnev continued created a cultural shift of its own. Fashion became a big issue, and Soviet leaders tried to rein in self-expression.

This chapter considers:

1. *Proletkult* and the avant-garde, 1917–29
2. Socialist Realism, 1930–53
3. Thaw and non-conformity, 1954–64
4. Clashes between artists and the government to 1985.

## 1 *Proletkult* and the avant-garde, 1917–29

Following the October Revolution, new forms of art flourished. The notion of a truly revolutionary art inspired painters, sculptors, film makers and artists of all kinds to create new kinds of art. What is more, there were disagreements among leading members of the Communist Party about what revolutionary art should actually mean. Even so, all the leading Communists agreed that art was of prime importance to the future of the revolution. Lenin was extremely interested in the potential and purposes of art. He was particularly interested in cinema, which he thought was the art of the future. Bukharin, who played a leading role in Soviet politics throughout the mid-1920s, was a champion of artistic expression. For these reasons, there was a vibrant and experimental Soviet art scene from 1917 to 1929.

### Note it down

Using a note-making style of your choice, make notes on the different attitudes towards art among senior Communists in the early 1920s. Make sure that you highlight the key differences and how each thinker justified their approach to art. Make notes on the consequences of these different views for Soviet art in the 1920s.

Finally, look up the works of art mentioned in this section on the internet and make a document containing images of these examples. Annotate the images, making sure you record the name of the artist, the title of the piece and the date it was produced.

### Proletarian art?

Communists believed that the October Revolution had ended **capitalism** and therefore had created a new kind of society where workers would increasingly be their own masters. However, Communists disagreed on what the new revolutionary culture should be like. Anatoly Lunacharsky, the new People's Commissar of Enlightenment, argued that following the revolution proletarian culture should flourish. Lenin, however, believed that the proletariat should learn from the best of bourgeois culture.

### Lunacharsky and *Proletkult*

Lunacharsky argued that just as capitalism had been dominated by bourgeois culture, so the new revolutionary society should be dominated by proletarian culture: art made by working people reflecting the concerns and experiences of working people. Additionally, Lunacharsky believed that a truly revolutionary society should foster artistic talent among working people, as artistic expression was an important part of a fulfilling life. Lunacharsky believed that proletarian culture would be fundamentally different to bourgeois culture. Proletarian culture, he argued, would naturally focus on collective experience and involve a wide range of people. However, Bourgeois culture, he argued, reflected the culture of capitalism. Therefore bourgeois culture was individualistic and dominated by an artistic elite.

In order to foster the growth of proletarian culture, Lunacharsky supported *Proletkult*: the proletarian culture movement. The new organisation was established prior to the October Revolution. From 1918 to 1920 it became a national movement with branches across Russia. Through *Proletkult*, working people had access to local studios where they could paint, sculpt, rehearse plays and put on exhibitions and shows. By 1920 there were around 84,000 members of *Proletkult* working in over 300 studios. *Proletkult* published *Gorn* (Furnace) a monthly magazine that showcased the work of proletarian artists. Crucially, *Proletkult* was an independent organisation, free of Communist Party control.

Bukharin was a champion of *Proletkult*. He used his position as editor of *Pravda* to promote the organisation throughout the Civil War.

## Lenin and revolutionary culture

Lenin was critical of Lunacharsky's philosophy and *Proletkult*. Lenin argued that the best culture was universal. It was neither bourgeois nor proletarian; rather it reflected the human spirit. Therefore he defended bourgeois culture and argued that working people should learn from the best bourgeois artists who had created a universal culture.

Lenin also had misgivings about *Proletkult*. He believed that in searching for a new culture, *Proletkult* was encouraging artists to embrace Futurism, a style that Lenin believed was the worst kind of bourgeois art. Lenin argued that Futurism was degenerate, in the sense that it celebrated individual self-expression, and most working people simply could not understand it.

### Futurism

Futurism was an international artistic movement that was inspired by urbanisation, youth and modern technology. Futurism emerged in the early twentieth century and influenced painting, sculpture and literature as well as other art forms. Futurist sculpture and painting was often influenced by angular industrial shapes. Futurists also attempted to capture the experience of travelling at high speed, which they associated with modern technologies such as cars and aeroplanes. Kazimir Malevich, best known for his painting 'Black Square' (1915), was the most famous Russian artist to be influenced by Futurism.

## The dissolution of *Proletkult*

*Proletkult* flourished from 1917 to 1920, which was a remarkable achievement in the context of the Civil War. However, Lenin was suspicious of the organisation. He believed that *Proletkult* was dominated by socialists associated with opposition movements such as anarchism. Moreover, he believed that working people needed a basic education rather than opportunities for artistic expression. Therefore he believed that the continued independence of *Proletkult* was a danger to the revolution.

Lunacharsky continued to defend the independence of *Proletkult*. However, Lenin sent representatives to the National Congress of *Proletkult*, which took place in October 1920. Following an appeal for *Proletkult* to support the Communist Government, the Congress voted and voluntarily merged with the Commissariat of Education. Dissenting artists who wanted to stay independent were criticised in the Soviet press.

Following the merger, government funds were diverted from local activities to supporting traditional arts such as ballet.

## Agitprop

Lenin and Trotsky believed that art could be used to inspire people to support the new government. In 1920, this led to the establishment of the Department of Agitation Propaganda (*agitprop*), a department within the Communist Party. In the same year, the Commissar of Enlightenment established a similar department: *Glavpolitprosvet*. Together these departments organised propaganda that was designed to support the government. The *agitprop* departments that were formed in 1920 built on propaganda work that had been going on since the revolution.

*Agitprop* was often produced by avant-garde artists working for the government. In this sense, the style of early *agitprop* was experimental, much more experimental than Lenin was happy with, and much more experimental than anything produced after 1929.

### The avant-garde

Avant-garde is a French term that can be translated as 'advance guard' or 'vanguard'. In terms of art, it was used in the early twentieth century to refer to artists who were on the cutting edge of experimental art and culture.

Avant-garde artists experimented with a variety of influences such as chance, geometric shapes, technology and the influence of dreams in order to create new kinds of art.

## Painting and sculpture

Russian artists associated with the avant-garde collaborated with the government to make posters, sculptures and paintings to encourage support for the new regime. El Lissitzky, a graphic designer and photographer, created the poster 'Beat the Whites with the Red Wedge' in 1918, one of the most famous experimental posters of the Civil War. The poster uses geometric shapes to represent the Red Army and the White Army. The style is reminiscent of the abstract art of the period, particularly kazimir Malevich's **Suprematist** work, which is also based on geometric shapes. Lissitzky's poster also formed the basis of a sculpture in which a red wedge splits a block of white stone. The sculpture was unveiled in Moscow in October 1918 to celebrate the anniversary of the October Revolution.

'Beat the Whites with the Red Wedge' was one of over 100 *agitprop* posters that were produced during the Civil War. The Russian Telegraph Agency (ROSTA) worked with artists to produce posters that were displayed in shop windows or on the side of *agitprop* trains. Vladimir Mayakovsky, a poet and designer, made a series of simple graphic posters reminding Russians of the horrors of Tsarism and encouraging them to support the Red Army.

Vladimir Tatlin was another artist who used sculpture to support the new regime. His 'Monument for the Third International' was designed to be the tallest monument in the world. The monument was designed to be made from a series of geometric shapes that moved at different rates so that the shape of the monument was continually shifting. A ten foot (3 metre) model of the monument was completed in 1920, but the final monument was never built.

▲ 'Beat the Whites with the Red Wedge', 1918. In what ways is this poster revolutionary?

## Revolutionary photography

Alexander Rodchenko was the most famous avant-garde photographer to collaborate with the Soviet Government in its early years. Rodchenko used techniques such as photomontage to make posters celebrating the revolution. He was one of the founders of Constructivism, a Russian artistic movement which sought to produce art with a clear purpose. Indeed, during the period of the NEP Rodchenko used his talents to create advertising posters for companies.

## Revolutionary cinema

Lenin believed that cinema was the most important art form of the twentieth century. He also argued that it should be used to inspire support for the new government.

During the Civil War cinematic equipment, such as cameras, films and projectors, were extremely scarce. Nonetheless, in the 1920s, Soviet cinema flourished. Experimental film makers such as Dziga Vertov and Sergei Eisenstein made films that supported the reigne.

### Dziga Vertov

Vertov was an experimental film maker. He rejected the Hollywood style, including the use of scripts, sets and actors. He preferred to make 'cinema of fact'. Therefore his technique was simply to film people as they worked, shopped or had fun. Vertov made a series of documentary films called *Kino-Pravda* (film-truth). He used mirrors, sped film up or slowed it down, ran film backwards and used montages to achieve experimental effects. Influenced by Futurism, he mounted cameras on cars and trains to capture the feeling of speed. He also spent a lot of time filming machines. His most famous film, *A man with a movie camera* (1929), was filmed in some of the Soviet Union's biggest cities and tells the story of a day in the life of a Soviet city. His films were so experimental that the Soviet newspaper *Pravda* described them as 'insane', 'puzzling' and 'laughable'.

### Sergei Eisenstein

Eisenstein made a series of **agitational** films in the 1920s, which combined a revolutionary message with experimental film making. Unlike Vertoz, he did use actors, scripts and sets, and his films told clear stories.

In the mid-1920s Eisenstein designed a series of seven films, entitled *Towards Dictatorship of the Proletariat*, which were designed to tell the story that led to the October Revolution. *Strike* (1925) was the first part of this series, and told the story of a strike set in 1903. Significantly, Eisenstein's film was influenced by Futurism and abstract art, and it contained many scenes dominated by circles or grids. Eisenstein also used special effects to combine human faces with the faces of animals. *Battleship Potemkin* tells the story of a naval mutiny which took place during the **1905 Revolution**, and *October: Ten Days That Shook the World* (1928) dramatised the events of the October Revolution.

By the late 1920s Eisenstein's experimental techniques were criticised as they could not be understood by workers and peasants. Moreover, in the 1930s the films were edited to take out references to Trotsky. Eisenstein continued to make films in a more traditional style under Stalin.

## Art under the NEP

During the period of the NEP, there was a relatively large degree of creative freedom. However, as the 1920s went on the Communist Party was able to assert a greater degree of artistic control.

From 1918 to late 1920, Lenin and senior Communists were preoccupied with winning the Civil War, and therefore there was relatively loose control of artists. Consequently, during this period *Proletkult* and avant-garde artists flourished. However, as the Civil War came to an end, Lenin began to enforce tighter control of artistic expression. The first victim was *Proletkult*. By the end of the 1920s, the Communist Party was firmly in control of art. According to most senior Communists, workers and peasants simply could not understand avant-garde art. Therefore, as the 1920s progressed, the avant-garde became less influential. Artists were forced to change their style and artistic institutions were attacked and in some cases closed. Kazimir Malevich, for example, sent his most radical paintings to Germany in 1927 and adopted a more conventional style at the end of his life. Moreover, the Petrograd State Institute of Artistic Culture was forced to close in 1926 following a campaign against avant-garde art in *Pravda*. The newspaper claimed that the art school was using government money to encourage individualism and debauchery.

Official concerns about contemporary art forms encouraging moral problems also extended to popular culture. From the mid-1920s the government was critical of the influence of American fashion and music on young people. Fashion from the USA, particularly clothes associated with the **flapper style**, and jazz were extremely popular with young people in Soviet cities. Party leaders claimed that the new fashion and the rhythmic new music encouraged sexual promiscuity and drunkenness. They were also concerned that young people would rather dance than attend lectures on revolutionary politics. From the mid-1920s, Communist Party bosses were using the OGPU to break up parties where Jazz was played.

A new group of artists, members of the Association of Artists of Revolutionary Russia, started to emerge in the late 1920s. These artists painted in the traditional style of nineteenth-century painters and produced pictures that obviously celebrated the achievements of the Soviet Government. Works such as Aleksandr Deyneka's 'The Defence of Petrograd' won the praise of Party officials.

### Conclusion

In the early stages of the revolution there was considerable room for creativity. Experimental and avant-garde artists flourished as long as they supported the Communist Party. There were also radical experiments in creating a new proletarian culture. However, as the Communists consolidated their power, they attempted to extend their control of artistic expression. Lenin considered independent artistic expression dangerous and encouraging creativity among workers a waste of time. During the 1920s Communist leaders became increasingly worried about the moral problems that they believed modern art and pop culture caused. Therefore, from the mid-1920s, independent creativity dwindled, the government criticised Vertov and Eisenstein for their experimental style and new more traditional artists emerged to satisfy the conservative tastes of Party officials.

## 2 Socialist Realism, 1930–53

Stalin had strong views on art and therefore initiated a significant shift in Soviet art. Like many Communists, Stalin was suspicious of the avant-garde and experimental techniques. In 1930, Stalin wrote an article in *The Bolshevik*, which argued that revolutionary art should reflect government priorities rather than individual creativity. He also criticised abstract art and non-narrative films arguing that ordinary Soviet citizens could not understand them.

Following the establishment of the Union of Soviet Writers (USW) in 1932, the new group of artists developed 'Socialist Realism'. The USW argued that the new style was genuinely revolutionary. Quickly this new style influenced other art forms. In many ways, this new style had been developing in the 1920s; the key change was the level of official support for the new traditionalism.

### Note it down

Make an index card for each of the artistic styles discussed in this section: *Futurism*, *avant-garde* and *Socialist Realism*. On each card, make detailed notes about:

- the key features of the style
- key examples of art in this genre
- arts associated with the genre.

### Defining the new style

Socialist Realism proved hard to define. Ivan Kulik, President of the Union of Soviet Writers, argued that Socialist Realism had two qualities:

- It contained a 'true reflection of reality'.
- It aimed to 'participate in the building of socialism'.

In painting, this came to mean art that was realistic, in the sense that pictures looked a lot like photographs, and socialist in the sense that they were paintings of factory construction or workers producing **raw materials**.

In terms of literature, the new style meant novels had to have a plot that ordinary people could follow and had to focus on a subject that was related to building socialism. Fyodor Gladkov's 1924 novel *Cement* was held up as an example. The novel tells the story of a group of workers who, having played a major role in the Civil War, reconstruct a cement factory.

Ballet changed too, to reflect the new style. In the 1920s Soviet ballet had been influenced by Constructivism and Futurism, therefore dance moves were angular. Additionally Soviet impresarios, such as Sergei Diaghilev commissioned experimental scores. For example in 1925 he commissioned world renowned Russian composer Sergei Prokofiev to write the music for *The Steel Step*, a Constructivist ballet. The ballet was designed to celebrate Soviet industrialisation and the used experimental techniques such as chromaticism. Under Stalin ballet became more traditional. From the early 1930s Soviet ballet became more about telling epic stories and much less about creative choriography. Leonid Lavrosky's version of *Romeo and Juliet*, staged in 1940, was praised by the Soviet press for telling stories that were accessible to working people.

### Artistic production

Under Stalin, art was produced in a similar way to other goods. Artists were set targets for the number of paintings or sculptures they were required to produce and sent to factories or collective farms to record what they saw. Equally, in 1936, during the Great Terror Soviet artists were purged. Nonetheless, according to Alexander Gerasimov, Stalin's favourite painter, the terror led to a new 'creative atmosphere of enthusiasm among the entire mass of artists'.

Socialist Realism focused on building socialism as Kulik intended. To celebrate the opening of a ball-bearing factory, Soviet sculptors working in 1932 produced a giant sculpture of a ball bearing ten metres in diameter. Many paintings focused on the Five-Year Plans. For example, Gustav Klutsis's 'In the Storm of the Third Year of the Five-Year Plan' portrays heroic workers mining, and Alexander

Lobanov's painting 'Training Workers for Magnitogorsk' depicts the daily occurrence at the new Soviet steelworks.

Soviet artists also celebrated Collectivisation. Samuil Adlivankin's painting 'Voting to Expel the Kulak from the Collective Farm', for example, showed popular enthusiasm for dekulakisation. The style continued into the 1940s and 1950s. Famous paintings from Stalin's later years include Fedor Shurpin's 'Morning of Our Motherland' (1949), which shows Stalin standing in a landscape transformed by collectivisation and industrialisation. The painting is full of the tractors, chimneys and pylons created by Stalin's rule. The painting presents the Soviet Union as a utopia, and yet Stalin looks into the future, apparently imagining even greater things. Aleksei Vasilev's painting 'They are Writing About Us in *Pravda*' (1951) focuses on the plentiful harvests and easy lives of peasants on collective farms. In that sense, Socialist Realism was deeply unrealistic. However, in part, these pictures were designed to show Soviet citizens the future that they were working towards, a utopian future of peace and plenty on efficient farms and in modern factories.

Sculpture focused on the people building socialism as well as the process of building socialism. The leading Socialist Realist sculptor, Sergey Merkurov, was famous for creating giant statues of Lenin and Stalin. He created the three largest sculptures of Stalin in the Soviet Union.

Musical style was also more traditional in the 1930s. Stalin wanted music that was rousing and heroic. He praised Shostakovich's music for the film *Maxim's Youth* (1953). The film is part of a trilogy telling the story of an ordinary worker. Shostakovich composed a revolutionary song for the film. The melody was so strong that Stalin sang along at the screening. Stalin liked the music because it could be sung by ordinary people. He also praised the use of accordions in the opening of the film because they were a common musical instrument that working people could relate to. Stalin also praised nationalistic music, and some of the music Shostakovich wrote under Stalin was based on melodies from traditional Russian folk music. Examples of Shostakovich's nationalistic music include his Suite on Finnish Themes, which celebrated the Soviet invasion of Finland in 1939.

### Dissenting artists

There was a small amount of room in Soviet art in the 1930s to dissent from Stalin's artistic vision. One way of doing this was to celebrate the achievements of Lenin rather than Stalin. The world famous Soviet film maker, Dziga vertov did this in his 1934 trilogy *Three Songs about Lenin*. The film focused on Lenin's vision and the achievements of ordinary people. Stalin was barely mentioned in the film.

### Conclusion

Stalinism led to conformity and government control in almost all areas of life. Art was no exception. The art of Stalin's period, however, did not simply reflect Stalin's views on art. Rather it reflected growing concerns among Communists during the 1920s about the impact of experimental art and pop culture on the Soviet people. For many Communists in the 1920s and 1930s Socialist Realism was the best form of art for the new society. It could be understood by the Soviet people, its style reflected the best traditions of Russian art and the heroic subject matter inspired the Soviet people to give themselves to the construction of socialism. Nonetheless, the conformity was stifling, and the new post-Stalin leadership were keen to allow greater **freedom of expression** following Stalin's death.

## 3 Thaw and non-conformity, 1954–64

Khrushchev's cultural policy went through a series of 'thaws' and 'freezes'. During the 'thaws' a degree of freedom of expression was encouraged, and during the 'freezes' government control was re-emphasised. This 'zig-zag' policy reflected the contradictions in Khrushchev's approach to art and the pressure Khrushchev was under from the Communist Party to maintain control and supress the truth about the true horrors of Stalin's policies.

#### Note it down

Draw a timeline of the period 1954–64. Using bullet points, make notes on Khrushchev's cultural policy during this period. You could use one colour for periods of thaw and another for periods when control over art was tightened up. Make sure you note down examples of the books that were written and published during this period.

### Khrushchev and art

Khrushchev wanted to forge an alliance between the Party and creative intellectuals. Successive Soviet Governments had invested in education. As a result of investment in Soviet universities there were a growing number of intellectuals in the Soviet Union. Moreover, improvements in education meant that the Soviet intelligentsia was the fastest growing section of society in the 1960s. Khrushchev believed that intellectuals should help the government build socialism. Moreover, he believed that true intellectuals would understand the benefits of Communism and therefore would willingly collaborate with Soviet leaders. He also believed that Communism should liberate artists. However, Khrushchev believed that ordinary Soviet workers were not ready for complete freedom, or even for the truth about Stalin's policies. Indeed, he believed that freedom could destabilise the Party by allowing criticism of the government. Therefore Khrushchev's policies lurched between his desire to increase freedom for some and his concern that too much freedom, especially for ordinary citizens, could undermine the regime.

## The 'thaws'

Under Khrushchev Soviet culture experienced a series of 'thaws':

- 1953–54: Following Stalin's death, the government authorised a series of novels which acknowledged generational differences between the new generation of the 1950s and the previous generation of Stalinists. The Soviet journal *New World* published Ilya Ehrenburg's story *The Thaw*. The novel was critical of various aspects of Stalinism, including mass terror.
- 1956–57: Following Khrushchev's Secret Speech (see page 31), there was another period of cultural liberalisation. *New World* published Vladimir Dudintsev's *Not by Bread Alone*. Again, the story was critical of the Stalin period. Dudintsev's novel tells the story of an innovative worker's battles with the unjust Party bureaucracy.
- 1961–62: Following the Twenty-Second Party Congress and the vote to remove Stalin's body from Red Square, a number of books were published that were critical of aspects of Stalin's rule. Aleksandr Solzhenitsyn's short story *One Day in the Life of Ivan Denisovich*, which tells of the life of a prisoner in the Gulag, is the best-known work published in the period. Additionally, Dmitri Shostakovich's opera, 'Lady Macbeth of Mtsensk', which had not been performed in the Soviet Union since Stalin criticised it in 1936, was performed again in 1962.

The 'thaws' were not purely about literature; there were other cultural innovations during these periods. For example, during the World Youth Festival, held in Moscow in 1957, young people danced to jazz music and African drumming. Equally, in terms of music the Soviet Union experienced a 'thaw' under Khrushchev. For example, the classical music of Western Europe and the US, which was not taught in schools under Stalin, was put back on the curriculum in 1957. For example the work of US composer George Gershwin, which was influenced by jazz, was taught in schools from the late 1950s.

However, at the end of each period there was a temporary freeze, as artistic expression went beyond the limits that the authorities were prepared to tolerate. For example, following the initial thaw in 1953–54, Boris Pasternak's novel *Doctor Zhivago* led to cultural restrictions. Pasternak's novel was critical of Lenin's period as leader and therefore unacceptable to Khrushchev's regime. The book was banned in the Soviet Union until the late 1980s. Equally, after the final thaw Khrushchev was horrified by an exhibition of Moscow artists. He reacted to the show with anger shouting loudly that the work of the abstract artist Ernst Neizvestny was 'dog shit'.

The final freeze led to the arrest and imprisonment of several artists. The poet Josef Brodsky, for example, was arrested in January 1964.

## Challenging non-conformity

In spite of the various 'thaws' the government was still keen to challenge **non-conformity**.

### Propaganda and 'popular oversight'

Under Khrushchev there was a significant change in Soviet propaganda. During Stalin's rule, Soviet people had been depicted as heroic and, in a conventional sense, beautiful. Soviet farms and factories had been depicted as modern, efficient and harmonious. However, after 1954 this changed. Increasingly, propaganda posters poked fun at Soviet people. Graphic designers such as V. Fomichev and N. Denisovski designed posters that showed Soviet people in a new light.

The new posters attempted to challenge non-conformity through 'popular oversight'. Posters presented non-conformist citizens as comically bald, fat or lazy. 'The Lazy Bureaucrat' (1961) shows a plump man sitting at a disorganised desk. 'The Alcoholic' (1959) depicts a drunk man lying in a pool of his own vomit. The posters were designed to encourage 'popular oversight'. Citizens were expected to keep other citizens under surveillance. However, rather than report misbehaving citizens to the police, good citizens were encouraged to intervene with helpful moral advice. For example, the poster 'When two girls met' (1963) tells the moral tale of how a good working-class upbringing leads to a disciplined child, whereas the children of indulgent intellectual parents grow up to be lazy, selfish and obsessed with fashion.

Khrushchev-era posters were also a break from the past in that they recognised the inefficiencies of Soviet farms and factories. For example, 'The Cowshed' (1958) pokes fun at the inefficiencies on Soviet farms by showing two cows living in a palace, complete with chandeliers. The poster also contained a quote from kruschev criticising waste and at the top of the poster a quote from Khrushchev criticises wasteful spending on farms.

Fomichev and Denisovski's artistic style was also a break with the past as they tended to produce work that was similar to US cartoons of the period.

▲ 'The Alcoholic' (1959).

## Disciplining 'style hunters'

Khrushchev's government went to great lengths to ensure that women conformed. The government was concerned that women would be seduced by consumerism into lives of wanton glamour and reckless shopping. Consequently, there was an official campaign against young women who adopted Western fashion, so called '*stilyaga*' (style hunters). Apparently, officials at Gosplan believed that women's natural desire to shop could lead to lasting economic problems in a consumer society. Female sexuality was also a cause of official concern. The government assumed that fashionable clothes implied sexual promiscuity. As a result there were official campaigns against Western fashion and 'loose women' in the late 1950s and early 1960s.

The 1957 World Youth Festival had raised concerns that young Soviet women were having sex with male delegates from other countries. Notably, the authorities did not consider Soviet men having sex with foreign women a problem. During the festival squads of Party members patrolled the streets and shaved the heads of young Soviet women that they found having sex with foreign men. In some cases, these women were deported and forced to work on farms in the Virgin Lands for their 'crimes'.

Women's lifestyles worried policy makers due to rising teen pregnancy, abortion rates and the many 'children of the festival'. Soviet officials were worried by what they considered to be the emergence of a new phenomenon: female sexual desire. Officials considered male heterosexual desire to be natural and normal, but female sexual desire, of any kind, was considered to be a sign of unhealthy influences. Welfare policies attempted to direct women towards marriage and childbearing as a more healthy expression of their sexuality.

Increased levels of consumer goods led to increased consumer choice. However, economic planners and government propaganda campaigns sought to guide women to make the 'right choices'. Planned production of consumer goods was used to constrain women's choices. Economic planners planned the production of cosmetics and clothes in accordance with semi-official standards of beauty. The *Teacher's Gazette*, a magazine aimed at female teachers, set out guidance on how to dress appropriately in the consumer age. The magazine argued that Soviet women should dress in a way that reflected the socialist consensus, rather than seeking to express their individuality. The advice was given to female teachers as they were considered role models for young women. The magazine advised 'overly bright lipstick, colour on the eyelids and red nail varnish make a woman look vulgar'.

Additionally, the Soviet Government went to great lengths to restrict public access to the 1959 American National Exhibition which contained an American beauty salon and fashion show. Government posters contrasted wholesome Soviet young women who wore knee-length skirts and plaits with young women who, following American fashions, wore **capri pants** and had shorter blow-dried hair. In essence, Khrushchev's government, like the Soviet Government of the 1920s, associated modern fashion with frivolity, wastefulness and decadence.

While the government and the Party encouraged women to adopt simple, contemporary, but conventional ways of dressing, they were unable to stop the rise of the *stilyagism* (fashion hunters). The government failed to constrain the Soviet desire for fashion. Between 1964 and 1970 consumer spending on clothes tripled. Moreover, in cities over half the clothes that were available in shops never sold, as shoppers considered them unfashionable. Rich city families employed private dressmakers, who worked from foreign fashion magazines to produce clothes that satisfied modern tastes. By 1985, 450 Western magazines were available on the black market in big Soviet cities.

The government continued to try to combat the 'Western influence' of fashion. However, during the 1970s trade with the West increased, so Soviet cinemas showed films from the US and Western Europe that effectively showcased Western fashion. Soviet directors followed the lead of popular US films. For example, the heroine of *The Blonde around the Corner* (1983) wears Western clothes and lives in a fashionable apartment. This strategy was clearly successful as it attracted 24 million people.

## The 1970s and early 1980s

During the 1970s and early 1980s the government was still concerned about Western styles. Therefore Soviet magazines continued to ridicule Western ways of dressing, and teachers were expected to discourage Western styles at school. Nonetheless, sometimes official attempts to discourage new fashions backfired. For example, the comedy film *An Office Romance* (1977) ridiculed a fashionable young female secretary for her love of 'provocative' clothes. Nonetheless, audiences identified with the secretary rather than her conservative poorly dressed boss.

Where women led, men followed. During the 1970s men too were approaching private tailors to get suits with the latest Western looks. In terms of pop culture, the government lost the battle against non-conformity, at least among women in the cities. By the mid-1970s the fashion hunters had won.

## Deviant artists

Khrushchev's 'thaws' did not allow all Soviet artists to publish their work through official government-owned publishing houses. Therefore, from the late 1950s, writers produced '*samizdat*' (self-published) magazines and books (see page 89). Alexander Ginzburg is the best-known figure in the underground *samizdat* movement. He edited the magazine *Syntax*, which circulated on the Soviet black market. *Doctor Zhivago* was refused publication in 1954 in the Soviet Union. Nonetheless, foreign editions were smuggled into the country and *samizdat* editions were also produced.

Artists who refused to submit to government control were sent to psychiatric institutions in order to be cured. Josef Brodsky, for example, was sent to the Serbsky Institute where he was confined with people who suffered from mental illnesses that made them violent. Some artists were forcibly medicated as part of their 'treatment'. Conditions in the hospitals were extremely poor. Inmates lived on watery soup, and in the cold and damp conditions their physical and often mental health deteriorated.

▲ British schoolboys from Forest Hill School in London visiting Moscow in 1961, being mobbed by young Russian women. In what ways is the fashion or style of the two British schoolboys in the centre of the picture different from the young Russians surrounding them?

# 4 Clashes between artists and the government to 1985

Some artists were optimistic following Khrushchev's fall, hoping that the new leadership would end the cultural 'freezes' and initiate a sustained thaw. However, Brezhnev proved less willing to allow criticism of Stalin than his predecessor.

### Note it down

Using a note-making style of your choice, make notes on Soviet art under Brezhnev. Make sure that you note down key examples of conflict between artists and the government, as well as developments of official art during this period.

## Art and culture under Brezhnev

Brezhnev was much less interested in the arts than Khrushchev. However, he was aware of the political impact of art and literature. He was extremely critical of Khrushchev's willingness to publish works that exposed the difficulties of life in the Soviet Union.

Art under Brezhnev became nostalgic. Khrushchev appealed to a bright future and shook faith in the past by criticising Stalin. Brezhnev attempted to revive faith and interest in the heroic days of the revolution.

Brezhnev's cultural conservatism did lead to the creation of some exceptional art, particularly in terms of ballet. During the 1970s and 1980s Soviet ballet was in demand around the world. The Bolshoi Ballet, the Soviet Union's most famous ballet company, was a source of huge national pride. The ballet Spartacus was one of the Soviet cultural triumphs of the era. The ballet, which celebrates an ancient slave rebellion was originally written in 1954. However, Yury Grigorovich's choreography for the 1968 production, won international praise for its beauty following tours of Western capitals in the 1970s. Moreover, the Soviet government supported the ballet as the story of slave revolution was in keeping with Soviet ideology and the story was accessible to ordinary Soviet workers.

Political scientist Piero Ostellino argues that under Brezhnev there were effectively three groups of artists and intellectuals:

- obedient functionaries: intellectuals and artists who were prepared to work with the system without question, whatever their personal opinions about the regime
- loyal oppositionists: intellectuals and artists who were critical of the system, but expressed their criticisms within official channels, trying to improve the system from within
- dissidents: intellectuals and artists who expressed their criticism publicly.

The final group presented consistent problems for Brezhnev.

## The Sinyavsky–Daniel trial

Initial hopes that Khrushchev's fall would lead to a complete thaw were dashed by the trial of authors Andrei Sinyavsky and Yuli Daniel, who were arrested for producing 'anti-Soviet agitation and propaganda' in September 1965.

The new post-Khrushchev leadership were extremely concerned about Khrushchev's 'cultural liberalism', which they believed was undermining faith in the Soviet Union. Indeed, in early 1965 they commissioned a KGB report which stated that there were 1292 anti-Soviet authors who had written almost 10,000 anti-Soviet documents. In order to send a clear message that the thaw was over, the new leadership ordered the arrest and trial of Sinyavsky and Daniel, two authors who had been allowed considerable freedom under Khrushchev.

The Sinyavsky–Daniel trial, which took place in 1966, was essentially a Show Trial. It was significant because the only evidence presented against them were their own writings, Daniel's *This is Moscow Speaking* and Sinyavsky's *The Trial Begins*. Worse still, both writers had enjoyed considerable freedom and some fame under Khrushchev. At the end of the trial the two authors were found guilty and sentenced to seven and five years in a labour camp.

The trial, which revived Stalinist methods, and the attack on writers who had flourished under Khrushchev led to fears that the new leadership were reviving Stalinism.

## The impact of international pressure

The new leadership were, however, aware of the international outrage that persecuting writers and artists provoked. Therefore some writers, who had been imprisoned in Khrushchev's last years, were released. Brodsky, for example, who had been subjected to forced psychiatric treatment and then imprisoned, was released in 1965.

International pressure led to a change in the approach of the new leadership to artist dissidents. After the Sinyavsky–Daniel trial, show trials and imprisonment became rare. Rather, well-known dissident artists were allowed to emigrate. Brodsky, for example, emigrated to the USA where he continued writing and won the Nobel Prize for Literature. The Russian cellist, Mstislav Rostropovich, a supporter of Boris Pasternak, also emigrated, as did Sinyavsky following his release.

Lesser-known artists who deviated from the Party line were sent to psychiatric institutions. They lacked the profile of major artists and psychiatric treatment was not as newsworthy as a prison sentence, therefore the Soviet authorities could use this tactic without provoking embarrassing international reaction. Exact figures are not known, but estimates suggest that by the early 1970s there were 7000 to 8000 dissidents receiving 'repressive psychiatric treatment'.

## The impact of the Prague Spring

The Prague Spring of 1968 led to further hardening of Brezhnev's attitude to art and culture. Reformers in Czechoslovakia had attempted to liberalise Communist rule and create 'socialism with a human face'. This entailed a rejection of Stalinism and much greater freedom of artistic expression. However, the reform led to popular pressure within Czechoslovakia to end Communist rule and break away from the Soviet Union. Brezhnev responded by sending the Soviet Army to crush the liberal regime.

The Prague Spring confirmed Brezhnev's view that cultural liberalisation was a danger to Communist rule. Therefore, following 1968, there was increasing pressure on artists to conform. For example, Solzhenitsyn, who published controversial work under Khrushchev, found it increasingly difficult to publish in the Soviet Union following 1968. Moreover, Alexander Tvardovsky, editor of *New World* and advocate of greater artistic freedom in the 1950s and 1960s, was finally forced to resign in 1970.

The Prague Spring had other cultural consequences for the Soviet Union. Following 1968, Soviet official culture became profoundly nostalgic. The trend towards nostalgia had been obvious since 1965, but from 1968 it became the dominant trend in Soviet art. This was clear in Soviet cinema with films like *Liberation* (1970) and its four sequels released between 1970 and 1971, which celebrated the Soviet victory in the Second World War.

## Dissident artists, 1968–85

In spite of Brezhnev's cultural conservatism and policy of repression, dissident artists continued to write, paint and perform in the Soviet Union throughout his premiership and into the mid-1980s. Nonna Goriunova's *Forest Ritual* (1968) was a live performance in which she posed naked in a forest. The performance was a direct attack on the prohibition of nudity in Soviet art, and a statement about female beauty – independent of male desire.

During the 1970s a group called the Moscow Conceptualists attempted to make art which was a 'rebellion against everyday life'. The art that they produced was supposed to expose the truth about Soviet society and therefore be an antidote to official propaganda.

Ilya Kabakov, one of the Moscow Conceptualists, created a fictional autobiography called *Ten Characters* to illustrate the dullness of Soviet life.

Finally, painter and writer Natalia Zhilina helped form Leningrad Underground Art. She was a member of the Mitki Collective, founded by Dmitry 'Mitya' Shagin in 1984. The initial inspiration for the group was Shagin's book *Mitki*, a series of essays about the absurdities of Soviet life. Shagin worked in a boiler room while making his work and encouraged his followers to drink cheap wine and dress shabbily in old military shirts in order to demonstrate their rejection of the system and their preference for 'warm and soulful pursuits'.

The official reaction to the underground art scene was inconsistent. On some occasions exhibitions took place without interference. The Mitki Collective's first exhibition took place in Leningrad in 1984, without any overt government intervention. However, on other occasions there was repression. The 'Bulldozer Exhibition' of September 1974, organised by artists Evgeny Rukhin and Oscar Rabin, for example, was broken up. Police driving bulldozers destroyed many of the paintings and sculptures displayed at the makeshift exhibition. Equally, the second Mitki exhibition of 1985 was raided by the police.

## Conclusion

Brezhnev was highly sceptical of Khrushchev's 'thaws'. Moreover, unlike Khrushchev he wanted to celebrate the achievements of the Stalin period, rather than expose its atrocities. Under Brezhnev official art became backward looking, focusing in particular on the Soviet triumph in the Second World War. The early Sinyavsky–Daniel trial sent a clear message that artistic dissent would not be tolerated and the thaw was over. Nonetheless, international pressure and the uncompromising spirit of Soviet dissident artists meant that by 1985 there was a thriving underground art scene that raids, bulldozers and the threat of psychiatric 'treatment' were unable to stamp out.

## Work together

Having read this chapter, copy and complete the following table:

| | Evidence of total control | Evidence of limited control |
|---|---|---|
| 1917–8 | | |
| 1929–53 | | |
| 1954–64 | | |
| 1965–85 | | |

Using your notes on Soviet politics, economics and culture, list evidence that the Soviet Government achieved total control in the left-hand column and evidence that government control was limited in the right-hand column.

Having completed the table, swap with a partner. Compare the tables and ensure that you note down any statements that you missed.

Discuss how far the Soviet Union truly established total control and in which periods control was at its most extreme.

Together write one sentence evaluating the extent of control in each era.

## Chapter summary

- Art in the Soviet Union went through a series of phases.
- In the early days avant-garde artists collaborated with the regime, using their revolutionary style to support the revolutionary regime.
- From the 1930s Socialist Realism became the dominant style.
- After Stalin's death dissident artists used new styles to promote new messages.
- The relationship between the Communist Party and artists was never easy.
- Communist officials and Party leaders recognised the power of art to inspire and direct the energies of the people.
- However, Lenin, Stalin, Khrushchev and Brezhnev were all wary of the potential of art to be used to undermine the government, to expose the flaws in the Soviet system and to form organisations which could challenge the government.

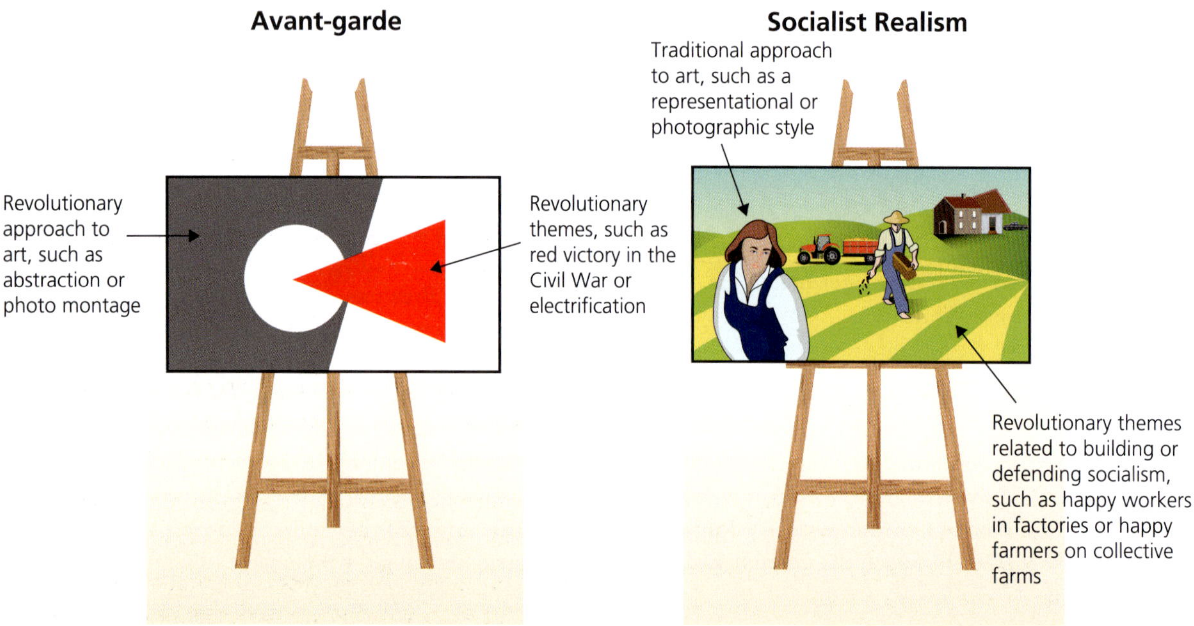


▲ Summary diagram: The state and art.

# Essay technique: Counter-argument

Essays that develop a good argument are more likely to reach the highest levels, because argumentative essays are more likely to develop sustained analysis (see page 59).

You can set up an argument in your introduction, but you should develop your argument throughout the essay. One way of doing this is to adopt an argument, counter-argument structure. A counter-argument is an argument that disagrees with the main argument of the essay. Setting up an argument and then challenging it with a counter-argument is one way of weighing up, or evaluating, the importance of the different factors that you discuss. Essays of this type will develop an argument in one paragraph and then set out an opposing argument in another paragraph.

Imagine you are answering the following question:

**How far did the Communist Government control art and culture in the Soviet Union in the years 1921–64?**

You could write an essay in which the first two paragraphs set out the arguments as in the example in the table below:

These two paragraphs could be developed into the beginning of a high-level answer. However, you will need to resolve the tension between the argument and the counter-argument (see page 136) and write a conclusion that weighs up the different aspects of the essay (see pages 142–143) in order to write a full essay.

| | |
|---|---|
| **Paragraph 1: Argument** | The Communist Party believed that art and propaganda had an important role to play in building and defending socialism. Therefore they had a high level of control through government control of the media, government commissioning of art and government-produced propaganda. |
| **Paragraph 2: Counter-argument** | However, there were periods in which there was relative artistic freedom, such as during the 1920s and Khrushchev's 'thaw'. Therefore the Communist Government did not always seek total control of art and culture. |

## Activity: Relative importance

Imagine you are answering the following question:

**To what extent were art and propaganda the main way in which the Communist Government consolidated its power in the years 1918–38?**

Using your notes from the previous chapters:

1 Draw the following diagram:

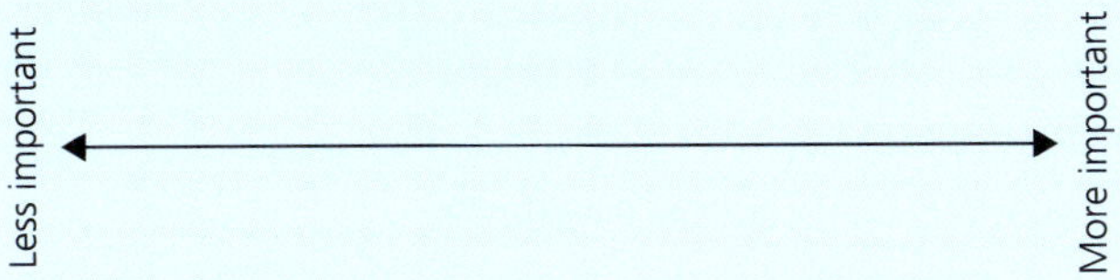


2 Write the following factors on cards or post-it notes and place them on the line according to their importance for the consolidation of Communist power (1918–38):
   - art and propaganda
   - the creation of a one-party state
   - terror
   - compromise.

3 Now write a short argument justifying the relative importance of each factor.

**TIP:** Remember, your argument must contain a statement and a reason.

4 Reverse the order of your first and second most important factors.

5 Write two sentences that explicitly argue that your second most important factor was actually the most important factor. This is your counter-argument.

**TIP:** Remember, your counter-argument must contain a statement and a reason.

6 Use your original argument and counter-argument as the basis for writing two paragraphs in answer to the question.

Paper 1 Russia, 1917–91: from Lenin to Yeltsin

# Theme 4 Social developments, 1917–85

In this theme you will consider the following:

- Social security: full employment, the provision of housing and social benefits, 1917–53; Khrushchev, Brezhnev, social security and social stability, 1953–85
- Women and the family: women's changing status in towns and the countryside; government attitudes towards women and the family
- Education and young people: the growth of education; literacy campaigns; state control of the curriculum.

## The Big Picture

Lenin and his fellow Bolsheviks believed that their revolution would transform society. Lenin's vision was that Communism would lead to the benefits created by capitalism being shared by all working people. Lenin looked forward to a society where everyone had a decent standard of living, where everyone was able to benefit from a good education and where there was genuine equality between the sexes.

Lenin's vision was not realised in his lifetime. Civil war and the economic pressures of industrialisation meant that many in the Soviet Union continued to live in poverty, and many were unable to get a decent education during Lenin's lifetime. Additionally, the ignorance and prejudice of many male Communists meant that sexual equality was never achieved.

Access to education improved significantly under Stalin, and social benefits of all kinds were much more widely available under Khrushchev and Brezhnev. However, achieving sexual equality proved more difficult. From 1930 successive governments failed to address the issue of sexual equality. The Communist Party was male dominated. Most senior Communists failed to understand the problems of sexism in the Soviet Union and believed that sexual equality had been achieved.

## TIMELINE

| | |
|---|---|
| 1918 | Compulsory labour introduced |
| 1918 | *Komsomol* founded |
| 1919 | *Zhenotdel* created |
| 1919 | The Decree on Illiteracy published |
| 1922 | The Young Pioneers established |
| 1927 | Fees for primary schools abolished |
| 1930 | *Zhenotdel* abolished |
| 1940 | Internal passports introduced |
| 1943 | Gender segregation introduced into secondary schools |
| 1947 | Vaccines for common diseases such as typhus and malaria made universally available |
| 1955 | Abortion legalised |
| 1963 | Valentina Tereshkova becomes the first woman in space |
| 1974 | Construction of the Baikal-Amur Mainline (BAM) initiated |
| 1979 | Almanac, a small feminist movement, established in Leningrad |

# 4a: Social security

## Overview

From 1917 to 1985 successive Soviet Governments tried to organise an economy in which everyone worked and everyone had a good standard of social security. To some extent this reflected an ideological commitment to run an economy in a way that reflected the values of socialism rather than capitalism. Under War Communism the government, for the first time, introduced compulsory labour. Rather than being paid, workers received free housing, free transport and food rations. The NEP's compromise with capitalism led to the re-emergence of unemployment. However, the commitment to social welfare continued, and industrial workers benefited from the most extensive benefit system in the world at that time. Stalin's Great Turn reintroduced compulsory labour. However, he prioritised economic construction over social welfare and therefore economic growth did not lead to a better quality of life. Housing, which was already a particular problem, turned into a crisis by the end of the 1930s. Khrushchev re-emphasised welfare. He initiated housing programmes and an extension of welfare that transformed the lives of Soviet citizens. Brezhnev continued with Khrushchev's policies, and although standards of living continued to improve, Brezhnev's 'social contract' led to a stagnant society and a declining economy.

This chapter considers:

1. Full employment and social benefits, 1917–53
2. Housing, 1917–53
3. Khrushchev, Brezhnev and the promotion of a stable society, 1953–85.

## 1 Full employment and social benefits, 1917–53

From 1917 to 1953 Lenin and Stalin tried to create economic systems that rewarded work and made sure that working people would receive benefits such as healthcare. However, economic problems undermined the system's capacity to provide benefits for all. Moreover, Party members received more substantial benefits than the rest of the population.

### Note it down

The provision of social benefits went through a series of phases between 1917 and 1953. Skim the text and the sub-headings and work out what the major phases were. Use a note-making style of your choice to make notes on healthcare provision in each phase. In each case begin by noting down a general statement about the availability of benefits in that period. Then take down specific details that demonstrate what was available and the limits of availability.

### Marxism and work

Marxism is, in part, a theory about work. One of Marx's central criticisms of **capitalism** was that capitalist economies do not reward work. Marx argued that under capitalism people grow rich because they own property allowing them to charge rent and to own anything that is produced in their property. Workers, however, stay poor because they have no property. Marx viewed capitalists as 'parasites' in the sense that they lived off the work of the working **class** without contributing to their well-being.

After the revolution Marx argued that parasitism should be abolished and that all able people should work. Marx also argued that the relationship between work and wealth would go through two phases after the revolution:

- Socialist economic organisation would be based on the principle: 'from each according to their ability, to each according to their ability.' Therefore work, rather than property, would be the key to gaining economic resources.
- Communist economic organisation would be based on a higher principle: 'from each according to their ability, to each according to their need.' Marx believed that during Communism, the final phase of human history, society would be so wealthy that everyone would be able to have what they needed. Therefore he argued that people would contribute in whatever way they could and get the resources they needed, regardless of the scale of the contribution they made.

### Work and benefits under Lenin

Lenin's view of work was influenced by Marx. Indeed, in 1918 he published the Declaration of the Rights of Toiling and Exploited People, which introduced two principles that were designed to transform work:

- The Declaration abolished the private ownership of land. Therefore capitalists could no longer make money simply by owning things.

- The Declaration introduced universal labour duty. This was designed 'to eliminate the parasitical layers of society' by ensuring that everybody worked and therefore capitalists could no longer simply live off the labour of others.

These principles were enshrined in every version of the Soviet Constitution. In many ways, the Soviet system failed to reflect these principles, but in some senses they continued to inspire policy makers until the end of the Soviet Union in 1991.

## Work 1917–18

Lenin's economic policy went through several phases but they all reflected the Communist Party's belief in the duty of all people to labour.

Ensuring stable employment was extremely difficult between October 1917 and mid-1918. The revolutions of 1917 had caused economic chaos. Around 570 industrial enterprises closed between March and August 1917. As a result, unemployment had increased to over 100,000 by October 1918. The situation worsened after the October Revolution. Lenin called a truce, effectively taking Russia out of the **First World War**. Consequently, war production ceased, leading to higher unemployment. By March 1918, 75 per cent of chemical and metal workers in Petrograd were unemployed.

During this period Lenin stressed the duty of labour discipline and collaboration between workers and their former bosses, who were employed as 'bourgeois specialists'. Importantly, the 'bourgeois specialists' no longer made money through property. Rather they received wages for their work running factories and organising production.

Lenin's early economic plans failed to stop the disintegration of the economy and rising unemployment. War Communism (see page 43), changed patterns of work again.

## Work and benefits, 1918–21

In theory, War Communism was based on a relationship between the government and workers. Workers had a duty to provide labour, and the government had a duty to provide food and basic amenities.

The widespread unemployment of early 1918 was ended by the introduction of compulsory labour. From September 1918 able-bodied men between 16 and 50 lost the right to refuse employment. People in work were issued a work card which entitled them to food rations.

War Communism also reflected the principle of allocating resources according to the value of work. After money was abolished, rations were allocated according to occupation. The population was divided into six groups according to their occupation. The rationing system was based on class, so that working-class people received the highest rations, but people working in middle-class occupations such as medical doctors received less. Aristocrats and former factory owners, 'the former people', were entitled to about 25 per cent of the food that working people received. At the height of the rationing system 36 products were rationed and there were 22 million people entitled to ration cards.

Rationing was organised by *Prodraspred* (Section of General Distribution), which had subsections which delivered rations to workers and a Community Section which tried to deliver food to schools and to people who could not work due to sickness or disability.

Workers also had access to other benefits, at least in Moscow and Petrograd. For example, a work card entitled workers to travel on public transport. Communal dining halls were set up in factories to feed workers. The government claimed that 93 per cent of people living in Moscow in 1920 were regularly fed in communal dining halls. Other communal facilities such as laundries and crèches were also provided in urban centres, in part to help women work in factories.

Party members also enjoyed special privileges. The government ran special shops where Party members could acquire food and goods that were scarce.

In practice, the system of compulsory work and government provision was unsuccessful:

- Compulsory labour proved unsustainable in the conditions of the Civil War. By July 1920 factories were beginning to close due to fuel shortages. The government responded by forcing unemployed people to search for fuel or join food detachments, groups of men organised in a similar way to the army who were responsible for searching villages for food.
- War Communism never provided more than 50 per cent of the food and fuel that people needed to live on. In the short term, people turned to the **black market**. In the longer term, workers fled the cities seeking work and food on farms. Between 1917 and 1921 the population of Petrograd dropped by 50 per cent. The total population of factory workers reduced by 25 per cent during the Civil War.

Factory closures and food scarcity meant that War Communism ultimately failed to create a system of full employment which provided social security for all those in work.

## Work and benefits in the 1920s

The relationship between compulsory work and government benefits disappeared under the New Economic Policy. Lenin conceived the NEP as a return to **state** capitalism, with the goal of promoting economic growth. Therefore a degree of capitalism and unemployment returned. Unemployment was a significant problem between 1921 and 1924 (see Table 1).

**Table 1: Unemployment figures, 1921–24.**

| Year | Percentage of the labour force unemployed |
|---|---|
| 1921 | 5.5 |
| 1922 | 8.6 |
| 1923 | 16.6 |
| 1924 | 18.0 |

Unemployment surged for a number of reasons:

- In 1921 and 1922 soldiers from the **Red Army** were demobilised and found it hard to get work.
- Urban workers who left the cities towards the end of the Civil War returned. Some were unable to get jobs.
- At the beginning of the NEP the government tried to 'rationalise' industry in order to make it profitable. Therefore the number of workers in government factories was reduced to lower labour costs.
- As War Communism ended, the government sacked around 225,000 administrators who had been employed administering the system.

Attempts to increase productivity in 1926 kept urban unemployment high in the mid-1920s. The government prioritised jobs for former members of the Red Army. Additionally, funding for crèches was ended. These policies, and traditional sexism, meant that women were far more likely to be unemployed than men. Indeed, in 1922, 62.2 per cent of unemployed people in the Soviet Union's towns and cities were women.

In spite of these problems, there were some attempts to make sure that workers benefited from work in the Soviet Union. During the 1920s an extensive system of benefits was created for urban workers. The system was administered by trades unions of local **soviets**:

- The 1922 Labour Law gave unions the right to negotiate binding agreements about pay and working conditions with employers.
- **Social insurance**, which paid disability benefits, maternity benefits, unemployment benefits and medical benefits covered nine million workers.
- The government invested in education for urban workers and their families (see page 133).

The system of social insurance for Soviet workers was the most comprehensive in the world. However, peasants were almost entirely excluded from these benefits due to the government's focus on the special position of the **proletariat**.

In conclusion, while unemployment was a major problem during the period of the NEP, urban workers were clearly better off in 1926 than they had been before the revolution in 1913. They were paid around ten per cent more and ate more meat and fish. Peasants, by contrast, did not benefit from the social insurance available in the cities.

## Work and benefits under Stalin

The link between compulsory work and social benefits, which had been eroded under the NEP, was re-established under Stalin. The Five-Year Plans and Collectivisation were deliberate attempts to move away from the compromise with capitalism that took place under the NEP. Therefore various aspects of capitalism that Communists saw as problematic, which had been tolerated in the 1920s, were ended following Stalin's Great Turn. For Stalin, Soviet workers were a crucial economic resource, central to building **socialism**. Therefore he wanted to ensure full employment in order to ensure rapid industrialisation.

### Employment and benefits in the 1930s

Rapid industrialisation led to full employment for men and women. Moreover, relatively well-paid jobs in the cities attracted peasants fleeing the horrors and poverty associated with Collectivisation. However, full employment did not lead to a rising standard of living.

Safety was not a benefit that Stalin prioritised for his workers. Therefore working conditions deteriorated as a result of the Five-Year Plans. Speedy construction was more important to Stalin than clean and safe workplaces. Equally, miners worked in dangerous conditions as meeting production targets was more important than the health and safety of workers.

Stalin introduced harsh labour discipline. Many measures that had been brought in as part of War Communism were revived:

- Lateness was criminalised.
- Unions lost the right to negotiate with factory managers.
- Damaging factory property was criminalised.
- Strikes were banned.

Stalin also introduced the 'continuous work week'. Workers still received one day off a week, but it changed from week to week. Consequently, factories and mines could work seven days a week, rather than closing down on Sundays.

In 1940 workers lost the right to change jobs. During the Five-Year Plans, demand for labour was very high as factory managers needed as many workers as possible to meet production targets. Therefore workers were able to move from job to job in search of better pay and conditions. This was stopped in 1940, and **internal passports** were introduced to prevent workers moving from town to town without permission.

Over time, the Five-Year Plans did lead to improved benefits:

- Workers were entitled to food rations.
- By 1933 most Soviet citizens had access to electricity.
- During the 1930s, 30,000 km of railways were built, increasing access to transport. Passenger traffic increased by 400 per cent in the 1930s.
- The Moscow Metro opened in the 1930s, providing underground transport to the population of the capital.
- There was a significant increase in healthcare provision, including mass vaccination campaigns dealing with smallpox, diphtheria, malaria and typhoid.
- Factory and farm canteens provided meals for workers.

There was a significant shift in how these benefits were administered. Under the NEP benefits were available through trades unions or through local soviets. However, during the 1930s benefits were increasingly available through factories or collective farms. This re-emphasised the link between work and social welfare. New factories became the heart of 'company towns', in which factories provided employment and administered benefits, including hospitals and housing (see page 115).

Peasants benefited much less than workers. For example, they were not entitled to rations, and food was much scarcer on farms than it was in cities as the government seized the vast majority of farm production. During the late 1930s farm workers would have to travel to towns to buy bread, as there was so little food available on the farms.

### Soviet healthcare under Stalin

Stalin's healthcare system was linked very closely to employment. Between 1929 and 1950 the government attempted to expand the system to all areas of society. However, healthcare was better in the cities than in small towns or on collective farms.

Stalin's healthcare system was designed to keep workers healthy enough to keep working. Therefore the doctors were based at factories and collective farms. Doctors were required to reduce days lost through sickness year on year. Moreover, doctors were expected to be very strict about allowing people to have time off due to illness.

In theory all Soviet citizens had rights to these benefits. However, in practice scarce resources meant that some benefited more than others. For example, Soviet healthcare operated a 'Party first' policy, where Party members were guaranteed vaccines and other workers could queue for any medicine that remained. Additionally, while all workers were entitled to rations, senior Party members could organise special events, such as banquets, which were paid for from government money. This system of privileged access to resources led to radical inequalities. For example, in Dnepropetrovsk, a city in the Ukraine, all Party officials were vaccinated against typhus, and yet there were 10,000 cases of malaria among the working population in 1932 and 26,000 in 1933.

## Employment and benefits, 1945–53

Full employment continued after the war. The industrial workforce increased from 8 million to 12.2 million between 1945 and 1950 largely as a result of returning soldiers.

Food shortages had a significant impact on the benefits workers received. Eating in communal canteens cost workers between 250 and 300 roubles a month in 1947, about half of a worker's monthly wages. Workers under 18 were entitled to three subsidised meals a day in factory or farm canteens. However, the subsidies only covered 2.3 kg of meat and six eggs a month, and most young workers, who earned low wages due to their junior positions, could not afford to pay for the meals. As a result there was a marked decline in communal eating following the war.

Conditions were better in Stalin's later years. In spite of the war, healthcare improved significantly from 1940:

- Infant mortality declined by 50 per cent between 1940 and 1950.
- The number of medical doctors increased by two-thirds between 1947 and 1952.
- Vaccines for common diseases such as typhus and malaria were made universally available from 1947. Malaria declined radically from 1949 onwards.

Nonetheless, the expansion of healthcare did not lead to an improvement in the health of the Soviet people. Food shortages, poor housing and the poverty caused by the war meant the sickness rates did not fall:

- The planned economy struggled to produce simple things like soap, warm clothing and shoes, which led to greater health problems.
- Food was a major problem. In order to make up for shortages, work canteens used rotten food, animal

feed and other products that were unfit for human consumption. This led to illness.

- Sanitation in factories and farms was often inadequate, leading to lice infestations and outbreaks of dysentery and vomiting.
- Hygiene education was poor. It was not until 1947 that there was a publicity campaign encouraging workers to 'use the toilet in a civilised fashion' and wash their hands after using toilets.

Indeed, the average Soviet worker took between ten and thirteen days off ill a year in 1946. This figure remained constant until the mid-1950s.

### Conclusion

In theory, Communists believed that all people had the duty to work and all people had the right to certain benefits. However, from 1918 to 1953 none of the economic systems that were tried delivered a satisfactory relationship between work and benefits. War Communism and the Five-Year Plans succeeded in making work compulsory, at least for the majority of the population, but consistently failed to ensure that workers benefited from the system. Under the NEP industrial workers were guaranteed a wide range of benefits. However, unemployment was widespread and the benefits were not available to peasants. Finally, the Communists never fully abolished parasitism. Capitalist parasites may have been liquidated in 1928, but Party members still enjoyed a privileged lifestyle that was based on their status rather than the work they did.

## 2 Housing, 1917–53

Housing was a continual problem for the Soviet people. Housing was destroyed in the Civil War and in the Second World War. Moreover, large numbers of people moved from the country to the cities at the beginning of the 1930s to get jobs in the new factories, putting pressure on already crowded cities. Additionally, housing was expensive to build, and the Soviet Government continually had other priorities.

In the 1920s, Soviet authorities redistributed existing housing, taking it away from rich property owners and allowing poor people to live in the houses of the 'former people'. Under Stalin house building did take place. However, with the exception of a few 'model' developments the housing was cheap and lacked facilities such as running water, electricity and sewerage.

#### Note it down

From 1917 to 1953 Soviet Governments had a range of policies regarding housing. Skim this section and work out what the main policies were. Then, using a note-making style of your choice, make notes on each of the different policies implemented during the period. Make sure your notes include all the appropriate technical terms, key details about the kinds of housing available, and the priorities of the government at the time and how this impacted on house building.

### Redistribution of property, 1918–28

From the beginning of 1918 working people in cities had forcibly taken property away from aristocrats and the middle class. Former owners were either killed, forced out of their homes or allowed to retain a single room for themselves and their families. Many others squatted in deserted buildings. Lenin issued a decree in August 1918 to try to bring the process under control. Local soviets were empowered to take property away from its owners and to redistribute it to the poor and homeless.

By the end of the Civil War workers were fleeing the cities in search of food as factories closed. Therefore the government authorised the destruction of houses in order to provide timber for fuel.

Under the NEP between 60 and 80 per cent of urban housing was denationalised. Redistribution of property was initially outlawed. However, after Lenin's death there were fresh attempts to redistribute housing. In 1923–24 large town houses were 'socialised'. Property owners were forced to live in a single room, while working-class families were moved into the other rooms. Often the authorities assumed that one room was enough for an entire family. At the same time, Church property was nationalised, priests were evicted from their cottages and Church buildings were turned into stores, civic centres or housing.

Experiments with rent-free housing came to an end in 1921 when rent was reintroduced. House building restarted after the Civil War in 1923. Under the conditions of the NEP 89 per cent of house building was undertaken by private companies. There were small attempts to create buildings that reflected the values of the revolution in the Soviet Union's major cities. These include the Zuev Club, the Rusakov Club and the Burevestnik Factory Club all built between 1927 and 1929. These were designed in a Constructivist style as social, educational and cultural centres for Soviet workers. Additionally, Constructivist houses were built, such as the Narkomfin Apartment House in Moscow. The building was designed to facilitate collective living through the provision of a collective kitchen, crèche, library, gym and laundry facilities, as well as a roof garden. The provision of a communal kitchen, crèche and laundry reflected a commitment to the liberation of women through sharing domestic duties. Four of these blocks were planned, construction started in 1928 and only two were built. Although these buildings were revolutionary and extremely well designed, only a few were built and therefore they made little impact on the lives of Soviet citizens.

### Constructivist architecture

Constructivism was an avant-garde style that was popular among artists in Russia in the late 1910s and continued to be influential into the 1920s (see page 117). In terms of architecture, Constructivism was deliberately futuristic. The design of buildings echoed the look of machines. Buildings tended to be based on dramatic geometric shapes, such as cylinders and cubes.

## Housing under Stalin

Under Stalin housing in cities became an acute problem. The urban population trebled between 1929 and 1940 as peasants escaped collective farms for jobs in the cities, and therefore demand for accommodation increased significantly. The government deliberately tried to keep the housing budget to a minimum and addressed the housing shortage in a number of ways.

▲ **The Zuyev Workers' Club in Moscow, a prominent work of Constructivist architecture. What is revolutionary about the Zuyev Workers' Club?**

## *Kommunalka*

In existing cities Soviet authorities divided buildings into small *kommunalka* (communal apartments). Entire families would share a single small room. Bathrooms, where they existed, and kitchens were shared. The average family *kommunalka* was 5.5 square metres in 1930. However, pressure for housing meant that over time *kommunalka* were redivided. By 1940 the average *kommunalka* was 4 square metres. Often buildings were divided up into barely useable spaces. For example, rooms would be divided, without being rewired. Therefore one light switch would control the lighting of several apartments.

The government also failed to invest in sewerage or communal facilities. For example, bathhouses were scarce. The 650,000 people in the Liubertsy district of Moscow, for example, did not have a single bathhouse.

The modernisation of urban centres was also a low priority. For example, during the 1930s electrification and the provision of street lights slowed. Similarly, the authorities made no attempt to introduce modern sewerage.

Coal sheds and under-stairs cupboards were converted into accommodation. In one case in Moscow a family of six lived in an under-stairs cupboard. The 1930s also saw the emergence of 'corner-dwellers': people who lived in corridors or communal kitchens within *kommunalka* buildings. Corner-living could be expensive; space in corridors could cost as much as half a month's wage. Moreover, corridor living was often permanent. One worker in Leningrad lived in a corridor for five years before being moved into a *kommunalka*.

## Factory towns

New buildings were constructed under Stalin to support the new factory towns like Magnitogorsk. However, construction of factories was prioritised over housing. Accommodation in the new factory towns was often inferior to the *kommunalka*. Rather than allowing one family per room, several families would occupy a barracks-style dormitory. The best of these were built of timber and insulated with straw. They did not have running water or bathrooms. New factory towns also lacked other basic necessities, such as paved streets and electric lights.

Magnitogorsk was initially designed as a model town. At the beginning of the project planners commissioned a radical German architect to design clean, modern, state-of-the-art accommodation. However, these houses proved too expensive. The few that were built were occupied by American specialists who came to advise on the project, and later by the managers of the factory. Even the initial designs provided no kitchens, assuming that all workers would eat in factory canteens. Within a year of the project starting the initial housing plans were abandoned. The majority of workers lived in barrack-style dormitories and around 20 per cent lived in mud huts. The combination of dormitory living and poor sanitation led to disease and lice.

New factory towns built outside the Ukrainian city of Dnepropetrovsk were similarly basic. They had no sewerage system, streets were not paved and there were no electrical lights, in spite of the fact that they were extremely close to the Dnieper hydroelectric power station.

## Housing, 1941–53

The Second World War made the housing situation much worse. The destruction caused by the war was immense. Approximately one-third of urban housing was damaged or destroyed between 1941 and 1945. However, Stalin continued to prioritise industrial buildings over housing. The official pre-war policy of cramming more people into smaller spaces continued. By 1947 the average worker in a *kommunalka* had four square metres of space, and the average worker living in a dormitory had three square metres. Conditions in dormitories were poor. Workers in the Moscow coalfields were housed in dormitories. However, there were only 15,000 beds for the 26,000 workers. All kinds of furniture were scarce. There was one table between every 10 workers, one wardrobe for every 27 workers and one wash basin for every 70 people.

The government did begin a scheme to encourage workers to build their own homes. However, building materials were scarce, there was a series of administrative obstacles and the process was expensive. Consequently the scheme proved largely unsuccessful.

House building was not a major priority under the Fourth Five-Year Plan (1945–50). Budgets were small, and management inefficient. Workers were often reassigned to other projects, which meant that even the small number of projects that were started progressed extremely slowly. For example, in the first half of 1948 housebuilding projects outside Moscow spent 40 per cent of their budget and were then suspended, meaning that not a single house was completed. Those houses that were constructed in the early 1950s, like much of what was produced under Stalin's Plans, were often extremely poor quality. Roofs leaked, plaster fell off walls and there was no gas, electricity or sewerage.

Housing on collective farms was prioritised. Stalin's indifference to agriculture and Khrushchev's energy led to a massive housing project in the Ukraine after the war. As a result, between 1945 and 1950, 4500 farming villages were built. This led to the construction or renovation of 919,000 houses, 250,000 agricultural production buildings and 31,000 communal buildings. Khrushchev came up with a similar plan for Moscow, but Stalin vetoed it due to its expense.

## Conclusion

Housing was never one of Stalin's priorities. Industrialisation always took precedence. In many ways, Stalin's policies created the housing crisis, which was exacerbated by the apalling destruction caused by the Second World War. His policies did little to solve the problems and therefore his workers were forced to live in squalid accommodation with no amenities or privacy.

# 3 Khrushchev, Brezhnev and the promotion of a stable society, 1953–85

Full employment continued, in theory, from Stalin's death until 1985. Indeed, full employment was part of the economic model of planned industry and collective agriculture that was at the heart of Soviet society from 1928 to the late 1980s.

However, the post-Stalin leadership had different objectives to Stalin. Whereas Stalin prioritised giant factories and the mass production of **raw materials**, Khrushchev and Brezhnev wanted the Soviet economy to produce a better standard of living for Soviet citizens.

### Note it down

Khrushchev and Brezhnev implemented radically different social policies to Stalin and Lenin. Begin your note making by taking down the key shift in priorities that took place around the time of Stalin's death. Next, using a note-making style of your choice, make notes on the key features of Khrushchev's and Brezhnev's social policies. Make sure you note down details relating to:

- their priorities
- their policy initiatives
- their achievements.

## Khrushchev, socialism and sausage

Khrushchev summarised his approach to socialist economics and politics with the phrase 'What sort of Communism is it that cannot produce *sausage*?' Communism, for Khrushchev, implied a better standard of living for working people. Therefore Communism was impossible without a plentiful supply of consumer goods and food. This focus on plenty was evident in his Virgin Lands Scheme and his policy of increasing the production of consumer goods. His welfare and housing policies also reflected this commitment.

### Health and welfare

Khrushchev believed that a socialist society should look after the welfare of all. Therefore he increased investment in healthcare. The Soviet healthcare budget more than doubled in Khrushchev's first years, from 21.4 billion roubles in 1950 to 44.0 billion roubles in 1959. Soviet health greatly improved, particularly in the countryside. Death rates and infant mortality rates both dropped (see Table 2).

**Table 2: Death rates and infant mortality rates, 1950 and 1965.**

| | 1950 | 1965 |
|---|---|---|
| Death rate (per thousand population | 9.7 | 7.3 |
| Infant mortality rate (per thousand live births) | 81 | 27 |

The pensions budget quadrupled from 1950 to 1965, partly because pensions were raised and partly because the number of pensioners increased from 1 million in 1950 to 4.4 million in 1965.

Major reforms introduced in 1961 improved social benefits significantly. New laws introduced:

- free lunches in schools, offices and factories
- free public transport
- full pensions and healthcare rights for farmers.

These social benefits reforms marked a significant improvement in the standard of living of the Soviet people.

### Housing

Khrushchev had similar success in terms of housing. Between 1950 and 1965 the amount of urban housing more than doubled. This was due to a deliberate policy initiative by Khrushchev to construct more urban homes.

First, Khrushchev ordered a halt to new government and communal buildings. Secondly, he invested in new materials and techniques in order to solve the problem of housing. He argued that cheap mass housing was necessary in the short term, and that in the 1980s, when Communism had been achieved, these houses could be replaced by more sophisticated housing. The result was a new kind of low-cost housing block nicknamed Khrushchyovka. Although they were designed as temporary buildings, Khrushchyovka became the standard model for all new homes. Construction of Khrushchyovka continued throughout the 1970s and 1980s.

Khrushchev ordered architects to abandon grand Stalinist architecture and to focus on low-cost functional buildings. The result was the K-7 apartment block, which could be constructed quickly and easily from large **prefabricated**

## Soviet architecture, 1929–1965

◀ **Lomonosov Moscow State University, one of the Seven Sisters.**

Under Stalin architecture moved away from the Constructivism of the 1920s. Stalinist architecture tended to be palatial or monumental. Rather than experimental or futuristic buildings, Stalin's architects built more traditional buildings. In this sense, Stalinist architecture was similar to the Stalinist artistic style Socialist Realism (see page 99). The Seven Sisters, a group of skyscrapers built in Moscow between 1947 and 1953, reflect this style. They resemble Russian architecture of the seventeenth century, but were constructed using techniques developed to build skyscrapers in cities like New York.

Khrushchev was highly critical of this style. Construction was expensive and tended to create grand government buildings rather than private housing. Under Khrushchev building became much more functional. Buildings were not decorated in traditional styles, as Khrushchev believed this wasted resources. Consequently, all Khrushchyovka apartment blocks tend to look the same.

concrete panels and standardised windows and doors, rather than being built slowly from brick.

The new blocks allowed families to have an entire apartment, rather than being forced to live in a single room, or to share a dormitory. Khrushchyovka apartments included a bathroom, a kitchen and at least two bedrooms to allow parents to sleep in a separate room from their children. Apartments tended to be small, but were, nonetheless, over ten times bigger than the *kommunalka* of the Stalin period. Khrushchyovkas tended to have five storeys; larger models were built in big cities and fitted with elevators.

The Khrushchyovka transformed Soviet family life. However, they also worried the authorities. The Khrushchyovka effectively recreated privacy. Soviet authorities were no longer able to keep a check on the population through informants in dormitories or in *kommunalka* blocks. Therefore the new type of accommodation led to a propaganda campaign encouraging citizens to live good socialist lives (see page 101).

## The 'social contract'

Social policy under Brezhnev continued to follow the direction set by Khrushchev. However, while the policies continued, the justification for the policies changed. For Khrushchev, an improved standard of living in the short term was the first step to Communism, a society in which everyone was wealthy. Brezhnev, however, abandoned Khrushchev's promise of reaching Communism by 1980. Brezhnev's goal was the promotion of a stable society.

Brezhnev's rule was based on the 'social contract' or 'Little Deal', a **tacit** bargain between the government and the Soviet people. In essence Brezhnev's government promised a rising standard of living and greater social benefits in return for obedience and conformity. In that sense, the Soviet people traded political rights for economic well-being. In essence, the 'social contract' was Brezhnev's formula for promoting social stability. Brezhnev's social contract contained five main elements. The government guaranteed:

- job security through guaranteed full employment
- low prices for essential goods
- a thriving second economy, free of government interference
- social benefits such as free healthcare
- some social mobility.

Under Brezhnev standards of living increased significantly. Social benefits included subsidised rent, and utilities such as electricity and water were provided practically free of charge. The government also provided healthcare and pensions. Indeed, spending on health and pensions grew by between four and five per cent a year under Brezhnev. From 1970 subsidies extended to holidays.

Generally, Brezhnev's 'social contract' succeeded in promoting social stability. During the late 1960s and 1970s Soviet citizens enjoyed an unprecedented standard of living. Through a combination of government benefits, work and trading on the black market, citizens were guaranteed a secure and comfortable life. Moreover, organised opposition to the government was extremely rare. By ensuring a relatively high and rising standard of living, Brezhnev's policies broadly succeeded in promoting social stability in the period 1964–85.

## Stagnation

The 'social contract' created a stable society, but it also led to stagnation. Brezhnev's refusal to tackle economic and social problems led to a re-emergence of old problems.

First, full employment led to serious economic inefficiencies. Estimates suggest that in the 1970s there was hidden unemployment of around 20 per cent. This means that 20 per cent of employees were being paid but were not doing a useful job. At the same time there were serious labour shortages. In the late 1970s there were at least 1 million vacancies in Soviet industry that went unfilled. This led to lower production rates in some industries.

Secondly, female unemployment was on the rise. This problem affected Central Asia and the Caucasus, where employment was still centred on mining and heavy industry and where women were refused jobs due to gender stereotypes. In these areas estimates suggest that as many as ten per cent of women were unemployed. Even in central Russia political dissidents were denied the right to work and were therefore disqualified from many social benefits. Around two per cent of Russians were out of work by 1985.

Finally, in spite of increased health spending, Soviet health declined. Infant mortality rates increased from three to seven per cent in the 1970s while life expectancy declined from 68 to 64 years for men in the same period. Alcoholism was one of the main causes.

## Conclusion

Ultimately, the model of full employment, social benefits and political conformity promoted social stability. However, it also led to economic stagnation. Although standards of living continued to rise into the late 1970s, the Soviet Union lagged behind the West. Moreover, full employment led to inefficient uses of labour which slowed economic growth, which in the long term threatened to lower living standards and therefore undermine Brezhnev's 'social contract'. Nonetheless, Brezhnev was more concerned with retaining power and creating a stable compliant society. In this sense his policies succeeded, even if they led to economic stagnation.

### Work together

Having read this chapter write a paragraph in answer to the following question:

**How far was the Soviet Government committed to the social security of Soviet citizens in the years 1917–53?**

Swap your paragraph with a partner, and discuss:

- Which paragraph demonstrates the clearest focus on the question?
- Which paragraph has the most detailed examples from the period?
- Which paragraph provides a better answer to the question, and why?

Make a note of at least two ways in which you could improve your writing.

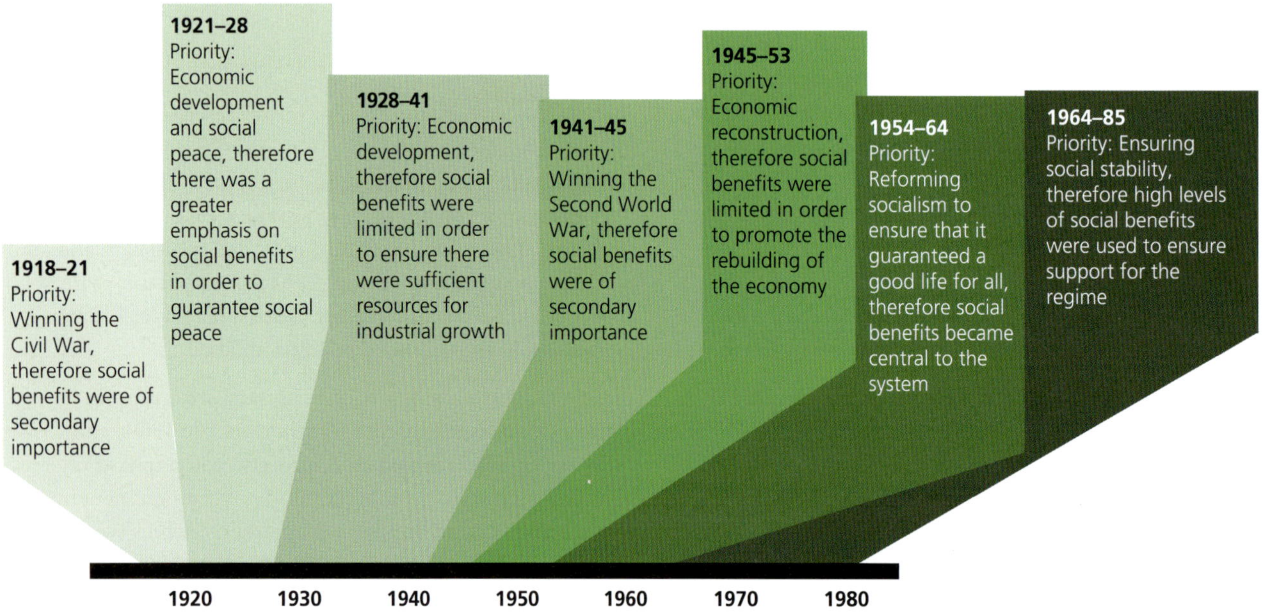


▲ Summary diagram: Government priorities and social benefits.

## Chapter summary

- Communists were ideologically committed to ensuring that working people enjoyed the full benefits of industrial society.
- From 1917 to 1953 this proved difficult to achieve as there were continual economic shortages and Stalin prioritised economic development over the well-being of the Soviet people.
- Khrushchev and Brezhnev re-emphasised the need for Communism to provide a decent standard of living for all people.
- For Khrushchev this meant better quality housing and greater availability of food.
- Under Brezhnev's 'social contract', social stability was built on the guarantee that the standards of living would continue to rise and that all Soviet citizens would enjoy economic security.

## Activity: Question practice

1. Was communist ideology the main reason for improvements in social security in the period 1953–85? Explain your answer. AS
2. How far did government policy towards art and culture change in the years 1928–85? AS
3. How accurate is it to say that the Soviet government successfully promoted social stability in the years 1953–82.
4. How accurate is it to say that the Soviet Government was stable and successful in the years 1945–82.

## Recommended reading

D. Filtzer, *Soviet Workers and Late Stalinism: Labour and the Restoration of the Stalinist System after World War II* (Cambridge, 2004), pages 91–116. This section of Filtzer's book looks at the problem of housing in the Soviet Union in Stalin's last years.

S. Malle, *The Economic Organization of War Communism, 1918–1921* (Cambridge, 1985), pages 322–37. This part of Malle's work looks at living standards during the period of War Communism.

R.G Suny, *The Cambridge History of Russia* (Cambridge, 2006), pages 300–5. This part of the book discusses the nature and significance of Brezhnev's social contract.

# 4b: Women and the family

## Overview

As the Soviet Union was a communist country, men and women were officially equal. However, Soviet Governments never wholly ended sexual inequality. Indeed, there were deliberate attempts to sustain traditional gender roles. For most of the period 1917–85 women were under-represented in the highest levels of government, expected to take low-paid and low-status jobs, and forced to work a 'double shift' comprising paid work and unpaid domestic labour.

Women in the country worked in the lowest paid and hardest jobs in Soviet society. Women in the cities had more opportunities in terms of education and they received higher pay. Nonetheless, by the 1950s women's working opportunities had narrowed and even within professional jobs women were expected to play roles that reflected their 'natural' desire to nurture.

Soviet family policy changed in a variety of ways between 1917 and 1985. Early Soviet thinkers embraced radical ideas about social and family change. However, by the mid-1920s the traditional family was held up as the best social model. From then on even Soviet leaders who took women's issues seriously assumed that women would always play a primarily domestic and nurturing role.

This chapter considers:

1 The changing status of women
2 Women at work
3 The Soviet family.

## 1 The changing status of women

The status of women changed throughout the period 1917–85. Government policy went through a series of phases. Sometimes there were initiatives that were designed to liberate women; on other occasions policy was much more conservative. The government's attitude can be seen through official propaganda and through women's changing legal rights.

### Note it down

Using the 1:2 method (see pages x), make notes on the different ways in which women were represented in Soviet propaganda in the years 1917–85. Look out for key changes in the presentation of women and use highlighters or different coloured pens to highlight key changes in the way that women were presented.

### Marxism and sexual equality

Marxists are committed to establishing a truly equal society. In traditional societies, Marx argued, there were a variety of different types of inequality, including sexual inequality, racial inequality and class inequality. For Marx, the most important type of inequality was class inequality, because Marx believed that destroying class inequality would lead to the destruction of all other kinds of inequality.

Lenin had a slightly different view. He argued that capitalism itself would lead to the destruction of sexual and racial inequalities. Class inequalities would persist under capitalism, but capitalism was based on economic efficiency and this required businesses to recognise talent wherever they found it, regardless of sex or race. Lenin's view was important to the early years of the revolution. Lenin argued that the Communist Government had to complete all of the tasks that capitalism should have completed in the Soviet Union. This included the industrialisation of the economy and the destruction of sexual and racial inequality.

## Women in government propaganda

Women feature prominently in Soviet **iconography**. Pictures, photographs, films and statues produced from 1917 to 1985 show how the government's view of women changed.

### Playing a supporting role, 1917–40

Between 1917 and 1940 women tended to play a supporting role in Soviet art. One of the most famous statues that symbolised the Soviet Union under Stalin was the 'Worker and Kolkhoz Woman' (1937). The 25-metre-high stainless steel statue comprises two figures, a male factory worker holding a hammer and a female collective farm worker holding a sickle. Soviet propaganda posters of this period often contain a male industrial worker and a female peasant representing the whole nation. The distinction between the two types of worker emphasises a difference in role between men and women.

According to Lenin's writings, industrial workers and peasants both played an important role in overthrowing capitalism. However, industrial workers played the leading and decisive role, whereas peasants played a supporting role. By routinely depicting men as industrial workers and women as peasants, the Soviet government believed that men played the primary role in society.

From 1917 to 1940 women were much less visible in propaganda then men. During the Civil War posters were dominated by male soldiers, and during the first three Five-Year Plans male workers were the focus of posters. Women represented in imagery of this period tend to be either mothers or children. Again, this indicates that women were expected to play a maternal role rather than fight or work on the front line of building socialism.

Some Soviet propaganda ridiculed women and femininity. Sergei Eisenstein's film *October* (1928) mocked female soldiers who fought against the **Bolsheviks** in the October Revolution. Moreover, it contrasted the masculine and decisive Bolsheviks with their effeminate, dithering political opponents.

Broadly, women who feature in Soviet art and propaganda from 1917–40 play similar roles to women in Russian religious art prior to the revolution, which also presents women as supportive mother figures, or weaker than men. In that sense, Soviet iconography indicates that attitudes to women changed little in the first few decades after the revolution.

### Women at war, women in space 1941–64

Women featured heavily in Soviet propaganda in the Second World War and the Cold War. The poster 'The Motherland is Calling' presented a woman as the symbol of the Russian nation and celebrated the vital work of women during the war. However, Soviet propaganda still presented women as vulnerable and in need of male protection during the war. For example, in 1942 *Pravda* media published a series of explicit pictures of Zoya Kosmodemyanskaya (widely known as 'Tanya'), an 18-year-old woman who was enslaved, tortured, mutilated and hanged by German soldiers. Her mother toured the country appealing to Soviet men to defend Soviet women and the motherland. Soviet propaganda linked defending the motherland with defending Soviet women regularly in this period.

After the war, heroic women were presented as symbols of the absolute sexual equality that Soviet leaders claimed had been achieved following the revolution. *Devushkivoiny* (girl-warriors) and *frontovichki* (women who served on the front line) were a feature of top level speeches, including

▲ Valentina Tereshkova.

Khrushchev's Secret Speech, and of Soviet war films all the way through to the 1980s. Additionally, in 1963 Valentina Tereshkova became the first woman in space and the Soviet Union's new woman hero. Born on a collective farm, she lost her father in the Second World War. Nonetheless, through Soviet education and the opportunities available in Soviet industry, she became an engineer and the first female **cosmonaut**. According to the head of the Soviet Space Programme she was nothing less than 'Yuri Gagarin in a skirt'.

At the same time, there was an official concern about women, and a campaign against young women who adopted Western fashion (see page 102).

### Good mothers and absent mothers, 1964–85

Under Brezhnev Soviet propaganda projected a more traditional view of women. Propaganda in the late 1960s and early 1970s emphasised that a true Soviet woman should be an exemplary worker and caring wife and mother. The tone of propaganda became even more conservative in the mid-1970s. Falling birth rates led to a campaign encouraging women to have babies. Brezhnev's **pronatal** campaign emphasised 'natural differences' between the sexes, stressing women's 'natural' ability to nurture and 'natural' need for a strong man. By the late 1970s this pronatalist message was coupled with official criticism of women who 'neglected' their children by going to work. According to Brezhnev's propaganda, working women were responsible for juvenile delinquency, rising crime, drug taking, alcoholism and family breakup. This view persisted into the 1980s and was reaffirmed by the last three Soviet leaders.

### Conclusion

Soviet propaganda did not present a consistent view of women; rather it reflected shifting official policies regarding women's roles and women's emancipation. It did, however, reflect the concerns of the male-dominated leadership of the Soviet Union, who were suspicious of women and who were therefore determined to keep female liberation within narrow bounds.

## 2 Women at work

Working women became a key feature of Soviet society in the 1930s. By 1955, 49 per cent of the Soviet workforce were women, a fact that Soviet leaders argued proved that sexual equality had been achieved. Nonetheless, promotions for women were rare, and there were significant inequalities in pay. Women working in the towns had many more opportunities than women who worked in the countryside. Finally, women tended to play a minor role in government throughout the whole period 1917–85.

#### Note it down

The lives of women in the towns were considerably different from the lives of women in the cities. Divide a large sheet of paper into two. Using a note-making style of your choice, make notes on the opportunities available to women and the limits of those opportunities (i) in the country (ii) in towns and cities. Additionally, make a note of the government's view on the nature and role of women and the way this affected policies towards women in the workplace.

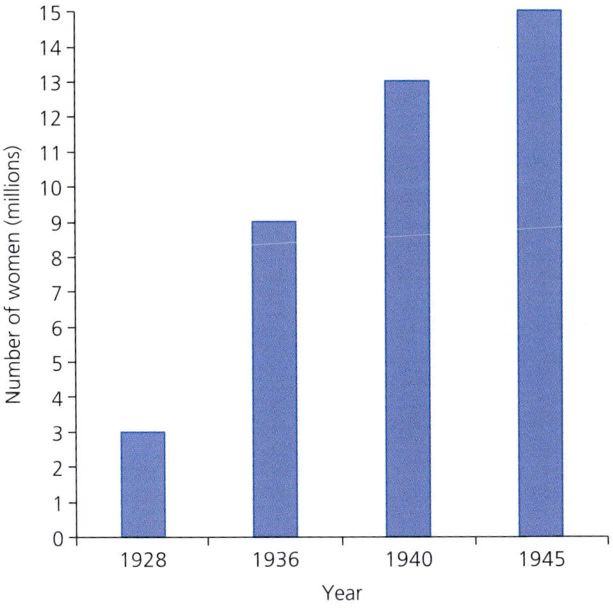


▲ **Figure 1: Number of women in the Soviet industrial workforce.**

## Working in the towns

During the Civil War, *Zhenotdel* – the women's department of the Communist Party – recruited women from the towns to fill jobs in nursing and food distribution. Alexandra Kollontai, head of *Zhenotdel*, believed that this reflected a natural division of labour: men should fight and rebuild industry once the war was over; women should lead the way in nurturing roles. Indeed, when the Civil War ended, women who had been working in industry were sacked so that men could take the industrial jobs.

Under the NEP opportunities for women in factories were limited. The NEP led to widespread unemployment. Female prostitution was also widespread, as it was legal and one way of making money. During the 1920s, it is estimated that 39 per cent of urban men used prostitutes, indicating that it was a large market.

Women joined the industrial labour force in large numbers due to the demands of the Five-Year Plans. In 1928, the last year of the NEP, only 3 million women worked in Soviet industry. By 1940 that figure had leapt to 13 million (see Figure 1). Indeed, by 1940, 41 per cent of workers in heavy industry were women. Soviet authorities recognised the importance of women in industry and therefore allocated an increasing number of places in higher or technical education to women: from 20 per cent in 1929 to 40 per cent in 1940. However, there were significant pay differentials. Women doing the same jobs as men were only paid 60–65 per cent of men's wages. Equally, women were subjected to verbal and physical abuse in factories. Some men refused to work on teams that included women, believing that working with women brought bad luck. Women's participation in the Five-Year Plans laid the foundation for greater participation during the Second World War. In some towns during the war women made up 75 per cent of the workforce.

### Leisure

Outside of work, women in cities also had access to various kinds of leisure. During the 1950s and 1960s, dancing became a big urban pastime. According to Soviet films and magazines, women loved to dance far more than men. Dancing became so popular that the government produced etiquette manuals advising men on how to ask women to dance and how to deal with rejection. According to official advice, men alone could initiate dancing; women could not ask men to dance. Women could, however, dance with other women if no male partners were available.

Official festivals were also organised in large urban centres to show off the latest fashions for women. 'Holiday of Girls', for example, was an event in which the headquarters of the Soviet Army was transformed for a fashion show, cookery show and grand ball. The event celebrated female beauty and domestication, establishing an ideal for Soviet women. Significantly, the emphasis was on beauty in order to please men. The 'Holiday of Girls' discouraged young women from discussing or engaging in sex. The Soviet Ministry of Health published reports 'scientifically proving' that women felt no sexual desire until their mid-20s.

After the war new trends developed in terms of women working in the cities. During the 1960s, around 45 per cent of industrial jobs went to women. However, women tended to be restricted to:

- production line work in **light industry**, which was intensive but required low levels of skill, such as textile production
- heavy manual labour, which was also low skilled.

In this sense, there was a change from the period 1928–41. Under Stalin, women tended to do all kinds of factory work, but be paid less. After the war, women tended to be employed in low-skill sectors of industry, whereas men were employed in high-skill sectors. Therefore women were paid less because they were doing less skilled work. Senior jobs within light industry, such as the job of foreman, routinely went to men. Indeed, between 1959 and 1965 less than one per cent of factory foremen in the textile industry were women.

During the 1960s another form of employment open to women was clerical or administrative work. In the mid-1960s, 74 per cent of people employed in clerical positions in health services and education were women. In towns around 50 per cent of working women worked in clerical positions, and the other half worked in industry. Finally, 90 per cent of the able-bodied population who did not work outside the home were female in the mid-1960s.

### BAM recruitment

The mid-1970s saw another major female recruitment campaign. In 1974, Brezhnev initiated the construction of the Baikal–Amur Mainline (BAM), a 4324-kilometre rail line across the north of the Soviet Union. Brezhnev was aware that the male workers and administrators who staffed the project would want female company, and therefore he initiated a campaign to recruit female workers from urban centres in their mid-20s. Remarkably, the campaign stressed that building the BAM was an opportunity for women to gain true liberation through work and establishing new homes in the north of the country. At the same time, the recruitment campaign stated that finding men would be easy. BAM construction was male dominated and therefore *bamovkas* (female BAM workers) would, the publicity implied, have the pick of the men. This was a contrast to Soviet society as a whole where men were in the minority. BAM publicity also emphasised other traditional aspects of Soviet womanhood. *Bamovkas* were expected to preserve their femininity by being caring, wise and maintaining, what BAM adverts called, their 'delicate female features'. Many *bamovkas* did do important construction work. However, others were employed in low-paid positions such as waitressing.

In many ways the BAM recruitment campaign exemplified the Soviet attitude to urban women: they were expected to be independent and equal, but in a way that served the interests of men.

### Educating female workers

Education was widely available to women in cities. By the 1960s women made up half of the Soviet Union's graduates. As a result of women's education, by the 1970s women dominated certain professions. By 1985 around 70 per cent of medical doctors were women, about 75 per cent of employees in universities were women and around 65 per cent of people employed in art and culture were women. Significantly, pay scales in these 'feminised' industries were lower than in factory management, which was dominated by men.

## Working in the countryside

During the 1920s, 1930s and 1940s a high proportion of women worked in agriculture. Women in the countryside performed a 'triple shift'. They provided agricultural labour on farms, they were responsible for household chores and they were often engaged in handicrafts to supplement the family income.

Some women on collective farms achieved a high social status. Specifically, female tractor drivers could earn a relatively high wage. During the period of the NEP there were only eight female tractor drivers across the whole of the Soviet Union. That figure had risen to 50,000 by 1940. However, female tractor drivers made up less than 0.5 per cent of the total rural female population. Most women did unskilled jobs and therefore had little wealth or social status.

### Women and the Virgin Lands

Women were specifically targeted in the campaign to recruit volunteers to work on the Virgin Lands. The recruitment campaign started in 1954 and continued to 1974. The campaign to recruit women focused on specific roles: women were required to act as milkmaids, gardeners and to start families. Women were not recruited to work with machinery or drive tractors; rather the emphasis was on women as manual labourers and carers. The official slogan for recruiting women was: 'Your caring hands are needed everywhere.' Government officials wanted to recruit 'girls' – young women of around 25 – rather than older women. They believed that young women would entice men to move to the Virgin Lands. A famous slogan that summarised this aspect of the campaign was: 'Join us, girls, in the Virgin Lands.' Single women over the age of 26 were turned down for the scheme, as were single mothers.

Women in the Virgin Lands tended to do the lowest paid and most demanding jobs. For example, of the 6400 women recruited in August 1958, less than 450 found work in well-paid professional jobs. The majority were haymakers and milkmaids, whose wage was about 15 per cent that of male tractor drivers. Women from Moscow were the most likely to complain about the conditions because they were used to a much more comfortable life in the capital. Equally, local women were horrified by the 'immorality' of the women from Moscow who enjoyed dancing and singing Western songs. Few women from cities stayed in the Virgin Lands long.

Finally, female farm workers in the Virgin Lands were often subject to sexual abuse and rape. Although there are no exact figures, apparently sexual violence was common. Farm managers tended to blame the women and on occasion force rapists to marry their victims.

Mechanisation of farming, an important goal of the Sixth Five-Year Plan (1956–59) and the Seven-Year Plan (1959–65), was supposed to make life for women on farms easier. However, even in 1964 machinery on farms was scarce.

Moreover, collective farms tended to give men priority in terms of access to machines. In this sense mechanisation failed to make a difference to the lives of women in rural areas.

### Farming in the 1970s and 1980s

Women continued to work in low-status, low-paid jobs in farming in the 1970s and 1980s. By 1983, around 65 per cent of work on farms was still unmechanised. Moreover, as industry expanded men left collective farms to get jobs in factories, leaving women over-represented in the lowest paid jobs. By 1970, 72 per cent of the lowest paid Soviet farmers were women. Professional opportunities also reflected the general prejudice that women played a nurturing role rather than a leadership role. Indeed, by 1980, 80 per cent of teachers in rural schools were women, whereas only 2 per cent of farm managers were women.

In short, the majority of women in Soviet agriculture worked in low-status and low-paid roles. In the worst cases, notably the Virgin Lands Scheme, women were recruited specifically to marry men and were subjected to sexual violence. Professional opportunities for women on Soviet farms were extremely limited, and those that did exist reflected widespread stereotypes regarding a woman's role.

## Fighting for the motherland

Women played a central role in the Soviet armed forces during the Second World War. In 1941, fighting was still considered a man's job and women who tried to enlist were turned away. However, by 1945, 800,000 women had served in combat roles. Female fighters included those in the three female flying regiments. Initially, female flyers were regarded with disdain by male pilots. However, as the war progressed the achievements of some women were considerable. For example, Lydia Litvyak shot down 12 German planes before being killed in combat. One female squadron were nicknamed the 'Night Witches' due to their deadly skill.

According to most accounts female soldiers and pilots enjoyed the respect of their male colleagues. Indeed, reports of sexual harassment are rare. However, after the war many male soldiers went on to have long careers in the military. Women, by contrast, were demobilised and denied entry to Soviet military academies. In that sense wartime sexual equality was short-lived.

## Female Party members

Women were consistently under-represented at the highest levels of the Party. Immediately following the revolution, women tended to get jobs in government that reflected traditional stereotypes of their role. During the Civil War, female Party members tended to work in the Commissariat of Social Welfare, the Commissariat of Health or the Commissariat of Education, whereas male Party members worked in government departments dealing with the economy or the military. Significantly, female communists did not play a significant role in the Party's most senior committees. In 1918, for example, only five per cent of delegates to the Party Congress were women. Nonetheless, during the 1920s it was usual for senior female Party members who had had children to employ nannies so that they could continue with their political work. Generally, in the first ten years of communist rule, female participation in politics stagnated. Around 10 per cent of Party members in 1918 were women; by 1928 that figure was 12 per cent, only a small increase.

Female Party members were expected to play a homemaking role in the 1930s. Party members were no longer encouraged to employ nannies. Rather they were expected to be exemplary wives and mothers who were devoted to creating and managing 'a well-ordered communist home'. Female Party members who married were expected to give up work and join the *obshchesttvennitsa* movement: the 'movement of wife activists'. 'Wife activists' were expected to help organise nurseries, engage in charity work and supervise factory canteens. Generally, 'wife activists' were expected to play a mothering role for the whole of Soviet society. At home they were expected to be perfect examples of 'order, warmth and feminine comfort', providing for all of the needs of their husbands and families.

From 1953, women played a slightly larger role in Soviet politics. However, as in the 1920s, women were expected to contribute to political work that concerned health, social services and education, reflecting their 'natural' role as nurturers. Women played a significant role in local soviets. Between 1959 and 1984 the proportion of women in the soviets grew from 27 per cent to 33 per cent. However, soviets played a very small social role, and in the most senior parts of the Soviet system, women never made up more than 10 per cent of deputies.

Larger numbers of women joined the Party after 1953. Between 1956 and 1983 the proportion of women in the Party increased from 19.7 per cent to 26 per cent. However, women were never more than 4 per cent of the Central Committee between 1953 and 1985.

Clearly, increased participation of women in the workforce and an increasingly educated female population did not lead to a rise in the proportion of women in government.

## 3 The Soviet family

Emphasis on the Soviet family changed over time. Moreover, as family policy changed, so did the legal rights of women. In some periods there was a deliberate attempt to reform the family and emancipate women; in other periods policy was much more conservative.

> ### Note it down
> Soviet policy towards the family changed overtime. Skim this section and work out the major periods of government policy. Using a note-making style of your choice, take down details of policies related to women and the family. Use different coloured pens to distinguish between policies that were designed to liberate women from their traditional roles and policies that were designed to reinforce their traditional roles.

### Families and women in the 1920s

Lenin's government did not have a consistent view on the family. Alexandra Kollontai believed that the family was an oppressive social organisation. She advocated replacing the family with communal living and **monogamous marriage** with **free love**. For Kollontai, the family encouraged selfishness and individualism. Kollontai advocated the 'withering away of the family' as an essential part of the emergence of the 'new woman' who was truly liberated. Lenin and Trotsky, however, were more conservative. Lenin was particularly critical of free love. Nonetheless, Lenin recognised the abuses that went on in traditional marriage and the need for reform to marriage and divorce laws.

Immediately after the revolution significant steps were taken to reform the traditional family and liberate women. Between its creation in 1919 and its abolition in 1930, *Zhenotdel* worked with a variety of government departments to advance women's rights:

- Education: *Zhenotdel* worked with the Commissariat of Education to introduce **co-education**. They also established women's reading rooms in urban centres where women could study. *Zhenotdel* established education schemes for women in factories and set quotas to ensure that women were represented at all levels of education. By 1930, around 28 per cent of university students were women, compared to 12 per cent in Germany and 20 per cent in Britain.
- Legal rights: *Zhenotdel* collaborated with the Commissariat of Justice to enshrine women's rights in law. From 1919 women were given a legal right to equal pay for equal work, and equal voting rights.
- Reproductive rights: The Soviet Union was the first country to introduce a legal right to abortion on demand. Contraception was also legal during the 1920s.
- Marital rights: During the 1920s 'postcard divorce' was available to men and women. From 1926 it was legal for one partner to end a marriage simply by sending a letter or postcard telling their partner that the relationship was over. The government looked on marriage as a simple contract that could be dissolved simply and easily by either husband or wife.
- Sexual rights: Lesbianism was not criminalised before the revolution and was never regarded as a criminal offence in the Soviet Union. Prostitution was also legalised. *Zhenotdel* worked with the Commissariat of Health to offer medical support to prostitutes.

Sadly, some of these early policies quickly became meaningless or were counterproductive. Legal and political equality was largely meaningless because democracy was suspended in mid-1918 and effectively abolished in 1921. Equally, legal rights were difficult to uphold because Soviet law courts had very little real authority.

Equally, men made use of the new divorce rights in order to divorce women soon after they became pregnant. Between 1917 and 1928, 70 per cent of divorces were initiated by men. This often left women without a home, unable to work as they needed to look after their new child and therefore without an income.

By 1925 experiments in communal living had ended. Kollontai's vision of the 'withering away of the family' had been formally abandoned. The 1926 Marriage Code reflected the official belief in the traditional family. It made adoption easier so that families could take care of children who had been orphaned during the Civil War. It also established de facto marriage: it gave men and women who were living together the same status as legally married couples. In both senses it underlined that the new government believed that marriage was the essential model for society.

*Zhenotdel* was also unwilling to help women who were victims of sexual harassment. Indeed, Soviet law did not recognise sexual harassment as a crime. Women organised themselves to protest against sexual abuse. In Leningrad in 1928, for example, women workers organised strikes and walkouts. However, male party officials viewed striking women as troublemakers and complaints from women as an 'anti-Soviet' activity. Therefore no changes were made and sexual harassment continued.

Finally, under the NEP the government did not fund crèches or day care facilities. Government money was used to modernise industry, not to emancipate women. Again, this was part of the reason for the government to re-emphasise marriage, as it provided a degree of security and did not require the government to spend money. As funding was cut from crèches and children's homes, street gangs developed. Groups of children who had lost their parents in the Civil War or who had been abandoned due to family breakup lived through petty crime.

### The Great Retreat, 1936–53

During the mid-1930s, government policy towards the family became much more conservative. Compared to the 'advance' of women's rights in the 1920s, Trotsky, writing in exile, described the new conservative policies of the 1930s as the 'Great Retreat'. In part, Stalin's policies were a reaction against the problems created by the liberal policies of the 1920s. However, they were also designed to create a stable society that could put all its energies into industrialisation.

Stalin's key aim was to increase birth rates and cut divorce rates. To achieve this, significant legal changes were introduced in 1936:

- Abortion was criminalised unless the life of the pregnant woman was in danger.
- Contraception was banned.
- Male homosexuality was criminalised. Consensual sex between men was punishable by five years in a labour camp.
- Lesbianism was treated as a 'disease'. Lesbian women could be subjected to hypnotherapy in an attempt to 'cure' them of their 'unnatural' desires.
- Sex outside of marriage was stigmatised. Collective farm managers carried out 'medical virginity checks' on young women to enforce sexual abstinence.
- Divorce was made expensive and difficult to obtain. A first divorce cost approximately one week's wages; subsequent divorces were more expensive.
- Following divorce, fathers were required to pay a minimum of one-third of their income to their former wives to support their children. Men were required to pay 60 per cent of their salary if they had left three or more children.

In addition to these policies, Stalin adopted a pronatalist policy of offering financial incentives for women to have children. Women with seven children received 2000 roubles a year for five years. This figure increased to 5000 roubles for mothers with eleven children. These policies were backed up by a media campaign which exposed unfaithful men. For example, the trades union newspaper *Trud* regularly carried stories about men who abandoned themselves to lives of 'wildness, degeneracy and baseness'.

In addition to working on collective farms or in Soviet industry, women were expected to perform essential family labour. On average, women spent five times longer on their domestic responsibilities than men during the 1930s.

In essence, Stalin's policies emphasised the importance of stable families based on monogamous heterosexual relationships. Stalin believed that these formed the basis of a successful socialist society as they provided a disciplined environment in which to bring up children.

## Women and the family, 1953–85

Women's rights were re-emphasised in the years following Stalin's death. However, Khrushchev focused on women's rights in the context of traditional families. Generally, Khrushchev wanted women to continue to perform their traditional roles as wives and mothers, but he wanted to make these roles easier.

Khrushchev's government made some attempt to recognise and address the problems facing women in the Soviet Union. By 1956 there were several national women's magazines including *Woman Worker*, *Peasant Woman*, *Women of the World*, and *Soviet Woman*. These magazines carried articles by women describing their lives and exposing the inequalities that persisted in Soviet society, particularly the poorly paid jobs and the 'double shift', and the government's failure to support women who had families.

Khrushchev's government was also aware of the impact of the Second World War on women. The war led to the deaths of over 10 million men. As a result, the proportion of women in Soviet society grew from 52 per cent in 1939 to 55 per cent in 1959. The war had also led to many lone-parent families. In this context the traditional Stalinist model of a heterosexual monogamous family in which the husband worked and the woman stayed at home no

#### Soviet women's magazines

The rise of Soviet women's magazines was an unexpected consequence of two of Khrushchev's policies. First, they were part of the new consumer socialism that Khrushchev advocated. Secondly, the publication of letters dealing with daily experience reflected his policy of cultural 'thaw'. Women took full advantage of these changes to write about their own experiences, and this soon spread from women's magazines into the mainstream press. Indeed, by the late 1950s newspapers were containing stories about rape and domestic violence which exposed major problems in Soviet society.

By the late 1950s the magazines were a forum in which women could discuss their own experiences of abortion, childbearing, motherhood, sex and work.

longer worked for many families. Therefore Khrushchev introduced a series of policies to change the legal status of women and make family life easier for married and unmarried women:

- In 1955 abortion was legalised.
- In 1956 state paid maternity leave increased from 77 days to 112 days.
- The Sixth Five-Year Plan, starting in 1956, contained a commitment to 'improve in every way the working and living conditions of women workers' including the expansion of crèches, childcare facilities and communal laundries.
- The Seven-Year Plan aimed to eliminate the 'double shift' by introducing convenience foods and mass-produced clothing, ending the need for women to cook and sew.
- The Seven-Year Plan also aimed to make refrigerators widely available, ending the need for daily shopping trips.

In spite of these changes problems remained. Contraception remained hard to acquire. Letters to women's magazines indicate that crèches opened late and closed early so that women were still unable to work full days. Also some employers refused to recognise the new legal entitlements regarding maternity leave and maternity pay.

Equally, the Sixth Five-Year Plan and the Seven-Year Plan failed to end the double shift. Domestic appliances were either less helpful than anticipated or less widely available. Surveys continued to show that women spent more time doing household chores than men and therefore had less access to leisure activities or education than men.

### Feminism in the Soviet Union

Feminist intellectuals and feminist groups were suppressed by the KGB. As a result the feminist movement in the Soviet Union remained small, particularly compared to the USA. However, in the period 1979–82 feminist groups began to emerge in the Soviet Union. For example, Almanac, a small feminist movement, was established in 1979 in Leningrad by Tatiana Mamonova. It attempted to raise questions about women's status through the publication of a magazine. However, the government supressed the magazine and members of the group were forced to emigrate following police harassment. The League for Emancipation from Stereotypes (LOTOS) was formed in Moscow in 1980. LOTOS was an informal network of female academics and teachers who attempted to influence public debate by publishing research. The group was finally supressed by the Soviet authorities in 1983.

Generally, although the government aimed to make domestic work easier, it still viewed housework as a woman's job. This was evident in the publication of a two-volume *Short Encyclopaedia of Housekeeping* published in 1959 in order to help women deal with their domestic role.

## Women under Brezhnev

Brezhnev continued to stress the centrality of the family to Soviet life. Under Brezhnev much less was done to try to improve the status of women. Officially, the government proclaimed that sexual equality had been achieved. The lack of women in the most senior jobs in industry, agriculture and government was explained by women's 'natural' desire to focus on their families. The government banned information about women's campaigns in the West being reported in the Soviet press in order to try to suppress debates about women's roles and sexual oppression. Brezhnev tended to think of women primarily as unskilled workers whose prime goal was having children. Sexual morality was strict: male homosexuality was a crime, lesbianism was a mental disorder and sex was about making babies rather than pleasure.

Within the home traditional roles endured. By 1982, official figures indicated that women spent twice as much time doing domestic chores as men. Brezhnev viewed this as part of the natural order and applauded women for their sacrifice. As noted above, Brezhnev's main concern was for women to have more babies and to look after them properly. Therefore the government did nothing to address sexual inequality in domestic labour. Brezhnev did introduce some reforms to make women's lives easier. For example, he lowered the pension age for women from 60 to 55.

## Conclusion

Soviet family policy changed over time. As family policy changed, so did the official status of women. Initial attempts to ensure the liberation of women were replaced by a more conservative policy. In the 1950s and early 1960s there was a renewed attempt to liberate women. However, Khrushchev's campaign never questioned the basic nature of the family or the assumption that women should be responsible for childcare and domestic labour. Under Brezhnev, policy towards women hardened again. Once again, the emphasis was on women having children, while men took the high-status jobs in the **public sphere**.

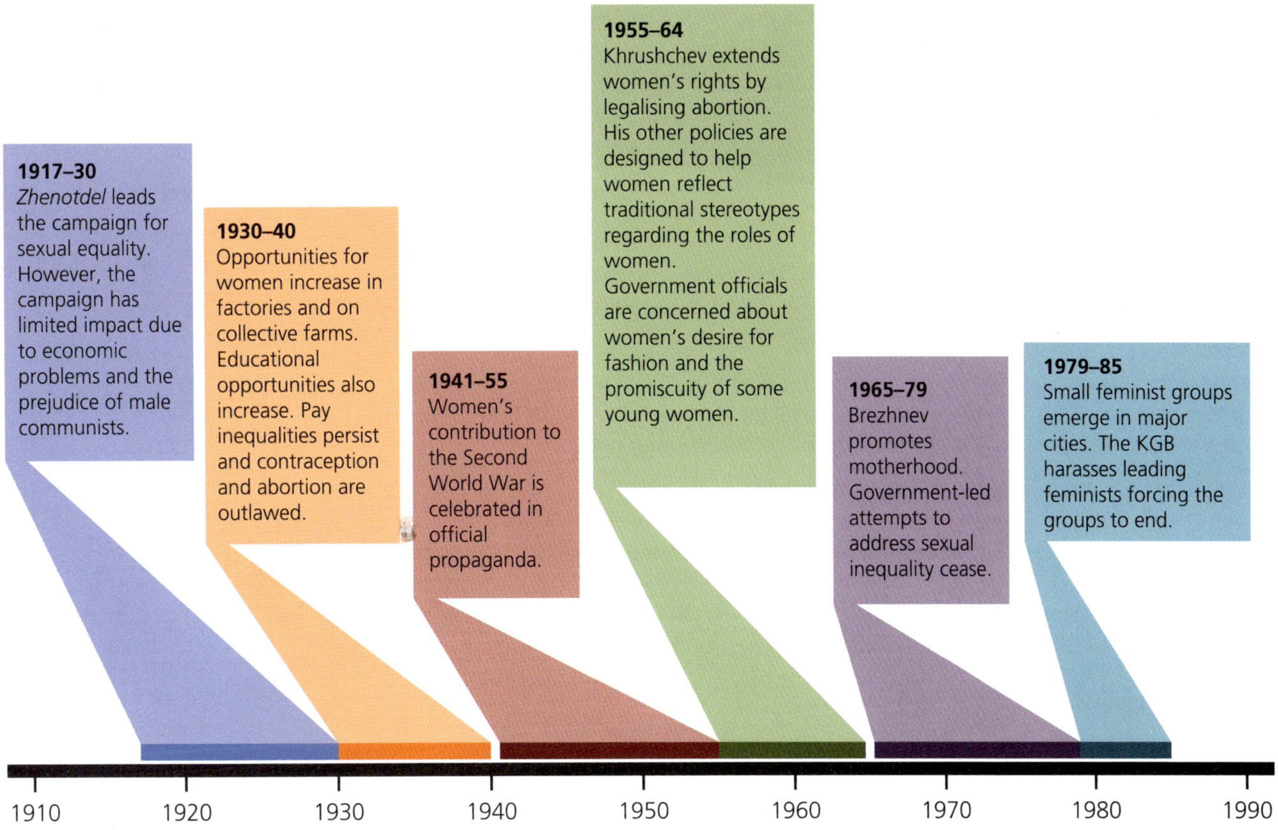


▲ **Summary diagram: Women and the family.**

## Chapter summary

- Between 1917 and 1985 there were considerable changes in the roles of women and the nature of the family.
- Revolutionary hope that the family and women's roles would be fundamentally transformed were quickly abandoned.
- Monogamous heterosexual families, where men and women played clearly defined roles, became the norm.
- However, women increasingly played a role in the Soviet workforce.
- In the country women tended to perform the low-paid, low-status work.
- In the cities, however, women were employed in all aspects of industry during the first three Five-Year Plans.
- As light industry grew, women were increasingly employed on production lines, while men worked in more highly skilled positions.
- After 1930 Soviet leaders never questioned the assumption that women played an essentially domestic and nurturing role.
- Therefore successive leaders developed policy that reflected a fundamental difference between the roles of men and the roles of women.

## Recommended reading

S. Fitzpatrick, *Everyday Stalinism: Ordinary Life in Extraordinary Times: Soviet Russia in the 1930s* (Oxford, 2000), pages 35–66. This part of Fitzpatrick's book discusses women in Stalin's Russia.

E. Casey and L. Martens (eds.), *Gender and Consumption: Domestic Cultures and the Commercialisation of Everyday Life* (Ashgate, 2007), pages 49–78. This section of Casey and Martens work analyses the government's concerns about young women in the Soviet Union during the 1960s.

N. Chernyshova, *Soviet Consumer Culture in the Brezhnev Era* (Routledge, 2013), pages 184–203. In this chapter Chernyshova examines the Soviet government's concern about the impact the role of women in a consumer economy.

# Essay technique: Resolution

The highest marks on Sections A and B of the exam are available for sustained analysis. One way of achieving this is to write an essay that develops a clear argument (see page 93) and counter-argument (see page 107).

Having set out an argument and a counter-argument you should resolve the tension between the two. One way of concluding an essay is to resolve the debate that you have established between the argument and the counter-argument.

Imagine you are answering the following question:

**How accurate is it to say that Communism failed to create sexual equality in the years 1918–53?**

Your essay plan could look like this:

| | |
|---|---|
| **Paragraph 1: Argument** | Soviet Communism failed to create sexual equality because after the abolition of *Zhenotdel* men dominated every aspect of government. |
| **Paragraph 2: Counter-argument** | Soviet Communism succeeded in creating greater sexual equality because of the new opportunities for women in factories and collective farms. |
| **Paragraph 3: Counter-argument** | Soviet Communism succeeded in creating greater sexual equality because of the new opportunities for women in education. |
| **Paragraph 4** | Soviet Communism's record on sexual equality was mixed because of the changing social policies regarding divorce, abortion and families. |

This essay has one clear paragraph arguing that Soviet Communism failed to create sexual equality, two arguing that there was some success and a final paragraph arguing that the record was mixed.

You can resolve the tension by weighing up the argument and counter-argument in the conclusion. In so doing, you can reach a supported overall judgement.

The conclusion on page 131 evaluates the argument and counter-argument. It resolves the tension by identifying a problem with the counter-argument, while also acknowledging that there is some truth in the counter-argument. Even so, ultimately it returns to the main argument that sexual equality was not achieved.

**TIP:** The process of evaluating the argument and the counter-argument is helped by the use of words like 'however' and 'nonetheless', which indicate that the paragraph is weighing up contrasting arguments.

The conclusion begins with the main argument, which summarises paragraphs 1 and 4.

In conclusion, Soviet Communism failed to create sexual equality in Russia in the years 1917–53 because under Lenin and Stalin, the government was dominated by men. Indeed, small early steps designed to represent women in government, such as the creation of *Zhenotdel*, and designed to give women rights to abortion and divorce were abolished by Stalin. However, there were new economic opportunities for women on Stalin's collective farms and in the factories created during the Five-Year Plans of the 1930s. Moreover, there were new opportunities for women in education too. Nonetheless, even in the economy men dominated. Women were routinely paid less than men, and more men than women gained places at university. Indeed, it is fair to say that the new opportunities for women were designed to improve the economy rather than liberate women. Therefore, although there were some steps towards sexual equality, Communism ultimately failed to create sexual equality in the Soviet Union in the years 1917–53.

The conclusion continues by contrasting this with the counter-argument – summarising paragraphs 2 and 3.

Identifies a problem with the counter-argument.

Finally, the conclusion resolves the tension, by evaluating the argument and the counter-argument, concluding that sexual equality was not achieved.

Acknowledges that there is some truth in the counter-argument.

## Activity: Resolving tensions

Imagine you are answering the following question:

**How accurate is it to say that the majority of Soviet citizens accepted limited political freedom in order to benefit from economic security in the years 1964–82?**

Here is a possible plan:

| | |
|---|---|
| **Paragraph 1: Argument** | In the years 1964–82 the majority of Soviet citizens accepted limited political freedom, because the standard of living was better than they had ever known it. |
| **Paragraph 2: Argument** | The majority of Soviet citizens clearly accepted limited political freedom because there was widespread participation in soviet politics and dissidents were in the minority. |
| **Paragraph 3: Counter-argument** | The majority of Soviet citizens did not wholly accept limited political freedom because cynicism, alcoholism and absenteeism were wide-spread, which indicates high levels of dissatisfaction with the regime. |
| **Paragraph 4: Counter-argument** | The majority of Soviet citizens did not wholly accept limited political freedom for the whole period because as the economy stagnated levels of dissatisfaction grew. |

1 Answer the following questions:
  **a)** Which is stronger, the argument or the counter-argument? Why is it stronger?
  **b)** What are the flaws in the weaker argument?
  **c)** What strengths does the weaker argument have?

2 Having answered these questions, write a conclusion that weighs up the argument and the counter-argument in order to reach an overall judgement.

**TIP:** Use the words 'however', 'nonetheless' and 'therefore' to structure the paragraph.

# 4c: Education and young people

## Overview

Education was a continual priority and a continual problem for Soviet leaders. All agreed that education was fundamentally liberating and therefore an essential part of the new society. However, there was disagreement concerning how education was supposed to liberate the Soviet people. Lunacharsky argued that new teaching methods and a general education that did not constrain the citizen's future was the key to a new revolutionary education. Lenin, by contrast, thought that the first job of Soviet education was to liberate the Soviet people from ignorance by teaching them to read and write. Stalin wanted to use education to help build socialism and in so doing liberate the Soviet Union from capitalism. Khrushchev attempted to revive some of the goals of Lunacharsky, whereas Brezhnev attempted to revive some of Stalin's educational approaches. In spite of these different approaches, Communism transformed education. Before the revolution education was the privilege of the few; by the 1960s it was the right of the many.

This chapter considers:

1 Education during a period of transition
2 The reduction of illiteracy
3 State control of the curriculum, 1932–53
4 Educational reform and expansion, 1953–85.

## 1 Education during a period of transition

Lenin and other Communists believed that the Soviet Union was in a period of transition, between capitalism and Communism. The transitional nature of this period affected the goals and development of Soviet policy.

### Note it down

Using a spider diagram, make notes on the goals that communists had for education and the problems that they faced in the first years of the revolution. Distinguish between different types of problems using different coloured pens.

### The goals of education

There were a variety of views about education within the Communist Party in 1917. These reflected different conceptions of what education had been and what it should be.

Communists tended to believe that education was important. Lenin, for example, believed that a high level of education, starting with basic literacy, was an essential part of building socialism. Socialism, according to Lenin and his followers, would require industrialisation, which in turn required an educated workforce who could understand the complex processes of industry. From this point of view education served the long-term goals of the revolution by helping to lay the foundation for industrialisation.

By contrast, other communists, like Anatoly Lunacharsky, People's Commissar of Enlightenment, believed that the primary goal of education was to allow individual students to flourish. Communists like Lunacharsky, therefore, believed that the revolution should liberate the student, rather than education serving the goals of the revolution.

### The problems of education

There was also disagreement over the nature of education in a revolutionary society. Education was traditionally associated with privilege and status in Russia, as only children from relatively rich backgrounds had access to schooling. This raised a series of questions:

- Should Communists continue with traditional forms of education, or create a new kind of revolutionary education?
- Should Communists work with educated people even though they were part of the traditional elite?
- How should Communists educate the millions of workers with little or no formal education?

These questions were complicated by the practical problems of organising education. These included:

- low levels of literacy – only around 32 per cent of the population could read and write in 1914
- educational inequalities – Russians tended to be better educated than non-Russians, and urban education was better than rural education.

Practical problems and ideological debates were further complicated by the notion that after 1918 Russia was in a 'period of transition', rather than being a socialist society. Therefore some Communists argued that in the short term compromises were necessary between socialist principles and the need to rebuild society after the Civil War. These kinds of questions and concerns led to a variety of twists and turns in educational policy between 1918 and 1936.

## The growth of education, 1918–28

Initially, educational policy was directed by Lunacharsky and Nadezhda Krupskaya – an educational theorist and Lenin's wife. During the Civil War there were attempts to institute a new polytechnic style of education and to deal with illiteracy.

### Unified labour schools

In October 1918, the Soviet Government issued a decree introducing a series of reforms which:

- established unified labour schools to provide free polytechnic education to all children aged 8 to 17
- banned religious instruction in schools
- introduced co-educational schools, ending gender segregation of schooling
- abolished **corporal punishment**, homework and exams
- promised free breakfasts for schoolchildren and free medical examinations
- allowed church buildings to be converted into schools
- made education compulsory.

Secondary schooling was designed to be vocational. The government proposed the creation of factory schools or professional schools in which young people spent four hours a day in factories learning skills and four hours a day being taught in school.

Lunacharsky favoured progressive teaching methods based on the theories of American educationalists such as John Dewey. These methods included learning through activities and through play, rather than rote-learning, using textbooks or traditional lecturing.

In reality, schooling fell short of Lunacharsky's vision in the early years of the revolution. Under the conditions of the Civil War there were insufficient resources to invest in education. Free compulsory education to the age of 16 was not achieved in the Soviet Union until the 1950s. Moreover, schools did not have the resources to provide free meals or medical check-ups. Finally, teachers continued to use traditional methods as there was no reliable system for training teachers.

### Polytechnic education

Marxists were critical of education that forced students to specialise. This, they argued, trapped a student in a specific area. Rather than offering specialist training, Marxists advocated a polytechnic education: a general education that taught many technical skills. This would allow students to enter whatever branch of industry they chose and to move between industries.

## Education under the NEP

The NEP was a period of compromise. This affected education as well as the economy as a whole. Educational provision declined in the first years of the NEP. Financial problems meant significant cuts in educational provision. In 1921 the government:

- forced some schools to close to save money.
- introduced fees to pay for primary and secondary education for all except the poorest children and the children of those unable to work due to war injuries
- scrapped plans for opening children's homes linked to schools for the 7 million children orphaned by the Civil War.

In the first 18 months of the NEP the number of children in education halved, as did the number of schools.

### Expansion in the mid-1920s

As the economy stabilised, education expanded. First, from 1927 fees for primary schools were abolished, and from then on the majority of children received a four-year primary education. By 1928 about 60 per cent of Soviet children of primary school age were in school, around 10 per cent more than prior to the revolution. However, there were significant inequalities in the system. For example, in towns and cities children in education tended to get the full four years of primary education, whereas in the countryside children were unlikely to complete three years of education.

Secondary education took a new direction during the 1920s. Under the NEP education was funded locally rather than by the Commissariat for Education. Therefore central government had difficulty controlling the development of education. Rather than follow the educational programme of polytechnic schools that had been outlined in 1918, local soviets simply took over existing gymnasia, schools that had been set up by the Tsarist regime. Around 97 per cent of students paid fees to attend. Therefore the schools tended to be dominated by the children of the wealthy. Around 90 per cent of middle-class students started secondary school and around 25 per cent finished secondary school, whereas only 40 per cent of working-class students started secondary school and only 3 per cent finished secondary school. Finally, the vast majority of teachers in the former gymnasia were trained before the revolution. Therefore they continued to teach in the traditional way. Additionally, their approach to subjects such as history remained traditional. The government wanted teachers to teach the history of class struggle and of the working class. However, teachers tended to continue to teach the history of Russia, particularly the achievements of the **Tsars**.

## Young people's groups in the 1920s

*Komsomol*, the Young Communists' League, and the Young Pioneers were youth organisations established in the early days of the revolution to provide a way for young people to express their support for the Communist Party, learn about political campaigning and enjoy communal recreation. The Young Pioneers was established in 1922 to cater for children between the ages of 10 and 15, whereas *Komsomol* was founded in 1918 for people between the ages of 16 and 28. Communist Party leaders assumed that young people would be naturally attracted to communist values as they believed that young people were likely to be naturally radical.

*Komsomol* members and the Young Pioneers wore a uniform and took part in activities such as camping and hiking. They also had talks from local factory workers, soldiers from the Red Army and farm workers. *Komsomol* distributed posters of Lenin, Trotsky and other leading members of the government, and *Komsomol* members took part in a variety of campaigns. For example, *Komsomol* members were sometimes sent into markets to monitor prices, were sometimes instructed to distribute Communist Party leaflets and were also involved in anti-religious campaigns.

In theory *Komsomol* members were meant to be disciplined and keen supporters of the Communist Party. However, in reality they often had a reputation for drunkenness, promiscuity and hooliganism. Moreover, young people rarely attended the political meetings organised by *Komsomol*, but *Komsomol* parties and dances were extremely popular. Party leaders were aware of the nature of *Komsomol* and therefore in 1926 issued a directive that *Komsomol* leaders should discourage drinking, dancing and sex, and encourage 'healthy forms of entertainment'.

## 2 The reduction of illiteracy

Lenin believed that ending illiteracy was crucial to building socialism. Therefore tackling illiteracy was Lenin's central educational aim. In 1919 the new government published the Decree on Illiteracy which required all illiterate people between the ages of 8 and 50 to learn to read and write. It also gave the government the right to conscript literate people into the education system to teach.

The literacy campaign continued throughout the 1920s with mixed results.

## Note it down

Create a timeline for illiteracy in this period. Make notes on the timeline on the policies used to tackle illiteracy and, using a different colour, on the consequences of these policies.

### The Red Army

Trotsky shared Lenin's view about the importance of literacy. Consequently, as leader of the Red Army, he introduced education for all soldiers. As a result, literacy rates increased from 50 per cent in 1918 to 86 per cent in 1921. The campaign continued after the war was won, and by 1925 100 per cent of soldiers in the Red Army could read and write.

### Literacy and the Civil War

Outside the Red Army the Civil War saw a decline in literacy. The Communist Government published 6.5 million textbooks containing simple rhymes that taught the alphabet. Therefore there was a rise in the number of people who could identify letters, but this campaign did not lead to an increase in genuine literacy. Lunacharsky also set up a network of reading rooms or *likpunkty* (liquidation points) in towns and villages. They offered six-week intensive courses in reading and writing, and were designed to 'liquidate' illiteracy. However, learning was not a priority for those trying to survive the Civil War.

The literacy campaign was set back by a series of factors:

- The majority of teachers in 1917 did not support the regime; they advocated Western-style democracy. Indeed, teachers went on strike in early 1918 in protest at the new government.
- The government prioritised military victory and economic survival over education.
- Many schools were requisitioned by the army and turned into stores or barracks; therefore education ceased.
- The war economy did not produce or distribute educational products. By 1920 the schools that were open reported that they had one pencil for every 60 students and one pen for every 22.
- The war disrupted education across the country.

### Literacy and the NEP

Initially economic conditions led to the scaling back of the already small literacy campaign. To save money the government closed 90 per cent of the reading room network established during the Civil War. However, in the mid-1920s there was a new campaign to 'liquidate illiteracy'. In May 1925 the government announced an initiative to ensure that all adults in the Soviet Union were literate by October 1927: the tenth anniversary of the revolution. Working with trades unions the government set up libraries and reading groups in factories to educate workers. There were some successes. For example, the Metal Workers Union reported an increase in literacy from 86 per cent in 1925 to 96 per cent in 1926, and the Transport Workers Union achieved 99 per cent literacy by 1927. However, educating peasants proved harder. Therefore the goal of the campaign was pushed back to 1933. Overall, literacy rates improved from 38 per cent in 1914 to 55 per cent in 1928. However, the achievement was extremely uneven and rates of illiteracy began to increase after the illiteracy liquidation campaign ended in 1927.

## Stalin's war against illiteracy

Under Stalin the campaign against illiteracy was relaunched. The Sixteenth Party Congress of 1930 adopted new targets to eliminate illiteracy and ensure that primary schooling was compulsory during the First Five-Year Plan.

The government recruited 3 million volunteers from *Komsomol* to educate workers and peasants. The campaign was organised in a military fashion. Volunteers were called 'cultural soldiers', organised in 'cultural battalions' and tasked with fighting a 'cultural war' against illiteracy. However, the campaign took place in the midst of Stalin's campaign to collectivise agriculture (see page 54). As a result, teachers were attacked as they were associated with the government and therefore considered the enemy. Around 40 per cent of teachers were physically attacked in the first year of the campaign. For example, some teachers were locked in schools that were then set on fire, while others were beaten to death or had acid thrown at them. There were also rumours that the teachers were really there to kidnap children and send young Soviet women to China as slaves.

Teachers were also poorly equipped and poorly supported. They often arrived with no textbooks or writing materials. Additionally, they had little to offer peasants who attended schools. For example, they were unable to provide free school meals.

In spite of this unpromising start the campaign was successful. During the first Five-Year Plan 90 per cent of Soviet adults had attended a literacy course. These courses were not wholly successful, but approximately 68 per cent of people were literate by the end of the First Five-Year Plan, a significant improvement from 1928. Stalin's campaign continued throughout the 1930s. By 1939 over 94 per cent of Soviet citizens were literate. Significantly, literacy rates

▲ Dawn of the Motherland (1949). What evidence does this picture contain of Stalin's modernisation of the Soviet Union?

reflected inequalities in society, so while around 97 per cent of men were literate only 90 per cent of women could read and write. Equally, educational culture became obsessed with statistics and centrally enforced targets. Therefore although literacy rates shot up, there was no focus on the full educational development of the students. Nor was there any official attempt to encourage students to read or write for pleasure. Nonetheless, mass literacy was one of the successes of Stalin's first decade in power.

## 3 State control of the curriculum, 1932–53

Under Stalin, the government established tight control of the curriculum. From 1932 to 1935 the government ordered extensive changes to what was taught in schools. Curriculum changes were a response to criticisms of the People's Commissariat for Education and educational standards in schools in the 1920s. The reforms also reflected the values and methods of Stalinist society. In order to ensure that young people became good workers on collective farms or in government factories, schools emphasised discipline, hard work and traditional skills. Additionally, in order to ensure that children became obedient citizens, schools began to emphasise patriotism and respect for great Russian leaders. Teachers too were expected to embrace the values and methods of the **command economy**.

### Note it down

Draw a timeline on a large sheet of paper covering the period 1932–53. Using bullet points, make notes on:

- the goals of educational policy under Stalin
- the educational reforms introduced under Stalin
- the consequences of Stalin's educational policy.

### Educating workers

Under Stalin, education was expected to turn young people into good workers. In 1931 a decree ordered curriculum reform. The decree abolished the polytechnic focus that had been put forward in 1918. Rather it stated that core subjects such as reading, writing, maths and science should form the basis of a socialist education system. The aim was to ensure that all people had a foundational level of education necessary for work in factories or farms. Moreover, the progressive methods that were advocated in the 1920s were abolished. Stalin's education system stressed regimented discipline. A 1932 decree introduced new standards of discipline. Teachers were required to ensure that students attended regularly and were punctual, and were also required to set regular homework. Moreover, there was a national code of conduct which covered the correct way to stand and sit in classes. Students could also be expelled from school for misconduct. In essence, school discipline was supposed to prepare students for the labour discipline that they would experience in Soviet factories under the Five-Year Plans.

In 1933 a new series of textbooks was launched to support the new curriculum. Finally, in 1935 a system of national examinations was introduced. These were designed to grade the workforce of the future so students with good grades could be identified and trained for management posts, and less successful students would be assigned more manual jobs.

### Educating citizens

During the 1930s education acquired a new focus on traditional Russian history. Following the Decree on the Teaching of Civic History, issued in May 1934, history lessons, and new Soviet history textbooks, focused on the achievement of great men such as Ivan the Terrible and Peter the Great. History teaching also became more nationalistic, stressing the history of the Russian nation rather than the history of class struggle or the international working-class movement. This emphasis emerged at the same time as the cult of Stalin. In that sense, the new focus on great Russian leaders was part of the hero-worship that was becoming a feature of Soviet culture at the time. The new educational focus was designed to make students respect Stalin and love their country.

### Stalinist teaching methods

Teachers were encouraged to set an example for their students by emulating Stakhanov (see page 53). For example, in 1936 Olga Fedorovna Leonova pledged that all of her students would gain excellent grades. When she had fulfilled this promise a media campaign made her an example for all Soviet teachers. Evidently, teaching and study in the Soviet Union reflected the aims and methods of Stalin's economy.

### Youth groups under Stalin

During the 1930s members of *Komsomol* and the Young Pioneers were expected to spy on their parents and report any criminal behaviour to the police. *Komsomolskaia Pravda*, the Soviet Union's young people's magazine, reinforced this message. The most famous member of *Komsomol* during the 1930s was Pavlik Morozov, who was supposedly killed by a kulak at the age of 14. *Komsomolskaia Pravda* described him as hard working and obedient, the model for other young people to follow.

## Educational expansion under Stalin

The expansion of primary education continued under Stalin. The government set the target that 100 per cent of children aged between 8 and 12 would be enrolled for primary schools by 1932. Official figures show that they achieved the enrolment of 95 per cent of children. Even though they missed their target, this was a dramatic increase from the 60 per cent enrolled in 1928.

Fees were still an important part of the education system outside primary school. Stalin's prime objective in the 1930s was industrialisation. Therefore the government was unwilling to spend money on education beyond what was necessary to ensure the workforce could operate government factories. For most workers primary education was enough. Fees were maintained in the higher levels of education to keep costs down. They also limited access. Significantly, the Communist Party and trades unions offered scholarships and grants to help students access higher education. However, the system favoured the sons and daughters of Party officials. Indeed, the scheme was part of Stalin's broader policy of rewarding loyal Party members.

In spite of educational fees, higher education grew significantly during the 1930s. The number of universities increased by around 800 per cent, from 105 in 1914 to 817 in 1939. The number of students receiving a university education increased by a similar proportion, from 127,000 in 1914 to 811,000 in 1939. Secondary education also expanded. By 1939 approximately 1.5 million Soviet citizens, seven per cent of the child population, completed their secondary education compared to just 216,000 in the last years of the NEP. Stalin's final attempt to ensure discipline at school came in July 1943 when a decree introduced gender segregation into secondary schools. Where possible, local soviets were encouraged to ensure that male and female students did not share the same buildings. Stalin felt that interaction between the adolescent male and female students was likely to lead to distraction and ill-discipline.

Expansion continued after the Second World War, and by 1953 official figures showed that:

- almost 100 per cent of children aged 8 to 12 gained the full four years of primary education
- around 65 per cent of children aged 12 to 17 gained some secondary education
- around 20 per cent of children aged 15 to 17 completed secondary education.

### Labour Reserve Schools

In addition to the network of primary schools, secondary schools and universities, the Soviet Union also established Labour Reserve Schools (LRS). These were established by the Ministry of Labour in 1940 in order to train young men between the ages of 14 and 17 in specialisms in industry. In a sense, the LRSs were a form of industrial conscription. Quotas for compulsory recruitment were issued. Recruits were then enrolled in training courses lasting between six months and two years, followed by a four-year work placement. For the period of their education they were provided with accommodation and food, but no pay.

During the Second World War the LRSs became an important part of Soviet industry. Young men could avoid military service by enrolling in a LRS and then be deployed to fulfil a specialist role in a factory in order to facilitate war production. Additionally, the LRSs started recruiting women. Conditions in the LRSs were harsh and students who deserted could face sentences of between one year in prison and ten years in a gulag.

During the Fourth and Fifth Five-Year Plans (see page 50), LRSs played an important part in providing the skilled labour necessary for economic reconstruction. For example, between 1946 and 1952, the LRSs recruited 4.2 million young people and trained them to work in metallurgy, electricity production, industrial and military construction, and as railway workers. LRSs were another feature of government control of the curriculum, as the government set the quotas for the number of people to be trained and the areas of industry they should study.

### University education under Stalin

Stalin's Great Turn required an expansion of Soviet universities. During the period of the NEP Soviet industry had been run by 'bourgeois specialists', people who had been born into privileged classes prior to the revolution. Stalin wanted to replace these people, who in his view were enemies of socialism, with a new generation of 'red specialists'. Therefore Soviet higher education had to be expanded. Stalin launched the new policy in 1928, and the number of university enrolments quickly increased. In 1927 enrolments totalled 170,000. By 1932 this had grown to 500,000 and in 1940 the number of enrolments stood at 812,000.

Between 1936 and 1938 a new examination system was introduced along with new standards of discipline. By the late 1930s the university staff who had been employed before 1928 were purged and replaced with red specialists. In spite of the purge, the number of academics increased from 29,000 in 1927 to 50,000 in 1940. University courses reflected the needs of the economy and there was a significant expansion of courses dealing with construction, transport and factory production.

The Second World War decimated the university sector, and by 1944 only 227,000 students remained at university. However, by 1953 the university sector had been extensively reconstructed with approximately 1.5 million students at Soviet universities.

# 4 Educational reform and expansion, 1953–85

While education grew under Stalin, the essential structure and curriculum stayed the same from the mid-1930s to 1953. Therefore Khrushchev believed that education, along with much else in the Soviet Union, was in need of reform. Khrushchev's reforms proved unpopular, and Brezhnev restored much of the Stalinist curriculum after Khrushchev's fall.

### Note it down

Draw a timeline covering the period 1953–85. Using bullet points, make notes on:

- educational reforms
- educational expansion
- the restoration of traditional educational policy.

You can use different coloured pens to distinguish between the three.

## Khrushchev's reorganisation and expansion

Between 1929 and 1953 schools in towns and cities improved considerably. Schools in the country were often much smaller and lacked resources. Teachers, for example, were often unwilling to give up the relative comfort of Soviet towns to work in the country. In order to address this, Khrushchev ordered the merger of small country schools and the establishment of new schools that would offer the full ten years of compulsory education. However, the scheme only affected certain areas, and the majority of country schools remained small and poorly resourced.

Khrushchev doubled the number of schools in towns and cities. He also invested in teacher training and recruitment. The number of teachers rose from 1.5 million in 1953 to 2.2 million in 1964. Moreover, the level of teachers' education also improved under Khrushchev. In 1953 only 19 per cent of teachers had a university education; that rose to 40 per cent in 1964.

Perhaps the most important reform in terms of improving access to education was the abolition of fees for students attending secondary school and university in 1956. This was followed in 1959 by the establishment of special funds to help maintain poor students who attended secondary schools. The fund paid for clothes, footwear, textbooks and school dinners.

As a result of these reforms, the proportion of 17 year olds who completed secondary education rose significantly from about 20 per cent in 1953 to about 75 per cent in 1959.

### Educational reform, 1956

By 1956 Khrushchev believed that the Soviet curriculum was in need of reform. The Soviet curriculum stayed much the same from 1931 to 1955. Indeed, of the 61 textbooks in use in 1958, 46 had been initially written in 1933.

Khrushchev's 1956 reforms reintroduced polytechnic education. This reflected the needs of Khrushchev's industrial policy. Whereas Stalin's economy needed disciplined and literate workers, Khrushchev's new light industries needed workers with more sophisticated skills. The reforms also reflected the impact of the war. High mortality rates in young men led to a shortage of skilled labour in the 1950s. As a result of the reforms, education became more practical. This is evident from the amount of time in class devoted to different subjects (see Table 3).

**Table 3: Percentage of time in class devoted to different subjects.**

| | Percentage of curriculum time | | |
|---|---|---|---|
| **Subject area** | **1947** | **1959** | **Change** |
| Humanities (including history, music and art) | 50 | 40 | –10 |
| Science (including mathematics) | 42 | 31 | –10 |
| Practical training | 8 | 28 | +20 |

In addition to the changes in the amount of time given to different subject areas, education was made more practical by increasing the practical focus of science and maths teaching. Finally, outside of lessons schools were expected to organise trips to factories and farms as well as work experience placements.

### The 1958 reforms

The reforms of December 1958 took Soviet schools further in the direction of polytechnic education. The 1958 reforms reflected Khrushchev's suspicion of the prejudice instilled by traditional education. He complained that academic education made students believe that they were too good to work in factories or on farms.

Khrushchev's reforms were set out in the December 1959 Education Law. The law:

- made education compulsory for children aged 7 to 15
- required schools to offer 11-year programmes rather than 10-year programmes so students could stay on to the age of 19
- restructured education for students aged 16 to 19, so that most students would complete their education through a combination of education in schools and vocational training in local factories or on local farms

- ensured the most academically gifted students would be given places at special schools that focused on academic education
- introduced a new course, 'the fundamentals of political knowledge', for all 15 year olds to ensure they knew the benefits of the Soviet system and the essentials of Marxism.

### Final reforms

Khrushchev continued to try to reform education. His final reforms were part of his broader policy of de-Stalinisation.

- Stalinist discipline was relaxed in November 1960 when a new code of conduct was introduced which abolished the rules about correct sitting and standing postures.
- In 1961 Khrushchev ordered a new emphasis on learning foreign languages. Again this reflected a rejection of Stalin's emphasis on cultural isolation.
- The requirement to set homework was also dropped, and final exams, introduced by Stalin in the 1930s, were replaced by **continuous assessment**.
- In June 1962 teachers lost the right to expel students who were underachieving.

### The impact of Khrushchev's reforms

Khrushchev's reforms were unpopular and a failure. They were unpopular because most parents wanted their children to get an academic education, rather than complete vocational courses. This view was particularly common among Communist Party members. The reforms were a failure because they were never fully implemented. By 1962, when all schools were supposed to offer courses to students up to the age of 19, only 65 per cent of schools had complied with government regulations. The slackening of discipline was generally ignored by teachers, who continued to set homework and insist on correct standing and sitting postures. Curriculum reforms were not implemented in 47 per cent of schools.

The most successful aspects of Khrushchev's reforms were those that improved education for the academic elite. These reforms were welcomed by Party officials, and the number of special schools increased significantly (see Table 4).

**Table 4: The number of special schools in 1959 and 1966.**

| Type of school | 1959 | 1966 |
|---|---|---|
| Academic | 5 | 24 |
| Art and Sculpture | 5 | 50 |
| Ballet | 16 | 18 |

Moreover, Khrushchev's reforms did not address some of the fundamental problems in Soviet education, such as poorly maintained or poorly built school buildings and the shortage of teachers in rural areas.

## Soviet education, 1964–85

Khrushchev's reforms were extremely unpopular with members of the Communist Party. Other leading Communists branded them 'crackpot' educational schemes. Therefore Brezhnev's top educational priority was to reverse Khrushchev's educational reforms.

### Repealing the Khrushchev reforms

The educational priority of the post-Khrushchev leadership was to repeal Khrushchev's reforms. Between 1964 and 1966 the Council of Ministers:

- ended the 11-year schooling policy in favour of a gradual shift from 8-year schooling to 10-year schooling
- drew up a temporary curriculum to restore the focus on academic education
- ended vocational training for students aged 16 to 19 in factories and on farms
- abandoned compulsory secondary education, replacing it with a target that 100 per cent of children would complete secondary education by 1970.

### Slowing expansion

Expansion of secondary schooling slowed from 1966. By 1976 only 60 per cent of students finished secondary education, far short of the 1970 target. The number of teachers remained roughly stable, but there was a continual increase in their level of qualifications. By 1978 almost 70 per cent of teachers had a university education.

### Small-scale reforms

Brezhnev introduced some small-scale reforms in the 1970s. The School Statute of September 1970 required textbooks to be updated to reflect the latest scientific knowledge and reintroduced compulsory homework. The Fundamental Law on Soviet Education, 1973, essentially consolidated the existing approach to education in a single document. During the 1970s attempts were made to increase peasant participation in schooling by requiring all schools to provide hot school meals. Free meals were available to poor students. Additionally, in the late 1970s textbooks were made available to students free of charge.

The curriculum remained largely unchanged under Brezhnev. Indeed, by 1985 students were still required to study the same mix of subjects as those established in 1947.

## University education, 1953–85

Soviet universities were one of the real successes of the Communist education system. Between 1953 and 1980 student numbers in higher education grew from about 1.5 million to over 5 million, around 19 per cent of the population.

Growth in student numbers took place following 1958. Moreover, the university curriculum expanded to reflect the diverse needs of Soviet light industry. From 1958 there were new courses, including electronics, radio, construction, agricultural chemistry and machine-building. Academic staff increased from 87,000 to 380,000 between 1958 and 1980 to teach the growing number of students.

There were attempts to serve the diverse communities that comprised the Soviet Union. For example, in 1954 Khrushchev initiated the building of five new universities to serve students from non-Russian ethnic backgrounds. Brezhnev continued this initiative by founding 18 universities in non-Russian Soviet republics including Kazakhstan, Tadzhikistan, Armenia and Azerbaijan.

Postgraduate education also grew. In 1953 only 9000 Soviet citizens had doctorates; by 1975 that figure had risen to 32,000. Soviet authorities were concerned about the impact of such high levels of education, fearing that advanced study would lead to political **non-conformity**. Therefore most postgraduate courses focused on sciences, which were considered politically less dangerous. Postgraduate students in the humanities were expected to write a chapter on how their research supported the established truths of Marxism-Leninism in order to show that they remained committed to the official ideology.

### *Komsomol*, 1954–85

Khrushchev and Brezhnev had different views of the role of *Komsomol*. Khrushchev seems to have had a lot of faith in the organisation and was keen to involve *Komsomol* members in his initiatives. For example, he instructed *Komsomol*'s leaders to recruit young volunteer workers to work on the Virgin Lands Scheme. Khrushchev hoped that *Komsomol* would play a leading role in holding factory managers and Party officials to account, reminding them of the vision that they were all working towards.

Brezhnev, by contrast, was suspicious of *Komsomol*. He viewed *Komsomol*'s leadership as young and ambitious, and therefore potentially dangerous. Brezhnev essentially wanted *Komsomol* to celebrate the achievements of the Party and the leadership. He believed that *Komsomol* should keep young people disciplined and obedient and should emphasise the values of working hard and respecting the government.

### Work together

1 Write a paragraph in answer to the following question:

**How far did the Soviet Government achieve its educational aims in the years 1917–53?**

Make sure your answer focuses clearly on the question, considers both sides of the question, considers media and religion, covers the whole time period and concludes with some genuine evaluation.

2 Having written the paragraph, swap it with a partner. Discuss which paragraph:

- focuses more clearly on the question
- uses the most appropriate evidence to support its points
- most effectively defines the educational aims of the government
- most effectively covers the whole period
- contains the most effective evaluation.

3 Having discussed these different aspects of your paragraphs, note down three things you could do to improve or maintain your essay technique.

4 Now repeat the activity focusing on the period 1953–85. Try to improve your paragraph based on your discussion of your original paragraph.

## Chapter summary

- From 1917 to 1985 education was radically reformed.
- Education reforms reflected the changing needs of the Soviet economy, the changing ideological emphasis of the leadership and the interests of policy makers.
- Lunacharsky wanted to ensure that Soviet education liberated students through progressive teaching methods and a polytechnic approach that allowed students to train for a variety of different economic roles.
- Lenin emphasised the liquidation of illiteracy as the greatest task facing Soviet education, arguing that true freedom began with the most basic education.
- Stalin continued Lenin's literacy drive, but refocused education on ensuring a disciplined workforce with the essential skills and the necessary loyalty to build socialism.
- Khrushchev revived polytechnic education stressing the dignity of factory and farm work. However, his own party rejected this, wanting an academic education for their children.
- Brezhnev revived a more traditional educational system but continued Khrushchev's drive to extend the benefits of education to the peasantry and the Soviet people outside Russia.
- By 1985 most Soviet citizens gained a world-class education, which, in itself, was a revolution from the experience of Russians in 1914.

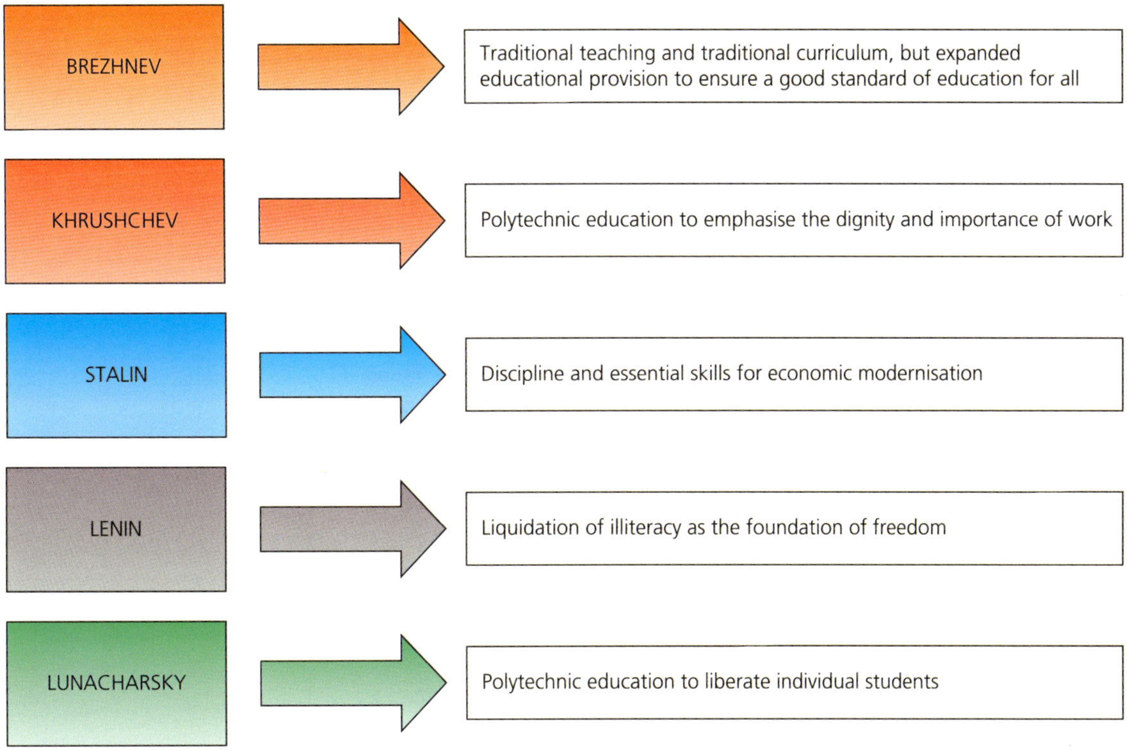


▲ **Summary diagram: Education and young people.**

## Recommended reading

V. Brovkin, *Russia after Lenin: Politics, Culture and Society, 1921–1929* (Routledge, 1998), pages 107–32. This chapter of Brovkin's book analyses youth culture in the Soviet Union in the 1920s.

S. Fitzpatrick, *Education and Social Mobility in the Soviet Union 1921–1934* (Cambridge, 2002), pages 113–36. In this chapter Fitzpatrick explores the change in education that took place under Stalin.

M. Ilič, S.E. Reid and L. Attwood (eds.), *Women in the Khrushchev Era* (Palgrave, 2004), pages 75–95. In this chapter the authors consider sex and youth culture in the early part of the Khrushchev era.

# Essay technique: Evaluation and relative significance

Reaching a supported overall judgement is an important part of doing well in Section A and B essays. One aspect of reaching the very highest level is to reach a supported overall judgement by evaluating the relative significance of different factors in the light of a valid criterion. This section examines how to evaluate and how to establish valid criteria.

## Evaluation

The purpose of evaluation is to weigh up and reach a judgement. Therefore evaluation needs to consider the importance of two or more different factors, weigh them against each other and then reach a judgement. Evaluation is a good skill to use at the end of an essay, because it helps support your overall judgement.

For example, imagine you are answering the following question:

**How accurate is it to say that the Soviet Government relied wholly on the secret police to retain its power in the years 1928–85?**

You might want to weigh up the extent to which the Soviet Government relied on the secret police on the one hand, and propaganda and economic incentives on the other. For example, your conclusion might read:

The first part of the paragraph focuses on the given factor, examining the importance of the secret police.

The first part of the paragraph weighs the given factor against other factors: propaganda and economic incentives.

The final part of the paragraph makes a judgement about the significance of the different factors.

In conclusion, clearly the Soviet Government was based on the secret police throughout the period 1928–85. For example, the secret police played a major role in supporting Stalin's government, particularly during the Great Terror, and Brezhnev reversed Khrushchev's attempts to reduce their role in Russian culture. However, other factors such as propaganda and economic incentives also helped support communist rule. During Stalin's Five-Year Plans, propaganda encouraged workers to make big sacrifices in order to build a better future, and economic incentives were also important during the Stakhanovite period, under Khrushchev and as part of Brezhnev's 'social contract'. Therefore, although the secret police played an important role supporting communist rule, they were not wholly responsible because propaganda and economic rewards were also important to the stability of the government.

In this example the evaluation is helped by using a series of words that weigh the importance of the secret police against the importance of terror. 'Clearly', 'however' and 'therefore' are useful words as they can help contrast the importance of the different factors. This conclusion could be improved by explicitly weighing the relative significance of the factors in the light of a valid criterion. An example of an improved conclusion can be found on page 143.

In conclusion, clearly the Soviet Government was based on secret police throughout the period between1928 and 1984. This was particularly true during the years 1935–38 when the Great Terror affected the whole of the Russian population. Terror continued under Khrushchev and Brezhnev, but it affected far fewer people. However, other factors such as propaganda and incentives also helped support communist rule. Propaganda was less important than the secret police, because after 1964 the Russian population became increasingly cynical and therefore propaganda was not very influential under Brezhnev. The most important factor was economic incentives. These became a feature of Russian life during the Second Five-Year Plan and became increasingly important to the Russian people due to Khrushchev's and Brezhnev's attempts to create a consumer society. Indeed, following 1964 Brezhnev's 'social contract' with the Russian people was based on economic incentives much more than on the secret police or inspirational visions of propaganda. Therefore, although the secret police played an important role supporting communist rule and were much more effective than the increasingly ineffectual propaganda, economic incentives were the most important factor because from 1953 and particularly after 1964 they were the main reason that the Russian people supported communist rule.

This part of the paragraph begins to evaluate the importance of the secret police by considering the criteria of duration and scope.

Here the paragraph argues that propaganda was less important than terror, by referring to the same criteria: duration (propaganda was increasingly ineffective from 1964 to 1984) and scope (most people stopped believing the propaganda from 1964 to 1984).

Using the same criteria, the paragraph argues that economic incentives were the most important factor.

The final sentence explicitly weighs the different factors in terms of the criteria and reaches an overall judgement.

## Relative significance

Clearly the Soviet Government relied on the secret police, propaganda and economic incentives. However, the best essays will make a judgement about which was most important based on a valid criterion.

It is up to you to come up with a valid criterion. Criteria can be very simple. The following criteria are often useful:

- Duration: which factor was important for the longest period of time?
- Scope: which factor affected the most people?
- Effectiveness: which factor achieved most?
- Impact: which factor led to the most fundamental change?

For example, in answer to the essay question on page 142. You could compare the factors in terms of their duration and their scope. For example, you could argue that economic incentives were more important than propaganda or terror because they affected more people for a longer time:

This conclusion is an example of high-level work because it reaches an overall judgement and supports it through evaluating the relative significance of different factors in the light of valid criteria.

## Activity: Weighing up the factors

Here is a plan in answer to the following question:

**How accurate is it to say that the Soviet Government was totalitarian in the period 1964–84?**

Plan:

- Paragraph 1: Communist political control – almost total
- Paragraph 2: Communist economic control – very large
- Paragraph 3: Communist cultural control – large, but not complete
- Paragraph 4: Increasing popular disenchantment with the government

1 Using your notes from previous chapters, decide on the criteria that you are going to use to judge how accurate it is to describe the Soviet Government as totalitarian in the period 1964–84.
2 Having established your criteria, write a sentence that summarises the extent to which the Russian Government was totalitarian in the period 1964–84.
3 Support this by writing three or four sentences that weigh up at least three of the factors mentioned in your plan.
4 Write a final summary sentence that explicitly weighs the different factors in terms of your criteria and reaches an overall judgement.

## Paper 1 Russia, 1917–91: from Lenin to Yeltsin

# Historical interpretations: What explains the fall of the USSR, c.1985–91?

## The Big Debate

Between 1985 and 1991 there was a fundamental shift in global politics. A series of profound changes, including the disintegration of the Eastern Bloc, the fall of the Berlin Wall and the end of the Cold War, climaxed with the fall of the Soviet Union. The collapse of European Communism was a deep shock. Few predicted it. In fact it was commonly assumed that the USSR and the Cold War would continue into the twenty-first century.

The fall of the Soviet Union has led to considerable historical debate. Historians have offered a variety of explanations for the collapse. The examination focuses on four of the key explanations:

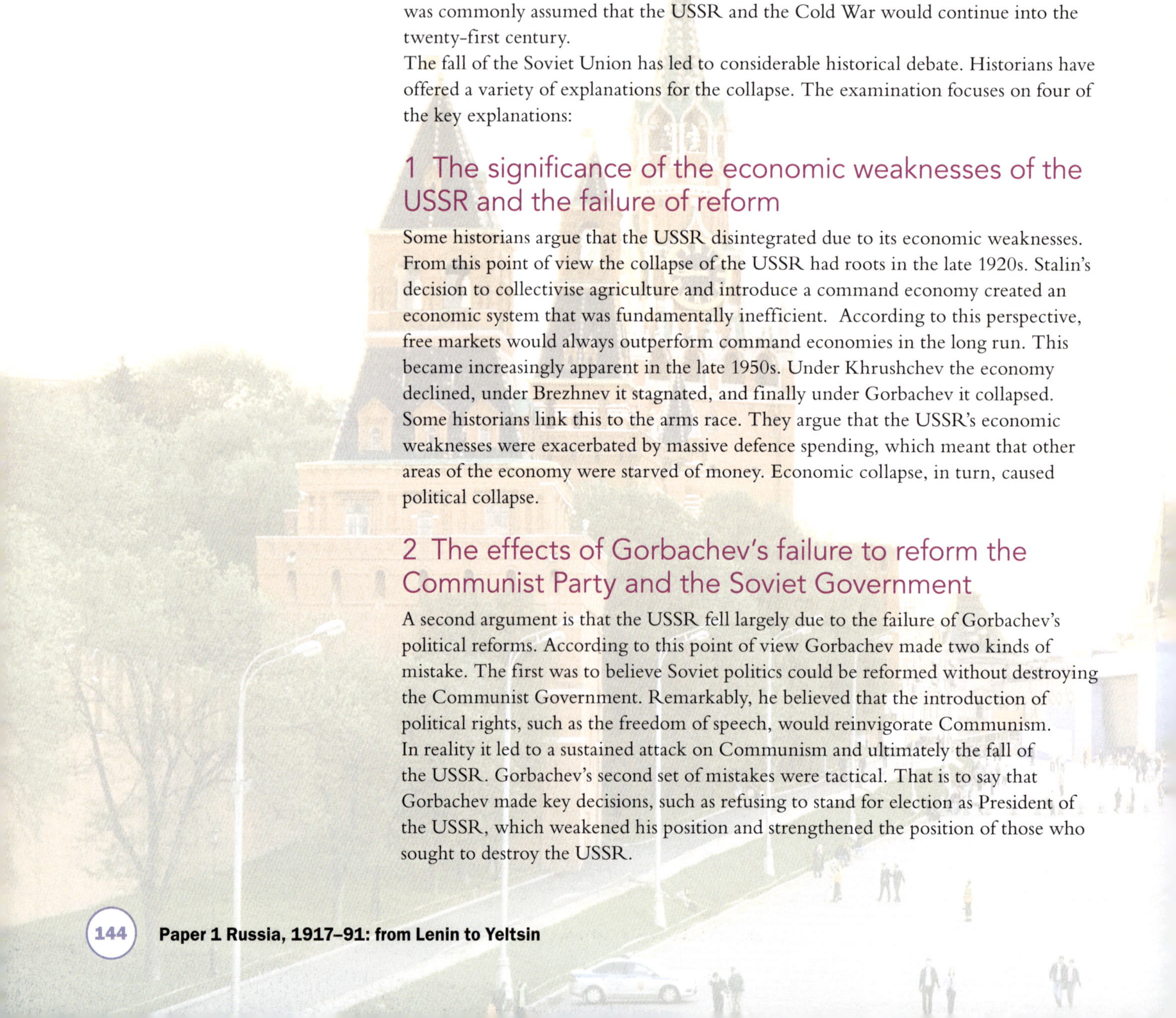

### 1 The significance of the economic weaknesses of the USSR and the failure of reform

Some historians argue that the USSR disintegrated due to its economic weaknesses. From this point of view the collapse of the USSR had roots in the late 1920s. Stalin's decision to collectivise agriculture and introduce a command economy created an economic system that was fundamentally inefficient. According to this perspective, free markets would always outperform command economies in the long run. This became increasingly apparent in the late 1950s. Under Khrushchev the economy declined, under Brezhnev it stagnated, and finally under Gorbachev it collapsed. Some historians link this to the arms race. They argue that the USSR's economic weaknesses were exacerbated by massive defence spending, which meant that other areas of the economy were starved of money. Economic collapse, in turn, caused political collapse.

### 2 The effects of Gorbachev's failure to reform the Communist Party and the Soviet Government

A second argument is that the USSR fell largely due to the failure of Gorbachev's political reforms. According to this point of view Gorbachev made two kinds of mistake. The first was to believe Soviet politics could be reformed without destroying the Communist Government. Remarkably, he believed that the introduction of political rights, such as the freedom of speech, would reinvigorate Communism. In reality it led to a sustained attack on Communism and ultimately the fall of the USSR. Gorbachev's second set of mistakes were tactical. That is to say that Gorbachev made key decisions, such as refusing to stand for election as President of the USSR, which weakened his position and strengthened the position of those who sought to destroy the USSR.

## 3 The impact of the nationalist resurgence in the late 1980s in the Soviet republics and in the communist states of Eastern Europe

Next, some historians argue that nationalism was to blame for the collapse of the USSR. From this perspective, historians argue that the new freedoms that Gorbachev introduced allowed nationalist groups to organise, set out their agendas, win elections and gain increasing independence. These trends emerged first in the Eastern Bloc. Starting in Poland and Hungary, communist governments across Eastern Europe were overthrown in anti-communist revolutions. The 15 Soviet republics followed, one by one leaving the USSR. From this point of view, however, Gorbachev's reforms were not the key issue. They were merely the short-term cause which allowed the expression of a long-standing desire for independence.

## 4 How far Gorbachev and Yeltsin can be seen as responsible for the collapse of the USSR in 1991

Finally, some historians argue that the fall of the Soviet Union was primarily due to Gorbachev and Yeltsin: the final leader of the Soviet Union and the first leader of post-Soviet Russia. Gorbachev, they argue, had a vision of a free, pluralistic Russia. He was willing to criticise the past and introduce radical reforms. Moreover, more often than not, Gorbachev refused to use force. Therefore there was nothing stopping Eastern European countries or the Soviet republics from rejecting communist rule. Yeltsin's role was more short term but, perhaps, no less important. Yeltsin's key achievements were to lead opposition to the coup of August 1991, to ban the Communist Party in Russia and to negotiate the Belavezha Accords, which abolished the USSR.

Significantly, all historians agree that the Soviet Union had serious economic problems; all agree that Gorbachev's reforms failed to achieve his aims; all agree that nationalism, Gorbachev and Yeltsin played major roles in the break-up of the USSR. They key issue is which factor was the prime reason for the dissolution of the USSR. This section considers each of these interpretations in turn.

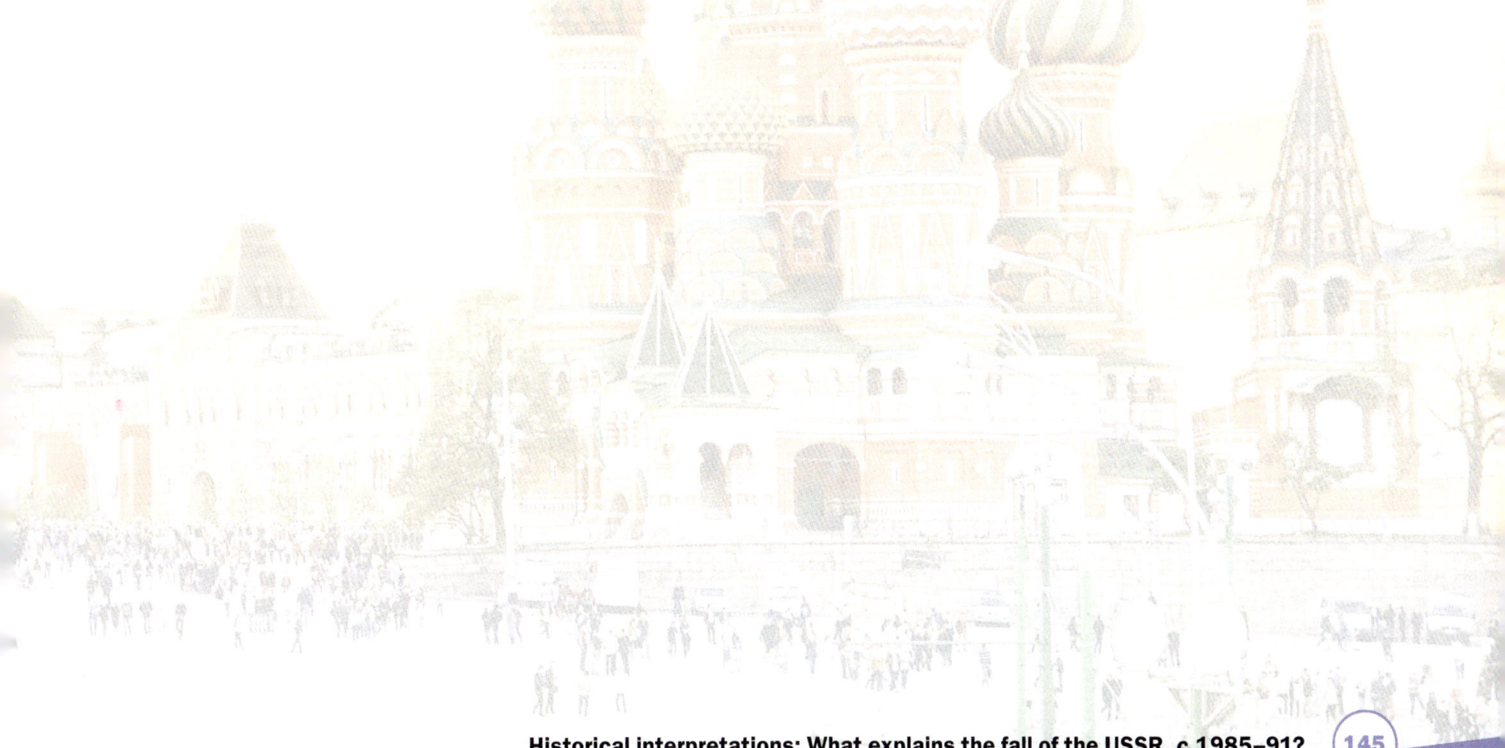

# 1 Economic weaknesses and the failure of reform

## Overview

The fall of the Soviet Union was due, in part, to long-term economic weaknesses and, in the short term, the failure of economic reforms. The long-term economic weaknesses were related to the command economy and collectivisation, which was inherently inefficient and wasteful. Additionally, the Soviet economy was under huge pressure because of the government's military spending commitments. However, these long-term problems did not threaten immediate economic collapse. Gorbachev's economic reforms exacerbated the economic weaknesses of the Soviet Union, causing an economic crisis which undermined the government.

This chapter considers:

1 Long-term economic weaknesses
2 Gorbachev and the Soviet economy
3 Transition to a market economy.

## 1 Long-term economic weaknesses

From 1928 until the late 1980s the Soviet economy was essentially a **command economy** (see page 42). Under Stalin this economic policy led to significant success. The First Five-Year Plan led to the industrialisation of Russia. Russia's economic might was a key factor in the Soviet victory against the Nazis in the Second World War, and by 1945 the Russian economy was the fastest growing in the world. During the mid-1950s the Soviet economy grew at an average annual rate of 7.1 per cent, whereas the US economy grew at a mere 2.9 per cent. Consequently, many politicians, economists and historians assumed that the Soviet economy would catch up and overtake Western economies. In fact, during the 1950s there was concern in the West that communist economic policy might be superior to capitalism, and that Communism might eventually become the dominant world system.

Khrushchev's economic reforms promoted growth in agriculture and raised living standards. However, growth rates declined. From 1958–63 the Soviet economy grew at 5.3 per cent annually. Moreover, from 1945 the Soviet economy had to compete in an **arms race**, producing ever more sophisticated weapons at huge expense. The decline that began under Khrushchev became worse under Brezhnev. In the 1970s annual growth averaged 2 per cent, and by 1980 this had dropped to 0.6 per cent. Brezhnev's successors were determined to reverse the decline, but their strategies ultimately failed.

### Note it down

Using a note-taking style of your choice, note down the key weaknesses of the Soviet economy. Remember, your notes need to record:

- the reasons for Soviet economic weakness
- the economic data that illustrates the extent of the weaknesses.

### Fundamental economic weaknesses

The Soviet economy was fundamentally flawed. One major problem was that the Soviet economy failed to create incentives for hard work or innovation. From 1945 to 1980 the Soviet Union was increasingly egalitarian – the difference between the richest and the poorest was much smaller than in the West. For example, in 1970, the richest ten per cent of American society were seven times wealthier than the bottom ten per cent. In Russia, in the same period, the richest ten per cent were only three times wealthier than Russia's poorest. As a result, there was less incentive for workers to improve. Consequently, labour productivity was much lower in the Soviet Union than it was in the West.

A second problem was waste. Gosplan, the **State** Planning Committee, measured and rewarded production. The quality of production was irrelevant, as was the proportion that was actually used. Therefore, although large amounts of goods were produced, they were often wasted. For example, by the early 1980s Gosplan demanded the production of 400,000 tractors every year. However, at least 20 per cent were never used, due to the shortage of tractor drivers. Waste in industry was also a problem. In 1986, for example, Gosplan estimated that 12 per cent of machinery was never used.

Next, the Soviet economy had never been fully modernised. This was a particular problem in agriculture. Although there were too many tractors, Soviet agriculture lacked more sophisticated machinery. This meant that Soviet agriculture required much more labour than American farming. In the 1960s, for example, 25.4 per cent of Soviet workers were employed on farms, compared to just 4.6 per cent in America. The Soviet transport system had also never been fully modernised. Therefore transporting food around the country was difficult. Finally, a lack of modern storage facilities meant that a lot of what was produced was wasted. Grain, for example, often rotted in inadequate storage facilities before it could be used. Therefore, while a much greater proportion of the Soviet population worked on farms, American farms were six times more productive.

The Soviet economy also struggled due to the arms race with the US. From 1945, Russia produced ever more expensive missiles, nuclear bombs, tanks and fighter planes. Between 1965 and 1985 the proportion of Soviet **gross domestic product** (GDP) spent on defence increased from around 12 per cent to 17 per cent. This was a much greater burden than American defence spending, which averaged around 6 per cent over the same period. Soviet defence spending was a huge economic problem because it starved other areas of the economy of much needed funds.

A final chronic problem was centralisation. The economy was controlled by government administrators. In farming, for example, the government set the timetable for planting and harvesting. As a result, farmers could not use their expertise to adjust the schedule to take weather conditions into account. Equally, central planners set schedules for the delivery of fertilisers used on farms. Often fertilisers arrived at the wrong time or were the wrong type for the crops grown. These problems explain why the production of important crops improved slowly. For example, Soviet sugar beet production increased by 28 per cent in the period 1956 to 1980, whereas production of sugar beet in North Dakota, which has a similar climate to the Soviet sugar farms, increased by 191 per cent. Centralisation caused significant problems because it meant that production could not be maximised.

## The road to serfdom (1944)

One of the first writers to analyse the problems of the Soviet economy was the Austrian-born economist Friedrich Hayek. Although Hayek was not a historian, his work became increasingly influential from the 1970s and affected the perspectives of many Western historians.

In his book *The Road to Serfdom*, Hayek believed that he had spotted a fundamental flaw in the Soviet economy. He contrasted market economies with planned economies. He argued that in a market economy everyone has an impact on what is produced, as we all make decisions about what we buy and where we work. Therefore a market economy is broadly efficient because economic decisions reflect the economic knowledge of everyone in the market. In a planned economy, by contrast, decisions are made by a few economic experts. Significantly, however good economic experts are they could never know as much as the market. Therefore decisions made in market economies tend to be more efficient. Over time, he argued, market economies would always outperform planned economies, and people who live in planned economies will be reduced to poverty compared to those who live in market economies. Hayek's theories were extremely influential from the 1970s and influenced those who argued for economic reform. Moreover, some historians and economists such as Theodore Burczak argue that Hayek's theory explains why the Soviet economy could not survive in the long term.

## Historical interpretation: Long-term economic problems

Historians have argued about the impact of long-term economic weaknesses on the Soviet Union. Richard Sakwa claims that the nature of the command economy meant that in the long term the Soviet economy was bound to stagnate.

Paul R. Gregory, by contrast, argues that even as late as 1988 the Soviet economy was far from collapse and that long-term weaknesses did not undermine the stability of the system.

**Extract 1** From Richard Sakwa, *Soviet Politics in Perspective*, published in 1998.

> In its final years the Soviet economy faced significant problems, including systemic difficulties arising from problems internal to the socialist economy, and which could be remedied by actions taken by the leadership itself. Most of the latter arose from the pattern of Stalinist super-industrialisation which created a vast top-heavy bureaucracy managing the country's economic life. At a certain stage the enormous costs and wastage involved in maintaining the managing mechanism, the heart of the command economy, condemned Soviet-type economies to relative stagnation. In the absence of the invisible hand of capitalist market forces, and the increasingly palsied condition of the visible hand of command planning, such economies had no self-sustaining mechanism to imbue them with dynamism. These problems were not new, and the issue of economic reform had been at or near the top of the agenda at least since the death of Stalin.

**Extract 2** From Paul R. Gregory, *The Political Economy of Stalinism*, published in 2004.

> The Soviet administrative-command economy continued to have positive economic growth until 1989. The negative growth thereafter is indicative of an economic system in collapse. Although the USSR began the postwar era with high rates of growth (which were matched by much of Europe and exceeded by the economic miracles in Germany and Japan), its growth declined steadily after 1970. Whereas growth in Western industrialized economies turned down in response to energy crises in the mid-1970s and early 1980s, they bounced back so that no long-term declining trend was evident.
>
> The fateful decision in favour of radical economic reform was not forced by outright collapse. The party elite were reasonably satisfied, and the Soviet population was not in open opposition. The administrative command system, on the eve of its radical change, was inefficient but stable. Gosplan's projections called for an annual growth rate of some 3 percent through the year 2000. Declining Soviet growth rate, coupled with the acceleration of growth in China, Southeast Asia, and the marked recovery of the U.S. economy, were troubling but do not fully explain the fateful steps that eventually spelled the demise of the system.

Having read the extracts:

1. Summarise the key argument of Extract 1 and Extract 2.
2. Select three details from your own knowledge that support the argument of Extract 1. Write these down as a list under your summaries.
3. Swap your summaries and discuss lists:
   - Which summary best captured the argument of Extract 1?
   - Which summary best captured the argument of Extract 2?
   - Which details most precisely supported the argument of Extract 1?

## 2 Gorbachev and *Perestroika*

### Note it down

Using a note-taking style of your choice, note down the following key details concerning Gorbachev's economic reforms:

- the goal of Gorbachev's policies
- Gorbachev's methods
- the reasons for failure.

Gorbachev's economic policy changed radically from 1985 to 1991. Initially, he attempted to stimulate economic growth within the existing system. When this failed he attempted to introduce some aspects of the free market, while retaining many of the essential features of the command economy. Finally, he abandoned central planning altogether in order to create a genuinely free market. Gorbachev referred to his economic and political reforms as '*Perestroika*', which means 'restructuring.' Historian Richard Sakwa argues that *perestroika* had three stages:

- Rationalisation, 1985–86: This was a period of *uskorenie*: initial economic reforms. Led by the Communist Party, the reforms were designed to stimulate economic modernisation, higher rates of economic growth and higher levels of production.
- Reform, 1987–March 1990: Gorbachev initiated reforms intended to introduce market forces into the Soviet economy. At the same time he initiated political reforms designed to build support for greater economic change.
- Transformation, March 1990–August 1991: During this stage of *perestroika* Gorbachev began to abandon the fundamental aspects of the system such as single-party rule and the command economy. Additionally, the Party lost control of the process.

Gorbachev's reforms consistently failed to increase economic growth. Indeed, under Gorbachev the economy stopped growing and began to shrink.

By 1985, the Soviet economy was not merely lagging further behind the West, it was beginning to be overtaken by developing countries in Asia. Gorbachev recognised that the economy was stagnating and embraced economic reform.

### Alcohol production

Gorbachev's first initiative continued Andropov's anti-alcohol campaign. In May 1985 Gorbachev reduced alcohol production at state-run factories by 50 per cent. In addition, 55,000 Party members were assigned to a new task force to stop the illegal production of alcohol.

In general terms, the policy failed. First, although there was a drop in alcohol consumption among moderate drinkers, alcohol consumption in 1987 was still double that of 1960. In 1987, Soviet citizens over the age of 15 were still consuming between 15 and 16 litres of alcohol every year and there were still 4.5 million registered alcoholics. However, Soviet citizens were now drinking *samogon*, illegally manufactured alcohol. Therefore the government made much less money out of vodka sales. Indeed, government alcohol revenues dropped by 67 billion roubles (9 per cent of GDP), making economic problems worse. As a result the campaign was abandoned in 1988.

### Mikhail Gorbachev, 1931–

Gorbachev was the last leader of the Soviet Union. Prior to his appointment as General Secretary in 1985 he had been promoted by Andropov, who believed he had talent and dynamism. His goal, like that of Andropov and Khrushchev, was to reform Communism in order to make it more successful. In this sense, his various policies were designed to save Communism rather than to destroy it. In spite of his commitment to revitalising Communism Gorbachev had no clear plan. Rather he improvised and was prepared to change direction. Gorbachev played a key role in ending the Cold War, in causing the break-up of the Eastern Bloc and in the collapse of the Soviet Union.

## Acceleration

Acceleration, or *uskorenie*, was an economic initiative designed to end economic stagnation and get the Soviet economy moving again. Acceleration was at the heart of the Twelfth, and final, Five-Year Plan (1986–90). In essence, acceleration meant a huge increase in investment which was designed to modernise the Soviet economy and therefore make it more efficient. Gorbachev predicted that the new investment would lead to a 20 per cent increase in industrial production in the next 15 years.

Acceleration failed. A major reason was the decline in the global price of oil. During the 1970s the Soviet economy had made a great deal of money from selling oil to the West. However, the oil price fell from $70 a barrel in 1981 to $20 a barrel in 1985. As a result, Soviet oil revenues dropped by more than two-thirds. Combined with the drop in alcohol revenues, the Soviet Government had significantly less money from the mid-1980s. Therefore Gorbachev financed acceleration from borrowing from Western countries. As a result, government debt rose from $18.1 billion in 1981 to $27.2 billion in 1988. Gorbachev invested in energy production, ignoring the advice of his economic experts who argued for more investment in high-tech machines. Therefore the investment did not lead to greater growth. Increasing levels of debt meant that the government was spending more and more money on interest payments. Consequently, there was less money for further modernisation or to produce consumer goods. In sum, rather than leading to economic growth, acceleration created an economic crisis.

## Partial market reform

Acceleration was the Soviet Government's last serious attempt to save the centrally planned system. From late 1986 senior Communist officials began to believe that only some degree of market reform could bring about economic recovery.

The first small reform was the Law on Individual Economic Activity of November 1986. This made it legal for families and individuals to make money from small-scale work such as private teaching or repair and maintenance jobs.

The 1987 Law on State Enterprise was much more radical. It was intended to devolve power from central government to factory management. For example, factory managers were allowed to set the prices for their production. This reform failed in two ways. Firstly, very little power was actually devolved as Gosplan found new ways of maintaining central control. Secondly, the ability to charge higher prices meant that the government had to pay more for goods, which further increased government debt.

The 1988 Law on Co-operatives made it legal to set up large-scale private companies. By 1990 nearly 200,000 private companies, or **co-operatives**, had been set up across the USSR. Many co-operatives were successful. In the first year, the turnover of the co-operatives increased from 29.2 million roubles to 1.04 billion roubles. Moreover, the incomes of co-operative members were between two and three times higher than people employed by state enterprises.

In addition to these reforms Gorbachev increasingly restricted the power of Gosplan. Initially, he devolved Gosplan's powers to the governments of the republics. In 1990 Gosplan was finally abolished.

## Problems with the market

From 1987 to 1990 Gorbachev's economic reforms created a partial market. Gorbachev hoped that he could combine the best features of the market with the best features of planning and in so doing revive the economy. However, the new market could not function properly and created greater problems. Markets require prices that accurately reflect the true value of goods and services – that is to say, prices that reflect how much it costs the producer to make the goods and services. However, the Communist Government subsidised prices – allowing consumers to buy goods at a price well below the market rate.

Initially, the new co-operatives could sell goods at a price of their choosing. However, free market prices were higher than state-subsidised prices, and therefore the free market goods were unpopular. The government responded by imposing low prices on the co-operatives. This 'price capping' made production uneconomic and therefore caused problems for the new co-operatives.

## Economic chaos and political problems

Partial market reform created economic chaos. The reforms undermined the central planning system, while at the same time failing to create an effective market alternative. As a result, there was no effective way of distributing goods, and shortages of essential goods increased. For example, during 1990 there were severe food shortages. Although Soviet farms had produced 218 million tons of grain, there was no longer an effective distribution system. The state distribution systems had been abolished and the market was still developing, therefore there were food shortages across the Soviet Union.

What is more, Gorbachev's economic reforms had been a failure. Figures for the Twelfth Five-Year Plan demonstrated the failure of the new policies. Government figures showed that between 1986 and 1990 GDP had shrunk by four per cent, although the official figures are likely to underestimate the drop. This was the worst economic performance in Soviet history.

In April, Gorbachev finally cut government subsidies for basic products, allowing prices to rise. He hoped that the cut in subsidies would reduce government spending and allow the economy to stabilise. Prices increased rapidly (see Table 1).

**Table 1: Price of goods in January 1990 and April 1990.**

| | Price in January 1990 (roubles) | Price in April 1990 (roubles) |
|---|---|---|
| Beef (kilo) | 2.00 | 7.00 |
| Pork (kilo) | 1.90 | 5.30 |
| Butter (kilo) | 3.50 | 8.80 |
| Rye bread (loaf) | 0.12 | 0.48 |
| Cotton cloth (metre) | 1.12 | 3.00 |

The economic chaos had political consequences. Price rises led to widespread dissatisfaction with the Communist Government:

- Gorbachev's **approval rating** dropped from 52 per cent in December 1989 to 21 per cent in November 1990.
- The number of strikes increased. In 1990 only 260 enterprises were affected by strikes; in 1991 that figure had risen to 1755.

As faith in the Communist Government declined there was a rise in support for nationalist movements demanding the break-up of the Soviet Union (see page 172).

## 3 Transition to a market economy

As a result of this chaos, and due to his growing conviction that market economies were superior to planned economies, Gorbachev accepted the need to abolish the centrally planned system and introduce a full market economy. Nonetheless, achieving this would be difficult, and Gorbachev was faced with increasing opposition from **hardliners** within the Communist Party (see page 161).

### The 500 Day Program

In order to minimise the economic problems that were expected during the transition to a market economy, Gorbachev and Boris Yeltsin commissioned two Soviet economists, Stanislav Shatalin and Grigorri Iavlinskii, to devise a plan for the economic transition. The result was the '500 Day Programme', published in August 1990. Shatalin and Iavlinskii proposed widespread privatisation and complete marketisation in less than two years.

Gorbachev initially supported the proposals, but under pressure from senior hardline communists he backed down. He remained committed to an economic transformation, but was persuaded that it should happen at a slower pace.

Ultimately, radical reform continued during 1991. However, the government did not adopt an overall plan, largely because of Gorbachev's refusal to act decisively.

### Reform and collapse, 1991

In January 1991, the Supreme Soviet introduced private property as an important step towards a free market economy. As a result, the Soviet people could own land and factories in a way that had been impossible since the 1920s. In April, a law was passed to allow citizens to trade **stocks and shares**. Again, this reform was designed to revitalise the economy through the introduction of market forces.

However, the economy continued to decline. Oil production fell by 9 per cent, while steel and tractor production both fell by 12 per cent. An official government report stated that the Soviet economy was moving beyond crisis to catastrophe.

By the summer of 1991, the Soviet Government and the republican governments were effectively bankrupt. Neither had the economic power to govern. Consequently, although Yeltsin announced a programme of full marketisation in October 1991, it was difficult to implement.

### Note it down

The transition to the market economy posed a series of problems for Gorbachev's government.

- Skim read the section, looking at the sub-headings and the key words. Make a list of the key aspects of the transition. Use these as main headings on a spider diagram.
- Read the section and make notes on the different aspects of:
  - the problems facing the Soviet economy
  - the solutions that were proposed
  - the policies that were introduced
  - the impact of these policies.
- As you read the section, you can add other headings to your diagram if you missed anything while skimming the text.

# Extended reading: Interpretation

**Historian Martin McCauley considers the Soviet economy and the impact of economic problems on the fall of the Soviet Union.**

Since the mid-1920s the Soviet economy was geared for war. The stupendous achievement in defeating Hitler's Army in 1941–45 strengthened what became known as the military-industrial complex. The onset of the Cold War in 1947 led to the conviction that only military might could save the country from an American attack. But as Lenin had pointed out the race between capitalism and Communism would be won by the system which achieved the higher labour productivity per worker.

By the mid-1970s Soviet leaders were aware of three major economic problems. The first was how to increase the supply of consumer goods in line with the aspirations of the population.

The second major problem was the need to accelerate technological development. The most advanced sectors were the military and the nuclear industry but, the country neglected electronics, lasers and other high tech sectors. It did not invest in computers to the extent the Americans did. It was slow to react to the computer revolution.

The third problem was low labour productivity, lack of discipline, drunkenness, theft and general inefficiency of the civilian economy.

Mikhail Gorbachev was aware of these problems when he became Party leader in March 1985. He regarded the number one problem to be the raising of living standards. His first initiative was called *uskorenie* or acceleration. This aimed at a rapid expansion of the machine building industry. This would permit more machinery to be used to produce consumer goods. As Gorbachev had a limited grasp of economics he left the problem of where the extra investment was to come from to the Ministry of Finance. Gosplan opposed the extra investment in machinery. It preferred more money for consumer goods production. It was overruled and this set the pattern for the Gorbachev era. He rarely saw eye to eye with Gosplan. National economic performance in 1985 was inflated to demonstrate that growth was greater than in 1984 under his predecessor.

In reality, the results of *uskorenie* were disappointing so a new policy, called *perestroika* or restructuring, was announced. Gorbachev toured the country and was received with great enthusiasm. The future is bright – the future is *perestroika* – was the message. Unfortunately when asked in factories what exactly *perestroika* meant, he was at a loss to define it succinctly. For those who favoured market-oriented solutions it did not touch on the most important topic – price reform.

This led to an even more radical reform, the Law on the State Enterprise of 1987. It was probably the most destructive of all the economic reforms. Enterprises were to go over to self-financing. This was putting the cart before the horse. The first step should have been price reform.

The first move to a market economy was the law on co-operatives and the law on leasing in 1988. The former permitted the setting up of co-ops by individuals and also

## Activity

Having read the essay on pages 152–153 answer the following questions.

### Comprehension

1 What does McCauley mean by the following phrases:
- 'military-industrial complex'
- 'the Party apparatus'
- 'Gorbachev removed the ideological and political pillars on which the Soviet Union was built'?

### Evidence

2 Make a list of the examples of Gorbachev's successes and failures in McCauley's essay.

### Interpretation

3 Identify the passage in which McCauley explains why, in his view, the Soviet Union collapsed.

4 Summarise McCauley's interpretation in 25 words or less.

### Evaluation

5 Using your own knowledge, write a paragraph explaining how far you agree with McCauley's interpretation of the fall of the Soviet Union.

companies. The law on leasing allowed workers to lease part of their own enterprises, set up their own co-ops and sell their own goods. The advantage was that prices were not controlled by the state so a market price could be charged. This led to consumers complaining about high prices and profiteering. Co-op tea shops were used to get around the vodka ban which Gorbachev had introduced to deal with drunkenness. The teapots contained vodka not tea! This reform left a large hole in state revenues as sales of alcohol had brought in the most revenue. Money was simply printed to fill the shortfall.

Gorbachev concluded that the main reason for the failure of *perestroika* was the opposition of the Party apparatus. *Glasnost* was to shake up the apparatus from below. Citizens could vent their anger about the deteriorating situation on the local Party bigwigs.

Gorbachev, in 1988, took the momentous decision to remove the Party apparatus from the industrial economy. The net result was that by the end of 1989 the Party and government had lost control. The USSR Supreme Soviet, the parliament, convened in 1989, passed a raft of economic legislation but had no way of forcing implementation.

The most dramatic move to the market economy was the 500 day programme in 1990. However, it was too radical for Gorbachev but Boris Yeltsin, in October 1990, declared it would be implemented in the Russian Federation. Hitherto there had been some co-operation between Gorbachev and Yeltsin on reform. Now it was open warfare between the Soviet Union, headed by Gorbachev, and the Russian Federation, led by Yeltsin. Politics took over and the economy headed for collapse. The other republics of the Soviet Union followed suit and claimed sovereignty. They declared that only those Soviet laws which benefited them would be implemented on their territory.

The astonishing conclusion is that Gorbachev did not understand how the Soviet planned economy functioned. His advisers were over confident and their recipes for growth often had the opposite effect. Moving from a command to a market economy was something which had previously never been considered. Gorbachev was perplexed by the failure of the reforms. There was a belief that a reform borrowed from a market economy – for example, enterprise self-financing – could be grafted on to a command economy and the result would be the best of both worlds, socialist and capitalist. A magic mix of the best of capitalist and socialist policies would work miracles. However, monetary (the emission of money and credit) and fiscal (taxation) policy was loose and inevitably led to high inflation. Hence financial reforms from the centre in 1990 and 1991 had little effect.

China and Vietnam have demonstrated that it is possible to move from a command to a market economy without undermining the power of the Communist Party. Hence the reasons for the failure of economic reform are political. Gorbachev removed the ideological and political pillars on which the Soviet Union was built. As a result the whole edifice collapsed.

**Martin McCauley is a historian who specialises in the Soviet Union, Eastern Europe and China. He studied at the Universities of Westminster, London, Paris (Sorbonne) and Perugia (Italy), The Teachers' University (Beijing) and the Timiryazev Agricultural Academy (Moscow). He taught at the School of Slavonic and East European Studies, University College, London, for over 30 years. Among his many publications are *The Rise and Fall of the Soviet Union*; *Gorbachev*; *Stalin and Stalinism*; *The Origins of the Cold War 1941–49*; and *Russia, America and the Cold War 1949–91*. He is at present working on a book entitled *Communism: The Whole Story*.**

## Work together

Having completed the activity, swap your notes with a partner. Consider the following questions:

1. Did you both spot the same evidence in McCauley's essay?
2. Has your partner missed anything?
3. Did you agree on which passage contained the interpretation? If not, who was right?
4. What was good about your partner's summary of McCauley's interpretation?
5. Can you learn anything about McCauley's interpretation from your partner's summary?
6. How far did you both agree with McCauley's interpretation?

Use these questions to feed back to each other and improve your analysis of the debate.

## Conclusion

Long-term weaknesses in the Soviet economy clearly undermined the Soviet Union. However, it is important to remember that in 1985 there was no economic crisis, and no indication that the Soviet Union was in danger of imminent collapse. Gorbachev's reforms created an economic crisis, which rapidly turned into a catastrophe. In so doing, he undermined the authority of the Communist Government and the government's economic power.

However, there are clearly other factors which explain the fall of the Soviet Union. Gorbachev's political reforms allowed Soviet citizens to express their dissatisfaction and to organise against the government (see page 162). Equally, Gorbachev and Yeltsin played key roles in the crucial period of crisis (see page 184).

### Historical interpretation Gorbachev's reforms

Historians disagree over the reasons for the failure of Gorbachev's economic reforms. Some historians, such as Archie Brown, believe that effective reform was possible but that Gorbachev's policies were poorly conceived. Other historians, such as Stephen Richards Graubard, argue that reform was inherently impossible. For Graubard, Gorbachev should either have stuck with the command economy or abandoned it and introduced a market economy. On this account, reform, the attempt to make the command economy work better, was impossible.

**Extract 3** From Archie Brown, *The Gorbachev Era*, published in 2006.

There is no doubt that the attempt to reform the Soviet economy ended in failure. Part of the reason for that was the tension between reforming an existing system to make it work better and replacing that system by one which had a quite different logic. In the early years of *perestroika* the first aim was being pursued - and with only very limited success. By 1990-1, while there was not a consensus, there was at least a broad body of support among specialists for the idea that the command economy had to give way to a market economy. It was clearer to Gorbachev than to Yeltsin that this would mean tens of millions of citizens becoming worse off for some years to come. Freeing prices would improve the supply of goods and services but would also raise those prices to a level the majority could ill afford.

Much of the economic legislation of the *perestroika* years - not least the Law on Co-operatives - had helped to pave the way for marketisation, but the Soviet economy remained in limbo at the end of the Gorbachev era. It was no longer a functioning command economy but not yet a market system.

**Extract 4** From Stephen Richards Graubard, *Exit from Communism*, published in 1998.

Gorbachev's major failure was economic reform. Keenly aware of the need for economic reform he never realised that no middle way existed. As a result, his economic policies tended to fall between two stools, leading to a completely inconsistent economic system, utterly out of balance. The Soviet economic system became far worse than it would have been under an ordinary command economy, or a bold step forward to complete market economy. Initially, Gorbachev was impeded by Communist conservatives, but from 1990 on he showed that he was unprepared to go very far himself. At the very end he insisted on slow change. He failed to grasp that disintegration and chaos had already been reached and that speedy action was the requirement of the day.

Having read Extracts 3 and 4:

1. Write a paragraph stating how far you agree, or disagree with Extract 3. Your paragraphs should contain:
   - a summary of the extract's argument
   - evidence that either supports or challenges that argument
   - a concluding sentence in which you analyse the extent to which the argument of the extract is valid.
2. Swap your paragraph with a partner, read them and then write two suggestions about how the paragraph could be improved.
3. Finally, repeat the process for Extract 4. Make sure you incorporate the advice you have received about how to improve your paragraph.

# Essay technique: Identifying the interpretation

Section C of the exam paper is different to Section A and B (see exam brief page vi). Unlike Section A and B it contains two extracts from the work of historians. Significantly, Section C tests different skills.

In essence, Section C tests your ability to analyse different historical interpretations. Therefore you must focus on the interpretations of the extracts.

## Interpretations and evidence

The extracts will contain a mixture of interpretations and evidence. The mark scheme rewards essays that focus on the *interpretations* offered by the extracts more highly than essays that focus on the *information* or *evidence* mentioned in the extracts. Therefore it is important to identify the interpretations.

- Interpretations are a specific kind of argument. Like all arguments, they tend to make general claims such as 'The Soviet Union was doomed to fail because of the fundamental flaws in its economic system.'
- Information or evidence tends to comprise of specific details. For example: 'Economic reforms failed to stimulate economic growth in key industries.'

Imagine you are answering the following question using Extract 1 below and Extract 2 on page 156:

**In the light of differing interpretations, how convincing do you find the view that the USSR collapsed because of 'policy errors or mistakes within Gorbachev's reforms' (Extract 1, lines 4–5).**

**To explain your answer, analyse and evaluate the material in both extracts using your own knowledge of the issues.**

**Extract 1** Robert Strayer, *Why Did the Soviet Union Collapse?: Understanding Historical Change*, published in 1998.

Counter-argument — To some observers, the Soviet system was unreformable and too far gone to respond to any treatment at all. Therefore, the Gorbachev program was doomed from the start. Other historians have pointed to various policy errors or mistakes within Gorbachev's reforms. On the economic front, some have criticised Gorbachev for neglecting agriculture. Others noted that his policy of raising wages while ignoring the importance of a balanced budget allowed inflation to get out of control thus undermining his reforms. Might a more sequenced approach of delaying political change until a market economy took hold have prevented the Soviet Union's disintegration?

Argument — (from "Other historians have pointed to various policy errors or mistakes within Gorbachev's reforms.")

Evidence that supports the argument — (from "On the economic front, some have criticised Gorbachev…" to "…thus undermining his reforms.")

Extract 1 contains two interpretations: a counter-argument (see page 107), and an argument (see page 93–4). Additionally, Extract 1 contains information and evidence that supports the argument.

While writing your essay it is important that you evaluate both the interpretations. You should evaluate the interpretations by introducing your own knowledge (see page 182–183).

**Extract 2** Anders Aslund, *Russia's Capitalist Revolution: Why Market Reform Succeeded and Democracy Failed*, published in 2007.

> The sudden burst of activity in the Soviet Union over 1985–87 broke two decades of stagnation. From the outset, Gorbachev's top priority was to revitalise the economy. His team tried all kinds of measures, but economic growth did not improve. Shortages became worse because tax revenues declined with the anti-alcohol campaign, and a larger share of GDP was diverted to inefficient investment. *Perestroika* fell miserably short of its main goal to boost economic growth.
>
> *Glasnost* took off later than the other policies and much more gradually. It came into its own in 1987 and freedom of speech was attained in 1989. Gorbachev unleashed *glasnost* in order to undermine hard-line communist opposition to his reforms. But *glasnost* turned into an unguided missile. It condemned not only the hard-liners but the very foundations of the Soviet state, especially its ruthless policies against various nationalities. Rather than strengthen the Soviet state, *glasnost* eventually suggested that the soviet government was no longer sustainable.

## Activity: Identifying the interpretation

Imagine you are answering the following question using Extract 1 (page 155) and Extract 2 on this page:

**In the light of differing interpretations, how convincing do you find the view that the USSR collapsed because 'Rather than strengthen the Soviet state, *glasnost* eventually suggested that the soviet government was no longer sustainable.' (Extract 2, lines 19–21).**

**To explain your answer, analyse and evaluate the material in both extracts using your own knowledge of the issues.**

1 Identify the following aspects of Extract 2:
- the argument
- information or evidence that supports the argument.

2 Having identified these extracts, share your answer with a partner. Consider the following questions:
- Did your partner correctly identify the interpretation?
- Did you both spot the same information in the extracts?
- Has your partner missed anything?
- Did you miss anything that you should note down?
- What can you learn from your partner's approach?

Use these questions to feed back to each other and improve your analysis of the extracts.

## Activity: AS-Style question

**Historians have different views about the reasons for the fall of the Soviet Union.**

**Analyse and evaluate the extracts and use your knowledge of the issues to explain your answer to the following question:**

**How far do you agree with the view that Gorbachev's economic reforms led to the collapse of the Soviet Union?**

# 2 Gorbachev's political reforms

## Overview

The collapse of the Soviet Union was due, at least in part, to the nature of Soviet politics and Gorbachev's political reforms. Gorbachev's political reforms started slowly. Nonetheless, his initial reforms led to pressure for greater freedom. By 1988 Gorbachev was willing to embrace more radical measures, including competitive elections. The elections of 1989 and 1990 transformed the Soviet system. These changes were profound. His policies allowed greater freedom than Russia had ever known. He ended some of the key features of communist rule, introducing competitive elections which ended the dominance of the Party leadership. However, by 1990 Gorbachev had lost control of the process of reform, and soon after he lost control of the Soviet Government.

This chapter considers:

1 The problems of political reform
2 Gorbachev's early political reforms, 1985–86
3 *Glasnost*, 1986–88
4 Democratisation, 1988–90
5 Constitutional reform.

## 1 The problems of political reform

### Note it down

Using a note-taking style of your choice, note down the key problems with the Soviet political system. Remember, your notes need to record:

- the basis of the Communist Government's authority
- the economic data that illustrates the extent of the weaknesses
- the reasons why reform posed a threat to the Soviet Union
- Gorbachev's initial objectives for reform.

The fundamental nature of Soviet politics had been established by Lenin and Stalin. Between them they had created a political system which included:

- a **centralised** party with control over the state across the whole of the Soviet Union
- regional parties in each of the republics that obeyed the Communist Party of the Soviet Union
- a disciplined party that obeyed the direction of the **Politburo**.

The Communist Party had become the government of the Soviet Union, controlling the economy, the army, the police and the media.

Crucially, any policy which weakened the authority or discipline of the Party risked weakening the Soviet Union, as the Communist Party held the Union together.

However, the communists remained ideologically committed to creating a genuine democracy based on the will of all of the working people in the Soviet Union. This tension between the reality of Soviet government and Communist ideals created discussion in the Party which periodically led to pressure for reform.

Over time, the tension between the official goals of the Party and the reality of life in the Soviet Union led to widespread cynicism. In essence, the Soviet people became increasingly aware of the corruption of Party officials. Nonetheless, in general terms, the Soviet people tolerated the government as the Party was improving living standards year on year. The cynicism of the people troubled **idealists** in the Party, who hoped that reform of the Party and some kind of democratisation would inspire the new generation to embrace Communism and finish the journey started by Lenin in 1917.

Nonetheless, reform was dangerous. True democracy could lead to the fall of Communism. Indeed, Khrushchev's reforms had threatened Soviet control of Hungary and Poland (see page 342). Therefore, under Brezhnev there was little meaningful reform and no attempts to democratise the government. Andropov essentially continued Brezhnev's policy of supressing political dissent. Nonetheless, Andropov allowed greater freedom within the Party leadership to discuss the Soviet Union's social and economic problems. His desire to deal with long-term problems such as economic decline and corruption meant that he promoted Communists who were prepared to question the system to senior positions. Indeed, Gorbachev owed his position on the Politburo to Andropov.

## Historical interpretations: Was the Soviet Union's fall inevitable?

Long-term economic weaknesses and the fundamental contradiction between the political goals of Communism and the political reality of the Soviet system have led some historians to argue that the fall of the Soviet Union was inevitable. In Extract 1, Jeremy Smith sets out an argument that the Soviet Union was bound to fall at some point. Archie Brown, in Extract 2, takes a different approach, arguing that in 1985 the Soviet Union was still strong enough to keep going into the twenty-first century.

**Extract 1** From Jeremy Smith, *The Fall of Soviet Communism, 1986–1991*, published in 2005.

Many historians adopt the long-term view that the Soviet system, while successful in transforming the former Russian Empire into a powerful industrial state, contained within itself the seeds of its own destruction. Systemic weaknesses, a redundant ideology, internal contradictions, and the absence of the flexibility required to adapt to changing environments and challenges meant that, even if its collapse need not have occurred exactly when it did, it was ultimately inevitable.

**Extract 2** From Archie Brown, *The Gorbachev Era*, published in 2006.

While there had been an accumulation of problems over several decades, including a secular decline in the rate of economic growth and rising rates of infant mortality and alcoholism, and though the gulf between Soviet rhetoric and reality had led to an increase in popular cynicism, there was no strong pressure from below for change in 1985. The dissident movement had been crushed and the atmosphere was primarily one of political apathy and fatalism. In Brezhnev's time there had been a lot of talk about the 'scientific and technological revolution', but technologically the Soviet Union was lagging far behind the advanced Western countries and not faring well in comparison with the newly industrialising countries of Asia. Moreover, the war in Afghanistan was proving costly and becoming increasingly unpopular. Yet all the mechanisms of political control were firmly in place and it is highly likely that the system – and, accordingly, the Soviet state – could have survived into the twenty-first century had not radical reform, or 'revolution from above', shaken its foundations. Although Gorbachev, with some justification, spoke of the presence of 'pre-crisis phenomena' in the Soviet Union he inherited, it was not so much a case of crisis forcing radical reform as of radical reform generating crisis.

Having read Extracts 1 and 2:

**1** Write a paragraph stating how far you agree, or disagree with Extract 1.

Your paragraphs should contain:

- a summary of the extract's argument
- evidence that either supports or challenges that argument
- a concluding sentence in which you analyse the extent to which the argument of the extract is valid.

**2** Swap your paragraph with a partner, read it and then write two suggestions about how the paragraph could be improved.

**3** Finally, repeat the process for Extract 2. Make sure you incorporate the advice you have received about how to improve your paragraph.

## Gorbachev's objectives

At the time of his appointment as General Secretary, Gorbachev's key political aim was to revitalise the Soviet Union. He wanted to end the stagnation of the Brezhnev period, including the corruption of senior members of the Party. He also wanted to end the cynicism and apathy of the Soviet people. He did not have a clear strategy for achieving these goals, but he consistently argued that the Soviet Union needed to return to the model that Lenin had outlined in 1917, with people playing a genuine role in politics through participation in local **soviets**.

Initially, Gorbachev believed that it was possible to reform the Soviet system and retain communist control. His original plans for reform were quite limited. He wanted to:

- open up debate within the Party
- allow intellectuals more **freedom of expression**
- allow the public to have more access to information.

However, Gorbachev's reforms had consequences that he did not foresee. Reform led to greater pressure for change.

## 2 Gorbachev's early political reforms, 1985–86

Gorbachev's appointment as General Secretary was the beginning of a shift of power from one generation to the next. Gorbachev was 20 years younger than his predecessor Chernenko. Indeed, whereas Chernenko, Andropov and Brezhnev had all been born before the revolution, Gorbachev was born during Stalin's reign.

Gorbachev's first priority as General Secretary was to replace the senior officials who had been close to Brezhnev. This was part of Gorbachev's desire to end the stagnation of the Brezhnev era, but also part of his desire to heighten his own authority through patronage. He appointed young communists, who supported reform, to senior positions. In his first year Gorbachev focused on economic reform (see pages 149–151). However, as economic reform failed Gorbachev became convinced that political reform was an essential part of reviving the economy. He argued that traditionalist Communist officials were standing in the way of his reforms because of their faith in old-fashioned economic methods. Gorbachev also argued that the Soviet economy was too highly centralised and that accurate information, which was essential for effective planning, was almost impossible to obtain due to official manipulation of economic data. His solution to these problems was democratisation and openness.

- He hoped that democratisation would limit the power of traditionalists and therefore speed up economic reform. He also hoped that democratisation would end strict centralisation by passing some power to the people.
- Gorbachev hoped openness would help economic recovery by ending the distortion of economic information.

### Gorbachev's 'reformers'

Gorbachev appointed a new generation of ministers who favoured reform. For example, he made Nikolai Ryzhkov Prime Minister, he appointed Viktor Chebrikov head of the KGB, and made Egor Ligachev a member of the Politburo and at the end of 1985 he made Boris Yeltsin head of the Communist Party of Moscow. At the same time Andrei Gromyko and Viktor Grishin, who had worked closely with Brezhnev, were removed from their posts.

These changes were significant because they gave power to communists who backed reform. However, many of Gorbachev's new appointees, like Ryzhkov, backed an extension of Andropov's reforms rather than anything more radical. Indeed, during 1985 and 1986, Gorbachev's policies looked much like a continuation of Andropov's initiatives.

## 3 *Glasnost*, 1986–88

Gorbachev spoke repeatedly about the need for the government to admit the truth. Gorbachev first spoke of the need for openness in December 1974. Indeed, from 1983 the term was used by supporters of Andropov who wanted to expose corruption within the Party. Initially, *glasnost* was primarily a commitment to being open about the state of the Soviet economy.

*Glasnost* became an increasingly important initiative from 1986. This was due, in part, to opposition to Gorbachev within the Communist Party. Hardline communists opposed Gorbachev's reforms. Therefore Gorbachev looked for support from outside the Party. He invited writers and intellectuals to criticise hardliners and support his reforms. Gorbachev believed that intellectuals, writers and artists were natural allies against Party hardliners.

### Note it down

Using a note-taking style of your choice, note down:

**1** the reasons for and nature of Gorbachev's early political reforms.

Make sure you note down:

- the key words that Gorbachev introduced to Soviet politics
- the changing meaning of Gorbachev's new words.

**2** note down the following aspects of *glasnost*:

- how Gorbachev understood *glasnost* between 1983 and 1985 and why he wanted to introduce *glasnost* in this period
- the political impact of the Twenty-Seventh Party Congress
- the impact on the Communist Party of Yakovlev's liberalisation of the press
- the political impact of the Nineteenth Party Conference
- the political significance of the Chernobyl disaster.

Don't forget to note down the key details: the names of key individuals and the dates of key events.

## The Twenty-Seventh Party Congress

The Twenty-Seventh Party Congress held in February and March 1986 set out a new programme for the Communist Party. This was the first time that the Party had adopted a new set of priorities since 1961. Gorbachev's new programme committed the Party to the 'systematic and all round improvement of **socialism**', including 'genuine democracy – power exercised for the people and by the people'. Gorbachev linked democratisation to *glasnost*. However, there were few signs of genuine openness at the Party Congress. Nor did Gorbachev set out detailed proposals for achieving the Party's new goals. Nonetheless, the adoption of a new programme was a symbol that Gorbachev wanted to break with the past.

## Liberalisation of the media

In order to help create an alliance between communists, reformers and Russian intellectuals Gorbachev allowed much greater freedom of expression in the Soviet media. He hoped that greater freedom would allow intellectuals to criticise the Party and develop new ideas.

Following the 1986 Congress, Gorbachev gave Aleksandr Yakovlev responsibility for the Soviet media. Yakovlev appointed new radical editors to head the *Moskovskie Novosti* (Moscow News) and *Ogonek,* a Communist Party newspaper. As a result, the Soviet media was liberalised. Newspapers began to publish accounts of the scale of Stalin's atrocities, as well as stories that admitted problems in the Soviet economy. Yakovlev permitted the publication of previously banned books, plays and films by anti-communist intellectuals. An important early example was the release of the film *Repentance.* The film, made in 1984 but only released two years later, was highly critical of Stalin's terror. Gorbachev also authorised the release of dissidents from prison. Indeed, in December 1986 he invited Andrei Sakharov to Moscow from exile in Gorky to support political reform (see page 89). This was a clear signal that Gorbachev wanted to work with intellectuals outside of the Communist Party to promote reform.

## The extension of *glasnost*

During 1987 and 1988 *glasnost* was extended. Initially, the media had criticised Stalin. These criticisms were not new. Khrushchev had initiated criticism of Stalin in 1957. However, in 1988 Aleksandr Tsipko, supported by Yakovlev, went much further, publicly criticising Marx and Lenin. Tsipko's criticisms attacked the foundations of Soviet Communism. Additionally, from 1988 citizens were permitted to listen to foreign radio broadcasts and read foreign newspapers.

The Nineteenth Party Conference of June 1988 took openness to a new level. Senior Party officials admitted the scale of the problems facing the Soviet Union, including the inadequacies in healthcare and education and the poverty of the rural populations. This was a huge contrast to traditional high profile meetings which claimed the Communist Party was improving all areas of life. Moreover, the scale of the problems that the Party now admitted shook the public's faith in communist rule.

## The consequences of *glasnost*

Gorbachev had hoped that *glasnost* would benefit him at the expense of his opponents. Certainly, *glasnost* allowed Gorbachev, communist radicals and Soviet intellectuals to criticise moderates in the Communist Party and aspects of communist government that were not working. However, Gorbachev did not escape criticism. He was accused of reforming too slowly or of reforming too little. Even more concerning were criticisms of the whole Soviet system. Revelations about Stalin's terror led some to question the foundations of the communist system. Moreover, groups in the Soviet republics began to demand not merely reform, but independence from the Soviet Union. Fundamentally, *glasnost* destabilised party rule because it permitted profound criticism of the Party that Gorbachev had not anticipated.

### Chernobyl

The explosion at the Chernobyl nuclear reactor was an early test of Gorbachev's commitment to *glasnost*. The accident, the largest nuclear accident on record, occurred in April 1986. Initially, local officials attempted to cover up the scale of the catastrophe. Indeed, the disaster was not reported to the central government for two days. The Soviet media were slow to report the accident, and initial reports played down the seriousness of what had happened. Gorbachev did not speak in public about the accident for over two weeks.

Although the government eventually acknowledged the scale of the problems, it continued to conceal the real cause of the disaster. The final report blamed the people who operated the power station rather than acknowledging fundamental problems with the design of Soviet nuclear power stations.

Chernobyl became a symbol for the problems of the Soviet Union. The disaster was caused by some of the fundamental failings of the communist system: the reactor's design was flawed; the authorities hid the design flaws from the operators; the power plant was constructed cheaply; the problems were covered up; and when disaster struck officials refused to acknowledge the scale of the problem.

## Divisions in the Party

Many Communist officials refused to support Gorbachev's political and economic reforms. Hardliners believed that *glasnost* and *perestroika* would end the power of the Party and the privileges of Party members. In short, they feared reform would risk destroying the communist system.

By 1988, there were at least two **factions** in the Party:

- Moderates: Party members, such as Ligachev and Ryzhkov who had supported Andropov, accepted the need to tackle corruption and promote limited economic reform. However, they believed that Gorbachev's reforms were undermining the power of the Party.
- Radicals such as Yeltsin and Yakovlev believed that exposing the Party to criticism and giving greater power to the Soviet people were an essential part of revitalising Communism.

Gorbachev attempted to balance both wings of the Party, but in so doing he often alienated both radicals and reformers.

## Historical interpretations: Gorbachev and the Party

Historians disagree about Gorbachev's relationship with the Communist Party during the 1980s. George W. Breslauer, for example, argues that Gorbachev antagonised and alienated the Communist Party. David Lane and Cameron Ross, on the other hand, argue that Gorbachev tried to work with the Communist Party and only turned his back on the Party in 1989.

**Extract 3** From George W. Breslauer, *Gorbachev and Yeltsin as Leaders*, published in 2002.

Gorbachev was engaged in a relentless process of destruction of the Brezhnevite order. He was in effect stripping the *apparat* and the official classes of immunity from public, systemic criticism and thereby also emboldening the intelligentsia and the masses to believe that such forceful criticism could now be safely advanced in public.

Such public criticism also assisted Gorbachev in his efforts to maintain the initiative against the Brezhnevites and conservative forces within the Central Committee and Politburo. Puritans such as Ligachev and technocrats such as Prime Minister Ryzhkov found themselves increasingly disillusioned with Gorbachev. Their alienation from Gorbachev's evolving definitions of *perestroika* only deepened as the General Secretary permitted civil liberties to expand in the areas of religion, travel, emigration, speech and mass media. As the bounds of the permissible grew, so too did the boldness of journalists, academics, writers, artists and political activists. Increasingly, Gorbachev's unwillingness to draw and enforce limits alienated those members of the Central Committee who had always assumed that the alternative to order would be anarchy.

**Extract 4** From David Lane and Cameron Ross, *The Transition from Communism to Capitalism*, published in 1999.

Gorbachev was the last Russian communist leader who believed that he could reform state socialism from within, that he could reassert the role of the Communist Party. In the early years of his regime, he increased the numbers of top Party officials who were moved into government posts. This policy failed.

After September 1989, he revoked this policy and began to move power away from the Party to the new executive presidency. At this stage, he was pushed into a more radical reform. He sought to move authority to executive bodies under his newly created executive presidency. Again, in similar vein to Khrushchev, he tried to gain the support of the masses against the bureaucracy. In 1989, he was able to direct the new and more democratically elected congress and Supreme Soviet (where ministers could no longer be elected deputies) to act as a check on the Party bureaucracy.

1. Having read Extracts 3 and 4, write short answers to the following questions:
   a) What is meant by the following terms:
      - Extract 3: 'Brezhnevite, 'Puritans', 'technocrats', 'the bounds of the permissible'
      - Extract 4: 'executive presidency', 'a check on the Party bureaucracy'?
   b) How does Extract 3 characterise Gorbachev's relationship with the Party? How does it support its characterisation?
   c) How does Extract 4 characterise Gorbachev's relationship with the Party? How does it support its characterisation?
2. Having answered these questions, discuss them with a partner. How far do you agree? Where you disagree, how can you use the extracts and the information in this section to resolve your disagreements?

# 4 Democratisation, 1988–90

> **Note it down**
>
> Using a note-taking style of your choice, note down the following aspects of democratisation:
>
> - the nature of Gorbachev's reforms
> - the impact of the 1989 and 1990 elections
> - how far the reforms of 1988–90 weakened the Soviet Union
> - the nature of constitutional reform in 1990
> - how far constitutional reform strengthened the Soviet Union.
>
> Don't forget to note down the key details: the names of key individuals and the dates of key events.

Gorbachev had committed the Party to creating a 'genuine democracy' in 1986. The turning point, however, came at the 1988 Party Conference, where Gorbachev set out his proposals for 'socialist democracy'.

## Soviet power

The Nineteenth Party Conference of 1988 embraced radical democratic reform. In essence, Gorbachev introduced multi-candidate elections to the Supreme Soviet. From 1989 onwards, Soviet citizens had the right to vote in elections where there was a choice of Communist Party candidates. Independent candidates could also stand for election.

Since 1917 Russian citizens had elected local soviets. However, since the 1920s citizens had no choice of candidate. Rather, single candidates had been appointed by the Communist Party. In this way, the Communist Party had gained control over the elections and guaranteed their control over the soviets. Gorbachev changed this. Multi-candidate elections stripped the Communist Party of its power to appoint the candidates. Therefore there was a considerable shift of power from the Party's leadership to the Soviet people.

The 1988 reforms were only partial:

- In multi-candidate elections 1500 of the Congress of People's Deputies would be elected.
- The remaining 750 would be appointed by the Communist Party and other official organisations.
- Equally, multi-candidate elections did not allow citizens to vote for different political parties.

Nonetheless, the reforms allowed them to make a real choice between radicals, moderates and independents. Gorbachev hoped that the Soviet people would back radical candidates and in so doing provide a mandate for further reform.

The new Congress of People's Deputies would elect the Supreme Soviet. The Supreme Soviet was also reformed. Rather than meeting once a year, the Supreme Soviet was given the right to meet for two three-month sessions every year. Gorbachev appointed himself Chair of the Supreme Soviet.

The reforms meant that, for the first time since 1921, the Supreme Soviet was, at least partly, independent of the Party's leadership. Therefore the reforms significantly weakened the Party.

## Election, 1989

The March–April election of 1989 was an important step in reducing the power of the Communist Party. During the campaign candidates were forced to engage in public debate in order to win votes. As a result of the election, the communists won 80 per cent of the seats in the Congress of People's Deputies. Nonetheless, several high-ranking communists were defeated, including five members of the Central Committee. Radicals, on the other hand, did well. Yeltsin won with 89 per cent of the vote in Moscow. Soon after the election a group of newly elected deputies, including Yeltsin and Sakharov, formed the Inter-regional Deputies' Group (IRDG), which embraced a radical anti-communist agenda including the introduction of private property and greater **autonomy** for the republics. The creation of the IRDG was an important step towards democracy because it became an organised opposition group with an official position within the Soviet system.

> **Congresses and Conference**
>
> Traditionally, big changes of Communist Party policy were agreed at meetings that represented the whole of the Soviet Communist Party.
>
> - Party Congress: The Communist Party's most important meetings were the Congresses. These were semi-regular meetings which elected the Central Committee. There were 28 Party Congresses between 1900 and 1990.
> - Party Conference: Conferences were smaller meetings called to discuss specific issues. They could be held between Congresses. Eighteen Party Conferences were held before 1941. The Nineteenth Party Conference of 1988 was the last.

## The consequences of the election

The election weakened the position of the moderates, as Gorbachev had hoped. However, it also led to consequences that he did not intend:

- Nationalists who wanted to break up the Soviet Union used the election to campaign for independence. In Georgia, these campaigns resulted in violence (see page 74).
- Yeltsin emerged from the election as a popular figure and a rival to Gorbachev. Indeed, Yeltsin's desire to replace the Soviet Union with a loose confederation of truly independent states was extremely popular with nationalists across the Soviet Union, and therefore a threat to the Soviet Union.

## Republic elections, 1990

Anti-communist trends were also obvious in the March 1990 elections in the republics. In Moscow, for example, a group called Democratic Russia won 85 per cent of the seats. Similarly, in Leningrad the group Democratic Elections 90, another new anti-communist group, took 80 per cent of the seats.

Gorbachev had assumed that democratisation would strengthen the radicals within the Communist Party. However, the soviet elections weakened the whole of the Party, increasing the authority of anti-Party and nationalist groups. The consequences of democratisation, like the consequences of *glasnost*, were much more radical than Gorbachev had anticipated.

### Historical interpretations: The significance of the 1989 elections

Historians have interpreted the 1989 elections in different ways. Robert Service, for example, sees them as a turning point: the moment when Gorbachev decisively broke with the past and embraced revolutionary change. However, Neil Robinson sees them quite differently. For Robinson, the elections were designed to reinvigorate the Party, not to transform it. In this sense, they were a development in Gorbachev's original programme rather than a major change in direction.

**Extract 5** From Robert Service, *Comrades! A History of World Communism*, published in 2007.

In 1985, Gorbachev was aiming not to terminate the one-party state but to enhance its effectiveness. Supremely optimistic, he genuinely believed that reforms in Moscow would create an order superior to the best on offer from advanced capitalism.

By 1989, he was no longer seeking to adjust and revitalise the Soviet order: he wanted to transform it. He was turning many of the basic features of the Soviet Union into their opposites. He did this with ingenuity and audacity. The first great step in constitutional change was to scrap the pyramid of appointed soviets in favour of elected ones. In 1990 he gave scope for the formation of rival political parties by repealing article six of the Soviet Constitution which guaranteed the leading role of the Communists. There had been nothing like this since the early years of the Soviet state.

**Extract 6** From Neil Robinson, *Ideology and the Collapse of the Soviet System: A Critical History of* Soviet Ideological Discourse, published in 1995.

It was inconceivable to the leadership that the Party would suffer during the March 1989 elections. As far as Gorbachev was concerned the Party's vanguard role and its acceptance by the people was the same thing. The people would inevitably recognise the true nature of the Party as a politica leader. The elections were definitely not supposed to be about altering the Soviet political system in any way. During the election Gorbachev claimed that the elections and the Party's leadership role proved that there was no need for the development of multi-party politics.

**1** Having read Extracts 5 and 6 write a short answer to the following questions:

**a)** Why did Gorbachev initiate the 1989 elections according to Extracts 5 and 6?

**b)** What is Extract 6 referring to when it mentions 'the Party's vanguard role'?

Having answered these questions, swap your answers with a partner. How far do you agree? Whose answers analyse Extracts 5 and 6's claims about Gorbachev's motives most clearly? What can you learn from each other's answers?

## Constitutional reform

Democratisation had succeeded in weakening the Communist Party. However, it had not produced a strong government. This posed problems for Gorbachev who needed a strong central authority in order to push through his economic reforms and maintain order.

Democratisation had also raised questions about the role of the Party. Yeltsin demanded a new constitution that officially stripped the Communist Party of its leading role. Gorbachev too wanted a constitutional change that would give him new powers to deal with the Soviet Union's growing economic and political problems.

### The presidency

In March 1990 Gorbachev was appointed as President of the Soviet Union. In the short term this was a victory, but in the longer term the appointment created huge problems for Gorbachev.

Gorbachev created the presidency for a number of reasons. First, he wanted to increase his power. Democratisation had weakened his position. He had hoped that democratisation would give him a power base independent of the Party. However, while democratisation had given the Supreme Soviet new authority, Gorbachev was not able to control the new institution. Therefore he decided to set up a new position, President of the Soviet Union, which would be independent of the Party and the Supreme Soviet.

Standing for election as President was a gamble. Yeltsin's popularity had been increasing since the election of 1989, and therefore it was possible that Yeltsin, rather than Gorbachev, would win the election. Consequently, Gorbachev decided that the President would be appointed by the Congress of People's Deputies, where he had a majority of support. While this ensured Gorbachev's appointment as President, it meant that Gorbachev lacked democratic legitimacy, unlike his rivals who, like Yeltsin, had been elected to their positions.

Following his appointment Gorbachev was given emergency powers for 18 months in order to deal with the economic crisis and with growing unrest in the republics. On occasion, Gorbachev used his new powers to censor the press, or to use Soviet troops to restore order, particularly in the non-Russian republics. As a result, Gorbachev was criticised by radicals for abandoning reform and introducing a new form of dictatorship. Indeed, Eduard Shevardnadze, a key supporter of Gorbachev in the 1980s, resigned from the government in December 1990. He claimed that Gorbachev had abandoned the path to democracy.

## Conclusion: Gorbachev in 1990

Gorbachev hoped that *glasnost* and democratisation would help revitalise the Party and the economy. However, the reform process failed to achieve either of these goals and contributed to the dissolution of the Soviet Union. Greater openness destroyed the authority of the Party, while simultaneously allowing the anti-communist opposition to criticise the government. Democratisation weakened the Communist Party by bringing its democratic legitimacy into question.

By 1990, Gorbachev's reforms had destroyed his power base, and therefore he had increasing difficulty pushing through his reforms. Significantly, although Gorbachev stressed the importance of democracy, he refused to stand for election. Therefore he never gained a mandate for his power or his reforms.

Gorbachev consistently hoped that the Soviet people would back his reform agenda. However, Gorbachev misunderstood the mood of the people. Ultimately, democratisation undermined the Soviet Union because the Soviet people had lost faith in the Communist Party and the Union.

# Essay technique: Structuring your essay

In order to do well, your essay needs to focus on the interpretations of both extracts. Although there are only two extracts, your essay may have to deal with several interpretations, as each extract might contain an argument and a counter-argument.

Your essay structure should allow you to:

- analyse all of the interpretations effectively
- deal with the different interpretations in turn
- deal with the different interpretations in a logical sequence.

Therefore your essay should be structured around the key interpretations contained in the extracts.

## Analysing the extracts

In order to deal with the different interpretations in a logical sequence, you should look for the ways in which they support and challenge each other.

Imagine you are answering the following question. Guidance on how to plan an essay in answer to this question is given on page 166.

**In the light of differing interpretations, how convincing do you find the view that the USSR collapsed because 'Gorbachev lost control of his political reforms'? (Extract 1, line 1)**

**To explain your answer, analyse and evaluate the material in both extracts using your own knowledge of the issues.**

**Extract 1** From George E. Breslauer, *Gorbachev and Yeltsin as Leaders*, published in 2002, page 293.

Gorbachev lost control of his political reforms and proved unable or unwilling to prevent things that he clearly hoped to avoid: the total collapse of Communism in Eastern Europe, the collapse of the USSR, and the abolition of the Communist Party. Gorbachev made a great start, but was a poor finisher. This was especially the case in those realms such as economic and ethnic policy. However, marketising the economy and federalising the Union were the two most intractable problems facing the Soviet regime. Perhaps nothing Gorbachev did would have averted the collapse of the economy and the Soviet Union – given the forces he had unleashed 1987–1989.

**Extract 2** From Alec Nove, *An Economic History of the USSR 1917–1991*, published in 1993, page 415.

By the summer of 1991 the process of disintegration was proceeding at an accelerated pace. Gorbachev's government had now neither money nor authority.

Looking back, one is struck by a fundamental problem. To carry through the fundamental *perestroika* of the economy required strong government. In the first three years of Gorbachev's rule the mechanism for imposing a policy did exist. So Gorbachev set about dismantling the apparatus, changing its personnel, allowing criticism of the privileges, putting the whole system into question. *Glasnost* and *demokratizatsiya* undermined the power to implement policy. So by the time the reform programme was radicalized, the means to enforce it no longer existed. This, as well as doubts and hesitations about how far and how fast the reform process should go, plus the disastrous economic policy led to failure. Add the forces of nationalism and regionalism, and one had collapse.

## Planning your essay

In order to plan your essay to the question on page 165, you need to analyse the two extracts, that is to say, you need to break down the extracts into the different arguments, counter-arguments and pieces of evidence they contain.

While you are doing this:

- look for contrasting arguments between the extracts – these can be the major sections of your essay
- look for aspects of the extracts that support each other, or aspects of the extracts that contradict each other.

For example, your plan could look like this:

| Extract 1 | |
|---|---|
| **Argument** | Gorbachev lost control of the process of reform, and therefore was unable to stop the Soviet Union's collapse.<br>Nonetheless, the reforms <u>started</u> well. |
| **Counter-argument** | The problems facing the Soviet Union were so big that once reform started the collapse of the Soviet Union was inevitable. |

1(a) Main argument

3(a) Resolution: there were many factors involved.

3(b) Both extracts agree that Gorbachev's early reforms were more successful.

1(b) Supports the main argument.

2(a) Counter-argument

2(b) Evidence extends the counter-argument.

| Extract 2 | |
|---|---|
| **Argument** | The failure of Gorbachev's <u>final</u> reforms plus a series of other factors led to the break-up of the Soviet Union.<br>Gorbachev's reforms failed because:<br>• they required a strong government to force them through<br>• the reforms themselves weakened the government. |
| **Evidence** | By 1991 Gorbachev's government had no real power. |

### Activity: Question practice

Plan an answer to the following question using the extracts on page 168,

**In the light of differing interpretations, how convincing do you find the view that 'without Gorbachev the rapid disintegration of the Soviet Union would not have occurred'? (Extract 1, lines 10–11)**

**To explain your answer, analyse and evaluate the material in both extracts using your own knowledge of the issues.**

Follow the steps below:

1. Read both extracts.
2. Analyse them by looking for:
   - the main arguments
   - counter-arguments
   - evidence.
3. Look for contrasting arguments between the extracts.
4. Look for aspects of the extracts that support each other.

**TIPS:**

- Your first main paragraph should analyse the interpretation set out in the question.
- Your second paragraph should analyse the interpretation that contrasts most strongly with the interpretation in the main paragraph.
- Other paragraphs should deal with other arguments that the extracts put forward.
- Try to use both extracts in each paragraph.
- Overall, you can try to achieve an argument – counter-argument – resolution structure.

**Extract 1** From Vladislav M. Zubok, *A Failed Empire: The Soviet Union in the Cold War from Stalin to Gorbachev*, published in 2007, pages 330–31.

Gorbachev's idealistic rush to bring the Soviet Union into the 'common European home' made him the grave digger of Soviet power. After the Soviet 'empire' in Central Europe collapsed, the Soviet Union itself became vulnerable. Growing domestic anarchy, deepening economic crisis, rise of nationalist separatists and the weakening of the existing state structures demanded action. Yet Gorbachev, as before, continued to believe he could create a new democratic Soviet Union. His over confidence let him down. In 1987 he refused to get rid of Boris Yeltsin, who had already emerged as a major trouble maker. He also kept hard-liners in charge of the army, the KGB and the military-industrial complex.

Without Gorbachev the rapid disintegration of the Soviet Union would not have occurred. At each stage Gorbachev made choices that destabilised and weakened the USSR. The unwitting destruction of the Soviet Union made him one of the most controversial figures in Russian history.

**Extract 2** From Martin McCauley, *The Rise and Fall of the Soviet Union*, published in 2007, page 450.

Poor leadership provoked political and economic collapse. A major weakness was the Party-state system. The Party never possessed the technical expertise to run the country. Gorbachev's attempts at economic reform provoked a collapse. One of the reasons for this was that economic reform needs time to produce positive results. Gorbachev was impatient and introduced more radical reforms to accelerate growth. He eventually wrecked the system. He was quite unqualified for the role he had to play. He had little understanding of economics. This meant he was swayed by economists who promised him success. When it did not materialise, he listened to more radical economists. None of these economists had ever worked in a market economy, let alone industry. They were all theoreticians.

They assumed that the planned economy was infinitely malleable. Reformers could pick and choose policies and the economy would improve as a result. Hence they had no understanding of the consequences of any of their reforms.

## Work together

Having completed the activity on page 166. Consider the following questions with a partner:

1. Did you both identify the same arguments and counter-arguments in the extracts?
2. Did you agree about which aspect of the extracts was the biggest contrast to the main argument of Extract 1?
3. How was your partner's plan different to your own?
4. Did you miss anything that you should note down?
5. What can you learn from your partner's approach?
6. Which plan better answers the question and why?

Use these questions to feed back to each other and improve your analysis of the extracts.

## Activity: AS-Style question

**Historians have different views about the reasons for the fall of the Soviet Union.**

**Analyse and evaluate the extracts and use your knowledge of the issues to explain your answer to the following question.**

**How far do you agree with the view that Gorbachev's political reforms led to the collapse of the Soviet Union?**

## Extended reading: Interpretation

**Richard Sakwa, Professor of Russian and European Politics at the University of Kent, considers the extent to which Gorbachev's political reforms led to the downfall of the Soviet Union.**

Why did a system that had defeated the world's most powerful military force in 1941–45, launched the world's first artificial satellite (Sputnik 1) into earth's orbit on 4 October 1957, achieved the first human spaceflight by Yuri Gagarin on 12 April 1961, gained nuclear parity with the United States in the mid-1970s, and attained standards of living typical of a mid-level developed country, collapse so quickly and suddenly?

The fundamental reason is Mikhail Gorbachev's botched attempt to reform the political system. The Soviet Union could have continued if Gorbachev had not removed the keystone in the arch, the Communist Party of the Soviet Union (CPSU) and its 'apparatus' (*apparat*), the gigantic machinery of government.

Gorbachev came to power in March 1985 not to destroy the Soviet system of governance but to save it. However, as *perestroika* gathered pace his reforms became increasingly radical, and instead of simply reforming Communism, Gorbachev sought to create a new system that is conventionally called 'reform Communism', which he defined as 'humane, democratic socialism'. This ended up provoking numerous contradictions. The overall principal aim was to create a 'socialist legal state', with the separation of powers and a genuine parliament. However, the system ended up trapped between a disrupted old Soviet system of governance and a new system that could not be established. The steering mechanism of the state was destroyed but no effective alternative system was put in place, and by the end of 1991 the whole order collapsed.

Gorbachev launched a number of political reforms. First, *glasnost* (openness) allowed the problems facing the country to be discussed, but the criticisms soon turned into a condemnation of the whole system that had allowed Stalin's crimes and the continuing repression.

Second, the Nineteenth Party Conference marked a turning point in reform of the CPSU, and from now on the Party was intended to guide rather than to lead. In September 1988 power was shifted away from the party machinery to ordinary members, and from the party to the state. The process began whereby the party was stripped of its supervisory machinery. Six new commissions responsible for party affairs, ideology, social and economic policy, agriculture, international affairs and legal reform were created, and following their reorganisation in October the powers of the Central Committee Secretariat were effectively transferred to them. The vast apparatus of the Central Committee was drastically reduced.

Third, and no less important, in 1990 at the CPSU's Twenty-Eighth Party Congress the Politburo's status was radically changed, with 15 of its 25 members *ex officio* becoming the leaders of the Union republics. Gorbachev was freed

### Activity

Having read the essay, answer the following questions.

#### Comprehension

1 What does Sakwa mean by the following phrases:
- 'The Soviet Union could have continued if Gorbachev had not removed the keystone in the arch.'
- 'Gorbachev sought to create a new system that is conventionally called "reform Communism", which he defined as "humane, democratic socialism". This ended up provoking numerous contradictions.'
- 'Gorbachev increasingly found that when he pulled the levers of power, they were not attached to anything.'

#### Evidence

2 Make a list of the examples of Gorbachev's failures in Sakwa's essay.

#### Interpretation

3 Identify the passage in which Sakwa explains why, in his view, the Soviet Union collapsed.

4 Summarise Sakwa's interpretation in 25 words or less.

#### Evaluation

5 Using your own knowledge, write a paragraph explaining how far you agree with Sakwa's interpretation of the fall of the Soviet Union.

from Politburo control, and the once-mighty body was marginalised. However, a genuinely competitive party system was not introduced – the old system was destroyed but nothing effective was put in its place.

Fourth, In December 1988 the USSR Supreme Soviet created a three-chamber Congress of People's Deputies (CPD), two chambers of which (the Soviet of the Union and the Soviet of Nationalities) were to be chosen in multi-candidate elections, while the third (the Soviet of Representatives) was to be made up of delegates from social organisations, including 100 guaranteed seats for the Communist Party. The full Congress was to meet twice a year while current parliamentary business was to be conducted by a smaller Supreme Soviet drawn from the CPD. This was a strange and unworkable body.

Fifth, competitive elections were introduced. In the first instance these affected the lowest levels of governance, but gradually the whole system became focused on competitive elections. The March 1989 elections to the new Soviet parliament were dramatic, as many of the old CPSU leaders were defeated. In March 1990 the elections to the new Russian parliament were even more democratic, and indeed in many ways these were the freest and fairest elections that Russia has ever seen.

Sixth, at the first convocation of the Soviet CPD in May 1989 Gorbachev was elected chairman of its new 542-member Supreme Soviet, a post he assumed without winning an election at any stage. Power began to shift from the Party to what would in the end become a fully-fledged presidency. However, the fact that Gorbachev did not put himself forward in a national election meant that he lacked electoral legitimacy. This would ultimately cripple Gorbachev's ambitions, especially when it came to facing the leader of Russia, Boris Yeltsin, who won a national election in June 1990.

In short, Gorbachev's political reforms made the whole system of governance unworkable. A full-scale constitutional reform should have been planned and implemented, and instead endless small-scale reforms destabilised the whole system of governance. This may not have been so dangerous in a time of calm, but with economic and nationality problems getting worse, and conflict with Yeltsin over the fate of the country, Gorbachev increasingly found that when he pulled the levers of power, they were not attached to anything.

No single cause can be identified that precipitated the fall, but a 'perfect storm' swept the Soviet Union away. Gorbachev's inept attempt to reform the Communist Party and Soviet government is certainly one of the key factors.

**Richard Sakwa is Professor of Russian and European Politics at the University of Kent and an Associate Fellow of the Russia and Eurasia Programme at Chatham House. He has published widely on Soviet, Russian and post-communist affairs. Recent books include The Crisis of Russian Democracy: The Dual State, Factionalism, and the Medvedev Succession (Cambridge University Press, 2011), Putin and the Oligarch: The Khodorkovsky-Yukos Affair (I. B. Tauris, 2014) and Putin Redux: Power and Contradiction in Contemporary Russia (Routledge, 2014).**

## Work together

Having completed the activity on page 168, swap your notes with a partner. Consider the following questions:

1. Did you both spot the same evidence in Sakwa's essay?
2. Has your partner missed anything?
3. Did you agree on which passage contained the interpretation? If not, who was right?
4. List three things that were good about your partner's summary of Sakwa's interpretation?
5. Can you learn anything about Sakwa's interpretation from your partner's summary?
6. How far did you both agree with Sakwa's interpretation?

Use these questions to feed back to each other and improve your analysis of the extracts.

# 3 The impact of the nationalist resurgence

## Overview

The Soviet Union comprised 15 republics. In this sense, the Soviet Union was a supranational organisation, rather than a nation. Gorbachev assumed that the Union was genuinely popular, that Soviet citizens felt loyal to the Soviet Union rather than to their individual republics. However, faith in the Soviet Union declined following 1985. A combination of economic crisis and revelations about the crimes of the Communist Party weakened the authority of the Soviet Union. Simultaneously, Gorbachev's political reforms allowed opposition groups to flourish. By 1988 there were popular nationalist groups in many of the Soviet republics. These groups claimed to represent the national identity, traditions and freedom of the various nations that made up the Soviet Union. By 1990 many of these nationalist groups had beaten the Communist Party in elections. Therefore they had more authority than the Communist Party or Gorbachev, who remained an unelected leader. The popularity of nationalist groups, the growing weakness of the Soviet Government and Gorbachev's reluctance to use force to hold the Union together were key aspects of the fall of the Soviet Union.

This chapter considers:

1. The Union and the republics before 1985
2. The impact of Gorbachev's reforms
3. Growing nationalist unrest 1988–90
4. The coup, 1991.

## 1 The Union and the republics before 1985

In 1985 Gorbachev became leader of the Soviet Union, a collection of republics controlled by the Communist Party. According to the Soviet Constitution each of the republics, which included the Soviet Republics of Russia, the Ukraine, Uzbekistan, Kyrgyzstan, Georgia and Latvia, was an independent nation. Indeed, each republic had its own Supreme Soviet and its own governmental **institutions**. However, in reality, the Soviet Communist Party, which was based in Moscow, governed the entire Soviet Union, and the republics had little real independence. Indeed, the Soviet Government was dominated by **Slavs**, the vast majority of which were Russians. In this sense, the Soviet Union was similar to an empire, with the non-Russian republics as Russia's **colonies**.

From 1917 to 1985 nationalism in the republics was managed by a mixture of economic and political incentives and repression.

### Note it down

Make notes in the form of a spider diagram showing the different ways that nationalism was understood and expressed in the Soviet Union prior to 1985. Use arrows to show the way in which the different powers conflicted or complemented each other.

### Nationalism

Many historians have argued that nationalism was one of the main causes of the fall of the Soviet Union. However, the term 'nationalism' has a number of different meanings, therefore it is important to clarify what it can mean. There are at least two different types of nationalism, and some writers distinguish between 'liberal nationalism' and 'chauvinistic nationalism'. In essence liberal nationalism is the view that all nations should be self-governing, that is to say independent of the control of other nations. This is the kind of nationalism that emerged as a powerful force in the Soviet Union in the 1980s and lead to campaigns for the Republics to break away from the Soviet Union. Chauvinistic nationalism, by contrast, is the view that a specific nation has the right to rule or play a guiding role in the development of other countries or nations. This view was common in the Empires that played a dominant global role in the nineteenth and early twentieth century. Nationalism of this kind was common in Russia before the October Revolution and influenced Soviet nationalism, justifying Soviet control of the Republics.

### The Soviet Union

Some historians refer to the Soviet Union simply as 'the Union'. Indeed, the term Union can be used to draw attention to the disputed relationship between the central Soviet authorities and the Republics. After all, it was the Union, that is to say control from Russia, which nationalists in the Republics objected to and wanted to end.

## Soviet politics and nationalism

Political opportunities and political organisation were one way in which the Soviet Union kept nationalism at bay between 1917 and 1985. First, each republic had its own government system. Stalin's purges wiped out the previous generation of leaders in each republic, therefore from 1938 energetic and talented people could gain powerful and well-paid positions in each republic. Republican governments tended to be dominated by people of each republic, so the government of Georgia, for example, was dominated by Georgians. These people owed their power and wealth to the Soviet system and therefore they tended to be loyal.

While governments were dominated by local people other important organisations were not. The secret police and the army were always dominated by Russians and kept under strict central control. Therefore the Soviet Government was always ready to deal with unrest through terror or military action. Moreover, under Andropov's leadership, the KGB kept nationalists under constant surveillance. By 1975 around half of the people in prison or subjected to repressive psychiatry were nationalists.

## 'Soviet nationalism'

Although the Soviet Union was not a nation, the government tried to inspire loyalty to the Union through the creation of 'Soviet nationalism'. In the 1920s and again after Stalin's death, citizens of the republics were encouraged to put loyalty to the Union ahead of loyalty to their own nation. The government argued that traditional nationalism encouraged division and competition, whereas 'Soviet nationalism' was superior because it was based on ethnic equality and unity. Moreover, from 1945 all Soviet citizens were encouraged to take pride in the Soviet Union's superpower status and the fact that they were part of one of the most powerful nations on earth.

'Soviet nationalism' was, however, unpopular in many of the non-Russian republics because, in reality, it was based on Russian values and traditions. Therefore non-Russians were expected to renounce their existing customs, traditions and language and assimilate by adopting Russian customs. In that sense, 'Soviet nationalism' was based on the assumption of Russian superiority and the inferiority of other cultures.

Significantly, Gorbachev did not understand the weaknesses of Soviet nationalism. He seems to have genuinely believed that Soviet citizens had renounced their national identity and become a united 'Soviet people'. Therefore he assumed that the Soviet Union was more stable than it really was and the strength of nationalism in the republics took him by surprise.

## The Soviet economy and nationalism

Economic benefits were another way in which nationalism was controlled prior to 1985. From 1953 economic planners targeted investment at the poorer regions of the Soviet Union. As these areas tended to be in the non-Russian republics, they led to an improved standard of living for the majority of people in the 13 non-Russian republics. Under Brezhnev the 'social contract' (see page 117) was as important to managing the republics as it was to managing Russia. In return for obedience, lives were transformed as areas of Central Asia were urbanised and modernised. Educational investment was also higher in the non-Russian republics, and it was easier for non-Russians to get university places. Under Brezhnev the system developed into what historian Terry Martin has called an 'affirmative action empire'. Consequently, non-Russians who made the most of the opportunities could get good jobs and improve their standard of living. Significantly, these benefits could only continue while the economy continued to grow. Economic decline in the 1980s threatened to reduce the standard of living and opportunities for people in the republics and therefore undermine the Union.

## Nationalism under Brezhnev

Under Brezhnev the government encouraged some forms of national self-expression. This increased tolerance of nationalism would later play a role in the emergence of anti-Soviet nationalist movements. Following 1964:

- Each of the republics had the right to introduce education in their own language.
- There was an increase in the publication of books and newspapers in non-Russian languages in the republics.
- Folk art, folk music and museums devoted to national culture were allowed in each of the republics.
- Brezhnev established new universities to educate non-Russian citizens of the Union.
- Brezhnev's 'trust in **cadres**' policy allowed local elites to consolidate their hold over the Communist Parties in the non-Russian republics.
- There was greater representation of Turkic people in the Central Committee and Politburo.

## 2 The impact of Gorbachev's reforms

### Note it down

Gorbachev's reforms led to the emergence of nationalism in a variety of ways. Make notes in any form you choose to dealing with:

- Gorbachev's policies
- the ways in which they encouraged nationalism.

### Cadre change and anti-corruption

Following Brezhnev's death there was a change in policy towards the republics. Andropov and Gorbachev both argued that effective government was more important than representative government. Therefore they were no longer committed to ensuring that the governments of the republics were staffed by local people. Rather they argued that all government posts should go to the best candidates. In practice this meant that Andropov and Gorbachev replaced existing leaders in the non-Russian republics with Russians. This process was linked to the anti-corruption campaign, which led to the sacking of many local leaders. Gorbachev's purges of the republican governments were particularly far reaching. For example, he removed relatively popular leaders in the Central Asian republics in 1986.

Moreover, at the top of the Soviet Government Brezhnev's appointments from the republics were replaced by Russians. Gorbachev's Politburo, for example, only had one non-Russian. As a result, following Brezhnev's death Soviet Government became more dominated by Russians at all levels. This created resentment in the non-Russian republics. Indeed, in Kazakhstan in 1986, for example, there were riots when the new Russian leader Gennadii Kolbin replaced local Kazak leader Dinmukhammed Kunaev.

### Acceleration

Gorbachev's economic reforms led to economic decline. Therefore standards of living in the republics either declined or stagnated. This change happened at the same time that Gorbachev was replacing local leaders with Russians. The economic decline became associated with the new Russian leadership, whereas economic growth was associated with the previous generation of local leaders.

Gorbachev did not challenge the privileges of Communist Party officials. This made matters worse. As the economy declined, the inequalities between the new privileged Russian leaders and the people they ruled became obvious. Therefore Gorbachev's reforms led to growing nationalism because of their failure and because they were associated with a new privileged Russian leadership.

### Glasnost

*Glasnost* and democratisation had led to problems that Gorbachev had not foreseen. The most significant of these issues was the demand for greater autonomy or full independence from the Soviet republics. *Glasnost* led to the rise of nationalism in a number of ways:

- It exposed the ways in which Stalin's government had persecuted non-Russian people.
- It allowed Soviet people to see how much higher Western standards of living were than those within the Soviet Union. This was a significant change. From the mid-1950s to the mid-1980s citizens in the republics were broadly happy with their standard of living. The Soviet economy had improved living standards compared to the 1920s or 1930s. However, compared to the West living standards were still poor. Therefore *Glasnost* undermined the perception that the Soviet Union had benefited people in the republics.
- It allowed nationalist groups to publish material that demanded greater autonomy.

### The Sinatra Doctrine

Gorbachev's foreign policy reforms also led to a rise in nationalism. The most significant change in this context was to redefine the relationship between the Soviet Union and the East European '**satellite states**' it had controlled since the late 1940s. Under Khrushchev and Brezhnev these states, which included East Germany, Czechoslovakia, Hungary and Poland, were only allowed very limited freedom. Reforms in Hungary and Czechoslovakia which threatened Soviet interests were crushed by the Soviet military.

The Soviet Union's relationship with the Eastern European satellite states was summed up in the 'Brezhnev Doctrine' of 1968. In essence, Brezhnev argued that the Soviet Union had a right to intervene in the affairs of other European socialist countries in order to protect socialism across the whole of Europe. Gorbachev rejected the Brezhnev Doctrine in August 1989, renouncing the Soviet Union's 'right' to intervene in the affairs of other socialist countries. Rather, he argued that different countries could all follow their own path to Communism. This new doctrine, nicknamed the 'Sinatra Doctrine' after Frank Sinatra's song 'My way', allowed much greater freedom in the Eastern European countries.

As a result, during October and November 1989 Communism fell across Eastern Europe (see Figure 1).

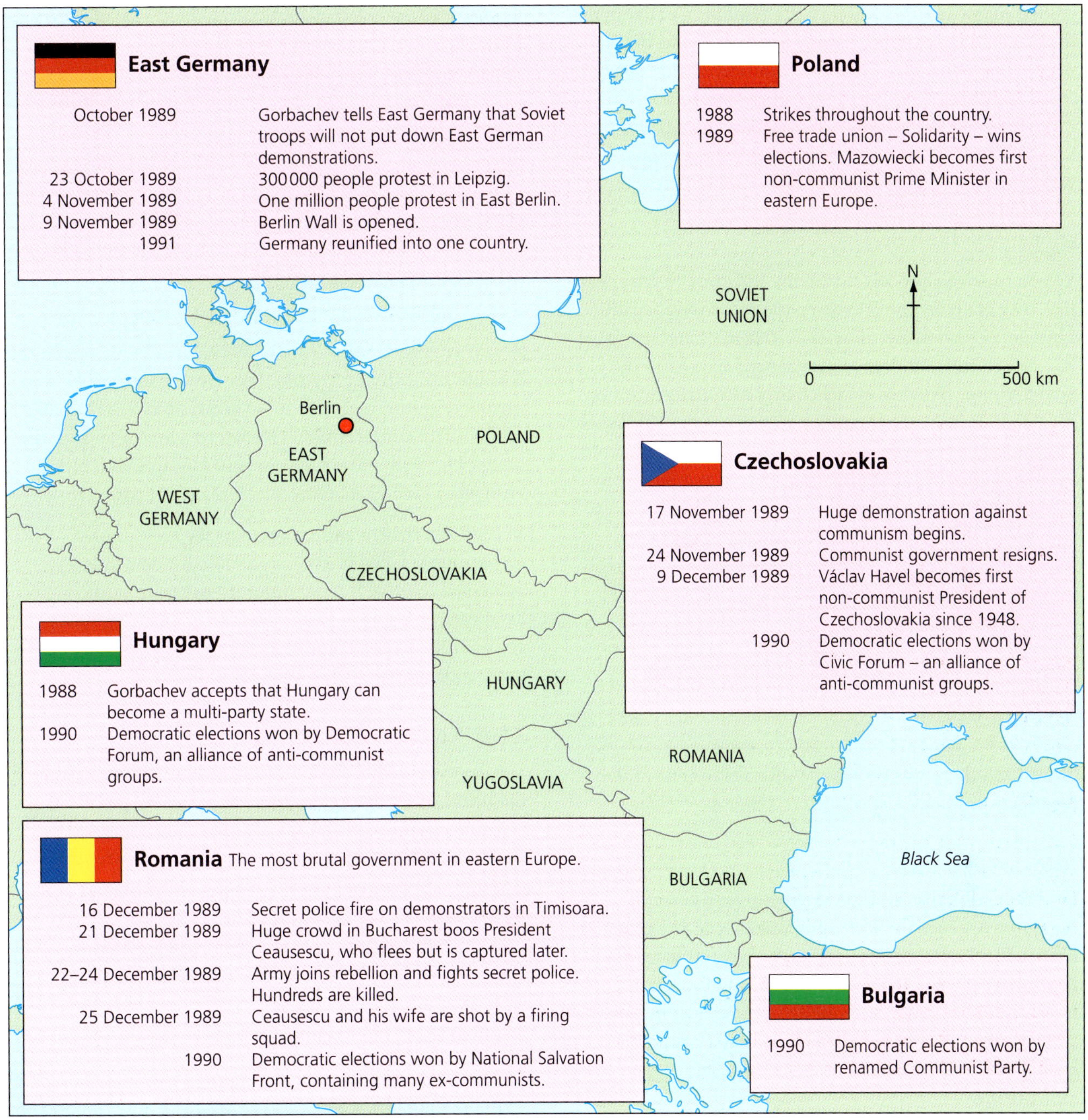


▲ **Figure 1: The break-up of the Soviet Empire in the years 1988–91.**

In Poland and Hungary new leaders won democratic elections; in Czechoslovakia and East Germany there were peaceful revolutions against communist rule. The destruction of the Berlin Wall, which began on 9 November 1989, symbolised the end of Soviet control of Eastern Europe. Once again, these changes went well beyond what Gorbachev had anticipated. Nonetheless, Gorbachev allowed them to happen, refusing to use Soviet troops to restore communist rule in the new democracies.

The revolutions in Eastern Europe clearly had implications for the Soviet republics. Across Eastern Europe countries had regained their independence from the Soviet Union. Nationalists in the non-Russian republics hoped that they could do the same.

## Democratisation

Democratisation further aided nationalists by allowing them to fight and win elections. Significantly, nationalists gained majorities in several of the republic's parliaments in the elections of 1990. These elections led to the first major nationalist challenge to the Soviet Union since 1921. In March 1990 the newly elected parliament of Lithuania declared Lithuanian independence from the Soviet Union. Gorbachev claimed that the declaration was illegal and imposed economic sanctions. Although the sanctions were lifted in the summer, there was no resolution to the issue.

Yeltsin took this process further by insisting, in May 1990, that laws made by the Russian parliament were legally superior to Soviet laws. In effect, Yeltsin's statement gave Russia a significant degree of independence from the Soviet Union. Further evidence that nationalism was on the rise in Russia was the re-emergence of the old Russian flag and the double headed eagle – the symbol of the old Russian monarchy. Both the flag and the symbol of the monarchy had been banned by the Soviet Government. The use of these symbols by Russians who supported Yeltsin indicated that nationalists in Russia wanted to break away from the Soviet Union and assert Russia's independence.

## 3 Growing nationalist unrest, 1988–90

From 1988 there was growing nationalist unrest in the republics. In some cases this led to religious violence.

### Nationalist violence

In 1988 nationalist protests broke out in Karabagh, a region of Azerbaijan. The crisis was caused by Armenian nationalists living in Karabagh who wanted to unite with Armenia. Armenian nationalists organised protests in favour of redrawing the republic's boundaries in February 1988. Azerbaijani nationalists organised a counter campaign, and by the end of the month there were violent riots.

> **Note it down**
>
> As you read this section, make notes on the following topics using the 1:2 method (see page x):
>
> - the nature of the new nationalisms
> - the impact of the new nationalisms on Gorbachev and the Soviet Union
> - government responses to the new nationalisms.
>
> **TIP:** Remember to make a note of the names of the places that were affected by the emergence of nationalism.

Gorbachev responded by introducing direct rule of Karabagh. However, this pleased neither side. New groups emerged fighting for their different national communities. The situation led to massacres and mass migration of Armenians. Both sides began to denounce the corruption of the Soviet Union.

The Soviet authorities failed to contain the crisis, and by the end of 1989 the Communist Party had lost control of the Republic of Azerbaijan. In January 1990 Azerbaijani nationalists, who now effectively controlled the republic, massacred Armenians. Mass Azerbaijani rallies demanded formal independence from the Soviet Union.

A year later in Central Asia in 1989, Uzbeks massacred the Muslim minority of Meshketians. Soviet authorities were unable to restore peace in these areas, nor were they able to negotiate compromise. This led to a loss of faith in the Soviet Government which appeared incapable of either ensuring peace or meeting the demands of nationalists.

In both Azerbaijan and Uzbekistan the Communist Government failed to contain nationalist demands and failed to solve intercommunity issues. In both cases nationalist protests that started against a minority community escalated into violence and demands for independence from the Soviet Union.

### The Tbilisi massacre

Similar events took place in Georgia, which demonstrated the limits of Gorbachev's real power. On 9 April 1989 Georgian nationalists protested against the rights of the Abkhazian minority. On this occasion Soviet troops attempted to restore order by force. Consequently, Soviet forces killed 19 Georgian protestors and wounded thousands more. The killings outraged Georgian nationalists. As in Uzbekistan the government's response turned Georgian nationalists against the Soviet authorities.

The killings in Georgia had two main consequences:

- The massacre led to concern among nationalists in all of the republics that the Soviet Government was prepared to use lethal force to stop nationalism.
- The government refused to take responsibility for the killings and blamed local military leaders. As a result, military commanders became increasingly unwilling to use force against protestors. This refusal to use force became known as 'Tbilisi syndrome' and weakened the government's position, because it could no longer rely on military support.

### Russian nationalism

During the late 1980s there was a growth in Russian nationalism. Traditionally, Russians had benefited from the Soviet Union, and many Russians had identified with the successes and world power that had been achieved under the communists. However, the Soviet Union and Soviet leaders were blamed for the onset of the economic crisis. Therefore, from 1988 there was a growing demand for a change that put Russia first.

Russian nationalism was also spurred on by a growing environmental or green movement. Russian citizens were first alerted to the environmental impact of Communism in 1986 due to the explosion of the Chernobyl nuclear reactor. As a result of *glasnost*, the government published environmental data that demonstrated that Russia was much more polluted by Soviet industry and farming than had been previously admitted. The green movement began to flourish in Armenia in the late 1980s. Indeed, in 1987 environmentalists organised mass demonstrations against the Soviet Government's environmental policies. These demonstrations were unprecedented and indicate how powerful the green movement was in some of the republics. In 1989 the State Committee for Environmental Protection published a report which acknowledged serious levels of pollution in 16 per cent of the Soviet Union's land. The report admitted that the Aral Sea was an area of 'ecological calamity' due to pollution from biological and chemical weapons testing and from oil and gas extraction. More generally, industrial pollution was affecting water and air quality, and extensive use of chemical fertilisers was poisoning some of the Soviet Union's great lakes.

Environmental groups in Russia tended to express their concerns in terms of saving the Russian landscape and saving the Russian environment. Therefore increasing support for green issues undermined the Soviet Union and aided the growth of Russian nationalism. Equally, Russian nationalists began to use some of the arguments that emerged from the green movement. Specifically, they argued that Soviet Communism was unnatural and had smothered and poisoned national culture like the chemicals from Soviet factories.

Nationalism also flourished among groups established to protect national monuments. Protecting national monuments and traditional buildings was part of a bigger movement to protect Russian culture and re-evaluate the past. Indeed, some Russians began to argue that Tsarism had been a better system than Communism. Moreover, as the economic and political crisis deepened a minority of Russians began to back extremist movements which were openly anti-Semitic and nationalistic.

## Baltic independence

The break-up of the Soviet Union started in the Baltic states of Latvia, Lithuania and Estonia. These states had been independent in the 1920s and 1930s, but had been conquered by Stalin in 1940. Nationalists in these states wanted a return to independence.

By 1988 large 'popular fronts', movements dedicated to gaining independence, were growing in all three Baltic states. Estonia declared itself **sovereign** from the Soviet Union in November 1988. Estonia did not leave the Union, but the government claimed the right to revive the old flag and begin educating citizens in the Estonian language.

Lithuania's declaration of independence, in March 1990, came after nationalist victories in the election of a new Lithuanian Supreme Soviet. Gorbachev refused to accept the declaration. However, criticisms of the Tbilisi massacre meant that Gorbachev was only prepared to use force against nationalists in the Baltic in extreme circumstances. Gorbachev imposed economic sanctions, rather than using force. Sanctions failed to force Lithuania to accept Soviet rule. Therefore, in January 1991 the Soviet Government sent in troops. Soviet forces occupied the press and television headquarters, killing 14 people. There was outrage across the Soviet Union at the use of force. Ukrainian miners in Donetsk organised protests at the government's action. Yeltsin also asked Russian soldiers to refuse to obey any orders from the Soviet Government that would suppress political protest. Yeltsin also started creating a Russian army to defend the Russian Republic from Soviet attack.

## Reforming the Soviet Union

Gorbachev's response to the growing nationalism was to propose a reformed union, in which the republics would have a greater degree of independence. Gorbachev first proposed a new union treaty in 1990. Negotiations were hampered by Gorbachev's declining authority. Whereas nationalist leaders had won elections and therefore had the authority to act as representatives of their people, Gorbachev was unelected. Therefore Gorbachev was unable to deal with nationalist leaders as an equal.

In March 1991, following the crisis in Lithuania, Gorbachev proposed a referendum of all the people in the Soviet Union, hoping to strengthen his position by winning popular support for a reformed union. Six of the republics, including the Baltic republics, refused to participate. However, 76 per cent of voters in the remaining nine republics backed a new union. On the basis of the referendum, Gorbachev reached a provisional agreement in April 1991. The so-called **9+1** agreement was designed to establish a federation of independent states with a single president.

In June 1991, Russia took another step away from the Soviet Union by electing its own president. Yeltsin

## Historical interpretations: The impact of nationalism

Historians have disagreed about the origins of the nationalism that emerged in the Soviet Union in the 1980s. Ronald Grigor Suny in Extract 1 argues that the weaknesses of the Soviet regime and Gorbachev's mistakes allowed nationalism to grow and threaten the Soviet Union, at least in Armenia, Georgia, and the Baltic republics. In Extract 2 Anatoly Michailovich Khazanov, by contrast, argues that nationalism emerged due to specific problems with Soviet policy, particularly the ecological problems created by the Soviet economy and the abuses of minority cultures within the Union.

**Extract 1** From Ronald Grigor Suny, *The Revenge of the Past: Nationalism, Revolution, and the Collapse of the Soviet Union*, published in 1993.

When Gorbachev came to power in March 1985, the Soviet state was already in a profoundly weakened condition. The Soviet Union had experienced not only years of political and economic stagnation but also a frustrating absence of able and stable leadership in the first half of the 1980s. Weakness in the centre had enabled the local ethnic and regional mafias within the Party-state apparatus to increase their power.

In nearly every Transcaucasian and Central Asian republic, a series of purges (1985–1988) eliminated the top leaders, although not without resistance. In Kazakhstan the removal of long-time party Chief Dinmukhammed Kunaev and his replacement by a Russian brought demonstrators onto the streets.

When these 'democratic' forces began to act, the emergence of nationalist politics burst the bounds of the old politics in a number of republics. In a number of republics – Armenia, Georgia, the Baltic – this rapidly undermined the power of local Communist parties. In other republics, however – in Central Asia most particularly – *perestroika* was contained and Communist apparatchiks maintained their hold on both state and society.

**Extract 2** From Anatoly Michailovich Khazanov, *After the USSR: Ethnicity, Nationalism, and Politics in the Commonwealth of Independent States*, published in 1995.

From the end of 1986, at the onset of a period of change, representatives of the non-Russian peoples began to express in the press complaints about the Soviet nationality policy, specifically its abuses of non-Russian cultures. Estonian economists and reform minded officials began to insist on economic and financial independence for their republics. In 1987, groups sprang up in various republics to address social, cultural and ecological problems that were often connected with national interests of these people. Ecological movements were particularly active in Armenia, Georgia, Azerbaijan, Estonia and Moldavia. In September and October of 1987 in Armenia, the Greens organised mass demonstrations – an uncommon phenomenon in the Soviet Union at the time. By 1988, the economic and political crisis in the Soviet Union began to be accompanied by an explosion of nationalism and tension in interethnic relations.

**1** Read Extracts 1 and 2 and write a brief answer to the following questions:

**a)** Extract 1 refers to 'a series of purges (1985–1988) eliminated the top leaders'. Which purges is this a reference to?

**b)** What reasons do the extracts give for growing nationalism in the period 1986–91?

**c)** How far do the two extracts agree about the extent to which Gorbachev's policies were responsible for growing nationalism in this period?

**2** Having answered these questions share your answers with a partner. How far do you agree? Where you disagree, can you resolve your disagreements referring to the interpretations of the extracts and the information in this chapter?

won the election with 57 per cent of the vote, beating the communist candidate who only gained 16 per cent. The victory clearly strengthened Yeltsin's position and weakened Gorbachev. Yeltsin's election gave him popular legitimacy. Indeed, as Russians made up 60 per cent of the Soviet population, Yeltsin could claim to be a truer representative of the Soviet Union than Gorbachev. Clearly, Gorbachev had never won a popular election and therefore lacked a democratic basis for his position.

Negotiations for a new treaty continued throughout the spring. In mid-July a complete draft of the treaty establishing a Union of Sovereign States had been agreed by the leaders of eight of the Soviet republics. Gorbachev announced that the treaty would be signed on 21 August.

## 4 The coup, 1991

### Note it down

Using a note-making style of your choice, make notes on:

- the causes of the coup
- what happened during the coup
- how far the coup weakened the Soviet Union.

Don't forget to note down the key details: the names of key individuals and the dates of key events.

Gorbachev's new Union Treaty did not have the support of hardliners in the Party. Gorbachev's conservative opponents thought that the new treaty allowed the republics to have too much power. Gorbachev's decision to go on holiday immediately prior to the signing of the new treaty allowed his hardline opponents to overthrow Gorbachev. On 18 August, eight senior Communists announced the establishment of an Emergency Committee, which would replace Gorbachev's government. The Emergency Committee was led by Gorbachev's deputy, the head of the army and the head of the KGB.

The plot to overthrow Gorbachev had been growing since the beginning of the year. The coup's leaders launched the coup when Gorbachev was on holiday, hoping that he would be unable to stop them as he was away from the centre of government. On 18 August, the Emergency Committee announced that Gorbachev had resigned due to poor health. However, Gorbachev refused to resign, and Yeltsin called a general strike to resist the coup.

The plotters stated that their goal was to stop the break-up of the Soviet Union and to restore law and order. Significantly, they recognised that Communism was deeply unpopular and therefore did not take power in the name of the Communist Party.

Yeltsin headed resistance to the coup. Army units were sent to the White House, the Russian parliament building, to arrest him. However, the soldiers refused to obey orders and Yeltsin demanded Gorbachev's return to power.

Without the support of the army the Emergency Committee could not continue, and the coup collapsed on 21 August.

## The consequences of the coup

The coup had a series of consequences:

- Gorbachev's position weakened. His statement following the coup indicated that he was significantly out of touch with majority opinion. On his return to Moscow, Gorbachev declared that he still had faith in the Communist Party, that he remained committed to renewing the Party, and that he still wanted the Party to play a key role in the future of the Soviet Union. However, due to *glasnost*, the public had lost faith in the Party. Moreover, the coup further weakened the Party as it showed that senior Party figures wanted to reverse democratisation. Gorbachev's statements demonstrated that he did not represent the aspirations of the majority of the public. Consequently, while Gorbachev was reinstated as President his authority did not recover.
- The Party, the army and the KGB were discredited as they were behind the coup.
- Yeltsin's authority grew. He emerged as the defender of democracy. His actions following the coup won him even greater support.
- The coup led to the end of the Communist Party. On 23 August Yeltsin suspended the Communist Party in Russia. As there was little popular opposition, Yeltsin went further and banned the Party on 6 November.
- The coup led to the break-up of the Soviet Union. Fear that the Emergency Committee would re-establish a communist dictatorship led the Republics of Ukraine, Moldova, Azerbaijan and Kyrgyzstan to declare their independence by the end of August. Armenia followed suit after a referendum in early September. Gorbachev was also forced to recognise the independence of the Baltic states. Consequently, the coup destroyed the treaty establishing a Union of Sovereign States. Gorbachev worked hard throughout October and November but could not revive the treaty.
- The coup led to the creation of the Commonwealth of Independent States (CIS). In December, Yeltsin and the leaders of Belorussia and the Ukraine signed the Minsk Agreement which stated that the Soviet Union had been replaced by the Commonwealth of Independent States (CIS). Eleven of the 15 former Soviet republics joined the CIS on 21 December 1991.

## Historical interpretations: The significance of the coup

Most historians agree that the coup was a significant moment in the fall of the Soviet Union. Nonetheless, there are differences of emphasis. Peter Kenez, for example, argues that the coup was significant because it exposed the bankruptcy and weakness of communist hardliners. Martin McCauley, by contrast, emphasises the way in which the coup strengthened Yeltsin and Russian nationalism at the expense of Gorbachev and the Communist Party.

**Extract 3** From Peter Kenez, *A History of the Soviet Union from the Beginning to the End*, published in 2006.

On August 19, 1991, the premier, the vice president, and the head of the KGB, among others – all Gorbachev appointees – formed a 'state committee on the state of emergency,' which assumed all governmental powers, banned strikes and demonstrations, and introduced censorship – that is to say, they staged a coup d'état. The conspirators were ludicrously inept, lacking both charisma and political sense. Beyond a dislike of Gorbachev's reforms and a desire for a return to the defunct Soviet order, they had no political program. Worst of all from their point of view, they took no serious measures to disarm the opposition. Within two days the coup had failed.

The putschists accomplished the opposite of what they had intended: by their actions they demonstrated that there was no force behind them, and that the old order could not be reconstructed. Their press conference, in which they allowed themselves to be ridiculed and showed themselves to be helpless, drunken, and fearful men, was a demonstration of the bankruptcy of the old order. Although the regime managed to hang on for four more months, this ill-considered conspiracy was the real end of the Soviet era.

**Extract 4** From Martin McCauley, *The Rise and Fall of the Soviet Union*, published in 2008.

Had Yeltsin and his aides been arrested on the first day of the coup, it would probably have succeeded. KGB officers watched him leave his dacha but did not arrest him because they had not been given a written order to do so. Yeltsin was a brilliant populist and knew how to arouse passions. He was astute enough to demand the return of Gorbachev. He avoided the impression of going for power himself. The legal, constitutional norms had to be observed. Yeltsin appealed to Russian patriotism. The coup was anti-Russian as the Committee wanted to force Russia back into the old Soviet Union. This message struck a responsive chord among the intelligentsia. They knew that their lives would be blighted if the Committee secured power. Many workers were indifferent. Things had been going from bad to worse in the late Gorbachev era. Why should they suddenly improve if the leader came back? Yeltsin's answer was that we Russians can do it, if we are permitted to. Let us regenerate Russia together.

**1** Having read Extracts 3 and 4:

- Summarise the argument of Extract 3 in one sentence.
- Write a paragraph arguing either for or against the argument in Extract 3. Use your own knowledge and Extract 4 to justify your claim.

**2** Swap paragraphs. Now write a counter-argument to your partner's argument.

**3** Having read the arguments and counter-arguments, discuss how far you agree with Extract 3.

### Ukrainian independence

Following the coup on 1 December 1991, 90 per cent of the people of Ukraine voted for independence from the Soviet Union. The Ukraine had the second largest population of any of the Soviet republics, containing almost 20 per cent of the Soviet population. Therefore the Ukrainian decision to leave the Soviet Union effectively ended Gorbachev's plan to save the Union.

The coup led to a series of fundamental changes. In essence it finally destroyed the authority of Gorbachev, the Communist Party and the army, the three forces holding the Soviet Union together. However, in many ways, the coup simply accelerated trends that were already obvious in mid-1991. Prior to the coup, Gorbachev's authority was declining and Yeltsin's was increasing, there were signs that at least six republics were going to leave the Union and the authority of the Communist Party was declining sharply.

▲ **Figure 2: The break-up of the Soviet Union into the Commonwealth of Independent States.**

## The end of the Soviet Union

The creation of the CIS effectively destroyed the Soviet Union (see Figure 2). In this sense, from 21 December Gorbachev was the President of a state that no longer existed. Gorbachev formally resigned as President of the Soviet Union four days after the creation of the CIS and declared that the Soviet Union would formally cease to exist on 31 December.

# Conclusion

Nationalism clearly played an important role in the demise of the Soviet Union. From 1985 the Soviet Government's economic failure, the revelations about the political and environmental crimes of the Soviet Government, and Gorbachev's refusal to seek a democratic mandate all weakened the Soviet Government. At the same time local leaders were able to present themselves as defenders of natural local traditions against the tyranny of the Union. Moreover, local leaders, like Yeltsin, had genuine authority, as they had been elected by the people. Therefore they had more respect and power than Gorbachev, who was associated with the failures and crimes of the Soviet Union. Gorbachev's attempts to save the larger part of the Union, however, were destroyed by the communist hardliners who led the coup. The coup finally destroyed the authority of the Soviet Union and ended Gorbachev's attempts to restrain the growing nationalism.

## Extended reading: Interpretation

**Historian Robert Hornsby considers the nature and significance of nationalism in the fall of the Soviet Union.**

By the time that Mikhail Gorbachev officially dissolved the Soviet Union in December 1991, most of the fifteen republics that made up the union had already declared their independence. Essentially, once the different republics that made up the Soviet Union decided to go their own way, there was no Soviet Union left for Gorbachev to rule over.

There had been a certain amount of nationalist dissent for years in parts of the USSR – most notably in the Baltic States of Latvia, Lithuania and Estonia, but also in the likes of Ukraine and Georgia – but it had never threatened the survival of the system as a whole. In large part, this was because the authorities had been willing and able to suppress it: by force if necessary. As economic decline became ever sharper by the 1980s, and then Gorbachev's reforms toward the end of that decade began to loosen the political shackles, it became far harder for the authorities in Moscow to control swelling nationalist sentiment. One commentator in the late 1980s even argued that, if the Russian Empire of the tsars had been a 'prison of nations' (as Karl Marx once claimed), then the Gorbachev-era Soviet Union had become a 'volcano of nations'.

As Gorbachev sought to reform the Soviet system, he inadvertently created more and more possibilities for those who simply wanted out. Then, when he tried to reassert control in those republics pursuing independence, his own credibility as a reformer nosedived. Introducing democratic elections to the Council of People's Deputies in 1988, for example, helped bring long-suppressed nationalism into the open: it created the possibility to organise, to hold rallies, and to campaign for independence.

Gorbachev fought hard to avoid Soviet disintegration, but he was mostly prepared to do so through compromise with the demands of nationalists. Plenty of others near the top of the Soviet system, however, were not so willing. As Gorbachev made concessions to one group, he alienated the other and eventually neither trusted him. When hardline conservatives tried to overthrow Gorbachev in August 1991 – largely because he was about to complete a new and looser agreement between the different republics – separatists became ever more convinced that it was time to leave, and leave quickly.

### Activity

Having read the essay, answer the following questions.

#### Comprehension

1 What is meant by the following phrases:
- 'a "prison of nations"'
- 'a "volcano of nations"'
- 'ethnic and national conflicts that marked its last days remain only frozen, not solved'?

#### Interpretation

2 Summarise Hornsby's interpretation of the causes of the growth of nationalism in the late 1980s and early 1990s.

3 Summarise Hornsby's interpretation of Gorbachev's role in the growth of nationalism.

#### Evaluation

4 Using your own knowledge, write a paragraph explaining how far you agree with Hornsby's interpretation of the role of nationalism in the break-up of the Soviet Union.

One of the key factors that quickly made nationalism a powerful force almost everywhere in the late 1980s was that so many leaders and elites in the different parts of the Soviet Union – most famously, Boris Yeltsin in Russia – decided that their ultimate allegiance was not to the Soviet Union but to their own republic, be that Russia, Ukraine, Georgia or anywhere else. Some surely made this decision based on genuine consideration of what was in the best interests of the people, others did so more cynically: with an eye on how best to protect their privileges and status in a post-Soviet world. After years in which they had mostly been left to their own devices under Brezhnev, and many had grown extraordinarily corrupt and wealthy in the process, local leaders did not take kindly to Gorbachev attempting to shake up and clean out the system. He, in turn, probably did not realise the extent to which such people commanded loyalty locally and held the power to derail orders coming from Moscow.

Public demonstrations for independence in cities like Minsk, Kiev and Tbilisi topped 100,000 people by the turn of the 1990s. In the Baltic States around two million people held hands in a human chain that stretched right across the region. In some places the public mood turned much uglier. Conflict between Armenia and Azerbaijan resulted in massacres of Armenians in Baku, ethnic riots broke out in Kyrgyzstan, and even individual republics faced breakaway movements from within their own territory, such as in Chechnya (Russia), Abkhazia (Georgia) and Transnistria (Moldova). While the Soviet Union is no more, most of these ethnic and national conflicts that marked its last days remain only frozen, not solved: proof enough that Gorbachev stood little chance of dealing with them as the Soviet system began to crumble around him.

No single factor caused the collapse of the Soviet Union. What made nationalism so significant, though, was the unique way in which it was fed from virtually every direction: by economic decline, by limitations on religion and culture, by both political reform and political retrenchment, by local and national problems, and by the popular mood among the masses and the manoeuvring of local elites. One only needs to look today at the fifteen countries that emerged from the Soviet collapse as independent states to see that holding them all together under one umbrella was a virtual impossibility without the use of force.

**Robert Hornsby is a Research Fellow at the School of History, University of Kent. His present research focuses on the *Komsomol* in the Soviet Union between the 1950s and the 1980s. More generally, he is interested in the relationship between conformity and non-conformity in dictatorships. This is also reflected in the title of his first book, Protest, Reform, and Repression in Khrushchev's Soviet Union.**

## Work together

Having completed the activity on page 180, swap your notes with a partner. Consider the following questions:

1 Did you identify the same causes of the growth of nationalism in the late 1980s and early 1990s?
2 Did you both agree with Hornsby's interpretation of Gorbachev's role in the growth of nationalism?
3 What was good about your partner's summary of Hornsby's interpretation?
4 Can you learn anything about Hornsby's interpretation from your partner's summary?
5 How far did you both agree with Hornsby's interpretation?

Use these questions to feed back to each other and improve your analysis of the debate.

# Essay technique: Integrating own knowledge

Section C of the exam requires you to evaluate the interpretations offered by the two extracts. You will need to consider the interpretations in the light of your own knowledge of the debate. Therefore, once you have identified the interpretations (see page 157) and worked out the structure of your essay (see page 165), you will need to integrate your own knowledge into your essay.

Imagine you are answering the following question:

**In the light of differing interpretations, how convincing do you find the view that the 'Soviet Union was brought down in large part by a remarkable explosion of nationalism'? (Extract 1, lines 14–16)**

**To explain your answer, analyse and evaluate the material in both extracts using your own knowledge of the issues.**

You should integrate your own knowledge to support and challenge different aspects of the extract. You can plan this quickly in the exam by annotating the extract. You could use different coloured pens to indicate support and challenge.

As you go through the extract consider the strengths and the weaknesses of the interpretation. It is a good idea to make a brief note of your overall judgement at the bottom of the extract. For example:

**Extract 1** From, Mark R. Beissinger, *Nationalist Mobilization and the Collapse of the Soviet State*, published in 2002.

A great deal of attention has been focused on Gorbachev's personal role in bringing down the Soviet state. Other historians, by contrast, have placed emphasis on political, economic or social conditions which prepared the way for both Soviet liberalisation and the eruptions of nationalism that precipitated Soviet collapse. Still others view the Soviet collapse as largely unrelated to the nationalist explosions that rocked the Soviet state in the *glasnost* years. Obviously, nationalism was both a cause of and consequence of the declining power of the Soviet state brought on by *glasnost* and failed reform. But in a period of revolution, insurrection, and major upheaval in which hundreds of thousands took to the street on a daily basis, explanations that focus solely on the elites lack the ring of authenticity. For the Soviet Union was brought down in large part by a remarkable explosion of nationalism, and the impact that explosion had on the ways in which both Russians and non-Russians thought about the Soviet state.

Challenge: Beissinger considers a series of alternative arguments.

Support: Beissinger argues that nationalism was central to the break-up of the Soviet Union.

**Extract 2** From Norman M. Naimark, Preface to *The Revenge of the Past,* published in 1993.

> The collapse of the Soviet Union was caused in good measure by nationalism, that is, by the demands of the subject nationalities of the Soviet Union for genuine independence and autonomy. Unified in their hostility to the Kremlin's authority, the fifteen constituent Union republics, including the Russian Republic, declared their sovereignty and began to build state institutions of their own. The demands of the nationalities of each republic became the dominant motif in the program of both Communist and non-Communist leaders. With the failure of the August 1991 putsch attempt, sovereign republics obtained their independence. Nationalism reigned supreme.

## Activity

Using the question on page 182 complete the following activity:

1 Read Extracts 1 (page 182) and 2.
2 Analyse them by looking for:
   - the main arguments
   - counter-arguments
   - evidence.
3 Look for contrasting arguments between the extracts.
4 Look for aspects of the extracts that support each other.
5 Identify where you can support or challenge different aspects of Extract 2 using your own knowledge.
6 Make a brief note of your overall judgement at the bottom of the extract.
7 Make a full plan, showing how you will structure your essay, where you will use the different aspects of both extracts and where you will bring in your own knowledge.

**TIP:** Own knowledge should be used to support or challenge the interpretations contained in the essays. It is best used to evaluate the extracts; it should not dominate the essay.

## Work together

Having completed the activity, consider the following questions with a partner:

1 Did you both identify the same arguments and counter-arguments in the extracts?
2 Did you agree about which aspect of the extracts was the biggest contrast to the main argument of Extract 1?
3 How did your partner's use of own knowledge differ from your own?
   - Did they use it to support the same things?
   - Did they use it to challenge the same things?
4 Did you miss anything that you should note down?
5 What can you learn from your partner's approach?
6 Whose use of own knowledge:
   - better analysed the interpretations contained in the extracts
   - better integrated own knowledge with the extracts?

Use these questions to feed back to each other and improve your essay planning.

## Activity: AS-Style question

**Historians have different views about the reasons for the fall of the Soviet Union.**

**Analyse and evaluate the extracts and use your knowledge of the issues to explain your answer to the following question.**

**How far do you agree with the view that Gorbachev's political reforms led to the collapse of the Soviet Union?**

# 4 Gorbachev and Yeltsin

## Overview

Two leaders, more than any others, are associated with the fall of the Soviet Union. Historian Archie Brown pointed to what he called the 'Gorbachev Factor', the significance of Gorbachev and his reforms in the transformation and fall of the Soviet Union. According to Brown, Gorbachev played an important early role in realising that reform was necessary, and by the early 1980s, in realising that reform was not enough and that the system had to be transformed. In many ways Gorbachev's reforms undermined the system he was trying to save and therefore led to the fall of the Soviet Union. Yeltsin also played an important role; indeed, Brown has also written of a 'Yeltsin Factor'. Yeltsin was consistently more radical than Gorbachev; by 1990 he was more popular and by 1991 he was more powerful. Yeltsin encouraged nationalism and took a series of decisive steps to strengthen the nations that made up the Soviet Union at the expense of the Union. Moreover, Yeltsin played a key role in defeating the coup with a counter-coup against the Communist Party.

This chapter considers:

1. Gorbachev: *perestroika*; Westernising; his missteps; China
2. Yeltsin: his role as a popular radical; nationalism; the coup; the Union.

## 1 Gorbachev

Gorbachev's goals emerged over time. Initially, he proposed economic reforms, later political reforms and finally reforms to the nature of the Union. Gorbachev's goal was to revitalise both Soviet Communism and the Soviet Union. He failed in both of these ambitions. His reforms, his political and economic failures, and his failure to foresee the outcomes of his policies all played a role in the destruction of the Soviet Union.

### Note it down

Using a note-making style of your choice, note down the different ways in which Gorbachev played a role in the fall of the Soviet Union.

### *Perestroika*

Gorbachev played an important role in the fall of the USSR by initiating *perestroika*, a series of economic and political reforms that led to the transformation of the Soviet Union (see page 149).

The three phases of *Perestroika*, Nationalism, Reform and Transformation (see page 149) weakened the Soviet Union:

- Rationalisation led to a decline in economic growth, making economic conditions worse and undermining faith in the Party. The failure of these reforms also led Gorbachev to initiate more radical economic and political reforms.
- Reform further weakened the Soviet Union. *Glasnost* exposed the crimes of previous Soviet Governments. Consequently, it undermined faith not only in the Communist Party but also in the ideology on which it was based. In this sense *glasnost* led to a more profound loss of faith in the system than rationalisation. Democratisation weakened the Communist Party by allowing alternative candidates to stand. It also weakened Gorbachev's control of the Party as Soviet voters chose their candidates; therefore the Party no longer had a monopoly of patronage.
- During the transformation stage Gorbachev abandoned the essential features of Soviet Communism. His reforms further weakened the Soviet Union and allowed rival national powerbases to emerge.

From this perspective Gorbachev's reforms were an important cause of the break-up of the Soviet Union for the following reasons:

- In 1985 extensive reform was not necessary. The Soviet Union was experiencing decline, not a crisis. Equally, between 1979 and 1982 Andropov had successfully eliminated the dissident movement. Finally, there was support for more conservative reform options within the Party. Therefore Gorbachev played an important role in the fall of the Soviet Union because he introduced reform in spite of the fact that he was not under immediate pressure to do so.
- Gorbachev's reforms themselves created the crisis that led to more reforms and the ultimate break-up of the Union.
- Gorbachev was prepared to embrace more radical reforms as time went on.
- By 1990 Gorbachev was prepared to abandon the essential features of Soviet Communism, the very features that held the Soviet Union together.

## New thinking: new vocabulary

One of Gorbachev's crucial achievements that underpinned his political reforms was introducing 'new thinking' to Soviet politics. The 'new thinking' was based on a new language of politics. The 'new thinking' helped erode the Soviet Union.

First, Gorbachev embraced the term '*perestroika*' rather than 'reform'. 'Reform' was associated with the failure of Khrushchev and policies that had destabilised the Soviet Union. Consequently, communists were suspicious of the notion of reform. *Perestroika*, by contrast, was a neutral word which implied scientific restructuring in order to achieve efficiency. Therefore the term did not arouse opposition.

Secondly, Gorbachev introduced words which had previously only been used critically. For example, Soviet politicians had traditionally rejected 'pluralism', which they associated with the weaknesses of Western democracy. Gorbachev, however, began to advocate 'socialist pluralism'. Adding the word 'socialist' allowed Gorbachev to suggest that pluralism was compatible with the values of the Soviet Union. Similarly, he spoke publicly about 'socialist markets', in so doing advocating political and economic approaches that socialists had traditionally rejected.

Gorbachev's new vocabulary included:

- *Glasnost* – literally 'openness'. Originally, Gorbachev used it to mean greater freedom of information, but quickly it became associated with freedom of speech.
- *Perestroika* – meaning 'reconstruction'. Initially, *perestroika* meant economic reform, but it too gained a new meaning and by the late 1980s implied economic and political reform.
- *Uskorenie* – 'acceleration' (see page 150).
- *Demokratizatsiya* – 'democratisation'. Democratisation too changed its meaning from 1985 to 1991. Early on, it meant giving workers a greater say in the running of their factories. By the late 1980s, Gorbachev used it to indicate that significant aspects of the government should be elected.

Gorbachev's willingness to embrace new ideas allowed radicals in the Party, intellectuals and members of the public to advocate radical alternatives to Communism such as freedom of speech, free market economics and democratic elections.

## Westernising

Gorbachev also played an important role in reorienting Soviet politics towards more Western values. At the beginning of his reign, Gorbachev stated that he wanted the Soviet Union to abandon isolation and re-enter 'our common European home'. Whereas previous leaders had rejected Western values as capitalist and argued that Soviet values were superior, Gorbachev believed that European standards could make the Soviet Union more humane.

Gorbachev endorsed a number of Western values that previous leaders had rejected. First, he embraced the importance of human rights. In 1985 he allowed 129 dissidents to move abroad in order to be united with their spouses. He also allowed Sakharov's wife to leave the Soviet Union to receive lifesaving medical treatment. In 1986 travel restrictions were eased for all Soviet citizens, Soviet authorities stopped jamming Western radio transmissions, Sakharov's internal exile was ended and *glasnost* allowed unprecedented freedom of speech.

Gorbachev also embraced pluralism by allowing Soviet citizens to form their own groups and stand for election. Pluralism was a step towards Western multi-party politics and a step away from the single-party state. Indeed, in March 1990 Gorbachev removed Article 6 of the Soviet Constitution. As a result the Communist Party lost its right to a leading role in Soviet society and other parties were legalised.

Finally, Gorbachev also renounced violence as a method for holding together both the Soviet Union and the Eastern Bloc. Gorbachev set out his vision at the Twenty-Eighth Party Congress in July 1990. He argued that 'a civil society of free people is replacing the Stalinist model of socialism' and that the Soviet Union was moving towards 'genuine democracy … with free elections, a multi-party system and human rights, real people's power is being reborn'. This commitment to Western values played a significant role in the fall of the Soviet Union because it weakened the power of the Party, which had held the Union together since its creation.

## Gorbachev's mistakes

Another way in which Gorbachev could be said to be responsible for the fall of the Soviet Union is through his mistakes and miscalculation.

Gorbachev's fundamental miscalculation was to believe that reform could save the Soviet Union. The aim of *perestroika* was to revive the Soviet system, to unleash its potential. However, the reforms ultimately created a crisis from which the Soviet Union could not recover.

Gorbachev failed to anticipate the effects of *glasnost*, the extent to which revelations about the past would undermine the claims of the Communist Party. He also failed to see the fragility of commitment to the Soviet Union. In this sense, he believed the Communist Party's own propaganda that Communism had created a new Soviet people who no longer felt the pull of nationalism.

Gorbachev not only made fundamental mistakes, he made policy mistakes that undermined his position. Having embraced democracy he refused to stand for election, and having survived the coup he failed to abandon the Communist Party. Moreover, he set competing goals and his policies were often inconsistent. For example, his initial policy of *uskorenie* was designed to restructure industry and increase output. Restructuring would disrupt production and increasing production would make it impossible to restructure. These competing objectives are one reason why the policy failed. Gorbachev was also inconsistent in his approach to the Communist Party. From 1985 to 1990 he sided with the radical reformists in the Communist Party, whereas in 1990 and 1991 he tended to side with conservatives and resist more radical reforms. In terms of the economy, he shifted from one plan to the next without allowing any to develop fully, further undermining the economy.

Finally, Gorbachev failed to win over the Communist Party. The Party was the only institution that was strong enough to introduce reform. However, in practice the Party resisted reform and therefore hampered Gorbachev's programme.

Gorbachev's mistakes undermined the authority of the Communist Party and his own position, thus weakening the Soviet Union. Specifically, as President of the Soviet Union, Gorbachev was in a position to hold the Union together. However, the failure of his political and economic policies led to a rapid decline in his authority and therefore he no longer had the power to hold the Union together.

## Gorbachev and China

Since 1992 historians have attempted to understand the fall of the Soviet Union by comparing it to the survival of Communism in China. Both communist regimes embarked on a reform process in the 1980s, yet while reform in the Soviet Union led to the fall of Communism, in China Communism grew stronger. The comparison highlights a number of Gorbachev's policies.

- China embraced market reform more quickly and comprehensively than the Soviet Union. As a result, China's economy continued to grow and therefore the Communist Party retained its political authority. By contrast, Gorbachev's economic reforms were slow and inconsistent. Gorbachev mistakenly tried to integrate markets into a command economy. This approach failed creating an economic crisis which led to widespread dissatisfaction with the Soviet Communist Party.
- The Chinese Communist Party was prepared to be more flexible than the Soviet Communist Party. Therefore economic reform in China had a high degree of support from the Communist Government. In the Soviet Union, by contrast, the majority of communists, including Gorbachev, were committed to the command economy and viewed markets with suspicion.
- Communist leaders in China introduced economic reform without increasing political freedom. The lack of political reform meant that China continued to be politically stable during the reform process. From this perspective, the Soviet Union collapsed because Gorbachev tried to introduce economic and political reform at the same time. Therefore when *perestroika* led to economic chaos, the government, which had been weakened by political reform, was not strong enough to retain control.

## Conclusion

Ultimately, Gorbachev's project of reviving and renewing the Soviet Union failed. Gorbachev's reforms led to economic chaos and a decline in faith in the Communist Party. His mistakes and his inability to see the consequences of his policies undermined his own position. Perhaps Gorbachev could have saved the Union if, like Chinese leaders, he had focused on the economy rather than trying to reform the political system, the economy, the relationship between the republics and foreign relations all at the same time.

## Historical interpretations: The Gorbachev Factor?

Historians have disagreed about the extent to which Gorbachev was responsible for the fall of the Soviet Union. Archie Brown's *The Gorbachev Factor* clearly argues that the appointment of Gorbachev was central to the destruction of Communism in the Soviet Union. However, Peter Kenez argues that Gorbachev was timid and lost control of the process well before the Soviet Union collapsed.

**Extract 1** From Archie Brown, *The Gorbachev Factor*, published in 1997.

The changes in what used to be the Soviet Union have been so great that it is easy to forget what the unreformed Soviet system was like and how modest were the expectations of significant innovation when Mikhail Gorbachev succeeded Konstantin Chernenko as top Soviet leader in March 1985. Neither Soviet citizens nor foreign observers imagined that the USSR was about to be transformed out of existence. If the scale of the change in the Soviet Union during the Gorbachev years is considered with dispassion, what is most remarkable is the extent to which it occurred peacefully. Given the failure of all who had openly attacked the system from within the country to make any positive impact on policy outcomes prior to the late 1980s, it is doubtful if change of such magnitude could have taken place with so little violence – especially in Russia – in any way other than through the elevation of a serious reformer to the highest political office within the country. Without the promotion of a genuine reformer and highly skilled politician to the top Communist Party post in 1985, fundamental change in the Soviet Union would certainly have been delayed and could well have been bloodier as well as slower than the relatively speedy political evolution which occurred while Gorbachev was at the helm.

There were many stimuli to the changes which followed the succession of Gorbachev to the Soviet leadership in March 1985, including (some two or more years into *perestroika*) the moral and intellectual legacy of the dissidents of the 1960s and 1970s. But the choice of Gorbachev, rather than of any of the other people in the Communist Party leadership who could aspire to the Party's (and at that time the country's) most powerful post, was of critical importance.

**Extract 2** From Peter Kenez, *A History of the Soviet Union from the Beginning to the End*, published in 2006.

Gorbachev's timid reforms not only did not bring about the desired results, but made matters worse. The reforms brought greater shortages to the Soviet people, a decline in productivity and production, inflation, and a black market controlled by criminals. The signs of deterioration were ever more visible. Liberal politicians and economists were telling Gorbachev that the way out of the crisis was to introduce more radical reforms. However, he knew that there was no constituency supporting such reforms, and indeed that the opponents of abandoning the foundations of the Soviet system were powerful, numerous, and well organized. Beginning in late 1989 his leadership became hesitant and erratic. He temporized, at one time supporting the reformers but then, a short time later, withdrawing his support. He became increasingly isolated.

The Gorbachev era was over at the end of 1990. From this point on, Gorbachev had no new ideas for reform. He was a spent force. In reorganizing the political system, just as in matters of economics, he temporized. The danger of spreading disorder - indeed, the possibility of civil war - brought him closer to the conservatives, and he adjusted his policies accordingly. On the one hand, he did not want to go further in reforming away the Soviet system; on the other, he wanted to protect his reforms but did not know how to restore stability.

**1** Having read Extracts 1 and 2:

- **a** Summarise the key argument of the two extracts.
- **b** Select three details from your own knowledge that support the argument of Extract 1. Write these down as a list under your summaries.

**2** Swap your summary with a partner and discuss your lists:

- **a** Which summary best captured the argument of Extract 1?
- **b** Which summary best captured the argument of Extract 2?
- **c** Which details most precisely supported the argument of Extract 1?

## 2 Yeltsin

Boris Yeltsin also played a crucial role in the fall of the USSR. Historians have focused on different aspects of his role, arguing that he was significant for a number of different reasons.

> **Note it down**
>
> Skim read this section and note down the different ways in which Yeltsin helped break up the Soviet Union. Use these as the headings in a note-making style of your choice.

### Popular radical

Yeltsin played an important role as a popular radical in a period in which Gorbachev was becoming increasingly unpopular and conservative. Yeltsin made a name for himself in 1986 at the Twenty-Seventh Party Congress by denouncing the privileges of Party leaders and advocating a renewed focus on equality. He also called for multi-candidate elections to all posts in the Party. Yeltsin continued his radical career by publicly attacking communists who opposed reforms in 1987. In doing so, he exposed the factionalism that existed in the Party, thus damaging the Party's reputation for unity. As a result of this, he was sacked as leader of the Moscow Communist Party.

In 1988 at the Nineteenth Party Conference, Yeltsin made another public attack on Party conservatives. The attack was broadcast to millions on Soviet television and again highlighted the deep splits in the Party.

Between 1986 and 1988 Yeltsin's attacks on the leadership made him popular with many Soviet people who hated the privileges of senior Party officials. Moreover, his call for multi-candidate elections attracted the support of middle- and low-ranking officials in the Party, who saw elections as a way of advancing their own careers. Consequently, during the 1989 Soviet elections Yeltsin won a massive victory in Moscow, gaining 89 per cent of the vote. Yeltsin was one of the founders and leader of the Inter-regional Deputies' Group, which functioned like an opposition political party. From this point, Yeltsin was important as he was the leading opponent of Gorbachev.

### Yeltsin in 1990

Yeltsin became more important throughout 1990. Indeed, 1990 was a turning point in the history of the Soviet Union. It was the year in which Gorbachev lost control of the reform agenda and was forced to react to popular protest calling for radical change.

During 1990 there were elections to soviets in all of the Soviet republics. Consequently, Yeltsin became Chair of the Russian Congress of People's Deputies, Russia's new parliament, in May 1990. A month later in June, the Congress declared Russia's sovereignty. In practice this meant that Russian laws were superior to Soviet laws. The Baltic republics had already declared themselves sovereign, but Russia's declaration was more significant as Russia contained 75 per cent of the Union's population. Yeltsin also moved to establish a Russian army, independent of the Soviet army, and started to build support for an elected Russian President. These moves towards Russian power led to the 'war of laws', a series of disputes between the Russian Government and Soviet authorities about who had the right to rule Russia.

Yeltsin publicly resigned from the Communist Party in July 1990. His resignation was highly dramatic and weakened support for the Party. Indeed, Yeltsin's resignation was part of a mass exodus from the Party: during 1990 Party membership dropped from 19.2 million members to 16.5 million. Party popularity also dropped to a mere 18.8 per cent.

### Boris Yeltsin, 1931–2007

Boris Yeltsin was the first President of the **Russian Federation** after the fall of the Soviet Union. He joined the Communist Party in the early 1960s. In 1985, Yeltsin was elected to the Central Committee. From 1985 to 1987, Yeltsin was a keen supporter of Gorbachev's reforms. Under Gorbachev Yeltsin became the leader of the Communist Party in Moscow, where he became popular for fighting Communist Party corruption. He was also appointed to the Politburo, but resigned in 1987 in protest at the slow pace of reform.

Following clashes with Gorbachev, Yeltsin lost his most important jobs within the Soviet Government. However, following Gorbachev's political reforms he was elected to the Russian Congress of People's Deputies.

Yeltsin played a key role in the destruction of the Soviet Union by using his power to advance radical political and economic reform.

During 1990 Yeltsin became increasingly popular. Gorbachev's policies seemed unsuccessful and confused. By June Yeltsin was more popular than Gorbachev among Russian voters. Moreover, from 1990 Gorbachev became more cautious about reform. Yeltsin, by contrast, clearly advocated market reform and democracy. Moreover, Russian people viewed Yeltsin as one of them, whereas they believed that Gorbachev was distant and had no idea of the problems facing the country, or how to solve them.

## Yeltsin and nationalism

Yeltsin was also significant because of his attitude to nationalism. Yeltsin encouraged non-Russian republics to establish their independence from the Soviet Union.

Yeltsin embraced nationalism, in part, to outmanoeuvre Gorbachev. By emphasising the rights of Russia, Yeltsin weakened the Soviet Union, which was Gorbachev's power base. His election as Chair of the Russian Congress was a symbol of the growing Russian nationalism. As Chair, Yeltsin was able to speak on behalf of the Russian nation. In that sense, Yeltsin becoming Chair was central to the process which led to the declaration of Russian sovereignty.

Yeltsin attempted to consolidate his own power base in Russia by being elected Russian President. Yeltsin's election as Russian President in June 1991 was significant because it gave him the right to speak and act on behalf of Russia. Moreover, it gave him a status within government that rivalled that of Gorbachev. From then on Gorbachev had to accept a secondary role in Russia and was forced to begin renegotiating the relationships between the republics.

Not only did Yeltsin embrace Russian nationalism, he also supported the growth of nationalism in other Soviet republics. During the summer of 1990 Yeltsin visited several Soviet republics advising their leaders to 'take as much sovereignty as you can swallow'. In 1991 Yeltsin supported the Baltic states' declarations of independence from the Soviet Union. He publicly denounced the actions of Soviet troops in Vilnius, the capital of Lithuania (see page 175). Gorbachev criticised Yeltsin for encouraging a 'parade of sovereignties' and in so doing threatening the survival of the Soviet Union.

## Yeltsin and new elite

Some historians argue that the break-up of the Soviet Union was the result of conflicts within the Communist Party, rather than conflict between the Communist Party and democrats. From this perspective Yeltsin was important because he represented and worked for the interests of middle-ranking Communist officials, against the interests of high-ranking Communist officials.

According to this interpretation, Gorbachev's Communist Party was never a united group. Rather, there were divisions within the Party between the senior levels and the lower levels. Senior Communists tended to want to preserve the Soviet Union because their status and power were tied up with the Communist Party and the Soviet system. Lower-ranking officials, however, saw Gorbachev's reforms as an opportunity to improve their position. For example, some Communist officials joined nationalist movements or bought state-owned factories that were privatised in the early 1990s in order to advance their own careers and safeguard their power and privilege.

Yeltsin had been a champion of lower-ranking Party officials since the mid-1980s. Indeed, one of the reasons for his sacking as Moscow Party Leader in 1987 was his decision to dismiss established Party officials and replace them with younger Party members. Gorbachev criticised this as a dangerous policy of 'instability of cadres'.

Yeltsin's rise to power, and the growing power of Russia over the Soviet Union, led to the emergence of a new elite at the expense of the old Soviet elite. For example, of the 230 people who were ministers under Gorbachev from 1985 to 1991, only nine were still at the top level of Yeltsin's government after the coup. At the same time Yeltsin's new government had relatively few 'new men', people who had no government experience at all. The vast majority of Yeltsin's new government, almost 70 per cent, had held middle-ranking positions in Gorbachev's government. Only around 13 per cent of Yeltsin's new government had been elected to any of Gorbachev's new democratic institutions.

In this sense, Yeltsin was able to contribute to the fall of the USSR because he had the support of a 'counter-elite' – middle-ranking Communists who supported the destruction of the Union in order to enhance their own power. Moreover, from this point of view Yeltsin's power base was made up of former Party officials and government officials rather than people associated with the Soviet Union's new democratic institutions.

## Yeltsin, the coup and counter-coup

Yeltsin also played a significant role in the destruction of the Soviet Union due to his handling of the coup.

First, the coup transformed Yeltsin's strategy. Prior to the coup Yeltsin had been trying to gain Russian independence from the Soviet Union by fighting small battles over the rights of the Union. Throughout 1991 Yeltsin was prepared for a long drawn-out battle with Gorbachev that might last many years. However, his strategy changed during the coup. Whereas Gorbachev did not understand the full significance of the coup and assumed that he could continue with the same policies once the coup had failed, Yeltsin realised that the coup had caused a radical shift in Soviet politics. From August 1991 Yeltsin saw the opportunity to establish Russian independence.

Secondly, Yeltsin's strategy for dealing with the coup was extremely successful. He publicly denounced the coup as unconstitutional. Moreover, while demanding Gorbachev's return as President, he was also encouraging popular risings against the Communist Party. As a result, statues of Lenin across Russia were demolished, often with the help of Russia's security services. In this sense, Yeltsin's response to the coup was to organise a counter-coup. Yeltsin ordered the suspension of the Communist Party and the closure of Communist Party newspapers including *Pravda*, and he surrounded the Communist Party headquarters with armed police. Yeltsin's counter-coup was extremely effective as it all but destroyed the Communist Party in Russia.

In the weeks after the coup Yeltsin pressed ahead to break up the Communist Party:

- At the end of August the Communist Party was suspended across the Soviet Union.
- In early November Yeltsin banned the Party in Russia, and seized all of its money and property.
- Yeltsin published extensive evidence of Party corruption seized from Communist Party files.
- In November Yeltsin announced that Russia was taking control of the Soviet oil and gold industries.

Significantly, Yeltsin tended to attack the Party rather than the Union. However, as the Party was the organisation that had traditionally held the Soviet Union together, Yeltsin's actions clearly weakened the already fragile Union. It was only in December that Yeltsin publicly advocated ending the Union.

Indeed, after the coup Yeltsin moved very slowly to consolidate his position. In essence, he had no plan for building democracy in Russia or for replacing the Soviet Union. Notably, after the coup had been crushed, Yeltsin went on holiday to consider his options rather than introducing reforms or demanding the end to the Union.

### Yeltsin and the Union

A final perspective on Yeltsin suggests that Yeltsin was important in the demise of the Soviet Union because he could have saved it and chose not to. From this perspective, Gorbachev simply did not have the authority to revive the negotiations to create a new Union after the coup. Yeltsin, by contrast, was more popular than ever and therefore could have tried to revive the Union. However, rather than back Gorbachev's negotiations, Yeltsin supported the creation of the Commonwealth of Independent States.

Yeltsin's choice to abandon the Union was partly a political decision, as it was one way to defeat Gorbachev. However, it was also a decision that Yeltsin thought was best for Russia. He believed that reconstructing the economy would be easier for Russia than for a whole Union. Russia was more developed than most of the rest of the Union, and without having to support the other republics, Yeltsin assumed economic reconstruction would be quicker and easier. Equally, he believed that he had a better chance of establishing democracy on a national scale, than he had across the whole Union. In this sense, he chose to build Russia rather than save the Union.

However, Yeltsin reached this decision only in December 1991 after the people of the Ukraine voted to leave the Union in a referendum. Immediately following the referendum Yeltsin organised a secret meeting with the leaders of Ukraine and Belorussia. The three leaders agreed to throw their weight behind the CIS, and in so doing destroyed Gorbachev's plan for a new Union treaty. Following the meeting he persuaded the leaders of the Soviet military to abandon the Soviet Union and form the new Russian army.

## Conclusion

A profound and revolutionary transformation took place between 1985 and 1991. In 1985 the Soviet Union was a mighty superpower, a rival to the USA symbolising an alternative to capitalist democracy. However, by 1991 single-party rule had been abolished, freedom of speech established, and countries such as Latvia, Lithuania, and the Ukraine had achieved independence. These developments were unthinkable in 1985. Gorbachev and Yeltsin both played important roles in the break-up of the Soviet Union. Clearly, Gorbachev was important in that he initiated reform which became a transformation and later a dissolution of the Soviet system. Yeltsin played an increasingly significant role from 1989, stimulating the growth of nationalism in Russia and the other republics, as well as attacking the Communist Party, and finally concluding a rival agreement that destroyed Gorbachev's hopes of creating a reformed Union.

## Historical interpretations: The Yeltsin Factor?

Historians have disputed Yeltsin's significance in the fall of the Soviet Union. Peter Kenez clearly argues that Yeltsin's actions during 1991 led to the collapse of the Soviet Union. George W. Breslauer, by contrast, argues that Yeltsin and Gorbachev both played important roles in bringing about the end of the Soviet Union.

**Extract 5** From Peter Kenez, *A History of the Soviet Union from the Beginning to the End*, published in 2006.

Boris Yeltsin came to be the standard bearer of the reformists. He had been dropped from the top leadership of the party and had openly clashed with the conservative Yegor Ligachev, and these facts may have contributed to his growing popularity. In March 1991 his conservative opponents attempted to get rid of him as head of the elected Russian parliament. He outmaneuvered them by creating the office of the president of the Russian republic, and stood for the election to the presidency of Russia in June 1991. For Yeltsin, the presidency of the Russian republic became a power base. He established contact with representatives of other republics and took a much more tolerant view of the nationalist aspirations of the minorities. He openly deplored the bloodletting in Vilnius in January 1991. Under Yeltsin's leadership Russia began to act independently of the Soviet government, behaving as if Russia really was just one of the republics. This development, more than any other, led to the dissolution of the union.

**Extract 6** From George W. Breslauer, *Gorbachev and Yeltsin as Leaders*, published in 2002.

In 1985, the Soviet Union appeared to be an entrenched entity, capable of defending itself against all challenges to the Communist Party's right to rule at home and in Eastern Europe, and determinedly pursuing a policy of great-power competition abroad. By the end of 1991, an oppositional figure had been elected president of Russia, both Communism and the Soviet Union had collapsed, and independent Russia had emerged as a seemingly helpless supplicant of the West.

Without presupposing that Gorbachev and Yeltsin made all these things happen, it is fair to say that things would have happened quite differently had different individuals been in charge. Their acts of leadership were crucial.

Khrushchev's reformism and Brezhnev's conservativism had long pedigrees within Soviet history, as did Gorbachev's initial strategy of reformism during 1985–1987. But Gorbachev's subsequent decision to push for transformation of the system, and Yeltsin's decision to try to destroy and replace the Leninist system, were unprecedented acts by political leaders of the system itself. One cannot explain these choices without reference to these leaders' personalities and beliefs.

Having read Extracts 5 and 6:

1. Compare Extract 2 (page 187) with Extract 5. Write a paragraph summarising Kenez's view of the relative importance of Gorbachev and Yeltsin to the fall of the Soviet Union.
2. Write a paragraph comparing Kenez's view of the relative significance of Gorbachev and Yeltsin with Breslauer's view (Extract 6) of the relative significance of the two leaders to the fall of the Soviet Union.
3. Swap your paragraphs with a partner. Discuss which summary most accurately reflects the contrast between Kenez and Breslauer's interpretation of the relative significance of the two leaders to the fall of the Soviet Union.

## Extended reading

**Historian Christopher Catherwood considers the roles played by Gorbachev and Yeltsin in the fall of the Soviet Union.**

The great nineteenth century French historian Alexis de Tocqueville said that a despotic regime is at its most dangerous point when it tries to reform. He was referring to the French Revolution in 1789 and the attempts of King Louis XVI to ameliorate royal absolutism before that event. But it could equally apply to the Soviet Union in 1991. And if that is the case, then in one sense the Soviet Union was doomed already in 1985 when the gerontocrats in the Kremlin decided that after two aged and infirm General Secretaries they would appoint the much younger and dynamic Mikhail Gorbachev in their place. It then became a question not of *whether* the Soviet structure would collapse but *when and how.*

Archie Brown is right to say that the key point about Gorbachev and his reforms – *perestroika* and *glasnost* – was that they happened with comparatively little bloodshed. Gorbachev was awarded the Nobel Peace Prize in 1990 for the peaceful way in which he permitted the end of the Soviet bloc in 1989. There were no massacres in Czechoslovakia and the other former Warsaw Pact countries. The decision of the Communist regime in the DDR (East Germany) *not* to shoot the pro-democracy protestors in Leipzig shows that unlike earlier repressions the new style of Marxist did not wish to stay in power by armed force.

This was surely the major difference between the collapse of the Soviet Union and the survival of the Communist Party in China. Tiananmen Square and the mass murder of the protestors showed that there, the Party *would* employ violence. Although Gorbachev's suppression of similar protests in Lithuania, a state within the USSR, suggests that he would use force if necessary, there was nothing on the Chinese scale in the last years of the Soviet Union.

The failure of the 1991 coup is therefore critical. In Beijing in 1989 the Army carried out the will of the Party. In 1991 in Moscow the plotters were unable to persuade the Red Army to do the same. It is possible, as some of our sources argue, that the USSR could have continued beyond 1991, despite the increasing disagreements between Gorbachev and Yeltsin. But the coup entirely delegitimised the Communist Party and showed that it was fatally split from inside. A house divided against itself cannot stand, and that was most certainly the case of the ruling elite of the USSR in 1991. It also undermined what was left of

### Activity

Having read the essay, answer the following questions.

#### Comprehension

**1** What does Catherwood mean by the following phrases:

- 'a despotic regime'
- 'gerontocrats in the Kremlin'
- 'Tiananmen Square'
- 'the coup entirely delegitimised the Communist Party'?

#### Evidence

**2** Make a list of the examples that indicate that Gorbachev played a significant role in bringing about the end of the Soviet Union.

#### Interpretation

**3** Identify the passage in which Catherwood sets out his main argument.

**4** Summarise Catherwood's interpretation of how far Gorbachev, on the one hand, and the 1991 coup, on the other, were responsible for the fall of the Soviet Union.

#### Evaluation

**5** Using your own knowledge, write a paragraph explaining how far you agree with Catherwood's interpretation of the causes of the fall of the Soviet Union.

Gorbachev's authority, since his return to Moscow was very much a product of Yeltsin's resistance and not that of the Soviet leadership.

Because we think of the USSR as an ideological regime, we forget the reality of how it began. The Soviet Union was, in fact, the Russian Empire under a new name, shorn after 1918 of some of its Western territories that it was to regain in 1940. In theory all the peoples of the Union were equal, and Stalin, for example, was a Georgian. But in practice it was Russian-dominated, and Stalin used the resettlement of ethnic Russians to the various Republics, from Latvia through to Kazakhstan, as a means of ensuring Soviet unity. This did not stop it from being the Tsarist in different guise however.

And in 1991 all this was to come undone, as the forces of Communism soon proved no match for renascent ethnic nationalism. As the sources remind us, 75% of the USSR was the Russian Federation.

Thus, when its new leader, Boris Yeltsin, sought to give the Russians predominant power in their own country, any chance that Communism could keep the component parts together, and overcome nationalist fervour, was therefore surely doomed to failure. Of course the role of Yeltsin as a Communist Party apparatchik and his sponsorship of middle-ranking functionaries was important, but the fact that he was the leader of *Russia* meant that if 75% of the USSR had no vested interest in the state, then the Soviet Union was finished.

So what can we conclude?

First, reform always puts a despotic regime at risk, and this was certainly the case for the USSR at the end of the twentieth century. Secondly, Gorbachev's decision not to use ultimate violence was morally the right choice but led to the ending of the Soviet bloc and then of the USSR. Thirdly, that the rivalry between Gorbachev and Yeltsin was critical for the collapse of the Soviet Union, but the coup was the fatal blow.

**Christopher Catherwood is a historian based at Churchill College, University of Cambridge. In 2001 he was appointed Rockefeller Fellow at the University of Virginia and in 2002 was briefly a consultant to the British Cabinet Office's former Strategic Futures Team of their Performance and Innovation Unit. Catherwood has written extensively on twentieth-century history and international relations. His books include *Why the Nations Rage* (1997), which deals with the consequences of the fall of Communism in Eastern Europe, and more recently a series of books on Winston Churchill including *Winston Churchill: The Flawed Genius of WWII* (2009).**

## Work together

Having completed the activity on page 192, swap your notes with a partner. Consider the following questions:

1. Did you both spot the same evidence in Catherwood's essay?
2. Has your partner missed anything?
3. Did you agree on the passage in which Catherwood sets out his main argument? If not, who was right?
4. How far did you both agree with Catherwood's interpretation?

Use these questions to feed back to each other and improve your analysis of the historiography.

# Essay technique: Overall judgement

Reaching a supported overall judgement is an important part of doing well in Section C. The judgement that you should reach in Section C is similar to the judgement that you should reach in the other sections of the exam (see page 68). However, in Section C, your judgement should be based on an evaluation of the interpretations offered by the extracts, as well as reflecting the overall argument of your essay.

Imagine you are answering the following question:

**In the light of differing interpretations, how convincing do you find the view that the USSR fell because of 'choices made by Gorbachev, particularly in regard to the pace and scope of reform'? (Extract 1, lines 23–4)**

**To explain your answer, analyse and evaluate the material in both extracts, using your own knowledge of the issues.**

**Extract 1** From Christopher Marsh, *Unparalleled Reforms: China's Rise, Russia's Fall* and the Interdependence of Transition, published in 2005.

> While the collapse of the Soviet Union was not inevitable prior to the launching of *perestroika*, it became increasingly likely as events unfolded and decisions were made about how to proceed. The first real phase of the collapse began between March and December 1989, from the initial elections to the Congress of People's Deputies to the collapse of Communist rule in Eastern Europe. By this time *perestroika* had run into trouble. Gorbachev attempted to reinvigorate his reform agenda by pushing ahead with democratisation. But in so doing Gorbachev gave the vote to a population largely in need of food.
>
> During the second phase of collapse, from January 1900 to August 1991, collapse of the system became an increasingly possible outcome of reform. Yeltsin's meteoric rise to power in Russia, and his call to the republics to swallow as much sovereignty as they could was a lethal blow to the Soviet Union. The failure of the coup led the country into the final phase of collapse, which saw the Soviet Union crumple piece by piece throughout the autumn of 1991.
>
> While long term conditions certainly contributed to the failure of Communism, the Soviet collapse was also due in great measure to the policy choices made by Gorbachev, particularly in regard to the pace and scope of reform.

**Extract 2** From Dick Combs, *Inside the Soviet Alternate Universe: The Cold War's End and the Soviet Union's Fall Reappraised*, published in 2008.

> It is generally agreed that Boris Yeltsin became a courageous opponent of Communist Party rule well before Gorbachev was prepared to abandon the party. Upon Yeltsin's selection as chairman of the Russian parliament in mid-1990, and then his popular election as President of Russia about a year later, he served as a rallying point for those who felt Gorbachev was too accommodating to regime conservatives or was otherwise lacking as a reformer. Most observers concur that Yeltsin played a vital role in defeating the right-wing forces behind the August 1991 coup against Gorbachev, in pushing aside the party nomenklatura in Russia, and then in pushing aside Gorbachev himself.
>
> In August 1991,Yeltsin and his supporters effectively destroyed the power of the USSR government. The Russian government then began to take over in its territory the institutions previously controlled by the USSR government.

## Planning your essay

Your essay plan might look like this:

| Paragraph | |
|---|---|
| 1: Main argument: Gorbachev's reforms | Extract 1: 'Soviet collapse was also due in great measure to the policy choices made by Gorbachev, particularly in regard to the pace and scope of reform.' e.g. Gorbachev chose to bring in political and economic reform, introducing democracy at a time when the 'population [were] largely in need of food.' This destabilised the country because people were able to express their discontent with economic problems by turning against the Communist Party and the Soviet Union. |
| 2: Counter-argument: Yeltsin's actions | Extract 2: 'Yeltsin and his supporters effectively destroyed the power of the USSR government.' Extract 1: 'Yeltsin's meteoric rise to power in Russia, and his call to the republics to swallow as much sovereignty as they could was a lethal blow to the Soviet Union.'<br>Extract 2: 'Yeltsin played a vital role in defeating the right-wing forces behind the August 1991 coup against Gorbachev.' |
| 3: Counter-argument: long-term factors | Extract 1: 'long term conditions certainly contributed to the failure of Communism', e.g. long-term economic decline, long-term disillusionment with the Communist Party (implied in Extract 2), and frustrated nationalist ambitions – particularly in the Baltic republics. |
| 4: Main argument: Gorbachev's reforms | However, long-term issues were not central to the collapse as 'the collapse of the Soviet Union was not≈inevitable prior to the launching of *perestroika*' (Extract 1). |

## The focus of your judgement

Your judgement should focus on the specific interpretation raised in the question. In this case, you need to focus on the extent to which the USSR fell because of 'choices made by Gorbachev, particularly in regard to the pace and scope of reform'.

Judgements that focus on the specific issue raised by the question are likely to do better than judgements that focus on the general issue of the fall of the USSR.

Therefore you could begin your conclusion like this:

> In conclusion, the view that the USSR fell because of 'choices made by Gorbachev, particularly in regard to the pace and scope of reform' is broadly convincing because *perestroika* destabilised the Soviet Union by introducing economic and political reforms.

Clear focus on the question

Clear argument

This is a good beginning as it focuses on the key interpretation, and therefore focuses precisely on the question. However, the judgement is not fully supported and therefore cannot be awarded marks in the highest levels. An improved introduction is given on page 196.

## Supporting your overall judgement

As in Sections A and B it is important to support your overall judgement. This can be achieved by evaluating the given interpretation. Specifically, you should weigh the given interpretation against the other interpretations you have examined in the essay. For example, the overall judgement you have just read on page 203 could be improved by adding the following evaluation of the different interpretations:

In conclusion, the view that the USSR fell because of 'choices made by Gorbachev, particularly in regard to the pace and scope of reform' (Extract 1) is broadly convincing because *perestroika* destabilised the Soviet Union by introducing economic and political reforms. In so doing, as Extract 1 argues, Gorbachev caused economic chaos and then democratised the system allowing the Soviet people to reject the Communist Party and the Soviet Union. Yeltsin and his supporters also played an important role. As Extract 2 argues, Yeltsin encouraged nationalists to declare sovereignty – which undermined the Soviet Union. Moreover, Yeltsin 'played a vital role in defeating the right-wing forces behind the August 1991 coup against Gorbachev' (Extract 2). However, Yeltsin was only able to play this important role because of the freedoms Gorbachev had introduced as part of *perestroika*, and because of the political changes that Gorbachev introduced as part of democratisation. Therefore, while Yeltsin played an important role in the last phase of collapse, and while there were clearly long-term issues (Extract 1) that also played a role, the pace and scope of Gorbachev's reforms were crucial to the Soviet collapse because having destabilised the economy he introduced democratisation and other political freedoms before the economy could recover and therefore allowed Soviet citizens to reject Communism and the Soviet Union.

Direct focus on the question.

Main argument from Extract 1 is supported with own knowledge.

Counter-arguments from Extract 2 are weighed against the main argument.

The final judgement is supported by a summary of the overall argument and is linked back to the question.

This conclusion is an example of high-level work because it reaches an overall judgement and supports it by evaluating the interpretations offered by the extracts.

### Activity

Plan and then write a conclusion for the question on page 197:

Try following these steps to make a plan:

1 Identify the interpretations offered by the two extracts – remember there may be more than two.
2 Look for contrasting arguments between the extracts, and look for aspects of the extracts that support each other.
3 Add own knowledge.
4 Note down a brief overall judgement.

Try following these steps to write a conclusion:

5 Start by giving a judgement that focuses on the given interpretation.
6 Support your judgement by weighing up the different interpretations contained in the extracts.

**TIPS:**

- Make sure you refer to both extracts in the conclusion.
- Make sure you use some details from your own knowledge to help weigh up the interpretations from the extracts.
- Use the words 'however', 'nonetheless', and 'therefore' to structure the paragraph.

**In the light of differing interpretations, how convincing do you find the view that the 'death of the Soviet Union in its 74th year represented a failure of Gorbachev's triple revolution? (Extract 1, lines 1–2).**

**To explain your answer, analyse and evaluate the material in both extracts using your own knowledge of the issues.**

**Extract 1** From Ronald Grigor Suny, *The Revenge of the Past*, published in 1993.

The death of the Soviet Union in its 74th year represented a failure of Gorbachev's triple revolution. The system fell because the leadership tried simultaneously to dismantle the old practices of the command economy and Communist Party dominance to construct a democratic multinational federation. Gorbachev's reforms had moved from a 'revolution from above' to a massive, multinational series of revolutions from below. Nations formed within the USSR tore that superpower into fragments, each with its competing interests and aspirations, and Gorbachev's program fell victim to the economic collapse and the rise of powerful nationalism. Once it became possible to break the imperial tie with Russia, nationalist leaders moved to take control of the destinies of their own peoples.

The forces of nationalism, which undermined the former Soviet Union and Gorbachev's plans for gradual economic and political reform initiated from above, were an understandable reaction to the hyper-centralism and bureaucratization of the old system. When Gorbachev loosened the controls from the centre, the effect in the Baltic republics, Armenia, Georgia, Moldavia, and the western Ukraine was an explosion of popular nationalism rooted in memories of life without the Soviet Union and a real sense that their cultures, even nature itself, were threatened if they did not strike out on their own.

**Extract 2** From Richard Sakwa, *Russian Politics and Society*, published in 2008.

The attempted coup of August 1991 sought to resolve by forceful means the crisis of power and end the struggle of conflicting ideologies. Yeltsin transformed the coup into a revolution. At a session of the Russian parliament the next day the CPSU was suspended in Russia by a stroke of Yeltsin's pen. The CC and Moscow City Communist Party offices in Old Square were sealed to stop documents being destroyed, and Yeltsin ordered a number of communist newspapers to stop publication. The retreat of the Party turned into a rout. On 24 August Gorbachev resigned as General Secretary of the CPSU and called for the dissolution of the Central Committee. On 29 August the USSR Supreme Soviet suspended the CPSU, and on 6 November 1991 Yeltsin banned the Party in Russia.

The attempt by conservatives to halt the tide of disintegration by staging a coup only accelerated the demise of the old system and the state. While the nature of the August coup remains controversial, its effect is clear: the collapse of the once all-powerful Communist Party and the disintegration of the Soviet Union itself. The coup was the final act of one of the cruellest regimes in human history.

## Activity: AS-Style question

**Historians have different views about the reasons for the fall of the Soviet Union.**

**Analyse and evaluate the extracts and use your knowledge of the issues to explain your answer to the following question.**

**How far do you agree with the view that the collapse of the Soviet Union came about because of the failure of Gorbachev's reforms?**

## Work together

Having written your conclusion in the activity on page 196, swap it with a partner. Consider the following questions:

1. Does your partner's conclusion begin by focusing clearly on the given interpretation?
2. Does your partner's conclusion mention both of the extracts?
3. Does your partner's conclusion use own knowledge to help evaluate the validity of the interpretations offered by the extracts?
4. Was your partner's overall judgement properly supported by an evaluation of the different interpretations offered by the extracts?
5. Does your partner's conclusion contain anything that you missed?
6. What can you learn from your partner's approach?
7. Whose conclusion better reached an overall judgement?

Use these questions to feed back to each other and improve your writing.

Paper 2

# Mao's China, 1949–76

## The Big Picture

Before the Second World War, the Chinese Communist Party (CCP) led by Mao Zedong had fought against the nationalists led by Chiang Kai-shek in a civil war for the control of China. Believing China to be an unequal and backward nation, Mao wanted to transform China according to the communist principles of Karl Marx. In contrast, Chiang Kai-shek advocated capitalist economic production and friendship with the West. The communists had been close to defeat, but were helped when the Japanese invaded China. In 1937 the communists and nationalists joined in an unequal alliance to fight against their shared enemy. In 1945 the Second World War ended and the two sides renewed their conflict. Although the nationalists were supported by the USA, the communists had greater support from the Chinese people and they were victorious, forcing the nationalists to flee to Taiwan.

### Establishing communist rule, 1949–57

In 1949 Mao Zedong announced the formation of the People's Republic of China. Although the communists possessed control of the government in the capital Beijing, China was shattered by war. Industrial plants had been damaged and infrastructure sabotaged. Farmland was ruined and crops destroyed; famine spread. The previous government had been corrupt and inefficient and parts of China far from Beijing were not controlled by the communists.

The communists moved quickly to consolidate their control. They created a new power structure comprised of three parts: the Communist Party, the Central Government and the People's Liberation Army (PLA). This new system gave the people of China the opportunity to vote in elections for the first time. In reality, Mao stood atop all three sources of authority and elections merely provided a superficial veneer of democracy in order to legitimise the creation of a one-party state. Campaigns were launched against enemies of the regime – opponents were intimidated, tortured or imprisoned in the new prison camp system, the laogai. The PLA was used to bring all areas of China under communist control. Mao also built up popular support. In 1950 China supported their North Korean communist allies and fought the United Nations to a standstill. After years of humiliation, China appeared to finally have a leader who would stand up to the foreign powers.

## Agriculture and industry, 1949–65

The communists had most support amongst China's poor farming communities. Peasant farmers made up 80 per cent of the population. The communists seized land owned by landlords and redistributed it to the peasants. This was hugely popular, as were CCP initiatives to encourage peasants to share resources and pool their labour. In 1953 the communists launched a Five-Year Plan that increased industrial production. These successes led Mao to try to transform China into a communist country more quickly, and in 1958 he launched the Great Leap Forward, an ambitious attempt to stimulate agricultural and industrial production simultaneously. Worked to exhaustion to meet unfeasible targets set by power hungry Party cadres, China suffered the greatest famine in human history. Only when more rational communist leaders like Liu Shaoqi and Deng Xiaoping ignored Mao's ideologically motivated ideas and allowed capitalist-style freedoms did the economy recover.

## The Cultural Revolution and its aftermath, 1966–76

After the failure of the Great Leap Forward Mao was pushed to the political margins. Worried that his communist revolution was being abandoned in favour of the 'capitalist road' advocated by his rivals within the CCP, in 1966 Mao launched the Cultural Revolution. His main motive was to remove his enemies, particularly Liu Shaoqi, and return to the political centre stage. Taking advantage of his popularity among China's young people, he encouraged them to destroy his opponents. China descended into anarchy as schools were closed and youths formed 'Red Guards' who attacked anyone they believed to be disloyal to Mao.

By 1969 Liu had died and the Party was completely loyal to Mao, but the all-powerful Chairman was aging and increasingly paranoid. A succession struggle ensued with the so-called Gang of Four radicals led by Mao's wife Jiang Qing hoping to take power. They were opposed by more pragmatic leaders like Deng Xiaoping. Mao believed that Jiang was obsessed with power and did not trust her, but he also feared that Deng wanted to introduce capitalist reforms. In 1976 Mao chose the little known Hua Guofeng to be his successor. Mao died that same year. Fearing a coup, Hua had the Gang of Four arrested but he was no match for the experienced and popular Deng. Eventually it was Deng who was able to use his support within the Party to overrule Hua.

## Social and cultural changes, 1949–76

Mao sought nothing less than the complete transformation of Chinese society. Traditional beliefs that denied women rights to divorce or to own property were challenged. Practices such as arranged marriages were forbidden. Education was similarly transformed – a national primary school system was created. A new form of written language, Pinyin, was created to improve literacy and communication. Health campaigns were launched to educate the masses on how to avoid spreading diseases while educated urban dwellers were encouraged to become 'barefoot doctors', who were sent to the villages to provide rudimentary medical care. Religions such as Buddhism and Islam represented rival beliefs to communism, while Christianity was considered to be an untrustworthy Western import. Temples were destroyed and monks and nuns forced into labour camps. Traditions such as ancestor worship were attacked as products of a feudal state, no longer of relevance in Mao's modern communist utopia.

# Key Topic 1 Establishing communist rule, 1949–57

## Overview

This chapter focuses on the situation in China at the formation of the People's Republic of China (PRC) in October 1949. Mao Zedong led his communist forces to victory in the Chinese Civil War over Chiang Kai-shek and the nationalists, but this was only the first step in the creation of a communist state. Mao had to deal with the legacy of poverty and destruction left from the Civil War. He still faced enemy forces at large in an ethnically and religiously diverse nation, large parts of which had resisted central government control for generations. This chapter examines the industrial and agricultural conditions that existed when Mao took power, as well as the problems with national infrastructure that made it extremely difficult for the Communist Government to consolidate its power. It also explains why, at a time when China was desperate for a period of peace and stability, Mao embroiled the PRC in a prolonged war with forces from the United States, the strongest military nation on Earth.

This chapter also helps you understand how and why Mao used a combination of popular policies and terror to impose communist rule. The condition of China in 1949 meant that the new government introduced a range of different policies, some of which were compatible with communist ideology, while others were not. Therefore it should make you think about how far Mao's policies were a reaction to the conditions that he faced, how much they were dictated by a desire to create communism, and finally how much they were a product of his own personal ideology. Did he seek to create a truly egalitarian communist system, or was he simply dedicated to consolidating his own power?

The overarching topic of establishing communist rule, 1949–57 is covered in four sections:

1 China in 1949
2 The new power structure
3 Defeating the CCP's opponents
4 China and the Korean War.

## TIMELINE

| | |
|---|---|
| 1949 September | Chinese People's Political Consultative Conference (CPPCC) convenes in Beijing to pass the Common Program |
| 1949 October | Mao announces the formation of the People's Republic of China (PRC) |
| 1949 December | Nationalist leader Chiang Kai-shek retreats to Taiwan |
| 1950 March | Campaign to Suppress Counter-Revolutionaries launched |
| 1950 June | The Korean War begins |
| 1950 October | United Nations (UN) troops drive into North Korea towards the Chinese border |
| 1950 October | People's Liberation Army (PLA) begins 'reunification' campaigns in Tibet and Xinjiang; PLA also deployed in Guangdong |
| 1950 November | China enters the Korean War in support of the communist North against the UN |
| 1951 February | 'Resist America, Aid Korea' campaign begins |
| 1951 May | 17-Point Agreement between Tibet and China signed |
| 1951-2 August-July | Three Antis Campaign |
| 1952 February -May | Five Antis Campaign |
| 1953 July | Truce signed between North and South Korea |
| 1954 September | China's first constitution introduced |
| 1957 May-June | The Hundred Flowers Campaign |
| June | The Anti-Rightist Campaign |

# 1 China in 1949

When the People's Republic of China was created in 1949, China was very far from the modern and powerful nation it is today. In fact, China was backward, lacking an organised central government and with an economy still reliant on small-scale agricultural production. Today China possesses huge urban centres, but in 1949 80 per cent of the population still lived in poor rural areas and survived by farming the land. China had been left behind in the **industrial revolution** that had transformed western Europe and the USA and, by the twentieth century, was far behind the West in terms of advanced production, technology and infrastructure. There was little healthcare outside the cities and education was very poor: the vast majority of peasants remained illiterate. Social attitudes were rooted in **Confucian** tradition. Women were not considered equal and they did not have the right to own property.

China had for many years been ruled by powerful Emperors or military warlords who ran their provinces as their own private **fiefdoms**. As a result, there was no history or experience of democratic rule. China's deeply rooted problems were further exacerbated by nearly forty years of conflict. Battles with the warlords, the Japanese who had invaded in 1937, and a civil war between **nationalists** and **communists** that started in 1927 had killed millions, destroyed infrastructure and spread poverty and malnutrition. Refugees clogged what remained of transport networks and filled the streets of the cities. Although they had been forced to flee to the island of Taiwan in December 1949, the nationalists continued to be a threat, bombing ships on the coast to prevent a communist attack, while killing hundreds in the cities on the **mainland**. It is clear that when the communists came to power in 1949, they faced huge challenges.

## Note it down

Using the 1:2 method of note taking in this section (see page x), write a list of the problems facing Mao in 1949 in the left-hand column and a bullet-point list of the solutions in the right-hand column. End by highlighting in different colours which ones you feel were:

- beneficial for the Chinese people
- beneficial for Mao's Government.

## The Civil War, 1946–49

In October 1949, Mao Zedong stood atop the entrance to the **Forbidden City**, the old imperial palace and historical centre of the Emperor's political power. He declared the creation of the People's Republic of China. The crowds in Tiananmen Square cheered, 'Long live Chairman Mao.' However, by the time Mao made his announcement, China had suffered decades of conflict. He promised the Chinese people that, after years of humiliation, the Chinese people had 'stood up'.

In 1911 a revolution took place against the **Qing** dynasty and, by the following year, the last great imperial dynasty had collapsed. The people had lost faith in the Emperors and the old system because it had proved unable to keep pace with the modern economic and military developments of the Western empires. Britain, France, Germany and Russia, seeking to expand their empires and gain access to China's wealth and resources, were all able to exploit China's weakness to their own benefit, forcing China to accept trade agreements that were very one-sided and controlling parts of its cites, like the vital port of Shanghai.

With the end of imperial rule, China descended into chaos. Lack of central government led to the country being partitioned by warlords who ran their regions as private fiefdoms. Two political groups sought to rebuild China. The

## Confucian thought

Born in 551BC, Confucius was a Chinese philosopher who argued that people should be loyal to figures of authority such as leaders, parents or ancestors. Rules had to be followed. Families were governed by a dominant male figure who had complete authority over his household and family: a father had power over his children and a husband controlled his wife. The same principles applied between a ruler and his people: the subjects were told to be obedient and loyal. In the past this had helped create a society that was very hierarchal and rigid, in which everybody knew their place and accepted their traditional place in society. In return, leaders should be righteous and live up to strict moral standards. If leaders were not virtuous, the people should be ready to sacrifice their lives in order to defeat them.

▲ Statue of Confucius, Confucius Temple, Shanghai.

nationalists (the **Guomindang** or **GMD**) under Chiang Kai-shek advocated **capitalist** economic development but rejected Western democratic values in favour of authoritarian rule. Its rival, the Communist Party of China (CCP), formed in 1921, advocated the development of a communist state based on the ideas of Karl Marx. They were led by Mao Zedong. Both sides fought for power, and although they did grudgingly co-operate to repel an invasion by the Japanese from 1937 until the end of the Second World War in 1945, they soon resumed fighting a bloody and costly civil war which lasted between 1946 and 1949.

The fighting was ferocious. As one communist general later reminisced, the Communist People's Liberation Army (**PLA**) wiped out village after village with blanket shelling: 'In fighting … we practically flattened the villages, using thousands of shells and countless bombs.' One pilot reported that every village he flew over was burning and 'the fields were covered with bodies'. Despite the nationalist armies possessing a four-to-one numerical superiority, the communists were more popular, especially among the poor peasants to whom communist promises of equality held great appeal. The war ended in communist victory.

## China at the end of the Civil War

Despite Mao's announcement in October 1949, formal establishment of a new communist China did not in reality represent either the consolidation of communist authority, nor herald the emergence of any sense of unified national identity. The condition of China at the end of the Civil War was nothing less than catastrophic. Tens of millions had been killed in the battle to suppress warlordism, the conflict between nationalists and the communists, and to repel the Japanese occupation. After years of humiliation by Western powers, China was ruined, bankrupt and chaotic.

Politically, the CCP had not come to power through a democratic election but had seized power as a result of its military success. Rather than winning over the people, they had won in large part by the ineptitude of the nationalists, whose generals were corrupt and incompetent. The Communist Party did have support in rural areas of the country, to whom their promises of land reform (see page 204) had appeal, but they were far less popular among businessmen and middle classes in large Chinese cities like Shanghai. Furthermore, the peasants had little understanding of Mao's communist ideas.

### Administrative chaos

It was only when the communist forces began to take control of the country, occupying region by region as the GMD retreated, that the extent of the problems facing the new regime became apparent.

Although the nationalists had fled, they vowed to return to reclaim power. Before they left they stripped the country of assets such as gold, silver and dollar reserves, alongside cultural treasures, including those from Beijing's Forbidden City. Many of the educated elite, including bureaucrats and businessmen, had left with them. There were few experienced officials left to run cities or with enough technological knowledge to rebuild the economy. The Communist Party members were ideologically committed and experienced at **guerrilla fighting** but lacked sufficient knowledge of civilian government. This was exacerbated by a lack of planning because of the speed with which the nationalist forces had collapsed in 1949. The war had become known as 'The battle of the feet' – not so much a military conflict but a race by the nationalists to flee from the advancing communists. Little preparation for running the country had taken place.

### Karl Marx, 1818–83

Karl Marx was a German philosopher. He believed that wealthy capitalists exploited the lower classes, making them work long hours and paying them very little. Marx predicted that the workers would eventually rise up and create a society where everyone was equal. Marx believed that this revolution would be led by the working class **industrial labourers**.

In 1917, the Russian Communist Party (Bolsheviks) seized power in Russia and set about trying to create a society based on Marx's ideas. While the CCP in China also wanted a communist revolution, China had so few factories and cities that there were not enough industrial labourers to support the revolution. They adapted Marx's ideas and instead tried to win over the peasants to support their revolution.

▲ Karl Marx monument at Chemnitz.

## Lawlessness

As law and order broke down, an estimated 1 million bandits began to roam the countryside preying on the refugees displaced by the Japanese invasion or fleeing from the atrocities in the Civil War. They clogged the transport system, wandered aimlessly, or crammed into the unsanitary cities. In many ways, China was living up to its old nickname as the '**Sick Man of Asia**'.

## Economic problems

China's economy was completely devastated. There was no stable or even unified currency. However, the biggest problem was **hyperinflation**. Unable to support itself through taxation, the GMD regime had sought to bankroll its armies through printing money. In places, the money economy had collapsed and people reverted to bartering. Shortages of consumer goods led to people hoarding scarce supplies, making the situation worse. In 1940, 100 Chinese yuan was enough to buy a pig. By 1945, it was only enough to buy a fish. By 1946, 100 yuan was needed just to pay for an egg! By 1949, people could be seen using a cart to transport their practically worthless banknotes through the city streets.

**Source A** From John Melby, *The Mandate of Heaven* (1968). Melby was an American diplomat in China during the Civil War.

> Mukden was never exactly a distinctive or beautiful city; now it is a mediocrity turned to ruins and shambles. It has been gutted by bombing, end of the war vandalism, Russian looting, and now Chinese neglect. The great factories and public works are empty and silent, the scars of fire are already beginning to be softened by the encroaching vegetation. The houses wear the tired look of disrepair and the streets are dangerous at night for lack of maintenance. Trade centres largely in stalls along the sidewalks or where sidewalks once were. There is little in them beyond a few art treasures which survived the looting and the cloth and iron tag-ends of a junk collection. The people move – or don't move – aimlessly, listlessly. They are shabby and the pinch of hunger begins to show in pale faces and defensive eyes. [The CCP] guerrilla activities had been especially successful in disrupting railroads ... there were long stretches ... where even the embankments have vanished. We could see that the entire railroad from horizon to horizon was on fire and the roadbed was visibly being obliterated. While I was away the exchange rate went to five million and prices followed suit. Money is becoming meaningless and you wonder how people eat. [The] Director says the Central Bank is flat broke.

What can you learn from Source A about the challenges facing the new communist regime?

## Key debate

### How revolutionary was the new government of China?

There is a debate among historians about the nature of the changes Mao's regime introduced between 1949 and 1957. Some **'revolutionary' historians** believe that Mao's policies represented a huge change from the rule of Chiang Kai-shek and the nationalists, while **'evolutionary' historians** stress the continuity between Mao's rule and his predecessors: in essence, they suggest that in the early years after the revolution, the new regime followed many of the same policies as the Nationalists. As you work through this chapter, make a note of policies, campaigns or laws that would have made life in China fundamentally different after 1949. In another colour, highlight those aspects of life that remained the same. Which school of historical thought do you agree with the most?

## The state of China's industry

Mao sought to make China a great power through transforming it from a nation dependent on a backward farming system to one possessing a modern industrial economy. However, when the communists came to power, China's industry had been badly damaged by the years of war and much of China's industrial equipment had been destroyed. In places, retreating nationalist forces had attempted to sabotage industrial sites to prevent them falling into the hands of the communists. Areas where local power stations had been bombed or coal stocks were low lacked electricity.

At the end of the Second World War, the **Soviet Union** controlled Manchuria in the north-east of China. They were meant to ensure that the defeated Japanese soldiers went back to Japan. However, this caused special problems. Many of China's steel mills were in Manchuria, as were huge reserves of iron ore and coal alongside fertile farmland. The Soviet Union dismantled industrial equipment in factories and mines, confiscated tools and gold and shipped them back to the **USSR**. One observer wrote that Shenyang, the largest city in the region, had 'been reduced from a great industrial city into a tragic, crowded **way station**'.

The situation had worsened during the Civil War. In 1949, factory output was 44 per cent below its level of 1937. Factories needed to be reconstructed before industrial production could be improved. Raw materials were scarce and it was difficult to get them to the factories. In 1949, one foreigner reported that in Shanghai 'Cotton spinning mills ... are working three days a week and have only six months' stock' left to operate. Many skilled personnel who had the knowledge required to rebuild industrial production had fled to Taiwan with the nationalists. Mao himself admitted the problem: 'China's modern industry still forms a very small proportion of the national economy ... only about ten per cent of the total value of output of the national economy.'

Finally, lack of industrial production posed an ideological problem. According to Marxist thinking the industrial workers were identified as the vanguard of **communism** (see box, page 202). Marxists believed that it was easier to mould them into a force in support of the communist revolution because they were more educated and could be organised more easily in the factories. However, this did not appear to apply to China: only five per cent of the population worked in industry. Many of them were illiterate and unable to read the Party propaganda. Even by 1953, only ten per cent of the Party membership were urban industrial workers.

## The state of China's agriculture

Communist Party popularity was greatest among the peasants in rural areas. In many ways it was a 'peasant party'. The communists had carefully cultivated support in rural areas, an astute policy given that 80 per cent of the population lived there. Mao himself clearly understood the importance of retaining their support. As he had said, the real force for change in China had been the 'struggle of the peasants, the peasant uprisings and peasant wars'.

However, this is not to suggest that many peasants were ideologically committed to the creation of a communist state. As the vast majority were illiterate and uneducated, they were incapable of understanding the complexities of Marxist thought. They had little interest in theories or political ideas. They yearned to escape poverty and own their own land. Many peasants felt unfairly exploited by their landlords who made the peasants pay very high rents or give much of their produce to them. To ensure their support, the Communist Party promised to introduce land reform. They used the slogan 'land to the tiller', meaning that the peasant who 'tilled' (ploughed) the land would own it and not rent it from landlords.

However, as with industry, Chinese agriculture suffered from long-term historical problems, exacerbated by years of war. In the middle of the twentieth century, the wealth produced per person in China was just half of that in England in the late seventeenth century. Agricultural tools and livestock were in short supply and the most common fertiliser used by the peasants remained human waste. This spread disease. During the Civil War, many peasants had been forcibly **conscripted** into the nationalist forces to replace soldiers lost in battle to the communists. Dragged from their fields, their farms were often left unattended. Crops wilted and died, reducing food supplies to dangerous levels. By 1949 food production was at **subsistence** level and in some parts of China, there was a famine.

### Land reform

The introduction of a nationwide policy of land reform (see page 232) was made more difficult by the size and diverse nature of China itself. In some areas occupied by the communists for a long time, Party organisations were well embedded in local society and as a result reforms such as the redistribution of land to peasants had already taken place, while in others, particularly in the north in areas only recently liberated by the communists, it had not yet started.

The vast areas of agricultural land made it physically impossible for the CCP to send trained Party activists or **cadres** to every village to organise land reform. Although committed communists, the cadres often lacked local knowledge of how land in the village was organised. Often they found it hard to communicate with the peasants because they did not speak the same dialect. Even if they could understand, most peasants were interested only in events in their own villages and local areas; they were not concerned with national political issues or revolutionary ideology.

### Redistribution of land to peasants

The Communist Party believed the poor Chinese peasants were being exploited by their rich landlords who forced them to pay high rents for land. The communists promised to undertake a policy of 'land redistribution'. Party cadres travelled to villages and encouraged the peasants to rise up against the oppressors, subjecting landlords to '**struggle meetings**' where they would be beaten while the mass of peasants shouted abuse and humiliated them. At the end of the meeting the landlord would be forced to sign a confession and hand over his land to the Party cadres who would redistribute it more fairly among the villagers. This policy was hugely popular and a source of great support for the communists during their war against the nationalists.

## National infrastructure

Although Mao had announced the formation of the People's Republic in 1949, China could barely be called a single, unified nation. Nationalist forces were still present on Chinese territory and while Chiang Kai-shek had been defeated, he had evaded capture and escaped to Taiwan, promising to return to remove the communists. He had a very powerful ally in the United States, who feared that a communist China would be a threat to US security and economic power and thus hoped that the nationalists would be able to remove

**Source B** From Sidney Rittenberg and Amanda Bennett, *The Man Who Stayed Behind*, 2001. Rittenberg was an American who converted to communism on the eve of the Second World War. Having studied Chinese, he was posted to China after the war. The first American citizen to join the CCP, he later worked as a translator for the Communist Party, translating Mao's works into English. He was imprisoned twice, falsely accused of being an American spy. The source is an extract from his memoirs written in 2001.

> A few days later, my companions and I set out southward by jeep. We drove up the dusty road and quickly realised that we were indeed driving into the famine. Bordering either side of the road in thin columns were the refugees, fathers and mothers with babies in their arms, pulling older children along behind them. Elderly peasant women with tiny bound feet hobbled along step after painful step. There were corpses too, lying by the side of the road where they had fallen.
>
> We drove on in complete silence. Once we got south of Hengyang, things got even worse. The corpses were so numerous that for the rest of the day they were almost never out of sight. The road was thick with refugees ... There were people with ox carts piled high with their own belongings, or pushing their household goods before them in barrows. They didn't beg for money. They demanded food. 'Yao mi,' the shout went up. 'Yao mi.' We want rice. The crowd took up the cry and surged forward against our jeep.
>
> We finally made it out of town and back onto the highway. Once we were safely out of the crowd [we looked] for signs of grain and hoarding. It didn't take long. Within a few minutes he returned, having discovered a full granary within a hundred yards of the starving crowds.
>
> 'Why?' I asked.
>
> 'They are waiting for prices to go higher before they sell.' There was plenty of grain all over the region. The main culprit ... was General Ou Guan ... a combination of prefect, warlord and bandit. One of the biggest grain hoarders and profiteers in the region, he seized the relief grain [provided by the United Nations] and sold it.
>
> [At a meeting one man declared]: 'When the Japanese were here ... we longed for the Nationalist government to return. Now we would rather have the Japanese.' 'They were foreigners,' another chimed in. 'These people are supposed to be Chinese, but their own countrymen mean nothing to them. I hate them.'

How valuable is Source B for historians seeking to learn about the conditions in China in 1949?

Mao from power. The previous nationalist government had been very corrupt. Bribery of officials was commonplace, while many leaders hoarded supplies or sold food meant for the people for their own profit. Warlords still controlled large areas, and bandits evaded the forces of law and order, making communication and travel between cities hazardous. Central government control had largely broken down. This lack of central control was further retarded by a lack of unified language. Instead, many areas had their own distinct dialect, unintelligible to outsiders. Although the majority of the people were **Han Chinese**, there were over 50 ethnic and religious groups each with their own customs and traditions.

## Transport

Transport networks were badly damaged; an estimated half of the railway network had been destroyed. Blowing up railway tracks and bridges had been a key tactic of the communists during the Civil War because it disrupted the nationalists' ability to move their troops into battle, but now it created a major problem for the new government. They had to quickly rebuild them in order to consolidate control over large expanses of the country, particularly isolated rural areas far from the capital, Beijing. Telephone lines had been damaged while rivers and harbours were clogged up with ships sunk during the years of conflict. For example, Hankou, the capital of Hubei province and the second largest port in China, had been the target of American B-29 strikes against the occupying Japanese and had been reduced to rubble. Similarly, the Japanese had developed Hainan in the south as a key port, but American bombing had destroyed it, leaving the iron mines in the surrounding hills that were vital for industrial production largely unattended.

### War against Japan

In 1931 Japan invaded Manchuria in an effort to secure raw materials and economic resources for its empire. This widened into a full-scale war in 1937. At first the Japanese easily defeated the disorganised Chinese armies, but the Chinese nationalists and the communists agreed to suspend the Civil War they were fighting against each other to band together to form a 'United Front' against the invaders. The invasion ended with Japan's defeat in the Second World War, but the impact had been devastating. Japanese occupation was extremely harsh. The most famous atrocity was the so-called 'Rape' of the city of Nanking where Japanese soldiers tortured and murdered thousands of civilians. The damage caused by the Japanese invasion, particularly to industry and national infrastructure, was considerable and represented a major problem for the new communist regime when it took power in 1949.

## Cities

The lack of established national infrastructure meant that rural and urban China were largely isolated from each other. The communist soldiers were mostly peasant farmers. When they took control of cities like Shanghai and Beijing, they became the source of jokes. One anecdote described a young soldier who found a white porcelain toilet and tried to wash the rice in it. Another soldier pulled the rope attached to the cistern, only to look on aghast as the rice vanished with the bubbles in the bowl. At the luxurious Cathay Hotel confused soldiers played with the elevators and tied up their mules in the marble floored lobby. Inexperienced, the communists simply were not well prepared to run China's cities or set up an efficient government administration.

## The nationalist threat

Establishing national, unified control would be extremely difficult. There was simply no effective administrative structure to co-ordinate the vast challenges of rebuilding.

**Source C** From John Melby, *The Mandate of Heaven* (1968). Melby was an American diplomat in China during the Civil War.

> Serious rice riots in major urban centres; stocks had run low and it was discovered that speculators were hoarding what was available. It is the first time the Communists have had to administer a city and they are finding that urban and rural skills are very different. A lot of racketeering groups are taking advantage of them. It is apparently the old story of the country boy who came to the big city. One pathetic note is the women in their country padded jackets and pants gawking in amazement at the painted ladies of the town. Chungking in a sense is a dying city. The foreign group is drifting away day by day, as are the universities, the intellectuals, the Government. Slowly the city drops back into the provincialism and insularity [isolation] of centuries past. It is like watching the recreation of an ancient order.
>
> Hankow, the second port of China, is still in the grip of an advanced stage of dry rot. The waterfront, once a showplace of wharves and commercial and office buildings, remains largely the rubble which our B-29 strikes made of it. The local administrations, both civil and military, are stagnant, corrupt and inept. Deterioration is the password.

What does Source C suggest were the major problems facing the new communist regime in its attempts to rebuild China?

Even after the formation of the PRC, the nationalists posed a threat. They sent spies and **saboteurs** to attack the new regime and US supplied planes to bomb coastal cities like Shanghai; one raid in February 1950 killed over 1000 people and damaged the electricity and water supply. Nationalist attacks also sunk PRC ships massed to prepare for the invasion of Taiwan.

## Conclusion: China in 1949

When Mao stood atop the Tiananmen gate in October 1949 and announced the creation of the People's Republic of China, he was greeted by enormous cheering crowds. Many Chinese were genuinely optimistic; after years of war, they hoped for an era of peace and prosperity. However, the communists clearly faced enormous challenges. Some had been caused by the recent warfare. The destruction of factories and lack of food production were problems that urgently needed to be addressed. Furthermore, lack of communications infrastructure made efficient government very difficult. The nationalists in Taiwan still posed a threat to the new regime. There were also problems that had been present throughout Chinese history. No government had ever successfully created a sense of unified national identity, or overcome the vast inequalities between rural and urban China. Finally, few people really understood or cared about Mao's ideology; they simply wanted to survive and live in peace. When Mao looked down at the crowds from the Forbidden City he knew that the struggle to create a modern and successful China had only just begun.

### Work together

- Put away your notes and take a blank piece of paper. Write the title 'The problems facing Mao in 1949'. Work with a partner and write down as many problems as you can remember. You might like to set yourself a time limit to test yourself.
- See if you can categorise them into types of problems. Industrial problems might be one example.
- Now imagine that you are the new ruler of China. Which problem would you try to solve first? Highlight your choice and write an explanation of why you have chosen that problem as the key priority.
- Explain your answer to another pair of students. Do you agree or do they have a different answer?
- Overall, how would you describe the situation in China at the start of the People's Republic? Write down three words to describe what China was like in 1949.

## 2 The new power structure

Mao set out the guiding principles of the new People's Republic in an essay written in 1949 entitled 'On the People's Democratic Dictatorship'. Rather than destroying his enemies, he declared that he wanted to 'arouse the masses of the people' to co-operate in a 'united front'. The system he introduced was termed '**democratic centralism**', again suggesting that the new regime would allow political freedoms and voting rights. However, it quickly became clear that the Communist Party sought to dominate the political decision making of the new China. Although the role of chairman was not one that officially afforded Mao massive personal authority, Mao's personal prestige meant that it was he who held the greatest power to dictate policy.

### The new constitution

The CCP organised the Chinese People's Political Consultative Conference (**CPPCC**) to meet in Beijing in September 1949. This body of 662 delegates created the **Common Program for China** (see box), to act as a provisional **constitution** to provide the legal basis for the new republic from 1949 to 1954. The delegates represented a wide cross section of social and political perspectives; only sixteen of them were formal members of the CCP. Left-wing members of the Guomindang were invited to participate as well as representatives from a range of organisations such as the Democratic League, which demanded that China take a middle path between nationalism and communism and advocated greater voting rights and freedoms. Also invited were a range of high-profile politicians termed 'democratic personalities'. Well known and popular, these individuals were treated well, though they had little real power. They were used for propaganda purposes: their inclusion made the new regime seem more open and democratic.

### Democratic centralism

A new constitution, introduced in 1954, declared that 'All power in the People's Republic belongs to the people.' An elected **legislature**, the **National People's Congress**, was to be a part of the Communist Party. It would represent the wishes of the people and meet once a year to make laws or amend the constitution. Its official powers included electing the chairman of the PRC, deciding on issues of war and setting out national economic policy. Mao termed his new form of government 'democratic centralism'. It meant that the voice of the people would be represented in central government through democratic elections to the legislature. There would also be democratically elected local congresses that would govern at a local and provincial level. They would pass information up to the 'Centre', the government in Beijing.

Officially, this organising principle was democratic in that those locally elected representatives, at first in villages and towns, up to provincial level and ultimately in the **legislature**, could discuss and debate issues. However, once the policy had been decided by the central government, and dictated back down the political structure, no deviation

### The Common Program for China

- All except 'political **reactionaries**' would enjoy freedom of 'thought, speech, publication, assembly, association, correspondence, person, domicile, moving from one place to another, religious belief, and freedom to hold processions and demonstrations'.
- Although it emphasised the leading role of the CCP, it accepted a multiparty system, within which eight political parties received legal status.
- It recognised the right to own private property and supported entrepreneurship and the mutually beneficial relations between workers and employees.
- It supported equal rights for women.
- It supported **universal education**.
- Soviet-style central economic planning was a goal. The program urged that the economy be 'centred on the planned, systematic rehabilitation of development of **heavy industry**' though this was a long-term objective.
- Mao was named as Head of State.

### Mao's early political vision

When he first came to power, Mao's political ideas appeared pragmatic and conciliatory. Many people feared that the communist regime would be repressive and would harshly punish their enemies, just as the communists in Russia had done when they first came to power. Instead, Mao said that he wanted to create a 'united front' formed by peasants and workers, and they would work in alliance with the middle classes. These would be defined as 'the people'. They would hold power in the new China. Working together with the Communist Party they would transform China into a modern, egalitarian nation. No mention was made of the massive use of terror and violence he would later introduce to control his opponents.

from the prescribed line was allowed. As he often did, Mao took advantage of Chinese history to enforce his power. The hierarchy and respect for authority and power that were principles of democratic centralism were found in the ideas of Confucius (see page 201) that had been so influential previously. For Mao these common characteristics provided a helpful historical point of reference to give an ideological justification of his overarching authority.

## The structure of the new government

The new government of the People's Republic was formed of three separate but tightly interwoven branches of government:

1. the Communist Party (CCP)
2. the Central People's Government
3. the People's Liberation Army (PLA).

### Mao's dominant position

The new political system greatly enhanced Mao's own personal authority. There was little distinction between the three branches of government, which overlapped and were interconnected. Leaders at the top of the Party, and therefore beholden to Mao as the Chairman, simultaneously held positions in the Central People's Government and the PLA. Furthermore, Mao was both Chairman of the CCP and Chairman of the People's Republic of China.

## The Communist Party (CCP)

The Communist Party (CCP) co-ordinated the government. At first this was difficult. The Party had fewer than 4.5 million members (in a population of over half a billion) and it was structurally impossible for it to instigate its rule, particularly in the more remote provinces. However, it quickly grew in size and by the end of 1950 it had 5.8 million members. It co-ordinated the other branches of government, organising education, the legal system and the military.

Political power rested with the Party and therefore Mao as its chairman. The Party had a Central Committee of 49 members in 1949, which in turn was dominated by the 25-man Politburo, which ultimately was controlled by a **Standing Committee** of five. As the Standing Committee's chairman, Mao held the real authority.

All the members of the Standing Committee were close revolutionary colleagues of Mao, including Liu Shaoqi, the Chairman of the Standing Committee of the National People's Congress, with the power to alter laws passed by the Congress, and Zhou Enlai, Premier of the People's Republic and Foreign Minister. Both had fought alongside Mao during the Civil War. These men ran the government. In reality the National People's Congress merely acted as a 'rubber stamp' to approve their decisions. Although Mao did not make every decision, and at times did not even attend all Politburo meetings, no policy that he did not approve of would be realised.

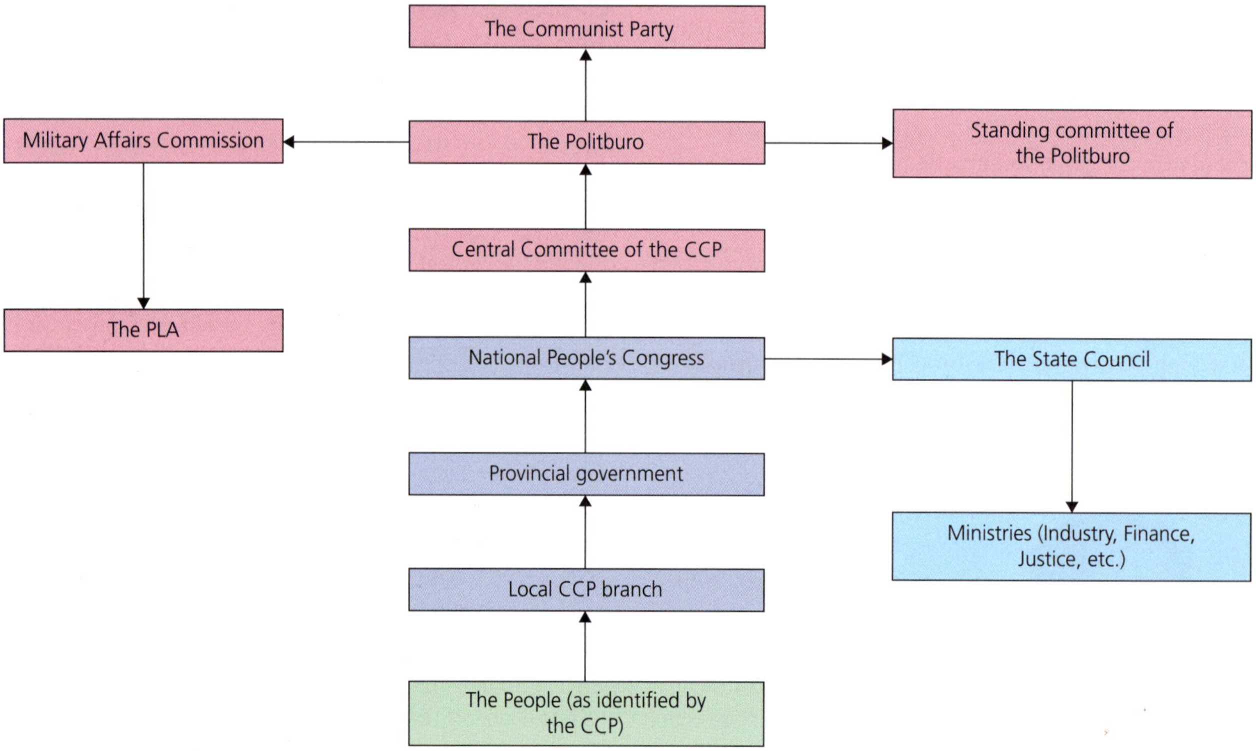


▲ Figure 1: The new political structure.

### The Central People's Government

The Central People's Government of China was also organised according to the principles of democratic centralism. In theory the government derived its authority from the Political Consultative Conference but in reality it held massive independent power. The power in the government was concentrated in the People's Government Council which combined legislative and executive powers. It interpreted and enacted laws, announced decrees and executed them. It made treaties, declared wars, controlled the budget and appointed all key government personnel. The Government Council, later called the State Council after 1954, was headed by Zhou Enlai. Zhou co-ordinated 24 new ministries such as Justice, Heavy Industry, Finance and Food.

## The People's Liberation Army (PLA)

When Mao announced the creation of the PRC in October 1949, the communists lacked an effective means of national control. How could Mao establish his authority? Perhaps his most famous quote suggested an answer: 'All political power,' he had said, 'lies in the barrel of a gun.' Only the gun, represented by the People's Liberation Army, could enable him to consolidate his power. The Party controlled the PLA through the Military Affairs Commission. The PLA greatly increased communist control through the **reunification campaigns** (see pages 213–214) and helped Mao enhance his personal political prestige while intimidating his opponents through the military achievements of the Korean War, 1950–53 (see page 219–220). Between 1950 and 1953, the PLA was also assigned responsibility for the suppression of bandits – 'a euphemism', suggests historian Linda Benson, 'for any opposition to the CCP'. Over 100,000 enemies of the communists were killed.

A conscription law passed in 1955 ensured 800,000 new recruits every year. Soldiers called the PLA the 'big university' because it was there that they were taught to read and write. Of course, this benefited the regime, too, because the new soldiers were indoctrinated with communist propaganda in order to create genuine ideological commitment. Many recruits from poor rural backgrounds welcomed the opportunities that a military career offered. One female soldier who had enlisted recalled 'the alternative was feeding pigs in the countryside'.

### Regional bureaux

The structure of the new government system helped increase the power of the PLA. In order to enable the central government to more easily control such a vast area of territory, the PRC was divided into six massive regions, governed by regional party bureaux, roughly corresponding to the areas under the control of the different communist armies at the end of the Civil War (see map, page 210). Each bureau had four officials:

- Government Chairman
- First Party Secretary
- Military Commander
- Army Political Commissar.

Two of the posts were military ones, filled by officers of the People's Liberation Army. This ensured military control of the country and the consolidation of the People's Liberation Army's influence. The military character of the regional bureaux was clear: these regions were initially called Military Administrative Commissions. 'Military' was later removed from their title, but, as Shaun Breslin notes, 'many of the new civilian leaders simply transferred out of the military into the new party-state. They were, in effect, soldiers into civvies.'

### 'Learn from the PLA'

The 'Learn from the PLA' campaign instructed the people to learn from the revolutionary and personal attributes the 'People's Soldiers' exemplified: discipline, bravery, resourcefulness, incorruptibility and, most importantly, commitment to the communist cause. So important was the loyalty of the PLA to Mao that they even received exemption from legal authority. When the divorce rate rose as a result of the 1950, Marriage Law (see page 289–90) New a special clause was added to make it more difficult for the wives of PLA soldiers to divorce their husbands.

### The PLA's economic role

The PLA had an economic role, too, helping to rebuild China's infrastructure. Officers' dependants were compelled to work in the **co-operative farms** (see page 234), while **work teams** of PLA soldiers contributed up to a week's free labour a year to help local construction or irrigation projects, teach in primary or night schools, or repair farm tools. Every fifty men were commanded to jointly raise at least one pig. Later, on holidays during the **Great Leap Forward** of 1958-61 (see page 242), the PLA were forced to join local peasants to hunt down the four pests – rats, sparrows, flies and mosquitoes. PLA men were even forced to collect their own excrement to be supplied to local co-operatives as fertiliser.

### A modern fighting force?

Losses incurred during the Korean War (see page 219) convinced Mao and his most successful general Peng

▲ **Figure 2: The regional bureaux of the PRC.**

Dehuai that the PLA needed to abandon its old-style **guerrilla tactics** and become a modern, technologically advanced army. The size of the army was reduced from 5 million in 1950 to 3.5 million in 1953. New military academies in Beijing and Nanjing trained an ideologically committed generation of officers, schooled in the techniques of modern combat and intensely loyal to the communists. Many were sent for advanced training in the USSR which provided weapons such as the MiG fighter jets. The advanced, professional army was a key tool in the consolidation of the communist regime.

## Conclusion: The new power structure

Although the new government promised greater liberty than previous rulers of China, in reality democratic centralism did not bring an era of freedoms and civil rights. In fact, it had much in common with previous imperial rulers of China. Power was restricted to the ruling elite and disagreement with government policy might incur harsh punishment. The influence of the Communist Party was vast. It controlled the government and China quickly developed into a one-party state. As head of the Party, Mao's personal authority was increasing rapidly. Not only was Mao Chairman of the Party but he was also China's first president and chair of the commission that controlled the armed forces. His influence over the PLA meant his power was secure. After spending his life railing against the excessive powers of the morally bankrupt leaders and dictators, he had himself become politically dominant; he was, in effect, the new Chinese Emperor.

### Work together

Take a large piece of paper. Draw a diagram to show the political structure of the PRC. Your partner does the same. You can use a few key words and simple images but no long explanations. Give your partner your version and ask them to use it to explain how the political structure of the PRC worked. Was your diagram straightforward and clear enough for them to be able to use it to explain the structure?

## 3 Defeating the CCP's opponents

Although the regime promised to free the Chinese people from oppression, it quickly began to use violence against them. The 'Campaign to Suppress **Counter-Revolutionaries**' was launched in March 1950 while the Three Antis Campaign (August 1951) and the Five Antis Campaign (February 1952) targeted opponents for intimidation, imprisonment and even execution. Mao was able to use the Korean War (1950–53) as an excuse to further increase the use of terror. By the end of the campaigns, Mao had greatly enhanced his control and effectively prevented anyone from challenging him.

### Note it down

Some historians argue that Mao was very similar to other communist leaders like Stalin. They point to the use of terror as evidence that they were bloodthirsty dictators. Other historians disagree. Although they agree that Mao did have his opponents imprisoned, he used terror in a very different way. As you work through this section, note down the different ways in which Mao used terror. If you have completed study of Russia 1917–91, highlight in one colour evidence that he used terror in the same way as Stalin and in another colour any ways in which terror in China was different.

### The campaign to suppress 'counter-revolutionaries'

This campaign, launched in March 1950, was openly aimed at preventing nationalist sympathisers and their spies from undermining the regime. Anyone who had the potential to cause trouble for the regime was at risk. Most vulnerable were anyone who had worked for the previous nationalist regime and academics who had worked with foreign universities, many of whom were denounced as saboteurs and spies. Western businessmen were forced to leave the country and had their property confiscated, while many **Christian missionaries** were arrested and charged on the suspicion of being imperialist agents.

The campaign was expanded by China's involvement in the Korean War (see page 219) that provided Mao with the justification for greater social control and purging his 'class enemies' on the pretence of hunting for traitors. Under the pretence of seeking to eradicate spies, Mao's decree of February 1951 entitled 'Regulations regarding the Punishments of Counter-Revolutionaries' extended the definition of 'counter-revolutionary activity' to include all forms of political dissent. In reality, this simply meant anyone the Party identified as undesirable. Those who had studied in the USA were suspected of being unpatriotic and anyone who had family in Taiwan was suspected of having nationalist tendencies.

### Self-registration

The regime tricked many victims into implicating themselves. The Ministry of Public Security, the organisation that ran the campaign, asked all those who had previously held positions within the nationalist regime to register in order to help those who had made 'political mistakes' to 'start life anew'. They were asked to submit autobiographies listing their friends and associates with the guarantee that everyone who confessed to having worked with the previous regime would be treated leniently. Afterwards they, along with the associates they had identified, were arrested. Just as in Stalin's Russia, many

### Key debate

#### Was Mao as big a murderer as Hitler and Stalin?

Mao Zedong is often placed alongside Hitler and Stalin as one of the most infamous dictators of the twentieth century. In 2005 Jung Chang and Jon Halliday's *Mao: The Unknown Story* reinforced this image, creating a picture of life in Mao's China as one of unremitting terror, and placing the death toll of the regime at well over 70 million, 'more than any other 20th century leader'. Mao himself seemed to welcome the comparison, declaring Hitler a fellow revolutionary because, Mao said, 'the more you kill, the more revolutionary you are'. However, there remains no consensus regarding the nature of the terror utilised during his rule. American historian Lee Feigon observes that Mao was 'ruthless ... but not bloodthirsty' and others have derided what they term as 'competitive body-counting' between dictators. Interestingly, some Chinese scholars have argued that Mao did not inflict the same amount of terror as other dictators. Jin Xiaoding has argued that many died only because of his 'bad judgement', while Professor Mobo Gao has declared 'it was public knowledge that Mao, unlike Stalin and Hitler, did not execute his political rivals'. No serious historian could argue that terror and repression was not a vital tool in Mao's' defeat of his opponents. However, its nature and the validity of the comparisons with the Hitler state and Stalin's Russia are still sources of historical debate.

people were rounded up by the police in midnight arrests. People found that their friends and family disappeared, never to be seen again.

## Mass participation

The Party also encouraged ordinary Chinese citizens to become involved in political activities with rallies organised to denounce 'counter-revolutionaries'. The victims were subjected to public struggle meetings where they were forced to admit their guilt in front of large crowds demanding retribution. They chanted, 'Kill the counter-revolutionaries! Kill! Kill! Kill!' Responding to 'the will of the masses' the sentence of death was often carried out there and then. However, this was clearly not the spontaneous act of an oppressed people. In April 1951 the Ministry of Public Security produced a manual entitled 'How to Hold an Accusation Meeting'.

Robert Loh, a factory manager who later fled to the West, wrote a book recalling his ordeal entitled *Escape from Red China* (Coward-McCann Inc., 1962). In it he recalled that:

> *'One of the execution grounds was near the university. Every day we would see truckloads of prisoners ... we would hear terrible shooting ... trucks carrying away the corpses dripped streams of blood onto the road ... Within the next few months, all the ex-Nationalists were wiped out.'*

However, unlike the terror in the Soviet Union (see pages 19–21), the secret police did not become overly powerful. Mao encouraged mass participation in the campaign. Non-Party members were invited to participate in committees helping to run it. Mao was also careful to prevent the use of terror against the Party at this stage. The campaign was carefully controlled by the Party itself. The *People's Daily* published long lists of political criminals alongside gruesome details of their punishment in order to intimidate anyone considering resisting the new regime. Although figures vary greatly, the government recorded 800,000 counter-revolutionary deaths during the first half of 1951. The moderate policies of the first years of the PRC were forgotten.

## The Three Antis Campaign (August 1951–July 1952)

In 1951 Mao called for a 'big clean up throughout the Party' and the Three Antis Campaign was launched. It was directed against:

- corruption
- waste
- **obstructionist bureaucracy** in government.

Many Chinese people, including the middle classes, supported this aim. They believed that the regime was going to discipline those within the CCP who had taken advantage of their new power for their own benefit. It quickly became clear that the regime was using public support for the campaign as an excuse to remove anyone in the civil service who they did not like. Many civil service employees had been in the same roles under the nationalists; the communists had needed them to help establish the new regime with jobs like collecting taxes, organising schools or co-ordinating the transport system. By late 1951, the communists had trained enough loyal Party cadres to do these jobs. Now the former employees were imprisoned or executed.

## The Five Antis Campaign (February–May 1952)

The CCP also used mass campaigns to remove possible opponents and seize control over economic assets. The 1952 Five Antis Campaign was dedicated to ending:

- bribery
- tax evasion
- theft of state property
- cheating on government contracts
- stealing state economic information.

The targets were the middle classes and private business owners. A variety of forms of pressure were used to round them up. Those who confessed were encouraged to believe that they might be treated leniently if they helped identify other guilty businessmen. Desperate, they became even more dedicated to hunting down and incriminating victims than the Party cadres, even if those they named were completely innocent of any real crime. After they had served their purposes the businessmen were executed.

Another form of pressure used was to tell a businessman's wife and children that he was guilty and that the only possible way out was to confess. Fearing that their husbands and fathers would be executed they pleaded with him to admit his guilt. Sometimes, in order to save themselves and avoid being implicated, wives and children denounced husbands and fathers, with bright red 'Denunciation Boxes' set up on street corners to help them to do so. Those found guilty were made to pay huge fines and had their property confiscated. Some were imprisoned.

Workers were encouraged to turn on their bosses and denounce them. In the cities loudspeakers were set up warning business owners: 'Evidence of all your misdeeds is now in our hands. Confess!' Banners were put up urging people to 'Sternly Punish Corruption Culprits'. So-called 'tiger beaters', selected employees of a firm, were organised by the Party cadres into a team of activists and ordered to gather incriminating evidence against their former managers and bosses. The beaters intimidated the 'capitalist tigers' torturing them until they were dragged before a mass struggle meeting and forced to confess their crimes. Robert Loh was forced to 'beg the masses to forgive my sins' while also thanking 'the great Communist Party which, under the wise and benevolent leadership of Chairman Mao, had instigated this great campaign'. Loh was spared and later escaped to the West. Others were not able to escape and chose suicide, the only possible act of defiance to the regime. Loh recalls that 'the sight of people jumping out of windows became commonplace' while 'coffin makers were sold out weeks ahead'. Funeral homes held several funerals at once in the same room in order to meet demand. Parks were patrolled by police to prevent people from hanging themselves from trees. Those who survived were sent to the Party's brutal new prison system, the *laogai* (see pages 215–216).

## Characteristics of the Campaigns

Both campaigns were very successful. According to one report, 30,000 people attended one meeting directed against local Party bosses accused of corruption, while in Shanghai 99 per cent of businessmen were found to be guilty of at least one of the 'Five Antis' called the 'five poisons'. The early days of the regime where private capitalism was tolerated was over. The campaigns helped establish the Party's control over private companies. Businesses found guilty during the Three and Five Antis Campaigns were forced to pay heavy fines and, in order to pay them, had to sell stock to the state, creating joint public-private enterprises. The Party sent cadres into the companies to take on leading management roles, enhancing their control.

The campaigns also greatly altered the social system in China. In this atmosphere of fear and repression, many chose to save themselves by denouncing others before they themselves could become a target. Friends were forced to betray friends to save themselves; family members denounced each other. Traditional relationships based on family, workplace or school background no longer mattered. The only way to protect oneself was utter loyalty to the CCP. Once his potential opponents were under control, Mao could more easily establish his one-party state and personal political control.

### The Yan'an rectification campaign

The campaigns of the early 1950s were not the first time that Mao had used violence to remove his opponents. During the Chinese Civil War, he had set up a base in remote Yan'an to escape Chiang Kai-shek. Once there he launched a 'Thought Reform Movement' to eradicate those who he feared were 'deviating' from 'correct thought', as he personally defined it. Party members were intimidated by struggle meetings to write self-criticisms in which they admitted any ways in which they had not been totally loyal. Anyone who deviated from Mao Zedong Thought was punished. Some were imprisoned and others were executed. Once in power over the PRC, he introduced exactly the same policies.

## The reunification campaigns

Alongside police terror, Mao also used his military force, the PLA, to consolidate his control within China's borders. Primary among Mao's aims was to establish his control of the peripheral regions of China. The seizure of these regions were entitled 'reunification campaigns' because the regime hoped to make the invasions appear more legitimate by trying to convince observers that all the areas had in fact once been part of a larger Chinese state. The campaigns were vitally important. Failure to control Tibet, Xinjiang, Guangdong and Taiwan presented a real threat to the CCP. Tibet and Xinjiang were border regions far from Beijing and vulnerable to foreign influence. With its large Muslim population, Xinjiang had more in common with Muslim areas in the Soviet Union than it did with China. Mao greatly feared that the Soviet Union might try to take advantage of the chaos in China during the Civil War to seize the province. Moreover, Tibet was led by the Buddhist **Dalai Lama**, a rival leader to Mao. Mao knew that control of these regions was vital if he were to protect the borders of his new republic.

### Religion in Tibet and Xinjiang

Control of Tibet and Xinjiang was important for the communist regime, particularly because of the importance of religion there. In both Tibet and Xinjiang, religion was fundamentally interwoven into the fabric of the society. Buddhist leaders in Tibet held great political influence, while in Xinjiang, Muslim ideas moulded attitudes to issues as wide ranging as politics, education and women's rights. Religious ideas represented a clear challenge to Mao's attempt to create a state based only upon communist principles which argued that God did not exist. As rival belief systems, they inevitably were targets for the new government.

## The invasion of Tibet (October 1950)

Mao declared that he sent the PLA to invade Tibet officially in order to 'liberate it from imperialist oppression'. 'Liberation from whom and what?' asked the Tibetans, who historically regarded themselves as culturally and racially different from the Chinese. In reality the invasion aimed to remove the threat of a rival belief system, Buddhism, and to control the loyalties to an alternative leadership, the Dalai Lama. Some 60,000 attempted to resist the invasion, but to no avail. Chinese troops entered the Tibetan capital Lhasa in November 1950. They set up a government that was superficially Tibetan but in reality was dominated by Beijing. With soldiers positioned in Lhasa, representatives of the Dalai Lama had little choice but to sign a 17-Point 'Agreement on Measures for the Peaceful Liberation of Tibet' which set out the terms of the merging of Tibet into the PRC.

Ignoring the promises of the agreement, the Chinese imposed policies aimed at wiping out all traces of separate Tibetan identity. Traditional religious practice was prohibited, as was the teaching of the Tibetan language and history in schools. Mandarin Chinese was enforced as the official language. Political meetings were prohibited with the threat of imprisonment for anyone who disobeyed. Part of the 17-Point Agreement guaranteed that Tibet would not be subject to the radical land reforms of other Chinese provinces (see page 232). However, boundaries were redrawn to ensure that many Tibetans now found they lived outside Tibetan borders, in the neighbouring Chinese province of Sichuan, and so were forced to take part in communal land reforms.

**Source D** On 23 May 1951, Representatives of the PRC and the Dalai Lama signed the Agreement on Measures for the Peaceful Liberation of Tibet, known as the '17-Point Agreement.' Quoted in Linda Benson, *China since 1949* (Pearson, 2002).

> The important content [of the agreement] was as follows: expel imperialist aggressors from Tibet; assist the Chinese People's Liberation Army to enter Tibet [in order to] strengthen border defence; merge all of Tibet's local government departments with the Central People's Government departments; put into practice minority district governments or autonomous government with the united leadership of the CCP; reform Tibet's social system; change the Tibetan military step by step; expand Tibetan government, economy and culture.
>
> In signing this agreement, Tibetans threw off forever imperialist aggression and returned to the motherland, thereby consolidating the unity of the motherland.

In what ways does Source D justify the Chinese invasion of Tibet?

**Source E** From Dalai Lama, *My Land and My People* (McGraw Hill, 1962), pages 88–89. In 1962, the Dalai Lama published his memoirs in which he recounted the circumstances and the content of the 17-Point Agreement.

> We were appalled at the mixture of Communist clichés, vainglorious assertions which were completely false, and bold statements which were only partly true. The preamble said that 'over the last one hundred years or more', imperialist forces had penetrated into China and Tibet and 'carried out all kinds of deceptions and provocations'. This was pure nonsense. Among the reasons given were that the influence of aggressive imperialist forces in Tibet might be successfully eliminated ... Reading this, we reflected bitterly that there had been no foreign forces whatever in Tibet since we drove out the last of the Chinese forces in 1912.

Compare Source E from the Dalai Lama's memoirs with Source D. In what ways do they differ? Which one has greater utility to a historian who was studying the reunification campaign in Tibet? (Hint: no source will be completely useless!)

### Migration of Han Chinese

In November 1952 Mao declared his desire to raise the population of Tibet from 3 million to 10 million. He did not mean to encourage the growth of the local population, but rather to promote the migration of the dominant Han Chinese ethnic group into Tibet. Once there, they would marginalise the indigenous population and replace their traditional culture and way of life. The PLA built a massive highway to help move migrants and military forces into Tibet, one of many construction and electrification projects that had the twin aims of improving infrastructure while destroying traditional ways of life.

### Propaganda and exile

Invading PLA forces were accompanied by propaganda units that spread communist ideas and tried to convince Tibetans that they needed liberation from their traditional 'feudal' society. Newspapers and magazines were distributed that explained the benefits of communism. Dances and dramas told tales of peasants liberating themselves from the repressive control of the Lamas and Buddhism. Outdoor cinemas showed propaganda films on the whitewashed walls while radio programmes that told Tibetans to be thankful to Chairman Mao were set up in town squares. Publicly Tibetan leaders had no choice but to offer thanks to Mao for having 'done so much for Tibet', but streams of Tibetan refugees began to pour into neighbouring India telling terrifying tales of persecution, exploitation and torture. When, in 1959, the Tibetans finally rebelled, they were brutally suppressed by the PLA, and the Dalai Lama fled into exile in India.

## Xinjiang

Xinjiang province in the west (see map, page 210) had a large Muslim population, and close ethnic ties with Muslims in the Soviet Union. The Mongols, the Turkic peoples and the Iranian peoples of Xinjiang had different written languages, starkly divergent cultural heritages and strong senses of ethnic identity. Mosques were commonplace and Arabic was the language used in religious services. As Xinjiang bordered Soviet-controlled Outer Mongolia, the Chinese regime feared the growth of **separatist** sentiment or Russian influence.

### The Uighurs

The Uighurs were the largest minority group in Xinjiang, accounting for three-quarters of the population of 4 million. They had a long history of opposition to central control, their violent resistance meaning that the region was not fully incorporated into the Chinese Empire until 1884. The CCP used a combination of military force and negotiation. Nationalist leaders were invited to the Political Consultative Conference in 1949, but on the way to Beijing their plane crashed, killing all on board. Rumours that Mao had had them murdered spread, and although never proven, their replacements agreed to submit to Chinese rule and were rewarded with key posts in the new government.

The PLA, led by Peng Dehuai, cleared all resistance and, by March 1950, secured territory to ensure safety for government-sponsored **in-migration** of Han Chinese settlers, sent to populate Xinjiang and to develop mining and industry. The government organised the settlers into PLA co-ordinated **militia**, the 'Production and Construction Corps', and they quickly became the wealthiest institution in the region.

## Guangdong

The southern province (see map, page 210) had traditionally been a pro-nationalist stronghold and the regime feared that enemy spies and saboteurs remained. A coastal region, its capital Canton (renamed Guangzhou by the communists) was a valuable trading port close to Hong Kong. The regime feared that anti-communist sentiment remained strong in the area and targeted it with great ferocity. An estimated 28,000 people were executed in Guangdong during the 'Suppress the Counter-Revolutionaries' campaign.

## Taiwan

The nationalists established a rival nation in Taiwan called the Republic of China (**ROC**). Chiang Kai-shek's new nation claimed to be the 'official' China and quickly set about preparing to re-invade the communist-controlled mainland. They sent spies and agents to attack and sabotage the new regime. The communists wanted to invade Taiwan but their involvement in the Korean War (1950–53) prevented this (see page 222).

## The *laogai*

Inspired by Stalin's **Gulag** in the Soviet Union, the Communist Party created a sprawling network of **labour camps** to imprison its enemies. They were called '*laogai*' meaning 'reform through labour'. The camps were first built in the nation's most inhospitable border regions such as Manchuria's mosquito-infested swamps and Qinghai's bleak mountains. They soon spread across the entire country.

The Communist Party had set up labour camps during the Civil War, putting prisoners to work to cover the cost of their imprisonment. Once in power the regime began to hunt down its enemies and the prison population expanded greatly. By the start of 1955 there were more than 1.3 million people undergoing forced labour. Some prisoners were common criminals like thieves, drug dealers and bandits. Members of criminal gangs like the Triads were hunted down and imprisoned. Most were 'political prisoners' including 300,000 doctors, engineers and experts who had been rounded up by the anti-counter-revolutionaries, and the Antis Campaigns. Their crimes included listening to foreign radio or not meeting work quotas.

## Conditions for inmates

Inmates were forced into back-breaking work like digging reservoirs or building roads. Some helped prepare land for cultivation. They were useful for dangerous work too, such as digging uranium mines. Conditions in the camps were appalling and diarrhoea and dysentery were common. In Sichuan inmates were made to build a railroad in the middle of winter, but were not issued with trousers; many froze to death. In the salt mines of Hebei, hundreds died each month. Torture and mistreatment were commonplace. Kept in unsanitary conditions and fed barely enough to stay alive, many prisoners took their own lives. For example, in the tin mines in Guangdong prisoners were treated so appallingly that one in three took their own lives or died of disease within a year of being incarcerated. Jung Chang and Jon Halliday estimate that 27 million people died in prisons and labour camps during Mao's rule. The inmates were entirely expendable. 'It is better for prisoners to die,' said the head of the **Public Security Bureau**, 'than to flee'.

As the prison population increased, the economic value of the *laogai* increased. By the mid-1950s the *laogai* were contributing over 700 million yuan in industrial products and 350,000 tons of grain to the economy. Another **purge** in 1955 added 770,000 prisoners. With this many inmates the prison system had to change. Forced Job Placement Camps (*jiuye*) kept inmates as slave labour while 'Re-Education through Labour' Camps (*laojiao*) developed in 1957 to hold victims of the Anti-Rightist Campaign (see pages 217–218). The *laojiao* were different from the *laogai* in that they abandoned all pretence of judicial procedure. Now inmates could be held indefinitely until it was decided by the police that they had been fully 're-educated'.

Accurate figures for inmates are not available but some estimates put the prison population at its peak at 10 million in any one year during Mao's dictatorship. That the population was not greater is likely to be down to the catastrophic death rates.

### Benefits to the regime of the *laogai*

As well as being an indispensable source of labour the *laogai* had other benefits for the new regime. They were a means to intimidate and terrorise the population, spreading fear and enforcing compliance to communist rule. They were also a way of converting former opponents by forcing them to attend study lessons where they would be bombarded with communist propaganda. All inmates were meant to be reformed through constant study sessions and indoctrination. Struggle meetings forced inmates to confess their crimes. Some were forced to denounce and physically abuse their fellow inmates in order to prove their ideological purity. Mao's doctor, Zhisui Li, observed that Mao believed 'opponents would be reformed within work units'. Mao declared, in his metaphorical style, 'An untrained horse can't be ridden.'

## The Hundred Flowers Campaign

When the communists took power, many educated intellectuals such as scientists, university professors, technical experts and engineers had not fled to Taiwan. Disillusioned with the nationalists, they had been swayed by the promise that the communists were trying to create a new, modern China. Those intellectuals who had previously been living abroad, returned to China to help out of a sense of patriotic duty. However, education had historically been extremely expensive in China so most intellectuals came from a wealthy background. Given that the communists publicly wanted to end privilege and create a greater sense of equality, this meant that they were damned as 'capitalist enemies'. During the Antis-Campaigns of the early 1950s public meetings were held where they were made to admit their guilt for their privileged past while abuse was hurled at them. Some were forced to undertake 'thought reform' to eradicate non-communist ideas. As Mao developed his dictatorship and his promises of a new, democratic China looked less and less likely to be realised, they became disillusioned and demoralised. Hoping to avoid punishment, the intellectuals stayed silent and hid their educated background.

### Asking the intellectuals for help

By 1956, Mao's power was well established and his ideas about the role intellectuals might play in the PRC changed. The reunification campaigns had been a success, his land reform policies had been popular and the Korean War (see page 222) had bolstered China's image abroad. However, economic production had stalled, particularly in agriculture and Mao believed that for the economy to catch up with the West, he would need the support of educated intellectuals and scientists. Most of the Party were uneducated peasants; they needed to enlist the help of those who could organise modern industries, develop advanced technology or provide innovative solutions for China's economic problems.

### Rectification of the Party

Alongside this Mao also feared that the Party was becoming less revolutionary. He feared that it had become **bureaucratic** and needed to be 'rectified' once again. The Party cadres were no longer revolutionary fighters but a new privileged class of managers. The 'revolutionaries had become rulers'. They had become lazy, said Mao. Taking advantage of their new status they had begun working for their own benefit and were now less interested in the needs of the people. Mao wanted to encourage intellectuals to point out the mistakes of Party members and force them to act in the interests of the people again. In particular, Mao believed that some members of the Party were not radical enough in introducing communist policies, especially economic reforms which Mao wanted to happen very quickly. He hoped that the intellectuals would criticise these more conservative communists giving him the opportunity to remove them.

### International concerns

Mao might also have been motivated by international events. In February 1956 the leader of the Soviet Union, Nikita Khrushchev, made a famous speech that denounced Stalin's **cult of personality** as well as the use of the secret police and terror to intimidate and repress opponents (see pages 31–2). Khrushchev called for an end to dictatorship and instead called for a sharing of power between leaders that he called Collective Leadership. This might have made Mao nervous. He had already begun to develop a strong personality cult and many of his terror policies, such as the creation of prison camps and campaigns against class enemies, had mirrored those of Stalin. Mao worried that he was being targeted for criticism too. He sought a way to prove that he was not a dictator.

## Was Mao over-confident?

Another possibility is that Mao acted not out of fear, but because he was feeling optimistic. The early years of the People's Republic had been a success. Communist control over the whole of China had been consolidated through a combination of popular policies and repression. Policies such as the rounding up of bandit gangs and drug dealers had been popular. Areas far from Beijing, such as Xinjiang and Tibet, had been brought under control by the PLA. After years of devastating civil war, the First Five-Year Plan had successfully stimulated industrial recovery (see pages 239–241). In foreign policy the new China had started to wipe away the memories of subservience and exploitation by successfully fighting the United Nations in Korea, a victory that had greatly bolstered Mao's personal popularity. By asking intellectuals to deliver a judgement on the regime, he expected a ringing endorsement of his policies that would give him even greater influence and allow him to advance his own personal policies that would introduce communism rapidly, against the wishes of less radical members of the Party.

## 'Let a hundred flowers bloom'

On 2 May 1956 Mao declared, 'Let a hundred flowers bloom, let a hundred schools contend.' Although he hoped to expose the Party to the criticisms of the people, his call for discussion, for new, even non-communist ideas to 'contend' had little impact. Remembering their earlier harsh treatment, most intellectuals were now unwilling to risk their freedom, and perhaps even their lives, by suggesting new policies or ideas that might lead them to be denounced as counter-revolutionary. Similarly, many Party leaders feared that they would be targeted for criticism and did not support the campaign, much to Mao's annoyance. 'Shit or get off the pot,' he shouted at the editor of the *People's Daily*, the Party newspaper, for not publishing documents in support of the new campaign.

Mao tried again in February 1957, making a speech to the Supreme State Council Conference entitled 'On the Correct Handling of Contradictions Among the People'.

He again asked for 'a hundred flowers to bloom.' He admitted that the CCP had made mistakes. Too often, he said, the Party had wrongly identified intellectuals as enemies of the regime and used too much force to control them. He admitted that 800,000 Chinese had been killed and implied that the time for violent class struggle was now over. He promised to release people from the labour camps. The speech was not published, but taped and played to audiences of Party officials who were tasked with encouraging intellectuals to speak up.

## Criticisms of the Party

Emboldened, the intellectuals began to criticise the Party. Big posters were put up on the walls of offices and factories denouncing the Party's failure to provide democratic rights or freedom of expression in arts and culture. Opponents compared the Party's use of violent methods to those used by the Nazis at **Auschwitz**. Many complained about economic inequalities, criticising their low wages and comparing them to the privileged lifestyle of the Party elites. 'Who are the people who enjoy a higher standard of living?' one critic asked. 'They are the party members and cadres who wore worn-out shoes in the past' but now 'travel in saloon cars.' Some Party headquarters were stormed by angry students who tied up officials and marched them through the streets. Some dared criticise Mao personally. Critical of his own personal power, one compared him to the Pope. One poster warned that 'dissatisfied peasants could throw Chairman Mao's portrait into the toilet'.

## Anti-Rightist Campaign

The personal criticism was a step too far for Mao. According to his doctor Zhisui Li, he 'stayed in bed … depressed'. Although 'apparently immobilised', Li writes, 'He was rethinking his strategy, plotting the revenge.' In June his speech on 'Handling Contradictions' was finally published in the *People's Daily* but there was no mention of compromise or moderation in this version. Instead it declared that 'poisonous weeds' had grown up among the 'fragrant flowers'. These '**right-wingers**' had abused their freedoms and he demanded a campaign of class struggle against them. In the resulting 'Anti-Rightist Campaign' these 'poisonous weeds' were defined very broadly so that they could include anyone who the regime wanted to get rid of. Crimes liable for punishment included 'opposing **socialist** culture' and 'opposing the fundamental policies of the state'. Simply 'denying the achievements of the revolution' could lead to arrest. Cadres were given a quota of five per cent of people in a *Danwei* or work unit to be damned as **rightist**, leading many officials to accuse innocent people just to ensure they met their target.

## Work units

It was compulsory for every Chinese worker in a city to register with a *Danwei* or 'work unit'. Controlled by the Party cadres, they kept information of every member in personal files and used it to decide who received housing, food and clothing, or whether to grant permits for marriage or to change job. They distributed permits to allow travel to other parts of China, and therefore played an important role in preventing free movement. Because everyone wanted access to the opportunities the *Danwei* controlled, the work units played a key role in the Party's control over the population.

### Victims of the campaign

More people were purged in the campaign than in previous campaigns. Although statistics vary, it is estimated that between 400,000 and 700,000 intellectuals were purged and sent to the countryside or the *laogai* for 'labour reform'. Others took their own lives to avoid such a terrifying fate. Even well-known Party members, such as Ding Ling, were expelled.

## Ding Ling, 1904–86

Ding Ling was a prestigious member of the CCP. Her commitment to communism was unquestionable. She had even been arrested by the nationalists in 1933 and imprisoned for three years. Even then she refused to abandon her beliefs. She wrote a glowing account of communist land reform, *The Sun Shines Over the Sanggan River* (1948). It won the coveted Stalin prize for literature in 1951, an award for a piece of writing that advanced the communist cause. In the early years of the PRC she was editor of a number of important literary journals. However, in 1957 she was denounced as part of the Anti-Rightist Campaign and she was exiled to a desolate part of northern China. All her writing was banned.

## Conclusion: Defeating the CCP's opponents

In the very first months of the new People's Republic the communists appeared to be making good on their promises of fair treatment to former enemies. Opponents, they said, would be given the chance to 'admit political mistakes' and 'start life anew'. It quickly became apparent that this leniency was born out of pragmatic need for established and trained personnel to help run the government and the economy. As soon as the CCP had trained enough loyal cadres to take over the running of the country, anyone that they deemed to be ideologically suspect was targeted for punishment. By 1952 they were feeling confident and secure enough to take over the economic assets of businessmen. Using the excuse of needing to hunt down spies and imperialists during the Korean War, they were able to mobilise the mass of the population to participate in this wave of terror. A combination of active enthusiasm for the repression alongside very public humiliation, torture and even executions, created an atmosphere of uncertainty, intimidation and fear that meant almost no one was willing to speak out against the new regime. Mao's consolidation of control finally culminated with the Hundred Flowers Campaign that purged intellectual opposition. The communist regime had effectively imposed its monopoly of power across the whole of mainland China. By 1957 Mao's power was absolute and he was free to legislate according to his own personal ideological whims. The consequences for the Chinese people would be truly catastrophic.

## Work together

Work in pairs or in a small group. Go through the reasons for the launching of the Hundred Flowers Campaign in 1956. You could make notes in support of the following interpretations:

- Mao was confident that he had consolidated communist control over China.
- The Chinese economy was not recovering fast enough.
- International worries forced Mao to launch the campaign.
- Mao had planned to trap the intellectuals all along.

Discuss how far you think each reason was important. When you have come to some sort of agreement, write down bullet points summarising your ideas. Having done this, you can compare them and expand on them where necessary. Which interpretation do you find most convincing? Which one best explains why he acted in 1956?

## Key debate

### Why did Mao launch the Hundred Flowers Campaign?

There is an ongoing debate about the answer to this question. Initially, Chinese writers believed that Mao had deliberately entrapped the intellectuals in order to purge them. Supporters of the regime, like Han Suyin, wrote in 1976 that the campaign was 'a deliberate strategy by Mao', believing that it was a justified attempt to remove enemies of communism who would have destroyed the People's Republic. Victims also agreed that it was a trap but were understandably less complimentary. Writing in 1986, Nien Cheng, who had been imprisoned by the regime, derided the 'treachery of Mao' for inviting frank and constructive criticism but then 'harshly punishing those who gave it'.

In 1990 Jonathan Spence argued that Mao launched the campaign out of a sense of security. He was feeling 'triumphant ... at the general success of his policies' and felt secure enough to be less authoritarian, and instead wanted to 'instil the idea of flexibility and openness' into the government.

In 1999 Philip Short called it nothing less than 'an ambitious attempt ... to combine a totalitarian system with checks and balances', and in 2002 American historian Lee Feigon agreed, calling it an 'effort to change the political climate ... to stimulate innovation and initiative'. These historians see Mao's attempt to encourage political discussion as genuine and argue that it only ended when Mao realised that the criticism had gone too far. Believing that the regime would be popular, they say he was shocked at the level of anger that included even complaints against him personally. He would not risk the intellectuals suggesting that he and the communists should share power, so he purged them.

In contrast, in 2005 Jung Chang and Jon Halliday returned to earlier analysis. They wrote that Mao had a 'devious plan' to 'set a trap' by encouraging non-communists to speak out so that the Party could use this as an excuse to purge them.

For historians who view the Hundred Flowers Campaign as a trap, Mao was a deeply paranoid leader who feared opponents plotting against him. They point to the fact that Mao's February 1957 speech asking for comments on the performance of the Party was never publicly published at the time in China. When it was finally published in June 1957 after the Anti-Rightist Campaign had begun, it was radically different. It had been edited and gone were the promises of a real and open discourse. Instead, the published transcript accused critics of 'trying to overthrow the CCP'. Had Mao succeeded in encouraging his opponents to implicate themselves as enemies, only for him now to reveal his true intention? This is certainly possible. Mao was certainly a devious leader who often changed his policies to confuse and trap his opponents. It is not clear if this was in fact a deliberate strategy. It is possible that the speech was changed not because of a clever plan but because Mao had realised he had made a mistake in giving people freedom to criticise the Party. Now he wanted people to believe he had been tricking them all along. If people did not believe that the ploy had been cleverly designed by Mao he would have looked foolish. Instead, Mao wanted people to believe that he had changed the speech deliberately to cleverly flush out his enemies.

## 4 China and the Korean War

At the end of the Second World War, Korea had been divided along the 38th parallel into the Soviet-dominated communist North and the South, allied to the USA. On 25 June 1950 North Korean dictator Kim Il Sung launched an attack on his southern enemy. The **United Nations Security Council** sanctioned military action to 'give such assistance' as may be necessary 'to repel the armed attack'. A UN force made up of soldiers from sixteen nations, most from the USA, was ordered to defend South Korea.

At first the communist forces prevailed but in a daring surprise attack, the UN forces landed at Inchon, more than 100 miles behind the enemy's lines. In September and October UN air power helped push the communist forces back across the 38th parallel and into North Korea itself. The crucial point came when UN forces advanced towards the Chinese border. In October Mao, against the advice of several key members of the Politburo and General Lin Biao, ordered the PLA to 'resist the attacks of United States imperialism'. The People's Republic of China was embroiled in its first **Cold War** conflict. The PLA successfully surprised the UN forces who did not believe China had the military capability to fight so soon after the end of the Chinese Civil War. The Chinese advanced into South Korea, but eventually the UN military superiority, especially its far larger air force, meant that the UN regained the upper hand. The Chinese were pushed back to the 38th parallel. The war dragged on for three years. It ended with an inconclusive stalemate. Korea remains divided between the communist North and capitalist South to this day. The human cost for China was huge – 400,000 men died – but the benefits for Mao's new regime, in terms of international prestige, domestic support and the removal of opposition, were profound and enduring.

## Note it down

### Why did China join the Korean War?

Try to imagine that you are Mao in 1950. Make a quick list of all the reasons why you think you might benefit from entering the Korean War. Which do you think would be the most important reason? Now imagine you are a member of the Party trying to dissuade Mao from ordering China into the war. What do you think your greatest fear would be? To help you, make notes on the questions below:

1. How could the war give Mao an excuse to purge more of his opponents? Which kind of opponents could Mao victimise?
2. China was a vast and diverse nation; this made it difficult to govern. How could success in war help solve this problem?
3. The communists had just come to power a year before the start of the war. Why do you think many communist leaders were opposed to entering the war?
4. China had previously been humiliated by the foreign, Western powers. How could the war help Mao develop his own personal popularity?
5. China desperately needed to borrow industrial equipment from the Soviet Union. How might the war help Mao convince the USSR to lend this equipment?

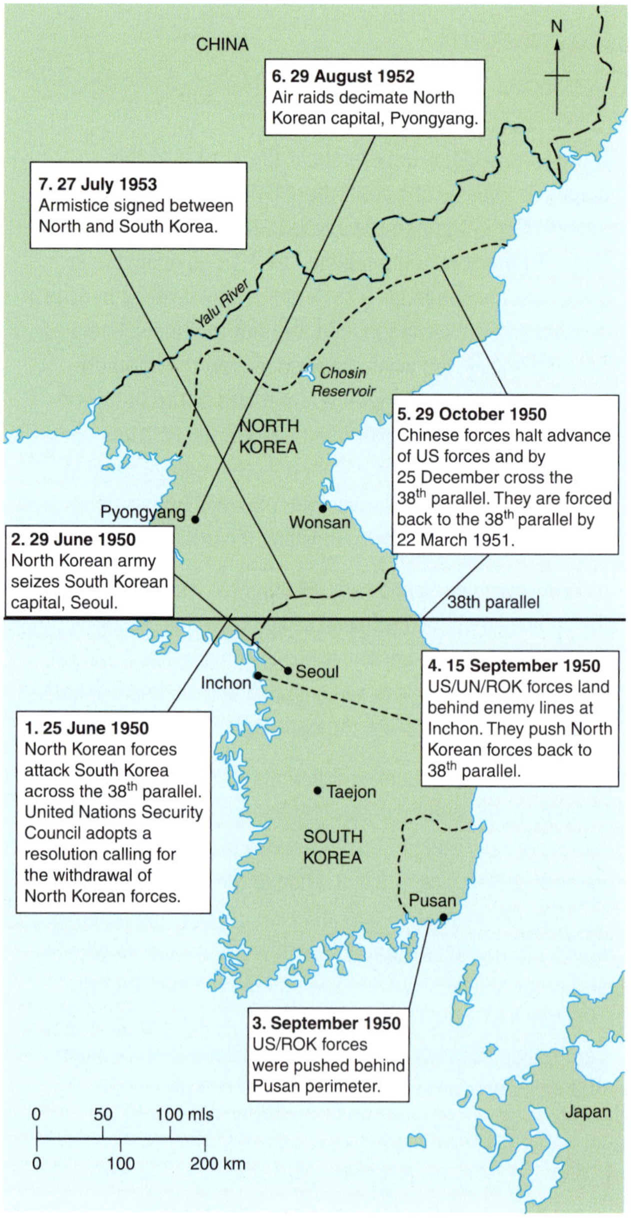


▲ Figure 3: Map showing course of events of Korean War.

## Role in enhancing CCP control

In 1950, China remained a republic conspicuously lacking a singular, unified national identity. It contained over 50 national groups, many with different languages, cultures and traditions. The Korean War offered the communists an opportunity to promote national unity through creating antipathy to the USA and a sense of collective endeavour which promoted the idea of the PLA soldier hero.

### 'Resist America, Aid Korea'

Mao was able to use the war as a rationale to purge his enemies on the pretence of them being spies or traitors. Collective spirit was forged in mass meetings that whipped up hatred for the USA. The 'Resist America, Aid Korea' campaign denounced the Americans as 'bandits, murderers and savages'. Posters were put up showing President Truman and General MacArthur as vampiric ghouls, their bestial claws dripping with blood. Mass meetings publicly denounced opponents and sentenced them to death, spreading an atmosphere of fear and suspicion. The *People's Daily* published long lists of political criminals alongside gruesome details of their punishment. Although figures vary greatly, the government recorded 800,000 counter-revolutionary and 135,000 official executions during the first half of 1951. The moderate policies of the first years of the PRC were forgotten.

The regime spread a rumour that the Americans were testing biological weapons. Insects infected with anthrax were being dropped on Chinese positions. Although later revealed to be false, the rumours were believed because the Japanese, now allies of the USA, were well known to have tried the same tactic in the Second World War. 'Preserve Our Homes, Defend the Nation' urged press and government broadcasts.

**Source G** From Zhisui Li, *The Private Life of Chairman Mao* (Arrow Books, 1996). This is a memoir by Zhisui Li, Mao's private doctor for over 20 years. The book is banned in China.

> I followed the war closely, surprised and thrilled that China was not only holding its own but was actually defeating the United States in battle after battle. It was the first time in more than a century that China was engaged in war with a foreign power without losing face. I was appalled, too, over reports that the United States was using bacteriological warfare in Korea. Even as the Korean War dragged on inconclusively, I was proud to be Chinese.

In what ways does Source G suggest the communist regime was able to benefit from the Korean War?

**A propaganda poster from 1950, during the Korean War. The figure on the right is General MacArthur, the US leader of the United Nations forces during the Korean War. How would the poster in Source F help Mao promote a sense of National Unity during the Korean War?**

## Model soldier hero

Although they fought with great bravery, the Chinese soldiers in Korea could not hope to defeat the UN forces with their advanced artillery and overwhelming air superiority. Chinese medical supplies were inadequate and their winter clothing unfit for the harsh Korean winter: almost 90 per cent of troops were reported to have suffered from frostbite. Despite this, the fact that the Chinese military was not defeated by the combined forces of the United Nations enabled the regime to regale the Chinese people with stirring propaganda tales of PLA bravery. One Chinese lady recalled being so impressed with the stories of PLA soldiers capturing American soldiers 'carrying them away while they slept in their sleeping bags' that she donated her whole week's wages to the war effort. Farmers pledged to increase production and donated surplus crops to the troops. Workers joined patriotic campaigns under the slogan 'Our factory is our battlefield and our machines are our weapons.' They increased production in key industries like coal, iron and steel. Even those Chinese who were wary of communism were caught up in the wave of patriotic pride. Businessmen and industrialists signed 'patriotic pacts' in which they promised to pay their taxes on time.

## International prestige

An inconclusive ceasefire was declared in 1953 but the value of the Korean War to the national unity of Mao's new regime was clear. After years of humiliation at the hands of the West, he had proved them to be, in his words, mere 'Paper Tigers' – fearsome looking and sounding, but easy to defeat. This greatly assisted his efforts to form a cohesive Chinese national sentiment. It showed that China was no longer a nation to be exploited or bullied by foreign powers. In turn, this enhanced Mao's personal prestige among the Chinese people. He had proved himself to be a tough leader who would stand up for China's interests and would defend his allies, even if it meant going to war against the most powerful nations in the world. This was particularly noted by other Asians. Mao hoped one day to rival Stalin as a leader of the communist movement in Asia and fellow Asian communists could not help but notice that it was Chinese soldiers fighting in Korea, not Russians.

# The impact of the Korean War

For all the benefits that Mao and his regime received, the costs of the war were real and personal. Much to their annoyance, Stalin made sure the USSR benefited from Chinese involvement in Korea, charging high interest on any money lent to the PRC. In total, the war cost the PRC $10 billion. Of the 3 million Chinese soldiers sent to the front, 400,000 died.

## Key debate

### Why did China enter the Korean War?

In June 1950, the new communist regime in China could scarcely afford to go to war. Still recovering from years of turmoil and violence, the leaders of the new People's Republic desperately needed a period of peace and stability in order to establish the regime. Instead, Mao embroiled China into a ferocious war against the United Nations, led by the world's greatest **superpower**. Why did Mao gamble the future of his regime in a war to protect Korea? During the 1950s the United States interpreted Mao's decision as evidence of a **Kremlin** co-ordinated plot to consolidate communist domination. They believed that such was Stalin's unrivalled power within the worldwide communist movement that China and North Korea simply followed Stalin's wishes in foreign policy. Writing in 2005, Jung Chang and Jon Halliday suggest that Mao helped plan the invasion because he was 'eager' to use the war as a proving ground to convince Stalin to provide him with technology and industrial equipment. The war 'was the only chance he had to claw out of Stalin what he needed to make China a world-class military power'. In contrast, others do not see Chinese involvement as the result of a premeditated plan. In 2013, Alexander Pantsov argued that Mao was manipulated into intervening because it suited Soviet Russia's Cold War agenda. He claims that Stalin secretly provoked Kim Il Sung's invasion to lure the United States into conflict not only with Korea, but with China too.

## The Republic of China

Furthermore, China would be forced to accept the presence of nationalist Taiwan. In June 1950 American President Truman had warned that the occupation of Taiwan by communist forces would be a direct threat to the security of the Pacific area and to the US forces performing their lawful and necessary functions. He sent the US Seventh Fleet to patrol the Taiwan Strait, the stretch of water between communist China and the capitalist ROC. If Mao's forces attacked Taiwan they would have been easily defeated by the United States massive navy. The impossibility of realising the promise of complete reunification was a great blow to China's national pride.

## Relations with the West

The Korean War had a profound impact upon Western attitudes to the new PRC. Chinese intervention reinforced the United States' mistaken belief in the existence of a monolithic communist plan for global conquest. After a period when accommodation appeared possible US policy became aggressive. Having killed thousands of American soldiers the Chinese were figures of hatred, accomplices in Stalin's evil communist empire. It was with the Korean War that the USA's harshly anti-communist Cold War policy became permanently entrenched. US commitment to realising **containment** through military force led US defence spending to reach $50 billion a year and, desperate to avoid a repeat of the criticism from right-wing Republicans engendered by the 'loss' of China to communism in 1949, President Truman set about building a system of alliances and bases in East Asia, while turning China's historical enemy Japan into nothing less than what he called an 'unsinkable aircraft carrier'.

## Relations with the Soviet Union

Before the war Mao had appeared open to support from both communist Russia and the capitalist West. He spoke only of 'leaning to the communist side'. Perhaps the most damaging impact of the war was that it left China securely on the Russian side of the Cold War. Certainly Mao hoped to extricate more economic and military support from Stalin for his new republic. Mao did succeed in impressing Stalin. China's Foreign Minister Chen Yi reported that Stalin shed tears upon hearing of China's intervention in Korea against the West. 'The Chinese comrades are so good!' he exclaimed. However, China was isolated. With Western diplomatic recognition of the Beijing regime now impossible, the isolation of the Chinese people from democratic influences was now complete. Now irreversibly a bitter foe of the USA, the PRC was totally dependent on Soviet economic aid and advice.

## Personal cost to Mao

Finally, the cost of the war was felt privately by Mao himself. His son, Anying, to whom Mao was very close, was killed by an attack on PLA headquarters. Upon hearing the news, Mao remained stoic. 'In revolutionary war, you always pay a price,' he said. However, others have highlighted Anying's death as a pivotal moment, particularly since Mao himself had urged him to go to Korea. 'When he died,' writes historian Philip Short in his biography of Mao, 'the one remaining human bond capable of invoking in Mao a deep, personal loyalty was severed.'

## Conclusion: China and the Korean War

After years of war, the majority of the Chinese people craved peace. They welcomed the formation of the PRC with optimism and hoped that the new regime would herald a period of calm and prosperity. These hopes were dashed when Mao intervened in the Korean War. Evidence that China was closely involved in the planning of the war is unconvincing. However, once war started Mao acted with a clear understanding of the benefits that could be accrued for his new regime. He used it to cultivate his previously inequitable relationship with Stalin, and then, crucially, to place himself as a rival to the Soviet Union as the leading revolutionary force in Asia. At home he used the war to build patriotic support to legitimise violent campaigns aimed at removing his opponents. He also consolidated his image as a military leader. The success of Chinese soldiers against overwhelming foreign forces affirmed his denunciation of China's enemies as 'Paper Tigers' and confirmed his promise that China had finally 'stood up' to Western imperialism in Asia. Unfortunately for the Chinese people, Mao took his successes in Korea as proof of his belief that force of will and mobilisation of the masses could overcome technological weakness, a mistaken idea that would later be harnessed for attempted economic advancement in the disastrous Great Leap Forward (see page 242).

### Work together

#### Was the Korean War worth fighting?

Work with a partner. One of you should collect evidence of all the benefits for China of their involvement in the Korean War. The other should note the costs of the war for China. When you have both finished, compare your lists. Was it worth the costs? Is your answer different if you think about the benefits for the Chinese people rather than the benefits for just Mao himself?

## Chapter summary

- In 1949, the Chinese Communist Party, led by Mao Zedong, defeated the capitalists, led by Chiang Kai-shek. Having won the Civil War, the communists formed a new nation, the People's Republic of China.
- China's economy had been very badly damaged by the Second World War and the Civil War. Much of China's industry had been destroyed or had been sabotaged by the Japanese or by the nationalists who had fled to Taiwan.
- China was still largely an agricultural nation. Its economy was still dependent on backward farming methods. Eighty per cent of the population were landless, illiterate peasants.
- The People's Republic was controlled by three interlocking institutions: the Communist Party of China (CCP), the Central People's Government of China and the People's Liberation Army (PLA).
- Mao's personal political prestige increased greatly during this period. The policies that he introduced in the early years of the PRC, such as land reform and attacks on criminal gangs, were largely popular and effective.
- The government of China was based on the concept of democratic centralism. This promised to provide democratic rights to the people of China for the first time while providing a strong central government that could solve China's problems. In reality, these democratic rights were for propaganda purposes; the Communist Party ruled as a one-party state.
- The Communist Party used the People's Liberation Army to control the border regions of China such as Tibet and Xinjiang. Declaring these areas to be a part of China, they launched invasions they termed 'reunification campaigns' to seize power there.
- The Communist Party launched campaigns of terror against their opponents. The Party encouraged the Chinese people themselves to identify and purge so-called 'class enemies' such as nationalist sympathisers, corrupt businessmen and anyone who had links with the West, such as Christian missionaries.
- The regime built a vast new network of prison camps, the *laogai*. Termed 'reform through labour' camps, enemies of the regime were imprisoned in brutal conditions and made to work while being subjected to communist propaganda. Many were tortured and died.
- In 1950 communist North Korea invaded capitalist South Korea. When the United Nations forces repelled the invasion, China entered the Korean War to help its communist ally.
- Mao used the Korean War as an excuse to round up enemies on the pretence of them being spies or enemy saboteurs.
- During the war Mao launched a campaign to generate a sense of patriotism. The 'Resist America, Aid Korea' campaign encouraged the Chinese people to donate money and resources to help the war effort. It helped to create a sense of national identity.
- The Korean War greatly increased Mao's personal prestige. By fighting the joint forces of the United Nations to a standstill, he had proved that the imperialists were, in his words, a 'Paper Tiger'. Communist parties in Asian nations began to look to China, not the Soviet Union, for inspiration.
- The Korean War isolated China internationally. The West was convinced that the PRC was an aggressive nation dedicated to communist revolution. As a result, China was forced to become more dependent on the Soviet Union.

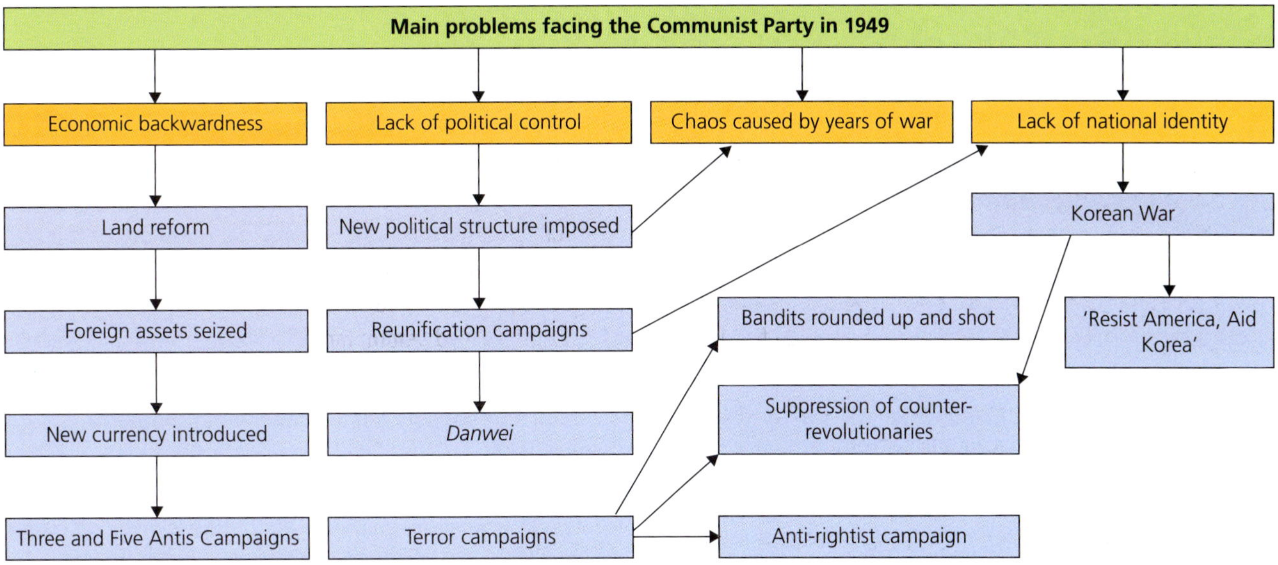


▲ **Summary diagram: Establishing communist rule, 1949–57.**

## Recommended reading


J. Brown and P. Pickowicz (eds.), *The Dilemmas of Victory: The Early Years of the People's Republic of China* (Harvard University Press, 2010). Rigorous analysis of the early years of the communist regime. Very challenging, but extremely detailed essays by top scholars in this field.

M. Burleigh, *Small Wars, Faraway Places* (Pan, 2013). Chapter 5 supplies an up-to-date analysis of the Korean War.

F. Dikotter, *The Tragedy of Liberation: A History of the Chinese Revolution, 1945–57* (Bloomsbury, 2013). Recent and detailed examination of the early consolidation of the communist regime.

J. Melby, *The Mandate of Heaven: Record of a Civil War, China 1945–49* (University of Toronto Press, 1968). Melby was an American diplomat stationed in China during the Civil War. His book is a collection of his diary extracts recording the coming to power of the CCP.

J. Spence, *The Search for Modern China*, 2nd edition (W.W. Norton, 1999). Especially Chapter 19 entitled 'The Birth of the People's Republic'. Also includes a very detailed account of the Civil War, not necessary for the exam but useful for understanding the background of the communist revolution.

D. Twitchett and John K. Fairbank (eds.), *The Cambridge History of China*, Volume 14 (Cambridge University Press, 1987). Especially Part I which deals with the consolidation of the new regime.

C. Tyler, *Wild West China: The Taming of Xinjiang* (John Murray, 2003). A history of Xinjiang, including an analysis of the difficulties faced by the People's Republic in suppressing the fiercely independent people of the region.

# Section A: Essay technique

## Focus on the question and understanding the sources

The A level Section A question requires you to deploy a variety of skills. The most important are source analysis and evaluation. In essence, the question asks how much a historian could learn about a specific issue from the two sources. This is a complex task, and requires a range of skills which will be covered in this section and at the end of Chapters 2–4. These include the ability to:

- understand the focus of the question and the sources (this section)
- structure an essay and write good introductions (Chapter 2, page 252)
- select information and make inferences from the sources (Chapter 2, pages 254–256)
- place the sources in their historical context (Chapter 3, page 283–284)
- evaluate and weigh the evidence of the sources (Chapter 4, page 313–315)
- reach and support a final judgement (Chapter 4, page 316).

The Section A question for AS level is different from that for A level, and some guidance about this is given on pages viii. However, you will need to develop very similar skills for the AS exam, therefore the activities will help with the AS exam as well. There are also some AS-style questions in every chapter.

### The focus of the question

In order to answer the question successfully you must understand how the question works. Below is a typical Section A-style question (the sources are on page 227). The question is written precisely in order to make sure that you understand the task. Each part of the question has a specific meaning:

'How far' indicates that you must evaluate the extent of something, rather than giving a simple 'yes' or 'no' answer.

They key word here is **together**. You must examine the sources as a pair and make a judgement about both sources, rather than separate judgements about each source.

This is the essence of the task. You must focus on what a historian could legitimately conclude from studying these sources.

The final part of the question focuses on a specific topic that a historian might investigate: in this case, the extent to which Mao launched the Hundred Flowers Campaign as a deliberate trick to trap his opponents.

> **Study Sources 1 and 2 before you answer this question.**
>
> **How far could the historian make use of Sources 1 and 2 together to investigate the extent to which Mao launched the Hundred Flowers Campaign as a deliberate trick to trap his opponents?**
>
> **Explain your answer, using both sources, the information given about them and your own knowledge of the historical context.**

This instruction lists the resources you should use:

- the sources
- the information given about the sources
- your own knowledge of historical context that you have learned during the course.

**Source 1** From Jung Chang's biography of Mao, *Mao: The untold story* (Jonathan Cape, 2005). Chang is of Chinese origin. She lived in China during the time Mao ruled and as a student was a strong supporter of Mao. Her family was a victim of Mao's terror and she later left China to live in the United States.

> On 27 February 1957, Mao delivered a four-hour speech to the rubber-stamp Supreme Council announcing that he was inviting criticism of the Communist Party. The Party, he said, needed to be accountable and 'under supervision.' But with the trend in the Communist world blowing towards de-Stalinisation(1), Mao decided it was not wise to be too blatant about launching a purge. To create a justification, he cooked up a devious plan ... Few guessed that Mao was setting a trap, and that he was inviting people to speak out so that he could then use what they said as an excuse to victimise them. Mao's targets were intellectuals and the educated, the people most likely to speak up. Mao confided his scheme only to a very few special cronies [loyal supporters]. In early April, he told these few cronies ... 'One day punishment will come down on their heads ... We want them to speak out.' Mao spelt out that he was 'casting a long line to bait big fish.' Mao's trap was extremely successful. Once the lid was loosened just a fraction, a deluge of dissent burst out. One of the very first things to be challenged was the Communists' monopoly of power.

(1) De-Stalinisation: the process of criticising Stalin's terroristic dictatorship and promising more freedoms and political rights.

**Source 2** From a speech made by Mao in February 1957 entitled 'On the correct handling of contradictions among the People', in Mark Selden (ed.), *The People's Republic of China: A Documentary History of Revolutionary Change* (Monthly Review Press, 1979), pages 232–40.

> Letting a hundred flowers blossom and a hundred schools of thought contend is the policy for promoting progress in the arts and sciences and a flourishing socialist culture in our land. Different forms and styles in art should develop freely and different schools in science should contend freely. Questions of right and wrong in the arts and sciences should be settled through free discussion in artist and scientific circles. We are against poisonous weeds of whatever kind, but we must carefully distinguish between what is really a poisonous weed and what is a fragrant flower.

Overall, all Section A questions ask you to make a judgement about how far two sources are useful to the historian. However, the second half of the question specifies what a historian is focusing on.

So, the first part of the question sets up **the general task**, which is true of all Section A questions:

'How far could the historian make use of Sources 1 and 2 together to investigate ...'

and the second part of the question establishes **the specific focus**, for example:

'... the extent to which Mao launched the Hundred Flowers Campaign as a deliberate trick to trap his opponents.'

As you write your essay, you need to focus on both aspects.

## How to focus in a source question

Source questions are different from questions that only require you to use your own knowledge. There are a variety of ways to ensure you maintain your focus on the question that are appropriate to this type of question:

- Use the phrases 'Source 1' and 'Source 2' when dealing with the sources so that it is clear which sources you are focusing on.
- Use words such as 'useful' or 'utility' to ensure that you are explicitly addressing the general task.
- Use comparative words and phrases such as 'Sources 1 and 2 disagree' to show that you are using the sources together.

### Activity: A focused introduction

1 Write a short introduction which provides a focused answer to the question on page 226. See pages 252–3 for advice on writing introductions. Also remember that this is a question about two sources.

2 Having written an introduction, swap it with a partner. Consider:

**a)** Which introduction best focuses on the question? Remember, your introduction needs to focus on the **general task** and the **specific focus**.

**b)** Which introduction best dealt with the sources *together*?

**c)** Which introduction gave the clearest answer to the question?

**d)** What can you learn from each other's approach to the question?

Use these questions to feed back to each other and improve your instructions.

### Activity: AS-style questions

1 Why is Source 1 valuable to the historian for an enquiry into the reasons for the Hundred Flowers Campaign?

2 How much weight do you give the evidence of Source 2 for an enquiry into the reasons why Mao launched the Hundred Flowers Campaign?

## Understanding the sources

Understanding the sources is crucial to doing well in Section A questions. The most important aid in this understanding is a detailed knowledge of the period. There are also techniques to aid understanding. Here are a few tips to get you started:

- Read the source word for word – if it helps, read it out loud when you are doing practice questions. This makes it much less likely that you will miss anything in the source.
- Think about the question as you are reading. You will then look out for relevant information within the source.
- Make index cards before your exam of the specific vocabulary for the topic you are studying, for example *intellectuals*, *Anti-Rightist Campaign*.
- Look up terms and definitions that you do not recognise in practice questions.
- Make index cards of the people who might be quoted in the sources, such as Mao Zedong, Liu Shaoqi or Zhou Enlai, and the documents that might be used as sources on the examination paper. Make notes on who they are and their attitudes to the key issues you have studied.

## Comprehension

Comprehension is the most basic source skill. It simply means understanding the source's meaning and you can demonstrate this by:

- **Copying**: writing out the words of the source in your essay.

**TIP:** Avoid copying any more than a sentence at any point in your essay.

- **Paraphrasing:** putting part of a source in your own words.

**TIP:** Avoid simply rewriting more than a sentence from the source in your own words, before using a higher-level skill.

- **Summarising:** summing up the meaning of the entire source, or a large part of the source, in a single sentence.

**TIP:** Summarising can be useful in introductions and conclusions.

These are low-level source skills. Therefore, they should not dominate your essay. However, small quotes, short paraphrases and occasional summaries can be useful to support higher-level skills.

## Higher-level skills

Higher-level skills include:

- using the sources together (see page 227)
- making inferences (see pages 255–256)
- analysing sources in their historical context (see pages 283–284)
- evaluating the evidence presented in the sources (see pages 313–315)
- reaching an overall judgement regarding the usefulness of the sources (see page 316).

### Activity: Test your understanding

Having read Source 1 and Source 2 on page 227:

1 a) Make a list of words and phrases that you do not understand.
  b) Look them up in the glossary of this book or online.
2 a) Study Source 1. **Copy** the sentence that best expresses the view that Mao was acting in a devious way in order to terrorise his opponents. Make sure you put the quote in 'quotation marks'.
  b) Study Source 1. **Paraphrase** what happened to the 'people who were likely to speak up'.
  c) Study Source 2. **Summarise** in no more than 30 words what Mao meant by 'Letting a hundred flowers blossom' and **why** he might want to encourage this.

You should repeat this activity regularly with the sources that you encounter. This will help with many of the sources you will examine as you study Mao's China, 1949–76, as sources from the same period, referring to the same topic, will tend to use a similar vocabulary.

### Work together

Having completed the 'Test your understanding' activities above, swap your answers with a partner. Consider the following questions:

1. Did you both identify the same words that needed to be defined?
2. Were your partner's definitions clear and accurate?
3. Did you both copy the same bit of Source 1? If not, which quote better expresses the view that Mao was acting deviously?
4. Is your partner's paraphrase clear? Does it accurately reflect the fate of those who 'were likely to speak up'?
5. Whose summary more precisely expressed what Mao meant by 'Letting a hundred flowers bloom' and why he might want to encourage this?
6. What can you learn from the approach of your partner to the two sources?

Use these questions to feed back to each other and improve your analysis of the sources.

# Section B: Essay technique

## Focus and structure

Section B essays, like all of your examined essays, will be judged on how far they focus on the question and the quality of their structure. You may have already considered advice on how to write a focused introduction and how to structure your essays in Paper 1 (see pages 26–7).

## Different types of question

Section B questions, like Section A and B questions in Paper 1, can focus on a variety of concepts. These include cause, consequence, change/continuity, similarity/difference and significance. These different concepts require slightly different approaches. Below are some examples of these concepts in questions.

1. How far was the PLA the most important factor in the consolidation of the communist regime in China, 1949–57?
2. 'The biggest challenges facing the CCP when they came to power in 1949 were economic.' How far do you agree with this statement?
3. 'The Korean War was a complete success for China.' How far do you agree with this statement?
4. How far was the Hundred Flowers Campaign a significant turning point in the consolidation of Mao's control over China?
5. How far did the international status of China change, 1949–57?

Question 1: This question requires you to evaluate the importance of the PLA in the consolidation of the communist regime in this period in comparison to other factors such as propaganda, popular policies or the use of terror and repression.

Question 2: This question asks you to evaluate how far economic problems such as damage to industry, the backwardness of agriculture and the lack of transportation and infrastructure were the biggest challenges facing the new communist regime in 1949.

Question 3: This question requires you to evaluate how far the Korean War was a success for China. Although Mao's personal popularity was increased and the PRC gained international prestige, China was viewed as a Cold War enemy by the West.

Question 4: This question requires you to evaluate the significance of the Hundred Flowers Campaign in the development of Mao's personal power and the lives of the Chinese people.

Question 5: This question requires you to evaluate how far China's international status changed over this period and how far it stayed the same.

## Structuring your essay

As in Paper 1, your essay should be made up of three or four paragraphs, each addressing a different factor (see page 26).

However, essays that focus on different concepts will need slightly different structures:

- **Cause essays** require you to explain why something happened. Therefore, each paragraph should deal with a different possible cause.
- **Evaluative essays** require you to weigh up the extent of something. Most essays will require you to evaluate at some point, as weighing up is essential to reaching a conclusion. In essays that focus on evaluation each paragraph should weigh a different factor. For example, if you were dealing with the question:

  'How far was the Hundred Flowers Campaign a significant turning point in the consolidation of Mao's control over China?'

  you would need to consider the impact of the Hundred Flowers Campaign and ask how far it reduced the freedoms of the Chinese people and helped Mao create a dictatorship. More importantly you need to make a judgement at the end based on what you have written in the essay.
- **Success or failure essays** require you to evaluate the extent to which something succeeded. Therefore, you will need to start by considering the aims in order to establish the criteria for success. You should go on to consider aspects that succeeded and weigh them against aspects that failed in order to reach a conclusion.
- **Continuity and change essays** require you to evaluate the extent of change. Therefore, your essay will have to weigh up what changed and what stayed the same.
- **Consequence essays** require you to evaluate which of a range of consequences was most important.

It is crucial to be able to distinguish between the different types of question. Confusing a causes essay with a consequences essay could seriously affect your grade.

### Activity: Question types

1 Below are five different Section B-style questions. Work out what types of question they are.

   a) How far did the international image of China change in the period 1949–57? AS

   b) 'The Chinese revolution brought widespread benefits to the Chinese people.' How far do you agree?

   c) 'The Korean War was a great success for China.' How far do you agree?

   d) 'The most important cause of Mao's personal political prestige was his use of propaganda.' How far do you agree with this statement?

   e) 'The use of terror and violence was the most important factor in Mao's consolidation of his regime, 1949–57.' How far do you agree with this statement?

2 Having worked out what types of question you are dealing with you should now write plans for each question. You can plan either as a spider diagram or a bullet-point list. Make sure your plan reflects the kind of essay that you are dealing with. For example, if you are dealing with a success or failure essay you should highlight which parts of the plan deal with success and which deal with failure. Complete one plan at a time, and after each discuss it with a partner.

### Work together

Having completed a plan in the 'question types' activity, swap it with a partner. Consider the following questions:

1 Did you agree on what type of question you were dealing with? If not, discuss it and work out who was right.
2 Whose plan most clearly focused on the specific type of question?
3 Did your partner's plan miss anything?
4 Did you miss anything that you should add to your plan?
5 What can you learn from your partner's approach?

Use these questions to feed back to each other and improve your question spotting and planning.

# **Key Topic 2** Agriculture and industry, 1949–65

## Overview

This chapter focuses on the main economic reforms introduced by the communist regime from the formation of the People's Republic to the beginning of the Cultural Revolution. It looks at the main agricultural and industrial policies and examines the dramatic changes that took place in both farmlands and urban areas as a result. It helps you understand why Mao introduced policies that in some ways improved the lives of the people, but had catastrophic results for many millions more. It should also make you think about what motivated Mao. Was he really interested in making China a more modern and prosperous nation or was he interested only in bolstering his own personal power at the expense of the lives of his people?

The overarching topic of agriculture and industry, 1949–65 is covered in four sections:

1 Early changes in agriculture, 1949–57
2 The communes
3 The First Five-Year Plan, 1952–56
4 The Second Five-Year Plan, 1958–62.

## TIMELINE

| | |
|---|---|
| 1950 February | Sino-Soviet Mutual Assistance Treaty |
| 1950 June | Agrarian Reform Law |
| 1953 January | First Five-Year Plan for industry begins |
| 1953 February | Plans to introduce Mutual Aid Teams announced |
| 1955 November | Membership in Agricultural Producers Co-operatives reaches 41 per cent of peasant farmers |
| 1956 December | Membership in Agricultural Producers Co-operatives reaches 96 per cent of peasant farmers |
| 1957 | Soviet Union launches first satellite, Sputnik, into orbit |
| 1958 May | The Great Leap Forward (The Second Five-Year Plan) begins |
| | The First People's Communes are formed |
| 1959 | The Great Famine begins and lasts until 1961 |
| 1959 June | Soviet Leader Nikita Khrushchev criticises the Great Leap Forward |
| | Soviet advisers are withdrawn from China |
| 1959 July | CCP meet at Lushan to discuss the Great Leap Forward |
| | Peng Dehuai's criticisms of communist policies leads to his purging |
| 1962 | A power struggle between Mao and Liu Shaoqi and Deng Xiaoping |
| | 'Little Red Book' of quotations of Mao published |
| 1964 | First successful test of Chinese atom bomb |

### Note it down

Using the 1:2 method (see page x) make notes on the following questions as you read this chapter:

- What were the aims of Mao's economic policies?
- How far were his policies inspired by the Soviet Union?
- How successful were his policies?
- How far did Mao's economic policies bring widespread benefits to the Chinese people?

# 1 Early changes in agriculture, 1949–57

The Chinese economy was largely dependent on agriculture, but it had been backward and inefficient. Mao desperately wanted China to be considered a modern **superpower** in order to avoid being exploited by other countries as it had been previously. To do this he knew that he had to improve both agriculture and industry as quickly as possible. But Mao was not motivated only by the desire to improve the standard of living of the Chinese people. As well as purely economic needs, Mao's reforms owed much to his ideology. Mao believed that modern industry was necessary to create a truly **socialist** nation. Therefore, food supplies needed to be increased not to improve the living standards of the peasantry, but instead to feed the growing urban population who would provide labour for the new factories. Similarly, the **collectivisation** of farmland was not only motivated by the economic benefits of large-scale production, but also by the belief that forcing the people to live together, to share everything and have no privacy would bring the creation of true **communism** that much closer to reality.

In 1949 Mao told the world that the 'Chinese people had stood up'. They would no longer be considered the '**Sick Man of Asia**', a feeble country victimised and manipulated by more powerful rivals. If Mao could truly transform China into a modern power, he would be lauded as a great and successful leader, truly the new 'Red Emperor'.

### Note it down

In this section use a spider diagram (see page x) to take notes on 'Early changes in Agriculture, 1949–57'. Draw a circle in the middle of your page with the heading 'Agricultural Change' inside it. Draw six lines coming out of the central circle that lead to these questions:

- What was the result of the attacks on landlords?
- How significant was the Agrarian Reform Law?
- How popular were the Mutual Aid Teams?
- What was the impact of the Agricultural Producers Co-operatives (APCs)?
- Why were there arguments about agricultural policy?
- To what extent was village life transformed between 1949 and 1957?

## Attacks on landlords and redistribution of land

Marx (see page 202) argued that a socialist transformation would take place in a nation where **capitalists** exploited the industrial working classes to a point that the workers rose up to seize power. Yet Mao knew that modern industry in China had not developed enough to make this possible. Marx had argued that peasants were too traditional and conservative to demand revolution, but Mao had previously been extremely impressed by the willingness of the peasants to support violent and revolutionary change. Sent to report on the peasants violent attempts to seize land in Hunan in 1927, Mao had come to believe that:

> *'The ruthless economic exploitation and political oppression of the peasantry by the landlord class could not fail to force the peasants to rise repeatedly in revolt against its rule.'*

In his unorthodox Marxist view it was the peasants, not the workers, who, he said, could act as 'vanguards of the revolution'. Their desperation to escape poverty made them useful. They were 'the most responsive to Communist Party leadership,' noted Mao.

## Agrarian Reform Law

In 1950 Mao decided to launch his major agricultural policy. With the introduction of the Agrarian Reform Law in June, land reform was introduced across the nation. The law's main aim was to destroy the 'gentry-landlord' class who had been the traditional rural elite for many generations. Landlords who exploited the poor peasants who rented their land would have their property seized. Many would be sentenced to death and their land redistributed 'to the tiller' (peasant who worked the land). The law stated, 'the system of peasant land ownership shall be introduced in order to set free the rural productive forces'. At this stage Mao viewed the process of socialist transformation of the countryside as a slow one. The movement towards collectivisation (see page 234), he said, should proceed according to the 'principles of voluntariness and mutual benefit'.

The introduction of a coherent national policy was problematic.

- In the north, where the **communists** had been in control even before 1949, land reform had already begun. However, only ten to fifteen per cent of farmers rented their land; exploitation by cruel, greedy and often absent landlords was not really a problem.

- In some areas occupied by the communists, many peasants already owned some land. They hoped that the new regime would provide the stability, peace, and rule of law that the **nationalists** had been unable to create in order to improve their standard of living. These peasants, who often had influence over other poorer farmers in their villages, were useful supporters for the Party and the regime did not want to alienate them.
- In the South, where the **GMD** had retained control before it had escaped to Taiwan, land reform had not yet begun. Communist Party organisation was weaker and the landlords more influential.
- Often land ownership and agricultural production was organised by **clans** with a wide range of members from different classes. The communist language of 'class conflict' and 'feudal exploitation' by greedy landlords had little meaning.
- A large number of clans were based on family ties or kinship relationships. Many peasants were not convinced of the need to seize the land of family members in the clan and certainly did not seek their death.

## Attacks on landlords

**Work teams**, sometimes including Party **cadres** and government officials but often only young people from the newly liberated cities, were hastily trained and sent out to the countryside to organise the land reform. For many, it was their first experience of rural life and they had little understanding of the conditions or particular local circumstances. The work teams organised peasants into Poor Peasant Associations to help determine the class of the different members of the village. The peasants were encouraged to round up their landlords. The landlords were then subjected to **struggle meetings** in front of the whole village where they would be forced to admit their crimes as 'class enemies' who had exploited their tenants. Often they were sentenced to death.

Mao himself was not always clear as to how much violence was necessary. At times he urged caution against what he called 'ultra-left deviations' and encouraged adherence to the social unity advocated in the Common Program (see page 207). Sometimes the violence escalated beyond that encouraged by the work teams with peasants seeing the opportunity to settle old scores and family feuds, or simply a chance to seize more land from a well-off neighbour and improve their standard of living.

Landlords made an easy target through which the communists could generate a sense of **class-consciousness** and conflict, vital for the sustaining of the revolution. Unlike many businessmen, they had not fled to Taiwan with the nationalists because their main assets, their land, could not be transferred. Many hoped that the GMD would return soon. The communists whipped up anger against them, in some cases releasing years of pent-up petty jealousy and long-festering resentments. In the past, the 'enemy' or 'outsiders' had been other villages, who often spoke different dialects or had different customs. Now the 'enemy' was another 'class' in the village who could be easily used as a scapegoat by the Party to generate popular enthusiasm for the communist cause.

## The impact of land reform

By the summer of 1952, the 'land to the tiller' movement had been largely completed. The work teams helped villagers measure out their new plots precisely to ensure fair redistribution. An estimated 88 per cent of households had taken part, with 43 per cent of the land redistributed to 60 per cent of the population. Rural production boomed. Between 1950 and 1952 total agricultural production increased at a rate of 15 per cent per annum. The gentry-landlord had been destroyed as a class but the human cost had been horrific, with an estimated 1 to 2 million landlords executed.

**Source A** From William Hinton, *Fanshen: A Documentary of Revolution in a Chinese Village* (Random House, 1968), pages 137–38. The source describes a 'struggle meeting' that took place in 1949. The victim was a local landlord, Ching-ho.

> Old women who had never spoken in public before stood up to accuse him. Even Li Mao's wife ... shook her fist before his nose and cried out, 'Once I went to glean [gather] wheat on your land. But you cursed me and drove me away.' Altogether over 180 opinions were raised. Ching-ho had no answer to them. He stood there with his head bowed. When the committee of our Association met to figure up what he owed, it came to 400 bags of milled grain. We went in to register his grain and altogether found but 200 bags of unmilled millet. [We] asked him what he intended to do since the grain was not nearly enough. He said, 'I have land and house.' 'But all this is not enough,' shouted the people. So then we began to beat him. Finally he said, 'I have 40 silver dollars.' We went in and dug it up. We beat him again. He told us where to find another hundred after that. Several militiamen began to heat an iron bar in one of the fires. Altogether we got $500 from Ching-ho. All said: 'In the past we never lived through a happy New Year because he always asked for his rent and interest then and cleaned our houses bare. This time we'll eat what we like' and everyone ate his fill and didn't even notice the cold.

Look carefully at Source A. What does the writer suggest was the main reason peasants supported the land reform movement? What can you infer from this source about the level of genuine ideological commitment to communism among the peasants?

## Agricultural co-operation

It soon became very clear that the CCP and the peasants had very different expectations of the land reform policy. For the peasants, it represented the realisation of their long-held dream of owning their own land free from landlord exploitation and indebtedness, a chance to create a better life, with greater security from threats like famine or drought that made their existence so precarious. Their support for land reform, therefore, did not necessarily represent communist ideological commitment.

On the other hand, the CCP saw land reform only as the very first step in the longer process of creating a truly socialist, modern and industrialised economy. According to Liu Shaoqi, the Vice Chairman of the Communist Party and a long-time colleague of Mao, the objective of land reform was 'to free the rural productive forces from the shackles of the landlords' feudal land-ownership system' in order to 'develop agricultural production and open the way for the new China's industrialisation'. The new system would be based on ending private ownership and production. At first agricultural co-operation between farmers would be encouraged by organising them to help them share tools, fertiliser and animals. Later agriculture would be 'collectivised' (see box below). The increased production would create a surplus that could be used to feed the urban industrial workforce in their modern factories. Mao knew that there would be resistance. 'The peasants want freedom, but we want socialism,' he admitted.

### Collectivisation of agriculture

Collectivisation of agriculture refers to the process of encouraging or forcing farmers to reorganise their individual private farms into much larger 'collective farms'. Instead of competing against each other, they would co-operate and work together. The sharing of materials, machines, animals and labour meant that production would be more efficient. Pooling resources would mean that the farmers could have access to more advanced machinery and share experience of new techniques to improve production. This would help meet the target of producing more food for the industrial workers.

### Mutual Aid Teams (MATs)

Changing the distribution of land ownership had not created the required increase in production. Although the landlords had been destroyed as a class, richer peasants still had more land and capital than poor peasants. Further reform was needed before the transformation towards a socialist economy could be completed. In December 1951 the CCP decided to introduce co-operative ownership of land. However, mindful of the tragic results of the rapid collectivisation undertaken in the **USSR** under its leader Stalin (see pages 55–57), the Chinese decided on a more gradual, moderate approach.

Voluntary Mutual Aid Teams (MATs), already set up in some communist-controlled parts of China before 1949, were introduced across the country. In these teams peasants pooled their resources such as tools, ploughs and their own labour. Animals were shared, as was knowledge and experience. This was rational: households with more land than they could farm efficiently could combine with those with more labour than they needed, and both would benefit. At first this was only at harvest time, but later it was all year round. MATs were on a small scale; most consisted of ten or fewer households, often from the same extended family. Richer peasants were excluded. MATs were enthusiastically accepted because, in part, they mirrored an already common practice in many villages where peasants helped each other for the benefit of the community. MATs were of particular benefit to the poorest peasants. By 1952 an estimated 40 per cent of all peasant households belonged to a MAT.

### Voluntary Agricultural Producers Co-operatives (APCs)

Mutual Aid Teams were pragmatic and popular. Yet communist leaders were worried that they still allowed the continued existence of capitalist ideas like the buying and selling of land, the hiring of labourers and the lending of money.

In order to reduce these economic freedoms, in 1953 the second stage towards collectivisation began. This was the setting up of voluntary Agricultural Producers Co-operatives (APCs). Now the land the peasants had just acquired during land reform as well as equipment and animals were shared. Land was reorganised into a single unit and the peasants were compensated using a points system according to the value of the land, labour and tools they had contributed. Once the harvest was collected and the state had taken its share, the peasants received either money or grain in payment. Although decisions about the management of the land were taken centrally by the local Party organisation, the land was still privately owned.

APCs were bigger than MATs; they comprised three to five MATs joined together, approximately 30 to 50 households. They gave the poorest peasants the chance to gain access to their wealthy neighbours' property but overall they were less popular than MATs. The peasants did not want to share their newly acquired land and only 14 per cent of peasants joined the new units. By June 1955 there were only 16.9 million peasant households in APCs out of a total of 110 million. Pace of development varied greatly too. In some areas they were started in 1951, but in the south, APCs did not appear until 1954.

Rich peasants were resistant to joining APCs, particularly where local cadres tried to speed the process up by moving peasants into APCs before organising them into MATs first. Some cadres undervalued property when deciding compensation and richer peasants slaughtered their animals rather than be forced to give them to the APC. The results in grain production were disappointing. The First Five-Year Plan (see page 239) assumed a 23 per cent increase in agricultural production, but output was falling far short of that. In 1953 and 1954 production had risen less than 2 per cent.

## Disagreements over collectivisation

An argument began within the Party. **Gradualists** like Liu Shaoqi and Premier Zhou Enlai claimed that China was not yet ready for large-scale farming; it lacked mechanised equipment like tractors and there was a shortage of chemical fertilisers. They denounced the 'premature' establishment of APCs. In mid-1955 Vice Premier Li Fuchun told the **National People's Congress**:

> *Only when agriculture ... turn[s] gradually from individual to collective management, and on this basis equips [itself] ... with modern techniques, can the productive forces of agriculture be greatly developed, its capacity for reproduction increased and output raised to meet the demands of the nation's industrialisation.*

Mao disagreed. In July 1955 he demanded an increase in the pace of reform towards full collectivisation, and an end to all private property. He argued that collectivisation was a key step in advancing the revolutionary process towards the creation of a socialist society. He declared that grassroots enthusiasm, what he called a 'high tide in new socialist mass movement' led by peasants, could make up for any shortfall in mechanical equipment. He also believed that slow agricultural growth would jeopardise his industrialisation programme because exporting food was the only way China could pay for imports of advanced technology from the Soviet Union. He feared that the disappointing results were caused by rich peasants and landlords using their influence to stop peasants joining APCs. He said his gradualist Party colleagues were 'tottering along like women with bound feet' constantly complaining 'You're going too fast! You're going too fast!' With his encouragement membership of peasant farmers in APCs reached 96 per cent in December 1956.

There are arguments among historians as to how fast Mao really wanted the process of agricultural change to be undertaken. Some argue that he was actually quite moderate and was worried that if the Party introduced collectivisation too quickly, it would be too big a shock to the peasants and they might resist it. He seemed to accept that the transformation towards socialism would take a long time. In February 1953 the Party's Central Committee declared that 'the peasants' individual economy will exist to a very large extent and for a considerable length of time'.

What is clear is that whatever Mao intended, the Party cadres working in rural areas enthusiastically increased the pace of collectivisation. Some were genuinely ideologically committed, but they had a personal vested interest in doing so. It was easier for them to extract grain from APCs than from individual farmers. They could exert their own personal authority over the co-operative. Lower-level Party cadres could also win favour and enhance their career by being seen to outstrip their quota for grain acquisition. Doing so enabled them to demonstrate their loyalty to Mao. Therefore the officials were understandably supportive of Mao's initiatives. This support meant Mao was able to override the concerns of the gradualists, taking the opportunity to remove some of them and replace them with some of his closest ideological allies in positions of key influence, such as Chen Boda.

### Chen Boda, 1904–89

Mao's political secretary at Yan'an, Chen Boda, was one of the Chairman's closest ideological experts and a trusted adviser. He played a key role in organising the regime's propaganda and was editor of the Party journal, *The Red Flag*. He was a radical, totally committed to Mao's vision. He called the victims of the famine (see pages 245-247) 'an unavoidable phenomenon of our onward march'. He later played a key role in supporting Mao during the **Cultural Revolution** (see Key Topic 3) as leader of the radical Cultural Revolution Group. At the height of his power, the Ninth **Party Congress** in 1969, he was ranked fourth in the Party leadership. Feared by other communist leaders, he was accused of being a 'revisionist secret agent' and was sentenced to eighteen years imprisonment in 1981 for political crimes. He was released early because of ill health. He died in 1989.

## Growth of APCs

The pace with which APCs began to form was impressive. In December 1955, 63.3 per cent of peasant households were part of APCs, with 4 per cent of those being higher-level APCs comprising 200 to 300 households, sometimes encompassing whole villages. Mao was greatly impressed by the apparent enthusiasm of the peasants for agricultural co-operation. 'We must guide the movement boldly,' he declared, and with a warning to his opponents within the Party, said that we 'must not fear dragons ahead and tigers behind'. Mao was convinced that peasant support meant that it was not necessary to wait for agricultural mechanisation before moving to large-scale production. 'Under the conditions prevailing in our country,' he said, 'co-operation must precede the use of big machinery.' Claiming that 'we underestimated our capacity,' he announced that it was 'possible that socialism will be realised in 1959'.

### Enforced collectivisation

By January 1956, 80.3 per cent of peasant households were in APCs, and by now 30.7 per cent of those were higher-level APCs. Now pragmatism was completely abandoned. Private ownership was abolished. Members would only be compensated for their labour; their land and equipment were simply taken over by the state. In these new APCs tools, equipment and all land were to be shared. Membership was now compulsory. Except for some very small private plots, privately owned land ceased to exist and no compensation was provided. By the end of 1956, almost 88 per cent of peasants were in higher-level APCs.

## Conclusion: Early changes in agriculture

Historians have talked of a 'New Mao' emerging during the process of collectivisation and it is certainly true that there were important precedents set that would have devastating side effects later on. By the mid-1950s such was Mao's personal prestige and authority that he was able to override the concerns of more moderate Party leaders in the Central Committee. Fearful of being denounced as 'rightist opportunists', they had little choice but to follow Mao's lead, even those of genuine stature like Liu Shaoqi and Zhou Enlai. Mao was able to ignore concerns over the unpopularity of increasing the pace of reforms in order to realise his own ideological goals. Finally, it saw Mao taking the side first of the peasants and then of lower-level cadres, consciously placing himself as their representative against his fellow Party leaders whom he derided as lacking the necessary revolutionary vigour. Some historians have referred to the beginning of a 'civil war' within the Party over the pace at which China could be transformed; a war that was not finally ended until the Cultural Revolution (see Key Topic 3). That he was convinced of the backing of the mass of the lower levels of the Party and succeeded in realising his personal radical vision would have dire consequences for the future of China.

# 2 The communes

According to orthodox Marxist ideology the socialist revolution would be supported most enthusiastically by the industrial working classes. Mao saw that in China it would be impossible to rely at this early stage on the industrial workers to create communism. Instead he built communism in the countryside first, forcing the peasants to live in communes. There, their property was taken away and every aspect of their lives was strictly monitored and controlled. As Mao himself put it: 'Without socialisation of agriculture, there can be no complete, consolidated socialism.'

By 1956 Mao was emboldened by the success of moving peasants into the co-operatives (see page 234), but agricultural production figures remained disappointing. Agricultural output had risen only 3.8 per cent over the previous year. Grain production rose only 1 per cent in 1957 and rationing of cotton cloth had to be implemented due to shortages. Seizing grain from the peasants by force might have provided enough food for the industrial workers, but the Party had to be careful. It could not follow the Soviet model of ruthless requisitioning, because unlike in the Soviet Union, almost 70 per cent of the Chinese Communist Party were from rural backgrounds. If the CCP took too much grain from the peasants it risked alienating the mass of its support. Instead, Mao believed that the best way to increase production was to move the peasants into communes. He believed that the experience of the MATs and the APCs showed that the peasants themselves wanted to move more quickly towards full communism.

The communes were to be vast in size and incorporate both agricultural and industrial production. Mao called this focus on both aspects of the economy 'Walking on Two Legs'. He believed that the communes would represent the final realisation of his goal to create a communist China but his overly ambitious **radicalism** proved disastrous. Between

### Note it down

Use the 1:2 method of note taking in this section (see page x). For example, write down the main aims of the communes in the left-hand column (as listed below) and a bullet-point list of factors relating to each aim:

- Create self-sufficiency in steel production
- Increase food production
- Make society more communist
- Improve the lives of Chinese women
- Enhance the control of the Communist Party over the people.

1958 and 1962 China suffered the greatest man-made famine in history (see pages 247–249). Perhaps as many as 30 million people died. By the end of the period Mao had been effectively side-lined from political decisions.

## The abolition of private farming

Mao judged that the early period of collective farming had been successfully completed. All private farming was to be abolished. In August 1958 a Politburo resolution declared people's communes to be 'the basic social units of communist society'. Once again, Mao did not personally direct commune policy, but his public endorsement was enough to quicken the pace of the movement.

The first commune was established in Henan province in July 1958. It was named 'Sputnik Commune' in honour of the Soviet satellite which, being the first ever satellite, appeared to represent the technological supremacy of the communist world. In August, Mao declared: 'The people's commune is great.' The next day his slogan was the headline in newspapers across the country, accelerating the transformation of co-operatives to communes. By the end of the year 740,000 co-operatives had been reorganised into 26,000 communes. The Party claimed that 99 per cent of the peasant population lived in communes – almost half a billion people.

## The organisation of the communes

With the average size of approximately 5500 households, communes organised both agricultural and industrial production as well as healthcare and education. Private ownership of land and livestock was abolished. Markets, denounced by the Party as evidence of rural capitalism, were banned.

Mao believed that the mass mobilisation of the people would allow industry and agriculture to be developed simultaneously within the communes. The peasants would no longer be dependent on urban industry; now industry would be developed within the commune itself, making it more self-reliant. Each commune would produce its own food as well as having its own factories producing industrial goods, such as tools and farm machinery, for use by the commune. Items that were in constant short supply, such as thermos flasks, toothbrushes, twine and rope, would be produced. The pooling of resources within the commune would be more efficient.

### Mass mobilisation

Mao believed that, although China lacked expertise and experience in organising economic and social change, it possessed a great asset: its massive population. By reducing central control by experts such as intellectuals and Party bureaucrats, the masses could become both 'Red and Expert': ideologically committed but also technically knowledgeable. Mao believed that human will, far more than rational planning or reliance on technology, could be harnessed to overcome any obstacle.

## Communal living: the vision

Mao believed that the communes moved life in China closer to the vision of a perfect communist society. Income, which in the APCs had been based on labour supplied, would now take into account the needs of the commune resident. Mess halls enabled communal eating, the theory being sharing meals would help to develop revolutionary fervour. Crèches and boarding schools were also provided.

Mao believed that with women no longer forced to toil in the kitchen to prepare meals, or spend time raising their children, they would be able to escape domestic drudgery and join the men in the fields and factories. Propaganda celebrated these 'iron women' for taking their full and equal role in economic production. An estimated 90 per cent of women laboured in agriculture between 1958 and 1959. Grandparents would no longer be forced to help care for grandchildren. They would be free to spend time with other elderly people in 'happiness homes'.

## Communal living: the reality

Forced into one location, the Party could easily target commune residents with propaganda, further forging their revolutionary and militaristic spirit. Communes were organised into 'brigades' and divided into production teams or 'platoons.' All able-bodied citizens between 15 and 50 years of age belonged to the commune **militia** who served as a police force to enforce the rules of the commune – they prevented people from taking too much food from the canteen and punished those who did not work hard enough.

These policies had devastating results for family life. The traditional family meal was replaced by eating in massive mess halls, surrounded by strangers. Parents lost influence over the raising of their children, grandparents became isolated from their relatives. Time was wasted travelling the often long distances to the mess hall while the food was of poor quality, causing diets to worsen. Far from liberating women, life in the communes was even harder. Women were forced to carry out harsh physical labour that had previously been the role of men. Still production did not rise enough. Mao sought reasons why. He became convinced that the grain was being eaten by sparrows. If he could remove them, production could be increased.

## The Four Pests Campaign

In 1958 Mao launched the Four Pests Campaign, dedicated to ridding China of sparrows that ate grain, as well as rats, flies and mosquitoes.

Party activists were sent to villages to encourage peasants to chase sparrows, making a noise by banging drums or pounding pots and pans to scare them from landing. If the sparrows could not find anywhere to rest, they would die of exhaustion. A small reward was paid for the bodies of the birds. Mao declared that children as young as five should climb trees to knock down nests. Crops lay rotting in the fields as villagers wasted their time desperately hunting for vermin or chasing sparrows. Worse still, the 'sparrowcide' reduced the number of birds who normally ate caterpillars. The greatly increased caterpillar population attacked and ate the crops, devouring the harvest.

**Source B** Quoted in Jonathan Fenby, *The Penguin History of Modern China: The Fall and Rise of a Great Power, 1850–2009* (Penguin, 2008). One peasant, then a schoolboy, recalls the frenzied efforts to eradicate sparrows during the Four Pests Campaign.

> 'Get the little thief!' some shouted.
>
> 'Don't let the little bastard get away!' others cried.
>
> 'Kill it! Kill it!'
>
> 'Our workers are strong, our workers are strong,' a voice intoned over a loudspeaker.
>
> The crowd surged forward screaming, 'Kill! Kill! Kill!' It then suddenly parted and the boy saw a large man holding a bird, its head covered with blood. The loudspeakers switched to a verse:
>
> You can fly, but stop you can't.
>
> The field is wide open.
>
> But you find no place to hide.
>
> You're hungry and tired.

What can historians infer from Source B about life in the communes?

## Lysenkoism

The effects of the Four Pests Campaign was exacerbated by the decision to follow the ideas of the Soviet scientist Trofim Lysenko.

Lysenko's theories were wholly fraudulent. He had manipulated his research in order to gain political influence in the Soviet Union and encouraged the **purging** of any scientist who disagreed with him. The slavish adherence to his theories, combined with the massive waste of time and labour caused by the **backyard furnaces** (see pages 246–247), led to a drop in agricultural production. Fearful that they would be dismissed from their posts, the cadres refused to report this failure, instead claiming that they had exceeded their production quotas. Overjoyed by the apparent success, the Party responded by simply increasing their already ambitious quotas even more.

### Trofim Lysenko, 1898–1976

A so-called **agrobiologist**, Lysenko had distorted his scientific research in order to gain influence in Stalin's Russia. By the 1950s, his claims that crop yields could be greatly increased through exposing seeds to moisture and low temperatures and planting them close together had been mistakenly lauded as promising the production breakthroughs that the Chinese regime desired. Greatly influenced by Soviet propaganda that declared Lysenko to be a genius, in 1958 Mao named his doctrine, Lysenkoism, to be official agricultural policy.

## Conclusion: The communes

The creation of the communes should have been a major turning point in the transformation of China into a truly communist society. They heralded the realisation of Mao's utopian vision, promising truly revolutionary changes. Economically they would end private production. They would totally revise long held and deeply engrained social attitudes on gender roles and parenting. For years Mao had railed against the dictatorial powers held by governments and dynasties in China's dark feudal past. Now he was attempting an act of coercion dedicated to remoulding China on a scale inconceivable to previous leaders. The communes marked the beginning of the ill-named **Great Leap Forward**. They would collapse in the nightmare of the Great Famine.

### Work together

Divide the sub-headings in this section between you. Re-read the notes you made on this section (see page 232), then put them away. Then take it in turns to explain a sub-heading to your partner. After you have finished each sub-heading, you can both look at your notes. Discuss what you missed out, and define any terms that either of you found difficult to understand or explain.

# 3 The First Five-Year Plan, 1952–56

In 1952 the CCP announced the beginning of the First Five-Year Plan for Industry. The Plan closely mirrored the Soviet model of industrialisation, most especially the Stalinist focus on the centralisation of **heavy industry** As in Soviet Russia, market forces would not influence how much was produced. Instead, clear production targets would be set and monitored by the Party. 'The Communist Party of the Soviet Union is our best teacher and we must learn from it,' said Mao. The decision to copy the Soviet Union may, in hindsight, appear to be a strange one. Yet Stalin's economic policies had very recently transformed Russia from a backward, agriculturally based nation to a modern industrialised superpower capable of defeating a technologically advanced Nazi Germany during the Second World War. Mao hoped to repeat a similar feat. 'The Soviet Union's today is our tomorrow,' promised one CCP slogan. After the years of humiliation by the West, the CCP considered industrialisation key to becoming an independent and respected nation. It declared: 'Because China did not have her own heavy industry and her own war industry, she was being trampled upon.'

The decision was not only ideological, but practical too. The Soviet Union was now China's only major ally. A **trade embargo** that had been imposed by the Western powers as a result of China's involvement in the Korean War (see page 219) meant China had few trading partners. It was forced to rely on economic help from the Soviet Union because no one in the West would trade with the **PRC**. Later Mao bitterly regretted adopting the Soviet model without adapting it to Chinese circumstances.

## Note it down

1. Before you start, read back over your notes from the previous chapter and write down a sentence that describes China's industry at the start of the communist regime.
2. Now, use an A3 piece of paper and write down at the top the main reasons why Mao launched the First Five-Year Plan. Then, as you read through this section, write down evidence that the plan:
   - successfully modernised the economy
   - failed and that the economy was still backward
   - helped China become a more communist society.
3. Overall, do you think Mao would have been happy with the results of the Five-Year Plan? What about the Chinese people? Would their opinion be any different?

**Source C** From the Communist Party newspaper, the *People's Daily*, 'How China Proceeds with the Task of Industrialisation', 23 May 1953, quoted in Mark Selden (ed.), *The People's Republic of China: A Documentary History of Revolutionary Change* (New York: Monthly Review Press, 1979).

> Industrialisation has been the goal sought by the Chinese people during the past one hundred years. But industry as a whole has never been developed in China ... It was just as Stalin said: 'Because China did not have her own heavy industry and her own war industry, she was being trampled upon by all the reckless and unruly elements. It is through the implementation of the policies of industrialization ... that the Soviet Union succeeded ... in turning a backward agricultural nation into a first class industrial power in the world. The foundation of socialism is large industrial development. Lenin said, 'There is only one real foundation for a socialist society, and it is large industry.' [Only] with self-produced capital goods, may economic independence be guaranteed and subservience to a capitalist state with great heavy industrial development be prevented. We are many years behind the economy of capitalist countries. We cannot afford to pursue the old path of the capitalist countries, but embark on a different course to catch up with the capitalist countries within a short time.

Look carefully at Source C. What can you infer were the key reasons that the CCP launched the First Five-Year Plan?

## The USSR's support

In the Sino-Soviet Mutual Assistance Treaty of February 1950 China and the Soviet Union had undertaken to 'render the other all possible economic assistance and carry out necessary co-operation'. Chinese involvement in the Korean War had disrupted the development of this economic relationship. After the armistice in Korea was signed in July 1953 the USSR began to support China's Five-Year Plan. The Soviet support was extensive and essential. It included:

- the construction or reconstruction of 156 major industrial enterprises, including seven iron and steel **plants**, 24 electric power stations and 63 machinery plants; some plants were constructed in the Soviet Union and shipped to China
- industrial experts to supply the technical knowledge and experience of organising a centrally planned economy that the Chinese lacked; 11,000 Soviet and Eastern European industrial experts were sent to China, helping to design the plants, construct them and train the workers

- inviting 28,000 Chinese technicians to study in Russia, in order to learn from 'elder brother'
- a loan of $300 million US dollars over the next five years.

## The Plan's targets

Declaring in 1953 that 'Industrialisation has been the goal sought by the Chinese people during the last one hundred years,' the Party announced that 'its basic objective is the gradual realisation of the industrialisation of the state.' The need to improve industrial production was pressing as it had fallen far behind the rest of the world. According to CCP statistics, industrial output in 1949 was just 10 to 20 per cent of its pre-Second World War peak, under 50 per cent in coal, roughly 75 per cent in electricity and 70–90 per cent in most consumer goods. The Plan aimed to achieve the following:

- A high rate of growth, particularly in heavy industry such as steel and coal production (see Table 1).
- Investment in advanced technology.
- The construction of modern industrial plants.
- Self-sufficiency: given China's lack of trading opportunities, Mao wanted China to become an **autarkic state**.
- A very high level of grain procurement at fixed prices from rural areas to fund the industrialisation in the cities. For example, in 1953 the state planned to procure 22 million tons of grain. Private grain sales were forbidden. Markets were controlled to prevent buying and selling before the state met its target.
- To stimulate the transformation towards a socialist society. As the former leader of the Russian Communist Party Vladimir **Lenin** had said, 'There is only one real foundation for a socialist society, and it is large industry.'

## The Plan's successes

Table 1 below shows the results of the Plan. In many respects it was a great success for the regime.

- The annual growth rate averaged 16 per cent.
- Industrial output grew 15.5 per cent per year, outstripping the target of 14.7 per cent.
- Heavy industrial output nearly tripled. For example, industrial production in Manchuria (see page 203) more than outstripped its pre-Civil War peak.
- Railway freight volume more than doubled, enabling raw materials, equipment and machines to be moved around the country to where they were needed more quickly and efficiently. The **PLA** could also be moved around China more quickly to control any opposition.
- Geological exploration discovered vital resources like oil, uranium and minerals in Xinjiang.
- The industrial working class grew from 6 million to 10 million. Investment was focused upon enormous industrial projects near cities. For example, the new steel centre at Anshan attracted 35,000 new workers. By 1957 it was producing two-thirds of China's steel.
- The regime wanted the Plan to accelerate the transformation towards socialism. In 1953 the state began to convert private firms into joint state-private ownership. By 1956 private sector industry had been abolished. Large retail firms also came under state ownership while small shops and services such as barbers and tailors were converted into co-operatives. Instead of competing for profit they pooled their resources and labour.
- The standard of living of industrial workers improved. They had greater job security. Work was guaranteed all year round. Given that many workers were simply peasants who had recently fled rural poverty this

**Table 1: The First Five-Year Plan, 1953–57 (mmt = million metric tons; tmt = thousand metric tons).**

| Indicator | 1952 Data | 1957 Plan target | 1957 Actual | Percentage of Plan achieved |
|---|---|---|---|---|
| Coal (mmt) | 68.50 | 113.00 | 130.00 | 115.00 |
| Crude oil (tmt) | 436.00 | 2012.00 | 1458.00 | 72.50 |
| Steel ingot (mmt) | 1.35 | 4.12 | 5.35 | 129.80 |
| Electric power (billion kwh) | 7.26 | 15.90 | 19.34 | 121.60 |
| Locomotives (units) | 20 | 200 | 167 | 83.50 |
| Merchant ships (thousand dwt tons) | 21.50 | 179.10 | 54.00 | 30.20 |
| Bicycles (thousand units) | 80 | 555 | 1174 | 211.50 |
| Trucks (units) | 0 | 4000 | 7500 | 187.50 |

Examine Table 1 above. How far does it suggest that the Plan was a success? (Remember to reflect on what kind of nation Mao was trying to transform China into.)

represented an escape from the precarious dependence on seasonal farm labouring. The living conditions in Shanghai were particularly improved.

- With greater urbanisation, the CCP was able to heighten its influence over the population. The large industrial plants could be organised on socialist lines, with committees of workers having an important say in how the factory was run. Housing, healthcare, education and even entertainment could be provided through subsidised cinemas set up by the Party. Workers were organised into *Danwei* or work units that controlled access to welfare support and provided permits for marriage and travel. This then was a success for the Party, but although the people in the cities did have steady employment and improved access to services, the cost was their freedom. They were completely controlled by the Party.

## The Plan's failures

- The Plan was dependent on loans from the Soviet Union which had very high interest rates. In order to meet the very demanding repayment schedules farmers were forced to sell their crops to the state at artificially low prices. This grain was needed to feed the growing industrial workforce and also to sell for currency to repay the loans. Although food prices were kept low, the peasantry paid the price, barely surviving at a **subsistence** level.
- The value of agricultural output grew only an average of 2.1 per cent per year, a sharp decline from the rate of 14.1 per cent achieved during 1949–52. Increases in factory production depended upon a co-operative and healthy working class, but not enough food was being imported into the cities to feed them.
- The supply of consumer goods was very low. This helped the Plan because the people saved more money and bought **government bonds** that provided funds for the Plan. However, there was little to buy in the shops.
- Despite Soviet advice, the Chinese still lacked organisational and management experience. Lack of co-operation between industries or between the central planners and the local producers created bottlenecks in production.
- Although the government **balanced the budget**, there was little investment in improving the healthcare or education systems. The standard of living, especially among the poorest peasants in rural China, was still very low. For example, there was still a huge shortage of trained doctors, particularly in rural areas, and many peasants received only a very basic education.

## Conclusion: The First Five-Year Plan

The First Five-Year Plan was a great success for the regime. Although not all targets were achieved, Chinese industry was dramatically transformed from its situation at the end of the Civil War. The Party established greater repressive control over the population and, given the importance of industrialisation in Marxist thinking, could point to the Plan being a genuine ideological success too.

For the people of China, however, the benefits were less clear cut. Living standards in the cities did improve, but this was at the cost of personal freedoms. As ever, it was the Chinese peasants who paid the biggest price. The Plan could only succeed if food prices for the workers were kept low, so they received little benefit for their hard work. Furthermore, there was so much food taken through **grain requisitioning** from the peasants that many rural areas could barely do more than simply subsist. They certainly did not see the great improvement in the standard of living the communists had promised. Soviet economic experts provided vital advice for their Chinese counterparts, but the harsh conditions imposed by the Soviet Union in return for their help exacerbated Chinese bitterness towards their supposed close ally. This strained the relationship between the Soviet Union and China that had already become tense during the Korean War (see page 223). Mao's distrust of Soviet methods, combined with an overconfidence borne out of the successes of the Plan, contributed greatly to his decision to quickly move the peasants into massive communes, the first step of his most catastrophic idea of all, the Great Leap Forward.

### Work together

Discuss the following statement in pairs:

**'The First Five-Year Plan brought widespread benefits to China.'**

How far do you agree with this statement? You could consider issues such as:

- the levels of industrial production created as a result of the Five-Year Plan
- the type of industrial goods that were produced
- the lives of people in the countryside as compared to the lives of people in the cities
- the impact on Mao's personal prestige.

## 4 The Second Five-Year Plan, 1958–62

The First Five-Year Plan had been a success for Mao. Industrial production had increased greatly. However, agricultural production still lagged behind. Obsessed with turning China into a modern nation in order to compete with the Western democracies, Mao sought a way to increase both agricultural and industrial production simultaneously. The Soviet model of central planning had not sufficiently increased agricultural production. He was also dismissive of what he termed a 'slave mentality' towards so-called experts. He found a fundamentally Maoist answer: he would rely on the mass mobilisation of the masses. Economic realities or technical expertise were irrelevant; force of human will would be enough to drag China's economy into modernity. Instead of centrally planned targets, local people would be self-sufficient and organise their own economic production. Under the campaign slogan 'More, faster, better, cheaper' the people of China were exhorted to focus all their energies on creating a massive increase in the production of both food and industrial goods. This policy, launched as the Second Five-Year Plan, became known as the Great Leap Forward. The result was an economic disaster and a human tragedy on an unprecedented scale. Mao's overly ambitious ideologically driven radicalism proved disastrous. Between 1958 and 1962 China suffered the greatest man-made famine in history. Perhaps as many as 30 million people died. By the end of the period Mao had been effectively sidelined from political decisions.

### The Soviet model of central planning

In a centrally planned economy, production levels are set by a central authority. In Russia, this was the Communist Party. Instead of the needs of the market dictating what and how much is produced, the economic experts at the central authority set specific targets for output, based on what they believed were the needs of the nation. Mao distrusted experts, seeking to rely on the initiative of the mass of the people. He believed that the efforts of ordinary people dedicated to communism, not educated planners and bureaucrats who lacked genuine ideological commitment, would make the Chinese economy powerful.

### Note it down

**1** This section focuses upon the Second Five-Year Plan, the so-called Great Leap Forward. Use a spider diagram to make notes on this (see page x). The body of the spider could be labelled 'Why did Mao launch the Great Leap Forward?' The legs could be labelled:

- Improve international prestige
- Modernise the Chinese economy
- Increase food yields
- Create communism.

Alternatively, you could draw a small visual metaphor to represent each of the reasons. Can you convert the text into a small cartoon to describe the essential points of each reason?

**2** Put numbers next to the reasons to show how you would rank them in order of importance to Mao personally.

**3** Then, as you read through the section on the results of the Second Five-Year Plan, note next to each aim any evidence that it was successfully achieved, and in a different colour any failures.

**4** Look at the ranking of the reasons. How successful was the Great Leap Forward for the Chinese people? How successful was it for Mao?

## Why did Mao launch the Great Leap Forward?

- Mao was desperate to transform China into a great economic power. He also wanted to place China as the leading communist nation in Asia. In 1957, the Soviet leader Nikita Khrushchev made a dramatic speech in which he promised that the USSR would overtake the United States in industrial production by 1980. Not to be outdone, Mao told the Party, 'We must start a technological revolution so that we may overtake Britain in fifteen or more years.'
- Mao had good reason to be optimistic. Although agriculture had faltered, industrial production had risen by 18.3 per cent during the First Five-Year Plan. This success had convinced him that very quick and very large improvements in agricultural production could be made.
- Mao's optimism was further enhanced because it appeared that the communists were winning the **Cold War**. Communist technology appeared to be ascendant

over that of the West. With the launching of Sputnik, in 1957, it looked as if the **space race** had been won. In a speech in Moscow in 1957 a confident Mao declared: 'The East wind is prevailing over the West wind.' (See Source D.)

- Mao wanted to achieve what was termed 'Walking on Two Legs': increasing both agricultural and industrial production at the same time. The regime declared that 'General Steel' and 'General Grain' were in charge of the economy.
- Mao believed that the people's sheer force of will would be enough to overcome all technological obstacles. The control of economic experts in the Party had to be loosened and control of the economy decentralised. Instead of targets and regulations set from central government, as happened in Soviet Russia, local people, in the individual communes, should have more control over what they produced.

**Source D** Translation of remarks made by Mao to Chinese students in Moscow, 17 November 1957. From Stuart R. Schram, *The Political Thoughts of Chairman Mao* (Frederick A. Praeger, 1969), pages 407–8.

> Chairman Mao pointed out first of all that the October Socialist Revolution [the coming to power of the communists in Russia] marks a turning point in world history. The forces of socialism surpass the forces of imperialism. Chairman Mao said it was an event of great significance that the communist and workers' parties of sixty-four countries attended the celebrations. It showed the solidarity of the socialist countries. Chairman Mao said that the direction of the wind in the world had changed. In the struggle between the socialist and capitalist camps, it was no longer the West wind that prevailed over the East wind, but the East wind that prevailed over the West wind.

What does Source D tell us about the reasons why Mao launched the Great Leap Forward in 1957?

**Source E** A poster celebrating the Great Leap Forward, published in 1958.

Look at the figures in the poster in Source E. In what ways does it suggest that the Great Leap Forward will bring positive benefits?

## Successes of the Plan

Economically, the Great Leap Forward had a few successes. Massive irrigation terracing helped make agricultural land more fertile, while construction projects changed the face of Chinese cities. Tiananmen Square was remodelled into a modern urban space, though many historical buildings had to be levelled to make this possible. Ideologically, the Party believed that the people in communes (see pages 236–238) lived more closely to a communistic model than ever before. Lacking private property, they pooled labour, food and even parenting responsibilities.

## Failures of the Plan

The Second Five-Year Plan was a spectacular failure:

- The targets of the Plan were simply absurd. Mao had created an atmosphere of competition. Government officials knew that the best way to advance their careers was to impress Mao, and they did this by telling him that his economic policies would achieve unheard-of economic improvements. For example, in January 1958 the Ministry of Metallurgy declared that it would more than double steel production to 20 million tonnes by 1962 and reach 100 million by 1977. Worried that his department would look slow in comparison, the chemicals minister claimed that it could construct thousands of chemical fertiliser factories.
- Mao let himself be convinced that the mobilisation of the masses could overcome all practical obstacles. He lost all sense of reality. When reviewing the steel production target to raise steel production from 6 million to 9 million tonnes, he announced, "Make it snappy! Let's just double it! Why dilly-dally? Let's make it 11 million tonnes!" He was overconfident and, after the **purges** of his enemies in the campaigns of the 1950s (see pages 211–213), no one would dare to challenge him and tell him the truth.
- The Anti-Rightist Campaign (see pages 217–218) meant that there were no intellectuals or experts left to offer advice or provide rational economic planning.
- He encouraged families to set up backyard furnaces (see Source F, page 246) through which they could contribute to steel production. Compelled by cadres who hoped to impress the Party leadership by meeting unrealistic production goals and driven by incessant propaganda, all possible sources of metal such as vital cooking implements and woks were melted in the furnaces. Wood from furniture, doors and roofs was burnt to keep the furnace hot. Inevitably, the steel was

▲ Tiananmen Square.

of extremely poor quality and useless. Much of it was taken away and buried. With so many people working the backyard furnaces, the economy began to break down and food was left to rot in the fields.

- Many factories were closed or reduced their production because of the shortage of raw materials. The famine (see below) meant that more and more workers died of starvation. By 1962, industrial production had declined by 40 per cent from the 1958–59 level.
- Table 2 provides statistical evidence of the economic results of the Great Leap Forward.

**Table 2: Economic results of the Great Leap Forward.**

| Grain output (million metric tons) | | | | | |
|---|---|---|---|---|---|
| Year | Total grain | Rice | Wheat | | |
| 1957 | 185.00 | 86.80 | 23.60 | | |
| 1958 | 200.00 | 80.80 | 22.60 | | |
| 1959 | 170.00 | 69.30 | 22.20 | | |
| 1960 | 143.30 | 59.70 | 22.20 | | |
| 1961 | 147.50 | 53.60 | 14.25 | | |
| **Other crops (million metric tons)** | | | | | |
| | 1958 | 1961 | | | |
| Sugar cane | 12.50 | 4.27 | | | |
| Beets | 3.00 | 0.80 | | | |
| Oil-bearing plants | 4.77 | 1.80 | | | |
| Cotton | 1.97 | 0.80 | | | |
| **Livestock (millions)** | 1958 | 1961 | | | |
| Pigs | 138.29 | 75.50 | | | |
| Draught animals | 53.60 | 38.10 | | | |
| **Steel, coal and cement, million metric tons** | | | | | |
| | 1958 | 1959 | 1960 | 1961 | 1962 |
| Steel | 8.80 | 13.87 | 18.66 | 8.70 | 6.67 |
| Coal | 270.00 | 369.00 | 397.00 | 278.00 | 220.00 |
| Cement | 9.30 | 12.27 | 15.65 | 6.21 | 6.00 |
| **Industrial output, billions yuan** | | | | | |
| 1958 | 1959 | 1960 | 1961 | 1962 | |
| 121 | 163 | 183 | 113 | 94 | |

What can you infer from Table 2 about the impact of the Great Leap Forward? What can you infer from the data about the likely social impacts?

### State-owned enterprises

The Great Leap Forward did not only create communes. Industrial firms were taken over to create state-owned enterprises. In one way they realised communist ideology. The Party dictated the prices the businesses could charge and the production targets that they had to meet, theoretically for the good of the nation, not for profit. Wages were set by the Party at a guaranteed level. Workers were given a home as well as healthcare and education. This meant that the Enterprises were inefficient. It did not matter how much effort a worker put in, he was still paid the same and had very little incentive to be productive. Managers were not rewarded for being efficient either. Any surplus they produced was taken away by the state anyway.

## The Great Famine, 1958–62

The communes and the Great Leap Forward were a disaster for agricultural production. The total announced for 1958 was 375 million tons. When it became clear that this was grossly exaggerated, it was revised down to 215 million tons. Fearful of being labelled as a 'rightist', local rural cadres refused to reveal the real conditions in the communes. Slogans like 'Go all-out', 'Aim high', 'Achieve better' and 'Faster results' imposed impossible pressures on cadres to outstrip their targets and they extravagantly exaggerated their production reports. As a result of the so-called 'wind of exaggeration', higher Party officials responded by demanding even greater results based on the inflated figures.

Falsely assuming that there existed a great surplus of grain in the countryside, in turn the officials in rural areas demanded that even higher quotas of grain be extracted and sold to the government at artificially low prices. Demands for food to be given to the government went up and up, even as agricultural production in reality dropped. Such was the expectation of a massive grain surplus that orders were given to leave a third of the farmland **fallow** because the storage facilities would be insufficient to contain it. Between 1958 and 1961, the amount of land in use for crop production was reduced by nine per cent. Grain exports to pay for more heavy industry from the Soviet Union continued to rise and grain was even sent abroad to fellow communist countries like North Korea and North Vietnam as a free gift.

### Life during the Great Famine

The Great Leap Forward created the greatest famine in human history. Before the famine the rural death rate was 11.07 people per 1000 inhabitants. By 1960 it was 28.68. Some provinces were even worse. In Anhui the death rate reached 68.6. Before the famine, Anhui was self-sufficient in food, but so much was taken away by the regime that 8 million people starved. In Henan 7.8 million people died and in Sichuan 9 million. In Tibet 1 million died; this was the greatest amount by proportion of the population. The regime deliberately took more grain away and handed out smaller rations in communes in order to deliberately kill more Tibetans who, as Buddhists loyal to the Lama religion, the communists did not trust.

Gangs of starving peasants launched attacks on grain reserves. Their punishment at the hands of the police was torture and death. Peasants resorted to scavenging for tree bark to make 'porridge' or grinding leaves for 'flour'. They scoured the communes for rats, but were often too exhausted to catch them. Instead they ate frogs, toads or worms. Birth rates dropped as women simply could not procreate. Malnourished and already physically exhausted from working their backyard furnaces, many people succumbed to disease. Children and the elderly were particularly vulnerable and died from malnutrition in vast numbers. Cases of cannibalism were reported: children were abducted, killed and boiled for food. In some cases parents killed and ate their own family members. Some men sold their wives into prostitution or servitude to raise money for food. Often the women wanted to be sold; it might offer their only chance to survive. Other women resorted to prostitution in order to survive. Peasant migrants fled the famine and swelled the overcrowded cities. Although finding accurate figures is difficult, it appears that at least 30 to 50 million people died.

## Why was the Great Famine so terrible?

Mao's policies were not solely responsible for the scale of the famine. Typhoons caused flooding in South China, while drought reduced the flow of the Yellow River by two-thirds. Eight of the twelve main rivers in Shandong dried up. More than 60 per cent of cultivated land was affected by either flood or drought and 2 million died through drowning or from starvation when their crops were destroyed.

**Source F** A photo of backyard furnaces

Look at the photo in Source F. Imagine you are a peasant in China, ordered by the Communist Party to build a backyard furnace and create steel. What problems and challenges do you think this would present to you?

Furthermore, the Party's ability to deal with the catastrophe was reduced by Soviet leader Nikita Khrushchev's decision in 1960 to recall Soviet economic and scientific advisers from China. Relations between the USSR and the PRC had been strained for some time. The Soviets had been upset by Mao's decision to abandon Soviet-style central economic planning while the CCP had been embarrassed by Khrushchev's public criticism of the communes. In the summer of 1960 there had been 1400 Soviet scientists and industrial specialists in China. By September, every single one had returned home. As one Soviet chemist who had worked in China put it, by 'the beginning of September, not a single Soviet citizen remained in China, apart from diplomats and a few trade officials'. With intellectuals unwilling or unable to provide advice after the purges of the Anti-Rightist Campaign (see pages 217–218), reliance on ideologically committed but economically illiterate rural local cadres only increased. Desperate to protect their positions, these cadres lied about the true failure of the Great Leap Forward. As a result, supplies that might have relieved suffering were never sent to some of the worst hit areas.

### How far were Mao's policies responsible?

Memories of Mao's terror campaigns certainly worsened the impact of the famine. After the Anti-Rightist Campaign, no expert dared suggest an end to the Great Leap Forward. Local officials concealed the true plight of the peasantry. As a result, aid that could have helped the famine-stricken areas was not sent. However, alongside Mao, individual Party leaders must also bear responsibility. As the people of Henan starved, the local Party boss built seven luxurious villas for high-ranking guests. In Sichuan, the population fell by 6 million between 1957 and 1961. The local Party Secretary, an enthusiastic supporter of Mao, was dismissive. 'Which dynasty has not witnessed death by starvation?' he asked.

## The Lushan Conference, 1959

In July 1959 the Party held a conference in the mountain town of Lushun in Jiangxi. Minister of Defence Peng Dehuai voiced doubts about the reports of a record grain harvest (375 million tons). Peng, a former peasant, had travelled to his home village in Hunan province and had witnessed the plight of the peasantry. He wrote a private letter to Mao in which he raised the issue of exaggerated reporting. He believed that his status in the Party would protect him. He had long been a close colleague of Mao's, a brilliant military leader, a hero of the struggle against the nationalists and of the Korean War (see Source G).

Despite this, Mao felt betrayed by the criticism, interpreting it as a personal attack on his policies. He circulated the private correspondence to other Party leaders and accused Peng of forming a 'right opportunist clique'. Knowing that Peng had recently visited the Soviet Union, Mao accused him of passing negative reports about the communes to the Soviets that had led Nikita Khrushchev to publicly ridicule anyone who advocated communes as having 'a poor understanding of what communism is and how it is to be built'. Mao denounced Peng for having gone 'behind the back of our fatherland to collude with a foreign country'. Peng was stripped of his ministerial post and barred from the Politburo. He was forced to leave his home and live in a run-down area of Beijing, where he spent his time gardening. During the Cultural Revolution he was attacked by **Red Guards**,

**Source G** Letter from Peng Dehuai to Mao Zedong, 1959, cited in Linda Benson, *China since 1949* (Pearson Education, 2002), pages 101–2.

> Dear Chairman:
>
> The Lushun meeting is important. Please consider whether what I am about to write is worth your attention, point out whatever is wrong and give me your instructions. The Great Leap Forward has basically proved the correctness of the General Line for building socialism with greater, quicker, better, and more economical results in a country like ours. But as we can see now, an excessive number of capital construction projects were hastily started in 1958. With part of the funds being dispersed, completion of some essential projects had to be postponed. This is a shortcoming, one caused mainly by lack of experience. So we continued with our Great Leap Forward in 1959 instead of putting on our brakes and slowing down our pace accordingly. As a result, imbalances were not corrected in time. In the nationwide campaign for the production of iron and steel, too many small blast furnaces were built with a waste of material, money, and manpower. This is, of course, a rather big loss. On the other hand, through the campaign we have been able to conduct a preliminary geological survey across the country, train many technicians, temper the vast numbers of cadres and raise their level. The exaggeration trend has become so common in various areas and departments that reports of unbelievable miracles have appeared to bring a great loss of prestige to the Party. Extravagance and waste grew in the wake of reports of extra-large grain and cotton harvests and a doubling of iron and steel output. As a result, the autumn harvest was done in a slipshod manner, and costs were not taken into consideration. Though we were poor, we lived as if we were rich.

What criticisms of the Great Leap Forward does Peng make in Source G?

tortured and imprisoned (see page 276). Mao announced a grave warning: if the criticism continued, he threatened to 'go to the countryside to lead the peasants to overthrow the government'. He would return to his life as a guerrilla fighter. 'If those of you in the Liberation Army won't follow me' he declared, 'then I will go and find a Red Army, and organise another Liberation Army.' Mao's power was further consolidated when he replaced Peng with subservient Lin Biao as Defence Minister and leader of the PLA.

### Mao withdraws from politics

Mao did take responsibility for some of the failings of the communes. 'The chaos caused was on a grand scale and I take responsibility,' he declared. He admitted that backyard furnaces had been a 'great catastrophe' but he encouraged other leaders to also take the blame. 'Comrades, you analyse your own responsibility.' He used scatological language arguably in order to emphasise his simple peasant background in comparison to the other leaders: 'If you have to take a shit, shit! If you have to fart, fart!' Despite his defiance, the failure of the Great Leap was too traumatic to ignore. Stung by the criticism, Mao chose to retire from day-to-day politics. Importantly, he never relinquished his role as Party Chairman.

## Liu, Deng and economic reform, 1962–65

Liu Shaoqi, as the new Head of State, and Deng Xiaoping, the General Secretary of the Party, took over from Mao as the key policy makers in charge of the daily management of the country. Pragmatism and rationality replaced fanaticism and **utopianism**. Mao's focus on local control of production and decentralisation were abandoned as central control and planning of national economic targets were reinstated.

In January 1962 Liu gave a speech to 7000 Party cadres that dismissed Mao's claim that successes outweighed failures by a ratio of 9 to 1 and rejected his argument that weather conditions had caused the Great Leap Forward to fail. He announced that the problems were due 30 per cent to natural disasters and 70 per cent to man-made disasters. 'Natural disasters hit only one region of the country,' he declared, 'man-made disasters strike the whole country. The policies of the Great Leap Forward were criticised, but never Mao personally. 'Everyone knew the policies were Mao's,' wrote Zhisui Li, the Chairman's personal physician, and therefore 'to criticise the policies was to criticise Mao.'

The new leaders announced a number of important reforms in order to restore agricultural production. This was clearly a retreat from the Great Leap Forward. Rather than a focus on 'Walking on Two Legs', the Party adopted the motto 'agriculture as the foundation of the economy'. Party leaders recognised that the economic priority was the revival of rural production, even if that meant reduced industrial growth. The following actions were taken:

- The communes were scaled back in favour of greater freedoms for peasants to produce what they wanted on small private plots. Although the peasants still had to meet quotas of food to give to the state, individual households were now able to make their own decisions about what to grow and how much fertiliser to use.

### Key debate

#### How far was Mao responsible for the Great Famine?

How far Mao was to blame for the Great Famine remains a source of debate between historians. Chang and Halliday (2005) have no doubt. They blame Mao for bringing 'utter misery'. He ordered grain requisitioning even when 'he knew perfectly well that the peasants had no food to hide'. By continuing to export grain during the height of the famine in order to fund his industrial modernisation programme, Mao 'knowingly starved and worked tens of millions of people to death'. Other historians are less convinced. Jin Xiaoding (2005) blames the exaggerated information regarding harvests given to Mao by ambitious Party cadres that caused the leader to believe that harvests made high levels of grain requisitioning possible. This might have been poor judgement, admits Jin, but 'bad judgement is not the same as starving people to death'. Although Jin has a valid point, it was Mao's own policies that created the political atmosphere in which there was incentive for the cadres to lie about the harvests. Even if he did not manage its minute details, he was the architect of the Great Leap Forward whose vision the cadres sought to realise. While it is also true that terrible weather conditions played a role in the famine, they exacerbated shortages rather than created them. Mao's motives might not have been to damn so many people to death, but his angry rejection of Peng, the one leader brave enough to tell Mao the truth, meant that his hubris and pride stopped those suffering from the famine from receiving the help that might have saved their lives. In the final analysis it was Mao's policies that led to the famine, his vision acting as a legitimating catalyst for what is arguably the single worst disaster in recorded human history.

- They were allowed to trade what they wanted on the free market.
- Peasants were allowed to claim any unused land, and cultivate it.
- Emergency aid was sent from the factories in the cities to the rural areas. Insecticides, chemical fertilisers and small farm tools were sent.
- In industry, profitability was emphasised. It was important for factories to make a profit, not just be run on strictly communist lines.
- Industrial production was changed to support agriculture. Materials like steel, wood and bamboo were used for producing hand tools, carts and boats.
- The role of the low-level rural cadres was downgraded in contrast to urban managers, and provincial and regional Party bosses.
- Those who possessed technical knowledge or administrative expertise to organise an efficient economy were promoted.
- Experts, intellectuals and Party bureaucrats had been purged or ignored because of Mao's trust in the power of the masses. Many had been imprisoned during the Anti-Rightist Campaign (see pages 217–218). Now they were returned to influence.
- Managers were given more control over the state-owned enterprises. The production targets set now had a focus on making sure factories were profitable.
- Urban Party cadres were sent to the countryside to replace the Maoist local rural cadres.
- Prisoners in **labour camp**s were put to work making cooking utensils to replace the ones melted in the backyard furnaces.

The reforms were a success.

- By 1965 agricultural production had recovered from the disastrous Great Leap Forward, back to the same level as 1957.
- The opportunity to work private plots provided an incentive for the harder working, more experienced and entrepreneurial peasants to improve their lives. They grasped this chance and by the mid-1960s private production accounted for approximately one-third of peasants' incomes.
- By the end of 1962 the availability of tools, boats and carts had been restored to the level that they had been before the communes.
- **Light industry** such as clothes and furniture was growing at a rate of 27 per cent per year and heavy industry at a rate of 17 per cent.
- Production of consumer goods was double the 1957 level.

## Conclusion: The Second Five-Year Plan

The Second Five-Year Plan was Mao's greatest failure. He was over-confident after his successes in land reform and the First Five-Year Plan. This was exacerbated by the fact that by now, after numerous campaigns to destroy the intellectual classes and to denounce economic experts as **capitalist roaders** and **counter-revolutionaries**, one was willing to stand up to him and tell him that his policies were creating a terrible famine. When Peng Dehuai did so, he was purged and later killed.

By 1962 it was clear that the Second Five-Year Plan had to end. The communes shrank and small-scale capitalist-style production was reintroduced. The peasants very quickly grasped the opportunity for greater freedoms to decide what to grow and how to live. Mao was appalled. He believed that policies to stimulate economic improvements such as wage differentials and advancement based on educational merit were re-establishing class inequalities. His fears were only heightened when, in 1961, Liu was publicly announced as his successor. He felt respected but marginalised, his policies ignored. 'They treat me like a dead ancestor,' he grumbled. He began to plot his political re-emergence.

### Work together

Historians have often debated the degree to which Mao was personally responsible for the Great Famine. Working in pairs, one of you should extract from your notes any points that suggest that it was Mao who was responsible for the Great Famine, while the other finds evidence that it was not his fault. Discuss the question:

**Could it be that Mao was responsible for the failures of agricultural production but not for the scale of the famine?**

## Chapter summary

- One of the communist regime's priorities was to introduce land reform. They passed the 1950 Agrarian Reform Law that redistributed land from landlords to the peasants.
- During the land reform movement, Party cadres were sent into the villages to encourage peasants to seize land from their owners and organise struggle meetings. Land lards were forced to admit that they had taken advantage of the poor peasants and to give up their land. It is likely that as many as 1 million were killed.
- Forms of agricultural co-operation like Mutual Aid Teams and Agricultural Producers Co-operatives were introduced. These encouraged peasants to pool resources. They were popular and successful.
- Mao believed that the success of agricultural co-operation meant that the peasants were ready to move quickly towards communism. He announced that the peasants should be organised into massive communes.
- The communes were meant to be self-sufficient, with both agricultural production and industry. They provided services for the members of the commune. The members of the commune ate together in shared dining halls. This sharing and equality meant that the communes represented a step towards true communism.
- The services provided by the communes had an economic rationale. Mao believed that people should not have to waste time with childcare or domestic chores; instend they could wash in the fields or factory longer.
- The First Five-Year Plan copied the economic plans introduced by Stalin in the Soviet Union. They were dedicated to improving heavy industry like coal, iron, steel and electricity. It was largely successful.
- The First Five-Year Plan had positive effects for the people of China. Many peasants moved to the cities and were given permanent jobs all the year round, instead of the unpredictable seasonal labour that they were used to.
- The Plan reduced the personal freedoms of the Chinese people. After they moved into the cities, the regime could control them more easily, denying them freedom of movement and dictating what work they did. The workers were forced to join a *Danwei* (see page 218).
- Mao launched the Great Leap Forward in 1958. He wanted to improve agricultural and industrial production. This policy was called 'Walking on Two Legs'. Mao was desperate to make China a great economic power.
- In order to produce more steel, Mao demanded that the people set up backyard furnaces in their villages or workplaces. Driven on by the Party cadres, the people used everything they could to keep the furnaces burning.
- The people were encouraged to support the Four Pests Campaign. They chased away birds and other vermin that spread disease or ate food supplies.
- Ambitious Party activists exaggerated the success of the Great Leap Forward to impress Mao. Desperate to meet ridiculously overambitious targets, they demanded more productivity from the people. They requisitioned huge quantities of food from the peasants.
- The Great Leap Forward resulted in the largest famine in human history. Upwards of 30–50 million people died.
- After the Great Leap Forward, Mao took a step back from frontline politics. Instead, Liu, Zhou and Deng ran China. They abandoned Mao's schemes and returned to rational and pragmatic policies. The Chinese economy recovered.

## Recommended reading


J. Becker, *Hungry Ghosts: Mao's Secret Famine* (Simon and Schuster, 1997). Based on interviews and archival documentation, Becker highlights the personal responsibility of Mao for the Great Famine.

F. Dikotter, *Mao's Great Famine* (Bloomsbury Publishing, 2010). Recent scholarly analysis of the causes and impact of the Great Famine utilising interviews with survivors and newly accessible archives in China.

L. Feigon, *Mao: A Re-Interpretation* (Ivan R. Dee, 2002). Especially Chapter 7, entitled tellingly 'The Great Leap into Cataclysm'. Revisionist account that seeks to reappraise Mao in a more positive light.

M. Selden (ed.), *The People's Republic of China: A Documentary History of Revolutionary Change* (Monthly Review Press, 1980). Primary documents charting the development of Chinese communism, 1946–78. Chapter 3 has documents on the Great Leap Forward.

D. Twitchett and John K. Fairbank (eds.), *The Cambridge History of China*, Volume 14 (Cambridge University Press, 1987). Especially Part II which features a detailed analysis of the Party's response to the Great Leap Forward and the economic recovery led by Liu and Deng.

Z. Xianliang, *Grass Soup* (Minerva, 1995). A first-hand account of a prisoner in the Chinese gulag during the Great Leap Forward.

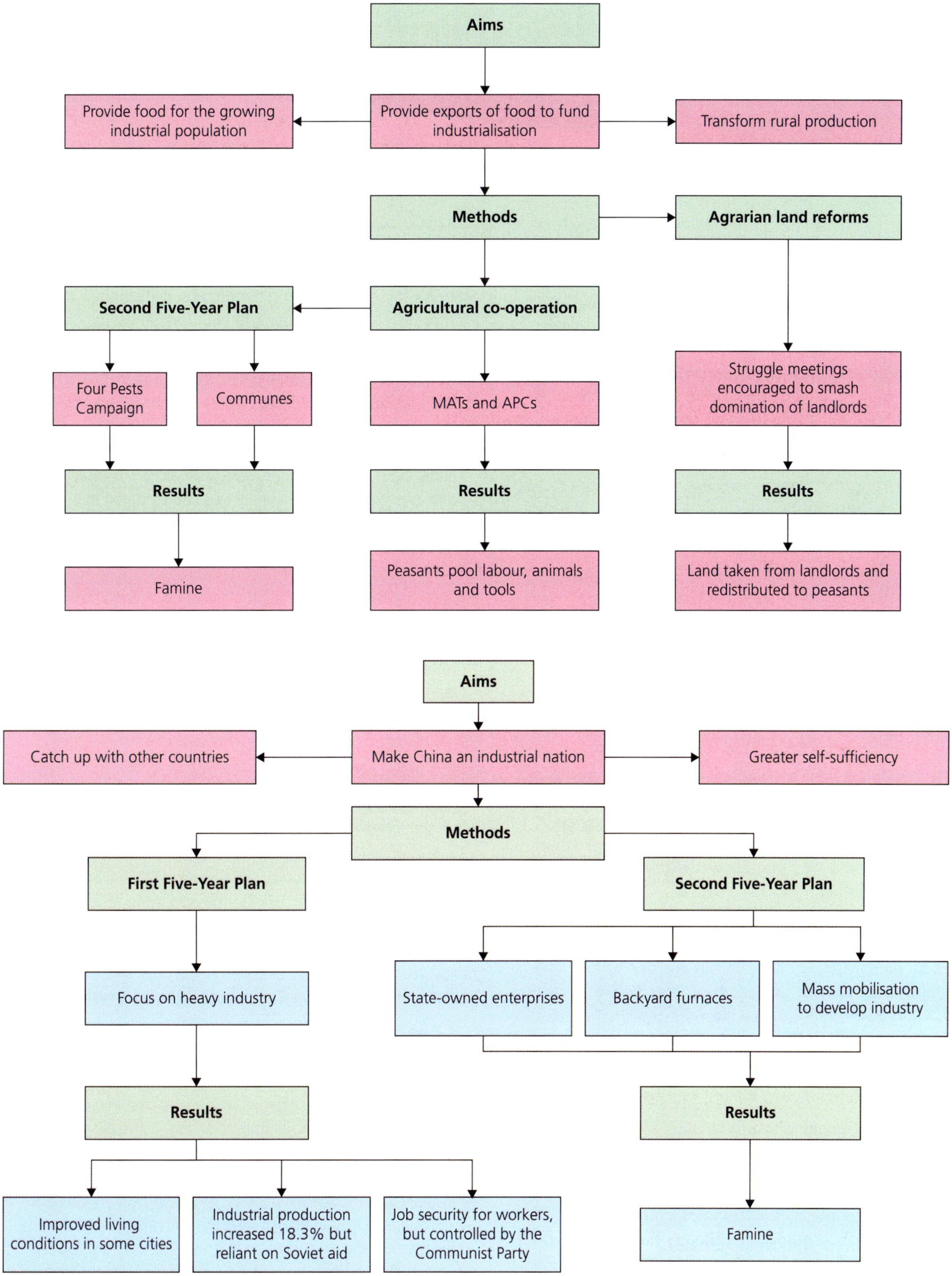


▲ Summary diagram: Agricultural and industrial changes, 1949–65.

# Section A: Essay technique

## Structuring an essay and writing introductions

Well-structured essays are likely to receive higher marks than essays in which the structure is unclear. The structure of your essay should reflect the nature of the task that you are performing. Therefore, it should help you evaluate how far the two sources together are useful to a historian who is investigating a specific topic.

### Macro structure

The overall structure of your essay should include:

- an introduction, which focuses on the question and sets out the essence of your answer
- a conclusion, which summarises your essay in order to weigh up the extent to which the evidence of the sources is useful, and reaches an overall judgement
- the main body, which should present a detailed evaluation of the evidence of the sources.

**TIP:** Remember, the question asks you to consider the sources *together*. Therefore, a structure which analyses Source 1, and then moves on to Source 2, is unlikely to do well. It would be better to structure your essay in a way that allows you to deal with the sources together.

### Micro structure

Each paragraph should set out an analysis of the usefulness of the evidence of the two sources. Therefore, you need to discuss both sources in every paragraph.

**TIP:** One way of doing this is to make sure that you discuss both sources in almost every sentence.

For example, imagine you are answering the following question:

> **How far could the historian make use of Sources 1 and 2 together to investigate how far Mao was responsible for the Great Famine?**

**Source 1** From Zhisui Li, *The Private Life of Chairman Mao* (Arrow Books, 1996). Li was Mao's former doctor. This source is an extract from his memoirs. It describes a train journey that he took across the countryside during the Great Leap Forward.

> What we are seeing from our windows ... was staged, a huge multi-act nationwide Chinese opera, performed especially for Mao. The party secretaries had ordered furnaces constructed everywhere along the rail route, stretching out for ten li[1] on either side, and the women were dressed so colourfully, in reds and greens, because they had been ordered to dress that way. In Hubei, party secretary Wang Renzhong had ordered the peasants to remove rice plants from far-away fields and transplant them along Mao's route, to give the impression of a wildly abundant crop. The rice was planted so closely together that electric fans had to be set up around the fields to circulate the air in order to prevent the plants from rotting. All of China was a stage, all the people performers in an extravaganza for Mao. The production figures were false. And what was coming out of the backyard steel furnaces was useless. 'This isn't what the newspapers are saying,' I protested. The newspapers, too, were filled with falsehoods ... printing only what they had been told.

[1] Li: a Chinese measurement of distance, approximately a third of a mile.

**Source 2** From Jung Chang, *Wild Swans: Three Daughters of China* (HarperCollins, 1992). The source is an extract from a memoir that describes life as a woman during Mao's rule. Her family were Party cadres. She was six years old at the start of the Great Leap Forward. The failure of Mao's policies led her to leave China and live in the West.

> A huge furnace was erected in the parking lot. At night the sky was lit up, and the noise of the crowds around the furnace could be heard 300 yards away in my room. My family's woks went into the furnace, together with all our cast-iron cooking utensils. We did not suffer from their loss, as we did not need them anymore. No private cooking was allowed now, and everyone had to eat in the canteen. The furnaces were insatiable. Gone was my parents' bed, a soft comfortable one with iron springs. Gone also were the iron railings from the city pavements, and anything else that was iron. I hardly saw my parents for months. They often did not come home at all, they had to make sure that the temperature in their office furnaces never dropped.

Here are three examples of introductions that could answer the question on page 252:

**Answer 1**

In Source 1 the author says, 'The party secretaries had ordered furnaces constructed everywhere along the rail route.' He also says that in Hubei, party secretary Wang Renzhong saw fields planted with crops taken from other areas 'to give the impression of a wildly abundant crop'. This was because the party secretaries wanted to look successful in order to win promotions and enhance their careers. Source 2 says that 'a huge furnace was erected in the parking lot'. Household items like cooking utensils were melted in it. They did this because Mao himself had declared that the Chinese people should overtake Great Britain in industrial production within fifteen years.

**Answer 2**

Source 1 is useful to a historian because it is from someone who travelled around China. Source 2 is also useful because it gives an eyewitness account of life during the Great Leap Forward.

**Answer 3**

Both Sources 1 and 2 are useful to a historian investigating the extent to which Mao was personally responsible for the Great Famine. Both are useful as eyewitness perspectives on the Great Leap Forward. Source 1 is of particular value. As Mao's personal doctor, Li would have had access to information and to areas of the country not available to ordinary Chinese citizens. While Source 1 provides a wider picture as the author has travelled across the country, in direct contrast Source 2 focuses on one area in which she and her family lived. However, there are problems with both sources. Source 1 relies too much on a personal experience while Source 2 offers a skewed picture from a young child whose experience of the Great Leap Forward and the famine that it caused may not have been very representative. Her family were Party cadres so their experience may not have been typical of all members of society.

## Activity: Analyse the introduction

Having read the three introductions, in pairs consider the following questions:

1. What skills do the different introductions demonstrate?
2. Which introduction focuses most clearly on the question?
3. Which introduction integrates Source 1 and Source 2 on page 252 most effectively?
4. How could you improve the best of the three introductions?
5. What can you learn from the three introductions?

## Activity: AS-style questions

1. Why is Source 1 (page 252) valuable to the historian for an enquiry into the impact of the Great Leap Forward?
2. How much weight do you give the evidence of Source 2 (page 252) for an enquiry into attitudes towards the Great Leap Forward?

## Selecting information

Another skill vital for success in Section A is that of selecting the right information from the sources. So what is the 'right' information? It is:

- information that is relevant to the question
- information that illustrates the main point of the source
- information that illustrates the points that you want to make.

In addition to the source material, the exam paper also contains a short description of the source's provenance printed immediately above the source. Selecting the important material from the provenance will also help you do well. You could select information that helps you evaluate the evidence, such as:

- information that would help explain the motives of the writer
- information that helps explain the purpose of the document
- information that helps contextualise the source (see pages 283–84).

**TIP:** Don't just copy information from the provenance; make sure you use the information to help weigh the evidence that the source presents.

Imagine you are answering the following question:

> **How far could the historian make use of Sources 3 and 4 together to investigate life during the Great Leap Forward?**

You need to think about the focus of the question – here the question is asking you about what these two sources can tell us, as historians, about life during the Great Leap Forward.

You could point out issues with both these sources. They both have a political purpose. Source 3 is an example of communist propaganda though it still has value for historians because it tells us what kind of society the regime was aiming to create and what messages it wanted the people of China to believe. Source 4 has the purpose of trying to convince the regime to change its policies in Tibet. It is written by a Buddhist anti-communist who opposed the communist invasion of Tibet.

**Source 3** From Wang Yin, 'Women's New Life in Rural People's Communes', China News Service, 1959. Quoted in Mark Selden (ed.), *The People's Republic of China: A Documentary History of Revolutionary Change* (Monthly Review Press, 1980). The China News Service was a news and information bureau owned and completely controlled by the communist state.

> During the Great Leap Forward of agricultural production last year, the broad mass of rural women in the country displayed tremendous revolutionary fervour and revolutionary vigour. By participating in all forms of agricultural production, they played an important part in securing the bumper harvest last year. Now that the people's communes are operating collective welfare undertakings, domestic labour has been socialised and the women are no longer compelled to attend at once to the two conflicting jobs of participation in social production and housekeeping. Because they are no longer tied down by household matters, they can work and study more attentively than before. Statistical returns show that to date, there are 2,650,000 dining halls in the rural people's communes in the country, serving meals to 90 percent of the total rural population. There are 4,750,000 nurseries and kindergartens, taking care of 24,000,000 children.

**Source 4** From the Panchem Lama's[1] 70,000-Character Petition to Zhou Enlai. Written in 1962, the 'petition' describes the impact of Chinese policies in Tibet. It was suppressed by the government and its contents were only revealed when the text was smuggled to London in 1996.

> During the big movement for competition in production [Great Leap Forward], because of a tendency to boast and exaggerate, there were false reports of increased production which were inconsistent with reality. Because the anguish of such severe hunger had never been experienced in Tibetan history and was such that people could not imagine it even in their dreams, the masses could not resist this kind of cruel torment, and their condition declined daily. Therefore, in some places, colds and other such minor infections and diseases caused a percentage of people to die easily. In some places, many people died because the food ran out; therefore in some places, there was the phenomenon of whole families dying out. The mortality rate was critical. Those abnormal deaths were all caused by the lack of food, and in fact they all should be counted as having starved to death.

[1] Panchem Lama: an important leader of Tibetan Buddhism, second only to the Dalai Lama.

### Activity: AS-style questions

1 Why is Source 3 valuable to the historian for an enquiry into the impact of the Great Leap Forward on women's lives?

2 How much weight do you give the evidence of Source 4 for an enquiry into the effects of the Great Leap Forward on Tibetan people?

## Activity: Selecting from the sources

Read the question and then the sources on page 254.

1 Make a bullet-point list of the information that you would select from Sources 3 and 4 to answer the question.
2 Now turn to page 454 and have a look at an example of the information that you could have selected for Source 3.
3 Check your notes – did you select the same kind of information for Source 3? Look back at the criteria for the successful selection of information. The selected information should all be relevant to the question, not merely giving facts of an event or date, and should be information that would help a historian investigating this issue.
4 Now read over your own notes again. Add anything into your notes on Source 3 that you might have missed, and check that your examination of Source 4 was as thorough. Add any new information you find.
5 Having read the sources, and selected pieces of information to use in your answer, consider the following questions with your partner:
   **a)** Did you both select the same information for the source? If not, whose selections were:
      **i)** most relevant to the question
      **ii)** most characteristic of the whole source?
   **b)** Did either of you select any information from the provenance?
   **c)** Did you both select the same information from the provenance? If not, whose selections were:
      **i)** most relevant to the question
      **ii)** most helpful to a historian evaluating the information contained in the source?
   **d)** Did you miss anything?
   **e)** What can you learn from this task?

# Making inferences

Making inferences from sources is one way to demonstrate your understanding of the source and of the period. An inference is a deduction or conclusion that comes from reading between the lines of a source – it is not about what lies on the surface but what is hinted at below the surface. It is not wild speculation but a conclusion that is drawn from reasoning or evidence. A detailed knowledge of the period is vital to making inferences.

Imagine you are answering the following question:

**How far could the historian make use of Sources 5 and 6 (page 256) together to investigate the impact of the Great Leap Forward on the Chinese people?**

There is a lot of information in Source 5 which is purely on the surface. But beyond that, you can use your own knowledge to draw out more complex and insightful conclusions as the annotations below show.

**Source 5** From an article written by Mao for the Party Journal, *Red Flag*, June 1958. The Great Leap Forward had been launched in spring 1958.

Throughout the country, the communist spirit is surging forward. The political consciousness of the masses is rising rapidly. Backward sections among the masses have roused themselves energetically to catch up with the more advanced [nations], proving that China is forging ahead in her socialist economic revolution, as well as in her political, ideological, technical, and cultural revolutions. In view of this, our country may not need as much time as previously thought to catch up with the big capitalist countries in industrial and agricultural production. China's 600 million people have two remarkable peculiarities; they are, first of all, poor, and secondly, blank. That may seem like a bad thing, but it is really a good thing. A clean sheet of paper has no blotches, and so the newest and most beautiful words can be written on it.

The Great Leap Forward has been a huge success in transforming China into a communist nation. The term 'spirit' suggests that communism has not been imposed by the Party but is actually very popular, leading to an upsurge of support from the masses. Mao believed that the CCP had succeeded in convincing the people to view themselves as an oppressed class engaged in class conflict against their enemies.

At the time, China was not an economic superpower. Previously it had appeared that it would take a very long time for China to catch up with the 'big capitalist countries', meaning the USA and Britain. However, the Great Leap Forward has been such a success in stimulating production that Mao is now very optimistic that it can catch up with the West much faster than before.

The most backward section of the masses was the peasants. Mao had been disappointed with the small increase in production created by his land reform policies. As a result of the Great Leap Forward the peasants were finally working hard.

Mao is suggesting that the Great Leap Forward could completely transform the lives of the Chinese people. When he describes them as 'blank' he means that they do not have an existing political ideology to wipe out before he can enforce his ideas and so they can be more easily converted to communism. Because they are poor Mao believes they will support the Great Leap Forward more readily because it offers them an opportunity to improve their situation.

Below is an example of how you could develop the inferences annotated around Source 5 (see page 255) into a paragraph in answer to the question on page 255.

We can infer from the source that Mao believes that the Great Leap Forward has spread support for communism among the Chinese people. It suggests that the 'backward' people, the peasants, are now working with great effort. The Great Leap Forward has completely transformed production to the point where China may be able to overtake the major economic powers like the USA and Britain very soon. Mao believes that it will have the effect of greatly improving the lives of the mass of poor people in China.

## Activity: Inferences

Having read the question and example on page 255 and above you can now practise making inferences from Source 6. Remember:

- Your inferences should help you answer the question.
- Inferences should be informed by your contextual knowledge of the period.

Answer the following questions:

1 What does Source 6 reveal about the scale of people's involvement in economic production during the Great Leap Forward?
2 What can you infer about changes in the role and status of women?
3 How has the influence of the Communist Party changed during the Great Leap Forward?
4 Compare Source 5 (page 255) and Source 6. Together, what do they imply about the way the lives of the Chinese people have changed during the Great Leap Forward?

## Activity: AS-style questions

1 Why is Source 6 valuable to the historian for an enquiry into the impact of the Great Leap Forward?
2 How much weight do you give the evidence of Source 5 (page 255) for an enquiry into the success of the Great Leap Forward in 1958?

**Source 6** From Tan Man-ni, 'Lushan's Pig-Iron "Sputnik"', an article in the magazine *China Reconstructs*, January 1959. The magazine was founded in 1949 to help spread a positive image of China around the world. This source describes the backyard furnace campaign.

> The river a few miles away from the county town is another scene of activity. Undaunted by a cold north wind, 25,000 students, women, and local government workers are ankle-deep in the water, washing for the iron-bearing sand that has been carried down from the nearby mountains. On the banks, groups of students off their working shift hold classes, and a crew of older women minds the children for the mothers beside the temporary living quarters made for workers from distant parts of the county. At night, lamps on the washing frames outline the river like two pearl necklaces.
>
> The office of the county Communist Party committee where I stayed in the county town of Lushan is like the headquarters of an army, for the party has taken direct leadership of the iron campaign. Any time of the day or night, one can hear someone shouting into the telephone, 'Long distance ... urgent ... coal ... tons.'

## Work together

Having completed the activity, consider the following questions with your partner:

1 Did you both make the same inferences from Source 6?
2 If you differed, look at the source again, discuss your points of view and try to work out which inference is more likely to be correct.
3 How can the inferences that you have made help you answer the question?

Having discussed these questions make a bullet-point list of three things that you can do to make sure you use inferences effectively in Section A questions. Review the list with your partner.

# Section B: Essay technique

## Detail and analysis

Paper 2 Section B questions, like Paper 1 Section A and B questions, need to be detailed and analytical. You may have already read the advice on how to write detailed and analytical essays for Paper 1 (see pages 39 and 59). Now is a chance to practise these skills in the context of the Great Famine.

### Activity: Detail and analysis

Imagine you are answering the following question:

**How far were Mao's agricultural policies the most important cause of the Great Famine?**

1 Identify the kind of question (see page 229).
2 Make an appropriate plan, writing down the main points of your three or four paragraphs.
3 Next to each of the points add three supporting details – you could use a different colour if you have one.
4 Write one analytical sentence to conclude each paragraph.

### Question practice

1 'Agrarian Land Reform brought widespread benefits to the people of China.' How far do you agree with this statement? AS
2 How successful was the First Five-Year Plan?

### Work together

Having finished the activity on detail and analysis, swap your work with a partner. Consider the following questions:

1 Did you agree on what type of question you were dealing with? If not, discuss it and work out who was right.
2 Whose plan most clearly focused on the specific type of question?
3 Were the details that your partner selected the most appropriate to support their points?
4 Could either of you have used detail that better supports the points that you wanted to make?
5 Were all of your partner's sentences truly analytical?
6 What can you learn from your partner's approach?

Use these questions to feed back to each other and improve your use of detail and analysis.

# **Key Topic 3** The Cultural Revolution and its aftermath, 1966–76

## Overview

This chapter focuses on the 'Great Proletarian Cultural Revolution'. It examines the motives behind this ten-year period of violence and upheaval that led to the denunciation, intimidation, torture and death of millions of Chinese people. It looks at the way in which Mao was able to mobilise millions of young Chinese students and workers into radical Red Guards to attack his enemies, the so-called 'capitalist roaders'. It explores how the violence got out of hand and dragged China into a devastating civil war as competing Red Guard factions fought themselves and the PLA. Finally, it evaluates the impact of the Cultural Revolution on Chinese society, its economy and its political situation, including the succession crisis leading up to and after the death of Mao in 1976.

The overarching topic of the Cultural Revolution and its aftermath, 1966–76 is covered in four sections:

1 Mao's reasons for launching the Cultural Revolution
2 The Red Guards and Red Terror
3 Attacks on Mao's political and class enemies
4 Winding down the Cultural Revolution, 1968–76.

## TIMELINE

| | |
|---|---|
| 1965 November | Yao Wenyuan publishes article that criticises Wu Han's play *Hai Rui Dismissed from Office* |
| 1966 March | Cultural Revolution Group formed |
| 1966 July | Mao re-emerges into public view |
| 1966 August | Mao calls for a 'Cultural Revolution' and millions of Red Guards travel to Beijing to attend rallies in praise of him |
| 1967 January | The 'January Storm' |
| 1967 February | 'February Adverse Current' |
| 1968 October | Liu Shaoqi officially removed from his post as Head of State |
| 1969 April | Ninth Party Congress officially declares the Cultural Revolution to be over |
| 1969 November | Liu Shaoqi dies |
| 1971 July | Lin Biao dies |
| 1976 January | Zhou Enlai dies |
| 1976 | Mao Zedong dies |

### Note it down

As you read this chapter, chart the relative power of the key leaders. Create a timeline noting the key events and their dates. With each event, note how it enhanced or reduced the political power of each of the leaders:

- Mao
- Lin Biao
- Liu Shaoqi
- Deng Xiaoping
- Jiang Qing.

## 1 Mao's reasons for launching the Cultural Revolution

The **Cultural Revolution** was a truly extraordinary event. After the failure of the **Great Leap Forward** Mao had retired from frontline politics. He let Liu Shaoqi and Deng Xiaoping run China. But Mao became suspicious of how committed they, and other Party leaders, truly were to creating **communism**. Concerned with their policies that appeared to be bringing capitalism back to China, Mao believed that '**capitalist roaders**' and 'bourgeois elements' had infiltrated the Party. These enemies lacked sufficient ideological commitment to communism. Chief among them were his rivals Liu Shaoqi and Deng Xiaoping.

Mao called on **Red Guards**, bands of violent young people, to rise up and **purge** them and their allies. Coupled with this attack on the Party he declared that the whole of traditional Chinese culture had to be destroyed and replaced with a new, communist culture. The Red Guards were encouraged to destroy old buildings and monuments, burn ancient books and attack anyone who believed in traditional ideas like religion. Soon the violence moved to attacks on people. During the so-called '**Red Terror**' anyone who the Red Guards deemed to lack loyalty to Mao was a target. The campaign of violence and terror soon got out of even his control. China descended into anarchy and near civil war until finally Mao was able to restore order using the **PLA** to control the Red Guards. When it was over Mao's enemies had been vanquished and Mao's power was again unrivalled.

The motives behind the Cultural Revolution have puzzled and been debated by historians ever since it ended.

- Why did Mao emerge from his political isolation to launch a campaign of violence and destruction?
- Why did he call on young people to attack the very same party he led into power in 1949?
- What motivated him to attack and purge some of his closest colleagues within his own party?

What is clear is that the Cultural Revolution was far more than an attempt to transform Chinese culture. Indeed, when Mao spoke of culture, he meant far more than just art, music, architecture and other expressions of cultural identity. For Mao, culture was fundamentally intertwined with politics. It was, he said, a tool used by a dominant ruling class to control the people. Un-communist culture had been 'fostered by the exploiting classes' and 'poisoned the minds of the people for thousands of years'. Now what was required was 'an entirely new ideology and culture and entirely new customs and habits – those of the proletariat'.

## Note it down

The beginning of the Cultural Revolution in 1966 was a highly significant development in Chinese history. Using the 1:2 method (see page x) make notes on the following questions:

- Why did Mao launch the Cultural Revolution?
- What conflicts were there within the Communist Party?
- Who were Mao's opponents between 1961 and 1965?

## Divisions within the CCP

Why did Mao attempt to destroy the Party that he had spent his entire life building up and leading into power? To truly understand why Mao wanted to propel China into a decade of anarchic chaos one must understand Mao's political position at the end of the Great Leap Forward. Mao had decided to retire to 'the second line', away from the arguments and debates of national politics. Instead, he spent his time in Zhongnanhai, a complex within the walls of the **Forbidden City** used by the ancient Emperors, surrounded only by bodyguards and servants. His third wife, Jiang Qing, lived in separate quarters in the compounds. He passed his time swimming in his private pool – distrusting modern medicine, he believed regular exercise would protect his health – or reading in his book-lined study. At night he availed himself of the sexual favours of young women sent to take part in the dance parties he held every week.

Increasingly remote and distant, he hardly saw his old colleagues and friends. He left the day-to-day running of the country to Deng Xiaoping and Liu Shaoqi. Although old colleagues from the days of revolutionary struggle and the Civil War, Mao increasingly began to distrust his old friends. Zhou had been highly critical of the overambitious targets of the Great Leap Forward. Liu had spoken out against it at the 7000 **cadres** conference in 1962, dismissing Mao's claim that the Great Famine had been caused by bad weather. In 1964 he argued for a reduction in the power of Party cadres in the countryside. Their attitude to Mao's revolutionary communism was summed up by Deng's famous declaration that 'It didn't matter if the cat is white or black, so long as it catches rats.' Pragmatism, not revolutionary fervour, was the order of the day. Mao's policies were being watered down. By now an old man, he felt threatened and was worried about what would happen to the revolution he had done so much to create once he was gone.

Mao was also jealous of China's new rulers. The new economic policies that had replaced his focus on mass mobilisation (see page 237) and 'Walking on Two Legs' (see page 243) seemed to be far more successful. The Party was increasingly split between ideologues and pragmatists.

## Personal slights

Alongside ideological arguments, Mao was also angered by what he perceived to be personal slights. A report by the Party's propaganda department in March 1960 warned against the use of Mao's writings to explain various achievements like medical breakthroughs or sporting victories. Liu Shaoqi declared that the phrase 'Thought of Mao' should not be used in propaganda that targeted foreign audiences. Party leaders publicly stated that Mao Zedong Thought should not be said to surpass Marxism-Leninism. Respected but without control over policy, he complained that he was 'treated as a dead ancestor' – shown respect but fundamentally ignored.

## Mao Zedong Thought

Mao's political theories, sometimes called Maoism, were the guiding principles of the Communist Party during this period. Mao believed that the Party should follow the 'mass line'- in other words uphold the needs and wishes of the mass of the population. These masses could be 'mobilised' to speed up the pace of transformation towards communism. He advocated a 'permanent revolution' to remove older members of the Party and replace them with more committed revolutionaries. As a revolutionary force, even the Communist Party, was in danger of becoming '**bureaucratic**' once it took power. Party cadres would become too accustomed to the benefits of power and simply become like the old elites that they had pledged to destroy.

## Ideologues versus pragmatists

Although members of the CCP wanted to transform China into a communist nation, there was an argument over the ways to do it and the pace at which this could happen. Mao was an ideologue. He remained the dedicated revolutionary he had always been. He believed that the communist ideology and the demands of class conflict had to be adhered to. According to these 'truly Red' believers, China must be transformed into a communist country as quickly as possible through mobilisation of the masses. Anyone who did not rigidly stick to *his* interpretation of communist ideology – so-called Mao Zedong Thought (see page 259) – was, he believed, a 'capitalist roader' who wanted to take 'the **capitalist** road' to development. Within the Party Mao was supported in this belief by his wife, Jiang Qing, and the leader of the PLA, Lin Biao.

In contrast, pragmatists like Zhou, Liu and Deng believed that if China attempted to move too fast towards communism, mistakes would be made, with terrible consequences. Their example of this was the Great Leap Forward. Its attempt to advance both agricultural development and industrial modernisation at the same time – to 'Walk on Two Legs' – had been overly ambitious and led to the Great Famine. Pragmatists argued for more caution. Instead of always doing what communist ideology suggested straight away, practical needs had to be taken into account. Instead of trust in the masses, economic experts and educational bureaucrats should be given the power to make rational decisions. For example, the pragmatists argued that the lack of infrastructure, skilled workers and modern technology needed to be factored into economic plans. In defence of their ideas they cited Mao's own dictum: instead of only doing what was ideologically correct the Party leadership should 'Seek truth from facts.'

◀ Deng Xiaoping

◀ Liu Shaoqi

◀ Zhou Enlai

▲ Pragmatists

◀ Mao Zedong

◀ Lin Biao

◀ Jiang Qing (Mao's wife)

▲ Ideologues

## The quest for permanent revolution

One reason why Mao launched the Cultural Revolution was his conviction that the Party that he had led into power in 1949 was no longer the force for revolutionary change. Instead of order and stability, he demanded 'permanent revolution'. Mao feared that the Party had become bureaucratised. He believed that after it had taken power in the revolution, some cadres had exploited their new power for their own advantage. After removing China's old rulers, they had become a new elite, taking advantage of the masses and living a life of luxury with better houses, cars, food and guaranteed access to the best schools for their children. The only way to prevent this was for revolution to be permanent, to constantly replace those in authority to prevent them from ever becoming comfortable and secure enough to take advantage of their authority. Comparing the CCP to a healthy body breathing air and exhaling carbon dioxide Mao later said, 'A proletarian party must also get rid of the stale and take in the fresh, for only thus can it be full of vitality.' Instead of stability Mao demanded constant class struggle to rid the Party of '**revisionists**', meaning anyone who wanted to 'revise' or change communist ideology.

### The Ten Points

Mao's fears about the Party were confirmed before the beginning of the Cultural Revolution. In 1962 Mao launched a new drive to reinvigorate China with revolutionary zeal. This '**Socialist Education Campaign**' hoped to return China to the path to communism. In February 1963 Mao drafted the 'Early Ten Points' that proposed that the masses should be mobilised to criticise corrupt Party cadres. This fitted into his belief in permanent revolution.

Mao introduced the so-called Four Clean Ups: the economy, organisation, politics and ideology should be cleansed of non-communist ideas. Peasants and workers were told to be critical of activists and Party leaders who had taken advantage of their authority and become bureaucratic. Mao told them to study his writings and to attend rallies in order to whip up revolutionary fervour. They were told to denounce corrupt officials as capitalist roaders and subject them to the same kind of 'struggle meeting' as had been used against landlords. The response was lukewarm; the people were still recovering from the famine.

In autumn 1963 Deng Xiaoping revised this plan in a document called the 'Later Ten Points' that ruled that any disruption should be kept to a minimum and that middle-class peasants should not be attacked. While Mao hoped the campaign would mobilise the masses directly, Liu and Deng wanted the campaign to be organised by **work teams** of Party cadres. They rewrote Mao's directives to de-emphasise class struggle. The campaign was not a success and Mao blamed Liu for what he perceived to be his unenthusiastic commitment to it. Mao became convinced that all that he had worked for during the revolution was in danger of being dismissed by 'revisionists'.

## Supporters and opponents

Mao might have wanted to be rid of his opponents, but he had to be careful. The pragmatic policies that had replaced the Great Leap Forward had been successful and popular. Liu, Deng and Zhou were well liked and had many friends and supporters within the Party. He had to be subtle. He began his attack on his opponents indirectly. A play called *Hai Rui Dismissed from Office* gave him his opportunity.

Written by historian and intellectual, Wu Han, it was the tale of a principled and loyal official during the **Ming era**. He had been critical of the Emperor for not preventing the corruption of state officials. Affronted, the Emperor had dismissed him. However, the play could have been perceived as an attack on Mao. the comparisons with the dismissal of Peng Dehuai for his criticism of the Great Leap Forward were clear (see page 247).

How much Mao believed that the play was a veiled attack on his power is unclear. First performed in 1961, Mao had at first praised the play. Now in 1965 he organised a negative review to be published, written by a loyal supporter named Yao Wenyuan. Wu Han was deputy mayor of Beijing, under Mayor Peng Zhen. Both were close allies of Liu and Deng. Peng Zhen at first defended Wu, but eventually both were forced to resign, damned as right-wing 'revisionists'. Mao had successfully got rid of two key allies of his enemies, leaving them more isolated and vulnerable.

### The Cultural Revolution Group

In March 1966, Mao formed the Cultural Revolution Group (CRG) to direct the Cultural Revolution. It was a seventeen-member sub-committee of the Politburo. It was dominated by ideologues:

- Chen Boda: Mao's propaganda chief. A colleague of Mao's since the Yan'an days, he was a key creator of Mao Zedong Thought.
- Yao Wenyuan: the writer of the article attacking Wu Han and his play *Hai Rui Dismissed from Office*.
- Zhang Chunqiao: Party Secretary of Shanghai.

- Jiang Qing: Mao's fourth wife and most influential member of the group. She became a self-styled 'cultural tsar' who bitterly attacked anyone whom she believed was not sufficiently loyal to Mao Zedong Thought. She was also a member of the Central Case Examination Group, whose task was to dig up damaging gossip about potential targets for the Cultural Revolution Group.

During the Cultural Revolution the CRG ran the **PRC**'s cultural policy. It was meant to be answerable to the Politburo. In reality it helped ferment criticism of what they called 'top Party people in authority who were taking the capitalist road'. Through their control of the media and propaganda, these **counter-revolutionaries** were, declared the Party's own journal, *Red Flag*, 'our most dangerous and our main enemy'. Although not named specifically, the targets of this propaganda campaign were Liu and Deng. Yao, Zhang, Wang Hongwen and Jiang Qing later became known as the 'Gang of Four' and were accused of attempting to launch a coup to seize power after Mao's death.

## Launching the Cultural Revolution

In July 1966 Mao swam in the dangerous Yangtze River. The event was widely publicised. Propaganda reports claimed that Mao, now 72 years old, swam nearly 9 miles in 65 minutes – a world record. The claim was laughable, but the message was clear: Mao was as fit and strong as ever. He had emerged from the political sidelines to once again establish his power. In August, Mao, now back in the public limelight, directed the Party's Central Committee to announce the 'sixteen-point directive on the Cultural Revolution' (see Source A). This called for 'a new stage in the socialist revolution' that 'touches people to their very soul'. Historian Roderick Macfarquhar calls it nothing less than 'Mao's blueprint' for the Cultural Revolution.

**Source A** The Sixteen Points: Guidelines for the Great Proletarian Cultural Revolution, quoted in Mark Selden (ed.), *The People's Republic of China: A Documentary History of Revolutionary Change* (Monthly Review Press, 1979), pages 549–56.

> Although the bourgeoisie has been overthrown, it is still trying to use the old ideas, culture, customs and habits of the exploiting classes to corrupt the masses, capture their minds and endeavour to stage a come-back. At present, our objective is to struggle against and overthrow those persons in authority who are taking the capitalist road, to criticise and repudiate the reactionary bourgeoisie academic 'authorities' and the ideology of the bourgeoisie and all other exploiting classes and to transform education, literature and art ... In the great proletarian Cultural Revolution, the only method is for the masses to liberate themselves ... Don't be afraid of disturbances. Chairman Mao has often told us that revolution cannot be so very refined, so gentle, so temperate, kind, courteous, restrained and magnanimous. Let the masses educate themselves. It is imperative to hold aloft the great banner of Mao Zedong's Thought. Mao Zedong Thought should be taken as the guide for action ... Party committees at all levels must abide by the directions given by Chairman Mao.

What does Source A suggest about the motives, targets and methods of the Cultural Revolution?

### Jiang Qing

An actress from Shanghai, Jiang Qing met Mao in the mid-1930s at Yan'an. She became his fourth wife in 1938. She stayed out of politics until he appointed her to a key role in the Cultural Revolution Group. She was given authority to control and remould Chinese culture in order to include a greater focus on communist ideology and class struggle. This backing by Mao gave her huge personal power. She revelled in it and became a feared enforcer for Mao, the terrifying 'Madame Mao'.

Hoping to one day take Mao's place as leader of China, during the Cultural Revolution she encouraged Red Guards to destroy anyone who might be a rival to her. She also used them to attack anyone who knew of her ideologically suspect past in cosmopolitan Shanghai, including accusations of sexual affairs. Because she benefited so much from the Cultural Revolution she did not want its violence to end. She belonged to the ultra-radical group called 'The Gang of Four' who wanted to continue it even after Mao wanted it to end. All of the gang were arrested after Mao's death. She became a scapegoat for the excesses of the Cultural Revolution and was sentenced to death for political crimes. She took her own life in 1991.

## Conclusion: Mao's reasons for launching the Cultural Revolution

Mao's motives for the Cultural Revolution are difficult to ascertain:

- How far was it a genuine attempt to destroy China's cultural heritage and replace it with one that glorified the proletariat?
- Did Mao really believe that the Party was being infiltrated by capitalist roaders dedicated to destroying the achievements of his revolution or was he motivated only by a desire for a return to power?
- Did he act out of petty jealousy in response to imagined slights by Liu and Deng?

Perhaps Mao himself did not have a clear plan in mind other than a commitment to ongoing revolution. He was certainly worried that the next generation of Party cadres lacked the revolutionary experience of himself and his colleagues from the Civil War days. Rather than one cause, it appears that all are true. Mao really did want a **rectification campaign** that returned the revolutionary vigour to a party grown increasingly bureaucratic; the cadres had been acting like a new 'elite'. Furthermore, there is no doubt that Mao saw culture not merely as social expression, but as a tool used by opponents to control the masses. It does, however, seem clear that Mao had one over-arching aim. Bitter, jealous and increasingly paranoid about what would happen to his achievements after he was dead, Mao was desperate to destroy his rivals within his own party. To do this, he mobilised his most loyal constituency: the young people of China.

### Work together

How far did the Cultural Revolution meet Mao's goals? Go through your notes (see page 259) and note down the reasons why Mao launched the Cultural Revolution. Swap them with a partner. When you are happy your notes are as comprehensive as possible, divide a large sheet of paper into two. On one side write down the aims of the policies described in this section. On the other write down the results of the Cultural Revolution all the way up to 1976. Did Mao achieve his aims?

# 2 The Red Guards and Red Terror

To restore his place at the political centre Mao launched a rectification campaign, the Cultural Revolution. Young people formed into violent groups called Red Guards. They clamoured to 'Smash the Four Olds' (see page 268), torturing and humiliating teachers and officials whom they deemed as disloyal, and murdering at least a million people. These young people were Mao's revolutionary soldiers. They had been indoctrinated by the propaganda they had been exposed to in schools. The young people of China had learned that Mao was like a God and when he told them to attack his opponents within the CCP they obeyed. In 1949, the Red Guards were told the CCP had been moderate in its treatment of class enemies. Now, 'everything which does not fit the socialist system and the proletarian dictatorship should be attacked.' Totally loyal to Mao, and not the Communist Party, they physically attacked Mao's enemies, beating, torturing and even murdering them. Why did so many young people join the Red Guards? Why did so many young people suddenly abandon their studies and leave their families to participate in violence against victims whom they had never met?

### Note it down

This section focuses upon the role of the Red Guards in the Cultural Revolution. Use the 1:2 method (see page x) to make your notes. The main headings should be:

- Propaganda: How effective was this in engendering support for Mao?
- The extent of genuine ideological commitment: What evidence is there that young people actively supported the regime?
- Personal self-interest: What personal benefits might motivate a young person to join the Red Guards?

When you have completed your notes discuss in pairs why you think young people were compliant in the violence of the Cultural Revolution.

## Mao's hold on young people

In the early years of the PRC Mao was lauded for his defeat of the **nationalists** and his establishment of the communist regime. During the Cultural Revolution this genuine appreciation for popular policies, such as land reform (see page 232) and success in the Korean War (see page 219), was replaced by a state-sponsored personality cult perhaps unrivalled in history. Mao himself justified the cult. In the aftermath of the discussion over Soviet Russian leader Nikita Khrushchev's denunciation of Stalin's **cult of personality** (see page 31) Mao announced: 'The question is not whether or not there should be a cult of the individual, but rather whether or not the individual concerned represents the truth. If he does, then he should be worshipped.'

The most likely people to believe in the cult of Mao were young people. He encouraged them to attack his enemies who were denounced as 'freaks and monsters'. They played a key revolutionary role. They had been indoctrinated by his control of the education system (see pages 296–297). Many of the younger ones had little recollection of his failures during the Great Leap Forward, nor did they blame him for the famine that had followed. They read the Little Red Book, the collection of Mao's comments that they recited. The Party's propaganda told them to believe it as they would the word of God. They were excited when Mao told them:

> *'The world is yours, as well as ours, but in the last analysis, it is yours. You young people, full of vigour and vitality, are in the bloom of life, like the sun at eight or nine in the morning. Our hope is placed on you … The world belongs to you. China's future belongs to you.'*

China had always been a hierarchal society. **Confucian** thought, taught in schools, told children to be obedient to their parents and not question authority. In May 1965 Mao called specifically to students: 'Dare to rebel against authority.' Here Mao was telling them to rise up and attack those in authority like their teachers, professors or Party cadres. The young people were excited and enthused and millions joined the revolution.

## Why did young join the Red Guards?

When attempting to understand the motives of the young people who joined the Red Guards it is important to note that the Red Guards were not a monolithic movement. Many young people joined for different reasons and participated with varying levels of ideological enthusiasm. At first the Red Guards were the children of Party cadres. Mao mobilised students of China's 'elite' **middle schools** that contained significant numbers of children of Party leaders of far greater status than their teachers. They were a cohesive group, drawn from small catchment areas, and had studied together since elementary school, thus ensuring peer pressure unified support for his violent aims. Having been regaled by their parents with stories of revolutionary heroism, Mao offered them a chance of glory. Pragmatic careerism undoubtedly played a part. Students whose employment opportunities were hindered by lack of Party connections took the chance to remove senior **communists** from the hierarchy, of vital importance given that there was no established retirement system.

At first the children of the so-called 'Black Elements' were not allowed to join. However, in autumn 1966, the restrictions were lifted. The young people who had been excluded were suddenly given the opportunity to prove their loyalty to Mao and they took their chance, throwing themselves into the campaign with frenzied revolutionary zeal. Shouting slogans like 'It is justified to rebel' and giving their groups names like 'Protectors of Mao Zedong Thought', they were the most violent and determined of all the Red Guards. They were, in effect, seeking to overcompensate for their family background.

### 'Five Red Types' and 'Five Black Elements'

People were categorised as members of the 'Five Red Types': workers, poor and lower middle-class peasants, revolutionary cadres, revolutionary soldiers and dependents of **revolutionary martyrs**. They were acclaimed for their ideological purity. On the other hand, to be categorised as one of the 'Five Black Elements' – landlords, rich peasants, counter-revolutionaries, bad elements and **rightists** – meant being ostracised. To be categorised as a 'Black Element' meant employment and educational opportunities were reduced, while the threat of being 'sent down' to do manual labour in the countryside was ever present.

## The cult of Mao

The cult reached bizarre degrees. One factory in Beijing created a ritual later known as 'asking for instructions in the morning and reporting back in the evening'. They wrote to Mao himself explaining how they organised their day. The ritual was split into four acts:

1. *At the start of the workday, turn to a portrait of Mao and 'ask for instructions' in order to 'see and think clearly and gain a sense of direction'.*
2. *At work, study the 'quotation board' featuring a selection of Mao's proclamations in order to derive 'a mighty increase in working enthusiasm'.*
3. *When changing shifts, exchange 'Mao-quotes' with fellow workers as a way of 'showing concern and offering help'.*
4. *At the end of the day, turn back to Mao's portrait and 'report back to him' reviewing one's work and thoughts critically in light of his teachings.*

Mao read the report and declared: 'I've read this, and it is very good. Thank you, comrades!' In an example of how ideas, if revolutionary enough, could spiral radically into policy the report was immediately distributed nationwide by the CCP.

## The Little Red Book

In 1964, head of the PLA, Lin Biao, commissioned the publication of a collection of Mao's most famous statements. He ordered every soldier to read it and learn to adhere to its every instruction. Soon it was not only the army that was reading the book. The young people in the Red Guards, who had been taught at school to revere Mao, also tried to decipher and follow its ideas, which took on a near religious power. Some believed that it could work miracles. Newspapers reported that doctors with the book had cured blind people. One disabled person declared that learning Mao Zedong Thought had enabled him to walk again. There was even a report that reading quotations from the book had raised a man from the dead. Historian Roderick Macfarquhar observes that the cult led to 'the transformation of even the most banal utterances by Mao into holy writ'.

The regime urged total and unthinking commitment to Maoist thought. At workplaces each morning people bowed to Mao's portrait and asked for 'instructions' for the day ahead. Mao's works were referred to as 'treasure books' and special ceremonies were held to celebrate their sale. Switchboard operators greeted callers with the words 'Long Live Chairman Mao'. Passengers at train stations had to perform a bizarre 'loyalty dance' before they could board their trains. Mao's thoughts were revered as the word of God.

The message of the cult, namely that Mao was a near-divine being worthy of worship, was encapsulated in the song, 'The East is Red', that became an unofficial national anthem during the Cultural Revolution. As Zhou Enlai put it simply, 'Whatever accords with Mao Zedong Thought is right, while whatever does not accord with Mao Zedong Thought is wrong.' Mao built a propaganda cult that effectively placed him above all other Party leaders. Whipped into a frenzy of adulation, Mao called the Red Guards to Beijing to personally encourage them to attack his enemies.

## The mass rallies of 1966

In July 1965 Red Guards from Tsinghua University in Beijing sent Mao a 'big character poster' entitled 'Long live the proletarian revolutionary spirit of rebellion!' Mao replied to them personally, writing, 'You say that it is right to rebel against **reactionaries**: I enthusiastically support you.' Mistrustful of the Party, Mao, recalled his secretary, consciously 'looked for backing among the students'.

**Source B** *The East Is Red* was a song that became the unofficial anthem of the PRC during the Cultural Revolution. It was played through loud speakers in towns and villages and students sang it every day at school.

> The east is red, the sun rises.
>
> From China arises Mao Zedong.
>
> He strives for the people's happiness,
>
> Hurrah, he is the people's great saviour!
>
> Chairman Mao loves the people.
>
> He is our guide
>
> to building a new China.
>
> Hurrah, lead us forward.

How would the song in Source B help Mao defeat his enemies during the Cultural Revolution?

## Big Character Posters

Big Character Posters were a popular way of communicating political ideas. They were used to level accusations at political enemies. They were easy and quick to make, requiring only ink, brush and paper. They could be anonymous and could be put up on walls and noticeboards quickly and cheaply. During the Cultural Revolution they enabled radical groups to seize control of the political debate, allowing their views to be spread, rather than the control of political messages being monopolised by those in authority who were in charge of more established forms of political media like radio and newspapers. They both represented and played a key aspect in generating exactly the kind of mass mobilisation that Mao hoped for.

On 5 August 1966, Mao heightened the revolutionary atmosphere when he had his own big character poster published in Beijing that urged the people to 'Bombard the Headquarters'. The message was clear: it was an encouragement to attack the leaders of the Communist Party who, in Mao's words, had 'taken the reactionary stand of the **bourgeoisie**' and 'enforced a bourgeois dictatorship'. He was, writes MacFarquhar, giving the young students 'a blank cheque' to attack his opponents.

In August Mao announced, 'Let the rest of the country come to Beijing, or Beijing go to the rest of the country. Train transport is free isn't it?' Mao's propaganda chief Chen Boda invited students to attend one of the eight massive rallies, where they were whipped into a revolutionary fervour by Mao. Most of the rallies were held in Tiananmen Square between mid-August and late November.

Mao was aided in organising the Cultural Revolution by Minister of Defence, Lin Biao, and the PLA. Lin was Mao's most loyal and subservient colleague. Lin Biao exalted Mao as 'our great teacher, great leader, great supreme commander and Great helmsman'. He also helped ensure Mao could always rely on the PLA to do his bidding. The PLA transported young people from across the country, erecting makeshift canteens and dormitories in Beijing. They arrived wearing 'Mao badges' (the more advanced included ones that glowed in the dark!) and clutching their Little Red Books, singing 'Sailing the Seas Depends on the Helmsman'.

Ecstatic to be able to catch a glimpse of their hero, and totally indoctrinated by Maoist propaganda, they worshipped Mao. In fact, close up, the leaders were less impressive than the propaganda imagery had led them to expect. One confused teenager recalled how Mao 'looked older than I had imagined' and that his face 'did not glow either, as it was supposed to'. Lin Biao 'was a small, thin, weak man'. Luckily for Mao, few in attendance got close enough to notice such inconsistencies.

**Source C** A 'Big Character Poster' in Beijing. This one is denouncing Deng Xiaoping as a counter-revolutionary.

Why do you think posters like Source C were used to win support during the Cultural Revolution?

**Source D** Song Binbin places a Red Guard armband on Mao during a rally in Beijing, August 1966. Binbin had come to the notice of Mao because she had led a protest against the education system that had led to the murder of her teacher.

What does Source D suggest about the attitude of Mao towards the Red Guards and their actions?

At the first rally, one of the student leaders, Song Binbin, was allowed to place a Red Guard armband on Mao himself. The exchange represented to the Red Guards Mao's personal legitimisation of their radical movement. When Mao learned that her name meant 'suave' he said that it should be changed to mean 'be martial', leading some to believe that he was implying that they had not been militaristic enough in their activities. When ordered to attack traditional Chinese culture and ideas, they rushed to obey.

## Other reasons for participating

The revolution also offered other opportunities. The Party ruled that anyone wearing the armband denoting them to be a Red Guard would be allowed to board a train. Many young people travelled to Beijing to cheer on Mao at vast rallies in Tiananmen Square, or visit the places that Mao had lived while he was fighting the Civil War against the nationalists. Others simply took the chance, after years of control and repression, to travel across the country, moved more by curiosity and the opportunity to experience freedom as much as revolutionary zeal. While some were committed enough to participate in the torture and intimidation of those denounced as 'class enemies', others simply chanted slogans and attended the rallies out of peer pressure.

## Red Guard attacks on the 'Four Olds'

In August 1966 Mao launched the 'Four Olds Campaign'. The intention was to destroy 'old ideas', 'old culture', 'old customs' and 'old habits', which, the Party Central Committee announced, were still being used by the 'exploiting classes to corrupt the masses, capture their minds and endeavour to stage a comeback'.

The 'old ideology and culture,' declared the Party, 'have poisoned the minds of the people for thousands of years.' It was necessary to 'subject them to thoroughgoing criticism' and instead create 'an entirely new ideology and culture and entirely new customs and habits'. To destroy the old habits would hinder the ability of the **bourgeois feudal classes** to endure.

The Red Guards had been told to 'put daring above everything else' and 'boldly arouse the masses' but their frenzied actions went far beyond that expected by the pragmatic Party leaders like Liu, Den and Zhou. The Red Guards ignored the orders to allow any who had made 'mistakes' the chance to 'turn over a new leaf'. Places and objects representing old-fashioned ideas were attacked.

Visitors to restaurants were forced to complete questionnaires declaring their class origin before they were served, while surgeons cancelled operations out of fear. If the procedure went badly they risked being accused of 'class revenge'. Simply owning a pet bird was enough to make one a target of the Red Guard violence. Bird keeping was a traditional past-time and therefore represented old-fashioned ideas.

Old 'feudal' shop signs were changed to read 'Defend Mao Zedong' or 'Permanent Revolution'. Children's names were changed to Red Glory or Face the East. Road signs were altered to read 'Anti-Revisionism Street' – the British embassy now stood on 'Anti-Imperialism Road', while Beijing University hospital became 'Anti-Imperialism hospital'. The Red Guards even changed the meaning of the traffic lights so that red meant 'Go' until, fearing chaos on the roads, Zhou Enlai stopped them. He also acted to prevent a move by one middle school Red Guard to rename Beijing 'East is Red City'.

## Cultural destruction

Temples were desecrated, the sculptures, statues and artefacts defaced and burned because they represented unsocialistic religious beliefs. The homes of people known to have Western books, traditionally designed gardens, classical musical instruments or even just records of old-fashioned music were ransacked. **Confucian** texts were burned. Zhou did send the PLA to protect the treasure of the Forbidden City from overexuberant Red Guards but, across China, priceless antiquities were destroyed. By the end of the Cultural Revolution one-third of China's 1100 libraries had been closed, and more than 7 million library books lost, stolen or destroyed in the provinces of Liaoning, Jilin, Henan, Jiangxi and Guizhou alone.

### The Confucius Temple in Shandong

The Confucius Temple in Shandong province, a priceless cultural relic and resting place of Confucius himself, was attacked by 200 teachers and students from Beijing Normal University. Personally encouraged by Chen Boda, they announced their intention to 'thoroughly demolish the Confucius Family Shop'. 'To be "nurtured" on the thoughts of Confucius never did anyone any good,' they said, 'and produced cowardly bastards who exploit, oppress, cruelly injure and bully other people.' Supporters of Confucius were 'monsters and freaks'. During their four-week stay, they joined with local activists to destroy 6618 registered cultural artefacts, including 929 paintings and 2700 books, while 2000 graves were defaced. Even then, other Red Guards attacked them for not being efficient enough in their destruction, denouncing them by saying they had 'just made a lot of noise, not mobilised the masses enough'.

### Hai Rui's burial site and Wu Xun

The ancient burial sight of Hai Rui, subject of the play by Wu Han that had sparked the entire Cultural Revolution, was defaced. Confucius and Hai Rui got off lightly. Nineteenth-century cultural hero Wu Xun was denounced as 'a propagator of feudal culture'. His corpse was exhumed from his Beijing grave by middle school students who walked with it to a public square, sentenced him for his failure to challenge the imperial system, broke the corpse into little pieces and burned it. One group of Red Guards took a state film crew with them to record their destruction of Buddhist statues and incense burners in a monastery in the hills outside Beijing.

### A Qing era archway

Historical sites that were linked to national embarrassment at the hands of the West were particularly vulnerable. One young student recalled that he marched behind a red column singing:

*We are Chairman Mao's Red Guards,*

*Tempering ourselves in great waves and winds;*

*Armed with Mao Zedong thought*

*We'll wipe out all pests and vermin.*

The climax of their march came with an attack on a 200-year-old **Qing** era archway. Although he had 'happy memories of playing under the shadow of the arches,' he 'did not feel too bad about destroying them' because it was 'under the Qing that the Western powers had begun to subjugate China with opium and gunboats'. They sang 'Smash the Four Olds' as the structure was smashed into a pile of broken stone.

## Tibet

The cultural destruction was particularly widespread in Tibet, where religious artefacts were a particular provocation to the Red Guards. Every aspect of Tibetan culture was targeted. The famous rooftop prayer flags that adorned Tibetan houses were taken down. Long hair was damned as an 'old custom' and ordered to be cut.

**Source E** From the autobiography of Rinbur Tulku, a Tibetan monk, reprinted from Warren W. Smith, *China's Tibet: Autonomy or Assimilation* (Rowman and Littlefield, 2008), pages 129–31.

> All the books in temples like the Tsuklakhang and Ramoche and in all the monasteries in Lhasa ... were burned, except for those few which some people managed to hide. Thus thousands of volumes accumulated at great cost over many generations and now very rare were surrendered at the orders of the Chinese officials in each section of the city and for a few days after the clouds of smoke in the sky over Lhasa blotted out the sun ... They employed blacksmiths to drive chisels into the statue's waist on either side of its cupped hands and pound them with hammers until it was broken into two halves, and the filling of powdered jewels and gold dust was scattered to the four winds. The statues from those temples and monasteries which were made of gold, silver, precious metal alloys, gilt or burnished copper, brass and suchlike, as well as offering utensils made of those materials, were all confiscated by the state and stored in the warehouse of the 'Cultural Relics Bureau'. Clay statues were thrown out in the street and their priceless contents scattered in the mud, and other heinous misdeeds were committed. Events similar to those just described in the Lhasa area took place all over Tibet.

How far does Source E suggest that the main reason for the Cultural Revolution in Tibet was to destroy Buddhism?

Local peasants were forced to help attack monasteries and shrines. Most were looted and destroyed. Unmovable artefacts like wall paintings or large clay statues were defaced. Buddhist scriptures were ripped up by the Chinese to use as inner-soles in their shoes or even as toilet paper. Evidence does suggest that apparent anarchy was far more organised in Tibet than in other regions. Before 'revolutionary masses' were allowed to attack the symbols of 'exploitative' Tibetan culture or Buddhist religion, Chinese soldiers were ordered to empty the contents of many monasteries of all valuables. Precious metals, rare scroll paintings and valuable statues were spirited away by corrupt officials who later sold them on the international art market. Traditional jewellery was to be handed over to the Chinese state bank. For all the communist's rhetoric about freeing Tibetans from their feudal past and backward religion, the Cultural Revolution in Tibet was little more than a greedy attempt to eradicate their entire way of life.

## The use of terror

During the autumn and winter of 1966 the violence of the Red Guards spiralled out of control. It became known as the 'Red Terror'. Some victims were targeted numerous times by rival Red Guard factions. Party members, former businessmen and landlords were subjected to denunciation and intimidation by the frenzied Red Guards, desperate to prove their ideological commitment. What started as intimidation and denunciation gave way to brutality. 'Class enemies' were sent for 're-education' through physical labour in prison camps. Intellectuals associated with liberal thoughts were ruthlessly targeted. Some were kidnapped; others were killed. Many took their own lives, unable to stand the unremitting threats. One such example was the renowned playwright Lao She. His house was burned by middle school Red Guards and he was denounced at **struggle meetings** where he was made to wear a dunce's hat. To escape the constant harassment he drowned himself in Taiping Lake near Beijing in late August 1966.

Ding Ling, who had been purged during the Hundred Flowers Campaign (see page 216–218), was once again targeted. She was denounced in struggle meetings and made to stand for hours in the painful 'airplane' position, her arms forced straight back behind her. At night she was made to sleep in a stable. Zheng Peidi, a teacher at Beijing University, was found guilty of criticising Jiang Qing. She was confined with her young baby in a building on the campus known as the 'cowshed'.

### Contract workers

Although the movement started with the students, by the end of 1966 it had spread to encompass workers. On 25 December workers on short-term contracts, angry at their poor pay, rose up to criticise their managers and well-paid workers and seized the Ministry of Labour. Jiang Qing arrived the next day to support them. Describing the Ministry as the 'Ministry of Lords' she declared it 'unbelievable' that 'even though the country has been liberated for so many years the workers are still suffering'. She berated the Vice Minister for Labour and told him, 'You, too, should work as a contract worker,' before bursting into tears. Contract workers across the country rose up to demand better treatment.

## The growth of anarchy

Urged on by Maoist indoctrination, rival groups of Red Guards began to fight and denounce each other. Red Guards of working class origin fought against different Red Guards with non-working class backgrounds. For example, they included children of intellectuals or former business owners. This group were desperate to prove their ideological worth, or simply to protect themselves. They argued that the original Red Guards were abusing their position, becoming exactly what Mao did not want: a new privileged class.

Radical groups sprang up in anarchic and unco-ordinated attempts to join the violent struggle. How far they were motivated by ideological commitment is hard to say. Political self-interest certainly played a part:

- In Heilongjiang province in Manchuria, one former opponent of the Great Leap Forward tried to seize power as a way to prove his revolutionary commitment to Mao.
- In Shanxi, the provincial vice governor joined the Red Guards as an attempt to purge rival Party leaders.

'Everywhere people were fighting, dividing into two factions,' recalled Mao, 'there were two factions in every factory, in every school, in every province.' Violence was not restricted to battles between the Red Guards. Violence broke out between Red Guards and farmers who resented idealistic young people arriving at their village or factory, telling them what to do and demanding food and lodging, without any real idea about practical realities. China stood on the edge of a civil war.

Even Mao found it difficult to control the anarchy because he had done so much to encourage it. 'It could not be controlled,' writes historian Shaun Breslin, 'because attempting to control it would undermine the movement's *raison d'être* … what had been unleashed could not easily be re-leashed.' Mao could not stop until he had purged the Party with his revolution from below. Indeed, at times he appeared to revel in the violence. At his birthday party on 26 December 1966, he proposed a toast 'To the unfolding of nationwide all-round civil war!' Besides, he later joked, although violence sometimes caused problems when 'good people beat up good people,' on the whole it was positive because 'they might otherwise not have got to know each other'.

For all Mao's encouragement of the anarchy, 'In reality,' he said, 'there will always be "Heads".' He observed that in Shanghai, 'There are people who wave the Red Flag to bring down the Red Flag.' In this wave of 'ultra-democracy' the radicals were calling for the abolition of the Party itself and, he said, 'that won't do'. He demanded that the commune in Shanghai be closed down.

### 'January Storm'

The biggest example of the anarchy spiralling out of control was in Shanghai in early 1967, the so-called 'January Storm'. Encouraged by Mao's calls to attack the Party, radical rebel Red Guard groups, made up not of students but of unprivileged workers in the city, destroyed the Party establishment and created their own form of control modelled on the **Paris Commune of 1871** when the city's labourers had seized control and created a new social order with democratic elections.

On 30 December 1966, 100,000 of these radical rebel Red Guards attacked and defeated 20,000 other Red Guards, known as the Scarlet Guards. The Scarlet Guards had been mobilised by the local Communist Party. The radical Reds declared that 'the time is ripe to seize power from the counter-revolutionary Party Committee and government' and proceeded to mete out exactly the same kind of violence and torture that the original Red Guards had inflicted on them. The radical Reds believed that they were doing Mao's bidding. The Sixteen Points (see page 262) had declared, 'It is necessary to institute a system of general elections, like that of the Paris Commune,' and at first Mao applauded their 'seizure of power from below'. It was anarchy.

## The February adverse current

The radicals and perhaps even members of his own Party had not understood Mao's true motives. It was not the destruction of the Party itself, but only the leaders of the Party, particularly Liu and Deng, that he believed were preventing him from instigating the correct policies. 'Bombard the Headquarters' did not mean the removal of the CCP from power, but rather only Mao's personal rivals. Indeed, when in February 1967 leaders of the establishment including Zhu De, former Commander in chief of the PLA, and Chen Yi, the Foreign Minister, protested against Mao's policy of encouraging chaos, he criticised them and dismissed their complaints as 'the February adverse current', meaning that they were 'flowing' against the correct 'tide' of revolutionary upheaval that Mao wanted to encourage.

## Further violence

In April Mao encouraged further violence when he told the Red Guards, 'Have no fear of chaos. The more chaos you dish out the better. Disorder and chaos are always good things.' This even led the Red Guards into battles with the PLA. The biggest example was in Wuhan in summer 1967. The army had sided with the local party organisation and was trying to defend it from radical Red

Guards. In the spring the PLA had arrested 500 leaders of radical Red Guards and worker groups for attacking the Party. This led to public protests and hunger strikes. In the summer there were armed clashes between radicals and the army. The PLA killed 1000 protestors. When members of the government flew to Wuhan and criticised the PLA for being too brutal in their suppression of the radicals, PLA supporters kidnapped them from the hotel while local soldiers did nothing to help them. They were only released when military reinforcements were sent. Opposing worker and student radical groups, both claiming to be the true defenders of Mao Zedong Thought, fought each other and the PLA, often raiding PLA depots to get hold of weapons. In August 1967 rebels seized power over the Foreign Ministry in Beijing for two weeks, declaring the creation of 'proletarian internationalism' and appointing radical diplomats to represent China around the world. Only the PLA kept the Red Guards from seizing the military facilities where scientists were working on China's hydrogen bomb.

### Revolutionary committees

By September 1967 Mao was concerned not to let the anarchy lead to a challenge to the legitimacy of the Party itself. Instead of autonomous communes advocated by the radicals in Shanghai, Mao called for the creation in provinces of a new form of organisation called the **revolutionary committee**. Based on a 'three-way alliance', these merged the role of the Party, state and army. However, the Party remained dominant. Mass organisations and radicals were represented but they were never in control. The committees were actually run by smaller '**standing committees**' and radicals only had token representation on these. Indeed, many previous personnel from the old power structures, who had been purged mere months before, now re-emerged to take control of the committees and re-establish their power.

## Restoration of order by the PLA

By 1968 Mao knew he had to curtail the violence of the Red Guards. He was worried that if the anarchy continued, foreign nations might take advantage of it to attack China and seize some of its territory. It was time, thought Mao, to put the Party back in control in order to re-establish law and order and get the economy going again. He realised that only the PLA could restore control. He ordered the PLA to systematically crush the Red Guards and to violently re-establish the control of the central party, which they did but only with great ruthlessness and bloodshed. The corpses that began to wash up on the shores of Hong Kong hinted at a massive bloodletting. When the Red Guards protested that a 'black hand' was seeking to suppress them, Mao admitted, 'I am the black hand.'

In that same year the Cultural Revolution Group, by now dominated by Jiang Qing, launched a campaign entitled 'cleansing the class ranks'. It was dedicated to 'eradicating once and for all any signs of capitalism'. The PLA launched a massive wave of terror, led by Mao's own security force, PLA Unit 8341. They used surveillance, mass rallies and struggle meetings to extract confessions. Some 1.84 million people were arrested for allegedly being 'spies', 'bad elements' or 'newly emerged counter-revolutionaries'. Thousands of people were imprisoned, beaten to death or took their own lives.

- In Jilin province in north-eastern China the campaign led to the death of 2127 and permanent injury of 3459 cadres.
- In eastern Hebei, more than 84,000 people, including many cadres, were persecuted; 2955 died and 765 suffered permanent disabilities.
- In Yunnan, a staggering 6979 died by what Party records showed as 'death from enforced suicide'.

In the harsh frontier lands of south and south-western China, the campaign was particularly brutal. In Binyang county, Guangxi, villagers were shot and thrown into mass graves. Once killed, some had their flesh and liver eaten. In one case in neighbouring Yunnan a victim had his skull removed and his brain eaten, while another had his testicles cut off, boiled and eaten. A later Party report noted, without irony, that this cannibalism 'certainly provides plenty of food for thought'.

### End to the violence

The violent phase of the Cultural Revolution ended in April 1969 with the Ninth **Party Congress**. There Lin Biao was officially confirmed as Mao's successor.

The terror was at an end, but the impact of the anarchy and terror endured. One son of a former banker denounced as a rightist recalled that the legacy of the terror lasted long beyond the end of the Cultural Revolution:

> *'The greatest tragedy of the Cultural Revolution was its torture of people's souls … My father suffered badly … in the seventies, after countless struggle sessions, he developed a strange problem. At night, he would awake from his nightmares and begin to scream. It was a small place. When he screamed, no one could sleep. But he dragged on until 1989.'*

## Key debate

### To what extent was Mao responsible for the Red Terror?

The violence of the Red Terror clearly spread beyond Mao's control into anarchy. How much the violence was his responsibility is a source of historical debate. It is clear that rival leaders had much to gain by manipulating violence to their own selfish ends. Jiang Qing targeted any who could reveal her past as a Shanghai actress of dubious repute. Lin Biao ensured the death of Marshal He Long in part because the hero of the revolution had expressed doubts about Lin's military acumen. This is not to exonerate Mao, however. As historians Jung Chang and Jon Halliday argued, while Mao might not have personally signed death warrants himself, 'Mao would simply indicate his intentions, and some people would volunteer to carry out the tormenting and improvise the gruesome details.' It was Mao who created the political conditions and the incentives that gave the violence meaning and legitimacy, all for his own selfish political ends.

## Conclusion: The Red Guards and the Red Terror

The violent attacks of the Red Guards, the cultural devastation they wrought and their frenzied public humiliation and torture of their victims remain the enduring image of the Cultural Revolution. Radicalised by Mao's pervasive **cult of personality** and convinced of his near-divine status, the young people provided a terrifying force that Mao could rely on to remove anyone he believed was not entirely committed to Mao Zedong Thought. Although many acted out of a desire to prove their revolutionary zeal, many took advantage of the Red Terror to improve their career prospects, take revenge for personal slights or indulge their violent tendencies. Many Red Guards took the chance to travel the country for the first time. In a society where Confucian structure dictated order, discipline and respect for authority, Mao's call to 'Bombard the Headquarters' represented an unprecedented opportunity for the young to challenge the establishment. Recent memoirs of former Red Guards have stressed the feelings of **emancipation**, optimism and freedom from a rigidly hierarchical society. However, the paradox is clear – the Red Guard attacks on political authority succeeded merely in consolidating the power of Mao's dictatorship over the Chinese people. A campaign waged against control had simply elevated Mao's dictatorial power to unprecedented heights.

## Work together

Posters were a vital method by which groups within the Cultural Revolution spread their ideas. With your partner, go to maopost.com to see some examples. Then create your own poster. One of you should create a poster from the perspective of Mao, the other from the perspective of the Red Guards.

- What do you think the main message of your poster should be?
- Who would your targets be? (Many posters did not name their targets specifically, using metaphors instead.)
- What would you try to convince your audience about your target?

Remember, many people were illiterate. You should not use more than one sentence - your message must be delivered visually.

When you have finished, pass your poster to your partner. Can they guess what the message of your poster is?

## 3 Attacks on Mao's political and class enemies

At the start of the Cultural Revolution, the identities of Mao's targets were not completely clear. The 'Sixteen Points' released in August 1966 referred only to 'those within the Party who are in authority and are taking the capitalist road'. As the Cultural Revolution went on it became clear that it was Liu Shaoqi and Deng Xiaoping who were the real focus of Mao's anger. Both had advocated the abandonment of Mao's utopian ideology based on mobilisation of the masses and a trust in the effectiveness of revolutionary zeal to solve China's problems. Instead, Liu and Deng advocated reliance on intellectuals and experts, and a belief in practical solutions over ideological visions.

> **Note it down**
>
> This section focuses upon the fate of Mao's opponents. Using the 1:2 method (see page x) write down Mao's opponents in the left-hand column:
>
> - Liu Shaoqi
> - Deng Xiaoping
> - The Party membership
> - Capitalist roaders
> - Foreigners living in China.
>
> For each sub-heading, make notes on what happened to them. Reflect on what you know Mao's aims were for the Cultural Revolution. How happy do you think Mao would be with the results, and why?

### Liu Shaoqi

Liu's pragmatic policies had helped rebuild China after the Great Leap Forward. He was popular. There had been talk of hanging Liu's portrait alongside Mao's on the gates of the Forbidden City. Mao may have been jealous. When Mao had first encouraged the students to rise up, Liu had supported the sending of Party work teams onto the campuses to control the violence. This was used as evidence of his traitorous rightist sentiments, though at the time Mao had not contradicted Liu. Perhaps Mao was looking to set him up.

It became clear that Liu was the main target of the Cultural Revolution. He was subjected to constant struggle meetings where he was abused and beaten. Even his family was targeted. In April 1967 his wife, Wang Guangmei, was forced to wear a fashionable dress, high-heels and a necklace made of ping-pong balls to represent a pearl necklace that she had worn on a state visit to Indonesia. Wearing this 'evidence' of her capitalist and imperialist sympathy, she was humiliated in front of a crowd of 300,000 Red Guards at Qinghua University and then sentenced to years of solitary confinement in prison. His children were sent to work as peasants in the countryside. In August Liu wrote to Mao to resign as Head of State. Mao did not reply. Liu was held in solitary confinement in his home in Beijing but he was not allowed to die. Jiang Qing specifically ordered him to be kept alive to act as a 'living target'.

In October 1968 she presented evidence to the Central Committee of the CCP of Liu's treachery. She had personally taken charge of the investigation into Liu. She charged him with betraying the Party, colluding with US secret agents and giving information to the CIA in Hong Kong. The evidence was extremely flimsy, some dating back to the 1920s. To get it, Jiang Qing and Kang Sheng interrogated over 28,000 people, collecting confessions through torture. Liu was denounced as a 'renegade, scab and in 1969 he was officially traitor'. He was stripped of all his posts and in 1969 he was officially replaced as successor to Mao by Lin Biao.

By this time Liu was no threat to Mao. Torture and neglect meant he could no longer speak. His hair had grown to a foot in length. Mao ordered that he be exiled from Beijing to the city of Kaifeng and held in an empty, unheated building. When he developed pneumonia Mao refused to allow him to be sent to hospital. He died on 12 November 1968. The former President of China was buried in an unmarked grave.

> **Kang Sheng**
>
> Kang joined the Party during the 1930s. He was trained in interrogation and torture techniques by the Soviet Secret Police, the NKVD. Loyal to Mao, he used these skills during the Cultural Revolution to persecute, arrest and purge Mao's enemies. He died of cancer in 1975. After his death he was condemned by the Party for his political crimes.

### Deng Xiaoping

Mao was also angered by Deng Xiaoping. His famous dictum about the irrelevance of the 'colour' of a policy (see page 259) was a direct affront to Mao's belief that it was better to be communist than practical. Deng had helped Liu introduce economic reforms without Mao's advice. Mao complained, 'Deng Xiaoping never came to consult me … from 1959 to the present he has never consulted me over anything at all.' Damned as 'the number two person in authority taking the capitalist road' he was accused of trying to establish his own 'Independent Kingdom'. Deng disappeared from public sight, sent to a tractor factory in rural Jiangxi to work. Like Liu, his family also suffered. Deng's son attempted to escape torture by jumping out of a window (some say he was pushed by Red Guards) and was paralysed from the waist down.

## 'Learn from the PLA'

The PLA provided a key propaganda figurehead that exhorted the people to be loyal to Mao. The 'Learn from the PLA' campaign was launched in 1963. Army propaganda turned one rank and file soldier, Lei Feng, into an ideological role model, a national hero to be revered. Described in Party propaganda as 'one of Chairman Mao's good warriors', Lei was a soldier who was deeply loyal to the Party and Mao. When he died in an accident while on duty, his diary was published and became, in historian Jung Chang's words, 'a moral textbook' for the PLA. Extracts from his diary recalled his service in washing the feet of his tired comrades and darning their socks while helping the cooks clean cabbages. The diary showed him to be unselfish in the service of the revolution. For example, on a train he would help the staff clean the carriages and in the barracks he would secretly mend his comrades' clothes. At night he might creep into the kitchen and prepare a meal for his hungry friends. Source F is an extract from Lei Feng's diary.

Posters showed Lei Feng digging wells for peasants and helping old ladies to cross the road, all the while exhorting greater commitment to the communist cause with the slogan, 'It is glorious to be a nameless hero'. Mao declared that the people should 'Be like Comrade Lei Feng' and exhorted them to follow his example of revolutionary zeal. In 1961 the PLA newspaper began to publish a quotation from Mao every day. Soldiers were ordered to cut them out and compile their own collections to study and learn by heart. The people were told that Mao's ideas could solve all problems.

**Source F** Lei Feng, quoted in *Mao: A Life*, by Philip Short (Hodder and Stoughton, 1999), page 517.

> I felt particularly happy this morning when I got up, because last night I had dreamed of our great leader, Chairman Mao. And it so happens that today is the Party's 40th anniversary. Today I have so much to tell the Party, so much gratitude to the Party ... I am like a toddler, and the Party is like my mother who helps me, leads me, and teaches me to walk ... My beloved Party, my loving mother, I am always your loyal son.

What image of the Communist Party is Lei Feng trying to spread according to Source F? How effective do you think this would be?

## Key debate

### How did Mao treat his political rivals?

Some scholars have rejected comparisons with other dictators regarding Mao's treatment of fellow Party members. 'Unlike Stalin and Hitler,' writes historian Mobo Gao, 'it was public knowledge that Mao did not execute his political rivals.' Similarly, Gao claims that, while Liu Shaoqi was removed from office, he died of natural causes, and points out that Zhou Enlai served as Premier of the PRC until he died. This **interpretation** is unsophisticated. During the Cultural Revolution Peng was subjected to struggle meetings and maimed. Liu's death was hastened by the torture. Before Liu died he personally pleaded with Mao for mercy and to be allowed to withdraw to the countryside to live out his life as a peasant. Mao refused. Although Zhou was not expelled from his political offices, Mao's denial of treatment for his cancer hastened his death.

## Lin Biao and the role of the PLA

At this time communist leaders were preparing for life after Mao. Who would succeed the 'Great Helmsman'? While Mao was losing faith in Liu and Deng, other communist leaders saw a chance to benefit and position themselves favourably for the succession struggle. One was Lin Biao (see also page 275), a sycophant who had impressed Mao enough to take over from Peng Dehuai as Minister of Defence when the great general had been purged for his criticism of the Great Leap Forward. Lin published the Little Red Book and made it compulsory reading for PLA soldiers. It demanded self-sacrifice, self-reliance and revolutionary fervour, all in the service of the Chairman. Distributed to millions of soldiers, this indoctrination assured that Mao could depend upon the loyalty of the army.

## The purging of the Party membership

Liu and Deng were only the most high profile leaders to suffer during the Cultural Revolution. The impact on the Party and government officials was devastating:

- At regional and provisional level 70–80 per cent of all Party cadres were purged, 60–70 per cent in the organs of central government.
- In Yunnan 14,000 Party cadres were executed as 'traitors'.
- Four out of six of the regional Party first secretaries and 23 of 29 provincial Party secretaries were removed.
- Only nine out of 23 Politburo members survived the purge.
- Two-thirds of the Central Committee had been deposed.

## Mao's political rivals

### Liu Shaoqi

Liu had been a communist since his youth. As a young student he had travelled to Moscow to study communism. He had supported Mao during the Civil War. At Yan'an he had written a political report entitled 'How to be a Good Communist'. He was Vice Chairman of the Communist Party and was named as President of the PRC in 1959. He was considered likely to succeed Mao. A pragmatist who introduced a wide range of economic reforms to help China recover from the Great Leap Forward, he was purged during the Cultural Revolution. He and his wife were beaten, humiliated and tortured. He was stripped of all his posts and imprisoned. Denied medical care, he died in his prison cell in 1968.

### Zhou Enlai

An experienced communist, Zhou founded the European branch of the CCP in France and became a member of the Politburo as early as 1928. He became Premier of the PRC in 1949 and held this post until his death. As such, he was 'principal administrator' of the bureaucracy running China. He was also Foreign Minister. Considered a pragmatist, he was an intelligent politician. He avoided purging during the Cultural Revolution by being careful not to cross Mao. Genuinely popular among the people who saw him as a moderating figure acting against the excesses of the Cultural Revolution, his death of cancer in 1976 (hastened by Mao who refused to allow him vital treatment) sparked an outpouring of public grief that led to demonstrations against the radicals during the so-called 'Tiananmen Square incident'.

### Deng Xiaoping

Deng was an experienced communist who had worked alongside Mao since the Civil War. At the Eighth Party Congress in 1956 he was chosen as Secretary-General of the Central Committee. He was more pragmatic than Mao, helping Liu Shaoqi to get the country back on its feet after the Great Leap Forward. This made him a target for the radicals during the Cultural Revolution and he was purged in 1969. He was sent to a tractor factory in Jiangxi to live as an ordinary worker. He was recalled to Beijing by Mao in 1974. Respected for his experience and practical knowledge, he outmanoeuvred his opponents and became the most influential leader of the PRC.

### Lin Biao

An experienced soldier, Lin led the Red Army to victories against the Japanese during the Second World War and against the nationalists in the Civil War. He replaced Peng Dehuai as Minister of Defence in 1959. Lin helped modernise the PLA, but was also a supporter of the radicals during the Cultural Revolution, helping to support the Red Guards and spreading Mao's ideology through the Little Red Book, which he had commissioned. Although he was officially named in 1969 as Mao's successor, by 1971 Lin was worried that he might be purged. He decided to flee but his plane crashed as he tried to escape and he died.

Many were sent for 'productive labour and political study' which in reality translated to a life of hard labour and indoctrination in the May Seventh Cadre Schools. The official purpose of these was to re-educate the inmates in 'correct' communist thinking. In fact, this 'education' really meant back-breaking agricultural labour combined with constant study of Mao's writing. Living conditions were very harsh. Families were split up in the camps and frail or elderly workers were expected to do the same work as the healthy. Often the work was pointless. The Party officials could not hope to work the fields as productively as the peasants, so instead they were given menial, mind-numbing jobs. Instead of learning about communism, most simply learned about the harsh realities of rural life. In total, 3 million bureaucrats and cadres were exiled to the countryside. Others were beaten and tortured. An estimated half a million Chinese were killed.

Zhou Enlai's plea to 'denounce with words, not violence' was ignored. Constant threats and intimidation caused the first secretaries of Shanxi and Yunnan to take their own lives while the leader of Anhui was driven through the centre of Beijing on the back of an open truck, beaten and abused. The Coal Minister was forced to wear an iron hat weighing 60 kilograms. He was then beaten to death by the Red Guards. Everyone and anyone apart from Mao was vulnerable. Military service to the Party was no defence. General He Long, a military hero who had fought in the war against Japan, was denounced as a rightist by Jiang Qing and placed under house arrest without heat or water. Refused medicine for his diabetes, he died in 1969. Peng Dehuai was brought back to Beijing from his exile after his criticism of Mao at Lushan in 1959. He was subjected to endless struggle meetings and beaten at public rallies. He was beaten so hard by jailers who demanded he confess that his ribs were broken. He finally died of medical neglect in 1974. The numbers of Party members killed are not known, but at their trial, the Gang of Four were charged with legitimising the death of over half a million CCP officials.

## The purging of capitalist roaders and foreigners living in China

As representatives of capitalist and imperialist nations, foreigners in China were vulnerable to being attacked or abused. The rules of diplomatic immunity were not respected by the Red Guards. Foreign embassies from both capitalist and communist countries were besieged by angry mobs.

- The Red Guards attacked three embassies in Beijing: those of Burma, Indonesia and India.
- The Dutch chargé d'affaires was imprisoned in the embassy by a mob for nearly six months. Dutch women and children were denied exit visas to leave China.
- A mob with loudspeakers blaring out Maoist slogans laid siege to the French, Soviet and Yugoslavian Embassies, trapping diplomats inside.
- Shops, restaurants and hotels put up signs declaring that Soviet citizens would no longer be served. Posters were put up at train stations declaring 'Smash Brezhnev's head' (Brezhnev was the Soviet leader after Khrushchev).
- Crowds trapped ambassadors in their cars for hours. On one occasion Soviet staff who had left the embassy to buy tickets for their families to leave China were trapped in their cars by a mob for sixteen hours.
- The French trade counsellor was confronted outside his embassy and made to stand in the freezing cold while being denounced for seven hours. The police watched and did nothing to assist him.
- Staff at the British Embassy in Beijing were manhandled and beaten. The embassy itself was set on fire.

Individual foreigners were also victimised:

- American Sidney Rittenberg was an avowed communist who took part in struggle meetings against Mao's enemies and spread propaganda criticising Liu Shaoqi on Chinese radio. Even this did not make him safe. In 1968 he was sent for 're-education' at a May Seventh Cadre School. He was only released in 1977.
- Some of the violence reached absurd levels. When a Chinese journalist was sentenced to two years' imprisonment in Hong Kong for encouraging anti-imperialist riots in the then British-held territory, in retaliation a British correspondent in Beijing, Anthony Grey, was put into solitary confinement for 26 months. Later Red Guards broke into the house and killed his cat!
- One odd target for denunciation was the Italian film director Michelangelo Antonioni. In 1972 he was invited to China by the government to make a documentary about the new China. But when the film was released it was criticised for focusing on traditional life and old buildings, and banned. Posters denouncing him were hung in factories and villages. The ban on the film in China was only lifted in 2004.

## Conclusion: Attacks on Mao's political opponents and class enemies

By the end of 1968 the most violent stage of the Cultural Revolution was over. Mao's power was once again unrivalled. His rivals within the Party had been purged and many older Party cadres had been removed, with younger cadres who were completely obedient to Mao taking their place. In the 1969 Party Congress, a new **constitution** placed Mao Zedong Thought as the official guiding ideology of the Party. Mao's most loyal servant, Lin Biao, was named as Mao's official successor. Mao had come to power promising to free the nation from political repression yet by the end of the 1960s the Chinese people were once again ruled by an 'Emperor' of absolute power.

### Work Together

Read this section again carefully. Working in pairs, divide the content into two. One of you should take the first half examining the fate of individual Party leaders, the other the second half examining the Party membership, capitalist roaders and foreigners living in China. After you have read it, put your notes and this book away and explain your 'half' to the other person. Note down any areas that you struggled to explain or where the explanation was unclear. These will serve as reminders for revision.

# 4 Winding down the Cultural Revolution, 1968–76

Mao had purged his enemies. Yet questions remained: How could the anarchy that Mao himself had done so much to encourage be brought to an end? How much political power would the PLA have? And, most pressing of all, who would succeed the now ageing Chairman? The Cultural Revolution was, proclaimed the *People's Daily*, 'without precedent in human history'. It had inevitably meant violence. 'Destruction comes first,' said Mao, 'and in the course of it there is construction.' But exactly what had Mao created?

### Note it down

Take a piece of A3 paper. Draw a graph with each year from 1966 to 1976 on the horizontal axis. Write 'Radical' at the top of the vertical axis. As you read through the chronology of the Cultural Revolution, note when it was radical in nature and also when it became less anarchic and less radical. Note on your graph the key turning points and then make sure you note when different individuals had more or less control over the event. What happened at the very end of the Cultural Revolution? What were the key turning points?

## 'Up to the mountains and down to the villages'

Eighteen million Red Guards were sent to 'cool off' in remote areas in the countryside as part of the 'up to the mountains and down to the villages campaign'. According to Party propaganda, to be chosen was a privilege because it offered them the chance to learn from the peasants by 'serving the people' through manual labour. Schools and universities remained closed as the young people travelled across China as part of this 'rustification campaign'. This was entirely in keeping with Mao's negative attitude to academic education and the value of learning from practical experience. 'I said to my own child,' referring to his daughter, 'You go down to the countryside and tell the poor and lower-middle peasants, my dad says that after studying a few years we became more and more stupid. Please … be my teachers. I want to learn from you.' Those sent to be 're-educated' in the realities of rural hardship were not welcomed. Although the peasantry was exhorted to partake in the Cultural Revolution, fear of disruption to agricultural production meant that in the main they were not directly involved. Peasants had little spare food to give the newcomers and they resented the fact they were forced to help the youngsters who had never done any manual work before in their lives.

The formerly ideologically committed young people were shocked and dismayed. The so-called 'lost generation' became disillusioned and cynical about politics, especially when it became clear that those with Party connections or influential families could quickly return to the cities. Those without faced the fact that their exile to the countryside was permanent.

## The rise and fall of Lin Biao

Mao's attempts to deradicalise the Cultural Revolution brought him into conflict with his most loyal supporter, Lin Biao. Lin had been a key figure in encouraging the radicalisation of the movement through his publication of the Little Red Book and the use of the PLA to help transport Red Guards to Mao's rallies. Lin did not want the radicalisation to end. He hoped to take power when Mao died and although Liu and Deng had been successfully purged (see page 273), other leaders, most notably Zhou Enlai, remained in his way.

Lin had been a clear winner in the Cultural Revolution. After the Ninth Party Congress he was the official successor to the ageing and increasingly infirm Chairman. However, events soon turned against the leader of the PLA. First, he tried to reinstate the post of Head of State, a role that had been vacant since the purging of Liu Shaoqi. Mao had already made it clear he did not want the post. Mao, it appears, interpreted Lin's move as an attempt to enable him to take the job for himself. Added to Lin's military command, he could challenge Mao.

Mao also began to be concerned about the power and independence of the army. Having been a key force in controlling the Cultural Revolution, the PLA had massive political influence. Of the 29 provincial revolutionary committees set up in 1967, 21 were headed by PLA officers. 'Why do we have so many soldiers around here?' Mao was heard to complain. Mao feared a military coup. He reversed his earlier slogans and now declared: 'Let the PLA learn from the People.'

### Lin's death

It may be that Lin was planning to seize power. Rumour has it that he and his son planned to attack Mao's private train with artillery or an assault by specially trained commandos, loyal only to Lin. Why would he do such a risky act? Some have suggested that he was working with the **Soviet Union**, others that his power hungry wife had persuaded him to seize power. Regardless, what seems likely is that Lin was convinced he was to be purged himself. He fled from Mao's security forces in such a panic that his escape plane was not fully fuelled before take-off and he was killed when it crashed, along with his wife and son. The death of Lin caused a major problem for the regime. For years propaganda had described him as Mao's 'closest comrade in arms' and no one had done more to spread the cult of Mao. Now he was denounced as having always secretly been a traitor who was working for the Soviet Union. For the first time, people began to question the regime.

## Deng Xiaoping's return to power

By the early 1970s, Mao's health was failing. He could no longer exercise properly. He trembled. His heart and eye-sight were failing. No longer able to read, he occupied his time watching Hong Kong kung-fu movies. His speech was barely decipherable. When he entertained visitors, he communicated through writing. Mao clearly had an eye on who would succeed him and was very concerned as to the long-term future of the revolution he had dedicated his life to (see Source G). Yet many of his friends were also sick. In late 1972, Zhou Enlai was diagnosed with lung cancer. His secret police chief, Kang Sheng, had bladder cancer. As his closest advisers from his revolutionary days became sick or died, they were replaced by young and less trusted bureaucrats.

**Source G** From one of Mao's last statements to the Politburo, quoted in Philip Short, *Mao: A Life* (Hodder and Stoughton, 1999), pages 624–25.

> In my life, I have done two things. First I fought Chiang Kai-shek for several decades, and drove him to a few small islands ... We fought our way to Beijing and at last to the Forbidden City. There are not many people who do not recognise those achievements ... The second thing I have done you all know. It was to launch the Cultural Revolution, which now has the support of few and is opposed by many. But this matter is not ended yet. It is a legacy which must be handed down to the next generation. How should it be handed down? If not in peace, then in turmoil. If this is not properly handled there will be bloodshed. Heaven alone knows what you will do.

What are the main arguments made in Source G? How far do you agree? Why might there be 'turmoil' after Mao was dead?

Mao decided that the time was right to call Deng Xiaoping back from his work repairing tractors in Jiangxi. Although associated with Liu, his 'capitalist' crimes had never been as serious and Mao respected his organisational skills, now vitally needed to re-establish normality after the Cultural Revolution. In 1975 Deng was picked to join the Politburo's Standing Committee (see page 208). He was also appointed PLA **chief of staff**.

### The Four Modernisations

Deng supported a programme that became known as the 'Four Modernisations': advancement in agriculture, industry, defence, and science and technology. This focus on technological development and reliance on scientific expertise was a direct reversal of Mao's trust in mass mobilisation. Hugely experienced and resourceful, Deng clearly understood that the people wanted a return to normalcy and pragmatism, not more campaigns calling for upheaval. 'Some say [we represent] ... the old order. Let them say what they like,' he told a meeting of senior Party cadres in October 1975. 'The worst that could happen is you could be overthrown a second time. Don't be afraid. If you've done a good job, its worth being overthrown for!'

## The Gang of Four

Mao had supported Deng over any of the candidates loyal to Jiang Qing. The infamous Madame Mao made her last attempt to gain control. In 1973 she and her allies, the so-called 'Gang of Four' radicals, used their influence over the media and propaganda to launch the 'criticise Lin [Biao], criticise Confucius' campaign.

Historians and intellectuals were forced to attempt to find linkages between Lin and Confucius in an attempt to prove that the former PLA chief had been attempting to subvert the revolution by instigating traditional and rightist ideas. Clearly the target was not in fact Lin, who had been dead for two years, but two other less radical leaders, Zhou Enlai and Deng. Jiang Qing knew they were her two main rivals to succeed Mao and she hoped that the campaign would mobilise revolutionary forces against them. The campaign failed. This time, the people clearly saw her personal political motives and dismissed the anti-rightist rhetoric as nonsense. However, she still had enough influence at the top of the Party to have Deng removed.

### Support for the Gang of Four

The Gang of Four had the support of many of the younger members of the Party who had benefited from the purging of older members, taking their jobs and influential positions. These younger cadres were mocked by older Party members for their lack of revolutionary experience because they had joined the Party after the struggles of the Civil War. However, what they lacked in experience they made up for in their thirst for political intrigue. The younger Party members knew that the best way to expand their influence was to force out the older cadres, so they backed the Gang of Four in their attempt to purge the more experienced leaders.

## Zhou Enlai's death

On 8 January 1976, Zhou Enlai died in a Beijing hospital. Zhou was treated with genuine affection by the public. When his body was taken to be cremated, a million people lined the streets to pay their respects. Mao was too sick to attend the funeral. Deng delivered the eulogy. Jiang attacked Deng as 'China's new Khrushchev' but again she had misread the feelings of the masses. In April, just before the traditional 'tomb sweeping festival' where Chinese people pay homage to their dead ancestors, the people of Beijing began laying wreaths at the base of the Monument to the People's Heroes in Tiananmen Square, honouring Zhou Enlai. Jiang Qing and the Gang of Four were particularly angered by this because mixed with the tributes were thinly disguised attacks on her and her colleagues, such as the poem in Source H.

**Source H** A poem written on a tribute to honour Zhou Enlai and placed in Tiananmen Square, quoted in Alan Lawrence, *China under Communism* (Routledge, 1998), page 97.

> You must be mad
> To want to be an empress
> Here's a mirror to look at yourself
> And see what you really are.
> You've got together a little gang
> To stir up trouble all the time,
> Hoodwinking the people, capering about.
> But your days are numbered ...

What criticisms does Source H make against the Gang of Four?

When the government sent trucks to remove the wreaths, clear evidence of traditional 'bourgeois' culture, tens of thousands arrived in the square to protest. Some had to be violently removed in what became known as the 'Tiananmen Square incident'.

## Deng's removal from power

The Gang of Four argued that Deng was to blame for this 'counter-revolutionary' move. They knew that he was popular and experienced and, using their influence over propaganda, hoped to brand Deng as a counter-revolutionary and have him purged. Deng was banished again, this time to a pig farm in the south. He was removed from all his political posts. The Gang of Four had hoped to ferment anti-rightist unrest against him, but the people were not interested in yet another political campaign. Unlike previous attempts to rouse the masses into action, they did not respond.

## Mao's death

Most concerned of all was Jiang Qing. When Mao died she knew that Deng would be a strong rival in the race to replace her husband as leader of China. Instead, Mao handpicked a little known bureaucrat, Hua Guofeng, to succeed him, reportedly handing him a note saying, 'With you in charge, I am at ease.' Mao presumably picked him because his obscure background meant that he had not made an enemy out of either the pragmatists or the ideologues. An amiable man, he would be a compromise between them. In July 1976, a massive earthquake shook northern China, killing a quarter of a million people. It was widely interpreted as a bad omen, further evidence of Mao's failure to eradicate traditional superstitions. This time, however, perhaps it did herald a change: on 9 September 1976, Mao died.

## Post-Mao

Hua Guofeng immediately called for total loyalty to Mao's ideas. He announced what became known as the 'two whatevers' policy: dedication to 'uphold whatever policy decisions Chairman Mao made' and 'follow whatever instructions Chairman Mao gave'.

Mao had wanted his body returned to his native province of Hunan but Hua ordered that it be embalmed and placed in a massive mausoleum in Tiananmen Square. As it lay in state, 300,000 people filed past it but there were few signs of genuine grief. Before Mao's death Jiang Qing had been treated with subservient respect, now she was ignored. She treated Hua with contempt and it was rumoured that she was organising a coup to seize power. After she criticised Hua at a State Council meeting in July 1976, Hua decided to act against her and the other members of the Gang of Four. On the night of 6 October 1976, a month after Mao had died, Hua ordered that they be arrested. They were accused of 'entering an anti-Party and anti-socialist alliance'. Zhang Chunqiao was sentenced to death, later changed to life imprisonment, Yao Wenyuan served twenty years in prison, Wang Hongwen was sentenced to life imprisonment, though he died of cancer in 1992. Jiang Qing remained unrepentant to the end of her life. She defended herself by saying, 'I was Chairman Mao's dog. I bit whomever he asked me to bite.' She was sentenced to death, but this was changed to life imprisonment. Suffering from cancer and depressed, she hanged herself in 1991.

### The return of Deng

Hua was Mao's handpicked successor, but would Mao have died a satisfied man? He was clearly worried that his policies would be reversed. 'What are you going to do without me?' he asked just before he died. It was quickly clear that Hua Guofeng was no match for Deng Xiaoping. The wily veteran returned to Beijing and quickly undermined Hua. Although he remained Party Chairman, it was Deng who had the strongest support within the Party. Deng became China's Paramount Leader. This was not an official title, but meant that Deng was the most powerful man in China. Deng introduced economic reforms that gave the people more freedoms.

Far from calling for left-wing revolution, the overwhelming number of Chinese people embraced Deng's new policies. The economy quickly recovered from the chaos of the Cultural Revolution. Some parts of China were untouched. When PLA soldiers went to the countryside to aid the peasants they found that many villagers had never heard of the Cultural Revolution.

'To be rich is glorious,' announced Deng and after years of repression and control, the Chinese people embraced the opportunity to improve their standard of living. Today the Chinese economy is one of the fastest growing in the world, firmly taking the so-called 'capitalist road' that Mao had fought so hard to avoid.

## Conclusion: Winding down the Cultural Revolution, 1968-76

Historians still argue about Mao's motives for the Cultural Revolution. Was it a serious attempt to remould Chinese culture or simply an attempt to remove rivals to his personal authority? Although the debate goes on, it is striking that once his primary opponents, Liu and Deng, had been purged, he moved quickly to restore order and end the chaos. His cult of personality and the support of Lin Biao ensured that he could rely upon the PLA to take control of the Red Guards. Fully 'rectified', the Party was restored to authority but by this point Mao himself was an elderly man. With one eye on his impending death, a power struggle broke out within the Party to control its future direction, with Jiang Qing and the ideologues seemingly well placed to seize power. By then, though, the people had tired of the endless campaigns and **radicalism** was rejected. The open antipathy towards Jiang Qing helped give Hua Guofeng the confidence to act against the Gang of Four. Their arrest and purging ended China's transformation towards a truly communist state, with Deng Xiaoping introducing economic freedoms. Perhaps Mao had been right to call Deng a 'capitalist roader' all along. Deng took China along exactly the kind of 'capitalist road' that Mao had feared.

### Work together

In 1981 the CCP Central Committee approved a resolution which affirmed that 'gross mistakes were made in the Cultural Revolution' but Mao's 'merits are primary and his errors secondary' in the proportion of seven to three.

In pairs, prepare for a debate. Look back through your notes. One of you should list evidence to support this judgement of Mao. The other should search for evidence that rejects it. At the end of the debate decide which point of view you agree with.

## Chapter summary

- After the Great Leap Forward it was clear that there was a split within the CCP. 'Ideologues' argued in favour of continued commitment to Mao Zedong Thought. The 'pragmatists' believed that ideological purity was less important than practical needs.
- By the mid-1960s Mao was increasingly worried that his colleagues within the Communist Party, particularly Liu Shaoqi and Deng Xiaoping, were not committed to his communism and really wanted to 'take the capitalist road' to development.
- Mao believed that once revolutionaries took power they inevitably became a new elite, taking advantage of their new authority and exploiting the masses. Mao advocated permanent, ongoing revolution to prevent this happening.
- During the Cultural Revolution Mao's cult of personality reached absurd heights. He used the fact that the young people of China had been taught to view him as having near-supernatural powers to convince them to attack his opponents.
- Urged on at massive rallies where the young people worshipped Mao like a god, the Red Guards launched attacks on the so-called 'Four Olds': culture, customs, habits and ideas.
- Soon Mao's urging them to 'Bombard the Headquarters' – in other words attack figures in authority – spiralled out of control. China descended into anarchy as rival Red Guards and worker groups battled against each other, each believing themselves to be the true defenders of Mao's revolution.
- The PLA was loyal to Mao. It was led by Lin Biao who served Mao without question. When the Red Guard violence got out of hand, Mao was able to use Lin and the PLA to end it.
- Ultimately, Mao's most important target was Liu Shaoqi. His former colleague and head of the Chinese state was publicly humiliated at huge struggle meetings, tortured and beaten. He died in 1969.
- After the PLA had restored order, Mao sent millions of former Red Guards into the countryside to help peasants in their villages. This had two effects: it was meant to teach the Red Guards about the hardships of their rural comrades' lives but also to disperse them across China so that they could not cause more unrest.
- One of the targets of the purge, Deng Xiaoping, was brought back to political power by Mao. Deng was an experienced and able administrator and Mao needed him to rebuild China.
- Mao died in September 1976. Before he died, he named a little-known bureaucrat, Hua Guofeng, as his successor.
- Mao's wife and her radical colleagues, damned later as 'The Gang of Four', had increased their power greatly through the Cultural Revolution. They did not want the violence to end. Knowing that Hua was inexperienced, they believed that they could also seize power from him.
- Fearing a coup, Hua ordered the arrest of the Gang of Four. They were sent to prison for their part in the violence and terror of the Cultural Revolution.
- Deng, crafty and popular, was then able to undermine Hua's influence. He became China's main leader and set the nation on the path to becoming the economic superpower that it is today.

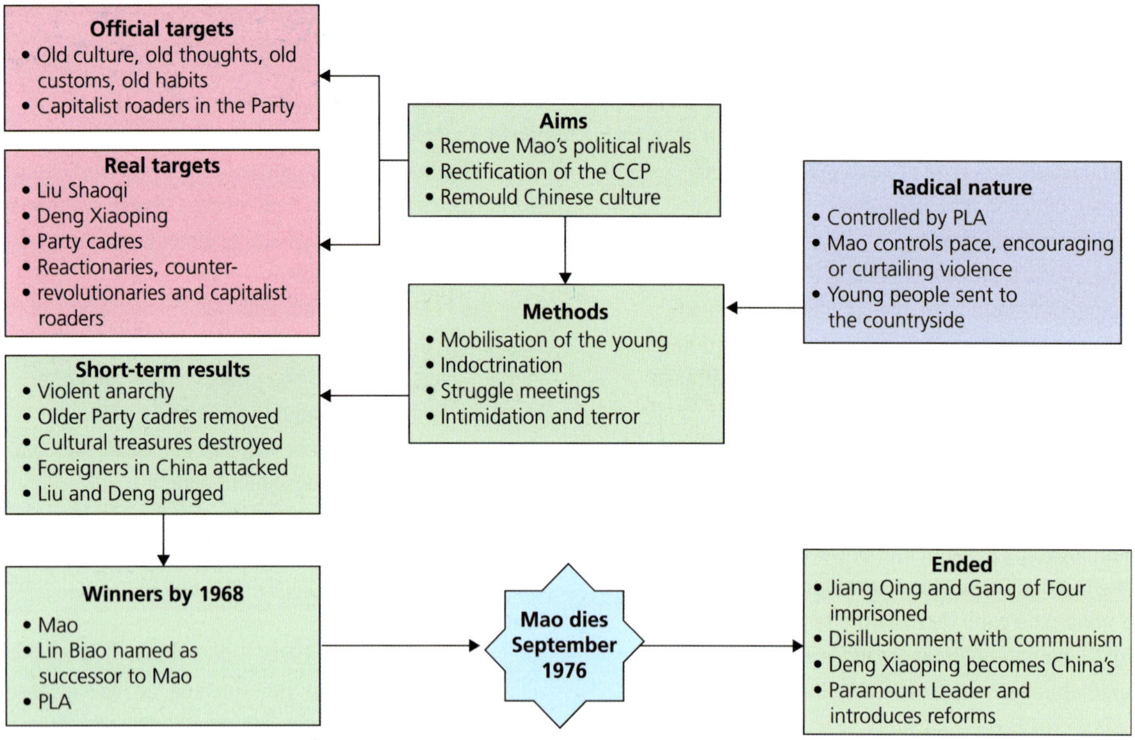


▲ **Summary diagram: The Cultural Revolution and its aftermath, 1966–76.**

## Recommended reading

L. Feigon, *Mao: A Re-Interpretation* (Ivan R. Dee, 2002). Revisionist account of Mao's rule, particularly Chapter 8 'The Cultural Revolution Revisited' that stresses the more positive aspects of the event.

G. Yuan, *Born Red: A Chronicle of the Cultural Revolution* (Stanford University Press, 1997). Recollections of a former Red Guard. Disturbing account of how the idealistic student movement quickly descended into jealousy and violence.

R. *Mao Zedong and China in the Twentieth-century World: A Concise History* (Duke University Press, 2010). Highly readable account. Chapters 8 and 9 focus upon the Cultural Revolution up to the death of Mao.

A. Lawrence, *China under Communism* (Routledge, 1998). Chapter 6 provides a concise and readable account of the Cultural Revolution. A good starting point for readers interested in the topic.

R. Macfarquhar and M. Schoenhals, *Mao's Last Revolution* (Harvard University Press, 2006). Expansive scholarly treatment, highly detailed but readable, authoritative text.

D. Priestland, *The Red Flag: Communism and the Making of the Modern World* (Penguin, 2009). Not focused solely on China, but on the whole of the communist world, Chapter 8 compares the Cultural Revolution to events in other communist countries.

R. Terrill, *Madame Mao: The White-Boned Demon* (Stanford University Press, 1992). Biography of Jiang Qing. Chapters 6 and 7 focus on her role in the Cultural Revolution and her attempt to succeed Mao as ruler of China.

# Section A: Essay technique

## Contextualising the sources

In order to understand the sources properly, you need to place them in the context in which they were written. Specifically, you need to consider the background or environment in which the source was produced. This may sound obvious, but twentieth-century sources were produced by twentieth-century people, and therefore reflect their experiences, beliefs and prejudices at the time they were written. This means that sources are never stand-alone documents – they should be understood within the context of the values and assumptions of the society that produced them.

In essence, your task when contextualising the sources is to try to understand the world in the same way as the writers of the sources. In short, you should try to see things their way.

Understanding the context is an important part of evaluating the evidence that the sources contain.

Imagine you are answering the following question:

**How far could the historian make use of Sources 1 and 2 (page 284) together to investigate the reasons why Mao launched the Cultural Revolution?**

You have read about the Cultural Revolution in this Key Topic. If you wish to remind yourself of this re-read the chapter or your notes. This is important before embarking on an exercise about context.

One way to contextualise the sources is to begin by asking the question: what issue is this source contributing to? The reason for this is that sources are written for specific purposes. In this case they may have been written for propaganda purposes or intended to boost support for the Cultural Revolution. Below is an example of an attempt to put Source 1 in context.

**Source 1** An article from the *People's Daily*, June 1966. The *People's Daily* is an official newspaper of the Chinese Government.

At present the representatives of the bourgeoisie, the bourgeois 'scholars' and 'authorities' in China are dreaming precisely of restoring capitalism. The Proletarian Cultural Revolution is aimed not only at demolishing all the old ideology and culture and all the old customs and habits which, fostered by the exploiting classes, have poisoned the minds of the people for thousands of years, but also at creating and fostering among the masses an entirely new ideology and culture and entirely new customs and habits – those of the proletariat. This great task of transforming customs and habits is without any precedent in human history. As for all the heritage, customs and habits of the feudal and bourgeois classes, the proletarian world outlook must be used to subject them to thoroughgoing criticism. Facts have eloquently proved that Mao Zedong's thought becomes a moral atom bomb of colossal power once it takes hold of the masses.

Mao launched the Cultural Revolution to inspire the masses to attack his opponents in the Communist Party who he believed wanted to abandon his policies and re-establish capitalism. They were the 'authorities' referred to here.

Mao wanted to replace these old ideas with new, communist ones in order to fundamentally transform the whole of Chinese society into one that believed in his ideology.

During the Cultural Revolution, Mao encouraged his supporters to view him as an almost divine being. People were taught to view everything he said as the word of God.

This article was written at the very start of the Cultural Revolution in order to explain to the Chinese people why it was necessary and generate support among the people for the campaign. The *People's Daily* was the official newspaper of the government. This source is propaganda, defending the Cultural Revolution and supporting the attack on Mao's enemies.

As part of the Cultural Revolution Mao launched the 'Four Olds Campaign' to encourage people to attack these old-fashioned ideas.

Mao encouraged the people to rise up and 'criticise' anyone who he accused of not supporting communist ideology. They were to be humiliated at struggle meetings and forced to write grovelling 'self-criticisms'.

It is crucial to relate your analysis of context to the question.

The context for Source 1 (see page 283) helps answer the question in the following ways:

- Mao encouraged articles like this to be published in the *People's Daily* to promote the Cultural Revolution through encouraging the mass mobilisation of the people against Mao's enemies.
- The bourgeoisie, meaning the educated and intellectual middle class, is singled out as a target of the Cultural Revolution.
- It is clear that the target of the Cultural Revolution was 'the authorities'. The only 'authority' in China was the Communist Party itself.
- The source makes clear that another target was those who wanted to return China to capitalism. Between 1961 and 1965, Liu Shaoqi and Deng Xiaoping had angered Mao by reversing his policies of the Great Leap Forward and introducing reforms like wage differentials and allowing peasants to buy and sell products at markets. To Mao, this sounded like capitalism and he launched the Cultural Revolution to crush these two rivals for power.
- Mao believed that traditional culture, ideas and traditions were being used by conservative forces to support un-communist beliefs. They acted as barriers to his vision of creating communism. He launched the Cultural Revolution to destroy old ideas and traditions.
- However, we should remember that the article does act as propaganda. It does not, for example, talk about how Mao wanted to get rid of Liu and Deng because he was worried that their economic policies were actually more popular than his own, or show that he was angry with them because of a number of personal slights that he felt indicated that they did not respect him anymore.

## Activity: AS-style questions

1 Why is Source 1 (page 283) valuable to the historian for an enquiry into the reasons why Mao launched the Cultural Revolution?

2 How much weight do you give the evidence of Source 2 for an enquiry into the behaviour of the Red Guards during the Cultural Revolution?

## Activity: Seeing things their way

Now try contextualising Source 2 below. Re-read the question on page 283 – remind yourself of the specific task you are focusing on.

1 Ask yourself the following questions and annotate a copy of the source with the answers:
   **a)** What was the purpose of the source?
   **b)** What attitudes does it display towards the Red Guards?
   **c)** Why does the author admire the Red Guards?
   **d)** What important role does the author say the Red Guards played?

2 Next write a series of bullet points outlining:
   **a)** the aspects of the source that are useful for answering the question
   **b)** the aspects of the source that are less useful
   **c)** a summary of the extent to which the source provides useful evidence concerning the reasons why Mao launched the Cultural Revolution.

**Source 2** From Han Suyin, *Wind in the Towers: Mao Zedong and the Chinese Revolution, 1949–75* (Jonathan Cape, 1976), pages 291–92. Han Suyin was born in China of a Chinese father and a Belgian mother. She was one of the few foreign writers to travel widely in China during the Cultural Revolution years.

> Everyone praised the 'little generals' [Red Guards] whose conduct was excellent, who sang 'The World belongs to Us,' and who were very clean, well behaved and polite. They began long marches, walking to places as far as Sinkiang, Manchuria, Tibet, to organise great linkups and 'exchange revolutionary experience' with other Red Guards. This enormous cavalcade through China was very well absorbed, and no Red Guard went hungry or without a bed. To pin point the few cases of bad conduct is to ignore the discipline and good example of the great majority of these youngsters. 'They left no dirt behind them ... they did not steal anything.' Never had China been so exuberant, so alive, so full of the sound of drums and cymbals and so colourful with Red Flags everywhere. Some of their actions were naïve, and some were brutal, especially when they began to conduct house searches among former capitalists ... But out of thirty million young people it would be unbelievable not to have a percentage of delinquents. The Red Guards performed a task no one else could have; they literally spring-cleaned the cities, turning up caches of gold and firearms, ferreting out many a secret agent and spy.

# Section B: Essay technique

## Overall judgement

An overall judgement is as important to a Paper 2 Section B essay as it is to essays in Paper 1. You may have already read advice about the characteristics of a good overall judgement (see pages 68–69). Remember, good judgements are supported, and the best judgements consider the relative significance of the key factors you have discussed in your essay.

Now you can practise writing an overall judgement to an essay concerning the reasons why Mao launched the Cultural Revolution.

### Activity: Detail and analysis

Imagine you are answering the following Section B-style question:

**'Mao launched the Cultural Revolution in order to remove his political rivals.' How far do you agree with this statement?**

1 Read the question and work out what type of question it is.
2 Make a plan that is appropriate to the specific question. Remember it should consist of three or four main points.
3 Add three pieces of detail to support each of your main points. Remember, use the detail that best supports the points you want to make.
4 Write an analytical sentence to conclude each of your main points.
5 Now write a conclusion to the essay.
   - Start by asserting an overall judgement.
   - Support this by weighing the different main points in your plan.
   - Summarise your overall judgement in the final sentence.

### Work together

Having completed a plan in the activity, swap it with a partner. Consider the following questions:

1 Did you agree on what type of question you were dealing with? If not, discuss it and work out who was right.
2 Whose plan most clearly focused on the specific type of question?
3 Did you both begin your conclusion with a clear judgement?
4 Did you both weigh up the different key points to support your judgement?
5 Whose overall judgement was better and why?
6 What can you learn from each other's work?

Use these questions to feed back to each other and improve your essay technique.

### Question practice

1 How far was the main reason that Mao launched the Cultural Revolution a genuine desire to remould Chinese culture? AS
2 How accurate is it to say that Mao's hold over young people was responsible for the Red Terror?

# Key Topic 4 Social and cultural changes, 1949–76

## Overview

This chapter focuses upon Mao's attempts to change Chinese society and culture. When, at the start of the Great Leap Forward, Mao spoke of the Chinese people as a 'blank sheet of paper' he was not referring only to his goal to dramatically alter their economic practices. In fact Mao aimed for nothing less than the creation of a 'New China' - a society completely transformed and a culture that represented a fundamental departure from previous traditions, attitudes, customs and morality.

This was a long cherished vision. Mao had been greatly influenced by the influx of Western and liberal ideas that had begun to challenge tradition-laden Chinese culture in the first decades of the twentieth century. This 'new culture' movement had railed against what it damned as a backward and insular society based on outdated Confucian thought, suffocating family hierarchy and entrenched patriarchy. As early as July 1919 he had declared, 'I venture to make a singular assertion: one day, the reform of the Chinese people will be more profound than that of any other people, and the society of the Chinese people will be more radiant than that of any other people.' Mao certainly attempted to make good on his transformative goals. The changes he wrought were extremely dramatic, radical and profound; their impact reverberates throughout China today. How far they brought positive and widespread benefits to the Chinese people themselves is a different matter entirely.

The overarching topic of social and cultural changes, 1949-76 is covered in four sections:

1. The changing status of women
2. Education and health provision
3. Cultural change
4. Religion.

## TIMELINE

| | |
|---|---|
| 1950 | New Marriage Law |
| 1958 | The Great Leap Forward |
| | New college entrance examinations adopted |
| 1959 | Tibetan revolt is suppressed by the PLA |
| 1963 | Emulate Lei Feng campaign introduced |
| 1964 | Mao criticises nature of education in primary and middle schools |
| 1965 | The barefoot doctors are sent out on a large scale |
| 1966 | Jiang Qing named cultural adviser to the military |
| | Cultural Revolution begins |
| | National unified college entrance examinations ended |
| 1967 | 'Up to the mountains and down to the villages' campaign |
| 1973 | Examinations for entrance to university resume |

### Note it down

Use a spider diagram to take notes for this chapter. You need a large piece of paper for this. Draw a central circle entitled 'Social and cultural changes, 1949-76'. Make 'legs' for the different sections: women's rights, education, healthcare, culture, religion. Read the different sections very carefully and add the key points for each section to your spider diagram.

# 1 The changing status of women

The traditional inferior position of women in society was a subject of great debate at the start of the twentieth century in Western democracies. This talk of equality spread to China as part of the 'new culture' intellectual movement that demanded reforms following the 1911 revolution (see page 201). At the same time as activists like the suffragettes in Britain were campaigning for voting rights, their Chinese counterparts were demanding female **emancipation** and reform.

Traditionally Chinese women were subject to the so-called 'three obediences':

- to their father when young
- to their husband when married
- to their son in old age.

Many women were forced into arranged marriages against their will. They could not own property and had no political voice.

From an early age, Mao had been critical of this subservient role that Chinese society and politics afforded to women. 'Women,' he said 'hold up half the sky', and the Communist Party called women 'an indispensable force in defeating the enemy and building a new China'.

This section focuses on the way women's lives changed under communist rule. It examines legal changes to marriage to make it more equal and reforms dedicated to freeing women from doing domestic chores, encouraging them instead to work. It evaluates the surprising impact of the **Cultural Revolution** on women's lives. It shows how these changes impacted upon the personal attitudes of the women themselves. Did communist rule really bring gender equality to China? And if it did make women more equal to men, did they really benefit?

## Note it down

Use the 1:2 method of note taking in this section (see page x). For example, write down each sub-heading in the left-hand column:

- Traditional attitudes towards women
- The Marriage Reform Law
- The impact of **collectivisation** and the communes
- The nature of change.

Then write a bullet-point list of factors relating to each.

## Traditional attitudes to women

Women held a low status in Chinese society. Many were forced into arranged marriages. Rich husbands married women to be pretty adornments, while poor men hoped to have another labourer join the household. Some were forced to marry to provide children for their new husbands. Women were not independent and not equal partners in marriage. Those married into more wealthy families might have to share their husbands with **concubines**. The poet Fu Hsuan wrote the poem in Source A in the third century.

These views still held in traditional Chinese culture 1700 years later.

**Source A** Fu Hsuan, *Woman*, third century, quoted in William Hinton, *Fanshen: A Documentary of Revolution in a Chinese Village* (Monthly Review Press, 1966), page 157.

How sad it is to be a woman.
Nothing on earth is held so cheep.
Boy stand leaning at the door
Like gods fallen out of heaven.
Their hearts brave the Four Oceans,
The wind and dust of a thousand miles.
No one is glad when a girl is born:
By her the family sets no store.

What can we learn about the attitude to women from the poem in Source A?

## Mao's views on marriage

Mao was an advocate of women's rights long before he came to power. In 1919 he was moved by the suicide of Miss Zhao, a young bride whose marriage had been arranged against her will. The bride slit her own throat on the way to the wedding ceremony and bled to death. Mao published a number of articles in local newspapers arguing that the tragedy had been caused by the 'rottenness of the marriage system'. He cited the proverb, 'Better a shattered piece of jade than an unbroken pot of clay,' and called her suicide 'an act of true courage'.

Mao complained that while 'A man in China is usually subjected to the domination of three systems of authority – political, clan and religious,' in addition women were 'also dominated by men' through 'the authority of the husband'. What he called 'the four authorities' were 'the embodiment of the whole **feudal-patriarchal ideology**'. They were 'the four thick ropes' that constrained women and he damned arranged marriage as 'indirect rape'.

Perhaps Mao's intense interest also resulted from the fact that Mao himself had been party to an arranged marriage against his will. When he was fourteen his parents had arranged for him to marry a woman seven years older from a local influential and wealthier family. Mao resisted the marriage and claimed later that he 'never lived with her' and that he 'did not consider her my wife'.

## Foot binding

Many women were physically crippled by foot binding, a practice begun by the ruling class in the court of the capital, but widely emulated throughout China. A girl would often have her feet bound at the age of six. Her toes were turned under her feet and held there by tightly wound bandages. This prevented feet from growing normally and the bone structure would become deformed. The small feet and the swaying gait that this induced was revered as beautiful and sexually appealing. 'My feet hurt so much that for two years I had to crawl on my hands and knees,' one woman recalls. 'Sometimes at night my feet hurt so much that I could not sleep.' Although the practice was officially banned in 1911, it continued, especially in northern villages. An anti-foot binding movement had begun in the 1880s, led in large part by **Christian missionaries**, but it was deeply rooted in traditional culture. A significant proportion of **Han Chinese**, the dominant racial group, practised foot binding.

**Source B** A Chinese woman's feet distorted by foot binding.

What can you learn from the photograph in Source B about the practice of foot binding and what it shows about women's status in traditional Chinese culture?

## Traditional attitudes to marriage

A woman's sense of inferiority was enforced from a young age. A girl baby was often not valued as highly as her more privileged brothers. This was in part because a daughter would often be married out of the family in her early teens. Once she left the family she would be forced to submit to her new husband's authority. Thus she would be lost to the family just when she might have become economically productive. This loss was increased by the practice of giving away a **dowry** with the bride for the benefit of the bridegroom's family. Jewellery might be given by wealthy families while peasant families might provide clothing, bedding or simple kitchen items like pots and pans. Such was the economic burden that when times were hard a daughter might be denied food in favour of her more valuable brothers. Desperate families sometimes even resorted to **infanticide** to escape the burden of raising a girl.

Sometimes gifts were given to the family of the bride by the bridegroom's family and this only reinforced the sense of the bride as property that had been purchased. Having paid for marriages, many husbands treated their wives as private property and expected them to carry out domestic work with a subservient attitude. Husbands objected to women speaking out of turn or leaving the home, and many were beaten. Even the death of the husband might not provide relief. Confucian ethics abhorred the remarriage of widows, leaving them economically vulnerable.

## Attitudes of mothers-in-law

Once married, the new bride was not only subservient to her husband but to all senior members of his family, most particularly her mother-in-law. In her study of women in China between 1949 and 1958, Delia Davin observes that because a traditional Confucian marriage was unlikely to provide emotional support, the mothers-in-law often compensated for this by staying close to their son, who would look after them in old age. This meant that they were very jealous of their son's wife and could be petty and spiteful. For example, the new bride would be given the most unpleasant or backbreaking chores by the mother-in-law. Mistakes often resulted in beatings.

## Educational opportunities

Gender discrimination extended to education. While boys were valued, girls were simply not provided with educational opportunities. There was no incentive to send them to school because they would soon be leaving home and the parents would experience no economic benefit from their education. One survey of rural China in the 1930s suggested that only 1 per cent of females over the age of seven had acquired a level of literacy required to read a simple letter, in comparison to 30 per cent for males, while 45.2 per cent of males and just 2.2 per cent of females had received schooling.

## Popular sayings

Discriminatory attitudes to wives were long held and deeply rooted in Chinese culture. Popular sayings such as this one summed up the situation:

*'When husbands are angry, they beat their wives; when wives are angry, their husbands beat them.'*

On the issue of mothers-in-law, one popular saying warned:

*'Daughter is heart and son is root; even the best daughter-in-law is of a different surname.'*

And another showed that daughters-in-law were expected to be wholly subservient:

*'No fighting back when beaten, no answering back when cursed.'*

## The 1950 New Marriage Law

So strong was Mao's commitment to improving women's rights that a New Marriage Law was one of the very first pieces of legislation that the new regime introduced when it took power.

- For the first time women received legal equality: they could hold property and seek divorce.
- The paying of dowries or bride-prices was forbidden, as was child marriage: women had to be 18 years old before they could marry.
- Marriages could not result from coercion: free-will was required.

Mao considered the New Marriage Law to be one of his greatest achievements. He declared:

> *'This democratic marriage system has burst the feudal shackles that have bound human beings, especially women, for thousands of years, and established a new pattern consistent with human nature.'*

However, for all Mao's optimism, it soon became clear that simple legal changes were not enough to transform the lives of China's women.

The regime also advocated later marriage and childbirth. Delaying marriage and childbirth meant that:

> *'the broad masses of the people have more time and energy to read and study, to participate in political activity ... it enables them to study Marxism, Leninism and the writings of Chairman Mao.'*

There is some evidence to suggest that the New Marriage Law and propaganda was effective. Statistics show that between 1946 and 1949, in 18.6 per cent of marriages the bride was aged 16 to 17. By 1958–65 this had dropped to 2.4 per cent. Similarly, in the late 1940s, 30.6 per cent of marriages were organised by parental arrangement. By 1966–76 this had dropped to 0.8 per cent.

**Source C** The New Marriage Law of the People's Republic of China (1950), Selected Articles. Quoted in Mark Selden (ed.), *The People's Republic of China: A Documentary History of Revolutionary Change* (Monthly Review Press, 1979), pages 193–200.

> *Article 2:* Bigamy, concubinage, child betrothal, interference with the remarriage of widows, and the extraction of money or gifts in connection with marriages, shall be prohibited.
>
> *Article 3:* Marriage shall be based upon the complete willingness of the two partners. Neither party shall use compulsion and no third party shall be allowed to interfere.
>
> *Article 7:* Husband and wife are companions living together and shall enjoy equal status in the home.
>
> *Article 10*: Both husband and wife shall have equal rights in the possession and management of family property.
>
> *Article 12*: Both husband and wife shall have the right to inherit each other's property.
>
> *Article 16:* Husband or wife shall not maltreat or discriminate against children born of a previous marriage.
>
> *Article 17:* Divorce shall be granted when husband and wife both desire it.
>
> *Article 18:* The husband shall not apply for a divorce when his wife is with child. He may apply for divorce only one year after the birth of the child. In the case of a woman applying for divorce, this restriction does not apply.
>
> *Article 19:* The consent of a member of the revolutionary army on active service who maintains correspondence with his or her family must first be obtained before his or her spouse can apply for divorce.

- Which of the articles in Source C represented the most radical change?
- Which one might have been the most popular?
- Which ones do you think may have created the most resistance?

### Impact of the New Marriage Law

Although rape, exploitation and domestic violence still clearly took place, in some cases women chose relationships based on calculated decisions to improve their quality of life. Women knew that the Party **cadres** had access to the commune bank and the village grain store. They could arrange the necessary travel documents to enable romantic visits to the opera. Many self-interested women sought to take advantage of New Marriage Law Article 1, that abolished the compulsory arranged marriages to overcome Article 19 that made it hard for spouses of **PLA** soldiers to obtain a divorce. 'My husband's out making revolution,' argued one woman to the local court officials, 'Because of this I'm at home and am so busy I have no spare time. How come this isn't considered work for the revolution?' PLA wives 'do not value their own honour,' lamented the Women's Federation. 'All they want to do is to eat and drink well and have fun.'

## Problems with the New Marriage Law

Enforcement of the New Marriage Law was problematic. Men who had paid a bride-price expected to be able to reap an economic reward from their marriage and they were extremely upset. The law led to rocketing divorce rates, with 1.4 million petitions filed in 1953.

As a result, many men lost what they perceived as a financial investment. This was particularly problematic in poor peasant families. The status of mothers-in-law was reduced. No longer could they force their will upon their son's wives. Widespread violence broke out as armed mobs attempted to violently reclaim divorced wives. Snubbed husbands attacked wives during divorce court proceedings. One man shackled his wife's ankles and forced her to cut firewood and dig for food. She was only released six weeks later when other people noticed what he had done.

### Attitudes of the cadres

Many cadres were ambivalent or hostile to the new law. Some feared that free choice in marriage would 'throw all under Heaven into turmoil' while others feared that only rich men would be able to find wives. A 1950 report observed that:

> *'Cadres with conservative views and backward feudal ideas are unwilling and fear to educate the masses ... [They] ... do not understand that we should take the position of women's liberation.'*

Such was the controversial nature of the new law that many Party cadres simply refused to uphold the law in their local areas, instead siding with the local population because they feared resistance and unrest.

### Attitudes to gender equality in Muslim areas

Traditional Muslim communities greatly resented the challenge to their long-held customs. In non-Han Chinese areas such as Xinjiang, far from Beijing, life for women in many rural communities continued largely unchallenged and unchanged. Although the Marriage Reform Law had been trumpeted through an extensive propaganda campaign, it is telling that such was the level of opposition that in 1953 the Party thought it necessary to launch a second campaign to try to promote it.

## The impact of collectivisation and the communes on women's lives

The success of the **Great Leap Forward** (see page 242) relied not only upon the mass mobilisation of men, but also upon the utilisation of women as productive labour. Although there were some regional differences, most women across the country did not work in the fields. Only the poorest peasant women were compelled to support their men in farm work out of economic necessity. As a result, in 1955 Mao warned, 'With the completion of agricultural co-operation, many co-operatives are finding themselves short of labour,' and now 'It has become necessary to arouse the great mass of women.' China's women were 'a vast reserve of labour power' that must be 'tapped in the struggle to build a great **socialist** country'.

Mao claimed that enabling women to work would bring them 'liberation through labour' and argued that this represented a form of equality because if women worked they could earn equal pay for equal work. Those who matched men in productivity were lauded as labour heroines, the so-called 'Iron Women', much like the propaganda in Soviet Russia that idolised factory workers who broke production records (see page 53). To enable them to join the workforce they had to be freed from their domestic roles. In the new communes created during the Great Leap Forward, childcare would be centralised by the creation of Party **kindergarten**, while the burden of food preparation would be alleviated through communal canteens (see page 237).

Mao hoped that the communes would release women from domestic servitude but this was not the case. Equality did not represent an improvement in the quality of life, for although more women now worked, they still largely took responsibility for domestic chores such as childcare and cleaning. Labour-intensive production relied on women taking on unfamiliar tasks such as ploughing fields, driving tractors or helping to run factories.

**Source D** Propaganda poster featuring a female agricultural worker.

What image of women in Mao's China is this poster in Source D trying to portray? How close to reality do you think this poster was?

## Kindergartens

Many mothers anguished over the marginalisation of their role when they gave up their child-rearing responsibilities to the mass kindergartens that were run by the Party. Mothers became distressed as, once they left their children at the communal kindergarten, they could be separated for weeks at a time. This sense of upset was exacerbated by the appalling level of care provided for their children. With priorities given to economically productive activity, the kindergartens were often housed in ramshackle buildings. In Daxing county children slept or ate on the floor. The kindergartens were staffed by hurriedly trained elderly or very young women, the only people left not mobilised for manual work in the fields.

Overwhelmed by the numbers of children suddenly under their supervision, standards of care were appalling. Diarrhoea, measles, chicken pox and worms spread quickly. In one kindergarten attached to a cotton factory in Beijing, 90 per cent of children got sick. In Shanghai nappies remained unchanged all day. The kindergartens reeked of urine. With the onset of famine (see page 245), the food supplies meant for the children were stolen by starving adults. Death rates were high. By the end of the Great Leap Forward, the kindergartens had collapsed, forcing starving villagers, mainly the already exhausted women, to try to care for their children as well as work and forage for food in order to survive.

## Communal canteens

The communal canteens were meant to release women from responsibility for feeding the family, but the poor quality of food and the length of time it took to get across the commune to get food actually increased women's hardship. With food allocated on the basis of the amount of physical labour performed, women were likely to receive less than men. Although women had not worked in the fields or factories, they had contributed to the household through selling handicrafts they made, such as shoes or hats. Worked to exhaustion in the fields and furnaces (see pages 245–246), this source of income was abandoned. When food ran low, it was often the women who were neglected on the grounds that men needed to have strength to go out and search for food for the family.

## The work points system

Despite public commitment to equal pay for equal work, women still received less 'work points' than men, regardless of their productivity or skill. This was because the realities of physical strength meant that while men could receive up to ten points, women were often limited to a maximum of eight. 'The result of this system,' writes historian Mark Selden, 'rooted in traditional notions of male superiority' was the 'reinforcing of the notion of women's inferiority'. It provided a disincentive for women to provide their labour to the collective economy. It also reinforced traditional gender roles because the lower earning power of wives meant that it made sense for them to sacrifice their paid labour in favour of domestic chores.

## Abuse and discrimination

Cadres took advantage of their position. In his analysis of newly accessible Party archives, historian Frank Dikotter has found overwhelming evidence of discrimination against women. Expectant mothers, forced to work throughout their pregnancy, miscarried. In one commune pregnant mothers who refused to work were forced to undress and break ice in the middle of winter. Sexual abuse was also rife. As families disintegrated during the Great Leap Forward, women were separated from husbands and became victims of the advances from cadres.

As the family unit collapsed, so did the boundaries of moral decency. Exhaustion through work and enfeeblement through starvation heightened women's vulnerability. Dikotter observes that 'rape spread like a contagion through a distressed moral landscape'. In one commune near Guangzhou, two Party secretaries of a commune forced themselves upon 34 women. In another northern village a secretary was investigated for 'taking liberties' with almost every unmarried woman in the village, raping 27 of them. Humiliation took other forms:

- In Hunan, local factory bosses forced females to work naked.
- In Zhejiang, women accused of crimes were forced to parade through the village unclothed.

## Despair

As the famine spread, many women were forced into prostitution, trading sex for food. Unsurprisingly, suicides were widespread. 'Collectivisation designed in part to liberate women from the shackles of patriarchy,' writes Dikotter, simply 'made matters worse,' while historian Rebecca Karl declares that as a result of collectivisation, the demands of work and family that she terms 'women's double burden' became 'intolerably difficult'.

# The nature and extent of change

While it is true that the regime was focused predominantly upon the need to maximise economic productivity by encouraging, then compelling, women into the workforce, it would be wrong to underemphasise the very real changes in gender relations that were transformative, though perhaps not as revolutionary as the regime proclaimed in its propaganda. The state may not have chosen to focus its resources on creating gender equality, but for the women themselves, the regime provided real and telling opportunities that they simply did not possess before. Many were determined to take advantage.

### *Woman Locomotive Driver*

The reformed status of women brought about by the **communists** was certainly trumpeted by Party propaganda. One film, *Woman Locomotive Driver*, was hailed as a 'heroic story of New China's first women locomotive drivers'. It told the story of the first woman locomotive engineer in China, trained at a technical school and assisted by a Soviet adviser. The heroine is distraught after failing her exam, but inspired by posters of labour heroines on her dormitory wall, she decides to plead to have another go. She is sent to see the Party administrator, who sits under a poster of Mao and next to a bust of the Chairman. He is impressed by her determination, and she eventually succeeds and is seen at her graduation ceremony in front of three locomotives bearing Mao's portrait.

## Changes in role: political activism

Mao's belief in mobilisation of the masses (see page 237) was applied to women.

### The Women's Association

The communists created mass organisations like the Women's Association to encourage political activism and mobilise the population behind the regime. The Central Committee appeared to be committed to a genuine role for the Association. It had 40,000 staff in 83 cities, and a publishing arm that produced books, pamphlets and newspapers proclaiming the accomplishments of the Party and exhorting women to even greater efforts for the communist cause. With an official membership of 76 million, it encouraged political activism.

The Women's Association set up ploughing lessons for women, organised classes to improve literacy and for the study of political ideas. Financial support was provided to help women weave uniforms or make shoes for the PLA, although, of course, these roles did reinforce traditional gender expectations. Wives and mothers were urged to encourage their husbands and sons to enlist for social benefit and economic progression. The Association clearly provided women with an avenue for social and political progression, as well as assisting in the campaigns against issues relevant to them, like prostitution.

### Finding a voice

The Women's Association did have some successes. One example of women's greater sense of self-confidence was their willingness to stand up and declare their grievances at the 'speak bitterness' meetings organised to denounce the regime's enemies. Often it was women, wrote William Hinton in his study of rural life in China, 'that had as many if not more grievances than the men' and that, given a chance to speak in public for the first time, found 'that they were as good at it as their fathers and husbands'. Hinton's study notes a number of occasions when women, encouraged by the local Women's Association, rose up to physically confront men who had beaten their wives. He recalls that at one meeting one 'panic-stricken husband' was attacked by women so aggressively that he was forced to cry out, 'Stop, I'll never beat her again.' The husband was 'sent home with a warning,' notes Hinton, that if he 'so much as lay a finger on his wife again ... he would receive more of the same.' Other women got together to write to abusers warning of the consequences if the domestic violence did not stop. Some women felt empowered to take matters into their own hands. In one case a woman was accused of poisoning her husband because he would not accept a divorce.

### The Cultural Revolution

Women were certainly politicised to the same extent as their male counterparts during the Cultural Revolution. Men and women wore the same Maoist uniform, representing a form of escape from gender expectations. Many women and girls led **Red Guards** in their violent denunciations. Once politicised, women stayed involved. In one study of Party cadres, women comprised between 8 and 12 per cent from 1958 to 1966, but between 16 and 21 per cent from 1970 to 1974. They were exalted as revolutionary heroes in ballets like 'Red Detachment of Women' that described female soldiers fighting against the Nationalists in the Civil War.

## Changes in education and employment

The communist state also succeeded in encouraging more families to send their daughters to school. One sample of rural girls who started school between 1929 and 1949 showed that only 38 per cent completed their primary education whereas 100 per cent did so for those starting after 1959. By 1978, 45 per cent of primary school children were girls.

Reforms also provided some more unusual opportunities. One was military service. In autumn 1949 the PLA enlisted unmarried, educated female students aged eighteen to nineteen for its military academies, specifically to be sent to the border region of Xinjiang (see map, page 210) in order to become wives for the soldiers stationed there. The Party was worried that PLA soldiers would find life on the frontiers too difficult without female companionship, but in order to avoid conflict with local men, the Han Chinese were strictly forbidden from marrying local, non-Han women. 'We want them to come and be good workers, good wives and good mothers,' said one military leader.

In February 1951 an advertisement in the *New Hunan Daily* aimed to recruit professionals, skilled workers and female students to form a female work team to go to Xinjiang to exploit its valuable natural resources like oil and gas reserves. The advertisement offered a range of formerly unattainable incentives such as paid study in the **Soviet Union**, teaching of advanced technology or becoming an actress in PLA entertainment troupes. The advertisement was answered enthusiastically. It offered the opportunity for rural women to escape the grinding poverty of their lives. The opportunity also held real appeal for educated women. The PLA promised that middle school graduates would be appointed as platoon leaders and college graduates would become company commanders. Finally, it was an opportunity for women who had been marginalised by their family background in the exploiting classes (see page 264). Under the communists, those from rich peasant or landlord families were discriminated against in employment and shunned socially. A military career was a chance to prove their commitment to the new regime.

## Women in the Party

Despite the New Marriage Law the Communist Party itself did not always live up to its own promises of gender equality. This failure did not go unnoticed by female Party members.

Ding Ling damned what she saw as the degraded status and exploitation of women by communist leaders. In 1942 she wrote an essay that noted that women were expected to be as 'hard as steel' but that women remained the source of gossip about relationships and conduct in their private lives in a way that men were not. In 1957 Ding Ling was denounced as part of the Anti-Rightist Campaign and her writing was banned.

Another leader, Song Qing-ling was the sister-in-law of Mao's Civil War opponent, Chiang Kai-shek, and in 1959 rose to become the Vice Chairman of the **PRC**. She complained that, despite her high status, she was not taken seriously by her fellow political leaders.

Indeed, most women at national government level owed their influence in large part to their husbands. Wang Guangmei became famous for her support of her husband Liu Shaoqi, travelling with him on diplomatic visits (see page 273). The most famous example is Jiang Qing who encouraged the violence and destruction of the Cultural Revolution (see page 262). How far she was able to act independently is unclear but her nickname, 'Madame Mao', suggests why this minor Shanghai actress was able to accrue such formidable influence.

One recruit recalled her mother's joy when she heard that she had joined the PLA because 'her bourgeois family now became a revolutionary soldier's family'. Even then, however, gender roles and expectations were not transformed for these women. When they finished their time in the PLA, home making and child rearing became again their primary focus.

However, the very fact that these opportunities for travel and study existed was important in beginning the process of changing attitudes of both men and women towards gender equality.

## The problems of changing traditional views

Many women understood that land ownership was the key to real equality. 'In the past men always said, "You depend on me for a living. You just stay home and eat the things I earn,"' recalled one Women's Association leader, 'But after women get their share they can say, "I got this grain from my own land and I can live without you by my own labour."' The collectivisation of land ended this possibility. After waiting so long to be able to hold property, all land ownership was banned.

Definitive judgements regarding the extent of change in women's lives after 1949 are problematic. This is particularly so with peasant women. These 'women were doubly marginalised,' writes historian Gail Hershatter, 'by virtue of both location and gender.' She notes that official, written records are inadequate evidence for the degree to which state policies changed their lives.

For all the campaigns and propaganda, it was clear that women still held the less influential jobs and still were expected to undertake most of the household and childcare chores. Divorcees often struggled, cut off from family support. With the focus on increasing the population to make China a strong nation, modern contraception methods were rare.

## Conclusion: The changing status of women

There remains no consensus among historians as to the impact of the CCP's reforms towards gender equality. It is clear that a simple change in the law could not change long-held attitudes or traditions overnight. There was a great deal of opposition to the Marriage Reform Law, particularly in isolated rural areas, and there are clear regional disparities. As recently as 2005, the situation of women in Xinjiang was described as 'like being a frog in a well: all they can see is a tiny bit of sky, so their outlook is very narrow. A woman is treated as a man's possession.' Even though life in the communes promised greater equality, women were never alleviated of the double burden of increased demands for economic productivity alongside domestic roles and childcare. Equality did not necessarily mean a better life.

However, Mao gave young Chinese, particularly women, a sense of personal identity and emancipation and equality. Their involvement in politics improved their self-esteem. Far from being simply victims of policy or unwitting targets of empty propaganda, from the perspective of the women themselves, the Chinese revolution represented an unequalled opportunity, if not one always realised, to achieve a level of economic security and social equity that was simply inconceivable under previous regimes.

## Work together

Divide the sub-headings in this section between you. Re-read your notes on the sub-headings you have made (see page 287), then put your notes away. Then take it in turns to explain a sub-heading to your partner. After you have finished each sub-heading, both look at your notes. Discuss what you missed out, and define any terms that either of you found difficult to understand or explain.

## 2 Education and health provision

Mao had long declared educational reform to be a key priority. He was particularly vexed by the inequality of educational opportunity. In his 1927 *Report on the investigation of the Peasant Movement in Hunan* he had declared that 'In China education has always been the exclusive preserve of the landlords,' and complained that 'the peasants have had no access to it', meaning that '90 per cent of the people have had no education.' What education they did have was from modern schools that the regime damned as 'foreign style schools' which did not serve the needs of workers and peasants. The attitude of the teachers 'towards the peasants was very bad, and far from being helpful to the peasants, they became objects of dislike.' The peasants preferred 'old style schooling' that taught Confucian morals, but neither type of education would realise the transformation towards **communism** that Mao sought.

Between 1949 and 1965 educational policy switched back and forth between the desire to replicate successful reforms introduced into communist held areas during the Civil War, the pressing needs of economic production and the constantly changing levels of commitment to follow the Soviet model. After 1965, the entire education system was thrown into chaos by the Cultural Revolution. Education was undoubtedly one of the most important tools used by the regime for transforming China into a communist nation. There is no doubt that the regime did make some progress in educational reforms across the entire period. How much the people of China themselves enjoyed the benefits remains a matter of historical debate.

### Note it down

- Take a piece of A3 paper and draw a graph. On the horizontal axis make a timeline with dates from 1949 to 1976. On the vertical axis, write 'Successes and failures of education policy'.
- As you read this section, write down the most important changes in educational policy on sticky notes.
- Use the horizontal axis to place the notes in time order on the graph. Place them towards the top of the page if they were successful and towards the bottom if they failed. You can complete this activity twice: first place them on the graph according to how successful they were for the Chinese people. Then repeat, but this time according to how successful they were for Mao and the Communist Party. For added complexity you could colour code to represent primary, secondary and higher education.
- When you have finished, reflect on the question: 'How successful were Mao's education policies?'

### Education before reform

Any evaluation of the success of the communist regime in ending educational inequalities must consider the very low educational levels that the regime inherited from the **nationalists** at the end of the Civil War. One contemporary study of education in rural China showed that:

- only 30 per cent of all males over seven years of age, and just 1 per cent of all females over the same age, could read a simple letter
- 45.2 per cent of males and only 2.2 per cent of females had received any schooling
- males attended on average four years of schooling; those females who did receive schooling attended for three years.

Two-thirds received education of a traditional style, learning fundamental Confucian concepts of morality and **filial piety** through the study of the same classical works used since AD400 to prepare students for the imperial examinations designed to become bureaucrats for the imperial dynasties.

### Subjects

Practical subjects required by a modern economy such as arithmetic and science were not included. Although the imperial examinations had been abolished in 1905 and more modern schools with Western-style curricula had been created, they were few in number and only in the cities. The system remained elitist: the best kindergartens and primary schools were located in the cities in wealthier neighbourhoods, charged prohibitive tuition fees and set entrance examinations that reduced access.

Within higher education humanities studies dominated: over 59 per cent of students enrolled on full-time degree programmes studied law, politics or the **liberal arts**. Just 10 per cent studied natural science, 11.5 per cent engineering and only 3 per cent agriculture.

#### Rote learning

Pedagogy was based on rote learning from books, which Mao had been openly dismissive of. 'Of the little progress I have made over these last few years,' he wrote in 1915, 'only the smaller part was achieved through books. The larger part of my solution was the result of questioning and seeking solutions to [practical] difficulties.' In 1917, seven of Mao's fellow students had died, apparently of overwork and excessive study. He wrote that:

> *'speculating on the intentions of the educators, one is led to wonder whether they did not design such an unwieldy curriculum in order to exhaust the students, to trample on their bodies and ruin their lives ... And if someone has an above-average intelligence, they give him all sorts of supplementary readings ... how stupid!'*

## Educational reform, 1949–58

Once in power, the communist regime sought to radically alter the situation.

### Improving literacy

A new form of written language was introduced in order to simplify the traditional and highly complex characters. Between 1949 and 1957 the number of primary school students increased from approximately 26 million to 64 million. In rural areas the *min-pan* 'run by the people' primary schools, financially supported and managed by the local village, were key to improving access. The Party aimed to establish a *min-pan* school in every village. Winter schools provided short courses for adult peasants. The Party claimed that 42 million peasants attended in the winter of 1951–52. For all these changes, the Higher Education Minister admitted that 78 per cent of the population remained illiterate and that only 52 per cent of school age children were attending primary schools.

### Higher education

University enrolments almost quadrupled from 117,000 to 441,000. The campaigns of the early 1950s had forced out most Western faculty and missionary educators (see page 211). Higher education was modelled closely on the Soviet Union (see page 137), with a separate Ministry of Education set up in November 1952, as in the USSR, to co-ordinate the introduction of prescribed teaching plans, materials and textbooks. They were adhered to, one administrator recalled, 'as though it was the law'. Between 1952 and 1958, 600 Russians taught in Chinese colleges and universities and, by 1959, 38,000 Chinese students had been trained in Russian universities, including teachers, students and workers. Instead of the liberal arts, the focus was upon training more students to undertake specialised technical jobs necessary for the running of a modern economy. Twenty new polytechnics and 26 new engineering institutes specialising in steelmaking, mining and geology were created. By 1953, 63 per cent of students were in engineering, medicine and agriculture. The imitation of the Soviet model reached absurd heights: college students took their oral examinations seated at cloth-covered tables upon which sat vases of flowers simply because 'that was the way the Russians did it'.

### The introduction of Pinyin

One handicap to the creation of a singular national identity in China was the issue of communication. Different groups and areas of China had very different languages and there was no standardised written alphabet. Words were written not with letters, but as different symbols. This was very complex: each word had a different symbol that had to be learned. In 1955 the government introduced a new written language with letters based on the Latin alphabet. Instead of symbols, the letters meant that words in Mandarin, the main language, could be pronounced phonetically. This greatly improved communication. It was one of the regime's most enduring reforms and remains the form of written language in China today.

### How did the regime use education to build belief in communism?

Creating commitment to communism was a priority of the education system. Attributes such as self-sacrifice for the nation, obedience and discipline were instilled. Students were taught that there existed a 'correct' solution or answer to every question, contained in Marxist thought, as defined by the Party. All competing ideas or past beliefs were rejected in favour of the new 'truth'. Reading lists included major speeches of Chinese communist leaders and works by **Lenin** and Marx, as well as the details of the Agrarian Reform Law and the **Common Program**.

### The failures of reform, 1949–58

Despite these changes the education system remained stubbornly elitist and inequitable. Although the CCP promised to make opportunities available to workers and peasants, the formal academic requirements needed for admission to **middle schools** and universities favoured both the children of the old **bourgeoisie** and the new privileged class: children of Party officials. Universities still serviced mainly urban students and many rural children still did not receive an education. Instead of the imperial bureaucracy, graduates now sought prestigious roles within the Party and government. A new communist elite had replaced the old imperial one. Although literacy programmes were introduced in many villages, the teaching was left to barely educated cadres, many of whom possessed only a rudimentary elementary level of education themselves. Available school places simply did not meet demand. The winter schools were not effective in creating literacy since many peasants forgot what they had learned from one winter to the next.

## The Great Leap Forward

The Great Leap Forward heralded the next change in educational policy. A 'Directive on education work' issued in September 1958 criticised bourgeois ideas such as 'education for education's sake' and a belief that 'education can only be led by experts'. In future, the promotion of teachers was to be dependent largely on their political qualifications and practical abilities, with their academic credentials as secondary concerns. Manual labour was introduced into the curriculum to prepare students to help expand China's economic power. The Ministry of Higher Education was abolished. The *min-pan* school principle was extended to secondary schools. Mao promoted a 'half work half study' curriculum that rejected the traditional rote-learning techniques. Instead, new agricultural middle schools ran vocational courses on agricultural techniques along with basic maths and languages in order to prepare peasants to be able to operate local rural industries and, in future, support the introduction of modern agricultural techniques.

Reducing the dependence on urban universities and schools would contribute to Mao's goal of reducing inequalities between town and country and 'foster students who are socialist minded and cultured labourers and ensure their moral, intellectual and physical development to produce new men of communism'. By 1960, there were approximately 30,000 schools, one per commune, with a total of 2.9 million students.

## Impact of the Great Leap Forward

The failure of the Great Leap Forward caused another change: the Education Minister was forced to admit that 'schools had cut too many classes for the sake of their productive labour activities'. Many potential students had not been able to attend school because they were needed to work on the **backyard furnaces**. In May 1959 the government placed strict limits on schools changing their curriculum or teaching methods. Guidelines were provided as to how much time should be given over to learning manual labour skills. A two-track educational system was developed. In rural areas children advanced from primary school to 'agricultural middle schools' for vocational training in agricultural techniques. In contrast, in the cities an elite school system was developed at all levels of the full-time education system from kindergarten to university. The so-called 'key point' schools received the best funding and the best teachers. Their primary function was to produce qualified applicants for higher education. Centred in the cities, young peasants were largely excluded from this elite college preparatory system. The old elitism had returned. The children of cadres took the places at the best schools' learning the same intellectual interests and developing the same career aspirations as the **capitalist** class the CCP had been trying to destroy.

The system had returned to its pre-Leap elitism. By the early 1960s, the educational system was even more elitist than it had been before.

## The collapse of education after 1966

By the mid-1960s the failure to create educational equality had convinced Mao that **capitalist roaders** had taken over the Party. In early 1964 Mao complained that the twelve-year education system was too long, examinations were too rigid and that students were not prepared for manual labour. 'At present,' he complained, 'there is too much studying going on, and this is exceedingly harmful.' He noted that 'when the intellectuals had power, things were in a bad state.' It was evident 'that to read too many books is harmful' because 'they petrify your mind in the end.'

As a part of the Socialist Education Campaign that later set the stage for the Cultural Revolution, politics and class background returned as a ground for admission to senior middle school and college. Education focused on Marxist-Leninist theory and class struggle. Socialist heroes like comrade Lei Feng (see page 374) played a central role in school.

## The Cultural Revolution

Mao made clear the importance of educational reform at the beginning of the Cultural Revolution. The May 1966 Central Committee's 'Decision on the Cultural Revolution' announced that 'The task of the Cultural Revolution is to reform the old educational system and educational philosophy and methodology.' Instead of schooling he offered students the opportunity to experience true revolutionary fervour. Schools and universities were closed as the Red Guards abandoned their education to travel to Beijing to attend the eight massive rallies led by Mao (see page 266). They chanted their support and wept hysterically at the sight of their beloved leader. Those lucky enough to get close enough to touch him would not wash for weeks. Whipped into a frenzy, the young people denounced and attacked their teachers. At Beijing University a wall poster urged students to 'eliminate all demons and monsters and carry the socialist revolution through to the end'.

Radical students intimidated their teachers at **struggle meetings**, forcing them to kneel for hours with their arms pulled out behind them in what became known as 'the aeroplane position'. Most radical of all were those students from 'bad class backgrounds' – children of the pre-revolutionary elites, landlords, business owners or those with family connections to nationalist Taiwan.

Abandoning their schooling to partake in 'revolutionary struggle' provided them with the opportunity to prove their ideological commitment. Sometimes their victims' forced apologies were accepted; on many occasions they were beaten or tortured to death. This violence completely shattered China's school system.

### The impact on education

The Cultural Revolution had a lasting impact on students' attitudes to learning. In one case, Zhang Tiesheng garnered national attention when he submitted a blank examination paper for his college admissions test. He wrote a note that declared he was too busy working eighteen-hour days on the commune to revise. He had 'no respect for the bookworms who for many years have been taking it easy' and declared it unfair that 'a few hours of written examination may disqualify me from enrolment in college.' The willingness to challenge the narrow focus on rote learning over practical skills and original thinking might be viewed as a success for Mao's vision of a more egalitarian education system.

At the end of the Cultural Revolution many young people were not sent back to school, but rather into the countryside as part of the 'up to the mountains and down to the villages' campaign (see page 277). There they would learn the value of hard labour, living among the peasants. They were sent in part because Mao wanted to force intellectuals to experience the harshness of rural life. It was also a convenient way to alleviate urban overcrowding. Finally seeing first-hand the realities of rural poverty, many became disillusioned with the regime and less trusting of its rulers. Uneducated and abandoned to a life of rural poverty, they became known as China's 'lost generation'.

**Source E** From J. Horn, *Away With All Pests* (1969). Dr Horn was a Western-trained doctor who worked as a surgeon in China for 15 years.

> Superstitious practices were widespread. Witch-doctors, usually unkempt semi-demented women with an awe-inspiring appearance, attributed illness to ghosts, devils and evil spirits which they tried either to exorcise or placate. Placation involved sacrifices of chickens or other luxuries which the poverty-stricken people couldn't afford, while the evil spirits could only be exorcised by incantations and weird antics, which, if they did not frighten the spirits, certainly frightened the patient and the spell-bound onlookers. Poverty and ignorance were reflected in a complete lack of sanitation as a result of which fly and water-borne diseases such as typhoid, cholera, dysentery, took a heavy toll. Worm infestation was practically universal, for untreated human and animal manure was the main and essential soil fertiliser. The people lived on the fringe of starvation and this so lowered their resistance to disease that epidemics carried off thousands every year.
>
> Many adolescent girls, lacking calcium and vitamin D, developed softening and narrowing of the pelvic bones, so that normal child-birth became either impossible or so dangerous that six to eight per cent of all deaths among women were due to childbirth. There were no preventative inoculations against infectious diseases. Military occupation and the licentiousness of the landlords and local gentry spread venereal diseases among the people and no treatment was available.

What are the main health problems for Chinese people that Dr Horn describes in Source E? Why would it be so difficult to solve them?

## Health provision

Public health provision in China was extremely rudimentary. In the nineteenth century Christian missionaries and charities had brought Western medicine to China and during the 1920s and 1930s more doctors were trained and hospitals opened. However, many still relied on traditional Chinese medical techniques like **acupuncture** and **herbalism**. Healthcare in rural China was practically non-existent and public health spending was not a priority for the regime. Spending on healthcare never rose above 2.6 per cent of the state budget up to 1956.

### How effective was the health policy?

To improve the situation without spending money needed for economic and military reconstruction the Party decided that the priority was in the prevention of disease rather than expensive cures. Cadres were trained to show the peasants how to prevent the spread of disease through improved sanitation and public hygiene. Patriotic Health Campaigns sent teams of Party workers into the countryside to educate illiterate peasants. One campaign focused on preventing disease spread by a microscopic worm carried by snails using lectures, film shows, posters and radio broadcasts. The campaigns were effective. Smallpox, cholera, typhus, typhoid fever, plague and leprosy were practically eliminated. Cases of tuberculosis and **parasitic diseases** were greatly reduced. Terror campaigns against drug suppliers and criminal gangs had the effect of greatly lowering the numbers of drug addicts.

Slowly the situation began to improve:

- During the Great Leap Forward communes established medical clinics.
- State investment built over 800 Western-type hospitals.
- The number of doctors trained in modern techniques rose from 40,000 in 1949 to 150,000 in 1965.
- By the 1960s medical schools were graduating 25,000 new doctors per year.

The results were impressive. In 1949 life expectancy was 36 years; by 1957 it was 57 years. Given the very low level of healthcare available prior to 1949, the Party was able to do enough to convince some Chinese people that they had realised their socialist goals. In his memoir of his life in China during the regime, American Sidney Rittenberg recalls the attitude of his mother-in-law when his young daughter became suddenly ill: '"Don't worry," she said serenely as we fearfully rushed off to hospital, "Children don't die in the New China."'

## The barefoot doctors

The work of doctors was greatly disrupted by the Antis Campaigns of the 1950s that labelled many in the medical profession as bourgeois while many others were denounced during the Cultural Revolution. Even Mao's personal physician Zhisui Li recalls the need to hide his family background. 'I knew I had to avoid the possibility of ever being interrogated and having my own past exposed,' he recalled, 'I would be destroyed.' As with education, there was a clear inequality between rural and urban China. Western hospitals were centred on the cities while in the countryside paramedics rather than fully trained doctors provided the first line of care. Mao denounced hospitals as 'hospitals for urban lords only'.

**Source F** Health Campaign Poster in the 1950s.

Why do you think the regime had to rely so much on posters to spread education about healthcare? How effective do you think the poster in Source F would be?

**Source G** 'Directive on Public Health', June 26, 1965, in Maurice Messier, *Mao's China and After: A History of the People's Republic* (Free Press, 1999), page 271.

> Tell the Ministry of Public Health that it only works for fifteen percent of the total population of the country and that this fifteen percent is mainly composed of gentlemen, while the broad masses of the peasants do not get any medical treatment. First, they don't have any doctors; second they don't have any medicine. The Ministry of Public Health is not a Ministry of Public Health for the people, so why not change the name to the Ministry of Urban Health, the Ministry of Gentlemen's Health, or even to the Ministry of Urban Gentlemen's Health? ... The methods of medical examination and treatment used by hospitals nowadays are not at all appropriate for the countryside, and the way doctors are trained is only for the benefit of the cities. And yet in China over five hundred million of our population are peasants.

What are Mao's main complaints about the health system in China in Source G?

Mao's answer was the barefoot doctor initiative. Many villages sent young people to receive medical training to become 'barefoot doctors', so named because they went to live with peasants so poor that shoes were too valuable to wear in the muddy fields. The new recruits worked in the village clinic. 'It is not at all necessary to have so much formal training,' Mao said. 'They should mainly learn and raise their standard in practice.' These 'doctors' were trained intensively for just six months. They could provide only rudimentary healthcare and the village clinic had little equipment and low supplies of medicine.

Jung Chang, the author of *Wild Swans*, was herself sent to provide medical aid. She recalls that 'The only medical book I had ever set eyes on was *A Barefoot Doctor's Manual*. I studied it avidly. There was no theory in it, just a summary of symptoms.' The peasants quickly realised that she was not knowledgeable. 'When I sat at my desk, with the other two doctors behind me,' she wrote, 'it was clear that the sick peasants who came in very sensibly wanted nothing to do with me.' She settled for providing nursing duties and giving injections. Calling the scheme 'propaganda' and one of 'Mao's political manoeuvres', she noted that in reality 'Out in the countryside, it was one's professional skills, rather than political rhetoric, that counted.'

## Impact of the barefoot doctors

For all its shortcomings, the scheme did provide the best healthcare that many rural peasants had ever experienced. Their training might not have been extensive, but it was adequate to treat the common problems that the peasants experienced. Simply put, doctors with rudimentary training were better than no doctors at all. They played an important part in challenging traditional practices and spreading modern medical knowledge and basic care to rural areas. In total, by 1973 over a million new doctors had been trained.

### Work of the Women's Federation

One health campaign led by Women's Federation workers (see page 293) was dedicated to improving midwifery and infant childcare in rural areas. Women's Federation **work teams** sent into the countryside found midwifery techniques to be backward. Few mothers had prenatal examinations. The need for sterile equipment was not understood. In Fujian it was common for cow dung to be used to dress the umbilical cord. In difficult births another report noted that midwives had 'fashion[ed] a hook from a nail or use[d] a fire-wood trimming knife to pull the baby out'.

**Postpartum** care was rudimentary, with mothers weak from childbirth barely fed. One Shaanxi folk saying summed up the attitude: 'We only see the mother hold her child, but not the child walking.' In one village they found that backward birthing practices led to an infant mortality rate of 38 per cent. Official literature damned these practices as 'feudal, superstitious and backward'.

The Women's Federation advocated new practices based on scientific methods. The new techniques emphasised hand washing, sterilisation, prenatal check-ups and having the mother lie down during labour. While propaganda damned them as inadequate, they knew that existing midwives had years of valuable experience if they could be retrained in the new techniques. As one Party slogan proclaimed: 'Promote new-style midwifery, reform old midwives, train new midwives.' The focus on midwifery continued with the onset of collectivisation (see page 234). Midwifery stations were established, and the tone of propaganda changed. One Women's Federation pamphlet advocated the new midwifery techniques based not only on the need to alleviate mothers' suffering during childbirth but also to ensure that they would be 'even better at joining in the work of socialist production'. Fertility rose and infant mortality declined.

## Conclusion: Education and healthcare provision

Mao sought to initiate a profound transformation in attitudes and access to education and public health. His ideas were nothing less, Lin Biao declared, than 'a Marxist-Leninism for remoulding the soul of the people'. Souls may not have been changed, but Mao's policy certainly influenced the bodies and minds of the Chinese people. But was it for the better?

Healthcare remained a low priority in the budget. The barefoot doctor scheme can be interpreted as a practical solution to China's shortage of doctors, but also as a hollow propaganda stopgap to win support without diverting funds from Mao's ambitious economic and military priorities. What advancements there were in healthcare provision were greatly disrupted by the upheavals of the Great Leap Forward and the Cultural Revolution. Similarly, access to educational opportunities did, at times, increase, but the line between education and indoctrination was frequently blurred. An education system that encouraged students to solve all problems by the use of predetermined formulae derived from Mao Zedong Thought certainly bolstered the regime's hold on power. However, it failed to open minds or encourage independent thought. It did not prepare students to supply the technological knowledge or innovative thinking urgently required to provide genuine and lasting benefits to the lives of the majority of the Chinese people.

### Work together

Working in pairs, attempt to summarise the arguments of the pragmatists and of Mao regarding social policy. One of you will represent the pragmatists. You need to explain the point of view of those who wanted an education system that would make China a modern, industrialised nation and healthcare modelled on the West that would better the lives of the people of China. The other person in the pair will represent Mao. You will explain his reasons for wanting to change education policy so it supported his revolutionary ideas and why he wanted to rely on untrained doctors to improve rural healthcare. When you have finished come together and re-read your notes. If there are any sections that you found difficult to explain then add more detail to your notes or work together on a better explanation.

# 3 Cultural change

For Mao, control of culture had been a way in which the previous ruling classes of China had imposed themselves upon their subjects. He meant to use it in the same way. According to Mao, culture was inherently political. 'There is no such thing as art for art's sake or art that is detached from or independent from politics,' he had declared at Yan'an (see page 213). Art and literature should further 'the proletarian revolutionary cause'.

Mao was in fact a great lover and collector of traditional Chinese culture. His quarters in the **Forbidden City** were lined with books of classical Chinese writings. However, during the period when he retired away from the centre of political decision making he became increasingly concerned about what he perceived as the bourgeois direction of Chinese culture. He used his concerns as an avenue through which to attack his political rivals within the Party (see page 273). He declared that in forms of art such as drama, music, cinema, poetry and literature traditional ideas still dominated and that 'very little has been achieved so far in socialist transformation'. The 'dead still rule today,' he declared. He sought to transform Chinese culture to correspond to communist ideology.

In August 1966 Mao launched the 'Four Olds Campaign' which the Red Guards enacted. The attacks on traditional culture in towns and countryside which this led to are detailed on pages 268–269. The imposition of revolutionary art and culture in its stead and Jiang Qing's role in this is discussed below.

## The role of Jiang Qing

Jiang Qing was Mao's fourth wife. Formerly an actress in Shanghai, she became involved romantically with Mao at Yan'an in the mid-1930s. She was specifically forbidden to have a role in politics until the launching of the Cultural Revolution (see page 262). Having previously had a career in the film industry and theatre, Mao named her as a so-called 'Cultural Tsarina' and chose her to personally oversee the purification of 'revisionist, **capitalist** and **feudalist**' influences in Chinese culture during the Cultural Revolution.

In 1966 Mao wrote to Jiang Qing that

> *'Great chaos will lead to great order. The cycle appears every seven or eight years. The demons and monsters will come out by themselves. Their class character dictates it.'*

She viewed this as a green light to carry out her aims to purify Chinese culture and an opportunity, with Mao now quite elderly, to launch her political career. In the same year Jiang Qing was given a place on the new Central Cultural Revolution Group (CCRG), an organisation tasked with helping Mao remould Chinese culture. With Mao's blessing the CCRG grew so powerful that it rivalled the Politburo. It controlled the pace and direction of the Cultural Revolution, even controlling the PLA. Its Art and Literature Group, personally controlled by Jiang Qing, replaced the Ministry of Culture in controlling art, music and literature. Its Central Case Examination Group, established in 1966, investigated the crimes of high-ranking Party members, gathering evidence against them that was passed directly to Mao. This helped Mao in his purging of Liu Shaoqi and Deng Xiaoping (see page 273).

## Key debate

### Was Jiang Qing following Mao's orders, or motivated by her own aims?

Jiang Qing remains a figure of derision among historians and the general public alike. Lee Feigon notes that she is vilified as a 'usurping concubine', Terrill calls her the 'White boned demon' while for Chang and Halliday, she was simply 'an evil woman'. But debate rages as to her true motives. Some argue that she was motivated by the desire to destroy any embarrassing remnants of her bourgeois past (she was rumoured to have had affairs with directors in order to win parts while an actress in Shanghai in the 1902s) that might hinder her personal rise to power. She certainly took advantage of the violent atmosphere of the Cultural Revolution as a cover to realise her own personal vendettas. Former friends who could reveal her embarrassing past in Shanghai were hunted down and **purged** on the pretence of representing 'revisionist elements'. She argued that she was simply following the orders of her husband. 'I was Chairman Mao's dog,' she claimed, 'Whoever Chairman Mao asked me to bite, I bit.' Regardless of her motives, her role in attacking anyone linked to pre-communist culture enabled and encouraged violence, terror and chaos on an unprecedented scale.

## Censorship of the theatre

Jiang Qing imposed strict censorship, vetting all theatre performances for evidence of revisionist content. As a result nearly all foreign works were banned. She angrily told officials from the Ministry of Culture that the food they ate 'came from the farmers!' so they should 'serve the farmers in your plays and operas!' Personally involved, she visited theatres to oversee and interfere with auditions, loudly contradicting the instructions of the directors with almost comic results. At one audition she instructed the actor how to dismount from a horse: 'Don't simply slide off his back,' she told him, 'That looks weak.' Revolutionary heroes should 'Spring over the horse's head.' 'Make it revolutionary or ban it' was her slogan.

### *Romance on the Milky Way*

Plays were changed to fit with Mao's revolutionary ideology. One popular play, *Romance on the Milky Way*, pictured happy marriages as preordained by the gods. When wedding arrangements were discussed in one scene the prospective groom declares, 'We must pick an auspicious day.' The sister-in-law scolds him, 'You are still a little superstitious. No day is as good as today.'

## Revolutionary opera

Jiang Qing's main target was traditional Chinese opera. She damned the storylines as bourgeois and feudal, full of superstitions such as 'cow ghosts and snake spirits'. Instead, communist writers should write new works removing 'feudal' characters – 'emperors, ministers, scholars and maidens' – and replacing them with heroic peasants, workers and revolutionary soldiers. Only eight official revolutionary 'performances' (five operas, two ballets and a symphony) were allowed. Although popular at first, audiences soon tired of the simplistic storylines and overbearing revolutionary propaganda. The shows featured revolutionary characters: *Red Detachment of Women* told the story of female Chinese soldiers battling against the nationalists, while *Taking Tiger Gorge by Strategy* featured an undercover communist soldier infiltrating and defeating bandits. Existing works were rewritten to include less romance which was replaced with more scenes of class conflict.

To add to the authenticity of the performances, Jiang sent dancers to live with army units in order to better portray the realities of military life. With only eight performances allowed, people were forced to watch the same opera again and again. One joke remarked that the culture of the Cultural Revolution was 'eight hundred million people watching eight shows.' Deng Xiaoping imprudently declared: 'After a week's work, people want to go to the theatre to relax. Instead ... you go to the theatre and find yourself in a battlefield.' The plays were 'a bunch of people running to and fro on the stage. Not a trace of art.' But Mao was happy. 'The orientation is right,' he pronounced, while loyal newspapers announced that the new works were 'shining pearls of proletarian literature and art, fostered personally by Comrade Jiang Qing.' The artistic results were not comedic. Cowed by terror and fear of denunciation, writers, painters and musicians either towed the Party line or stopped producing. By the time she was finished, writes Terrill, 'the minds of Chinese theatre goers were reduced to mashed potatoes.' So boring had broadcasts become that second-hand radio sets could be bought for less than a quarter of their original price.

## Key debate

### Jiang Qing's legacy

Historians debate the cultural contribution of Jiang Qing. As a result of her censorship and intimidation China became, writes Michael Lynch, 'an artistically barren land'. The result of her campaign to eliminate what she perceived as 'bourgeois' and 'revisionist' elements was, he writes, 'dross ... nothing of genuine quality was produced.' After the 'terrible physical famine' China was now 'subjected to an equally devastating spiritual deprivation'. Chang and Halliday agree: she destroyed the lives of millions of people and turned China into 'a cultural desert'. However, other historians disagree. Lee Feigon points out that although it became a matter of faith that Mao had sought to replace the rich culture of China with 'revolutionary slop' much of this 'backlash against the art of the Cultural Revolution lingered' because they were identified to the much hated Jiang Qing. Feigon encourages what he calls a more balanced judgement. He argues that in fact much of the music of the Cultural Revolution, far from monolithic, was varied, complicated and incorporated foreign, even Western influences. The Cultural Revolution was more than just pointless violence and propaganda. Despite the control, writers and artists found a way to express their creativity.

## Conclusion: Cultural change

Mao not only sought to alter the nature of political power and the economic system in China, he desired nothing less than a complete transformation of Chinese cultural traditions and the wiping away of centuries of art, music and literature, some of the greatest contributions in their fields in world history. For Mao, culture was a political tool. In the past it had been used to defend repressive feudal beliefs – he now sought to remould it to the benefit of his regime. In doing so he had a willing accomplice in Jiang Qing. How far the dreaded 'Madame Mao' acted out of genuine commitment to the regime and how much she was using the Cultural Revolution as a means to her own power remains unclear. What is without doubt is that Mao's regime brought massive, fundamental and at times catastrophic changes to China's culture.

## Work together

1. In pairs, make notes on the aims of Jiang Qing's cultural policy.
2. Then, watch one of the eight performances that she helped authorise: *Red Detachment of Women*. It is easy to find online. As you watch, think about the imagery, language and use of music. Individually note down how the performance meets the aims you have listed. Once you have finished, compare your notes and discuss how far you think the performance met her aims.
3. Imagine you were a Chinese person living at the time. What do you think your reaction to the performance would be?

## 4 Religion

In the immediate aftermath of the communist seizure of power in 1949, the Party was quick to guarantee religious freedom. In his study of the peasant movement in Yunan, Mao himself had declared that religious sentiment could not be destroyed by force. Article 5 of the PRC's Common Program (see page 207) promised 'freedom of religious belief' and this was later reaffirmed in Article 88 of the 1954 **Constitution** (see page 207). It quickly became clear that the regime would not allow such legal restraints to control their actions. This section examines the different ways in which the regime dealt with China's religions and how far they succeeded in destroying them and replacing them with belief in communist ideology.

### Note it down

1. Draw a spider diagram, with the spider's body labelled 'How did the CCP treat religious groups in China?' Label five 'legs':
   - Confucianism
   - Ancestor worship
   - Christianity
   - Buddhism
   - Islam.
2. Make notes in different colours on each leg on the following questions:
   **a)** Why was it targeted?
   **b)** What actions did the CCP take?
   **c)** How far did the CCP achieve its aims?
3. Note where policies changed. Can you identify the key turning points in religious policy? Highlight them on your diagram.

### Religion in 1949

In 1949 religious faith was a mainstay of many people's lives. Ceremonies to honour Confucius and festivals at New Year and Ch'ing Ming, when families tended the graves of their ancestors and gave offerings to the gods, were widely observed. Protestant and Catholic Christianity was spread across China by missionaries sent from the Western nations to save the souls of the unbelieving Asian peoples. There were 3 million Catholics and 1 million Protestants in China before 1949. In isolated Xinjiang, far from the influence of Beijing, Islam was a defining characteristic of society and culture, controlling schools and defining attitudes to women. Muslim leaders held great power there.

### Communist attitudes to religion

The Communist Party denounced religious attitudes as feudal superstitions with no place in the New China. Confucianism was seen as having upheld the old imperial system with its hierarchy and acceptance of inequality. Celebrating festivals and honouring ancestors were derided as old thoughts, to be swept away. Christian belief in God was derided as myth. In addition, because Christianity had been introduced to China by missionaries from Western nations, it was attacked as deriving from Western thought and for being supported by imperialist enemies. The Islamic **mullahs**, with their influence over their societies, were seen as a rival to communist rule, as were the Buddhist lamas. The Communist Party acted with different strategies towards these faiths and traditions, attacking some and replacing others, but the ideological premise was consistent: religion had no place in Mao's China.

### Confucianism

Confucius was a philosopher whose writings had become elevated to the status of Holy Scripture. Public ceremonies honoured him and temples and shrines were dedicated to him. The communists marked Confucian ethical code and ideas as 'old culture', with no relevance in the New China. All public ceremonies honouring him were ended in 1949. At first temples and shrines dedicated to him were not destroyed; they simply became museum pieces. Some philosophers did attempt to defend Confucian thought by arguing that it was compatible with communist ideology. One pointed out that Confucius had set up a private school at a time when access to learning was the preserve of the aristocratic elites, and therefore made education available to the masses.

During the Cultural Revolution the attack on Confucianism became violent. The temple at Confucius' birthplace was attacked (see page 268). By this time being associated with Confucianism was politically dangerous:

- One reason given for purging Liu Shaoqi (see page 273) was that he had preached Confucian ideas.
- When the Gang of Four radicals (see page 278) wanted to attack their enemies, they launched the 'criticise Confucius campaign' which tried to tie his 'feudal' thought to the policies of the pragmatists in the Party like Deng Xiaoping.

### Ancestor worship

For Mao, traditional beliefs such as ancestor worship represented old-fashioned thought, totally at odds with his revolutionary desire to create a 'New China'. One example was the New Year Festival, called Chinese New Year in the West. During this time, families returned to the ancestral home to burn joss sticks to honour their ancestors, making offerings to the Kitchen God in the hope of receiving his blessings and giving small packets of money, *hongbao*, to children – the red colour of the envelopes denoting wishes of good luck.

The communists first discouraged and then condemned these traditions, encouraging instead new practices and attitudes. Workers journeying home to pay respects to their ancestors were urged not to take home what were damned as 'superstitious articles' such as joss sticks or red paper for envelopes. They were told to stop honouring the Kitchen God because, in the traditional ceremonies, common people always made their sacrifices last – a symbol of feudal oppression.

## Replacing old traditions

Instead of these old traditions, workers in one Shanghai dock suggested that they erect a portrait of Chairman Mao, with banners reading 'Long live the People's Government!' Instead of banquets, they proposed that the holiday be marked by celebrating thriftiness: no heavy drinking or eating and no new clothes. They suggested that instead of traditional folktales, the younger generation should be told stories of the struggle for liberation. The Party encouraged people to buy pictures with slogans such as 'We and Chairman Mao are of one heart.' Religious shrines in peasant houses were destroyed and replaced by pictures of Mao. Street names that derived from folk traditions such as 'Fortune and Longevity Road' were renamed.

### National Memorial Day

For centuries, the Ch'ing Ming festival had been marked by people returning to tend the graves and make offerings to their ancestors, burning paper 'spirit money' as a gift to the dead. A new communist festival was announced to take its place. By 1966, the Qingming festival had become National Memorial Day and was focused on commemorating those who had died during liberation. Delegations of communist youths and workers marched to the graves of fallen revolutionary heroes to lay wreaths.

### How successful was the regime in destroying old attitudes?

It is impossible to know how effective the communists were at discouraging old traditions. Certainly many temples, shrines and religious statues were destroyed but this did not necessarily equate to the destruction of long-held beliefs. The Party was embarrassed when it was discovered that one director of a commune health clinic had an image of the God of Wealth in his home and was making offerings to it. It was reported that even some cadres were carrying around holy symbols to ward off ghosts. This evidence suggests that, for all the regime's efforts, the Chinese people did not entirely abandon their old beliefs.

## Early religious policy

[AQ]

The new regime was initially less immediately militant with the more institutionalised and organised religions. Worried by the sheer number of followers and their foreign support the new rulers of China adopted a careful and conciliatory approach to the major religions. Unlike their counterparts in Russia who had immediately launched an ideologically driven wave of terror against the Christian Church (see page 10), the CCP initially tried to win over and control the leaders of the major religions. They hoped that they could convince religious leaders to work with the regime. For example, the Party invited hand-picked representatives to attend the First National Political Consultative Conference (NPCC) in September 1949. The representatives included four Protestants, two Buddhists and one Muslim. Although the regime promised co-operation, this was an attempt to gain the support of sympathetic leaders who could then convince members of the religious groups to cut off their ties with the outside world and support the purging of non-communists.

## Christianity

Christian groups were targeted because the communists believed that the Church was representative of Western, imperialist ideas. In January 1951, a formal Religious Affairs Department in the Commission of Culture and Education (RAD) was created. In 1954 the RAD was upgraded and expanded to become the Religious Affairs Bureau. Some of its first main tasks were to force out foreign Christian missionaries, coerce Christians to cut ties with foreign countries and take over Church-run schools that received funding from Western Churches.

## Protestant Church

Protestant leaders were pressurised into organising a 'Patriotic Church Movement' for Chinese Protestant churches to support the regime. Leaders of the Patriotic Churches sought to convince their congregations to be loyal to China and the Communist Party. They argued that the Protestant Church should be organised according to the 'Three-Self' principle:

- self-ruling
- self-supporting
- self-propagating.

## Patriotic Churches

The Patriotic Church Movement was created to convince members of the Christian Churches to comply with the Party line. Individual priests were coerced into joining the movement and told to ensure that their congregations were loyal to the new regime. These churches could remain open as long as they supported Mao. This gave the image of religious toleration, but in reality it was part of Mao's system of enforcing communist control. One church in Beijing draped red communist flags over the altar and streamers proclaiming 'Long Live Chairman Mao' were hung from church columns. Portraits of Mao replaced pictures of the Virgin Mary. Another church installed a red star above the cross on its tower. However, the new churches did not completely succeed. Congregation sizes at patriotic churches were low, while congregations at churches where the priest was independent of the regime increased in number. Some priests gave services in private homes. Pilgrims still met to celebrate Easter Sunday. In Kangding, the church was one of the few buildings to survive an earthquake in 1955. Interpreting this as a sign from God, followers flocked to pray there.

In reality the 'Three Selfs' meant complete obedience to the government. While the principle appeared to suggest a level of autonomy from the regime, in practice it meant that Protestant Churches were pressurised to cut all ties with foreign organisations and leaders. Christian schools, universities and hospitals were closed down or taken over by the government. The leaders of the Patriotic Churches were told to drive out foreign missionaries and refuse to accept foreign financial aid from Protestants in other countries. Schools, universities and hospitals set up and run by the Protestant Church were taken over by the government. In 1949 there had been more than 3000 Protestant missionaries in China; by April 1952 there were fewer than 100 left.

## Catholic Church

The government tried the same tactics with the Catholic Church but they met more resistance. The **Vatican** refused to accept that the 'Patriotic Church' was truly Catholic. With tensions exacerbated by the Korean War (see page 219), the Party launched a crackdown on clergy and expelled the representative of the Vatican in Nanjing. Accusations were created to rally public sentiment against Catholicism:

- The Sacred Heart Home for Children was described as 'Little Buchenwald' (a Nazi prison camp) and the Chinese people told that the sisters working at the home had deliberately starved and tortured the children. Some children, said *People's China* magazine, had been sold into slavery.

**Source H** From *The Christian Manifesto*, September 1950, quoted in Richard L. Walker, *China under Communism: The First Five Years* (Yale University Press, 1955), pages 190–91.

> The Church must teach the evils of past imperialism, purge itself of the influences of imperialism, especially American imperialism which is plotting to use the Church for its own ends. The Church should 'oppose war and uphold peace' and support the government's land reform policy. Through self-criticism, austerity measures and thorough reform of itself, the Church should instil a 'patriotic and democratic' spirit among its members and aim at self-reliance.

**Source I** 'How did Imperialism use religion for aggression in China?' from the *People's Daily*, 13 April 1951, quoted in Richard L. Walker, *China under Communism: The First Five Years* (Yale University Press, 1955), pages 190–91.

> In the past hundred years, churches have been the bastion of the aggressors, while the latter have served as the background for the former. Whenever chances occurred for diplomatic negotiations, certain missionaries came to meddle in affairs. For instance, J. Leighton Stuart, former president of Yenching University, had posed as a religious leader and educator for many years. Outwardly he was one of the most important secret agents for American aggression on China. Unveiling himself, he became the American ambassador to China in order to carry out America's aggressive policy towards China.

What do Sources H and I suggest were the main reasons why the communists wanted to rid China of Christian belief?

- Catholic hospitals were charged with using patients as human guinea pigs to try out new medicines.
- Catholic schools were attacked as centres of 'cultural aggression' for providing support for the espionage carried out on behalf of the United States Army.
- In Canton the PLA banned the Legion of Mary, the international organisation of Catholic volunteers who carried out charitable work. It was derided as an 'international anti-Communist and anti-people reactionary organisation in the guise of religion and manipulated by imperialism'.
- In Shanghai, a special exhibition was created to demonstrate 'Catholic espionage activities'.

Catholics were subject to surveillance, threatened and forced to attend study meetings and write self-criticism. The wearing of religious symbols such as rosaries or crucifixes was banned in some provinces. In January 1951 there were 3222 Catholic missionaries in China. By November 1953 there were just 364 left. In 1955 a further crackdown on the Catholic 'counter-revolutionary clique' was launched and 1500 believers were jailed for crimes such as imperialism and attempting to spread non-communist ideas to young people.

### Conclusion: Christianity

Although the regime was initially nervous about attacking the Christian Churches, after the success of the campaigns of the early 1950s and the isolation from the West completed by the Korean War, Christians were targeted with special ferocity by the regime. Clergy were converted to physical labourers. Churches were closed down, the buildings converted to other uses. Christian leaders who resisted were sent to the **labour camps**. The Red Guards destroyed what was left of the Christian churches, statues and symbols during the Cultural Revolution. Any religious leaders who had managed to escape the previous purges were imprisoned. Public Christian worship in China was effectively ended.

## Islam

Muslims were also targeted. Mosques were seized and converted into meeting halls for struggle meetings. Muslim schools were converted into barns for livestock. Unlike the Christian Churches, followers of Islam fought back with force. In one battle over a thousand people were killed in Gansu. Armed rebellions against Chinese domination were common. In response, the regime ordered that cadres be more respectful of Islamic customs. The Islamic Association of China was set up by the regime officially to encourage co-operation between Muslims and the regime and to protect the traditions of Islam.

▲ Tanjiaping Catholic Church in Shaanxi. It was built in 1906 by a spanish missionary. During the Cultural Revolution the body of the missionary was dug up by Red Guards and thrown into the Yellow River. The Church was then converted into an office for the Grain distribution bureau. It was returned to the Catholic Church in 1989.

## Xinjiang

In Xinjiang, many Uighur people who were Muslim had welcomed the 'peaceful liberation' by the PLA in 1949. They had been promised full autonomy by Mao over a decade before. Their demands for greater independence were recognised when Xinjiang became named as an Autonomous Region in October 1955, meaning that it had greater local government.

In reality, the granting of autonomous status did not mean independence. The new regime, controlled by Beijing, compelled Muslim children to leave mosque schools and attend government schools instead. Marxism, not the Qur'an, was on the curriculum. Muslim religious leaders, the Imams, held real authority in their communities and therefore represented a clear challenge to communist rule. Their judicial authority was removed and they were forced to attend 'thought reform' for indoctrination in communist ideas. The religious tithe (*zakat*) was abolished and mosque land redistributed to the poor. Those who did not comply were sent to the *laogai* (see pages 215–216). During the Great Leap Forward activities such as worshipping or reading scripture were reduced in order to devote more time to economic production. The regime encouraged the mass migration of Han people into the region in order to dilute the influence of traditional religious beliefs. 'There is no such thing as a good Muslim,' declared one Party official.

### The Cultural Revolution in Xinjiang

During the Cultural Revolution, Muslims were targeted. Attacks on mosques were renewed with many turned into stables or slaughterhouses. Religious leaders were tortured and given menial jobs like cleaning sewers. They were forced to write self-denunciations and swear loyalty to the regime. Muslims were ordered to raise and eat pigs, a direct challenge to religious sentiment and an attempt to make them more like Han Chinese. As in the rest of China, Islamic intellectuals were targeted. A famous linguist, Ibrahim Mutte'i, was tortured by having the heavy volumes of a multilingual dictionary he had edited dropped on his head. Muslim men were forced to shave their beards. Uighurs learned to recite the greeting 'Long Live Chairman Mao' in Chinese in order to avoid punishment. Traditional dress was abandoned in favour of the drab workers' overalls that became known as 'Mao suits'.

## Conclusion: Islam

Despite the attacks on Islamic traditions, the Muslim identity endured communist rule better than the other religious groups. The regime's attitude to Islam was shaped by fears that the Uighur peoples sought independence for Xinjiang. Given that Xinjiang bordered other Muslim countries, like Pakistan, and had links with Muslim minorities in the Soviet Union, the CCP were concerned that Xinjiang might attempt to ally itself with them. This meant a more conciliatory approach. Mosques remained open and festival celebrations continued in public. Muslim culture remains there today.

▲ A mosque at Xinjiang

## Buddhism

Buddhism was far less organised than Christianity and Islam and therefore easier to attack. As soon as the communists took power monks, denounced as 'parasites' by the regime, were sent back to their homes and ordered to work. Some were forcibly enlisted in military academies. Others were denounced as **counter-revolutionaries** and killed at struggle meetings.

During the 'Resist America, Aid Korea' campaign (see page 221) the Buddhist Association exhorted members to undergo 'thought reform' and to abandon their 'feudal ideology'. Ancient temples were converted into barracks, prisons, schools and hospitals for wounded soldiers from Korea, although the Yonghegong Temple in Beijing was restored at great cost in case foreigners visited. The regime still wanted to keep up the pretence of religious tolerance. Buddhist landholdings were redistributed by the 1950 Agrarian Reform Law (see page 232). The regime organised a Chinese Buddhist Association in 1953 officially to speak up for Buddhists, but, in reality, like the Patriotic Church Movement, it was a form of government control. Its objectives were to 'unite the Buddhists of China so that they might participate under the leadership of the People's Government'.

### Buddhism in Tibet

The most important Buddhist community was in Tibet. The PLA invaded Tibet during the 'reunification campaign' in 1950 (see pages 213–214). The Tibetan people resisted with sabotage and guerrilla warfare. The resistance was so committed that Tibet was targeted during the Anti-Rightist Campaign of 1958 when an intense anti-Buddhist propaganda campaign was launched. The Great Leap

### Pilgrims

Despite government action, in rural China villagers still turned to religion for comfort in times of deprivation. In 1953 disease and famine caused thousands of pilgrims to travel to the White Horse Temple in Luoyang, a key Buddhist temple. More than 20,000 queued at the temple to receive the healing touch of the monks.

▲ White Horse Temple, Luoyang

Forward heralded a renewed attack on Buddhist monks. With the regime focused on increasing productivity, monks were converted into physical labourers and forced into communes. Lamas, Tibet's religious leaders, were stripped of their traditional sources of income: providing shelter for travellers, medical care and organising ceremonies and festivals. Temple land was added to the communes. Often forced to work the worst quality land, many starved. Many joined the PLA out of desperation. In 1959 the **Dalai Lama** was ordered to report to communist officials. Fearing that he would be imprisoned, the Tibetan people helped smuggle him out to safety in India.

### The impact of the Cultural Revolution

Buddhism was denounced as one of the 'Four Olds' during the Cultural Revolution (see page 268). Monasteries were burned, religious relics destroyed and monks beaten or arrested and sent to the *laogai* for 'labour reform'. By the end of the Cultural Revolution, few temples or shrines remained. The lamas had been forced into labour. Religious schools were closed and were no longer able to spread Buddhist ideas. An entire generation of monks, nuns and Buddhist followers had been wiped out.

## Conclusion: Religion

Religion, as a symbol of the old culture of China, was targeted by the regime from its earliest days. Despite these efforts, the regime's record in eradicating religious belief was mixed. Buddhism in Tibet might have been repressed, but isolation from Beijing and international concerns handicapped the campaign to alter the traditional Muslim culture of Xinjiang. Public Christian worship was banned, but clergy continued to minister to the faithful in private. Traditional practices such as ancestor worship were only partially controlled. The honouring of Zhou Enlai during the Qingming festival in 1976 (see page 279) was further proof that for all the legal controls, propaganda and terror inflicted on religious communities, religiosity and long-cherished cultural traditions privately endured.

## Conclusion: Social and cultural changes, 1949–76

Mao made it clear that the victory over the nationalists in 1949 was not the end, but the beginning of a process to revolutionise Chinese society. The Civil War had achieved only 'basic victory in the revolutionary war'. He promised continuous, and radical, revolution: 'Our past work is only the first step in a long march of 10,000 **li**.' There were undoubtedly successes. Many Chinese people saw a doctor for the first time, with even those in remote rural areas receiving access to basic healthcare. The introduction of Pinyin helped the literacy rate. Despite the suffering, some women did feel genuinely empowered and look back on the Maoist period as one of social advancement and opportunity.

As in all nations, healthcare, education and attitudes to religious, linguistic and cultural diversity were subject to change in government attitudes. What marked the Maoist regime as different was the scale and rapidity of the changing direction: at one point slavishly following the Soviet model, then abandoning it; at one time handing women their long-cherished aspiration of land ownership only quickly to collectivise property. While traditional religions were targeted, Mao himself became a focus of spiritual devotion. While the Party told the people that ceremonies and rituals represented 'feudal ideology', during the Cultural Revolution many people performed confessions in front of Mao's portrait or listened to daily 'sermons' at their schools or factories, extolling Mao's supernatural authority. Education at times valued intellectual and technological expertise; at others, such skills might make people vulnerable to denunciation, imprisonment or even torture. In the final analysis social policy in this period was dictated in large part by Mao's personal whim and political ambitions. As he became increasingly paranoid and irrational, the changes in policy only became more radical and terrifyingly violent.

### Work together

Firstly, compare the notes that you have made on this chapter with a partner. Add anything that you have missed and check anything that you have disagreed on. Next, divide your paper into three columns. In one column work together to list the main aims of Mao's social policies. Then, one of you should identify positive aspects of Mao's social policies. The other should note the negative aspects, drawing lines to show how the successes and failures link to the aims. After you have finished, combine your findings. Overall, how would you describe Mao's social policies in this period? How far did he successfully achieve his aims? Finally, reviewing your diagram, discuss how far Mao's policies improved or worsened the lives of the Chinese people. Remember that successes for the regime may not be successes for the people!

## Chapter summary

- Traditional attitudes to women in China were highly negative. Women had no voting rights and many were not educated.
- The 1950 Marriage Reform Law gave women the right to divorce and to own property. It banned arranged marriages.
- Mao declared that living in communes would free women from the domestic drudgery of housework and childcare. However, they were forced to undertake harsh physical labour, so the quality of their lives did not improve.
- Traditional attitudes took a long time to change. In isolated rural areas arranged marriages continued.
- Some women were empowered by the reforms introduced by the regime.
- In 1949 access to education in China was very unequal. The regime made education available for children of a lower-class background.
- Education suffered during the Cultural Revolution. The schools were closed and the students were encouraged to abandon their studies and join the Red Guards.
- Mao introduced Pinyin: a simplified written language. This improved communication across the country.
- Healthcare in China in 1949 was very backward; many peasants did not have access to a doctor. Mao introduced the 'Patriotic Health Campaigns' to educate them on how to prevent diseases spreading. Later the 'barefoot doctor' scheme encouraged young students to go to the countryside and provide basic healthcare.
- Mao believed that culture was a tool used by the 'feudal' ruling classes to control the masses. He wanted to rid China of the 'old' culture and replace it with a new communist culture.
- Jiang Qing, Mao's wife, was given the job of ridding China of its old culture and instead creating new art which would glorify the communist revolution.
- For the communists, religion was an outdated idea. Christianity was hated because it had been brought to China from the West. Religious leaders were arrested and churches and temples attacked.

## Recommended reading


A. D. Barnett, *Communist China: The Early Years, 1949–55* (Pall Mall Press, 1964). An account by an American journalist and academic who lived in China and Hong Kong during the early years of the regime.

J. Chang, *Wild Swans* (HarperCollins, 1991). Best-selling autobiography of three generations of Chinese women. The author grew up during Mao's rule and later became a Red Guard. Includes a chapter on the famine.

J. Chang and J. Halliday, *Mao: The Unknown Story* (Jonathan Cape, 2005). Chapter 50 focuses on the role of Madame Mao in the Cultural Revolution.

D. Davin, *Women-Work: Women and the Party in Revolutionary China* (Oxford University Press, 1976). A pioneering study of the impact of the communist regime on China's women.

F. Dikotter, *Mao's Great Famine* (Bloomsbury Publishing, 2010). Recent scholarly analysis of the Great Famine; includes a chapter on its impact on women.

F. Dikotter, *The Tragedy of Liberation: A History of the Chinese Revolution, 1945–57* (Bloomsbury Publishing, 2013). Evaluates the treatment of religious groups.

G. Hershatter, *The Gender of Memory: Rural Women in China's Collective Past* (University of California Press, 2011). Based on the recollections of women who lived in Mao's China, very detailed exploration of the impact of Party policies on their lives.

M. Lynch, *Mao* (Routledge, 2004). Chapter 8 describes Mao's attitude towards the status of women and includes an evaluation of his relationships with Jiang Qing.

R. Keith Schoppa, *The Columbia Guide to Modern Chinese History* (Columbia University Press, 2000). As well as concise narratives of key events, this guide provides a wide range of socio-economic data.

D. Twitchett and J.K. Fairbank, *The Cambridge History of China. Volume 14: The People's Republic Part I: The Emergence of Revolutionary China, 1949–1965* (Cambridge University Press, 1987). Chapter 4 'Education for the new order' and Chapter 9 'New directions in education' are detailed accounts of changes in educational policy.

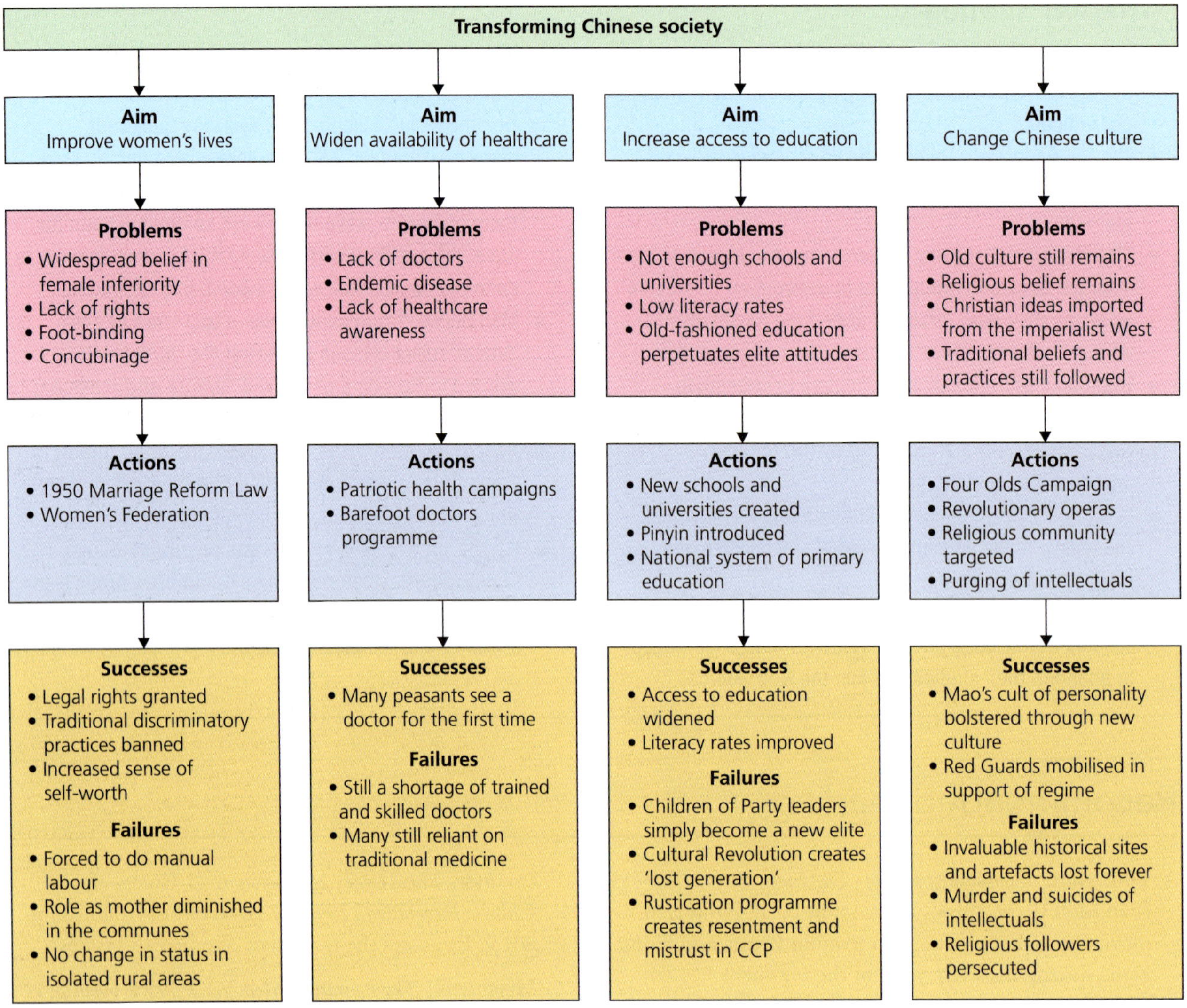


▲ Summary diagram: Social and cultural changes, 1949–76

# Section A: Essay technique

## Evaluating the sources

Evaluating the sources is essential to doing well in the exam. It means working out how far the sources contain evidence that is useful to a historian doing a specific task. There are different levels of evaluation, which are rewarded to different extents.

First, your source evaluation must be relevant to the question:

- Source evaluation that is not clearly linked to the question will be awarded marks in the lower levels.
- Source evaluation which is clearly relevant to the question will be awarded marks in the higher levels.

Secondly, there is the issue of the criteria you use to evaluate the sources (see table below).

| | |
|---|---|
| Level 1 | **No criteria** – evaluation is extremely superficial, it does not relate to any criteria. |
| Level 2 | **Questionable criteria** – evaluation is based on a criterion, but the criterion is invalid, simplistic or poorly understood. |
| Level 3 | **Formulaic criteria** – evaluation is based on a discussion of the **nature, origin and purpose** (NOP) of the source. |
| Level 4/5 | Valid criteria – at this level responses will use criteria that reflect the kind of source and the kind of specific task that the question focuses on. In this sense the evaluation will be tailored to the question.<br>At Level4 the criteria will not be applied rigorously.<br>At Level 5 the criteria will be applied rigorously. |

## Evaluating the sources: the criteria

Imagine you are answering the following question:

**How far could the historian make use of Sources 1 and 2 together to investigate the role and status of women in Mao's China, 1949–76?**

**Source 1** From 'Women's Life in Rural People's Communes', an article by the China News Service, a state-owned news agency, 24 February, 1959.

> Many women, since they ceased to be illiterate, have joined part-time schools. When the women are asked to describe their new life after the building of the people's communes, they say that such description will take more than three days and three nights. They are now leading the life for which they have long yearned. In the morning, the whole family goes to the mess hall for breakfast. The children are then sent to the nursery or the kindergarten as the case may be. The adults are free to attend to their own work. In the afternoon, after work is finished, the whole family is reunited to enjoy the comfort of home. The women have participated in social productive labour and have been earning their own wages. In family life, their position has been raised to that of the other adult members of the family. This has removed the last vestige of the feudal family system left behind by history. In production as well as in studies, women's political consciousness and cultural and technical level are rising higher every day. The difference between women and men politically, culturally and technologically is being reduced.

**Source 2** From an interview with a female Party cadre. She recalled attending a meeting for cadres in 1950 on the new grain policy less than a month after giving birth for the first time. Quoted in Gail Hershatter, *The Gender of Memory: Rural Women and China's Collective* Past (University of California Press: Berkeley, 2013), page 76.

> I was having my month of postpartum confinement [maternity leave], but I had to set an example. I thought, they have put me in charge of a township. How can I go down to the countryside and lead others if I don't understand the policy. I am a person of rather strong character. I don't want to show weakness. When the meeting was over, I went down [to the countryside] immediately. It was a dozen li [four miles] from where I lived. I found a pull cart and brought a temporary wet nurse and my child and my mother along with me. At that time my enthusiasm for work was very high. As soon as I got them settled in the afternoon, I shuttled back and forth between the township and the district. I left the child behind with a temporary wet nurse. She was a woman with a child who had a lot of milk and a fat baby. But at night she had no milk. The next day, my mother arranged for someone to bring me a message that the baby had almost cried herself to death because she hadn't gotten anything to eat.

## Simplistic source analysis

Having read the sources on page 313, it is clear that both sources suggest that the lives of women in China have changed a lot. **Source 1** argues that there has been a very big improvement. It talks about them being much happier and more equal with men, which was a big change from the situation before Mao came to power.

This is a low-level response because there is no indication of why the authors think their lives have been improved, nor why **Source 1** is biased. The evidence offered is very superficial, taking **Source 1** at face value in terms of what it literally says without looking for the deeper meaning.

You could say that **Source 2** is unreliable because it is only about one area of China and only one type of person: Party cadre. However, these comments are based on questionable criteria. The source sheds light on a significant part of the population and an important part of Mao's support in the countryside. The very fact that women could become Party cadres is itself revealing. It can be used to illustrate the lifestyle of female Party cadres to which further evidence may be added as to its typicality.

Based on this, here are three basic tips:

- Avoid simply saying '**Source 1** is biased'. Statements like this are very simplistic and are therefore unlikely to get you a good mark.
- Avoid assuming that the only useful sources are eyewitness accounts.
- Avoid assuming that sources relating to only one area are not very reliable.

## Nature, origin and purpose

One way of evaluating the sources is to ask questions about the nature, origin and purpose of the sources:

- Nature: what type of source is this?
- Origin: when and where does the source come from?
- Purpose: why did the author write the source?

This approach is a good place to start. It is also better than making simplistic statements about sources. However, it can lead to formulaic responses, which are unlikely to gain top marks. See below for how to evaluate the sources in their own terms.

## Evaluating sources in their own terms

The best way of evaluating sources on page 313 is to try to understand them in their own terms. Reading the sources in the context of the time is a good way of evaluating their usefulness. By situating the sources in their context, we can argue the following:

- First **Source 1** argues in support of Mao's policies. It was written during the Great Leap Forward and is an example of propaganda whose purpose is to convince the Chinese people that Mao's policies have greatly improved the lives of women. The source is arguing that life in the communes has freed women from childcare and housework, enabling them to undertake economically productive work. At the time, Mao was attempting to transform China into a modern, industrial power but he did not have the technology that this required. Instead of advanced machines, he had to rely on his policy of 'mass mobilisation' – exhorting the people to work as hard as they could. He needed to ensure that all available sources of labour, such as women, worked as hard as they could for the benefit of the regime. The source is trying to convince the Chinese people that this has brought great improvements to women's standard of living.
- **Source 2** meanwhile gives a snapshot of a woman's life during the introduction of land reform that shows that despite the political opportunity for women to become Party cadre, the expectation that they would work meant that their lives were very hard. It shows that although the woman is doing an important job for the Party, she is still expected to be responsible for the care of her new-born baby.
- Therefore, both sources are useful in the sense that they reveal what the regime wanted people to believe about the lives of women, while showing that although there might be political opportunities for women in Mao's China, there was still a social expectation that women would be the primary carers of children.
- However, the two sources do not give the full picture. **Source 1** is an idealised image presented by the regime to generate support, while **Source 2** gives the view of a Party cadre. We do not hear the voices of the ordinary Chinese peasant, whose life would be very different, nor of female workers in the cities. The sources do not provide any information about how far men supported or attempted to block the advances made by women during this period.

**TIPS:**

- Use what you have already learned to help you understand the sources.
- The dates of the sources are often significant. Note, for example, the date of Source 2, which is in the immediate post-liberation period. Use what you already know to explore the possible significance of the dates, places and people mentioned in the sources.
- Remember that sources are contributing to a debate. Use your knowledge to situate the sources in the wider debate.

Having read the advice on evaluating the sources on page 314, try to evaluate the sources in order to formulate an answer to this question:

**How far could the historian make use of Sources 3 and 4 together to investigate the attitude of the communist policies towards Buddhism in Tibet?**

**Source 3** A party propaganda announcement that claims to describe the reaction of the Tibetan people to the Chinese invasion of 1950. Quoted in Warren W. Smith, *China's Tibet?: Autonomy or Assimilation* (Rowman & Littlefield Publishers, 2008), page 44.

> In this violent class struggle, after a campaign of propaganda and education was carried out and after contrasting the old and new societies, the class consciousness of the vast labouring herdsmen was rapidly promoted. After they perceived the reactionary essence of the feudalistic exploiting class, they were all greatly surprised; and rose up with set teeth to accuse the exploiting class of their heinous crimes. After stripping off the religious cloak of the counterrevolutionary elements in religious circles, they exposed their fraud; and the masses say: 'We shall never permit these man-eating wolves to do evil things while riding on the neck of the people waving religious banners.' At the debate meetings, the masses were so excited that they shouted continuously: Long Live Chairman Mao! Long Live the Communist Party! We are liberated!

**Source 4** An extract from a report written by the Panchem Lama, the second most important Buddhist leader in Tibet. It was part of a petition the Panchem Lama personally submitted to Zhou Enlai, the Premier of the PRC. It describes the situation in Tibet after the introduction of changes made by the communists that the CCP termed 'democratic reforms'.

> Before democratic reform in Tibet there were over 2,500 large, medium and small monasteries in Tibet. After democratic reforms, only 70 or so monasteries were kept in existence by the government. This was a reduction of more than 97 percent. Because there were no people living in most of the monasteries, there was no one to look after their Great Prayer Halls and other divine halls and the monks' housing. There was great damage and destruction, both by men and otherwise, and they were reduced to the condition of having collapsed or being on the point of collapse. In the whole of Tibet in the past there was a total of about 110,000 monks and nuns. Of those, possibly 10,000 fled abroad, leaving about 100,000. After democratic reform was concluded, this number of monks and nuns living in the monasteries was about 7,000 people, which is a reduction of 93 percent.

## Activity: AS-style questions

1. Why is Source 3 valuable to the historian for an enquiry into CCP policies towards Buddhism in Tibet in 1950?
2. How much weight do you give the evidence of Source 4 for an enquiry into the realities of life in Tibet after the communist invasion?

## Activity: Evaluating the sources

1. Having read Sources 3 and 4 above, try to put them in context by answering the following questions:
   **a)** What events were taking place at the time that Source 3 was written?
   **b)** What debate are the sources contributing to?
   **c)** What is the purpose of each author of the sources?
2. Now try to evaluate the usefulness of the sources by answering the following questions:
   **a)** What does each of the sources argue about communist rule in Tibet?
   **b)** How similar and different are their arguments?
   **c)** How far do the sources reflect the full range of debate over the nature of communist rule in Tibet? Is there anything that the sources do not tell you?
3. Summarise the extent to which the sources are useful to the historian studying the attitude of the communist regime to Buddhism in Tibet. Make sure you deal with the ways in which they are useful and the limits of their usefulness.

## Reaching an overall judgement

Having understood, contextualised and evaluated the sources you should finish your essay with an overall judgement. Reaching a supported overall judgement is an important part of doing well in Section A. Your judgement in Section A is similar to the judgement that you should reach in the other sections of the exam (see page 68). However, in Section A, your judgement should be based on an evaluation of the evidence offered by the sources.

Your judgement should:

- clearly answer the question
- be supported by weighing the evidence of the sources.

In addition to this, the very best essays will distinguish between the levels of certainty of the different aspects of the conclusion.

Having already read the sources and evaluated them in their context as you did in the activity on page 315, it is possible to reach the following overall conclusion to the question on page 315. This is a high-level conclusion as it focuses on the question, reaches a supported judgement and discusses the different levels of certainty of the different claims it makes.

Both sources are useful to some extent to a historian investigating the policies of the communist regime towards Buddhism in Tibet. Both show that the regime was dedicated to the eradication of Buddhist ideas, buildings and the community of Buddhist monks. Source 1 reveals that the people of Tibet were exposed to a programme of propaganda and education that encouraged them to attack Buddhists who the source describes as 'counterrevolutionaries'. The policy of the regime is clearly to encourage attacks on Buddhism. Source 2 goes some way to providing evidence of the results of this attack: the temples and monasteries have been destroyed and the monks and nuns have fled. During this time Tibet was the target of a 're-unification campaign'. Although the communists had come to power in 1949, there were still parts of China, like Tibet, that were beyond their control. Tibet was a specific focus for repressive policies because its Buddhist culture provided an alternative belief system to communism and its religious leaders, the lamas, provided rivals to the Communist Party.

However, Source 1 is clearly created by the CCP to encourage the people of Tibet to rise up and attack the Buddhists. It is an example of propaganda and it does not really provide an insight into how far the policies were supported by the Tibetan people or how far the attacks on the Buddhists were carried out by communist soldiers. Although it claims that the people themselves rose up to attack the 'counterrevolutionaries', its origin and purpose mean that this claim cannot be taken at face value. It aims to provide an excuse for the attack on Buddhism by claiming that the people, not the Party, are the source of the attacks. Similarly, Source 2 also has a purpose: written by a Buddhist leader to attempt to alert the Chinese premier to the damage caused by Chinese occupation of Tibet, the author hopes to convince him to change Chinese policies. However, the Panchem Lama was travelling in Tibet at the time and was an eyewitness to the destruction, while Source 1 is written in emotive language with a tone that seeks to generate support for the CCP. The tone of Source 2 could be considered to be more measured: it uses statistics to support its argument without trying to be overly emotional or aggressive. Overall, although their purposes are very different, both sources are of some use: one provides the perspective of the communist regime, the other the viewpoint of the victims.

This focuses directly on the question.

The sources are used explicitly and together.

Contextual knowledge is used to explore the sources' usefulness.

The limits of the sources are summarised.

A conclusion is reached which is supported by the rest of the paragraph.

## Work together

Conclusions are made up of a series of claims (a claim is a statement). In the example conclusion on page 316:

1. Count the number of claims made in the conclusion.
2. Do you agree on the number of claims – if not discuss your different views and try to resolve the disagreement.
3. The different claims deal with a series of issues that are not all certain. List the words and phrases that are used to describe the different degrees of certainty.
4. Did you both spot the same words and phrases?

Use the list and your discussion to make a note of how you could improve your writing.

Imagine you are answering the following question and carry at the activity in page 318:

**How far could the historian make use of Sources 5 and 6 together to investigate the impact of the communist regime on healthcare in China?**

**Source 5** From Dongping Han, *The Unknown Cultural Revolution: Life and Change in a Chinese Village* (Monthly Review Press, 2008). The author is a Chinese academic who grew up in Jimo county, Shangdong province, during the Cultural Revolution. His work stresses the positive impacts of the Cultural Revolution, challenging the idea that it was a period of senseless violence and economic disaster.

> To be sure the rural cooperative medical system was of low quality. The barefoot doctors did not have much professional training, and the village clinic did not have much medical equipment, supplies or medicine. But it was the best system of medical care villages in Jimo had ever had and it provided villagers with important services and peace of mind. The value of the barefoot doctors to Jimo villagers cannot simply be measured by the formal training they received. They were from the same villages as their patients. They were available 24 hours a day in all weather conditions, even during the Chinese New Year or during a big snowstorm. Their medical training was adequate to treat common problems, and for big problems they could get help from regular doctors from the commune or county hospitals. For common problems like colds and tracheitis, the barefoot doctors had a standard treatment. Of course it would have been better if villages had doctors with more professional training, but they were not available at the time. Doctors with rudimentary training were better than no doctors.

**Source 6** From Jung Chang, *Wild Swans: Three Daughters of China* (HarperCollins, 1992). Jung Chang grew up in Mao's China, the daughter of parents who were both communist officials. During the Cultural Revolution she joined the Red Guards before being sent to the countryside to be a barefoot doctor.

> The propaganda about barefoot doctors was one of Mao's political manoeuvres. He had condemned the pre-Cultural Revolution Health Ministry for not looking after peasants and concerning itself only with city dwellers, especially Party officials. Mao offered a magic cure to the peasants: 'doctors' who could be turned out en masse – barefoot doctors. 'It is not at all necessary to have so much formal training,' he said. I went to work with absolutely no training. The only medical book I had ever set eyes on was *A Barefoot Doctor's Manual*. I studied it avidly. There was no theory in it, just a summary of symptoms. When I sat at my desk, with the other two doctors behind me, all wearing our dusty everyday clothes, it was clear that the sick peasants who came in very sensibly wanted nothing to do with me, an inexperienced eighteen-year old ... They went straight past me to the other two desks. I was more relieved than offended.

## Activity: Write your own conclusion

1 Read the question on page 317, the sources and the information about the sources.

2 Put the sources in context:

**a)** What is significant about the background of the two authors?

**b)** What debate or debates are the sources contributing to?

**c)** How far do the sources agree on the impact of the communist regime on healthcare in China?

**d)** Why do you think each source was written?

3 Read the question again.

**a)** Write a series of bullet points outlining:

- the aspects of the sources that are useful for answering the question
- the aspects of the sources that are less useful
- a summary of the extent to which the sources provide useful evidence about the changes in healthcare in China.

**b)** Now write the conclusion. Remember:

- You need to weigh the evidence, and therefore you should use words that help you to do that such as 'clearly', 'however', and 'nonetheless'.
- You should weigh the sources *together*, rather than separately. Make sure you use words and phrases that make it clear that this is what you are doing.
- You should try to specify how certain you are about your various concluding claims. Look at the example of a conclusion you have just read and try to use similar words and phrases to show which of your concluding claims are certain and which are less definite.

## Work together

Having completed your conclusion in the activity above, swap it with a partner. Consider the following questions:

1 How far did you agree on the context of the sources?

2 How far did you agree on the usefulness of the sources?

3 Which conclusion most effectively weighed the evidence of the sources? How was this achieved?

4 Did both conclusions really consider the sources *together*? How could you improve this aspect of your writing?

5 Which conclusion most effectively expressed the different degrees of certainty? How was this achieved?

6 Which conclusion most effectively focused on the question?

Use this discussion to make notes on how you can improve your Section A technique.

## Activity: AS-style questions

1 Why is Source 5 (page 317) valuable to the historian for an enquiry into the changes in healthcare in China during Mao's rule?

2 How much weight do you give the evidence of Source 6 (page 317) for an enquiry into the success of the 'barefoot doctors' programme?

# Section B: Essay technique

## Argument, counter-argument and resolution

The highest marks in Section B of the exam are available for sustained analysis. One way of achieving this is to write an essay that develops a clear argument and counter-argument, and then reaches a resolution. This approach is outlined in the activities that support Paper 1 (see page 107). This kind of structure is equally applicable to Paper 2 Section B.

### Activity: Detail and analysis

Imagine you are answering the following question:

**To what extent did the lives of the Chinese people improve in the period 1949–57?**

1 Read the question and work out what type of question it is.
2 Make a plan that is appropriate to the specific question. Rather than simply picking four relevant factors, develop an argument, a counter-argument and a resolution to the argument.
3 Add three pieces of detail to support each aspect of your essay. Remember, use the detail that best supports the argument you are creating.
4 Write an introduction that sets out the essential aspects of your argument, counter-argument and resolution.
5 Now write a conclusion to the essay.
   **a)** Start by asserting an overall judgement.
   **b)** Support this by writing an evaluative summary of your argument, counter-argument and resolution.
   **c)** Summarise your overall judgement in the final sentence.

### Work together

Having written your introduction and conclusion in the 'Detail and analysis' activity swap them with a partner. Consider the following questions:

1 Did you agree on what type of question you were dealing with? If not, discuss it and work out who was right.
2 Whose plan set out the most compelling overall argument?
3 Which introduction most clearly set out the key claims of your essay?
4 Which conclusion best summarised and evaluated the argument, counter-argument and resolution?
5 What can you learn from each other's work?

Use these questions to feed back to each other and improve your essay technique.

### Question practice

1 How far did the role and status of women change in the period 1949–65? AS
2 'Healthcare for Chinese people was extremely limited in the period 1949–76.' How far do you agree with this statement? AS
3 How far was Jiang Qing personally responsible for the impact of the Cultural Revolution, 1965–76?
4 How far did the CCP successfully replace traditional beliefs and attitudes in the period 1965–76?

Paper 2

# The German Democratic Republic, 1949–90

## The Big Picture

After the end of the Second World War in 1945, Germany and its capital city, Berlin, were each divided into four zones of occupation. Each of the victorious powers – the USA, the Soviet Union, Britain and France – took responsibility for one zone. As the 1940s progressed the three Western zones began to co-operate more while the Soviet zone took on more trappings of communism. It was becoming evident that two Germanies were being created.

Berlin lay geographically within the Russian zone and various crises developed which could have led to the Russians taking control of all of it. After the Berlin Blockade and Airlift of 1948–49, the western half of the city remained in the hands of the Western powers. The year 1949, however, saw the formal division of Germany into two states, the Federal Republic of Germany (FRG) and German Democratic Republic (GDR). The GDR owed its creation and survival to the support of the USSR which was very influential in its decision-making processes. It was a Russian satellite country, part of its Eastern and Central European sphere of influence.

### Establishing and consolidating communist rule

The GDR, ruled by the Communist Party (SED) and its leader Walter Ulbricht, developed along communist lines. Industry was taken under state control and farms were collectivised. When the Russian leader, Joseph Stalin, died in March 1953 there began a period of uncertainty, and there was a rebellion within the GDR. This was suppressed with Russian help and Ulbricht felt more confident to impose authoritarian rule. The existence of West Berlin within the heart of the GDR, however, allowed millions of its citizens to move west. These were often the best-educated and most skilled citizens whom the country could ill afford to lose. In August 1961 the decision was taken to build a wall through and around Berlin to stem this tide of migration.

### The development of the East German state

In a sense the Berlin Wall stabilised relations with the West, although the GDR remained at the interface of the Cold War, and Berlin in particular became a symbol of divided Europe. The SED, meanwhile, tried to modernise the GDR through the New Economic Policy and raise living standards through the introduction of more consumer goods. It always lagged behind the West, however; its citizens could see this through the widely available FRG television.

One of the biggest challenges for the GDR leadership was to create a national identity. This was attempted through the media promoting GDR achievements and in particular through international sporting success. The astonishing achievements of GDR athletes have since been soured by the exposure of widespread doping.

The GDR also sought international recognition. This hinged in particular on building a relationship with the FRG which had hitherto refused to recognise it. The policy of Ostpolitik began in the late 1960s which saw closer relationships developing with the FRG to the extent that it almost became the GDR's prime backer. The Soviet Union looked askance at this and supported the removal of Ulbricht whom it feared was seeking too much independence from the USSR. Ostpolitik continued, however, under his successor Erich Honecker and during the course of the early 1970s the GDR won the international recognition it craved, culminating in membership of the United Nations in 1973. It also experienced something of an economic renaissance with its citizens enjoying the highest living standards in the Eastern bloc. This came, however, at a price and the country found itself more and more in debt.

## Life in East Germany

The GDR prided itself on extensive social welfare programmes which it hoped would bind its citizens to it. Citizens were also encouraged to participate in SED controlled mass movements in which communist ideology was promoted. One in five of its citizens joined the SED. However, there is much debate about the actual extent of support for the regime, whether genuine or simply acquiescence. The Stasi or State Security Service was very powerful spying on millions of citizens and there was always a fear of repression. However, Honecker also tried to widen support, for example through his 1978 Concordat with the Protestant Churches.

The GDR was susceptible to Western influences in part because of the proximity of the FRG and the availability of its media.

## Growing crises and collapse

In the 1980s economic hardship became more apparent and conditions grew worse. This can be seen within the context of economic malaise throughout the communist bloc and the appointment of Mikhail Gorbachev as Soviet leader. Gorbachev sought reform and more open discussion but it soon became apparent he was embarking on major changes. He also said that his communist allies must sort out their own problems; the Soviet Union would neither bail them out nor intervene militarily to support them. Protests and unrest grew in the GDR, and emigration became possible through relaxation of border controls in Hungary. Faced with mass exodus of citizens, the SED dismissed old leaders such as Honecker and opened the Berlin Wall in November 1989. Events gathered their own momentum and, quite unexpectedly, within a few months the GDR had collapsed and Germany was reunited.

# Key Topic 1 Establishing and consolidating communist rule in the GDR, 1949–61

## Overview

After the end of the Second World War, Germany faced military occupation with the four victorious Allies each taking one zone. The capital city Berlin was also divided. In the next few years the three Western zones developed along capitalist lines while the Soviet zone increasingly became communist. While there was no overriding plan as to how Germany should develop, the Soviet leader Stalin sought to control all of Berlin by blockading its Western zones in 1948. This resulted in a massive airlift of supplies to the Western zones in Berlin which provided enough supplies to keep the people of West Berlin fed and with enough fuel to survive the winter of 1948–49. As a result the blockade failed and Berlin remained divided. Germany itself was divided into two countries – the FRG and GDR – in 1949. The GDR became a satellite of the Soviet Union, joining the economic alliance COMECON.

Although non-communist political parties remained, the GDR was ruled by the Socialist Unity Party (SED) through its Politburo. In a semblance of democracy there was an elected national parliament – the *Volkskammer* – and an upper House representing the states – the *Länderkammer.* However, these bodies merely rubber-stamped SED policy which, in its turn, often originated in the USSR. The GDR developed along communist lines with an emphasis on industrial development and collectivisation of agriculture.

After Stalin died in March 1953 there was a time of uncertainty during which the SED adopted the New Course. This slowed down the pace of socialism and promised to produce more consumer goods. However, a failed rebellion in June 1953, largely about working conditions, allowed Walter Ulbricht, First Secretary of the SED, to assume dictatorial control. He rescinded the New Course and resumed collectivisation and industrial development. Millions of East Germans moved to the FRG. Often these were the most highly qualified people. Ulbricht used various international crises in the late 1950s and early 1960s concerning Berlin to build a wall to keep GDR citizens in. This stabilised the situation but was a propaganda disaster for the GDR, signifying comparatively few would remain there by choice.

The overarching topic of establishing and consolidating communist rule in the GDR, 1949–61 is covered in four sections:

1. The post-war division of Germany
2. The system of government
3. Economic developments, 1949–61
4. Defending the GDR, 1949–61.

## TIMELINE

| | |
|---|---|
| 1943 November | Teheran Conference |
| 1945 May | End of the Second World War |
| 1945 June | Soviet Military Administration in Germany (SMAD) established in Berlin |
| 1946 April | Formation of the Socialist Unity Party of Germany (SED) |
| 1948 June | Beginning of Berlin Blockade and Airlift |
| 1949 January | Council for Mutual Economic Aid and Co-operation (COMECON) founded |
| 1949 April | North Atlantic Treaty Organization (NATO) founded |
| 1949 May | Creation of Federal Republic of Germany (FRG) |
| 1949 June | End of Berlin Blockade |
| 1949 September | End of Berlin Airlift |
| 1949 October | German Democratic Republic (GDR) founded |
| 1950 February | Ministry of State Security set up |
| 1953 March | Death of Stalin |
| 1953 April | USSR recommends SED becomes more conciliatory; beginning of the New Course |
| 1953 June | Rebellions in the GDR |
| 1955 May | Warsaw Pact founded |
| 1955 September | Creation of GDR's army (NVA) |
| 1961 August | Creation of the Berlin Wall |

# 1 The post-war division of Germany

Germany surrendered to the victorious Allies on 8 May 1945. It appeared a country in ruins. Its wartime leader Adolf Hitler was dead and many members of its government were either in hiding or under arrest. Hitler's expansionist aims and genocidal policies against Jews and others had brought the country to catastrophe. Four million Germans were dead and a further 10 million would shortly be expelled as refugees from areas of Eastern Europe it had previously controlled. Many of its cities were destroyed by mass bombing or battle. It had no functioning institutions or economy. Its currency had collapsed. There was widespread fear of starvation and the outbreak of disease among its inhabitants, many of whom were living in cellars or in the open, their homes having been destroyed. Adult men were noticeable by their absence; as many as 7 million of them were dead, missing or prisoners of war. Many of those captured by the Russians would either die or not reappear for ten years.

The four major Allies (Britain, France, the **Soviet Union** and the USA) had no coherent long-term strategy for how to deal with Germany. The four zones of occupation initially focused on **demilitarisation** and **denazification**, then later on economic development. As economic recovery from the war was slow, the three Western zones increasingly merged together to facilitate development while the Soviet zone increasingly became **communist**.

### Note it down

Use the 1:2 method of note taking in this section (see page x). For example, write down these sub-heading in the left-hand column:

- Allied policies
- The Soviet zone
- The creation of the Socialist Unity Party (SED)
- Developments within the Soviet zone
- Growing divisions
- The formation of the GDR

and a bullet-point list of factors relating to each.

You could also begin your collection of index cards (see page xi). Write a term that you need to define (for example, denazification) on the front of the card and the definition on the back. Specialist words are in red type the first time they are used and the definitions are found in the glossary (pages 441–48). Swap your notes with a partner afterwards to ensure you have covered all the main points.

Once it seemed inevitable that separate German states would be created, the emphasis turned to control of Berlin, also divided into four zones. Stalin provoked a crisis by blockading the Western zones of the city, to which the USA and UK responded with an airlift of supplies. By the time Stalin reopened the borders, the Federal Republic of Germany (FRG) had been created. This was followed by the foundation of the German Democratic Republic (GDR) as a socialist state in October 1949.

## Allied policies

The Allies had agreed policies about what to do with Germany in the short term but had not decided on longer-term strategies. Their thinking during wartime had understandably been dominated by a determination that Germany could never again become an aggressive military power. Hence in the Teheran Conference of winter 1943 there was a plan to divide Germany into zones of military occupation with key industrial areas such as the Ruhr controlled by the proposed **United Nations**. In 1944 the Morgenthau Plan to destroy its industrial capacity and refashion it as an agricultural state was favoured. However, by early 1945 this was regarded as impractical. What actually happened to Germany was decided at two key conferences held at Yalta in February and Potsdam in June 1945.

### Yalta

- The Allies agreed to divide Germany into four military zones – one governed by each of them (see figure 2, page 325). This would be overseen by an Allied Control Council comprised of members from each of the four victorious Allies.
- The Soviet leader Joseph Stalin sought a redrawing of Germany's eastern borders. Poland would be given all the land to the east of the Oder and Neisse Rivers as compensation for the **USSR** keeping land it had taken from the west of Poland in 1939 (see figure 1, page 324).

### Potsdam

The Allies agreed to the following policies:

- Denazification – former Nazi leaders would be brought to justice in post-war trials. The most famous of these was held at Nuremberg in 1945–46.
- Demilitarisation – military reductions would ensure Germany could never wage aggressive wars again.
- Deindustrialisation – large German industrial concerns would be dismantled partly to keep Germany weak but also to ship them to the Soviet Union to help pay **reparations** (see page 324).
- Democratisation – it was agreed that Germany should be prepared for democracy.

▲ **Figure 1: Germany and Poland in 1945.**

The idea of military zones of occupation was approved, with the capital city, Berlin, to be similarly subdivided (see figure 2, page 325). Berlin, however, lay geographically in the east of the country, within the proposed Soviet zone and there was no formal agreement about how the Western Allies would access their zones in Berlin beyond Soviet goodwill in allowing them to travel through territory it controlled.

### Reparations

The Allies were not so successful, however, in agreeing the issue of reparations. Stalin, whose country had lost over 20 million of its citizens and was in many regions a wasteland, wanted $20 billion whereas the USA refused to agree a fixed sum. They were reluctant to see the Soviet Union facilitate its recovery through further pauperising the Western zones. It was finally agreed that each occupying power would take reparations from their own zones, but Stalin could in addition have ten per cent of the industrial machinery in each of the three Western zones and a further fifteen per cent in return for food and raw materials from the Soviet zone.

It is important to note that this was a short-term strategy. There was no plan to permanently divide Germany. It was assumed that Germany would eventually be reunited; the Western Allies saw it as a **capitalist democracy**, while Stalin emphasised the demilitarised, neutral aspect. The priorities in 1945 were to denazify Germany and get it functioning again to ward off **humanitarian crises**.

## The Soviet zone

The Soviet zone consisted of five German states: Thuringia, Saxony-Anhalt, Brandenburg, Mecklenburg and Saxony. The population, 17 million in 1939, had dipped as a result of war losses but rose again to 19 million by 1947, swollen by 4 million refugees. Again, as a result of war losses, the ratio of women to men was 135:100 and for every 100 persons of employment age, there were 58 who were not. This meant there were a lot of young and elderly people as opposed to wage earners.

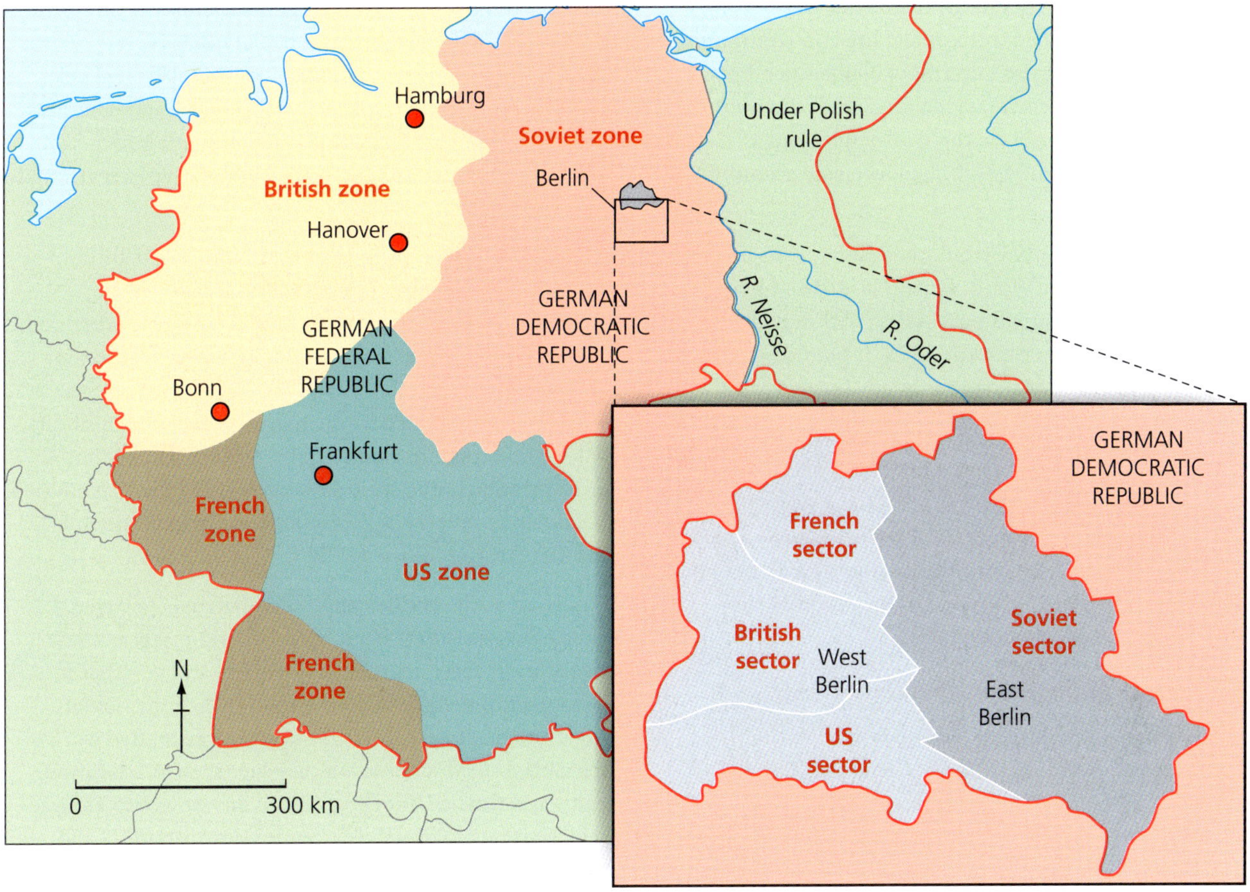


▲ Figure 2: Germany and Berlin divided into zones of occupation.

Historians now agree that the claims of war damage were over-exaggerated; most large-scale enterprises had been able to resume production shortly after the end of hostilities. Certainly there was nowhere near the 40 per cent reduction in industrial capacity claimed by the East German authorities in an attempt to minimise Soviet demands for reparations.

### Saxony-Anhalt

While much of the Soviet zone was agricultural in nature, Saxony-Anhalt in particular was an industrial centre, accounting for almost 50 per cent of the **machine tool** production in the zone. In 1939 Saxony-Anhalt had the biggest percentage of its **labour force** working in industry in all Germany. There was, however, a shortage of raw materials, especially good quality coal and iron ore. Before the post-war division, it had been dependent on exports from western Germany and eastern regions now in Poland such as Upper Silesia.

## Soviet policy

Stalin was inconsistent in his policies towards the Soviet zone. He had no desire initially to transform it into a communist **republic** separate from the other zones. He was not even sure that **communism** would work in Germany; he once said that communism fits Germany like a saddle fits a cow. Having said this, he ideally wanted to see a reunited Germany, preferably under communist control, so his aim was to achieve something he doubted was possible.

Clearly Stalin needed to control the Soviet zone and felt he could best do this by deploying German communists in key positions under the Soviet administration. Stalin chose, therefore, to create an 'anti-fascist democracy' to provide a model for the rest of Germany. The idea was for German communists to help run the Soviet zone largely under Russian supervision, and their anticipated success would lead to widespread support from the working classes in the other three zones. They would agitate for revolution in their zones and eventually a united communist-controlled

Germany would be achieved. In the Soviet zone, former Nazis would be excluded from public life and communists would govern on Marxist-Leninist principles (see box below). The idea of democracy derived from the notion that workers would embrace these principles and a communist government would therefore rule according to the common will.

Stalin also hoped the USA would withdraw from Europe as it had after the First World War (1914–1918). He was encouraged in this by a US proposal to withdraw by 1947. Stalin thought that, without the USA, it would be easier to create the desired form of a reunited Germany in the future.

It is essential to emphasise that no one knew how events would develop. Stalin's priority at this stage was to keep Germany weak and ensure ideas of **nationalism** did not re-emerge. However, by keeping Germany weak he would not get the reparations he needed to help rebuild the USSR. Here was another dilemma.

## The Soviet Military Administration

The Soviet zone of Germany was governed by the Soviet Military Administration (SMAD) and a group of experienced German communists. Some of these Germans, for example Walter Ulbricht and Wilhelm Pieck, had spent the Nazi years (1933–1945) in the USSR being prepared for this eventuality. In February 1945, when it was clear that Germany would be divided into four zones of occupation, Pieck was told to select 150 reliable German communists to help administer the Soviet zone. In April, he and nine colleagues were sent from the USSR to Berlin to help in its reconstruction. Other communist leaders from the 150 were sent to the other regions within the zone. The idea was to ensure communists held key positions, such as responsibility for security and education. Ulbricht, who was to become the dominant leader, said 'It's got to look democratic but we must have everything in our control.'

SMAD was created in June 1945. It comprised almost 50,000 Soviet and German members by November including 21 generals, and was supported by hundreds of thousands of Russian troops. Its role was to ensure the Soviet zone evolved in the ways Stalin wanted and to supervise all German administrators. It had responsibility for four key areas: military affairs, the economy, civil administration and political questions. Officially it advised; effectively it governed the Soviet zone until its demise with the creation of the GDR in October 1949.

It was rent with rivalries and incompetence, partly as a result of vague orders from Moscow and partly because of confusion about its role in Germany and whether it held a greater weight of power than that of the Soviet Government. It appointed administrations staffed by Germans to deal with domestic issues such as education, health and finance but these lacked any power to enforce their decisions. Nevertheless some administrations did develop a degree of autonomy from the central power. The German Economic Commission, set up in June 1947, was one such agency. It was responsible for co-ordinating the work of the central administration and drawing up economic plans, and later became the basis for the East German administration.

### Marxist-Leninism

Karl Marx was a nineteenth-century German philosopher who lived and worked for much of his life in Britain. He believed that the working classes would rise up to overthrow the bourgeoisie who ruled over them. He believed they were exploited by the system of capitalism in which they did all the work, but their employers enjoyed all the profits. Once in power they would create communism, for example by the abolition of private ownership. The state would control resources and concerns on the workers' behalf until they learned to manage everything themselves. Then gradually the state would wither away.

▲ **Karl Marx monument at Chemnitz**

Marxist ideas were first applied after the 1917 **Bolshevik** Revolution in Russia. Vladimir Lenin, the most important Bolshevik leader, adapted Marxist ideas to the situation in Russia, supporting rapid modernisation through the development of industry. Lenin's period of rule was too swamped with civil war and subsequent dislocation for much to be achieved, but his successor, Joseph Stalin, claimed to follow Lenin's lead through central planning, **collectivisation** or forced state ownership of farms and massive industrialisation. It was anticipated that all Soviet Union **satellite countries** would follow this model of communism – Marxist-Leninism. However, Stalin recognised this could not be achieved overnight; countries such as Poland and Hungary and the Soviet zone of Germany would inevitably be behind the USSR in terms of communist understanding and development. Therefore the application of Marxism should be more gradual.

## The creation of the Socialist Unity Party

In June 1945 the SMAD authorised political parties within the Soviet zone in part to develop and influence those in the Western sectors. In the Soviet zone there were two socialist parties surviving from the pre-Nazi years, the Socialist Party of Germany (**SPD**) and the Communist Party (KPD). These sought state control over key industries and the abolition of private ownership. In addition two other parties broadly sympathetic to their goals were authorised – the Christian Democrat Union (**CDU**) and Liberal Democratic Party (**LPD**).

In June, the KPD launched a manifesto which played down communism but focused very much on the **expropriation** of property belonging to former Nazis. Denazification was a popular policy because it implied that ordinary Germans did not share collective guilt but that the Nazis were solely to blame for its ills. By isolating former Nazis, the KPD set out its stall as the party which would allow Germans to move forward from the evils of the past for which the active Nazis had been solely responsible.

## Merger of KPD and SPD

The communist theorist Anton Ackermann wrote an influential article in 1946 in which he argued Germany needed to take a peaceful path towards socialism – there would be no Russian-style revolution but rather a democratic vote. This paved the way for the proposed merger between the KPD and SPD throughout Germany, not just in the Soviet zone. The thinking was still focused on a reunited Germany. The idea was that a merger between the two socialist parties would create a party big enough to win in future elections.

SMAD was very much in favour of the merger because it would create one large Communist Party. Some local organisations in the Soviet zone, for example in Thuringia, were very enthusiastic. While the KPD followed the line of the SMAD, SPD leaders often saw the merger as a way of attaining power and preventing the rise of any future Nazi-type party. Following a conference in April 1946 in East Berlin, the merger was agreed and the Socialist Unity Party of Germany (SED) was born. At first it had about 1,200,000 members comprised equally of former SPD and KPD members. By summer 1948 its membership was 2,000,000.

However, outside the Soviet sector of Berlin, and in the Western zones in particular, there was little support for the merger. For example, in a referendum held in the Western zones of Berlin on 31 March 1946 almost 20,000 members voted against it and only 3000 in favour. In the Western zones of Germany and indeed of Berlin there was no merger and the two parties remained separate.

Historians have argued that the merger was forced and East German archives have shown that the Russians were very influential in its creation. However, it is also true that the SPD leader Otto Grotewohl, who had been imprisoned during the Nazi years, did feel that disunity and indeed mutual hostility had weakened the socialist parties during the Nazi rise to power, and therefore he did not oppose the merger. It seemed sensible to have one strong united socialist party, not least in the eventuality of any future threats from the extreme right.

One thing was quickly made apparent: whether in the guise of the KPD or the SED, communists could not win free elections. In the October 1946 elections to create a Berlin administration, the SED won less than 20 per cent of the popular vote. In the 1946 elections for the regional administrations they failed to get over 50 per cent in a single province.

# Developments within the Soviet zone

The priorities for the authorities were to eradicate both Nazism and what were perceived as the preconditions which gave rise to it, and to organise reparations.

## Eradication of Nazism

Thousands of former Nazi Party members and officials were arrested and often sent to **concentration camps** such as Buchenwald and Sachsenhausen where conditions were as bad as during the Nazi period. Here inmates were beaten, worked as slaves and lived in inhumane conditions. They were joined by **dissident** communists and any who might potentially oppose the new regime, including former members of the SPD. It is estimated that between 1945 and 1950, 43,000 died in these camps. This figure does not include those who were sent to the USSR, executed or imprisoned within the **gulag system**. The eradication of Nazism was therefore widened to effectively purge the Soviet zone of any potential opposition.

It was felt that the elitist nature of pre-war Germany, with its wealthy classes and inequalities, gave rise to Nazism. The removal of these preconditions took various forms, including land reforms, the confiscation of property and reforms in the education system. The aim was to reduce elitism and widen equality of opportunity, binding beneficiaries to the new regime.

- Land reforms: In September 1945 all landowners who were tainted with support for Nazism with holdings exceeding 100 hectares lost their land without compensation. This affected 3.3 million hectares, or 33 per cent of all the useful agricultural land in the

Soviet zone. Two million hectares were redistributed to formerly landless peasants or smallholders. The average size of a holding was small, however – 0.6 hectares – and in the absence of machinery and livestock, many were subsequently abandoned by their new owners.

- Confiscation of property: In October 1945, property and firms belonging to former Nazis or leading officers in the wartime armed forces were confiscated by the regional administrations; some went to the USSR as reparations but the rest were maintained as new public enterprises. The managers were recruited from the working classes, although members of the SED featured heavily. Many became dependent on the success of the new regime as a result of these opportunities.
- Education: Higher education was opened up to members of the working class, thus creating a new graduate class dependent on the new state. In 1945 members of the working classes comprised three per cent of university students; by 1950 this figure had risen to 58 per cent. Schools within the Soviet zone taught a curriculum designed to promote communist ideas (see page 362) and engender support for the Russians. In Source A one student rebels against having to learn Russian.

**Source** A From Wolfgang W.E. Samuel, *German Boy* (Sceptre, 2002), page 252. A memoir of growing up in Germany in the years following the Second World War. The author has been caught truanting from Russian lessons to play soccer and has been hauled up before the *Rektor* (Headmaster) for punishment.

> He screamed about the greatness of Communism, about how he had suffered under Hitler and had escaped the Nazis and about how he had found asylum among his Russian brothers: now he was back to set things right. Part of setting things right was that we Germans would learn the language of our brothers [the students were beaten] ... From that time on we played no more soccer during breaks, all of us were punctual to our classes, and we studied our Russian lessons diligently. The brutal experience was demonstration enough for me that a new regime was in power and that it would react quickly and cruelly, regardless of the level at which it was challenged.

Source A was written many years after the events it described. How useful is it as evidence of making people conform within the Soviet zone?

## Payment of reparations

The Soviet Union exacted harsh reparations in part to help rebuild its shattered economy but also to keep Germany weak. Reparations took various forms to encompass the paying for damages perpetrated by Germany in the Soviet Union during the war, and the actual cost of the Soviet occupation of its zone in Germany:

- dismantling **industrial plants** and equipment for shipment to the USSR
- actual monetary payments.

It is estimated that the total cost between 1945 and 1954 was in excess of 54 billion **Ostmarks**; of this 16.8 billion were for occupation costs. This figure did not include plunder – theft, looting and so on – the costs of which are unknown.

That the reparations were in part to keep Germany weak is evidenced by the fact that the disassembled plants were often left to rust by railway sidings. The system only became more efficient once the Russians realised they were not benefiting from such wastage and that it was not in their interests to preside over an economically crippled zone – especially when the Western zones began to improve economically. By the time dismantling ended in 1948, however, the Soviet zone had lost 11,800 km of railway track, torn up for metal to send to the Soviet Union, and had suffered a 29 per cent loss in its wartime industrial capacity.

**Table 1: Cost of reparations as a percentage of GNP**

| Year | Soviet zone | Western zones |
|---|---|---|
| 1946 | 48.1% | 14.6% |
| 1947 | 38.4% | 12.8% |
| 1948 | 31.2% | 9.0% |
| 1953 | 12.9% | 3.8% |

Historian Peter Grieder has emphasised that many Germans at this time were too busy trying to survive to get overly concerned about politics and would have supported any regime that assured them sufficient food and shelter. However, there is no doubt that the cost of reparations was bitterly resented, and this, together with the repression of the concentration camps, made the Soviet Union deeply unpopular. Many, as we shall see, fled the Soviet zone. Others were apathetic, some were opportunists, but comparatively few were active supporters as the regime moved in different directions to the Western zone and tensions mounted.

## Growing divisions

The USA, Britain and France became increasingly at variance with the USSR as to how Germany should develop. These divisions should be seen in the context of wider divisions in Europe.

## The development of the Cold War

The USA was increasingly concerned that communism might spread throughout Europe, particularly as economic recovery was slow and the ensuing poverty seemed to offer the right conditions for communism to grow. In Western Europe, communist parties were sharing power in Italy and France and Eastern Europe was increasingly coming under Soviet control. US President Truman was influenced by the Domino Theory that suggested if one country became communist, its neighbours would follow. He introduced the Truman Doctrine in 1947 in which he seemed to suggest that the USA would help countries fight communist insurgency. In the same year, Truman committed US troops to Greece where Britain could no longer afford to maintain its military presence to fight communist rebels. It seemed increasingly likely that Europe was being divided into two rival armed camps dominated by the USA and the USSR. People began to explain this situation in terms of a Cold War - hostility without actually fighting each other directly.

## The Western zones' co-operation

The costs of rebuilding and reparations were destroying the German economy in the immediate post-war years. Western Germany was dependent on food imports from the east and, as these dried up, conditions of semi-starvation ensued. Many Germans existed on fewer than a thousand calories per day. Increasingly the USA and Britain realised that a poverty-stricken, starving Germany benefited no one, and the country had to recover. The most efficient way to achieve this was co-operation, so in summer 1946 they merged their zones economically into 'Bizonia'. The French joined their zone to Bizonia in April 1949 to create 'Trizonia'. With the three Western zones joined economically, political unification seemed more likely. The impact of this was the possibility of two distinct Germanies – one capitalist and Western, the other communist and dominated by the Soviet Union.

## Tensions in the Allied Control Council

Co-operation between the Russians and the Western powers was breaking down in the **Allied Control Council** (**ACC**). For example, the American zone suspended reparations payments to the USSR in May 1946 in retaliation for the Russians' refusal to deliver foodstuffs and there were disputes about the distribution of coal across the four zones. This situation was exacerbated by external tensions such as the communist takeover of Czechoslovakia in February 1948, and the Treaty of Brussels in March which set up a military alliance – the Western European Union. The final straw came in March 1948 when the Russian representative walked out of the ACC over plans to introduce a new currency, the Deutschmark, in the three Western zones. He argued that as the Western powers had no interest in decision making for the whole of Germany, the council had no future.

As tensions between the Soviet Union and the USA grew, the USA cancelled plans to reduce its military forces and announced they would remain in Germany. This was the period which saw the development of the **Cold War**.

## Marshall Aid

Meanwhile, following the harsh winter of 1946–47, influential Americans such as Secretary of State General George Marshall realised that the continent could not recover without help. In June 1947 the Marshall Plan was introduced to provide the finance Europe needed to aid recovery. This financial support was known as Marshall Aid. The USSR and most of its satellite countries did not attend the July Conference in Paris in which the plan was discussed. Many historians see this event as the formal division of Europe into Soviet and capitalist zones of influence; the two sides represented by those countries which did send delegates and those which did not.

## The Berlin Crisis

We have seen that internal and external tensions led the Soviet representative to withdraw from the ACC, which in turn enabled the Western powers to introduce a new currency (the Deutschmark) into their zones in June and make preparations for the creation of a new state from their three zones. This was to become the Federal Republic of Germany (FRG) in May 1949.

Historians disagree about Stalin's motives in the ensuing Berlin Crisis. He still appeared to favour a reunited Germany, but the Western powers had stolen the initiative. The Deutschmark was an immediate success. Most price controls and rationing were abolished in the Western zones and, benefiting from Marshall Aid, they began to make rapid economic progress. The Soviet zone, meanwhile, still languished in comparative poverty, even though the Soviets had retaliated by introducing a new currency of their own, the Ostmark.

## The Berlin Blockade and Airlift

Berlin lay geographically within the Soviet zone with no guarantees of access for the Western powers. Faced with a *fait accompli* that Germany would be divided, Stalin appears to have decided to take control of all Berlin for inclusion in the Soviet zone. As he said to Pieck, 'Let's try with all our might and maybe we can drive them out.' He therefore ordered a blockade of West Berlin. He ordered electricity supplies, which were generated in the East, to be cut off to the West, and on 24 June 1948 all land and canal routes from the Western zones to West Berlin were blocked. It was intended that the West Berlin authorities would face the alternatives of starvation or agreeing to join the Soviet zone. However, the Western powers organised an airlift. By September they were flying 4641 tons of supplies in every day. In April 1949, a month before the blockade was called off, they were managing almost 8000 tons, including items such as coal. Altogether 2,325,808 tons were flown into Berlin. In May, Stalin, realising that the Allies would not give in, restored electricity supplies and allowed convoys to use land and canal routes again.

The blockade had failed and the airlift showed the Allies would not abandon Berlin. It appeared that Germany, like Europe, had become divided.

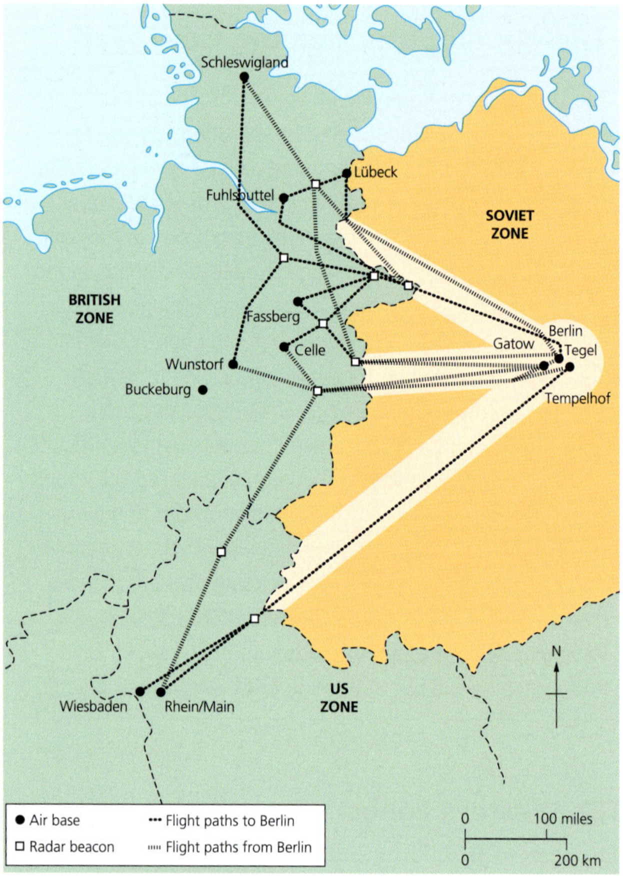


▲ **Figure 3: The Berlin Airlift.**

## The formation of the GDR, 1949

The GDR has been variously referred to as 'Stalin's unwanted child' and 'the unloved country'. Historian Mike Dennis has emphasised that it was created more out of default than design. After the creation of the FRG in May 1949 in the Western zones, there seemed little alternative. Even then, Stalin was reluctant to give the go ahead; when SED leaders spoke of creating a **People's Democracy** along the lines of other communist states, Stalin insisted on a gradual route to communism. Not only did he doubt the SED had the power to impose a communist regime, but he worried about international reactions to the formation of a communist state, and still hankered after a united Germany. The creation therefore of a communist state in the Soviet zone was very much the second best solution. Soviet leaders were realistic enough to know that it would take a communist regime years to catch up economically with the FRG and, as such, the latter would act as a magnet to dissatisfied East Germans.

Nevertheless the state was created. In 1947 a People's Congress had been set up supposedly to work towards German unity, although the few delegates from the Western zones were members of the KPD. The key decision to create a new state was ratified at the Third People's Congress in May 1949. In electing members to this Congress voters were presented for the first time with a single list of candidates; they either had to vote for them all or reject them all. In the relatively free vote, only 66.1 per cent approved it. Voting for subsequent single lists would not be so open.

The 330 members of this Congress agreed a draft Constitution of the German Democratic Republic and announced the formation of the new state on 7 October. In fact they were rubber-stamping a decision made in Moscow in September in which Pieck had already been appointed as President and Grotewohl as **Minister-President** of a provisional government which would undertake the responsibilities of the SMAD. The SMAD was technically abolished, but in fact transformed itself into the **Soviet Control Commission** whose role was to supervise the new state's implementation of any Allied directives relating to all of Germany as officially Germany was still under the overall control of the wartime allies. In this way 'Stalin's unloved child' was born but remained firmly under the control of its parents.

### International recognition

The GDR faced problems with recognition, particularly from the FRG and its Chancellor Konrad Adenauer who insisted the FRG spoke for all Germany. At the GDR's inception the only countries to recognise it were fellow communist countries. One of Ulbricht's, and indeed his successor Honecker's, greatest challenges was the quest for international recognition. This will be an important theme to which we shall return throughout this unit.

## Conclusion: The post-war division of Germany

The Allies had no long-term strategies for Germany in the post-war world. Stalin favoured reunification albeit as a socialist state. However, he recognised that communism might not fit Germany. The creation of the GDR therefore was not his most desired outcome. At best he hoped that the success of communism in the Soviet zone would give impetus to its spread throughout Germany.

Hence the GDR has been termed 'Stalin's unloved child'. It was born out of external factors such as the development of the Cold War and internal factors such as the growing co-operation of the three Western zones. There was also a dedicated group of communists who governed through the SED who wished to see the GDR become a fully fledged communist state. However, the GDR was not recognised by any countries except the USSR and other communist regimes in Eastern Europe.

### Stalin's notes

Stalin's notes exemplify how the GDR may have been a pawn in diplomatic games. On 10 March 1952 Stalin offered to sign a peace treaty with a reunited Germany. In his initial note he emphasised that the reforms that had taken place in the GDR would have to be extended to all Germany, so creating a communist Germany. The Western Governments replied by insisting on free all-German elections to which Stalin agreed in a second note dated 2 April 1952. Stalin of course did not really accept free elections because he knew the communists would not win. For this reason he rejected the West's proposal for independent United Nations monitors. After this rejection the notes came to nothing.

### Stalin's motivation: the debate

Historians have long debated Stalin's intentions. The German authority on the Cold War Wilfried Loch insisted that Stalin's offer was genuine, that Stalin saw a reunited Germany as the best guarantee of Soviet security. Others, for example Hermann Graml, have seen it as little more than a publicity stunt. Gerhard Wetting believes it was all part of a wider plot to bring down Adenauer's Government and destabilise the FRG. Mike Dennis argues that Stalin wanted to create confusion and use the offer of reunification to prevent the FRG joining the proposed Western military alliance, the European Defence Community.

### Work together

Work in pairs or in a small group. Go through the reasons for the creation of the GDR. You could consider issues such as:

- Allied strategies for Germany in the post-war period
- the creation of the SED
- the differing development of the three Western zones on the one hand and the Soviet zone on the other
- the Berlin Blockade and Airlift.

Discuss how far you think each reason was important. When you have come to some sort of agreement, write down bullet points summarising your ideas. Having done this, you can compare them and expand on them where necessary.

## 2 The system of government

The 1949 Constitution founded a **federal republic** with a People's Chamber – the ***Volkskammer*** – and the ***Länderkammer*** which represented the states. However, supreme authority resided with the **Politburo** of the SED. While the Constitution offered guarantees of free speech and religious toleration, Article 6 was a catch-all which could be used for repression. In March 1950 the Ministry of State Security was formed, from which emerged the **Stasi** or secret police. Other extensive security forces were also created. Elections took the form of single lists of candidates all vetted by the SED which voters had to accept or reject in its entirety. The SED was effectively the government of the GDR at all levels and its head Walter Ulbricht became dictator.

### Note it down

This section focuses on how the GDR was governed. Use a spider diagram (see page x) with 'The Political Structure of the GDR' as the body. Its legs should have the notes on the following headings:

- The system of government
- 1949 Constitution
- *Volkskammer*
- *Länderkammer*
- Political Controls – how Articles 6 and 8 could be interpreted
- Security Forces – how the security forces were set up and their role
- Elections in the GDR – how elections were conducted
- Political Control and the SED – how the SED controlled politics in the GDR (including the role of Walter Ulbricht)
- The SED and the state – how the SED dominated the state.

### The system of government and myth of democracy

The People's Congress which had rubber-stamped the creation of the GDR on 7 October 1949 turned itself into the *Volkskammer*, the parliament of the GDR, and passed the new constitution.

- The *Volkskammer* or People's Chamber was to be the supreme authority within the GDR. Its members were to be elected by secret ballot, with the weighting of parties represented by **proportional representation**. Its head was the Minister-President elected by the largest party in the People's Chamber.
- Personal rights such as freedom of speech, religion and assembly were assured, as was freedom to send letters uncensored through the mail.
- Trade unions were recognised and given the authority to call industrial action.
- Religious intolerance was outlawed. People were free to worship as they chose.

The five states were represented in the *Länderkammer* – the States' Chamber.

### Council of Ministers and *Volkskammer*

The supreme organ of legislation was the *Volkskammer* whose members were elected by direct and secret ballot. All citizens over the age of 18 could vote and those over 21 could apply for political office.

The highest authority was the Council of Ministers with a Minister-President at its head. Ministers were elected by members of the *Volkskammer* and were supposed to represent members of all the political parties. The Council of Ministers was officially the government although it was not formally recognised as such until the Constitution was amended in 1972. Its role in fact was to implement the wishes of the *Volkskammer* which had the responsibility of determining policy, organising finance and so on.

### *Länderkammer*

The *Länderkammer* was the legislative body which represented the five *Länder* or states of the GDR. Its delegates were selected from the five legislative bodies (the *Landtage*) which determined policy at *Land* level. Their job was to reflect the interests of the *Landtage* which had selected them. The *Länderkammer* could veto legislation but the *Volkskammer* could always override this.

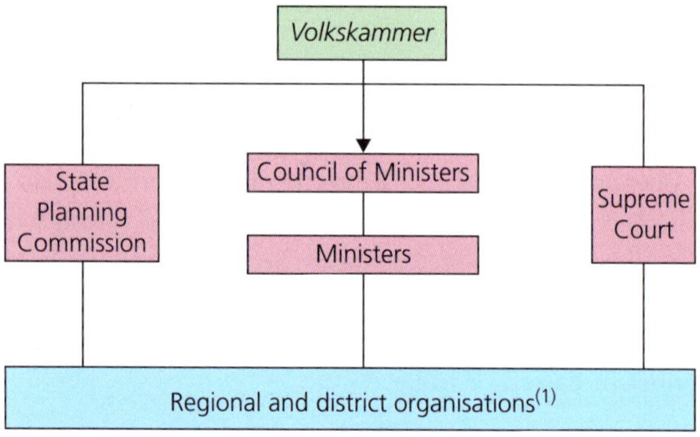


*(1) Länderkammer abolished* 1958.

▲ **Figure 4: Political structure of the GDR.**

## Political control

While the Constitution may have seemed democratic with civil rights guaranteed, there were important provisos. However reasonable these seemed, they could be and were very loosely adapted and rigorously enforced. The most significant were Articles 6 and 8. These articles effectively gave the authorities the power to act as ruthlessly as they chose to curb behaviour they considered undesirable and enabled the GDR to be run as a dictatorship. (see source B).

**Source B** Articles 6 and 8 from the 1949 Constitution of the GDR.

Article 6

All citizens have equal rights before the law.

Incitement to boycott [1] of democratic institutions or organizations, incitement to attempts on the life of democratic politicians, the manifestation of religious and racial hatred and of hatred against other peoples, militaristic propaganda and warmongering as well as any other discriminatory acts are felonious crimes within the meaning of the Penal Code. The exercise of democratic rights within the meaning of the Constitution is not an incitement to boycott.

Whoever has been convicted of such a crime is disqualified from holding public office or a leading position in economic or cultural life. He also loses the right to vote and to stand for election.

Article 8

Personal liberty, inviolability of the home, secrecy of the mail, and the right to take up residence at any place are guaranteed. State authority may restrict or revoke these freedoms only on the basis of a law applicable to all citizens.

[1] Incitement to boycott refers to attempts to dissuade people from participating in elections or taking part in state-run activities or organisations.

How could the security forces interpret the articles in Source B to curb individual freedoms within the GDR?

Various measures were introduced to ensure the state could control its citizens.

- On 7 December 1949, the GDR Supreme Court and Department of Public Prosecutions were created. Among other powers such as trying all cases of 'great significance', the Supreme Court was given the authority to interpret Article 6 as it chose. The Department of Public Prosecutions was tasked with prosecuting those who broke the law.
- The Central Commission for State Control, responsible to the Minister-President, was set up to order the investigation of those felt to pose any threat to the regime. Ultimately this was the group responsible for overseeing the security forces.
- The **People's Police** (**KVP**) stood at 50,000 strong by 1950 and formed the basis for the future National People's Army, which was formed in 1955 as the army of the GDR.
- The Ministry of State Security – the notorious Stasi – was set up in February 1950. Its duties were deliberately left vague. Tellingly it reported not to any state organisation but to the Politburo of the SED. It was all-powerful and outside the Constitution. Its remit was essentially threefold:
  - to detect all internal opposition to the state
  - to conduct espionage abroad
  - to provide security for political institutions, installations, public buildings and so on.

### Constitutions of the GDR

The 1949 Constitution was something of a compromise. In its emphasis on a States' Chamber and People's Chamber from which most legislation emanated, it resembled that of a democracy. In April 1967, Ulbricht recognised that this constitution no longer fitted the socialist republic of the GDR. A new constitution dating from April 1968 reflected the central role of the SED. In 1949, power had been said to be derived from the people; in 1968 it was from 'working people implementing socialism under the leadership of the Marxist-Leninist party', i.e. the SED. While still recognising civil rights, Article 21 rather ominously linked them with 'corresponding obligations'. The amendments of 1974 downplayed the increasing ties with the FRG (see page 175) and emphasised eternal ties with the USSR.

## Elections in the GDR

A further body, The National Front for a Democratic Germany, was set up by the *Volkskammer* in February 1950. Its role was to speak for all parties and institutions within the GDR and draw up candidate lists in elections; effectively it controlled elections.

The first elections to establish a permanent *Volkskammer* and *Länderkammer* took place in October 1950. As a blueprint for future elections the National Front drew up a single list of candidates on the basis of selection meetings at local level. Most non-SED candidates were rejected at these selection meetings. Over 400 were rejected in the state of Saxony-Anhalt, for example. As with all single lists of candidates, voters had to either approve or reject all the names on the list; they could not approve some and reject others.

The electoral turnout was 87.4 per cent and, of these, 99.7 per cent approved the single list of candidates. While the voting was meant to be secret, often it was not. Elections were carried out in a climate of fear as a result of mass purges and bribery. The elections coincided with laws providing credit for small farmers and benefits for disabled people. Historian Peter Grieder emphasises the point that there was from the outset a link between support for the state and welfare provision, and the timing here no doubt had some element of electoral bribery.

The SED took 110 seats in the *Volkskammer*, with the CDU and LPD each taking over 60. Two smaller parties, the Democratic Farmer's Party of Germany (DBD) and National Democratic Party of Germany (NDPD) took a further 60 between them, while mass organisations such as the **FDJ**, the communist youth organisation, also supplied delegates depending on their size. All these mass organisations were dominated by the SED, so whatever the actual political make-up suggested, the SED could dominate proceedings. It also took control of the most important committees. (see Table 2).

**Table 2: October 1950 election results to the *Volkskammer*.**

| Party/Organisation | Number of seats |
|---|---|
| SED | 110 |
| CDU | 67 |
| LDP | 66 |
| NDPD | 35 |
| DBD | 33 |
| Mass organisations | 155 |

The *Länderkammer*, meanwhile, was completely dominated by the SED as were each of the *Länder*.

## The dominance of the SED

The SED dominated the GDR with the *Volkskammer* simply rubber-stamping its proposals. The **Secretary-General** of the SED, Walter Ulbricht, was effectively the ruler of the GDR even though, officially, he only held the post of Deputy Prime Minister. Ulbricht ruled in part through the Ministry of State Security (the Stasi) which quickly made its presence felt.

### Walter Ulbricht, 1893–1973

Walter Ulbricht was born in Leipzig in 1893 and served in the First World War mainly on the Eastern Front, although he deserted in 1917 and spent some time in prison. On his release, he joined the KPD and in 1924 was sent to Moscow to the Lenin School, established to train future leaders of world revolution. Ulbricht was a **functionary**. With a thin, reedy voice and lack of charisma he would always appear the background player while often surreptitiously directing events. One of his contemporaries noted that he did not smoke, drink or socialise. He was hard working, very observant and gave nothing of himself away. He was also completely loyal to the line taken by Moscow.

On his return to Germany in 1925 he gained a seat in the **Reichstag** but spent much of his time back in the USSR as the German representative in the **Comintern**. Then, in 1929, he was elected to the Politburo, the supreme decision-making body of the KPD. As the KPD leader in Berlin, he became known for organising battles with the Nazis as each vied for power and once, during a brief period of truce when both Nazis and communists supported a transport workers' strike, shared a platform with Joseph Goebbels, later to become the Nazi Minister of Propaganda.

Clearly Ulbricht was a hunted man once the Nazis came to power and ordered the purges of all their political opponents. He spent the next twelve years in exile, first in Paris and then in the USSR. With over 70 per cent of the German KPD exiles being killed in the Stalinist purges of the 1930s, it is assumed that Ulbricht must have co-operated with the Soviet secret police to escape persecution. Certainly he accepted the central control of the USSR Communist Party (CPSU) and sought to replicate it in post-war Germany. By the establishment of the SED as the dominant force in the GDR it appeared he now had the opportunity to do so.

Some argue that the juxtaposition of the words 'personality' and 'Walter Ulbricht' are oxymoronic. He was the **apparatchik** par excellence, the man in the background who eschewed being noticed but was all powerful. Later in his career Ulbricht still pretended to disdain any notion of a **personality cult** but was rather pleased as one developed. He became known as the father of the GDR.

## The purges

The Stasi, whose workforce grew eightfold from 1100 to 8800 between 1950 and 1952, began to arrest potential opponents, including members of the SED. These specifically included:

- anyone who had spent time in the West and may have been contaminated by capitalist attitudes
- anyone who had been in contact with Noel Field, an American communist accused of working for the CIA
- anyone who appeared too worldly or supported **Zionism**.

This latter category was a replication of **anti-Semitic** policies in the USSR. Because there were few Jews in the GDR, it was felt that they would be easy targets and could be arrested without many people standing up for them. Communists tended to associate Jewish people with support for capitalism and it was easy to accuse them of **internationalism** or **imperialism** without needing to define what the terms actually meant.

Arrests could, however, be quite arbitrary, possibly a way of settling old scores or playing to prejudices. Ulbricht, who had spent the Nazi years in the Soviet Union, where unlike most of his colleagues, he had survived the mass Stalinist purges of the 1930s (see page 334), disliked SED members who had suffered under the Nazis. He ordered the arrest of Franz Dahlem, who had survived the concentration camps but favoured German reunification more than Ulbricht. Paul Merker, a Politburo member, was accused of supporting Zionism; certainly he had argued for the creation of Israel and opposed anti-Semitism. This was enough for him to be accused of being an imperialist agent and sentenced to eight years in prison.

Ulbricht did not organise show trials along the lines or scale of those which were happening in other communist countries. One of the reasons was the GDR was too close to the West and Western journalists could possibly infiltrate to cover the trials. More cynically it has been argued that Stalin wanted to keep rival leaders alive in case Ulbricht failed. Show trials almost always resulted in the execution of the accused. The trials in the GDR took place in secret and led to arrest and exile.

## The SED and the state

The SED dominated the state at all levels.

- The Council of Ministers, the main executive organ of government, had to comply with SED decisions. The Council was dominated by SED members such as Grotewohl and Ulbricht.
- The SED dominated public sector jobs at all levels and promoted the employment of members of the working classes. By the end of the 1940s, 49 per cent of public officials had a working class background. This grew in the following decade through the directives that 60 per cent of those in secondary school and centres of higher education had to come from the working classes; there were even special courses to bring members of the working classes up to higher education standards. This also, of course, had the effect of binding many officials to the communist system. It did, nevertheless, appear fairer. The SED selected potential public official personnel and even trained them through their own courses. The emphasis was on ideological purity as much as on skills such as administrative efficiency.

## The SED's governance

The SED itself was governed by a Central Committee or Politburo, and a Central Committee Executive of 80 members. These elected the Politburo which was made up of 14 full members in 1947 and candidate members who had less influence. The emphasis was on centrally made decisions. Ulbricht as Secretary-General was the most

### Noel Field, 1904–70

Noel Field was a Soviet spy working for the US State Department in the 1930s. During the Second World War he had involved himself with considerable humanitarian work while remaining a staunch communist. He was arrested in Prague in 1949 by the communist authorities apparently suspected of being a double agent who had recruited influential communists across Europe to work for the CIA. Although imprisoned and tortured for five years, Field was never actually accused of anything and was eventually released in October 1954. It may be that he was simply used as an excuse to arrest people who appeared in **show trials** in Hungary and Czechoslovakia. They were accused of being US spies with little or no evidence beyond the assertion that Field had recruited them for his spy network. In the GDR many prominent functionaries, including the head of Radio Berlin, were arrested as a result of alleged associations with Field, at least one of whom died in prison.

influential member and all the others were aware from the recent purges of what might happen to those he saw as potential rivals. The Party believed that socialism was inevitable according to scientific laws of history. Socialism and the Party which adopted its precepts were therefore infallible. In extreme examples in the Soviet Union purges had been used to blame opponents for sabotage if any policies failed, although in the GDR simple resignations were usually sufficient – as Ulbricht himself would discover (see page 369).

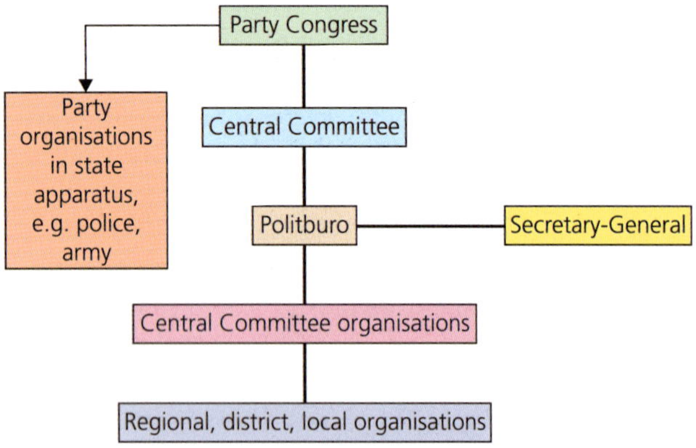


**▲ Figure 5: Structure of the SED.**

## The construction of socialism

It was only when all attempts to create a united Germany had failed that Stalin accepted the road of the GDR towards full-blown communism. He gave the go-ahead on 8 August 1950. In his speech to the third SED Conference, Ulbricht signalled this through the need to intensify the **class struggle** and equip the state to deal with internal and external enemies. The tasks of the state, he said, should be to destroy any resistance of capitalists and landowners, establish an army for defence and construct socialism.

By the end of July 1952, the five *Länder* dissolved themselves to be replaced by 15 regional organisations known as *Bezirke* controlled by the SED. The idea was that the *Länder* were unnecessary as the lower organisations could represent their citizens. This was clearly a process in the growing centralisation of power of the SED under the guise of greater democracy at lower levels. The *Länderkammer*, its members nominated by members of the new district assemblies or *Bezirkstage*, remained in existence until December 1958, but its powers were severely diminished.

Apart from the influence of the USSR, the SED was now effectively in control of the GDR which became a non-federal centralised state. The main personality was Walter Ulbricht, as Secretary-General of the SED and Deputy Minister-President.

## Conclusion: The system of government

The GDR was a police state from its inception. While the Constitution appeared to offer guarantees of free speech and other rights, this was an illusion. Article 6 could be widely interpreted to outlaw any activities the Government disliked. True power resided with the leadership of the SED aided by a fearsome security apparatus. There was a purge early on of SED leaders who were felt to be unreliable. By 1950 Ulbricht had been given the go-ahead by the USSR to develop full-blown communism in the GDR and he had the political power and security apparatus to enable this to take place.

### Work together

Take a large piece of paper. Draw a diagram to show the political structure of the GDR. Use it to explain to a partner how the political structure of the GDR worked. Discuss whose diagram was the most straightforward and easiest to explain, and why this was so.

## 3 Economic developments, 1949–61

As the GDR moved to developed socialism, it centralised economic planning and concentrated on the development of heavy industry and the **collectivisation** of agriculture. This involved cuts in production of consumer goods and social welfare provision, wage reductions and the introduction of new **work norms**. The death of Stalin led to instability in the leadership in Moscow and the introduction of the New Course which promised some improvements in living conditions in the GDR. The work norms remained, however, and stimulated the July 1953 rebellion.

### Note it down

Make notes in the section to address the following questions:

1. How did the central control and planning system work?
2. What developments took place in agriculture and industry?
3. What were the problems with living standards and work norms?
4. How effective was the New Course?
5. What factors led to the June 1953 revolt and why did it fail?
6. How did Ulbricht regain control of the SED?
7. How did the GDR develop under Ulbricht's control?

The rebellion was defeated by Soviet forces within the GDR. Back in control the SED leadership tightened and extended security and imposed more of a dictatorship. However, social welfare schemes were extended to try to gather more support for the regime.

### Socialist economics and planning

The GDR operated a centralised system of economic planning based on the Soviet model. In 1950, a State Planning Commission was created as the supreme planning authority. This drew up a series of **Five-Year Plans** in which targets were set and labour and resources allocated to meet them. Production, prices, quantity were all centrally planned. All production managers had to do in the various industries was ensure the targets were met. There were in theory many advantages to this system, although they tended to be ideological rather than necessarily economic in nature:

- The Government could harness the economy to the perceived needs of the state and desired outcomes – for example a concentration on public transport rather than private cars.
- Social rather than personal needs were emphasised – items were produced for the good of the community such as housing rather than consumer goods which may have been unnecessary.

However, there were also significant disadvantages which tended to be economic rather than ideological:

- Emphasis tended to be on quantity rather than quality.
- Too centralised a system stifled innovation and creativity; managers produced what the central planners told them to.
- The system was inefficient; it was difficult to plan needs five years hence and often goods were produced which were not required at the expense of those that were.
- As all production was planned and resources provided, there was no profit motive. The goods would still be produced whether they were cost effective or not.

Prices did not always reflect economic value or even costs of production; economic rules of **supply and demand** were not always considered.

### The First Five-Year Plan

The aim of the First Five-Year Plan was:

- to develop heavy industry in key industries such as iron and steel, energy and chemicals
- to increase living standards significantly above pre-war levels
- to overtake the living standards in the FRG to make the GDR more appealing to all German workers.

It anticipated hugely ambitious increases as Table 3 shows.

**Table 3: Projected increases in the First Five-Year Plan (1951–55).**

| Measure | Projected increase over 1950 level |
|---|---|
| National income | 60% |
| Labour productivity in industry | 72% |
| Agriculture | 25% |
| Metallurgy | 153.6% |
| Heavy machine building | 114.8% |

These targets were to be met by central planning throughout, including the provision of resources and work norms or expected output by the workers. The planners decided what should be produced and, to a large degree, how it should be done. Ideas such as the profit motive and the workings of supply and demand were not considered as important.

Clearly we can see with hindsight that these targets were unrealistic but it appeared planners were genuine in their beliefs because, as they saw it, the laws of history were on their side. They believed communism worked.

On the surface the plan achieved some impressive success in terms of industrial production. In a copy of the USSR **Stakhanovite movement** (see page 53), a miner, Adolf Henneke, was celebrated for increasing his daily output by a staggering 380 per cent. According to GDR statistics, pig iron production rose from 37,000 tons in 1950 to 1,517,000 tons in 1955; steel expanded from 999,000 to 2,508,000 tons. However, the increases were at the expense of living standards. The GDR always faced conflict between increased heavy industrial output and the provision of consumer goods. They could not produce both, and the economic history of the GDR is a story of shifting emphasis between the two. During the 1950s the emphasis was on the former. The dilemma was exacerbated by the GDR's membership of **COMECON** (see page 359). COMECON was the economic alliance of communist countries in which each was given its own area of productive specialisation with the concomitant need to buy goods from the other members.

## Problems with central planning

The SED had overestimated the economic capacity of the GDR and in their calculations for the Five-Year Plan had failed to account for the development of the armed forces or the continuing reparation payments to the USSR. It was proposed to pay for these through reductions in the welfare budget and cuts in consumption. However, this was insufficient. The state budget was 700 billion Ostmarks in deficit by 1952. The GDR bought goods to the value of 600 million Ostmarks in excess of what it sold to its Eastern European partners. The further burden of the development of heavy industry, which saw a 60 per cent increase in mining and iron and steel compared with a two per cent increase in the production of consumer goods, annoyed consumers who complained of shortages. Consumers found it difficult to buy items as varied as paper, clothes and basic foodstuffs such as butter, potatoes, fruit and rice. Nevertheless further cuts to the welfare budget had to be made, for example:

- cuts in cheap transport – although it was still heavily subsidised
- cancellation of working mothers' monthly day off work to catch up on domestic chores
- price rises in subsidised foodstuffs including jam, bread and confectionery.

This still was not enough to reduce the deficit and by 1953 shortages were beginning to appear, not only of foodstuffs but also of construction materials such as bricks. Whatever the official figures said, people could see that there were economic problems.

The planners could not be wrong; if the system was not working, the first reason must be sabotage or opponents deliberately limiting production, vandalising equipment and so on. Those with wealth such as owners of rented property were blamed and the Council of Ministers decided to withdraw their food ration cards – about 2 million were affected. Then they decided to cut wages and introduce new work norms. Workers were expected to increase production by ten per cent, a target that they could not meet often because essential tools and equipment were unavailable. This meant they missed out on bonus payments for meeting targets through no fault of their own, which was akin to a 25 per cent wage reduction for many employees. April 1953 saw prices rises in essential goods. Many people felt with some justification that conditions were worsening rather than getting better. They were working harder for essentially the same wages which were buying less.

The authorities worried about unrest and in particular the growing numbers who were thinking with their feet and leaving for the FRG. This rose from 165,648 in 1951 to 182,393 in 1952 and 120,000 in the first four months of 1953. There were criticisms and grumbling which the authorities often translated as a form of sabotage. Repression increased in line with unrest – the prison population grew by over 30,000 between July 1952 and May 1953.

# Agricultural collectivisation

The development of agriculture, particularly through collectivisation, was a key component of the planning process. The idea was that more could be achieved through large farms which could afford more machinery to operate in bigger fields and more animals, and would achieve more **economies of scale**. The leaders of the GDR had emphasised that collectivisation of agriculture should be a voluntary process; in fact it was far from this. Collectivisation was promoted by offering tax relief and such essentials as equipment and seed – and by way of contrast, higher tax rates and the non-availability of equipment to those who refused. As a result the number of collectives (**LPGs**) increased from 1999 covering 200,000 hectares in 1952 to 6000 covering 1.2 million hectares by 1955.

## The Socialist Spring

The process of collectivisation soared between 1959 and 1960, giving rise to the term 'The Socialist Spring'. By May 1960, there were 19,345 collective farms, working 83.9 per cent of the productive land. The intention was to make the GDR self-sufficient in food production.

By the late 1950s, 29 per cent of agricultural land was farmed by collectives. However, the leadership thought this was insufficient. Grotewohl announced at the Central Committee in December 1959 that collectives were superior to private farming and initiated a hurried campaign to bring all private farmers into collectives. This was effectively a forced campaign and they wanted it complete before the planting season began in spring 1960. The goal was to overtake the FRG in terms of agricultural production. However, the process led to disruption and resentment – and often to farmers leaving for the West.

**Table 4: Growth of collectives as a result of the forced campaign. (Note that even as the number of farms fell in the early 1960s, the amount of land under cultivation by collectives grew – because the farms became bigger.)**

| Year | No of LPGs | Area in millions of acres | Total % area of arable land |
|---|---|---|---|
| 1957 | 6,691 | 1.63 | 25.2 |
| 1958 | 9,637 | 2.39 | 37.0 |
| 1959 | 10,132 | 2.80 | 43.5 |
| 1960 | 19,345 | 5.39 | 85.0 |
| 1961 | 17,860 | 5.43 | 84.6 |
| 1962 | 16,625 | 5.46 | 85.4 |
| 1963 | 16,314 | 5.46 | 85.6 |

### Agriculture in the Erfurt area

George Last in his study of the Erfurt area has shown that the local SED launched a furious campaign during the Socialist Spring to hurry the collectivisation of agriculture. This was not only met with reluctance, but he also was able to show a correlation between the campaign and emigration to the West. The region had been more unwilling than other areas to collectivise its agriculture – by 1958 only 18 per cent of farms had done so. When the SED pressed for collectivisation, many farmers left. Once the Berlin Wall (see page 343) had stopped migration most of those who remained accepted collectivisation, however unenthusiastically – an example perhaps of the normalisation thesis (see page 357). In 1968, the SED Institute of Research found only 5.5 per cent of farmers surveyed preferred collectivisation to private farming. But they had no choice but to make the best of a bad job.

## Opposition to socialist economics

There was considerable opposition to socialist economics. Many farmers resented collectivisation and remained outside the system for as long as they could. Many left the GDR: by mid-1953 750,000 hectares were unused as landowners fled. The removal of the profit motive in industry led to disincentives to innovate and take risks. Many managers did not try very hard to improve production while their workers grumbled and did as little as possible. Their lack of motivation was worsened by shortages of essential foodstuffs and goods such as clothing, shoes and paper. Unofficial strikes were common, particularly over unrealistic work norms, poor quality equipment, and health and safety issues. This discontent continued throughout the lifetime of the GDR although came to a head in June 1953 (see below).

It should be remembered too that most people in the GDR did not actively support communism and remembered the capitalist system. They were slow to adapt to socialist economics because they were unused to it.

## The New Course

Stalin died in March 1953. This led to a period of uncertainty with Soviet leaders jostling for power and a lack of guidance for countries in the **Soviet bloc**. At Stalin's funeral Ulbricht asked his Soviet colleagues for advice on how to proceed but was left dissatisfied. The GDR may have hoped for reduced reparations, but what they got from the new Soviet leaders was a document dated 27 May 1953 entitled 'Measures for restoring the political situation in the German Democratic Republic', which was more commonly known as the New Course. This followed a Soviet initiative to slow down socialist development and called for a more conciliatory policy aimed at engendering more support and easing the population into socialist development rather than having it imposed upon them suddenly. On 9 June, the Politburo accepted the document, followed on 11 June by the Council of Ministers – an example of where decisions were actually made in the GDR. The New Course had the following effects:

- withdrawal of the April price rises
- restoration of the confiscated ration cards
- end to discrimination against Christians (see page 208)
- discontinuation of the collectivisation process
- restoration of property to returning emigrants which had been confiscated when they left
- production of more consumer goods.

This retraction was to some extent a self-criticism, and the SED publicly recognised it may have been unjust and had made mistakes. One gesture on 14 June saw 4000 political prisoners being released. However, it was too little too late.

## Challenges to Ulbricht and the Soviet power struggle

Ulbricht was worried about events in the USSR. The power struggle in Moscow added to his uncertainties. The former **hardliner** Beria was talking of abandoning the GDR entirely; his rival Khrushchev opposed this because the GDR was too important strategically. Nonetheless the discussions showed the GDR only really existed through the support of the Russians. It was a pawn. Ulbricht moreover refused to liberalise. He remained a hardliner who did not approve of the New Course and was biding his time to rescind it. Meanwhile, he became aware that various colleagues such as Rudolf Herrnstadt, editor of the SED newspaper *Neues Deutschland*, and Wilhelm Zaisser, Minister of State Security, who had close links with Beria, were taking advantage of the uncertainties to plot against him, hoping to create a collective leadership in the GDR.

## June revolt

In June 1953 the first revolt against communist control in the Soviet bloc took place in the GDR. This was followed by rebellions in other countries, for example Poland, but they tended to be spontaneous and localised while that in the GDR spread to much of the country. The authorities in the GDR were quick to blame Western Governments and infiltrators, but there was no conspiracy or plan to replace the Government with a specific regime. When the revolt began it was about living and working conditions and in particular the hated work norms. Having said this, the rebellions both in the GDR and elsewhere followed the death of Stalin and uncertainties concerning which new leaders would emerge in the USSR. Some possibly hoped the USSR would relinquish its control of Eastern Europe. However, there was little evidence to afford any hope of this.

In the GDR, the work norms, which were the biggest bone of contention among most people, remained in force. In protest there were strikes and demonstrations both in towns and the countryside and calls for the Government to resign. In Berlin on 16 June, building workers in the Stalinallee Project, a huge residential building project, went on strike and marched to SED headquarters demanding to speak to Pieck and Grotewohl. By the time of their arrival the protestors' numbers had swelled to 2000. In the face of government intransigence they called for a **general strike** the next day – 17 June. US radio stations such as RIAS (see page 404) in West Berlin encouraged them to rebel. On 17 June, 25,000 or more converged on the Council of Ministers headquarters and their demands widened to include free elections and the resignation of the Government.

Historian Mike Dennis has explained how the Government was ill equipped to deal with protests, not least because they had come to believe their own propaganda that people were happy and satisfied with socialism. More practically they were reluctant to call out the KVP as they could not be sure of their loyalty; some members of SED organisations such as the FDJ had already joined the protests. It was the Russians who showed firmness. The Soviet Military Administration had declared a state of emergency by 1 p.m., banned assemblies of more than three people and sent in troops and tanks. This strengthened the determination of the KVP. By evening order was restored.

Outside Berlin, the revolt spread to much of the country. There was unrest in 373 urban centres and, between 17 and 23 June, 497,000 workers throughout the GDR went on strike, with 418,000 taking part in demonstrations. The region most affected was Halle where 148,681 went on strike. In the countryside, SED and LPG officials were beaten up and members of collectives refused to meet their targets. One protest in the rural district of Jessen was ended by Soviet tanks. Demonstrations throughout the GDR called for free elections and denounced the Government. There seemed a real threat to the existence of the GDR.

### Support for the regime

Many of those who did not join in the June 1953 protests had their own reasons of apathy, fear of repression or allegiance to the regime on the basis of what they got out of it – for example economic position or welfare. Many historians have discussed the symbiosis in the GDR between repression and welfare. The state did ensure that basic essentials were provided and East Germans came to enjoy the highest standard of living in the communist bloc. Following the 1953 rebellion, 3.8 billion Ostmarks were spent on welfare provision and subsidised housing, foodstuffs and utilities. It is in fact an axiom that care and repression were the two sides of the GDR; if people left the politics to the politicians, the politicians would ensure that they had basic necessities, equal opportunities in education, reasonable housing, healthcare and so on.

It has been observed that even in open elections, the fact that 99.46 per cent voted for the single lists in the October 1954 elections showed there must be some support for the regime beyond indifference – although as we shall see the escape route to the West remained open and catered for the most disaffected citizens.

## Reasons for the failure of the revolt

There were various reasons for the ultimate failure of the revolt.

### Role of the USSR

This was probably the most important reason. USSR troops were deployed to help the GDR authorities restore order. Officially this resulted in the deaths of 50 East Germans, although it may have been considerably more. The point was, however, that the swift Russian response ended the protests before they got out of hand.

### Motives of demonstrators

The revolts were triggered by economic grievances. While they soon became political there was no co-ordinated leadership or blueprint for regime change. Indeed the protesters themselves were disunited: some showed their support for Nazism by displaying swastikas while others simply wanted the work norms reduced.

### Attitude of the West

Beyond incitement, the West did nothing to support the rebellion. The FRG indeed may have preferred to see a stable GDR to dissuade the growing influx of penniless refugees who, it was feared, might destabilise their own recovery.

**Source C** *The Solution* by Bertolt Brecht.

After the uprising of the 17th of June
The Secretary of the Writers Union
Had leaflets distributed in the Stalinallee
Stating that the people
Had forfeited the confidence of the government
And could win it back only
By redoubled efforts. Would it not be easier
In that case for the government
To dissolve the people
And elect another?

Brecht wrote the poem in 1953. Explain what the poem in Source C is saying in no more than 20 words. What can be inferred from the source?

## Government response

On the one hand the response of the Government was conciliatory. On 17 June they had announced wage rises. Rises in pensions followed. There was a certain amount of self-criticism. 'If large numbers of workers don't understand the party's position, then it is the party which is to blame not the workers.' The 15th SED **Plenum** on 24 to 26 June announced the goal of the Party was to raise living standards. It ordered that the numbers of consumer goods be increased by 30 per cent over the second half of 1953 and 10 per cent in each of the following two years. In October it reduced the price of some foodstuffs although those of bread, sugar and butter were maintained. The Government could afford these measures as a result of the ending of reparations payments to the Soviet Union on 1 January 1954 and an increase of 231 million roubles worth of food and raw material imports from the USSR to be paid on credit.

This was, however, largely window dressing. The Government response to the unrest was harsh, reflecting how shaken they had been by it. Inevitably the revolt was blamed on Western provocateurs but the 1300 imprisoned all came from the GDR. At least 18 were executed. At the same time that the SED criticised itself it insisted its general line was correct. The SED, meanwhile, was purged as Ulbricht used the 1953 rebellion to exact retribution against those who had plotted against him.

## Ulbricht in control

Ulbricht was back firmly in control, especially after the fall of Beria in Moscow (see page 340) and the selection of Khrushchev as the new Soviet leader. There was no more talk of abandoning the GDR.

There was a further purge of the SED to rid it of any whose criticisms may have encouraged the revolt, equating all those who wanted Ulbricht to resign in favour of collective leadership with those responsible for the rebellions. Wilhelm Zaisser and Herrnstadt, who had shared the wartime exile in the Soviet Union with Ulbricht but had endorsed the New Course, were expelled from the Politburo in July 1953 and from the Party itself the following January. One of the most noted casualties was Justice Minister Max Fischer who had called for leniency towards protesters and supported their right to strike. He was replaced by the hardliner Hilde Benjamin. The purges continued below leadership levels. By 1954, 62.2 per cent of the members of local SED committees elected in 1952 had been removed. The Politburo also announced that as many as 1.2 million rank and file SED members had no real political commitment and many were expelled from the Party.

The leadership of the SED never again trusted the population. Security was tightened and developed because there was always the fear of another rebellion. Many observers have remarked that paranoia breeds paranoia; that a state which employs a vast network to uncover disaffection will inevitably find evidence of it whether real or not. Nevertheless the events of 1953 remained with the SED until its demise in 1990.

In June 1955, the New Course was abandoned. Ulbricht claimed unequivocally in an SED meeting on 1 June that, 'It was never our intention to choose such a false course and we will never choose it.' It was announced that the task was now to build a socialist society, in which consumer goods associated with bourgeois values would no longer have priority. The Party and state organisations were also reorganised to afford more internal security. The Stasi was incorporated into the Interior Ministry and its numbers grew – from 10,000 in 1952 to 14,900 in 1954 and 17,400 by November 1957. By contrast the Nazi **Gestapo** had 20,000 agents covering the whole of Germany in 1939. The Stasi had one officer per 320 citizens; the Nazi Gestapo had had one per 3500. Factory Combat Groups were established for national defence and by 1955 they numbered 400,000. The KVP, meanwhile, became more militarised and formed the basis of the National People's Army (NVA) in January 1956 – this was after the GDR had joined the communist military alliance the Warsaw Pact in May 1955.

### The Warsaw Pact

The **Warsaw Pact** was founded in May 1955 ostensibly as a reaction to the integration of the FRG into **NATO**, the Western military alliance formed in 1949. Many historians argue, however, that the real reason was the desire by the Soviet Union to control the military forces of its communist allies. Eight countries including the GDR formed a military alliance of mutual defence against Western attack, but it was also deployed against member states who threatened to leave, for example Hungary in 1956. The Supreme Commander and other leaders were always Soviet.

## De-Stalinisation

In February 1956 the Russian leader Khrushchev made a withering denunciation of Stalin, the personality cult he had encouraged and the terror of his regime. This led to the policy of **de-Stalinisation** in which many of Stalin's ideas, particularly in terms of repression, were denounced and other communist leaders throughout the Soviet bloc removed. This caused shock waves throughout the communist world, but Ulbricht was lukewarm. Beyond agreeing that leaders should not indulge in personality cults, his response was muted at best. Khrushchev's imagined liberalisation fuelled rebellions against communist rule in Poland and Hungary, where the Russians invaded to restore order. There was no such rebellion in the GDR and Ulbricht may have prided himself in that his refusal to liberalise his regime kept it trouble free.

## Conclusion: Economic developments, 1949–61

With the GDR concentrating on the development of heavy industry in its first central economic plans, living standards were cut and there were shortages of consumer goods. More was expected of the labour force for less reward. Particularly resented were the extended work norms. These coincided with uncertainty as a result of Stalin's death and the introduction of the New Course and stimulated the June 1953 rebellion throughout the GDR. The role of the USSR in putting down these rebellions convinced the SED leadership that the Soviets would not abandon the GDR and led to extended security arrangements and a tightening of control. The New Course was abandoned. Social welfare was developed, however, in the hope of binding more people to the regime, but the leadership would never trust the population again.

### Work together

First, compare the notes that you have made on this section (see page 337). Add anything that you have missed and check anything that you have disagreed on. Next, divide your paper into two. One of you should extract from your notes the positive aspects of economic developments - for example the New Course - and the other the negative - for example forced collectivisation. After you have finished, combine your findings. Are there more positives than negatives? Overall, how would you rate the economic performance of the GDR in the 1950s?

# 4 Defending the GDR; 1949–61

The GDR was losing millions of its citizens who could travel to West Berlin and from there on to the FRG. Although Ulbricht had said the GDR would overtake the FRG economically, this was impossible and he told his own colleagues not to believe GDR statistics. Berlin, meanwhile, became the centre of international debate with Khrushchev's offer for it to become an **international city** and ultimatums for the Western forces to leave. Reluctantly Khrushchev agreed to the building of the Berlin Wall. This had the effect of stemming the migration and also stabilising relations by the removal of a pressure point in the Cold War, but had devastating human consequences for many who lost their jobs in the West and were separated from their families. There was some resentment towards emigrants and escapers, particularly those who had learned skills in the GDR which they were now taking elsewhere.

### Note it down

Using bullet points (see page ix) make notes on how the GDR defended itself. You should frame your notes around your answers to the following key questions:

- How successful was Ulbricht in promoting economic growth during the 1950s?
- What was the impact of continued emigration to the FRG?
- How did the Berlin Crises of 1958 to 1961 develop?
- What was Operation Rose and what was its immediate impact?
- How important was the role of Nikita Khrushchev in the building of the Berlin Wall?
- What were the advantages and problems associated with the effects of building the Wall?

Compare your bullet points with those of a partner. Then try to put them together so you are adding each other's information to your own.

## Emigration in the 1950s and its impact

The major event in the early history of the GDR was the building of the Berlin Wall in August 1961 (see page 343), called by the leaders the 'Anti-Fascist Protection Rampart'. Some historians in fact see this as the real beginning of the GDR as a **sovereign state**. The Wall was built as a result of both internal and external developments. The most immediate was the haemorrhaging of the GDR's citizens in ever-greater numbers. This was in turn due to dissatisfaction with the comparatively poor performance of the GDR compared with the FRG, the lack of essential freedoms and the open border within Berlin which made it possible to leave.

## Internal developments

Following his assertion of control after the 1953 rebellion, Ulbricht was the undisputed ruler of the GDR and felt confident enough to set a bold agenda at the July 1958 SED Congress. The GDR would, he asserted, promote accelerated economic growth which, coupled with developments in science and technology, would see it overtake the FRG by 1961. While this appeared a tall order given that the FRG produced over 25 per cent more goods than the GDR and had far more raw materials at its disposal, it fitted in with Khrushchev's strategy that the USSR would overtake the USA. These seemed heady days for the development of communism – in theory.

## Economic problems

The GDR faced continuing economic problems. There were frequent shortages, especially of foodstuffs and high quality products. Increasingly the GDR became economically dependent on the USSR and faced a perennial shortage in its **currency reserves**. The Soviet Union faced economic problems of its own and imposed a new Seven-Year Plan from 1959 to 1965. It expected its satellite countries to dovetail into this. Priorities were to be given to the production of energy, electrical engineering, chemicals and machine building in the GDR. Worker productivity, meanwhile, was to be increased by 58 per cent over the seven-year period. Consumer goods and rises in living standards were no longer felt to be a priority. The emphasis was to be the development of a fully-fledged socialist economy based on heavy industry.

Rather than overtake the FRG, the GDR seemed to be lagging further and further behind. Ulbricht told his colleagues not to believe the doctored production reports written for those outside the leadership; the GDR was in economic trouble. This was compounded by the decision of the FRG to cut its trade with the GDR in retaliation for restrictions on West German citizens seeking entry into East Berlin. The question of continued migration was the underlying issue. Indeed it has been suggested that it was the quality of migrants from the GDR that in part accounted for the economic performance of the FRG and growth rates of 8 per cent per year in the 1950s. In the GDR by comparison annual industrial growth rates were 2.9 per cent, with consumer goods well below that.

## Continued emigration

There were surges in emigration west (see Table 5, page 344) until it was stopped on 13 August 1961. This emigration was principally of young and well-educated people whom the GDR could not afford to lose. One-quarter of all the doctors left. The Government investigated the reasons why they were leaving in such numbers: while one might have expected these to be overwhelmingly pull factors such as the search for a better life in the more prosperous West or the desire to reunite with family there, a surprising number were negative factors pushing them away from the GDR – for example unrealistic targets, inefficiencies, shortages of goods and a heartless and labyrinthine bureaucracy.

**Table 5: Emigration from the GDR to FRG, 1949–61.**

| Year | Numbers moving from GDR to FRG |
|---|---|
| 1949 | 129,245 |
| 1950 | 197,887 |
| 1951 | 165,648 |
| 1952 | 182,393 |
| 1953 | 331,390 |
| 1954 | 184,198 |
| 1955 | 252,870 |
| 1956 | 279,189 |
| 1957 | 261,622 |
| 1958 | 204,092 |
| 1959 | 143,917 |
| 1960 | 199,188 |
| 1961 (until August) | 155,402 |

Clearly this volume had a huge impact on the GDR. The result was a shortage of the very same skilled personnel who were contributing to the economic success of the FRG. If its economic processes seemed ossified it was often because the people who could have improved them had been driven out in despair by the unwieldy bureaucracy, unrealistic planning and poor quality equipment.

## The Crisis of 1960–61

Berlin, meanwhile, became a factor in external developments relating to **superpower relations**. From the late 1950s to August 1961 it became the front line in the Cold War.

### The 1958 Crisis

In November 1958, Khrushchev gave an ultimatum to the West – that Berlin should become an international city, governed by the United Nations. If the West did not agree within six months, he asserted that the USSR and GDR would implement the plan anyway. In February 1959 Khrushchev further announced that the USSR would sign a peace treaty with the GDR unless West Germany signed one with the GDR – thereby recognising the GDR as an independent nation. This rekindled the post-war controversy about the recognition of two Germanies rather than, as the FRG saw it, a temporary arrangement before they were reunited (see page 365)

Historians have disputed Khrushchev's motives for this sudden aggressive action. It appears that having asserted his own control after the 1956 de-Stalinisation speech (see page 342), Khrushchev had grown confident of USSR superiority over the West:

- The USSR launched the first satellite – Sputnik – in 1957, taking the USA by surprise.
- Khrushchev mistakenly believed that the USSR had nuclear superiority over the USA.

### Nikita Khrushchev, 1894–1971

Nikita Khrushchev was born in the Ukraine in 1894 and became a Bolshevik after the October 1917 Revolution. He rose quickly through the ranks partly because of his organisational skills which saw him responsible for the construction of the prestigious Moscow underground system. After Stalin's death Khrushchev fought for the party leadership eventually emerging the victor in 1955. He denounced Stalin particularly for the repression of his regime, and genuinely believed that communism had to make itself popular.

However, Khrushchev could be as ruthless as any of his predecessors as shown by his invasion of Hungary in November 1956 as a result of the reform programme which threatened to take the country out of the Warsaw Pact.

Khrushchev's relationship with the GDR was always complex. He understood that if the GDR absorbed all Berlin this would undermine the international agreements which were still in force and restrict USSR movements in West Berlin - their forces were allowed to guard their War Memorial and they rotated guards with the Western powers in Spandau prison. Khrushchev refused to support the SED when it demanded that Western officials visiting the East should present their identification to GDR border guards. This was to lead to crisis incidents shortly after the Wall was built (see page 347).

His aims were straightforward:

- to neutralise Berlin as a centre of subversion against the GDR and a means by which emigrants could flee to the FRG
- to secure Western recognition of the GDR
- to forestall what he feared were NATO's plans to deploy nuclear missiles in West Germany.

While Khrushchev hoped eventually to absorb all of Berlin into the GDR, he saw the internationalisation of the city as a first step. This would involve first the withdrawal of Western troops from West Berlin and then the reunification of Berlin as one city, possibly under United Nations stewardship. If this happened Khrushchev no doubt felt the absorption of all Berlin into the GDR would one day be possible.

The USA had a new president, John F. Kennedy, whom Khrushchev saw as inexperienced and weak, especially after the failed **Bay of Pigs invasion of Cuba** in April 1961. At the Vienna Summit between the two leaders in June 1961, Khrushchev again insisted the West should withdraw its troops from Berlin within six months. He was possibly surprised by the venom of Kennedy's response that the USA was prepared to defend the freedom of West Berlin by nuclear weapons if necessary. This precise reference to West Berlin told Khrushchev that the USA recognised Soviet hegemony over the east of the city.

Khrushchev never intended to risk war over Berlin. Moreover, he appeared skeptical when Ulbricht insisted that the GDR could not survive unless its borders were sealed, and it was with reluctance that Khrushchev agreed to the building of the Berlin Wall.

## Operation Rose, August 1961

Operation Rose was the codename given to the building of the Berlin Wall in August 1961. It was an operation shrouded in secrecy. Many top SED officials were not informed until the night of its official construction. As late as June, Ulbricht assured his audience at a press conference that no one had any intention of building a wall. In the event he had tasked one of his most loyal colleagues, Erich Honecker, with carrying out Operation Rose.

Operation Rose began during the night of 12–13 August 1961, when a barrier was built initially with little more than barbed wire which Berliners woke to find both through and around their city. Those dwelling in the West but visiting the East because of its vibrant nightlife were escorted back across the border. Any visiting the West could choose to remain there. By next day Berliners found travel was no longer possible between the Eastern and Western zones. People who lived in the East but worked in the West – the so-called **border crossers** – could not get to work. People could no longer visit their relatives – or, in the case of one woman, visit her desperately sick child in a West Berlin hospital. The border was firmly closed.

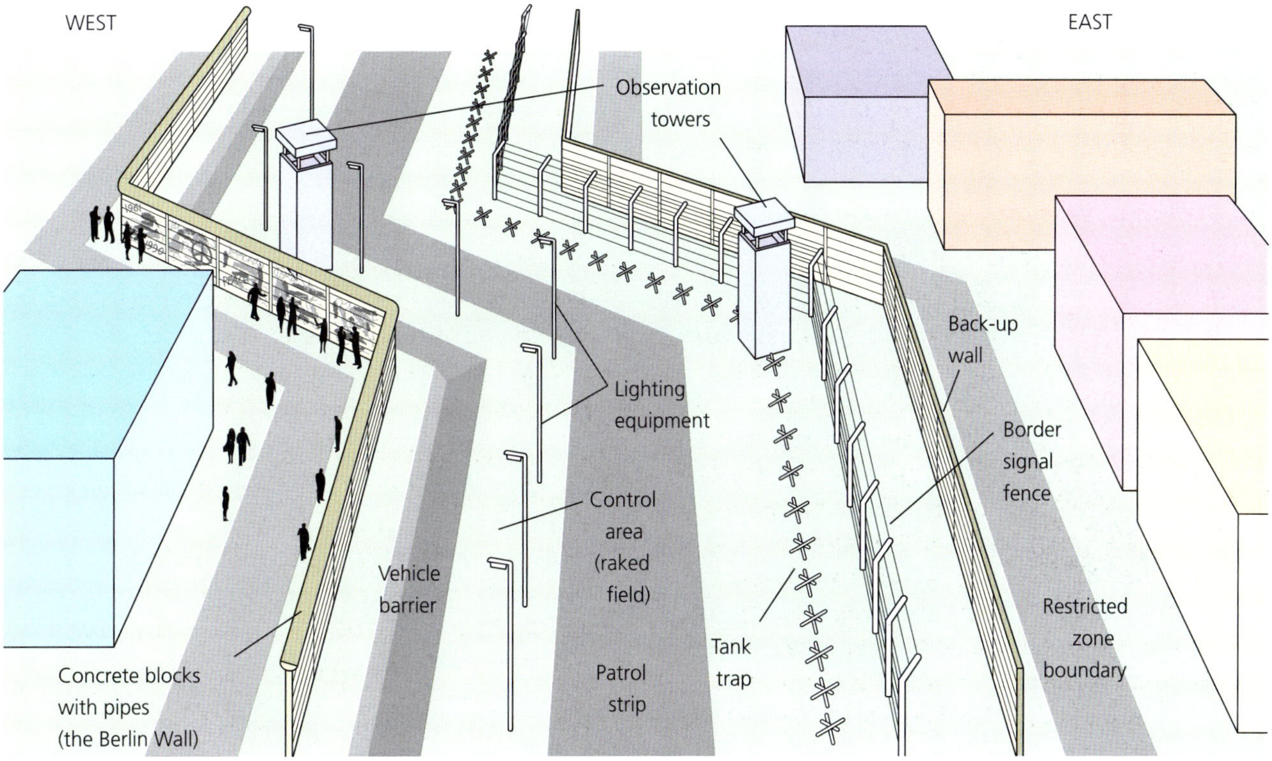


▲ **Figure 6: Diagram of the Berlin Wall.**

The Berlin Wall was developed in ensuing weeks as a barrier of concrete blocks and watchtowers. It became more and more elaborate as time went on, eventually running for 97 miles around the three Western sectors and 27 miles through the centre of Berlin. It was comprised of a four-metre high concrete wall, 30 watchtowers, guard dog tracks, tripwires and floodlights. Eventually it was made up of 45,000 separate blocks of concrete.

The construction of the Wall was more significant than simply stopping emigration:

- There were many border crossers who lived in the East but worked in the West. They were often resented because they were paid in valuable Western currency and could take advantage of subsidised housing and cheap goods (when available) in the East.
- Many children who lived in the East were educated in schools and colleges in the West.
- Westerners often travelled to the East to take advantage of the cheaper goods and more vibrant nightlife.
- Families were split; quite poignant were those in the West who had partners in the East and vice versa.

It is important to note that the building of the Wall was not an act of aggression against the West, rather one of defence, designed to keep people in; it was built wholly in East German territory. It was only aggressive against those who wanted to leave the East.

## Impact of the Wall

Behind the scenes many regarded the Wall as a solution to problems. As Kennedy said at the time:

> *'Why would Khrushchev put up a wall if he really intended to seize Berlin? There wouldn't be need of a wall if he occupied the whole city. This is his way out of his predicament. It's not a very nice solution, but a wall is a hell of a lot better than a war.'*

The Wall offered a stable border. It also meant that the leaders of the USA and USSR no longer needed to respond to the demands of their **clients**. Kennedy could refuse to place nuclear weapons in West Germany and Khrushchev could assure Ulbricht that the West **de facto** recognised the right of the GDR to exist. At worst it maintained the status quo. West Germany still did not recognise the GDR but had to accept its presence.

The cost to the GDR of the open border had been an estimated 2.5 to 3 billion Ostmarks in lost skills, although Ulbricht had exaggerated its impact to gain Khrushchev's support for the Wall. The GDR had paid for the education of its most skilled citizens. Now they were no longer

**Source D** An East German soldier helping a boy cross the 'Berlin Wall', on the day it was first built in August 1961. The soldier was helping a child who had become separated from his family. He was disciplined by his superiors, but it is not known what happened to him afterwards.

Why is Source D useful to a historian investigating the construction of the Berlin Wall?

## Checkpoint Charlie incidents, October 1961

Historian Peter Grieder has argued that although neither side wanted to risk war over Berlin, this was not fully understood at the time, certainly not by troops on the ground, and any misunderstanding or accident at the Wall could have led to hostilities. He gives the example of US diplomat Allan Lighter who, on the evening of 22 October, wanted to attend the opera in East Berlin. Representatives of the occupying forces were usually just waved through at Checkpoint Charlie but on this occasion officious GDR border guards demanded to see his passport. Lighter refused; to accede would have been to recognise the GDR and its right to examine diplomats' papers. At the time the USA did not recognise the GDR as a separate country. The standoff was only ended when, in face of the GDR guards, US troops escorted Lighter over the border – although he did miss the opera.

More seriously, three days later President Kennedy's representative in Berlin, General Lucius Clay, decided to test GDR resolve by lining up US tanks along the Wall. This time Soviet tanks and jet fighter aircraft confronted them. They were eyeball to eyeball. Then on 28 October Khrushchev ordered the Soviet forces to withdraw. It may have been posturing – but it was dangerous posturing nonetheless.

▲ Checkpoint Charlie, the most famous Berlin Wall crossing and a tourist attraction today.

free to sell their services elsewhere. It should be noted, moreover, that this had been and remained a source of resentment with working people in the GDR. Having paid through their taxes for the training of doctors and so on, people expected them to repay the state through their expertise, not practise elsewhere. This reason has also been offered as a common justification among border guards for preventing escapes even if they resulted in fatalities.

## Problems

Clearly, however, there were human problems following the closure of the frontier. Border crossers were regarded with suspicion. Those who had worked in the West lost their jobs as a result of the Wall and often found themselves directed to the most unpleasant vacancies in the East. There were restrictions on the education of those who had been to school in the West:

- Numbers were restricted in classes lest they contaminate their classmates with talk of the freedoms in the West, so many had to travel on long journeys to their new schools.
- Those in their final years who may have expected to go to university were directed to menial jobs.

Those who had been involved in any way in the West found discrimination throughout their lives.

### Escapers

People tried to escape across the frontier; it is estimated that about one in fifteen attempts was successful. Clearly escape became harder as the Wall became more sophisticated. In the early 1960s there were various networks which built tunnels; other escapers swam across rivers and canals or crashed vehicles through the barriers. One intrepid train driver drove his train through barriers at Anbrechtshof station and on to the safety of Spandau.

There were fatalities. In the earliest days of the Wall two people died while jumping from upper storey windows; their apartments looked out onto streets in the West. One died while attempting to abseil from a roof. On 17 August 1962 one young man, Peter Fechter, was shot by border guards and allowed to die in agony in **no-man's-land**. In retaliation Soviet troops guarding their War Memorial in West Berlin were stoned. They threatened to open fire, the West German police had to use water cannon on protesters and for the next few days the Soviet troops endured the indignity of being protected by British soldiers as they stood guard.

There may have been as many as 223 fatalities among would-be escapers. The last was in March 1989 when a balloonist escaped into West Berlin but crashed into a power line. There is still controversy over whether or not there was a shoot-to-kill policy, although, as we shall see, one may not have been necessary when penalties for border guards allowing escapes on their watch were all too apparent (see page 391).

## Key debate

### Khrushchev's role in the Berlin Wall

Historians have long debated the role of Khrushchev in the decision to build the Berlin Wall. Writing in 2003, Hope M. Harrison argued that Khrushchev was reluctant to agree because he feared it would on the one hand provoke the West and on the other show how unpopular communism was. Khrushchev would have preferred the SED to be more amenable and work harder to gain the support of its citizens. It was a GDR initiative.

Gerard De Groot places it more within an international context. He quotes a Khrushchev aide, Fyodor Burlatsky, who argued that the international city option was genuine. Adenauer, the FRG leader (see page 365), however, would not countenance it because he still supported the idea of a united Germany. However, Ulbricht was insistent. Burlatsky wrote, 'You had Adenauer, we had Ulbricht. At least two or three times each month he would harass Khrushchev about his ability and willingness to support the GDR in its quest for construction of the Berlin Wall.' De Groot asserts that Khrushchev visited the West in disguise and was shocked at the differences between East and West. He saw the Wall as a test of US resolve, which is why he agreed at first that it should be simply barbed wire. If the opposition was fierce it should be removed. Mary Fulbrook also spoke of the Wall inaugurating greater international stability. Writing in 2012, however, Peter Grieder has asserted the Wall remained a dangerous border and was a propaganda disaster for the GDR.

## Conclusion: Defending the GDR, 1949–61

The building of the Berlin Wall is best seen within the context of superpower relations in the late 1950s and early 1960s, when Berlin became a focus of attention. The GDR authorities wanted to build a wall to stop the emigration which lost them millions of their most skilled citizens. Khrushchev was reluctant to accede to this because he feared how the West would respond. However, after the failure of his own proposals for the future of Berlin and his lack of respect for the new US president, John F. Kennedy, Khrushchev gave the go-ahead in August 1961.

The Wall brought some stability to the Cold War because it removed one crisis point, although the events of October 1961 showed how volatile the situation could be. Overall, whatever the reasons offered and whatever the advantages, the Wall was a propaganda disaster for the GDR – it had effectively to imprison its own population to stop them from leaving en masse.

## Work together

Having checked each other's notes (see page 343), you should now be in a position to analyse in depth:

- the long- and short-term reasons why the Berlin Wall was built
- the short-term effects of its construction.

Which reasons and effects do you consider the most significant? Discuss your ideas with a partner. Can you come to any consensus about which were the most important reasons why the Wall was built and the effects of its having been built?

## Recommended reading


A. Applebaum, *Iron Curtain: The Crushing of Eastern Europe* (Penguin, 2012). Thorough account of the development of communist control in post-war Eastern Europe with excellent sections on East Germany.

M. Dennis, *The Rise and Fall of the German Democratic Republic 1945–1990* (Pearson, 2000). Readable and thorough analysis of the GDR from creation to demise.

F. Taylor, *The Berlin Wall* (Bloomsbury, 2006). Engrossing account of the building of the Berlin Wall and its impact on the GDR.

A. Tusa and J. Tusa, *The Berlin Blockade* (Coronet, 1989). Descriptive account of the blockade and airlift and their effects.

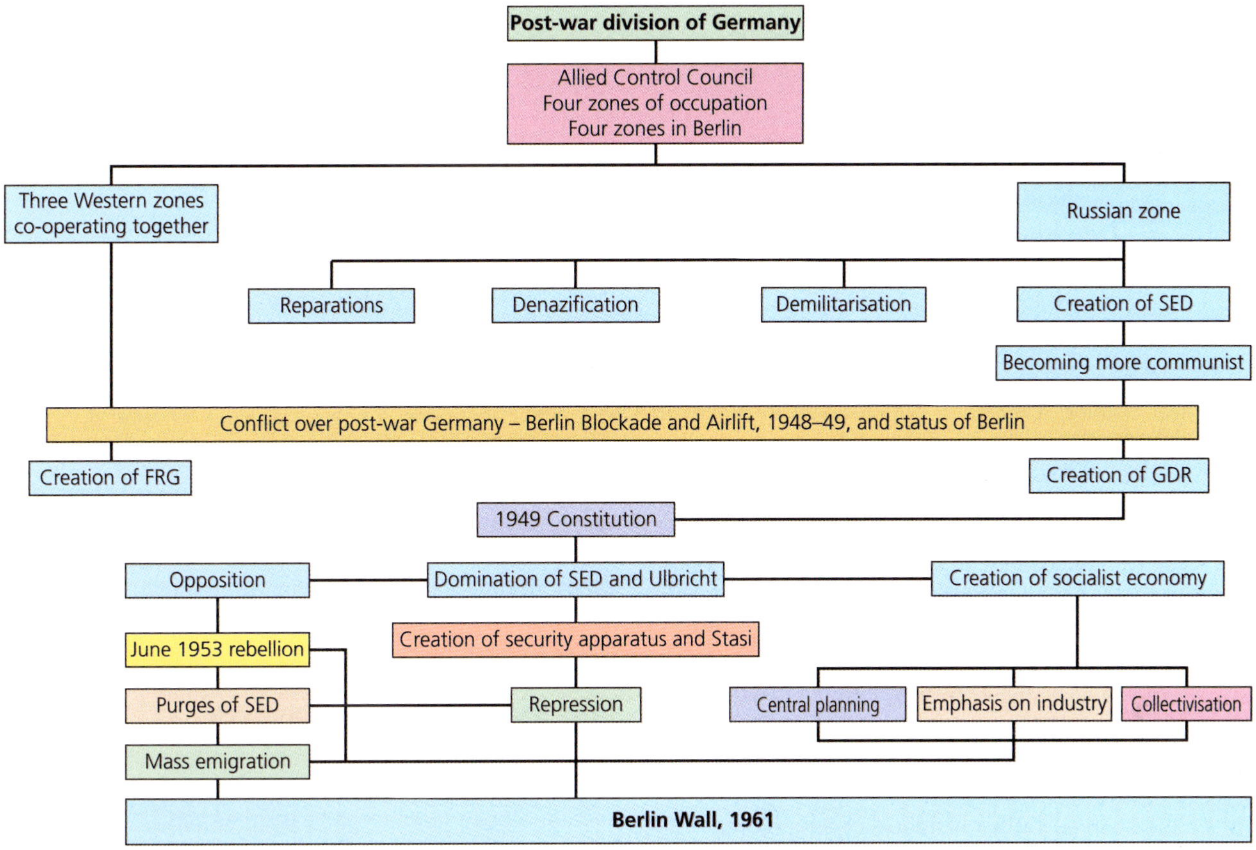


▲ Summary diagram: Establishing and consolidating communist rule in the GDR, 1949–61.

## Chapter summary

- At the end of the Second World War, Germany and its capital, Berlin, were each divided into four zones of occupation administered by each of the victorious powers.
- As the three Western zones moved closer together economically and the Soviet zone embraced communism, it increasingly seemed likely that Germany would be split into two states.
- This was formalised after the Berlin Crises of 1948–49 with the creation of the FRG and GDR.
- The GDR lacked formal recognition by any but fellow communist countries.
- The GDR became a communist state governed by the SED and its leader Walter Ulbricht.
- The death of Stalin in 1953 brought some uncertainty which saw the GDR leadership embrace the New Course to try to win more popularity.
- Continuing poor economic conditions and the introduction of tough work norms in 1953 led to the June 1953 rebellions.
- These rebellions were put down by Russian forces, and the SED responded by extending the security apparatus, abandoning the New Course and enforcing tighter controls over the population. The SED never again trusted the population.
- Agriculture was often forcibly collectivised.
- The GDR could be treated as a pawn in international relations as exemplified by Stalin's offer for a reunited Germany in 1952 and Khrushchev's 1958 idea that Berlin should become an international city.
- With Berlin still an open city, the GDR suffered millions of its citizens emigrating.
- In August 1961 the Berlin Wall was built to prevent this emigration. It also had the effect of stabilising tensions between the superpowers.

# Section A: Essay technique

## Focus on the question and understanding the sources

The A level Section A question requires you to deploy a variety of skills. The most important are source analysis and evaluation. In essence, the question asks how much a historian could learn about a specific issue from the two sources. This is a complex task and requires a range of skills which will be covered in this section and at the end of Chapters 2–4. These include the ability to:

- understand the focus of the question and the sources (this section)
- structure an essay and write good introductions (Chapter 2, page 376)
- select information and make inferences from the sources (Chapter 2, page 379)
- place the sources in their historical context (Chapter 3, page 407)
- evaluate and weigh the evidence of the sources (Chapter 4, page 434)
- reach and support a final judgement (Chapter 4, page 438).

The Section A question for AS level is different from that for A level, and some guidance about this is given on page viii. However, you will need to develop very similar skills for the AS exam, therefore the activities will help with the AS exam as well. There are also some AS-style questions in every chapter.

### The focus of the question

In order to answer the question successfully you must understand how the question works. Below is a typical Section A-style question (the sources are on page 351). The question is written precisely in order to make sure that you understand the task. Each part of the question has a specific meaning:

**Study Sources 1 and 2 before you answer this question.**

**How far could the historian make use of Sources 1 and 2 together to investigate the reasons for the building of the Berlin Wall in August 1961?**

**Explain your answer, using both sources, the information given about them and your own knowledge of the historical context.**

'How far' indicates that you must evaluate the extent of something, rather than giving a simple 'yes' or 'no' answer.

The final part of the question focuses on a specific topic that a historian might investigate: in this case, the reasons for the building of the Berlin Wall in August 1961.

This is the essence of the task. You must focus on what a historian could legitimately conclude from studying these sources.

The key word here is **together**. You must examine the sources as a pair and make a judgement about both sources, rather than separate judgements about each source.

This instruction lists the resources you should use:

- the sources
- the information given about the sources
- your own knowledge of historical context that you have learned during the course.

**Source 1** From Erich Honecker, *From My Life*, published in 1981. Honecker was the SED leader given the responsibility of organising the building of the Berlin Wall. Here he justifies its construction, having explained the existing border between East and West Berlin.

> ... Until August 1961 this border was neither secured nor could it be controlled by us at all. It ran through the middle of streets, through apartment blocks, allotments and waterways. Up to half a million people crossed it daily ... No less than 80 espionage and terror organisations carried out their dark activities from there. Large-scale currency speculations were directed from there to destroy the GDR economy. Centres for the recruitment of skilled labour from the GDR had established themselves in Berlin-West. It could justifiably be called a transit centre for a regular trade in human beings, out of which unscrupulous managers made large amounts of money per head.
>
> We followed these menacing events with due vigilance. Could we afford to look on passively while an open border was exploited to bleed our republic to death by means of an unprecedented economic war?

**Source 2** From Arthur M. Hanhardt Jr, *The German Democratic Republic*, published in 1968. Hanhardt, an American political scientist, here explains the reasons why the Berlin Wall was constructed.

> That ugly but nonetheless effective engineering exercise known as the Berlin Wall is the backdrop for the present stage. Two of the most important problems facing the GDR were rationalising Party and economic organisation and stemming the outflow of important segments of the population. [East Germany] had accomplished nothing by way of rallying the people to the purposes and goals of the Socialist Unity Party. Consequently more drastic measures were required if the system was to survive.
>
> Beyond the problems of organisation and popularity were the severe economic dislocations brought on by the forced collectivisation of 1960 and the economic difficulties that hit the rest of the Soviet bloc at about the same time. The Soviet Union was forced to cut off raw materials on which the East German economy had come to depend. These factors were combined with chronic labour shortages and worker productivity. All of this added up to the decision to close the sector boundaries in Berlin.

Overall, all Section A questions ask you to make a judgement about how far two sources are useful to the historian. However, the second half of the question specifies what a historian is focusing on.

So, the first part of the question sets up **the general task**, which is true of all Section A questions:

**How far could the historian make use of Sources 1 and 2 together to investigate...**

And the second part of the question establishes **the specific focus**, for example:

**...the reasons for the building of the Berlin Wall in August 1961?**

As you write your essay, you need to focus on both aspects.

## How to focus in a source question

Source questions are different from questions that only require you to use your own knowledge. There are a variety of ways to ensure you maintain your focus on the question that are appropriate to this type of question:

- Use the phrases 'Source 1' and 'Source 2' when dealing with the sources so that it is clear which sources you are focusing on.
- Use words such as 'useful' or 'utility' to ensure that you are explicitly addressing the general task.
- Use comparative words and phrases such as 'Sources 1 and 2 disagree' to show that you are using the sources together.

## Activity: A focused introduction

1 Write a short introduction which provides a focused answer to the question on page 350. See page 377 for advice on writing introductions. Also remember that this is a question about two sources.

2 Having written an introduction, swap it with a partner. Consider:

   **a)** Which introduction best focuses on the question? Remember, your introduction needs to focus on the **general task** and the **specific focus**.

   **b)** Which introduction best deals with the sources *together*?

   **c)** Which introduction gives the clearest answer to the question?

   **d)** What can you learn from each other's approach to the question?

Use these questions to feed back to each other and improve your instructions.

## Activity: AS-style questions

1 Why is Source 1 valuable to the historian for an enquiry into the reasons for the construction of the Berlin Wall in August 1961?

2 How much weight do you give the evidence of Source 2 for an enquiry into why the Berlin Wall was built?

## Understanding the sources

Understanding the sources is crucial to doing well in Section A questions. The most important aid in this understanding is a detailed knowledge of the period. There are also techniques to aid understanding. Here are a few tips to get you started:

- Read the source word for word – if it helps, read it out loud when you are doing practice questions. This makes it much less likely that you will miss anything in the source.
- Think about the question as you are reading. You will then look out for relevant information within the source.
- Make index cards before your exam of the specific vocabulary for the topic you are studying, for example *currency speculations*, *transit centre*, *collectivisation*.
- Look up terms and definitions that you do not recognise in practice questions.
- Make index cards of the people who might be quoted in the sources, such as Walter Ulbricht and Erich Honecker, and the documents that might be used as sources on the examination paper. Make notes on who they are and their attitudes to the key issues you have studied.

### Comprehension

Comprehension is the most basic source skill. It simply means understanding the source's meaning and you can demonstrate this by:

- **Copying**: writing out the words of the source in your essay.

  **TIP:** Avoid copying any more than a sentence at any point in your essay.

- **Paraphrasing**: putting part of a source in your own words.

  **TIP:** Avoid simply rewriting more than a sentence from the sources in your own words, before using a higher-level skill.

- **Summarising**: summing up the meaning of the entire source, or a large part of the source, in a single sentence.

  **TIP:** Summarising can be useful in introductions and conclusions.

These are low-level source skills. Therefore they should not dominate your essay. However, small quotes, short paraphrases and occasional summaries can be useful to support higher-level skills.

### Higher-level skills

Higher-level skills include:

- using the sources together (see page 351)
- making inferences (see page 379)
- analysing sources in their historical context (see page 407)
- evaluating the evidence presented in the sources (see page 434)
- reaching an overall judgement regarding the usefulness of the sources (see page 438).

### Activity: Test your understanding

Having read Source 1 and Source 2 on page 351:

1. Make a list of words and phrases that you do not understand and look them up in the glossary of this book or online.
2. a) Study Source 1. **Copy** the sentence that best expresses the reasons why the border between East and West Berlin could not be controlled. Make sure you put the quote in 'quotation marks'.
   b) Study Source 2. **Paraphrase** the economic problems outlined by Arthur M. Hanhardt Jnr.
   c) Study Source 2. **Summarise** in no more than 30 words **why**, according to the author, the Berlin Wall was built.

You should repeat this activity regularly with the sources that you encounter. This will help with many of the sources you will examine as sources from the same period, referring to the same topic, will tend to use a similar vocabulary.

### Work together

Having completed Activities 1 and 2 above, swap your answers with a partner. Consider the following questions:

1. Did you both identify the same words that needed to be defined?
2. Were your partner's definitions clear and accurate?
3. Did you both copy the same bit of Source 1? If not, which quote better summarises why the border between East and West Berlin could not be controlled.
4. Is your partner's paraphrase clear? Does it accurately reflect the economic problems outlined by Arthur M. Hanhardt Jnr?
5. Whose summary more precisely expressed why, according to the author, the Berlin Wall was built?

Use these questions to feed back to each other and improve your analysis of the sources.

# Section B: Essay technique

## Focus and structure

Section B essays, like all of your examined essays, will be judged on how far they focus on the question, and the quality of their structure. You may have already considered advice on how to write a focused introduction and how to structure your essays in Paper 1 (see pages 26–7).

## Different types of question

Section B questions, like Section A and B questions in Paper 1, can focus on a variety of concepts. These include:

- cause
- consequence
- change/continuity
- similarity/difference
- significance.

These different concepts require slightly different approaches. Below are some examples of these concepts in questions.

1. **How important was the creation of the Socialist Unity Party in 1946 in making the Soviet zone of Germany communist?**

   This question requires you to explain how important the creation of the SED was in turning East Germany into a communist country. You might consider other factors, for example the pressure from the Soviet Union.

2. **How far was the Berlin Blockade and Airlift of 1948/9 a significant turning point in the decision to create the GDR?**

   This question asks you to evaluate how significant the Berlin Blockade and Airlift were in the creation of the GDR – you could consider the relative importance of other factors such as the failure of Stalin to control all of Berlin and the creation of the FRG in coming to a judgement.

3. **How far were economic concerns the main cause of the 1953 rebellion?**

   This question requires you to evaluate how far economic factors sparked off the 1953 rebellions. You might consider other factors such as uncertainties following Stalin's death and political factors such as the demand for greater democracy.

4. **What was 'New' about the New Course adopted in 1953?**

   This question requires you to consider similarity and difference. How far was the New Course a radical departure and how far was it similar to the existing system?

5. **'The main purpose of the Berlin Wall was to imprison its citizens within the GDR.' How far do you agree with this statement?**

   This question requires you to evaluate how far the need to prevent emigration was a significant factor in the building of the Berlin Wall. You might consider other factors such as espionage and the influx of West Berliners buying GDR products.

## Structuring your essay

As in Paper 1, your essay should be made up of three or four paragraphs, each addressing a different factor (see page 26).

However, essays that focus on different concepts will need slightly different structures:

- **Cause essays** require you to explain why something happened. Therefore, each paragraph should deal with a different possible cause.
- **Evaluative essays** require you to weigh up the extent of something. Most essays will require you to evaluate at some point, as weighing up is essential to reaching a conclusion. In essays that focus on evaluation each paragraph should weigh a different factor. For example, if you were dealing with the question:

  **To what extent did the failure of the 1953 rebellion enable Ulbricht to accelerate the development of communist economic policies in the GDR?**

  you would need to show how Ulbricht was able to exploit the failures of the 1953 rebellion to consolidate his own position and drive communist policies, for example collectivisation. Most importantly you need to make a judgement at the end based upon what you have written in the essay.
- **Success or failure essays** require you to evaluate the extent to which something succeeded. Therefore, you will need to start by considering the aims in order to establish the criteria for success. You should go on to consider aspects that succeeded and weigh them against aspects that failed in order to reach a conclusion.
- **Continuity and change essays** require you to evaluate the extent of change. Therefore, your essay will have to weigh up what changed and what stayed the same.
- **Consequence essays** require you to evaluate which of a range of consequences was most important.

It is crucial to be able to distinguish between the different types of question. Confusing a causes essay with a consequences essay could seriously affect your grade.

### Activity: Question types

1 Below are six different Section B-style questions. Work out what types of question they are.

  a) 'The Berlin Blockade and Airlift was the most important reason for the creation of the GDR.' How far do you agree with this statement?

  b) How far were tensions between the USA and the Soviet Union responsible for the creation of the GDR in 1949? AS

  c) How far did the SED dominate the political system of the GDR?

  d) 'The 1953 rebellion was a turning point in the attitude of the SED to citizens of the GDR.' How far do you agree?

  e) 'Mass emigration was the main reason for the construction of the Berlin Wall.' How far do you agree?

  f) How significant was Khrushchev's de-Stalinisation speech in 1956 in changing the attitudes of SED leaders to control of their citizens?

2 Having worked out what types of question you are dealing with you should now write plans for each question. You can plan either as spider diagrams or a bullet-point list. Make sure your plan reflects the kind of essay that you are dealing with. For example, if you are dealing with a success or failure essay you should highlight which parts of the plan deal with success and which deal with failure.

  Complete one plan at a time, and after each discuss it with a partner.

### Work together

Having completed a plan in the activity above, swap it with a partner's. Consider the following questions:

1 Did you agree on what type of question you were dealing with? If not, discuss it and work out who was right.
2 Whose plan most clearly focused on the specific type of question?
3 Did your partner's plan miss anything?
4 Did you miss anything that you should add to your plan?
5 What can you learn from your partner's approach?

Use these questions to feed back to each other and improve your question spotting and planning.

# **Key Topic 2** The development of the East German state, 1961–85

## Overview

The early 1960s saw the introduction of the New Economic System through which the GDR tried to modernise and expand its economy with the aim of overtaking that of the FRG. The building of the Berlin Wall had stopped emigration so the workforce was now more stable and resigned to life in the GDR. The New Economic System gave more initiative to actual producers rather than planners and sought to raise living standards. It was opposed by more conservative elements, who feared that it was too akin to capitalism. The economy of the GDR always lagged behind the West, however. Its citizens could see this through the widely available FRG television.

The SED leadership tried to create a sense of national identity through manipulation of the media and organisation of mass rallies and parades to encourage a sense of participation and belonging. National identity was enhanced through astonishing international sporting success. At the time it was not understood that this came as a result of extensive cheating.

The GDR achieved greater international recognition, not least through the onset of Ostpolitik or rapprochement with the FRG. The 1970s saw the GDR join the United Nations and grow closer to the FRG, albeit reluctantly on the part of its leaders. It also continued close ties with the Soviet Union. This is shown by the influence of the USSR in the removal of Walter Ulbricht in 1971 and the 1975 Treaty of Friendship between the two countries. The high point of Ostpolitik may have been the visit of Erich Honecker to the FRG in September 1987. His Soviet allies had not allowed him to visit before this time. The GDR spent much of the 1970s and 1980s juggling its position between the USSR and the FRG and was increasingly in serious debt to both.

The overarching topic of the development of the East German state, 1961–85 is covered in four sections:

1. Economic stabilisation after 1961
2. The development of a GDR identity
3. Relations with West Germany
4. Growing international prestige.

## TIMELINE

| | |
|---|---|
| 1961 August | Creation of the Berlin Wall |
| 1964 February–March | Introduction of New Economic System (NES) |
| 1964 October | Overthrow of Khrushchev |
| 1965 October | Unrest in Leipzig concerning the banning of beat music |
| 1968 April | Introduction of Economic System of Socialism (ESS) |
| 1968 August | Russian invasion of Czechoslovakia |
| 1969 October | Beginnings of Ostpolitik with FRG |
| 1971 November | Overthrow of Walter Ulbricht as head of SED; replaced by Erich Honecker |
| 1971 December | Four Power Agreement over Berlin |
| 1973 June | Basic Treaty with FRG |
| 1973 September | GDR joins United Nations |
| 1975 July–August | Helsinki Accords |
| 1975 October | New accord with USSR |
| 1981 December | FRG Chancellor Helmut Schmidt visits GDR |
| 1987 September | Honecker's visit to the FRG |

## 1 Economic stabilisation after 1961

By 1960 it was clear that the centralised system of economic planning was failing to achieve the desired results not only in the GDR but throughout the **Soviet bloc**. In addition, following the construction of the Berlin Wall, the GDR had to absorb the people who could no longer migrate and exploit their skills. Ulbricht favoured a reform model developed by Soviet economists whereby emphasis would be on profitability and quality rather than quantity. This involved giving more responsibility to middle managers and producers themselves. Ulbricht announced the New Economic System (NES) in January 1963. Even though he insisted that central planners still had responsibility for overall targets, pricing structures and so on, critics felt the system was too close to capitalism and opposed it. There was a fundamental clash between political ideology and economic realities.

The results of the New Economic System were mixed in the sense that more quality goods were produced but still not enough to compete with the West. In 1968 Ulbricht emphasised scientific and technological development and relaunched the policy as the Economic System of Socialism (ESS). The GDR was constrained, however, by its membership of **COMECON** which encouraged specialisation in particular areas and always operated to the advantage of the **USSR**.

### Note it down

In this section use a spider diagram to take notes (see page x) on economic stabilisation after 1961. Draw a circle in the middle of your page with the heading 'Economic Stabilisation' inside it. Draw six lines coming out of the central circle that lead to these questions:

- What was the impact of the ending of mass emigration?
- How significant were problems associated with central planning?
- How successful were the NES and ESS?
- What challenges did membership of COMECON bring?
- To what extent was 'Overtaking without catching up' an acknowledgement of failure?
- How successful was the economy in the 1970s?

Write important points coming out from the questions which would be used in answer to them.

When Ulbricht was replaced by Erich Honecker centralised planning was returned to its former position and much of the ESS was abandoned, although the emphasis was still on modernisation and improvement in living standards. The 1973 oil crisis (see page 361) and subsequent price rises affected the GDR badly and accelerated the indebtedness which would eventually contribute to its demise.

## The end of mass emigration

If the real purpose of the Berlin Wall was to prevent mass emigration then it succeeded admirably. Those who might have fled west now had to come to terms with the regime. The SED in its turn had to make the regime more appealing for those who otherwise would have deserted it. While there was a wave of repression against perceived opponents and while those who had worked in the West did face discrimination (see page 346), the regime could nevertheless now rely on skilled people who had no choice but to comply. This was actually a significant shift. Before the building of the Wall, many people literally had no idea if their work colleagues or professionals on whom they depended would be there tomorrow. Skilled engineers might leave halfway through a crucial project; doctors' surgeries might be abandoned. Now the Berlin Wall offered stability. The retention of people with technical understanding and know-how stimulated the economic reform programme (see page 358). It meant that the GDR had a reservoir of skilled people to carry out the developments in industry, science and technology necessary for the NES to have a chance of success.

### 'Normalisation'

The period following the building of the Berlin Wall until the late 1970s when severe economic problems emerged is most commonly associated with the 'normalisation' theories of historians such as Mary Fulbrook (see page 357). With emigration halted it was the period when more people not only made the best of a bad job but actually saw advantages to life in the GDR, not least the provision of social welfare. Most people wanted to get on with their lives in the situation in which they found themselves. As a result the **labour force** needed for economic expansion was largely reliable. It is important to note that there was no significant opposition to the regime in the GDR at this time, and certainly little deliberate large-scale sabotage.

**Source A** From an interview with journalist Walter Leonhardt and George Schmidt, a Professor of Chemistry at the University of Leipzig, shortly after the building of the Berlin Wall. Quoted in Walter Leonhardt, *This Germany: The Story since the Third Reich* (Penguin Books, 1964), pages 57–58.

> Outside a uniformly grey mass of workers and employees was streaming out of dozens of railway cars and buses, seeping into streets and alleyways, in a steady flow as they changed shifts. The sight was incredibly depressing.
>
> 'Tell me one thing - if you were called to a West German university today, would you go?'
>
> 'I don't know what I'd have answered to that three years ago. Such an offer would have been very unlikely anyway. Today I know the answer - no.'
>
> 'Why?'
>
> 'I can even tell you that', said George '... things are looking up here. You can work decently here now, as long as you respect a few taboos. You can eat decently and live with a semblance of comfort. Social security and vacation benefits in the various holiday homes ...'

What is the value of Source A to a historian studying everyday life in the GDR?

## Key debate

### The normalisation thesis

One thesis particularly associated with historian Mary Fulbrook is the **'normalisation' thesis** which asserts that the GDR survived for so long because many of its citizens accepted it as part of everyday life. Writing in 2002, historians Corey Ross and Jonathan Grix argued that in the GDR there was mutual dependence between rulers and ruled, whose co-operation was necessary for the country to function. They pointed out that by the 1980s most GDR citizens had never known anything else - but the rulers accepted that most just went through the motions of support. They were satisfied with that. In 2006 Jeanette Z. Madarsaz, writing specifically about the period 1961 to 1979, argued that as the Wall closed off any avenues of escape, people just got on with their everyday lives. She described this in terms of routinisation.

While many historians agree to varying degrees with these ideas, there are some qualifications. Peter Grieder, for example, reminds us that a repressive state with a fortified border and wall to keep its citizens in is not normal and citizens knew this. Others, such as Clemens Vollnals and Jurgen Weber writing together in 2002, argue that fear pervaded the state. The **Stasi** were, after all, a fearsome presence. In any event many who accept the normalisation thesis feel it is most appropriate until the 1980s when dissent grew as the regime faced greater problems.

## Opposition

This is not to suggest that the workforce was entirely docile. Fulbrook quotes Federation of Free German Trade Unions (**FDGB**) reports on the reasons for industrial unrest. This mainly took the form of localised unofficial strikes usually for reasons relating to working conditions – raising of **work norms**, poor quality equipment, health and safety issues and rates of pay. However, the authorities were quick to attribute political reasons for unrest – particularly if strikers were known to have contacts within the **FRG**. In November 1961 three workers who were judged to be drunk at work at the VEB Waggonbau Goerlitz, which built rolling stock and locomotives, were arrested because they were found to have connections in West Berlin and must therefore be guilty of sabotage.

Forms of protest often appeared petty. Fulbrook gives examples of defacement of posters of SED leaders, mass whistling to drown out leaders' speeches on the radio and even women workers ostentatiously wrapping scarves around their ears to avoid having to listen to political exhortations in the workplace – although reports also speak of more serious defiance such as cutting cables and emptying the fuel tanks in SED leaders' cars. One common form of rebellion mentioned in the reports was overconsumption of alcohol.

It is also true that many workers were reluctant to strike because of the possible consequences. Many were old enough to remember the 1953 revolt and the repression which followed it (see page 340). It seemed after the building of the Wall that the GDR was a permanent fixture and there was no exit in sight and so most people acquiesced in it. Moreover, their living conditions, while not matching those of the FRG, were better overall than in other Eastern European countries.

## The New Economic System, 1963–68

By the 1960s it was clear that the economic performance of the GDR was faltering and growth rates were falling. Table 1 shows returns on investment.

**Table 1: Amount of investment and growth of national income.**

| Years | Amount of investment (millions of Ostmarks) | Growth in national income (millions of Ostmarks) |
|---|---|---|
| 1951–55 | 32,000 | 21,000 |
| 1956–60 | 63,000 | 21,000 |
| 1961–64 | 66,000 | 10,700 |

Ulbricht and the SED leadership knew living standards had to be improved, not least because repression could not continue forever, and they needed people to want to remain part of the GDR. The debate which took place within the GDR about economic policies mirrored that in other **communist** economies in Eastern Europe and was based on ideas promoted by the USSR economist Evsie Libermann, calling for more enterprise and initiative, with incentives to produce more quality goods as opposed to quantity. Ulbricht understood the failings within the system with its emphasis on bureaucracy and the fulfilling of targets without recourse to quality. As a result production was often expensive and inefficient. While Khrushchev in the USSR was doubtful about any system which paid bonuses and promoted local initiative, Ulbricht was more supportive.

It is possible that Khrushchev gave the go-ahead to economic reform in the GDR because he wanted to see if it could work before applying it to the USSR, and fell from power before he could do so. In any event Ulbricht announced the New Economic System of Planning and Management (NES) at the sixth SED Congress in January 1963. Quite simply it aimed to improve economic efficiency by developing procedures in which managers would be driven more by initiative and technology than by Marxist-Leninist ideology. The level of central planning was reduced so planners could concentrate on the big picture rather than the minutiae of the planning process. This did not imply any reversion to capitalism, however. The planners retained control over targets, resources and prices. The State Planning Commission and SED were still in overall control. Having decided what should be produced, they left the producers, those who best knew how to go about it, to get on with their jobs without unnecessary bureaucratic interference.

Libermann's original article in the Russian magazine *Pravda* in September 1962 had been entitled, 'Plan, Profit, Bonus'; profitability should be the yardstick for measuring economic success and calculating bonuses for the labour force. Libermann above all wanted to see an end to shoddy articles nobody wanted to buy or that were unusable.

### Associations of National Enterprises

Associations of National Enterprises (V VBs) were set up to facilitate improvements in economic performance, providing links between central bodies and enterprises to plan tasks. Each V VB was responsible for the development of its particular industry. The goal, it was emphasised, was profit. No longer would plans be based on how much they produced on paper, but on how much profit they made in reality. Initially the NES was applied to key sectors of the economy such as chemicals, electrical, engineering, machine building and transport, followed by building and construction, agriculture and trade. The intention was to get the infrastructure correct and to reform the sectors most valuable to the economy. The emphasis was on the development of science and technology, to facilitate research and development (R and D) and to compete with the West.

While elements of the NES may have smacked of capitalism, Ulbricht had no intention of weakening fundamental communist structures. For this reason there was no effective price mechanism to determine **supply and demand**. This was still centrally controlled. There were, for example, three stages of price rises between 1964 and 1967 for raw materials and semi-finished and finished products to enterprises, but the prices of the actual goods to consumers remained unchanged – so producers, even if they operated more efficiently, found it difficult to make profits.

### Opposition

Many party functionaries opposed the NES because they feared it weakened central control and the ideological underpinning of economic development. At the Central Planning **Plenum** of spring 1964 concern was expressed about incentives and bonuses which were making researchers 'socialist millionaires'. Critics were waiting for the policy to fail – which it threatened to do as a combination of factors such as state interference and technical difficulties stymied profit.

### Weaknesses of the NES

In 1963 Ulbricht had originally believed it would take the NES two to three years to embed itself. He was wrong. By 1965 he was adding at least two years onto this target. The reasons for this were the following:

- Labour force: Many people simply did not have the skills to work in a new way, and found it difficult breaking past practices. They had never had to worry about accurate costings, for example, or concentration on quality. Many lacked technical expertise.

- Pricing structure: As prices were still set by central planners, they tended to be too low in goods the planners promoted, such as essential non-luxury items. In these cases, producers either had to accept less profit, thus negating the point of the NES, or produce fewer goods – which led, of course, to shortages.

## Key debate

### Problems with the New Economic Policy

Writing in 1965 'a reliable western source' acknowledged the advantages of the NES but anticipated it would falter due to the central as opposed to market-based pricing decisions. It was suggested that any contradiction between political ideology and economic sense would be solved in favour of the former every time. German economic historian André Steiner emphasised the structural inefficiencies. It was impossible to accurately anticipate consumer demand through central planning. It seems that the NES was something of a hybrid, hoping for Western-type success using socialist methods. Peter Grieder has qualified the criticism of others by arguing that the NES failed to fulfil high expectations rather than fail in itself. He shows that growth did take place – it just was not sufficient.

## The Economic System of Socialism, 1968–71

In October 1964 Khrushchev was overthrown in the **Soviet Union** and his successors were more doctrinaire and less enamoured with the NES policy. Nevertheless Ulbricht persisted with it. At the seventh SED Congress in August 1967 it was rechristened the Economic System of Socialism (ESS) with a call for closer ties between scientific and technology researchers and industrialists to facilitate industrial development.

The programme did see results, although those who spoke of a second German economic miracle were overstating the case.

- If 1950 equals a figure of 100, national income rose to 310 in 1965 and 410 by 1970. Gross production in industry rose from 392 to 535 in the same period. Growth was particularly impressive in targeted industries such as chemicals, metallurgy and building materials.
- Private consumption per household rose 24 per cent between 1965 and 1970, while in the same period the average monthly income of **white collar workers** rose from 491 to 619 **Ostmarks**.
- As Table 2 shows, the numbers owning consumer goods rose. Of course while this could not compare favourably with countries in the West, it did with other communist countries.

**Table 2: Ownership of consumer items.**

| Item | % of population ownership 1960 | % of population ownership 1970 |
|---|---|---|
| Television | 16.7 | 61.1 |
| Refrigerator | 6.1 | 56.4 |
| Washing machine | 6.2 | 53.6 |
| Car | 3.2 | 15.6 |

Having said this, there were periodic and unexplained shortages in household goods from toilet paper to toothbrushes, and certain foodstuffs were often in short supply. East Germans were often seen carrying '*perhaps*' bags – as they passed a shop it may perhaps have something unexpected on sale.

## Membership of COMECON

The GDR joined the communist economic partnership, COMECON, in September 1950. Its original intention was for countries to work together to increase economic performance through planning and co-operation. However, it was dominated by the USSR with whom the other members were major trading partners. In theory the GDR supplied the Soviet Union with manufactured goods such as machine tools while the Soviet Union offered raw materials. Given that the GDR became dependent on these raw materials, particularly oil – 87 per cent of the GDR's oil was supplied by the USSR – any problems with supply seriously hampered its ability to provide the manufactured goods. This happened particularly after the Oil Crisis of 1973 (see page 361). The USSR also maintained privileges such as recruiting economic experts from member countries. The 'Sofia Principle' meanwhile, signed in the Bulgarian capital city in August 1949, allowed all members access to the technology of the others at little cost. As a result the USSR 'pillaged' the better-educated experts in more technologically developed countries such as the GDR throughout the period of its existence.

In 1954, COMECON widened its remit. It felt it would function more efficiently if countries specialised – concentrating on production of a limited range of goods to trade for others. It fell to the GDR to concentrate initially on **heavy plant machinery** and motor vehicles. In 1957 it was asked to develop the mining of brown coal or lignite, which was to lead to huge environmental problems (see page 413) and textile machinery in addition to heavy plant.

By the early 1980s, the USSR and COMECON accounted for 65 to 75 per cent of GDR trade. It provided the USSR with 25 per cent of its machinery imports. Many have compared the USSR's relations with other members as colonial exploitation. In the late 1970s and early 1980s as the USSR economy faltered, it cut supplies of raw materials and raised prices, which had significant knock-on effects on the GDR (see page 411). Even without this, COMECON procedures led to systematic shortages of consumer goods and difficulties in supply. It also led to massive foreign debts for the GDR whose living standards and welfare benefits tended to be higher than elsewhere but still had to be paid for.

## 'Overtaking without catching up'

In July 1970, FRG Journalist Werner Barm considered the reasons why the GDR had not caught up with the FRG as was its stated aim. He argued that, having realised that the goal was unattainable, the GDR had recently changed its tack. It now spoke of 'overtaking without catching up'.

This was a rather torturous idea which meant that as it could not catch up using its present outdated technology and equipping itself with comparable technology would simply maintain the existing gap, it should start anew with new and innovative ideas and pioneering technologies.

This would help it to overtake the FRG without having had to catch up with it first. Unfortunately its adoption led to even more economic problems for the GDR.

Barm showed that the GDR was centralising development in key areas of heavy industry and chemicals – what it termed 'structurally determining products' or crucial drivers in economic development. This meant in effect that about one hundred **industrial plants** received the lion's share of investment. The chemical industry, for example, which was only 40 per cent as efficient as that of the FRG was to receive a 50 per cent increase in investment. The result of course was other areas, such as the production of consumer goods, faced neglect in terms of development.

### Price comparison between the GDR and FRG

Interestingly Barm also compared costs of living in the FRG and GDR and found overall it was higher in the GDR. If costs in the FRG equal 100, food, drink and tobacco products in the GDR equalled 127. This was because while basic foodstuffs were much cheaper, more exotic and less available items such as citrus fruit were 314, and real coffee made from coffee beans, a staggering 450. Rent was much cheaper at 43 but clothing reached 152. Overall the cost of living in the GDR as compared to 100 in the FRG was 121. The Workers' and Peasants' State was more expensive to live in than its capitalist neighbour.

## The economy in the 1970s

By the mid-1970s the GDR saw itself as an advanced socialist society and stated in the 1974 Constitution that the primary goal was to improve the standard of living of its citizens. Many of the ESS policies were abandoned in favour of more central control. However, as an advanced society, the GDR leadership realised that it had to make modern goods including consumer items which were complex and expensive to produce. One solution was to expand enterprises into larger units called *Kombinate*. By 1985 there were 132 centrally managed *Kombinate*, each employing up to 25,000 people. Their role was to manage and co-ordinate the whole productive process – from research to actual manufacture to distribution and sales. While the economy was centrally controlled, it was hoped that productive responsibility would lie with middle management – again, as with the V VB, the people who knew best what they were doing. Collective farms also became larger – the total number of farms declined by two-thirds between 1960 and 1980.

### Examples of growth rates

While many statistics emanating from the GDR are unreliable, sources often quote growth rates in private consumption of 4.8 per cent between 1970 and 1975 and 4 per cent in the five years thereafter. The 1976–80 **Five-Year Plan** claimed an average annual growth rate of 4.1 per cent. On the basis of these figures there is little doubt that, on the surface at least, the GDR developed as a modern industrial society:

- By 1975 38 per cent of the labour force was employed in industry.
- The percentage of university graduates rose from 4.3 per cent in 1971 to 5.5 per cent by 1975.
- In the same period the percentage of skilled workers rose from 44.9 per cent to 53 per cent; the biggest rise was in young people – 80 per cent of 25 to 30 year olds were classed as skilled.

However, the economy failed to keep up with these percentages. At least 20 per cent of skilled workers were doing jobs incommensurate with their skills. Overall therefore the seeds of the problems of the 1980s were well germinated in the 1970s and statistics tended to mask the realities.

## Economic problems

While it would be the 1980s before the malaise really became apparent, there were earlier key indicators that the economy was in trouble. One problem was as simple as poor weather. Winters in the late 1960s were harsh and followed by hot, dry summers; as a result long-term underinvestment in water, transport and energy caused problems. The Oil Crisis of 1973 and subsequent price rise also had negative effects even though the GDR was insulated by USSR subsidies. Honecker claimed that the 1980 prices paid for Soviet oil were only 50 per cent of the world market level. However, the GDR struggled to maintain its payments even at that level. The price of GDR imports rose by 34 per cent and its exports by 17 per cent. This contributed to the growing trade deficit which was to do more than anything to undermine the economy in the 1980s (see page 411).

### The Oil Crisis of 1973

In the post-war era developed countries came to rely on cheap oil imports mainly from the Middle East. In October 1973 the Organization of the Petroleum Exporting Countries (**OPEC**) announced a 70 per cent increase in the price of oil and a five per cent reduction in output. This was partly due to price rises in goods they bought from the West, such as a 300 per cent increase in the cost of wheat, and partly due to the West's perceived support for the state of Israel which had defeated its Arab neighbours in the Yom Kippur War in October 1973. When supplies normalised early in 1974, oil prices had risen from $3 to $12 a barrel. This not only led to recession in the West but had knock-on effects in the communist world, too, as prices rose significantly even when subsidised by the Soviet Union.

## Conclusion: Economic stabilisation after 1961

The NES and its successor the ESS promoted modernisation through initiative and creativity among producers. While there were some improvements in economic performance, there was always a conflict between the continuation of central planning and how much could actually be produced. In debates between political ideology and economic realities, the former always won.

Erich Honecker abandoned the ESS and returned to former Marxist-Leninist models of centrally planned development although the goals of increased efficiency, modernisation and improved living standards were the same. Nevertheless, while some gains were apparent, the Oil Crisis of 1973 hit the GDR badly.

# 2 The development of a GDR identity

One of the biggest challenges for the leadership of the GDR was to create a sense of national identity. During the Honecker years this was attempted through media attacks on the West, reinterpreting German history to view the GDR as the logical conclusion of German achievement, propaganda promoting GDR success, and sport which came to the fore as a means of uniting the population in pride at international achievements.

The GDR enjoyed astonishing sporting success which afforded a real pride among its citizens. This has been subsequently soured by evidence of extensive doping which destroyed the lives of many of the athletes concerned.

### Note it down

In this section use index cards as a form of note-taking (see page x). Here, rather than using them to note definitions, use them to explain ideas. This does not mean that you should stop adding to your glossary of index cards but just provides a different way to use them. The overriding issue in this section is how SED leaders tried to engender a sense of national identity in the GDR. The main sub-headings are:

- Erich Honecker and the creation of a national identity
- Sport
- Mass media.

Put the sub-heading on one side of the card and an explanation of the main points on the other side. Bullet point your explanation and use abbreviations if it will help you fit all your notes on one topic onto one card. You can then use these for revision.

## Honecker and the creation of a national identity

In 1971 Erich Honecker replaced Walter Ulbricht as **Secretary-General** of the SED and effective leader of the GDR. He sought to create a distinct national identity for the GDR, particularly at a time when ties with the FRG were growing rather than diminishing (see pages 365–69). Honecker's idea to achieve this was two pronged: to reduce contact with the FRG – **demarcation** (see page 372) – and to extend ties to the Soviet Union and the GDR's communist allies. He believed that the FRG and GDR were two very different states between which there could be no real **rapprochement**, but that the GDR had much in common with other Central and Eastern European countries.

This approach was developed in various ways, again building on ideas already prevalent in the Ulbricht era:

- using the media to attack the West, particularly the FRG
- developing an identity through selective interpretation of German history
- propaganda, parades and rallies (see Section 2, page 394)
- creating national pride through the use of sporting success and the promotion of sporting heroes as role models.

## Using the media to attack the West

Journalist Anne McElroy has argued that the existence of the FRG was the single biggest concern to leaders of the GDR and propaganda was a crucial weapon in its armoury against it – even when **Ostpolitik** was taking place (see page 173) and the GDR became more financially dependent on the FRG. Military conscripts were told from day one that the FRG was their enemy and were forbidden contact (see page 179). Much propaganda was devoted to telling GDR citizens how miserable life was in the FRG, despite the fact that they could gain their own impressions from watching its television. The most infamous propaganda programme on television was probably *The Black Channel*, shown on Monday evenings for over thirty years. It was rumoured that as it came on there was always a power surge from people turning off their screens, and its presenter Karl-Eduard von Schnitzler was said to be more hated than anyone in the GDR. Von Schnitzler's regular opening gambit was: 'Poverty, unemployment, breached human rights, lies and state sanctioned murder, the FRG today'. The programme would continue with predictable content on the basis of this. People did watch, perhaps fascinated by the lies and fabrications it contained, but were not noticeably swayed against the FRG as a result of viewing it.

## GDR broadcasts

This is not to suggest, however, that television in the GDR was simply a diet of biased reportage and propaganda. Although the Chairman of the Radio Committee had asserted in 1960 that the primary function of radio and television was to achieve the socialist victory by ideological and educational programming, the amount of screen time given to entertainment was always far greater than any other genre. In 1965, 1274 hours were given over to entertainment and 1101 to information and current affairs while in 1989 the figures were 3651 and 2270 respectively. It was not even that the news programmes were necessarily crude propaganda. The current affairs programme 'Current Camera' began transmission in 1952 and was well respected; it survived the demise of the GDR.

It was true that Honecker told television programmers to avoid 'a certain boredom' in 1971, particularly when it was obvious that GDR television was competing with that of the FRG. However, much of the television diet was far from tedious. GDR drama and crime series were often well regarded and received.

### Some popular GDR programmes

- *Police Call 110* – a popular police series that ran from 1972 to 1990
- *A Kettle of Fun* – a Saturday evening variety show which became a national institution
- *Our Sandman* – a very popular children's show which began transmission in 1959 and survived into the reunified Germany
- *Eleven 99* – a lively vibrant programme aimed at young people which some argue was subversive enough to influence the 1989 protest movements (see page 422).

## Interpreting German history

GDR leaders were anxious to show a continuity in German history to illustrate that the creation and development of the GDR was the logical outcome of a historical process. For this reason they emphasised **class struggles** in history such as the sixteenth-century Peasants' Revolt, creating a hero out of one of its leaders, Thomas Mutzer, and the class struggles of the industrial revolution. They particularly applauded communist heroes of the 1920s such as Rosa Luxemburg and Karl Liebknecht, whose murders were commemorated on one of the most solemn days in the GDR calendar. All this was taught in schools and mass organisations to create a sense of national identity. They were initially anxious to downplay the militarism in German history seeing this as an aberration which led to the abomination of Nazi Germany. For example, they removed the equestrian statue of **Frederick the Great** from East Berlin. The FRG, meanwhile, was associated with militarism and Nazism, a false Germany.

Later in the 1970s Honecker changed tack and began to applaud former German leaders such as Frederick the Great and **Bismarck** because, if the GDR laid claim to be the heir to German development, these powerful forces could not be ignored. The thesis now developed along the lines that the GDR was a socialist nation embodying all that was good about German history. Positive traits were emphasised in German leaders formerly much criticised – such as

Frederick the Great's reforms and religious toleration and Bismarck's role in the unification of Germany.

This interpretation and reinterpretation of history may have led to many GDR citizens being confused as to what they were supposed to believe about their national identity. It is emblematic of the confusion and contradictions that can arise when leaders select events from the past to interpret the present – but the intention was plain: to create a sense of national identity within the GDR.

This became even more developed with the example of sport.

## Sport

From its inception, the GDR encouraged sport both to improve health and productivity and, at elite level, to enhance national prestige and identity. There was therefore a two-pronged programme to encourage sport at all levels and to develop elite athletes. The latter was achieved through a strategy of early identification through skilled scouting procedures and enrolling of promising young athletes in special schools. Here the emphasis was not only on developing the sporting techniques but strict discipline and political education. In 1952 there were four such institutions; in 1989 there were 25 with over 10,000 pupils. Many of the elite sports clubs which athletes joined after graduation were affiliated either to the military or the Stasi and they were given **sinecure jobs** to maintain their amateur status while being free to train as professionals. The idea was to produce an elite of disciplined communists who could demonstrate the superiority of **communism** while acting as heroes and role models for the East Germans who would therefore take more pride and identify more closely with the regime.

### Elite athletes

On the surface the success of the programme was evident. At the 1964 Olympics, East German athletes won a commendable 23 medals in an all-German team. However, it was when they were allowed to compete in the 1968 tournament in Mexico as a discrete GDR team that their success became evident, coming third in the medal table. This seemed astonishing for a small country. Between 1976 and 1986 the GDR won more medals than any other country in three Olympic Games and two World Championships. In the 1988 Seoul Olympics their medal tally of 102 compared very favourably with the 40 of the FRG. East German athletes were unfailingly sporting and polite; Ulbricht called them 'diplomats in tracksuits'. Reports suggest that citizens' pride in GDR sporting achievements was genuine, although there were criticisms of the limited opportunities to follow athletes to events abroad. There is some evidence, too, that GDR citizens were also proud of sporting success in the FRG; there was pride in German rather than specifically GDR success, which was the opposite of what had actually been intended.

### Doping

Since reunification in 1989 and the availability of information, the GDR has become synonymous with doping in sport. As early as the 1964 Olympics, steroids and hormones were being given to athletes. One has since reported they were told they were simply vitamin pills to replace the nutritional deficiencies in their diet due to a lack of fresh fruit in the GDR. The doping programme, known as State Plan 14.25, was costing 400 million Ostmarks by 1989. It was organised by the Leipzig Research Institute for Physical Culture and Sport, the Academy of Sciences in East Berlin and the Jenapharm drugs company.

It is noticeable that in team sports such as football, where skills of creativity and working together do not lend themselves to such doping methods, the GDR had less success – although they did beat West Germany 1–0 in their only meeting in the 1974 World Cup Finals.

### The 1954 World Cup

When West Germany won the World Cup in 1954, the GDR authorities found themselves in a difficult position. Most East Germans were very pleased and stars such as Fritz Walter were as popular in the GDR as in the West. However, West Germany had beaten Hungary 3-2. Hungary was a communist country and its team, one of the best of the post-war period, clear favourites to win. The SED had hoped a Hungarian victory would show the superiority of socialist sport and, by implication, communism over capitalism. When Helmut Rahn scored the winning goal, the East German commentator Wolfgang Hempel remained silent because he did not know how he was supposed to respond.

### Women and sport

The GDR's avowed belief in sexual equality (see page 388) ensured women would be encouraged to participate in sport as much as men – although they were discouraged from taking part in what were considered male preserves such as football and contact sports such as judo. Examples of the sports in which women excelled were track events, gymnastics, figure skating, swimming and diving. On the surface women athletes were hugely successful. In the 1980 Olympics, they constituted 36 per cent of the GDR team but won 47 per cent of the GDR medals. Individual performers such as swimmer Kornelia Ender, who won four gold medals and one silver at the 1968 Montreal

**Source B** The German Democratic Republic took a gold medal in the women's 4x100-metre medley relay finals in 1976, and set a new world record of 4:07.95 in doing it. Left to Right are Ulrike Richter, Hannelore Anke, Andrea Pollack, and Kornelia Ender.

How useful is this source to a historian investigating the impact of success in international women's sport in the GDR?

Olympic Games, earned international acclaim. However, all this came at a price.

International women's sport was favoured by the regime because, in the 1960s, it was in the early stages of development so could be more easily dominated as the competition was not as fierce as in men's events. In addition, gender equality notwithstanding, it was thought that women would be more compliant than men when it came to doping; it was also found that steroids developed muscles more readily in women. As with their male counterparts, girls were selected for elite training at a young age and given intensive training and were doped. The drug of choice given to female athletes was Oral-Turninabol which achieved particularly speedy results. The signs of steroid abuse were noted early on. When commentators remarked on Ender's muscular body and deep voice, her coach retorted, 'They're supposed to swim not sing.' Many of the athletes have subsequently suffered considerable physical and mental problems including, in at least one instance, the need for a sex change operation. One of the most respected researchers into the scandal, Professor Werner Frank, has called it a crime against humanity.

### Role models

Athletes were intended to engender pride in their sporting success and act as role models for GDR citizens. This was as true for women as for men, and female athletes were cast as ideals of GDR womanhood. There was huge emphasis in the GDR on family (see page 388) so athletes were shown as contented wives and mothers. Comments on their appearances notwithstanding, they were shown in the media as being very feminine, particularly in sports such as figure skating and gymnastics where presentation was important. They were taught to smile even when undertaking the most difficult manoeuvres and wore the most chic and fashionable outfits.

Statistics show that women did not participate in sport for leisure in the GDR as readily as men. Some 56 per cent of men participated in organised sport as opposed to 37 per cent of women – although women did enjoy sports such as gymnastics, swimming and aerobics where the female athletes had excelled.

## Mass participation

Officially the GDR encouraged mass participation in sport because of its beneficial effects. Ulbricht himself remained keen on exercise and even appeared on television leading workout routines. It is estimated that 9 million people took part in mass sporting festivals in 1963 alone. Children in particular were encouraged to participate in fiercely competitive sporting contests. In 1980, as many as 5 million East Germans may have participated in 28,500 sporting competitions, with 340,000 taking part in a mass table tennis tournament.

However, historians Mike Dennis and Jonathan Grix have shown that overall the reality of encouraging mass participation in sport (as opposed to exercise) was different. Most funds were channelled into the programme for elite athletes and sports provision was usually cut in times of economic difficulties. While the 'Joint Sports Programme' of **DTSB**, **FDGB** and **FDJ** (see page 397) encouraged mass participation in sport and awarded over 4 million sporting medals in 1983, the reality was that adults were often sedentary in their pursuits and the poor quality of sporting facilities impeded participation. A Sports Federation survey of 1992 after the demise of the GDR found only 11.3 per cent of sports fields, 10.6 per cent of sports halls and 8.6 per cent of swimming pools were adequate for use in its former territory. The sports which were really encouraged were those for which few state-run facilities were necessary – rambling, jogging, fishing, football and amateur gymnastics. Also encouraged, however, were activities such as shooting and amateur radio – so more people were prepared, if necessary, for paramilitary activities.

## Conclusion: The development of a GDR identity

The aim of the media and sporting success was to promote identity with the GDR. Honecker used the media to attack the FRG while promoting the GDR. German history was reinterpreted to acclaim the GDR, while citizens were encouraged to take pride in the GDR through rallies and parades.

International success at sport was judged a sure-fire way of engendering pride in GDR achievements, and to some extent it worked. However, evidence has since emerged of widespread doping using illegal, performance-enhancing drugs. Sport is another example in the GDR where illusion was not matched by reality.

### Work together

One of you should take the role of a critic who thinks the leadership failed to engender a sense of national identity in the GDR from the 1950s to 1970s, the other the role of an apologist for the regime who feels they did succeed. There are arguments to support each case. Extract arguments from your notes to justify your relative positions. Then discuss them together. Which side of the debate do you incline to? Which side has the most reliable evidence?

# 3 Relations with West Germany

The late 1960s saw the emergence of Ostpolitik or rapprochement between the GDR and FRG. Although this worried the USSR and led indirectly to the overthrow of Ulbricht, it continued as part of the overall trend of **détente** between the superpowers. There were various visits and agreements drawn up culminating in the Basic Treaty of 1973 when the countries formally recognised each other for the first time.

Ostpolitik gained some tangible benefit for the GDR including wider international recognition – in 1973 it joined the **United Nations** – and the sale of political prisoners and members of families divided by the border (see page 368). On a personal level it led to greater contact between the respective citizens of the two Germanies. Despite the close ties between the GDR and USSR, its relationship with the FRG became the most important for both German countries.

### Note it down

Using the 1:2 method (see page x) make notes on the following topics:

- Relations with West Germany and Ostpolitik – why did Ostpolitik take place?
- Preconditions for Ostpolitik – what needed to be addressed before Ostpolitik could take place?
- The effects of Ostpolitik – how significant was Ostpolitik?
- The fall of Ulbricht – why did Ulbricht fall from power?

Use index cards (see page xi) to make a note of all the treaties and international agreements mentioned in the text.

## Ostpolitik

Willi Brandt, a **Social Democrat**, became Chancellor of the FRG in 1969 and began a policy of reconciliation with the GDR. This became known as Ostpolitik and was perhaps the most important foreign policy venture for both German states.

Hitherto FRG policy towards the GDR had been clear: no recognition. Indeed Adenauer, the post-war Chancellor of the FRG, had gone further with the Hallstein Doctrine of 1955 which threatened to break off diplomatic relations with any country except the USSR which recognised the GDR. Adenauer had insisted that only the FRG represented Germany on the world stage; the GDR was simply an interloper. Although most communist countries had recognised the GDR by 1968, no developed capitalist countries recognised the GDR at this time.

The West German Government had always insisted at the very minimum that the division of Germany and any frontier disputes must be resolved before there could be any military disengagement from **NATO**, let alone diplomatic recognition of the GDR. However, the 1961 crisis over Berlin had taught them that the USA would not go to war over the issue of German reunification, and eight years on the Wall was not only a fact of life but had in fact settled many issues. Similarly the refusal of the West to intervene in the USSR invasion of Czechoslovakia in 1968 showed it both recognised and would not interfere in the USSR's **sphere of influence**.

### Reactions to the Russian invasion of Czechoslovakia

In Czechoslovakia, the regime led by Alexander Dubček initiated reforms such as more freedom of speech and promised free elections – the so-called **Prague Spring**. Like the leaders of other communist countries in Eastern Europe, Ulbricht opposed these developments and feared reformist ideas might spread to the GDR. At a meeting at Dresden in March 1968, Dubček was firmly censored by his **Warsaw Pact** colleagues. Ulbricht in particular warned of Western plots to destabilise both Czechoslovakia and the Warsaw Pact. He may have been one of the fiercest critics and he wholeheartedly supported the August 1968 Russian invasion to stop the reforms and replace Dubček's regime with one more pliable. However, GDR troops were not involved except to control the border (see page 367). There were some protests in the GDR against the invasion, noticeably in Erfurt on 22 August. These were put down brutally by the security forces and the hunt for participants continued into the 1970s. Ulbricht justified the invasion in the following terms:

- It preserved peace.
- It secured the GDR border.
- It prevented the spread of reformist ideas into the GDR.
- It prevented any democratisation within the SED.

The invasion convinced GDR citizens that there was little to hope for from the ruling SED in terms of reform.

## Reasons for Ostpolitik

Given that reunification was far from an international priority, many West German leaders adopted a pragmatic line that division was a fact of life which needed to be accommodated. Brandt and his advisers understood that more would be gained by negotiating with the GDR directly. They began to speak of 'change through convergence', by which they meant normalising relations without threatening the peace of Europe – in other words recognising the situation as it was and dealing with it accordingly. They sought to develop more friendly relations with the GDR. The two countries could not avoid close natural ties – they shared a common language, common traditions, common history, common families – and while recognising that two Germanies were a fact of life for the present, there seemed no reason why they could not co-operate together in the interests of both international harmony and restoring human contacts.

## The process of Ostpolitik

Brandt quietly abandoned FRG insistence on non-recognition of the GDR and began to speak of 'One nation but two Germanies' – by which he acknowledged that the people were divided into two countries, each of which had a right to exist. This made it possible for Ostpolitik to take shape:

- In 1969 a draft treaty was prepared including recognition of both countries and the entry of the GDR to the United Nations as a **sovereign state**.
- In 1970 Brandt visited the GDR city of Erfurt, the first FRG leader to do so. Although no agreements were reached, it was the fact of his visit that was important. He received a rapturous welcome. This convinced him that rapprochement was possible and worth proceeding with.
- Willi Stoph, the East German **Minister-President**, visited the FRG city Cassel by way of reciprocation. Again the fact that this visit took place was more important than any agreements. Stoph, a **hardliner**, had insisted at the meeting at Erfurt that the FRG must recognise the GDR before any agreement could be reached and at Cassel demanded DM 100 million in compensation owed to the GDR economy by emigrants leaving before the building of the Berlin Wall.
- Between 1970 and 1974, Brandt and Foreign Minister Walter Scheel negotiated major diplomatic agreements with the USSR and Poland to recognise their existing frontiers.
- The status of Berlin was formalised by the Four Power Treaty of December 1971 (see box).

- In the Basic Treaty of June 1973 the two Germanies recognised each other's right to exist and made the practicalities of Ostpolitik possible. The FRG relinquished its claim to be the sole representation of the German nation but continued to offer FRG citizenship to any GDR citizens who emigrated – either legally or otherwise. The treaty spoke of normalising relations through developing commercial, tourist, cultural and communications links. This effectively gave the green light for citizens of the FRG to travel freely to the GDR – but not the other way round.
- In May 1974, the two countries exchanged diplomats – effectively formally recognising each other.

### The Four Power Treaty

The status of Berlin needed to be settled before any agreement was possible between the FRG and GDR. The situation in Berlin in 1970 was still technically the same as it had been at the end of the Second World War. The USSR saw East Berlin as part of the GDR while the three western powers saw all Berlin as still subject to four-power control and therefore neither part of the FRG nor GDR. However, by 1971 the USSR prioritized a general settlement concerning Berlin over accommodating the wishes of the GDR. It wanted to improve relations with the FRG as part of detente and was also looking with concern at the USA's increasingly friendly relations with its communist rival China.

In December 1971 the Four Power Treaty was signed between the four wartimeAllies-USSR, USA, Britain and France - in which it was acknowledged:

- that West Berlin remained under four-power control, and was politically not part of the FRG
- that the FRG could maintain its ties with the city
- that the GDR had to accept transit arrangements through its territory so visitors could get to West Berlin
- that the actual sovereignty of Berlin itself was deliberately left vague.

The importance of the Treaty was that it formalized arrangements already in place and deferred any contentious issues, thereby helping to make possible rapprochement between the FRG and GDR.

## Effects of Ostpolitik

Although there were difficulties in the relations between the GDR and FRG, during the course of the 1980s contacts grew ever closer, most notably in the economy.

### Economic dependence

The GDR became ever more reliant on the FRG economically. By the 1980s it was its main trading partner and benefited from the fact that **European Union (EU) quotas** and **tariffs** did not apply to trade between the two German states. By the end of the decade there was widespread co-operation between firms from the FRG and GDR.

Such was the increased contact between the GDR and FRG that items such as tolls, postal payments and visa charges became important to the GDR economy. Visa charges alone brought in DM 16 billion between 1968 and 1989. DM 4.5 billion was raised simply through the compulsory exchange rate of DM 1 to 1 Ostmark introduced in 1964. It is estimated that the total value of financial transfers from the FRG to the GDR until 1989 was DM 91 billion, of which DM 21 billion went directly to the state. Currency obtained from the FRG was free of interest payments and vital for servicing the GDR's foreign debt. In return the FRG demanded improved emigration, postal and telecommunication services and an end to minefields and automatic firing devices on the border. Historians have noted linkages between an infusion of Deutschmarks and emigration as in 1984 when the two loans raised from the FRG coincided with 35,000 exit permits.

### Relaxation of travel restrictions

As far as ordinary people were concerned the most obvious manifestation of Ostpolitik was more contact between each other despite the legendary surliness of GDR border officials. During the 1960s, visits from West Germans were largely restricted to Christmas and for urgent family business. However, by the time of the Basic Treaty, over 2 million West Germans could visit the GDR for extended periods. In 1969 there had been 500,000 telephone calls between the GDR and FRG as a result of restrictions; by 1989 this number had risen to 40 million. In 1988, there were 10 million calls between East and West Berlin alone whereas until 1970 there had been no telephone links at all between the two halves of the city.

West Germans could now travel freely to the East although day-trippers had to return by midnight. The main crossing point in Berlin, Friedrichstrasse station, was labelled 'the Palace of Tears' as families and friends said their farewells. It was important that families could meet and exchange news and gifts – which is why many East Germans seemed more aware of life in the West than in other communist countries. It also tended to create disadvantages for those without Western contacts, who did not have access to the latest consumer goods or foodstuffs that might be in short supply in the GDR.

## Sale of political prisoners

The GDR had been selling political prisoners for cash since 1963. While still secret, this process intensified. By 1977, the FRG was paying DM 96,000 for each prisoner. In addition they paid DM 4500 to allow families, separated by the border or the Berlin Wall, to be reunited. It is estimated that by 1989, the FRG had paid DM 3 billion to buy 34,000 prisoners, reunite 2000 children with their parents and facilitate 250,000 cases of family reunification.

## The fall of Ulbricht

Ostpolitik was identified with Ulbricht and was distrusted by others who feared it would draw the GDR too close to the West and away from the USSR. The Soviet leader Leonid Brezhnev was more ambivalent. He was pursuing a policy of détente with the West and saw that closer relations between the two Germanies might be useful in this. However, there developed something of a power battle between him and Ulbricht, mainly about formal recognition of the GDR and the status of Berlin. He insisted the USSR was in control – talks had to be agreed in advance by the **Kremlin**, and Moscow's own negotiations with Western countries, including the FRG, took priority. Brezhnev insisted the GDR was more likely to achieve its goals by having the USSR negotiating on its behalf.

It became a question of GDR hegemony over its own affairs. Ulbricht wanted to control negotiations while the USSR saw the GDR as a satellite which would have to accede to its policies. The USSR had no intention of jeopardising the wider global policies of détente with what it considered the localised issue of inter-German relations. It has since been ascertained that Brezhnev laid out realities in a tense meeting with Erich Honecker on 28 July 1970 (see source C).

**Source C** From a secret transcript from archives released by the Kremlin after the collapse of the USSR, quoted in Anne McElvoy, *The Saddled Cow* (Faber and Faber, 1992), page 82.

> You can believe me, Erich, the situation which has developed in your country disturbs me deeply. Things have reached the stage where they are no longer simply your own affair. The GDR is for us a socialist brother country, an important outpost. It is the result of the Second World War, our conquest won with the blood of the Soviet people ... I will tell you quite honestly that we will not allow him to go his own way ... After all, we have troops on your soil, Erich. I say to you finally, never forget that.

What can be inferred from Source C about the relationship between the GDR and the Soviet Union?

### Erich Honecker, 1912–94

Erich Honecker was born one of six children into a coal mining family in the Saarland area of Germany in 1912. He followed his father into the KPD, joining the youth wing at the age of ten in 1922 and becoming an adult member in 1929. Honecker studied for two years at the International Lenin School in Moscow which gave him a great affinity with the USSR whose leadership he believed in absolutely. He was never to be less than a USSR loyalist.

Honecker was arrested by the Nazis for underground activity and spent the years from 1937 to 1945 in captivity. He briefly escaped from Brandenburg-Görden Prison during an Allied air raid in March 1945. When Ulbricht and his colleagues returned to the USSR Honecker soon made contact and proved himself useful in the role of recruiting young people to communism. In 1946 he became co-founder of the FDJ and organised mass youth festivals in Berlin in 1950 and 1951.

In 1950 Honecker became a candidate member of the Politburo, achieving full membership status in 1958. In 1953 he proved loyal to Ulbricht in the tension following the June revolt (see page 340), although he made enemies among Ulbricht's opponents. Ulbricht trusted him and his stature grew as Ulbricht reasserted control. Having resigned from the FDJ in 1958, Honecker undertook further study in Moscow and returned to be given responsibility for the construction of the Berlin Wall. It was his success here that really made him indispensable. However, during the 1960s he became more and more uneasy with Ulbricht's economic reforms and liberalism. By the end of the decade he was conspiring to oust him. He achieved this in 1971 and subsequently succeeded him as leader of the GDR.

Honecker and his colleagues had been requesting Moscow's permission to move against Ulbricht. Having been given the green light, it was a simple **Politburo** decision in April 1971: Ulbricht resigned as leader of the SED but accepted the purely symbolic title of Chairman of the State Council which he kept until his death, largely unmourned in August 1973.

### Key debate

#### The fall of Ulbricht

The fall of Ulbricht took many by surprise. The GDR news agency ADN attributed it to ill health which many at the time accepted. In the 1980s Martin McCauley argued that it was the GDR's poor economic performance which saw it neither able to significantly improve the standard of living of its citizens nor meet its international obligations to COMECON which led colleagues to plot against him. Historians of late have focused more on the USSR. Mike Dennis, for example, has shown that Brezhnev actually disliked Ulbricht's arrogance and wanted him replaced but was slightly reluctant to give the go-ahead because of his stature. Brezhnev acted only when he feared that Ulbricht might wreck détente through showing too much independence. It may also be that the USSR was surprised at the hostility towards Ulbricht among his own colleagues; after all it was they who requested his removal. Frederick Taylor may have summarised the debate with his comment that Brezhnev had decided his German satellite needed 'new blood at the top'.

## Conclusion: Relations with West Germany

While the GDR had followed the USSR lead in foreign policy in the 1960s, it showed independence in Ostpolitik whereby it and the FRG recognised each other's right to exist and developed much closer contacts. The GDR gained greater international prestige and revenue from the sale of political prisoners, while families and friends in the two Germanies could re-establish contact. The policy may, however, have led directly to the fall of Ulbricht in 1971.

### Work together

Historians have often debated the significance of Ostpolitik on the internal policies of the GDR. Working in pairs, one of you should extract from your notes any points that suggest it enabled the economy of the GDR to improve while the other finds evidence that it had little impact.

## 4 Growing international prestige

One of the most important payoffs of Ostpolitik as far as the GDR was concerned was the international recognition it so craved. In 1973 it was admitted to the United Nations and by 1974 it had diplomatic relations with over 80 countries including the USA. In 1974, too, it amended its constitution to remove the commitment to reunification – although it did reaffirm its eternal alliance with the USSR.

The GDR, while acknowledging its position within the Soviet sphere, nevertheless gained in international prestige and recognition during the 1970s. One highlight was the signing of the Helsinki Accords in 1975 which recognised all existing European frontiers and committed signatories to various human rights. Honecker hoped largely to ignore these.

The GDR signed a new Treaty of Friendship with the USSR in 1975 and tried to limit contacts with the FRG through the policy of demarcation. This had little success. The momentum generated by Ostpolitik was too great even when threatened by external developments such as a return to **Cold War**. FRG Chancellor Helmut Schmidt visited the GDR in 1981 but the reciprocal visit by Honecker to the FRG was delayed largely because the Russians did not think the time was right. Nevertheless the GDR was becoming more and more financially dependent on the FRG through extensive loans in 1983 and 1984 and an ever-increasing trade imbalance. Honecker finally visited the FRG in September 1987, leading many to ask whether the Berlin Wall was still necessary.

### Note it down

Use a spider diagram to make notes on this section. The body of the spider could be labelled 'Growing international prestige'. The legs could be labelled:

- Helsinki Accords – how important were they?
- The GDR and USSR, COMECON and Warsaw Pact countries in the 1970s – how did their relationship develop?
- The GDR and FRG in the 1970s – how effective was the policy of demarcation?
- External developments – how far did these threaten the growing relationship between the GDR and FRG?
- State visits – how significant was Honecker's state visit to the FRG in September 1987?

## The Helsinki Accords

The GDR always needed to balance its relations with the USSR and FRG. While recognising the benefits of Ostpolitik, it had to acknowledge that it was essentially a **satellite state** of the Soviet Union and ultimately it had to bow to USSR policies. Nevertheless, as we have seen, Ostpolitik paved the way for international recognition, and the GDR was a key player in the 1975 Helsinki Accords. The Helsinki Accords were signed in August 1975 between 35 countries including the USA and USSR and aimed at reducing tensions between them through agreements on issues in four 'baskets'.

- Basket 1: Agreement to settle disputes peacefully, acceptance of existing boundaries, agreements not to get involved in countries' internal affairs.
- Basket 2: Agreements on economic issues such as scientific and technological co-operation.
- Basket 3: Agreements on human rights including free migration of peoples and reunification of people divided by international borders.
- Basket 4: Agreements to continue to meet to implement and monitor the proposals.

Of course while these agreements removed any areas of contention over borders, they would also return to haunt countries such as the GDR which signed the human rights elements without any real intention of abiding by them. After all, most were already enshrined in the GDR Constitutions of 1949, 1968 and 1974 and negated by catch-all national security clauses (see page 333). However, the issue of migration was significant not least because 100,000 people applied for exit visas as a result of the Agreements (and usually were refused them). One group led by a doctor Karl-Heinz Nitsche signed a petition demanding the implementation of Basket 3 including the right to emigrate. As the 1980s developed the number of applications rose from two per thousand under pensionable age (pensioners usually had no trouble in being allowed to emigrate to the West!) to twelve by 1989. Many faced interrogation, imprisonment and loss of employment while ultimately being refused permission.

The GDR signed the Helsinki Accords but like other communist allies had little intention of keeping to them. As far as the SED leadership was concerned it was the significance of their involvement and how this demonstrated their international recognition as a major country which was important – not what they actually signed to say they would do.

## The GDR and USSR in the 1970s

While Ulbricht had been more inclined to assert independence, Honecker sought a closer relationship with the USSR and the two countries signed a new accord in October 1975. The Treaty of Friendship and Mutual Assistance not only promised friendship for 25 years but recognised that while the USSR was now a fully developed socialist state, the GDR was still on the journey. The USSR remained therefore its role model and mentor. It also asserted that GDR troops could be used anywhere to protect Warsaw Pact interests. The treaty may only have formalised existing realities but the fact that it did so showed that the GDR remained firmly in the Soviet camp.

### Relations with COMECON and the Warsaw Pact countries

In the 1960s and 1970s, the GDR proved a loyal ally to the Soviet Union. The same was true of COMECON and Warsaw Pact countries. The GDR fulfilled its military obligations to the latter to provide troops and military equipment to defend the Soviet bloc, which led to it having a highly professional army and requiring all its male citizens to undertake military training (see page 387). The GDR was perhaps the Warsaw Pact member to most strongly advocate intervention in Czechoslovakia in 1968 and it also urged the Soviet Union to take action against the **Solidarity movement** in Poland in 1980 (see page 372). The GDR earnestly felt that any process of liberalisation within the Soviet bloc would threaten all its members. In this it followed a consistent policy throughout its history, wholeheartedly embracing the **Brezhnev Doctrine** of 1968, and being particularly lukewarm to Gorbachev's reformist policies of the 1980s (see pages 417–18).

### The Brezhnev Doctrine

The Brezhnev Doctrine was the name given to a policy outlined in the Soviet periodical *Pravda* in September 1968. It was used initially to justify the invasion of Czechoslovakia, but expanded to suggest Warsaw Pact countries had the right to intervene in the internal affairs of any of their members if they threatened their unity by developing systems of capitalism or democracy or threatened to leave the alliance. The Soviet Union was to sign treaties with all Warsaw Pact countries to affirm its principles, for example with the GDR in 1975.

▲ **Figure 1: Warsaw Pact and NATO countries.**

### COMECON

The GDR followed the Soviet lead in COMECON. It consistently advocated closer co-operation between COMECON members and supported the specialisation policies where different members produced and sold specific items to each other, even though this may not have worked to the GDR's advantage. It saw itself as one of the most sophisticated and developed members of the economic alliance but firmly entwined with the international family of communist countries. Indeed, in July 1976, when the SED hosted an international meeting of communist parties, it saw itself as the role model for other communist countries to emulate in its loyalty to the Soviet Union and development of the socialist state.

It was possibly because the GDR felt so loyal to the policies of the Soviet Union that it felt so disappointed not to gain the support of Gorbachev in the 1980s (see pages 417–18).

## The GDR and FRG in the 1970s

In keeping with the Treaty of Friendship and Mutual Assistance with the USSR, the GDR limited contacts with the FRG. Party and state officials and military conscripts – the so-called 'secret carriers' – were actually forbidden contact with the FRG altogether for fear they would be contaminated by Western ideas or shed state secrets. The SED leadership undoubtedly believed greater contact with the FRG was reducing loyalty among its population. SED internal opinion polls in 1972 and 1973 saw a reduced allegiance. They were even afraid of the impact of too much FRG television on their citizens.

This led, in November 1973, to doubling the amount of the currency citizens of the FRG were made to exchange for Ostmarks when visiting the GDR – to 10 Ostmarks for day visitors and 20 for longer stays. The intention was to reduce the numbers of visitors. In this they succeeded – the numbers of West Berliners visiting fell by a third in

1974. The GDR was anxious to emphasise the differences and downplay commonalities between the FRG and GDR. Even mention of common German history was frowned upon – although, as we have seen, the GDR had appropriated most German achievements in history as developments leading to the creation of the GDR (see pages 362–63). Honecker commented that any talk of unification was 'twaddle'. The SED insisted that a new type of socialist nation had been created; it was the future while the **nation-state** as exemplified by the FRG was the past. Most people did not accept or even understand what precisely was meant by this. Many no doubt wondered if it was Honecker himself who was espousing 'twaddle'.

## Demarcation

The policy of contact limitation was known as demarcation. This policy flew in the face of the reality of what was happening – an example of the conflict between appearance and reality in the GDR. The policy was modified when polls showed a majority of GDR citizens believed there was a special relationship with the FRG and 16.1 per cent opposed any form of demarcation. The problem was compounded by the fact that contacts were both so extensive and so profitable. Some have argued that it was the FRG which effectively kept the GDR afloat, particularly during the 1980s when the USSR and COMECON economies were in tailspin (see page 411).

Talks took place to solve the dispute over currency restrictions. The FRG had a strong bargaining counter – the provision of credits to the GDR. In 1972 the GDR had received over DM 585 million in credits or loans to facilitate their growing trade with the FRG. While the FRG was anxious not to suggest blackmail, the GDR nevertheless quietly retracted the new currency arrangements after a year of protracted discussions. Even so they only reduced them by one-third so they remained higher than before November 1973, and in return they were offered credits to the annual value of DM 750 million. The GDR availed themselves of this upper limit until 1981 when their debt began to reach crisis proportions and their credit allowances were limited (see page 411).

It might be argued that the GDR was getting the best of its agreements with the FRG. Certainly the FRG Government seemed patient and willing to accommodate it. However, all the time it knew the GDR was becoming more dependent and, despite the bluster, more subservient. The GDR had long been the junior partner of the Soviet Union. After Ostpolitik it was also the junior partner of the FRG.

## External developments

In the 1970s many in the SED had feared that closer contacts with the FRG would destroy the fabric of socialist society and even threaten the existence of the GDR. By 1980, it seemed to many citizens throughout the GDR that the opposite appeared to be true. Both sides gained considerable benefits from the stabilisation of their relations. However, by the end of the 1970s, the relationship was threatened by external developments as various factors polarised attitudes and people spoke of a new Cold War:

- In December 1979, NATO decided to deploy medium-range Pershing and Cruise missiles in the FRG in retaliation for the movement of Russian medium-range missiles to western USSR.
- In December 1979, the USSR invaded Afghanistan. It feared the growth of Islam on its southern borders and sought to impose a communist regime on Afghanistan to counter this. There was widespread condemnation in the West and the USA began to support Afghan opponents of the invasion.
- There was repression of the Solidarity movement in Poland. Solidarity was advocating greater democracy and economic reform. The Soviet Union opposed it and feared demands for more freedoms may spread to the USSR. Many expected the Warsaw Pact to invade as they had in Czechoslovakia in 1968. However, when the Polish Government declared martial law and arrested members of Solidarity, the Soviet Union appeared satisfied. Despite the urgings of many of its allies including the SED in the GDR, it ruled out military force. The reasons why Warsaw Pact countries allowed the Polish authorities to put their own house in order are still unclear.
- In January 1981 Ronald Reagan became President of the USA with a more anti-communist agenda exemplified by his **'evil empire' speech** in 1983.

In keeping with this new mood of tension, Honecker laid out preconditions for continued friendship with the FRG. These included a full exchange of ambassadors.

## State visits

In December 1981, Chancellor Helmut Schmidt visited the GDR and reaffirmed the agreements made by Brandt a decade earlier, notably that both sides wanted peace. Both genuinely wanted to see the reduction of armaments on German soil. Again some SED hardliners such as Willi Stoph and Erich Mielke worried that too friendly relations with the FRG would drive a wedge between the GDR and the USSR, but the USSR had few objections to the relationship. Schmidt invited Honecker to visit the FRG and his successor Helmut Kohl repeated the invitation in autumn 1982. By this time, however, the Russians were more critical. When the FRG Parliament had agreed to the deployment of NATO medium-range nuclear missiles on their soil, and the Russians retaliated by placing their missiles both in the GDR and in Czechoslovakia, they decided this friendship was incompatible with international realities and told Honecker he could not go – a telling example of GDR's junior status. Honecker finally visited the FRG in September 1987.

### Honecker's state visit to the FRG

Perhaps the high point of both Ostpolitik and the career of Erich Honecker was his visit to the FRG from 7 to 11 September 1987. He had to wait for years until relations between the USSR and FRG thawed sufficiently for Gorbachev to allow it. While it was officially classed as a 'working' rather than a formal **state visit**, Honecker was nevertheless afforded most of the privileges of a head of state including motorcycle escorts. He acted as an equal to Helmut Kohl. Kohl spoke of German reunification but Honecker lamented that relations were bound by political realities and went on to assert that **socialism** and capitalism could no more be combined than fire and water. If he found the ceremonies and speeches at Bonn discomforting, he relaxed more as he toured the provinces and showed emotion when he visited his former home in the Saarland still inhabited by his sister.

The visit seemed a great success in normalising relations between the GDR and FRG.

The visit seemed to confirm Honecker as an international statesman. However, Stasi reports suggested many GDR citizens, particularly the young, thought if the FRG was a friend, then the Berlin Wall must be obsolete. If the visit was Honecker's greatest achievement on the world stage, it would nevertheless come back to haunt him.

## International prestige

The visit of Erich Honecker to the FRG in autumn 1987 saw the apex of his power. It appeared he had achieved all his objectives. At home the regime seemed stable and secure. Abroad the GDR had achieved widespread recognition and good relations with the FRG. Indeed Honecker realised that the maintenance of such relations was an important foundation of FRG policy.

There were various examples of diplomatic success:

- Honecker paid official visits to Belgium in October 1987, France in January 1988 and Spain in October 1988. In each he was afforded the respect due to a head of state. Preparations began for official visits to the UK and USA.
- Foreign heads of state from non-communist countries made official visits to the GDR – the Greek Prime Minister in January 1988, the Austrian Chancellor in June 1988 and the Danish premier in September 1988.
- The GDR over-exaggerated its role as a world player in the promotion of peace. In December 1987 the Soviet Union and USA signed the Intermediate-Range Nuclear Forces Treaty (INF) which effectively eliminated medium-range nuclear missiles. On 16 December an SED Plenum meeting suggested this would not have been possible without GDR help: 'It is recognised internationally that the constructive position of our country helped to make possible the treaty.'

**Source D** From the Joint Communiqué by Erich Honecker and Helmut Kohl (September 8, 1987) translated by Jeremiah Riemer.

> In consideration of the current circumstances, and irrespective of differences of opinion on fundamental questions, including the national question, it is the intention of both states, in the spirit of the Basic Treaty, to develop normal neighbourly relations with each other on the basis of equality, and to continue exhausting the possibilities of the treaty.
>
> It was agreed that what has already been achieved should be preserved and extended, being mindful of the principle that both states respect the independence and autonomy of the other in domestic and foreign matters. A willingness to communicate and realism should be the guiding principles for a constructive, practical-minded cooperation between the two states.
>
> Both sides paid tribute to the ongoing positive effect of the Quadripartite Agreement of September 3, 1971 on the situation in Europe's centre and on East-West relations, and affirmed the necessity of adhering to the Agreement and applying it as fully as possible.
>
> General Secretary Honecker and Chancellor Kohl dealt thoroughly with questions regarding holiday travel and visitor traffic, including travel in the event of pressing family matters. They acknowledged the progress made thus far, and affirmed their intention to continue working toward improvements and simplifications in the interests of the people. [...] They welcomed the establishment of partnerships between cities in the German Democratic Republic and the Federal Republic of Germany as important contributions to the facilitation of meetings between citizens - including cultural events - and thereby toward the extension of friendly neighbourly relations between the two states. In the future, they will continue to support such efforts. [...]

How useful is Source D to a historian studying the relations between the GDR and FRG in the late 1980s?

While the SED seemed confident in its role as leader now that the GDR had international recognition and respect, this confidence bred weaknesses that made it unable to adapt to the crisis which would soon be apparent. It became complacent and blind to the need to reform. Its very success accounted for its downfall. Various factors in the 1980s came together to threaten its complacency.

## Conclusion: Growing international prestige

The GDR always had to balance its relationship between the FRG and USSR. In 1973 the GDR joined the United Nations and the following year was recognised by the USA: the GDR had finally won international recognition of its right to exist. It went on to win international prestige, for example for its role in the 1975 Helsinki Accords, but equally it remained firmly in the Soviet sphere as exemplified by its 1975 Treaty with the USSR. In keeping with this, Honecker tried to limit contacts with the FRG through the policy of demarcation. This had only a limited effect, however. Despite a return to conditions of Cold War by the early 1980s, the relationship between the two Germanies grew ever closer and the GDR was becoming more and more dependent on FRG financing. In 1987 Honecker finally visited the FRG, but more and more of his citizens were now asking, if the two Germanies were friends, why was the Berlin Wall necessary?

### Work together

Discuss the following statement in pairs:

**'The GDR's relationship with the USSR was more important than its relationship with the FRG in the years 1961–87.'**

How far do you agree with this? You could consider issues such as:

- the loyalty of the SED leadership to the USSR and their support
- the impact of Ostpolitik including how far demarcation was practical
- the significance of Honecker's visit to the FRG in September 1987.

What conclusions have you arrived at?

### Chapter summary

- By 1960 it was apparent throughout the Soviet bloc that centrally planned economies were failing to achieve their targets.
- The Berlin Wall ended migration from the GDR and stabilised the workforce.
- In January 1963 the New Economic System (NES) was introduced with emphasis on profitability, quality and more initiative from the actual producers.
- Conservative elements within the SED opposed the NES because it smacked too much of capitalism.
- The NES faced problems because the economy was still centrally planned and pricing structures were decided centrally with little consideration of economic realities.
- In 1968 the NES was relaunched as the Economic System of Socialism (ESS) with a focus on science and technology.
- The GDR's economy was constrained within COMECON which operated to the advantage of the USSR.
- Walter Ulbricht resigned in May 1971, to be replaced by Erich Honecker.
- Honecker attempted to engender a sense of national identity through promoting the GDR as the natural progression of German achievement.
- The GDR enjoyed amazing sporting success but its athletes were subsequently found to have been widely doped.
- Ostpolitik or rapprochement with the FRG was the key foreign policy of the 1970s.
- The GDR became more recognised internationally and in 1973 joined the United Nations.
- Honecker maintained ties with the USSR and attempted to limit contacts with the FRG but the process was irreversible.
- The GDR remained loyal to its Soviet and Warsaw Pact allies, particularly the Soviet Union.
- The high point of Ostpolitik was Honecker's visit to the FRG in September 1987.

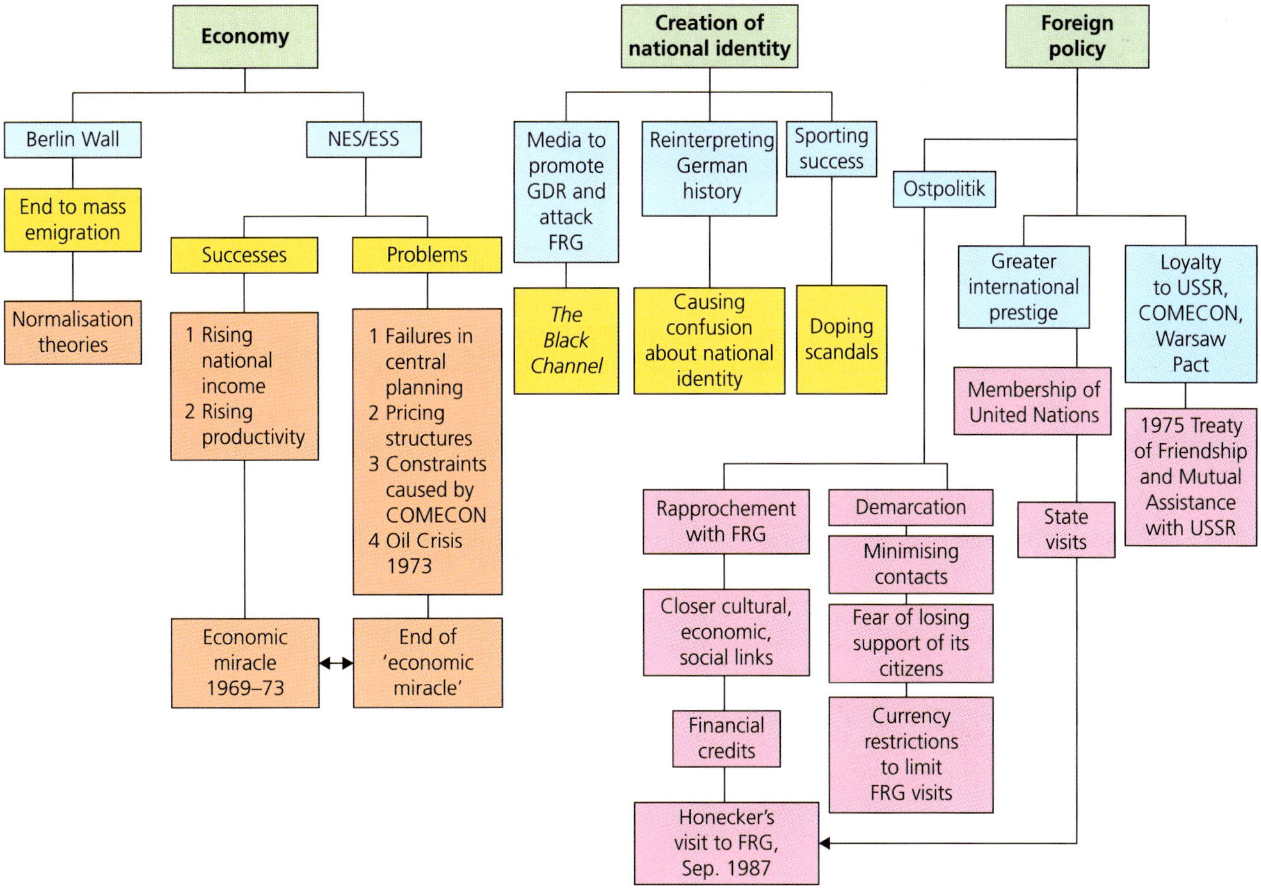


▲ **Summary diagram: The development of the East German state 1961–85.**

## Recommended reading

M. Fulbrook, *Anatomy of a Dictatorship: Inside the GDR 1949–1989* (Oxford University Press, 1995). Very perceptive study of the power structures of the GDR and why it remained stable for so long.

H. Haftendorn, *Coming of Age: German Foreign Policy Since 1945* (Oxford University Press, 2004). Examination of German foreign policy. Chapter 5 focuses on the GDR.

M. McCauley, *The German Democratic Republic Since 1945* (Macmillan, 1983). Very thorough examination of the GDR, particularly good on economic aspects.

A. Steiner, *The Plans That Failed: An Economic History of the GDR* (translated from German by Ewald Osers) (Berghahn, 2010). Thorough and readable account for students who seek to dig deeper.

# Section A: Essay technique

## Structuring an essay and writing introductions

Well-structured essays are likely to receive higher marks than essays in which the structure is unclear. The structure of your essay should reflect the nature of the task that you are performing. Therefore, it should help you evaluate how far the two sources together are useful to a historian who is investigating a specific topic.

### Macro structure

The overall structure of your essay should include:

- an introduction, which focuses on the question and sets out the essence of your answer
- a conclusion, which summarises your essay in order to weigh up the extent to which the evidence of the sources is useful, and reaches an overall judgement
- the main body, which should present a detailed evaluation of the evidence of the sources.

**TIP:** Remember, the question asks you to consider the sources *together*. Therefore, a structure which analyses Source 1, and then moves on to Source 2, is unlikely to do well. It would be better to structure your essay in a way that allows you to deal with the sources together.

### Micro structure

Each paragraph should set out an analysis of the usefulness of the evidence of the two sources. Therefore, you need to discuss both sources in every paragraph.

**TIP:** One way of doing this is to make sure that you discuss both sources in almost every sentence.

For example, imagine you are answering the following question:

**How far could the historian make use of Sources 1 and 2 together to investigate the role of international sporting success in engendering pride in the GDR?**

**Source 1** From Erich Honecker, *From My Life*, published in 1981. Honecker was First Secretary of the SED and ruler of the GDR from 1971. Here he is writing about international sporting success.

> Some people maintain that we unleashed a 'chase for medals' and that we were thus pursuing aims which did not have much to do with sports. I should like to reply that sports and games are of interest to us Communists mainly because they help to convince people to lead a healthier life and live longer – not to mention the fact that going to a sports field often makes it unnecessary for you to go to the doctor. It enhances better features in a person's character which are as important to an all-round person as healthy physical development ...
>
> It goes without saying that many talented youngsters are discovered ... thanks to the wide scope of our sports movement. All we do is encourage their natural striving for perfection and excellence. If they win top honours at world championships or the Olympic Games one day, they become examples to others, winning over new generations for sport.

**Source 2** 'State Aid as Price for Gold', an article by Neil Allen, a journalist, in *The Times*, 7 November 1971.

> East Germany is undoubtedly the most sports conscious country in the world and only a political innocent could fail to see that they pursue sporting success to gain the recognition which has not been granted them by the West. But the East Germans also genuinely believe in raising the standard of health of their whole population and many members of their teams, athletics in particular, must be numbered among the most educated young Europeans.

Here are three examples of introductions that could answer the question on page 376:

**Answer 1**

In Source 1 Honecker says 'sports and games are of interest to us Communists because they help to convince people to lead a healthier life'. He even suggests if you do sports you do not need to go to the doctor. Source 2 agrees. The author says East Germans genuinely believe in raising the standard of health of the whole population. Their athletes moreover are very well educated.

**Answer 2**

Source 1 is useful to a historian because it was from the leader of the GDR and tells us what he thinks about the value of sport. Source 2 is useful because it is from a journalist writing at the time.

**Answer 3**

Both Sources 1 and 2 are useful to a historian investigating the role of sporting success in engendering pride in the GDR although they take a different focus. Source 1 suggests that sporting heroes act as role models for others while Source 2 asserts that the GDR pursues sporting success to enhance its international reputation. Both agree, however, that participation in sports helps the healthy lifestyle which the Government finds desirable in its citizens. There are, however, problems with both sources. Source 1 is biased as the memoir of the leader who encouraged this policy, while Source 2 offers little evidence in support of its claims. Neither focuses on the problems accruing from the sporting success such as the doping of athletes – although writing in 1971 Neil Allen would not have known about this.

## Activity: Analyse the introduction

Having read the three introductions, in pairs consider the following questions:

1 What skills do the different introductions demonstrate?
2 Which introduction focuses most clearly on the question?
3 Which introduction integrates Source 1 and Source 2 most effectively?
4 How could you improve the best of the three introductions?
5 What can you learn from the three samples?

## Activity: AS-style questions

1 Why is Source 1 (page 76) valuable to the historian for an enquiry into the promotion of sporting success in the GDR?
2 How much weight do you give the evidence of Source 2 (page 76) for an enquiry into the promotion of sport in the GDR?

# Selecting information

Another skill vital for success in Section A is that of selecting the right information from the sources. So what is the 'right' information? It is:

- information that is relevant to the question
- information that illustrates the main point of the source
- information that illustrates the points that you want to make.

In addition to the source material, the exam paper also contains a short description of the source's provenance printed immediately above the source. Selecting the important material from the provenance will also help you do well. You could select information that helps you evaluate the evidence:

- information that would help explain the motives of the writer
- information that helps explain the purpose of the document
- information that helps contextualise the source (see page 216).

**TIP:** Don't just copy information from the provenance; make sure you use the information to help weigh the evidence that the source presents.

## Selection

Imagine you are answering the following question:

**How far could the historian make use of Sources 3 and 4 together to investigate the success of economic policies in the GDR in the 1960s?**

**Source 3** From a speech by Walter Ulbricht, First Secretary of the SED, on the 'New Economic System' of the GDR on 16 December 1965, translated by Alison Brown. Ulbricht acclaims the success of his policies.

The new economic system of planning and management is our instrument – with whose help we are tackling the tasks involved in the comprehensive build-up of socialism and the technological revolution in the German Democratic Republic and completing the transition from capitalism to socialism with the total victory of socialism in the German Democratic Republic.

With the new economic system of planning and management, we are creating, on the basis of the economic laws of socialism, the fundamental economic system of socialism in the German Democratic Republic. It is the economic system of a highly developed socialist industrial state with intensive modern agriculture. It is the economic system of a socialist state that has essentially mastered the unheard-of burdens imposed by the imperialist past, especially by the fascist world war and the division of the country.

It is an ideological task of the first order to insure that everyone understands the scope of this qualitative change in our economy and society. Understanding this qualitative change and its relationship to the new economic system of planning and management is a criterion for the maturity of leadership **cadres**, not only in the economy. *The most important conclusion is: take a stand for innovation and learn!* The two are inextricably connected. No comrade in any responsible position should ever forget that. Only those who take a stand and learn will live up to the new demands.

**Source 4** From an article by Werner Barm in *Die Welt*, 30 July 1970, translated by Alison Brown. The article is on the GDR's failure to catch up with economic progress in the FRG.

The Slogan: Overtaking without Catching Up

The economic problems of the 'GDR' stem, among other things, from the shortcomings of the New Economic System of Planning and Management (NES). Three important elements are missing from this system: a free, self-regulating market that is freely regulated, prices that react flexibly, and local initiative instead of centralized regulation attempts. Even NES ideologues are well aware of these drawbacks.

The 'serious shortfalls' in the production of industrial consumer goods are also described in the 'GDR' press as being 'caused by the weather'. Horst Werner, deputy minister for light industry, reported to the alarmed Volkskammer committee for trade and supply that production in fifty light industry plants had been temporarily suspended, and he estimated the plan deficits at 195 million marks. How this relates to the 'weather' – when the consumer goods factories have problems not with volume, but with assortment, quality, delivery dates, and contracts – remained unanswered. Committee members expressed doubts regarding the clothing, furniture, shoe, knitwear, and stocking industries – a bad omen for what will soon await central German shoppers in stores.

### Activity: AS-style questions

1. Why is Source 3 valuable to the historian for an enquiry into the purposes of the New Economic System?
2. How much weight do you give the evidence of Source 4 for an enquiry into the economic problems faced by the GDR?

### Activity: Selecting from the sources

Read the question and then the sources.

1. Make a list of the information that you would select from the sources to answer the question.
2. Look at an example of the information that you could have selected for Source 3 on page 454.
3. Did you select the same kind of information for Source 3? Look back at the criteria for the successful selection of information. The selected information should be relevant to the question, not merely giving facts of an event or date, and information that would help a historian investigating this issue.
4. Add anything into your notes on Source 3 that you might have missed, and check that your examination of Source 4 was as thorough. Add any new information you find to your notes.

## Work together

Having read the sources and selected pieces of information to use in your answer in the activity on page 378, consider the following questions with your partner:

**1** Did you both select the same information for the source? If not, whose selections were:
- **i)** most relevant to the question
- **ii)** most characteristic of the whole source?

**2** Did either of you select any information from the provenance?

**3** Did you both select the same information from the provenance? If not, whose selections were:
- **i)** most relevant to the question
- **ii)** most helpful to a historian evaluating the information contained in the source?

**4** Did you miss anything?

**5** What can you learn from this task?

Having discussed these questions, make a bullet-point list of three things that you can do to make sure you answer Section A questions effectively. Review the list with your partner.

# Making inferences

Making inferences from sources is one way to demonstrate your understanding of the source and of the period. An inference is a deduction or conclusion that comes from reading between the lines of a source – it is not about what lies on the surface but what is hinted at below the surface. It is not wild speculation but a conclusion that is drawn from reasoning or evidence. A detailed knowledge of the period is vital to making inferences.

Imagine you are answering the following question:

**How far could the historian make use of Sources 5 and 6 (page 380) together to investigate the relationship between the GDR and Soviet Union in the 1970s?**

There is a lot of information in the sources which is purely on the surface. But beyond that, you can use your own knowledge to draw out more complex and insightful conclusions as the annotations below show.

**Source 5** From Melvin Croan, *East Germany Soviet Connection,* in Washington Paper 36, Centre for Strategic and International Studies, Sage Policy Paper, 1976. This was a specialist study for people interested in international relations.

> Despite the GDR's breakthrough onto the international arena and despite (or, because of) the proliferation of East German-West German contacts, the accent now belongs to East German 'integration' into the Soviet bloc in Europe rather than GDR self-assertion ... This is certainly not to suggest there are now no differences between the GDR and the Soviet Union. Differences in roles, perceptions and even interests do persist and they could again become important in the future. Still the primary focus must be on the present stage of the relationship. Only by understanding the extent of East Germany's integration with the Soviet Union and the 'Socialist community', a process in which its own ruling elite has played an active and often eager part, can one appreciate the constraints imposed on the GDR's manoeuvrability in foreign policy.

Despite Ostpolitik, the GDR has become closer to the Soviet bloc countries.

The GDR and Soviet Union still have differences which could reassert themselves in future.

Only by appreciating its closeness to the Soviet Union can one understand how constrained it is in terms of an independent foreign policy.

The current rulers of the GDR have been important in developing the close relationship with the Soviet Union.

Below is an example of how you could develop the inferences annotated around Source 5 into a paragraph in answer to the question on page 379:

Source 5 confirms that while Ostpolitik had brought the two Germanies closer, the GDR was still primarily allied with the Soviet Union. Although there may be differences in policies, this closeness was promoted by the current GDR leaders. It further explains the lack of flexibility of the GDR in terms of foreign policies: effectively they had to follow the Soviet Union line.

## Activity: Inferences

Having read the question and example above you can now practise making inferences from Source 6. Remember:

- Your inferences should help you answer the question.
- Inferences should be informed by your contextual knowledge of the period.

Answer the following questions:

1 In Source 6, what is Fischer insisting upon in the first paragraph?
2 In Source 6, what evidence does Honecker use to emphasise continued GDR-Soviet Union friendship?

## Work together

Having completed the activity above, consider the following questions with your partner.

1 Did you both make the same inferences from Source 6?
2 If you differed, look at the source again, discuss your points of view and try to work out which inference is more likely to be correct.
3 How can the inferences that you have made help you answer the question?

Having discussed these questions, make a bullet-point list of three things that you can do to make sure you use inferences effectively in Section A questions. Review the list with your partner.

**Source 6** From Oskar Fischer, Foreign Minister of the GDR, 'Cooperation with the Fraternal Socialist States', in (ed.) Arthur W. McCardle and A. Bruce Boenau, *East Germany: A New German Nation under Socialism?* (University Press of America, 1984), pages 36–47. This is a collection of articles by GDR leaders about their areas of expertise and responsibility.

> A precondition for the solution of all problems as various as they may be is the strengthening of the German Democratic Republic as a sovereign socialist state while remaining anchored in the community of socialist states and in firm fraternal alliance with the land of Lenin[1].
>
> In his formal address on the 30th anniversary of the founding of the GDR ... Erich Honecker emphasised that cooperation with the Soviet Union has logically become more closely bound up with the further advance of socialist production in the GDR. It is the best testimony of the qualitatively new types of fraternal relations possible only between socialist states ... In international law, this is expressed in the treaty of friendship, cooperation and mutual aid of 7 October 1975.

[1] Land of Lenin – Soviet Union.

## Activity: AS-style questions

1 Why is Source 5 (page 379) valuable to the historian for an enquiry into the relationship between the GDR and the Soviet Union?
2 How much weight do you give the evidence of Source 6 for an enquiry into the reasons behind the Treaty of Friendship between the GDR and Soviet Union in 1975?

# Section B: Essay technique

## Detail and analysis

Paper 2 Section B questions, like Paper 1 Section A and B questions, need to be detailed and analytical. You may have already read the advice on how to write detailed and analytical essays for Paper 1 (see pages 39 and 59). Now is a chance to practise these skills in the context of the economic policy of the GDR.

### Activity: Detail and analysis

Imagine you are answering the following question:

**How far was the New Economic System a change in the economic policy of the GDR?**

1 Identify the kind of question (see page 353).
2 Make an appropriate plan, writing down the main points of your three or four paragraphs.
3 Next to each of the points add three supporting details – you could use a different colour if you have one.
4 Write one analytical sentence to conclude each paragraph.

### Question practice

1 How accurate is it to say that the consequences of the New Economics System were beneficial for the GDR in the years 1963–1970? AS
2 To what extent did the economy of the GDR change in the years 1963 to 1970? AS
3 'Celebrating sporting success was Erich Honecker's primary method for creating national identity in the GDR in the years 1971 to 1985.' How for do you agree with statement?
4 'Ostpolitik completely changed the GDR's attitude to the FRG.' How far do you agree with this statement?

### Work together

Having finished the activity 'Detail and analysis', swap your work with a partner. Consider the following questions:

1 Did you agree on what type of question you were dealing with? If not, discuss it and work out who was right.
2 Whose plan most clearly focused on the specific type of question?
3 Were the details that your partner selected the most appropriate to support their points?
4 Could either of you have used detail that better supports the points that you wanted to make?
5 Were all of your partner's sentences truly analytical?
6 What can you learn from your partner's approach?

Use these questions to feed back to each other and improve your use of detail and analysis.

# **Key Topic 3** Life in East Germany, 1949–85

## Overview

Most people in the GDR just got on with their lives. In the 1970s Honecker spoke of a Social Contract which offered generous welfare provision and subsidised housing. It was hoped not only that this provision would earn the loyalty of citizens but that their lives would genuinely be improved from it. The family was placed at the heart of life in the GDR and there were generous maternity benefits and childcare arrangements. Women were afforded complete equality in law although often still faced discrimination in practice. Education was geared towards producing a skilled workforce loyal to communist ideals.

However, there was extensive repression for those who rebelled against the system and the Stasi in particular were feared. They employed a vast army of informers and infiltrated most groups in society. There were many other types of security force, not least border troops and a Soviet army of occupation. Nevertheless most people avoided falling foul of the authorities. Their loyalty was also gained through mass organisations which attempted indoctrination but also provided benefits such as cheap holidays. While twenty per cent of the adult population joined the SED there is much debate about the actual level of support for the regime, although the welfare benefits were genuinely appreciated.

The relationship between the state and Protestant Churches appeared to change over time, although there was always an overarching desire by the authorities to undermine the Churches. Nevertheless the state realised they had to be accommodated and could be useful in engendering support for the regime. As a result, in 1978, Honecker agreed a Concordat with the Protestant Churches.

The GDR was susceptible to Western influences through both extensive contacts with the FRG and the availability of FRG media. Its own media often saw the FRG as an enemy but its television in particular was widely viewed. However, GDR citizens were not beguiled by it; they enjoyed their own television too.

The overarching topic of life in East Germany, 1949-85 is covered in four sections:

1. Social change and welfare programmes
2. Repression and control
3. The SED and the Protestant Churches
4. Western influences on the GDR.

## TIMELINE

| | |
|---|---|
| 1962 April | Conscription introduced |
| 1965 October | Beat music banned |
| 1965 December | Family State Law |
| 1971 8 June | SED conference announces 'Main Task' |
| 1972 March | Abortion Law |
| 1972 April | Announcement of social welfare measures such as increased pensions |
| 1973 September | Military training made compulsory for year 9 and 10 students |
| 1974 October | Exposure of Günter Guillaume as Stasi **spy** in FRG |
| 1976 October | The minimum monthly wage is raised from 350 to 400 Ostmarks |
| 1976 November | Wolf Biermann expelled from the GDR |
| 1978 March | Concordat with Protestant Churches |

## 1 Social change and welfare programmes

In the 1970s social welfare was developed to the point where many spoke of a **Social Contract**. Living standards would be guaranteed in return for at least outward acceptance of the regime. Problems emerged, however, in financing improved welfare provision and in shortages of goods. This was compounded by the introduction of **hard currency** shops where those wealthy enough could buy Western goods. This highlighted the inequalities in a supposedly equal society.

With the family placed at the heart of life there were genuine attempts to facilitate family life with generous maternity benefits. Housing, too, underwent reform, although ambitious targets could not be met and by 1990 much was in need of renovation and repair. Nevertheless huge suburbs sprang up featuring the high-rise accommodation found in other developed countries.

Schools were geared towards a combination of political indoctrination and providing the skills necessary to thrive in a developed country. **Vocational education** was well developed. However, there was always a tension between the desire to encourage creativity and initiative and the need for political conformity. There was also a problem in that the educational system produced too many skilled people whom the workforce could not accommodate.

A larger percentage of women worked in the GDR than in any other country in the world and officially there was complete gender equality. In reality this was not true. There were comparatively few top women managers and even fewer leaders in the political sphere. At home women tended to lead traditional lives, taking responsibility for domestic chores and childcare. However, what advantages they did derive from the GDR were dissipated after reunification.

### Note it down

Use the 1:2 method (see page x) in this section which focuses on social welfare programmes. You need to consider:

- the impact of the Social Contract: break it down into its component parts such as welfare benefits, housing, healthcare and education and consider the effectiveness of the provision of each of these
- how far the problems of social welfare outweighed the benefits
- how far the policies towards women and the family matched the rhetoric, i.e. consider theory and reality.

If you are revising or you are organising your notes thematically you could colour code the different points as to whether they are political, economic or social. This may help you later when trying to answer questions about reasons for the events that you are studying.

## The Social Contract

The SED supported social and welfare programmes to provide not just a minimum but a satisfactory standard of living for all the citizens of the GDR. It realised that as the economy developed these standards should commensurately improve. In 1971 Erich Honecker had spoken of the connection between the economy and social policy in establishing harmony in society. One aim of social policy was to ensure no one got left behind as society developed. This, it might be argued, was the difference between **socialism** and capitalism where groups could suffer in the face of overall developments.

The Honecker regime during the 1970s and 1980s hoped to secure popular support through social and welfare programmes. There was a genuine desire to improve living conditions without giving up any power. Honecker in particular had a genuine sympathy with the working classes derived from witnessing the poverty of his earlier life. Social welfare programmes were introduced in the 1960s (see page 342), but Honecker developed them into an informal Social Contract in which minimum standards would be guaranteed in return for at least tacit support for the regime – and the social welfare programmes were generally appreciated. This policy came to be known as '**really existing socialism**', a phrase first used in 1973.

According to figures from the International Labour Office, the amount of its **GDP** the GDR spent on social welfare rose from 12.7 per cent in 1970 to 16.8 per cent by 1979. However, these figures do not include aspects such as subsidised housing and the cost of guaranteed job security – so the actual figures would be higher. In 1971, state subsidies spent on food, industrial goods and wages amounted to 8500 million **Ostmarks**.

The central features of the Social Contract were outlined in the 'Main Task' announced by Honecker at the 1971 SED Conference. The Party committed itself to improvements in living standards on the understanding that these would lead to greater labour productivity and the development of greater scientific and technical developments – to modernise society within a socialist framework. In practice, 'really existing socialism' meant abandoning unrealistic visions and targets; it was more concerned with what could be achieved in reality – and even this was often found to be unrealistic.

Improvements in social welfare were announced throughout the 1970s:

- Honecker's first social policy programme was launched in April 1972 with the promise that pensions and welfare benefits would be increased.
- The **minimum wage** was increased in 1976.
- Housing provision was to be prioritised.
- Healthcare was to be improved from September 1973.
- Education was to be expanded.

### Pensions

Pensions had been comparatively neglected during the Ulbricht years simply because pensioners were non-productive. However, with an ageing population and, after 1968, an increase in voluntary contributions, pensions increased – by 20 per cent between 1971 and 1972, for example. Indeed with overall increases of 6.5 per cent between 1965 and 1972, old age pensions increased faster than benefits for any other group.

The minimum monthly pension was raised from 230 to 300 Ostmarks in December 1976 and to 327 by 1979. This was less than 33 per cent of the average wage – so people were encouraged to remain in paid employment as long as they could. Public servants such as teachers, police and doctors and SED officials had occupational pensions at 60 to 80 per cent of their final salaries, which were far more generous than those paid to workers in industry.

## The minimum wage

In October 1976, the monthly minimum wage was raised from 350 to 400 Ostmarks with smaller increases for those earning between 400 and 500 Ostmarks. The fact that 1 million people benefited, or one in seven of the workforce, shows that many were on comparatively low incomes. It was hoped that improved wages would lead to improved productivity, but there is little evidence to show this. The Government had been reluctant to call for increased **work norms** since the June 1953 rebellions (see page 340), and with greater job security coupled with continuing problems such as inadequate equipment and poor working conditions, many people simply were not incentivised to work harder.

## Housing

The provision of adequate housing was a key prerequisite of a socialist state. However, the GDR had faced critical housing problems predating its inception. As much as two-thirds of the housing stock in major cities such as Berlin and Dresden had been either destroyed or severely damaged during the war. Where it had been renovated, by the 1970s it was often dilapidated and falling once more into disrepair. Most complaints in ***Eingaben*** (see page 396) throughout the existence of the GDR related to poor quality housing.

Ulbricht's policy had been to renovate existing stock wherever possible. While he took a personal interest in architectural design and the development of new satellite towns, he did not like the 'barracks' nature of large new housing estates although his Government did build them (see below). Honecker, in contrast, was more concerned with quantity and the 1970s saw extensive building of accommodation. This was a popular policy:

- In a Leipzig survey of people's goals in October 1984, 53 per cent of respondents replied that their priority was to acquire a decent home.
- In Dresden in 1980 a survey of living standard satisfaction found that only 35 per cent were happy in older accommodation while the figure rose to 76 per cent of those living in newer housing.

There was no getting away from the fact that most people preferred new homes. Having said this, some would have welcomed any homes of their own. By 1986 it was estimated that seven per cent of families still lacked their own homes and had to share with parents or others.

### Rents

Rents, subsidised by the state, were cheap – often no more than four per cent of income. This was often offered as one of the big advantages of living in the GDR. Journalist Rudolf Walter Leonhardt, writing in 1964, reports of a Dresden resident favourably comparing rents of 38 Ostmarks a month to DM 400 per month in Hamburg in the FRG. 'You see? Not even a tenth of what you pay.'

Residents of Berlin paid 1.00 to 1.25 Ostmarks per square metre of living space. This was a problem in that rents did not cover the costs of repair in many of the older buildings. Private homes comprised ten per cent of the housing market in the 1980s; they were built at a rate of 11,000 to 12,000 per year and mainly catered for wealthier citizens, who, as in the West, often lived in spacious homes in the outskirts of cities or in 'gentrified' flats in well-modernised old inner-city buildings.

### New towns and new estates

Many new homes and indeed towns needed to be built at the centre of new industrial development, for example the chemical industries around Frankfurt-an-der-Oder near the border with Poland, which also therefore attracted Polish migrant workers. In the three new towns of Schwedt, Eisenhüttenstadt and Guben, 75 to 83 per cent of residents worked in the massive new chemical and petrochemical factories around this area. Many of the new constructions here and throughout the GDR were huge, often featureless concrete complexes with all the attendant problems of loneliness and isolation which residents experienced elsewhere in the developed world. Berlin-Marzahn comprised 64,000 dwelling units, Leipzig-Grunau 34,000 and Halle-Neustadt 33,000. In addition much of the accommodation was shoddily built with damp conditions, unreliable lifts and so on. Some eight-story blocks had no lifts at all. Crime rates tended to be higher than in older areas; the new accommodation at Halle-Neustadt had a 20 per cent higher crime rate than in Halle itself, while some new towns such as Schwedt had the highest crime rates in all the GDR. Often people called the new towns and estates 'stone deserts'. Nevertheless many were relatively happy to live in them if the amenities worked. Facilities such as schools and shops were usually within reach and the subsidised transport made it relatively easy to get to work. About 15 per cent of the units constructed up to 1981 were privately built and owned.

## Growth in house building

In 1971 the results of the **housing census**, which showed lots of substandard and antiquated accommodation, genuinely shocked the SED and a comprehensive programme was launched which thrust housing into the centre of social policy. No statistics on housing had been kept before 1958 but between that date and 1971 between 60,000 and 70,000 new homes had been produced annually. It was intended that over 3 million dwellings would be constructed or renovated by 1990. In the course of the 1970s the number of dwellings with inside toilets rose from 36 per cent to 60 per cent – but this was still very low compared to the West. Overall between 1971 and 1975, 400,000 new homes were built and 290,000 refurbished. Most new building was either in urban areas or extending them; less than one-third of either new building or renovation took place in rural areas where the population was more static.

### Continuing problems with housing

The overall target of 3 million new builds was not attained, however. Figures of new construction between 1971 and 1990 vary from 1.7 to 1.9 million, but nevertheless in 1990, 34 per cent of the housing stock predated 1919 and much of it had not been renovated. By the 1980s, 44 per cent of older homes had no hot water, while 60 per cent lacked a bath or shower and 65 per cent an indoor toilet. In 1984 one in seven of older homes in Leipzig lacked any of those amenities. Too many people were living in comparative squalor. By 1989, there was a waiting list of 800,000 for repairs to accommodation and a thriving **black market** in circumventing this.

**Source A** The wonders of socialism. An East German apartment building (*Plattenbau*) in the 1970s.

What impression does Source A give of life in the GDR?

## Healthcare

Healthcare in the GDR was comprehensive and based on two principles:

- Communities needed to be healthy for the strength of the nation.
- Individuals needed to be healthy so they could produce more.

Healthcare was largely funded through a system of National Insurance for which employees contributed ten per cent of their gross income and employers an equivalent amount.

During the 1970s and 1980s healthcare provision improved in terms of numbers of personnel as can be seen in Table 1.

**Table 1: Numbers of doctors and dentists in the GDR.**

| Profession | 1970 | 1989 |
|---|---|---|
| Doctors | 27,555 | 40,193 |
| Dentists | 7,345 | 12,011 |

The GDR was immensely proud that its **infant mortality rate** fell as a result of better ante- and post-natal care. However, the 1959 rate, when the GDR actually overtook the FRG where 10.83 babies per thousand died, rose slightly over the subsequent decades (see Table 2).

**Table 2: Infant mortality rate.**

| Year | Deaths per thousand of live births |
|---|---|
| 1950 | 20.57 |
| 1959 | 9.86 |
| 1978 | 13.1 |
| 1985 | 11.4 |

### Problems with healthcare

The overarching problems with healthcare were increased costs, an ageing population and greater expectations. While the GDR shared these with most developed nations, they may have been exacerbated through the growing economic problems and the more unhealthy nature of society as compared, for example, to western countries. The problems with the quality of healthcare included the following:

- The emphasis was always on prevention of illness so comparatively more was spent on preventative medicine and promotion of healthy lifestyles than on clinical medicine. As a result the number of hospital beds was actually cut – from 190,025 in 1970 to 163,305 in 1989. The GDR had slightly fewer beds available than the FRG – in 1977 the GDR had 107.5 beds available per 100,000 inhabitants and the FRG 118.8.
- As with most European countries in the 1970s and 1980s, care for those with mental illness was less robust than in other areas. The GDR in particular had some grim care homes and mental institutions; many predated the Nazi period. Ideologically, too, a society which supposedly operated in the interests of all its citizens was reluctant to address issues such as mental illness, alcoholism, suicide and domestic violence.
- The economy could not afford the quality of care it sought. Much specialist equipment had to be imported and the state lacked the resources to pay. It was estimated in 1988 that only 30 per cent of the equipment needed for successful heart surgery and transplants was available in the GDR. Even the largest hospital, Berlin-Buch, faced shortages while there were also shortfalls of different drugs and medicines throughout the GDR at different times. Basic items such as rubber gloves and sterile syringes could be in short supply. GPs often complained of shortages of equipment and medicines.
- Provision was not equal. The political elite and those felt to be more valuable to the state, for example scientists, received better treatment than the rest of the population – although they were expected to pay ten per cent more from their salaries.
- The environmental pollution (see page 413) took a fierce toll of health with more bronchial disorders and worse.

Healthcare, as in so many other areas within the GDR, is an example where the reality of everyday life was at variance with the rhetoric. The same might be said of education.

## Education

Education was crucial not only to give young people the necessary skills to flourish in a modern technological society but also for purposes of political indoctrination. The overall aim was conformity combined with initiative and channelled creativity – which always led to tension.

### Schools

The state sought to control the intake of all schools, which would be based on equality of opportunity rather than privilege. As early as 1946, the Law for the Democratisation of German Schools had begun to remove the influence of religion and abolish privileges for the children of wealthy parents. In the 1950s schools were entirely reorganised into a comprehensive system, except for elite schools for athletes (see page 363) and others for students gifted, for example, in foreign languages or mathematics. In 1959 the system of secondary schools called polytechnics was completed. These accommodated children from the ages of 6 to 16 and were the basic unit of secondary education in the GDR. More academic children left these in their final two years to attend 'Extended Upper Schools' (EOS) where they took, at the age of 18, the final leaving examination – the Abitur – which was essential for university entrance. While this was enough in theory to get students into university, they also in practice needed a good political record through the **FDJ**. It helped if potential students belonged to politically compliant families and showed little or no religious conviction. Needless to say the **Stasi** heavily infiltrated the universities which could otherwise have been a breeding ground for **dissidents**.

However, the GDR also adopted an informal system whereby children would only be selected for the Extended Upper Schools according to the number of university places available. Some years as few as 12 per cent of 18-year-olds received the Abitur necessary for university entrance.

### Vocational education

For less academic students there were developed links with industry which offered work placements and training schemes. There were annual 'Fairs of Tomorrow's Masters', which encouraged young people into careers in science, technology, engineering and so on. Children on work placements were often given real responsibility in developing new projects. Research discovered since German reunification found that many were shocked by poor working conditions, inefficiency and even drunkenness among the workforce. Nevertheless places were readily available and in theory students had plentiful choice of careers in industry – although there were never enough places for skilled applicants and many had to undertake work beneath the level of their qualifications. Links were tightened between enterprises and universities particularly after the introduction of the ESS in 1968 (see page 358), for example between the Friedrich Schiller University in Jena and Carl Zeiss optics firm. There were also endless opportunities for further education for adults; many complained that the pressure to attend evening classes was too great and made too many inroads into leisure time – this may indeed have been a deliberate intention on the part of the authorities.

### Military training

From September 1973 students in Years 9 and 10 (aged 13 to 15) had to undergo military instruction. This largely involved firing practice and survival techniques one afternoon per week. Those on vocational training were also included. The military even developed relationships with **kindergartens**, coming in to talk to classes of children and show off military equipment.

### Problems in education

In 1951–52, 16 per cent of students spent more than eight years in school. By 1971–72 this had risen to 72 per cent.

There were, however, two fundamental problems in education:

- The huge pressure for ideological conformity caused resentment among many.
- The workforce became over-qualified; there simply were not the skilled jobs for the numbers of skilled workers. One sociological survey in the 1970s suggested 70 per cent of workers were skilled but there were only suitable opportunities for 55 per cent of them. Other data suggests 20 per cent of workers were doing jobs for which they were overqualified.

## Problems in social welfare

We have seen there was a genuine effort to raise living standards through social welfare in the 1970s. The SED had recognised the correlation between higher economic growth and improvements in living standards. Expenditure of social welfare per head of the population rose 90 per cent between 1971 and 1979. While this may seem impressive the problem was that national income only rose by 46 per cent during the same period. The state could not afford its programmes of social welfare. This led to significant problems.

### Finance

The cost of subsidising items such as food, rents and transport rose from 16.9 billion Ostmarks in 1980 to 49.8 billion by 1989. By this time, for every 100 Ostmarks spent on foodstuffs, the state was subsidising it to the tune of 89 Ostmarks. Economists understood the problem early on: in 1972, the president of the State Bank had worried that this level of subsidy would exacerbate the external debt problem to an unacceptable degree. When officials had raised this issue with Honecker, however, he had accused them of sabotage. The policy was not for discussion.

### Investment

The Government spent on social welfare at the expense of investment. In the 1970s public investment accounted for 24.4 per cent of national income; by 1979 this had fallen to 20.1 per cent, the lowest in all the **Soviet bloc**. This meant quite simply that the Government lacked money for investment in economic and technological improvements which were significant in the 1970s but would become critical in the following decade.

### Shortages

The policy led to shortages. Essential minimum standards were prioritised and items considered luxuries had to wait. People could wait 12 to 17 years for the delivery of a new car and up to 13 to be connected to a telephone. Shoppers often queued for up to four hours a day and choice was limited when goods were available. The system of supply was also unfair. There were hard currency shops known as Intershops where high quality goods were available; food and drink, for example, in Delikit and stylish clothing at Exquisit. Originally these had been mainly for foreign visitors, but in 1974 East Germans were allowed to shop in them too – if they could afford to. Again contacts in the West could be a deciding factor and heightened the divisions in society supposedly based on equality.

## Living standards

However, there is little doubt that living standards did generally improve, certainly in the early 1970s. We have already seen how the minimum wage and pensions increased during the 1970s (see page 383). With cheap basic foodstuffs and rents and a well-developed welfare system, most people, if they could find everyday items to buy in the normal shops, could generally afford to buy them.

# The changing status and role of women

In theory women were treated on a basis of complete equality with men in the GDR. The 1949 Constitution guaranteed equality of opportunity and pay – almost 30 years before the UK did so. Unfortunately the practice did not always match the theory. Women often received what was termed 'double-burden' – a full-time job plus full responsibility for childcare and domestic arrangements. Some historians have argued that the role and status of women can be neatly divided between the Ulbricht and Honecker regimes, from a genuinely progressive effort to move women out of the home and into work in the 1950s and 1960s to the reversal to more traditional domestic and childcare roles in the 1970s and 1980s in addition to work. This is too simplistic a division since overall the **Politburo** had no single cohesive policy beyond ensuring women, like men, fulfilled their roles in building a socialist society.

## Women and family

According to the 1966 Family Code, the family was at the heart of life in the GDR, based on love, trust and gender equality. The GDR supported traditional values based on marriage; sexual relations, for example, were only socially acceptable between husband and wife. By the 1970s support for the family was extensive. There was a birth allowance of 1000 Ostmarks per child and a marriage loan of 5000 Ostmarks which was reduced as children were born and after three would be wiped out altogether. Maternity leave was very generous. In 1976, mothers having given birth to their second child were given a year's leave with 65 to 90 per cent of their salary paid. They were also exempted from shift work and given extra paid holidays.

Kindergarten provision was extensive – between 1970 and 1982 the provision of places per 1000 children rose from 645 to 922 and places in **crèches** from 291 to 612. At the same time the percentage of children placed in nursery schools rose from 59.7 per cent to 76.3 per cent.

However, the birth rate remained comparatively low, at 10.5 per 1000 inhabitants in 1975. This was partly due to the pressures on women. While so many had jobs, they were also mainly responsible for childcare and housework – in 1972, for example, it was estimated that 52 per cent of women had no help from their partners with this at all.

### Divorce

Although the state supported the idea of the **nuclear family**, the GDR had a comparatively high divorce rate – in the mid-1980s, 30 per cent of marriages ended in divorce after an average length of nine years. Reasons offered included the greater economic independence and greater assertiveness of women. They had higher expectations of marriage than men and were less likely to accept disappointment; wives initiated most divorces – 69 per cent by 1989. Similarly many did not need men to share their lives; in 1989 33 per cent of births were to single parents. The 1981 Census reported that 358,000 single women were raising children of under 17 years of age. It was more possible to do this in the GDR than the West because of the generous childcare arrangements and maternity benefits. Having said this, most people sought partners at some point in their lives. Cohabitation increased and, in 1981, 50 per cent of all cohabitees had at least one child.

## Women and employment

Women made up half the **labour force**. In 1984, 80 per cent of women had jobs. They expected to have paid employment. Similarly 50 per cent of university students were female; this percentage had risen from 25 per cent in 1960 to 35 per cent ten years later. The state provided facilities for women to improve their professional and technical skills and might send them to college with 80 per cent of their pay. One was far more likely to come across female engineers and scientists in the GDR than in the West.

Equal pay was real. By the 1970s women who had never known any regime but the GDR were often confident in their roles and would not have accepted anything but equal rights with men in the workplace. By this time working women tended to operate via the **FDGB** (see page 397) on equal terms with men to improve working conditions and so on.

However, women were noticeably absent from senior managerial roles in all professions. They comprised 82 per cent of teachers but never more than four per cent of departmental heads in the Ministry of Education, even though it had a female boss, Margot Honecker. There were no female **Rectors** of **Institutes of Education** in 1986 and only three Directors of Teacher Training Institutions or ten per cent of the total. Less than a third of secondary schools had female head teachers. The same trend was evident in healthcare where 86 per cent of employees were female and 52.6 per cent of doctors, but only 12.8 per cent of top positions were filled by women. To be fair, the authorities regularly tried to discover why this was so. They denied any **glass ceiling**. It may have simply been that women did not apply for senior roles because they were too busy juggling work and home; or that traditional gender roles of male domination of senior positions were too ensconced.

## Women and politics

Women were far less represented than men in the political system. In 1984, 33 per cent of deputies to the People's Chamber were female and only 19 of the SED Central Committee. At the very top only two out of the 27 members of the Politburo were women and they were candidates who never achieved full member status. Erich Honecker's wife, Margot, was Minister of Education from 1958 to the demise of the GDR but never a member of the Politburo.

It was difficult to believe the ageing male political leaders really had enlightened views of gender equality. Most wives were hidden from view. It was alleged that the Minister for Women's Affairs, Inge Lange, was never taken seriously. When gender issues came up in Politburo discussions they were treated with levity. In a sense this demonstrates a double standard; in theory the Politburo promoted women's equality and many members no doubt genuinely believed they were doing so. A key Politburo communiqué dated December 1961, 'Women – Peace and Socialism', for example, exhorted people at all levels to promote women's achievements and address any impediments to their progress. This led to a nationwide debate and to many of the social welfare measures already discussed (see page 382).

### The Democratic Women's League of Germany

The Democratic Women's League of Germany (DVD) was the only mass organisation for women. It had been founded in 1947 with the job of promoting equal rights but also tried to politicise women to actively work for socialist goals and support the regime. By 1985 it had 1.5 million members and over 17,000 local organisations. Its leadership was strictly SED controlled. By the 1980s its work was concentrated on those women who did not work, leaving many to think it a vehicle for housewives with concentration on domestic issues.

## Female expectations

Expectations of traditional roles persisted despite the rhetoric. An official encyclopaedia for women in 1987 focused on fashion, homecare, cooking, women's health issues – although there was also material on legal and occupational concerns for women.

This is not to suggest that women had no voice. They were instrumental, for example, in the passing of the 1972 Abortion Law. Mainly female members of the medical profession promoted its passage, offering as evidence in support as many as 100,000 illegal abortions per year. The law, which initially allowed women to abort at up to 12 weeks, may seem at variance with the drive to produce more children, but it was accompanied by free contraception and advice on birth control. The state which attempted to control minds at least allowed women some control over their bodies.

## Women at home

Historian Mary Fulbrook has argued that overall policy was geared to making women act more like men in the labour force but had little influence in the domestic sphere where women largely maintained responsibility for home and childcare. This was little different from elsewhere in the developed world. One survey in 1970 found that 24 per cent of wives and 43 per cent of husbands in the GDR thought they shared domestic chores equally. It also estimated that of 47.1 hours per week on average spent on housework, men were unlikely to contribute more than 6.1 hours. Similar surveys would discover similar results in many other countries. The point is that many women appreciated the employment opportunities and childcare provision that gave them a greater independence than elsewhere. It was found during the reunification process that 70 per cent of women in the GDR feared employment opportunities and childcare provision would diminish. Largely they were correct. As employment was cut back they were often the first to be dismissed while the generous childcare arrangements were reduced. Even the existing abortion law was changed to the tighter FRG model. This coincided with a resurgence of more traditional views on the role of women and less independence.

In the GDR, as elsewhere, the legal equality of women did not always match everyday realities. Many women testified to the problems of juggling work with domestic chores and indeed the prejudice that women with small children faced in the workplace (see Source B). This is supported by the terse prose of Rudolf Walter Leonhardt writing of a woman he interviewed in Dresden. 'Officially she enjoys equality with her husband; in private life she is devoted and submissive to him.'

**Source B** From Martina Daske, *A Female Engineer Reports*, 1986. Daske was a 27-year-old engineer in the Bad Salzungen Cold Rolling Mill.

> I was trained on the roller and got my college entrance certification in Henningsdorf; I rose from the ranks doing sheet metal profiling. I found my husband – he's from Halle – during my studies and we looked for a place where we could go together, with his mining skills and mine in rolling technology. We didn't care where, as long as we were together. He started at the potassium mine and I reported here. The department head did not look very enthusiastic; he asked, 'So, a woman?' As if he couldn't tell. I said, 'Yes, a woman!' He asked: 'With a child, too?' – 'Yes,' I said, 'with a child, too ... and we need daycare and an apartment as well ... and I also get my day to do housekeeping each month and if anyone at the daycare centre gets chicken pox then I'll have to stay home. ...'
>
> And then he turned around without a word. I was probably so cocky because never before, neither in my apprenticeship nor in my studies, had I felt that a difference was ever made between the performance of a woman and that of a man.

How useful would Source B be to a historian researching the lives of working women in the GDR in the 1980s?

## Conclusion: Social change and welfare programmes

While there were genuine efforts to improve living standards, provide first-class education and create gender equality, the difference between theory and reality in the GDR was as wide as ever. There were improvements in living standards but nowhere near as much as in the West. There was also a problem of financing them. Economic inequalities, moreover, were apparent by the presence of hard currency shops for those who could afford their merchandise. The housing problem was so great that targets could not be met.

Education faced tensions between the need to produce on the one hand political conformity and on the other initiative and independence of thought. While vocational education was well advanced, some students became disillusioned by the poor conditions in their work placements. Women, meanwhile, had legal equality and were encouraged to work, but were under-represented in top management positions and noticeable by their absence in positions of political leadership.

### Work together

This section lends itself to issues of theory and practice. How far did the GDR meet its goals in terms of social welfare policies and policies towards women and the family?

Go through your notes (see page 383) and then swap them with a partner. When you are happy your notes are as comprehensive as possible, divide a large sheet of paper into two. On one side write down the aims of the policies described in this section; on the other write down the realities of how well they operated in practice. How divergent are they?

## 2 Repression and control

There was a wide variety of organisations of state control in the GDR: it was a police state. The most feared was the Stasi, a vast network of security police headed by Erich Mielke who appeared paranoid that no one could be trusted. This led to a vast network of informers and surveillance that far outdid the Nazi **Gestapo**. Among other forces, border guards prevented escapes and the **USSR** maintained a huge military presence. If, by the 1970s and 1980s, most people did not feel repressed it may be a testimony to the efficiency of the security forces in preventing unrest.

Propaganda was deployed to generate enthusiasm for the regime but its effects cannot be measured. Censorship continued with critics often expelled or demoted from their positions if not arrested and imprisoned. Newspapers were heavily limited in the stories they could run and attitudes they could discuss. The media was all geared to conformity. The GDR canvassed the opinions of its citizens but it is difficult to judge in a dictatorship how accurate the responses were. Nevertheless there appears genuine support for welfare measures. It may be that the regime was satisfied with outward conformity.

There were mass organisations such as the FDGB and FDJ which organised people's lives and attempted to engender enthusiasm for the regime. The FDJ in particular was important in gaining the support of young people for the future of the GDR, although membership tailed off as children grew older.

### Note it down

This section focuses on institutions of repression and methods of control. Use the 1:2 method (see page x) to make your notes. The main headings should be:

- Repression: How far was the GDR a repressive society?
- Propaganda and censorship: How effective was this in engendering support for the regime?
- The extent of popular support: How far did people actively support the regime?
- Mass organisations: How effective were these in engendering support for the regime?

When you have completed your notes discuss in pairs why you think people generally seemed compliant in the GDR.

### Repression

The GDR was a police state with a vast apparatus of repression. If comparatively few by the 1980s were aware of this in their daily lives, it must be a testimony to its efficiency and how it circumvented rebellion by anticipating problems and addressing them by arresting suspected dissidents before they had actually done anything. This preventative system of security was partly achieved through an extensive system of surveillance and informers.

We have seen that the security forces were extensive (see page 342) – far more so than in Nazi Germany. Generally they worked harmoniously with the state and SED – there were no rivalries that threatened its competency. As with many dictatorships, the security forces essentially took military forms.

### National People's Army (NVA)

The NVA was the East German military force formed in 1956 out of the **People's Police**. It was noted for its efficiency and professionalism and could in theory be called out to address protest within the GDR. It was subordinated to the **Warsaw Pact** (see page 342) but its troops had not taken significant part in any of the interventions, such as in Czechoslovakia in 1968 (see page 174). Recruitment was sluggish and conscription was introduced in 1962 to counter this. Surprisingly, perhaps, there was provision for **conscientious objectors** who could serve in construction units rather than the military – in 1964, 12,000 to 15,000 recruits chose this option. By the late 1980s the numerical strength of the NVA was 179,000 with 123,000 in the army itself. It was controlled by the SED; virtually all the officers and 33 per cent of **NCOs** were members of the SED and subjected to party discipline and implementation of its policies.

### Border troops

By the late 1980s border troops numbered 50,000 – 30,000 policed the border with the West, 8000 were stationed in Berlin and 12,000 were stationed elsewhere. From the 1970s their connections with the Stasi increased. While they were ostensibly responsible for external threats to security, in reality their day-to-day job was preventing escapes. There remains controversy over whether there was in fact a shoot-to-kill policy (see page 348), but undoubtedly they could be punished if any escapes were successful in a sector while they were on duty, and preventing such escapes could be well rewarded.

### Police

The police had various branches:

- **KVP**: the paramilitary police were responsible for internal security – they had been called out in June 1953 (see page 340) and policed demonstrations and so on.
- Criminal police: the usual criminal police investigated robberies, violent crime and so on.

- Special police: discreet units were responsible for border protection, transport, security around sensitive buildings and so on.
- Voluntary police: largely organised around workplaces, they acted as auxiliary police when disorder threatened – there may have been as many as 400,000 of them.

The visibility of the police deterred protests. But the police were not in themselves repressive. The important fact is that most people accepted their presence and were not significantly affected by them.

## State Security Service

The notorious Stasi was formed in February 1950. From 1957 to the end of the GDR in 1989 their head was Erich Mielke, who became one of the most feared men in the country. The Stasi was organised along military lines, with up to 27 Generals heading specialised divisions. It was divided into 13 Major Departments each of which supervised 20 Independent Departments. Major Department XX, for example, was responsible for observation and control of the domestic population, with Independent Departments such as XX/4 for the control of the Churches and XX/9 for suppressing underground activities. The Stasi's budget in total in 1989 was 4 billion Ostmarks.

### The role of the Stasi

The Stasi's brief was clearly defined in a 1958 guideline after Mielke took charge. It was to prevent or throttle at the earliest stages – using whatever means and methods may be necessary – all attempts to delay or hinder the victory of socialism, in other words to anticipate and suppress political opposition before it manifested itself. This was why it had such a complex network of informers who enabled it by 1989 to keep files on 6 million citizens, 33 per cent of the population. Mielke himself preferred paper to computers: index cards could still be used in power failures which were common in the GDR. Given that the Stasi began to shred files as the demise of the GDR loomed, the numbers under surveillance must have been even greater.

### Surveillance methods

Surveillance itself was quite sophisticated with the usual phone tapping, video surveillance and agents following suspects – they even bottled smells of suspects to give to tracker dogs. Stasi officers have been accused of using radiation tags to track people. This could be responsible for some unusual cancers in some of their quarries. They were also expert in dirty tricks such as defaming opponents, setting **honey traps** – many prostitutes worked for the Stasi – and blackmail.

## Key debate

### The Stasi and SED

When called to account before the first democratic GDR parliament in November 1989 (see page 426), Erich Mielke insisted that the Stasi was simply there to protect the people. No one believed this. The Stasi was traditionally regarded as the 'sword and shield of the SED'. However, historians have debated its precise relationship with the SED. Mike Dennis has argued that on occasion it went beyond accountability to the SED through secret operations in which it was a law unto itself. It was obsessed by the fact that everyone was a potential security risk. Peter Grieder felt that the SED offered it a long leash but ultimately controlled it. Mary Fulbrook argued that the Stasi was the nerve system and brain of the GDR. It gathered information, evaluated it and advised the SED; it did this in collaboration with all the other security forces. Grieder, however, felt the Stasi was too all-embracing. It simply could not process all the mass of information it generated, so was inefficient in its briefing of the SED. David Childs and Richard Popperwell, in their 1999 work on the Stasi, also made the point that, highly motivated though they were, the Stasi was divorced from realities and could not accurately judge the public mood; therefore their advice to the SED was faulty. The Stasi may not have been a 'state within a state' as some have suggested, but its relationship with the SED was crucial.

### Informers

Inevitably, perhaps, because of the nature and volume of its work, members of the Stasi often became suspicious of everyone, even paranoid. One category of informers spied on the Stasi itself. The most common category of informers was Unofficial Collaborators (IMs); possibly 500,000 people worked in this capacity at some time in their lives, or one in 30 of the population. Most had a short career as an informer and turnover was high. Motivation was varied – it might be greed, desire for promotion at work, a feeling of power over others, personal grudges, blackmail by the authorities, or even political ideology – but some were informers by accident, for example talking injudiciously about someone to work colleagues who were in fact informers. Monetary reward was unlikely to be a consideration. One former senior Stasi officer assured journalist Anna Funder that IMs were paid only very occasionally – 'sometimes they were given a birthday present.'

The vast majority of informers were IMs, but there were more active categories: Unoffical Collaborators for Special Duties (IMBs ) infiltrated suspect organisations and

## Erich Mielke, 1907–2000

Erich Mielke was born into considerable poverty in the working-class Wedding suburb of Berlin, the heartland of **communism**. He joined the KPD in 1925 and worked as a journalist in **communist** papers but was also a member of the Party Self Defence Unit. This protected rallies, fought opponents and generally instilled a sense of lawlessness and terror in Berlin. After his involvement in the murder of two police officers in August 1931, Mielke fled to the USSR where he became implicated in Stalin's purges. He served as a political officer during the Spanish Civil War between 1936 and 1939. Here he was also involved in political violence and assassination. There is still confusion about Mielke's role in the Second World War, although he fought the Nazis with **partisan groups** for which he was decorated. After the war he undertook various roles in the Soviet zone before finding his niche in the Ministry for State Security. From 1958 until the end of the GDR he led the ministry, involving himself in all the roles of the Stasi including foreign espionage and domestic repression.

Mielke was one of the few GDR leaders who was arrested after the collapse of the GDR. Eventually in 1993 he faced justice over the 1931 murders for which he was sentenced to six years in prison. Released on grounds of compassion two years later, he died in May 2000 at 92 - a longevity he denied countless others.

Officers on Special Duties (OibEs) were active in spying on the leadership itself.

Mary Fulbrook makes the point that, while this system of informing and infiltration was efficient, it unwittingly helped destabilise the GDR, especially towards the end. By infiltrating opposition groups some informers inevitably aided their work to maintain their credibility. Funder quotes one Stasi file from 1989 in which an officer alerts his superiors to the fact that there were so many informers in Church opposition groups that at demonstrations their numbers suggested the groups were more popular than they were, which gave heart to other demonstrators. There is, however, little evidence of some conspiracy theorists that the Stasi, acting under orders from the **Kremlin**, deliberately undermined the regime as it increasingly lost credibility in the late 1980s.

### Prisons and interrogation

While some aspects of the work of the Stasi may seem almost comical with the benefit of hindsight, it should be remembered that they were a force of repression. People who fell foul of them were often treated brutally. They operated a series of prisons and labour camps throughout the GDR, the most infamous of which was Hohenschönhausen in the East Berlin suburb of Lichtenberg. This was in fact a complex of prison, interrogation centre and Stasi offices half a kilometre square which was blanked out from street maps – officially it did not exist, although most people suspected that it did. People brought there were subject to interrogation techniques of sleep deprivation and psychological pressure such as threats to have members of their families arrested. Stasi officers were experts in extracting information. One woman was sentenced to four years' hard labour when, shortly after the building of the Berlin Wall, she became involved in an escape group. She wanted to escape because her seriously ill child was being treated in a West Berlin hospital and she was no longer able to visit him. When interviewed today, former Stasi officers often say that the people they arrested were criminals. This, of course, depends on one's definition of criminality – but they were always particularly tough on those who helped would-be escapers, sometimes more so than on the would-be escapers themselves.

## Foreign espionage

The Stasi was charged with foreign intelligence - to collect information about potential enemies, undertake activities to undermine them and promote the GDR. The main Department Reconnaissance (HVA) was headed from 1952 until his retirement in 1986 by the urbane, charismatic Markus Wolf, who is widely regarded as being responsible for its success. Its full-time staff was relatively small at 4126 operatives in 1989, but their coverage of the USA, Western Europe, **NATO** and in particular the FRG was comprehensive. It is estimated that up to 20,000 FRG citizens were recruited as spies at different times, while many areas of the FRG Government including the security service were infiltrated. Perhaps the greatest success was the planting of Günter Guillaume as a top aide to Willi Brandt (see page 382). When Guillaume was exposed in October 1974, Brandt was forced out of office.

## Soviet forces

The USSR maintained its highest concentration of troops outside its own borders in the GDR – by the 1980s there were approximately 400,000 troops stationed there. Until the abandonment of the **Brezhnev Doctrine** in the late 1980s, it was assumed that these troops would act to defend the regime as they did in June 1953 (see page 340). If the SED called a state of emergency, the Soviet forces could intervene. Brezhnev, moreover, used the presence of the troops to threaten Honecker in their meeting of 28 July 1970 (see page 368).

# Propaganda and censorship

The leadership of the GDR attempted to gain the support of their citizens through propaganda. However, with the proximity of Western media this was increasingly difficult to achieve as the East German people saw the alternatives on their television screens.

## Propaganda

The GDR had used propaganda since its inception to engender support for the regime. This entailed the use of parades, media, promotion of national pride through sporting success and so on. Posters and banners acclaiming the regime and GDR successes were everywhere to be seen and the flag appeared ubiquitous, both being widely flown and its design often decorating household goods.

▲ The GDR flag.

## Parades

Parades and marches applauded the regime. There were celebrations of **labour days**, anniversaries of the creation of the GDR, homages to early communist pioneers and martyrs, Rosa Luxembourg and Karl Liebknecht – all geared to promote the current regime. The FDJ in particular was encouraged to participate in festivals and torchlight parades, which reminded many of the **Hitler Youth**. This was clearly not what was intended.

It was, moreover, difficult to assess the impact of parades on the largely well-ordered crowds. Festivals rarely seemed to achieve their propaganda objectives in the GDR possibly because of its Nazi past. In the 1950s officials often complained that crowds were sparse and participants unenthusiastic. Furthermore parades could be an opportunity for protest, as in the Olaf Palme peace march of 1987 (see page 420), while the celebrations to commemorate 40 years of the GDR were instrumental in the downfall of the regime (see page 424).

**Source C** From a speech by Erich Honecker to members of the Free German Youth (FDJ) movement, June 1984.

> Today this square, the scene of so many historic events, carries the names of Karl Marx and Friedrich Engels, the founders of scientific socialism. Also in the heart of Europe, on German soul, their revolutionary ideas are becoming reality. Our German Democratic Republic, a state of workers and farmers, proves this. So does your powerful demonstration on the 35th anniversary of its existence. *(Long-lasting strong applause, chants: 'FDJ-SED')*
>
> 35 years of the German Democratic Republic have been 35 years of hard struggle for peace and socialism. Our people, under the leadership of the Socialist Unity Party of Germany, has truly done great things during these years. We are filled with joy that you, under the sign of the rising sun, display the same revolutionary spirit for the strengthening and defense of socialism. *(Enthusiastic applause, cheers for the SED)*

How useful is Source C to a historian studying the attempts by Erich Honecker to create a sense of national identity within the GDR?

### Newspapers

The GDR had 38 newspapers read by 8.3 million of its citizens; 66 per cent of them were controlled directly by the SED but all of their content was subject to SED scrutiny. The Central Committee's Department for Agitation and Propaganda issued orders to editors. Erich Honecker was known to get personally involved in this process from time to time. Propaganda could be crude, as, for example, the newspaper headline: 'Workers Gather Crops Tirelessly Until Early Evening', but the different newspapers did cater for different audiences – for example the *Junge Welt* for the FDJ – with different content accordingly. The main SED newspaper was *Neues Deutschland* with a circulation of a million. All international news was channelled to newspapers from one news agency, ADN, under the control of the Chairman of Ministers.

**Source D** Reiner Oschmann, the *Neues Deutschland* correspondent in the UK, told Anne McElroy about the difficulties of being a journalist in the GDR, quoted in Anne McElroy, *The Saddled Cow* (Faber and Faber, 1992), pages 170–171.

> The brief of a foreign correspondent for *Neues Deutschland* was unlike any other even in the socialist world. On the one hand we were expected to deliver socially critical reports about life under a capitalist system; on the other, the GDR had a massive inferiority complex about its standing in the diplomatic community and a belated grudging recognition that any targeted criticism of the other country's rules was taboo ... We were doubly censored: first by our prevailing ideology and second by being required to be bland about that of our hosts.

What can you infer from Source D about the role of a journalist in the GDR?

## Censorship

Post from the FRG was censored and telephone calls tapped as a matter of course. In schools, Russian was the main foreign language taught. Students were encouraged to embrace it with enthusiasm: 'Learn the language of our friends!' English and French were far less widespread. Foreign newspapers and magazines were often available to buy as it was assumed few could read them. However, as the GDR came under threat of collapse in the late 1980s even USSR periodicals were censored (see page 418).

In 1952 Otto Grotewohl had stated that art and culture must be subordinate to politics. Their purpose was to engender support for the regime. This manifested itself negatively with the removal of politically suspect books and paintings from libraries, museums and galleries. Some work which had been banned by the Nazis now found itself banned again. Art was expected to follow the '**Socialist realism**' model – heroic peasants, workers and soldiers bringing in the harvest, breaking production records, defeating state enemies. Muhlen attended a major art exhibition in 1951 and counted 87 portraits of muscular men at work, 38 of women working in the fields and 55 scenes of the Russian Revolution with Stalin as the central figure in 48 of them. The paintings and sculptures of socialist Kaethe Kollwitz, one of Germany's greatest artists, were banned meanwhile because she had made her workers look too miserable.

### Literature

Books too were heavily censored or banned. In 1952 alone, 8 million books were purged. The Eisler Index of prohibited books listed 19,562 forbidden volumes. Copies were pulped or burned; only three copies of each banned title were allowed for the special use of top SED leaders. The Leipzig Municipal Library removed 59,000 of its 69,000 stock. They were replaced by Russian translations and acceptable works by SED members such as Bodo Uhse and Hans Marchwitza. The result was that people read less.

### Theatre

The situation was equally dire in the theatre, notwithstanding the presence of the world famous German playwright Berthold Brecht who was directing, writing poetry and indeed schooling a new generation of writers and directors. Although the SED itself recognised that there must be 'joy and gladness' in entertainment, much on offer nevertheless smacked of boredom. One musical comedy, 'The heart as meeting place', was about improving railway timetables with one song having the lyrics, 'Don't work more hastily but more efficiently. Let us all think how this can be done.' 'He who loves his wife' was a comedy about whether or not one should take one's spouse to a works social event, while 'From now on we will work' had an SED official admonish a courting couple to spend their time together more wisely than simply walking hand in hand by joining in the wheat harvest. The whole process was called 'Production Literature' or work produced for a political end of socialisation and support for the regime. Creativity was generally noticeable by its absence.

This is not to suggest the entire media was sterile. Of course there was some quality work within the tolerance of the regime.

## Extent of popular support

It is always difficult to judge the extent of popular support in a dictatorship. Many people outwardly conformed while putting more emphasis on their private and family life. Hobbies were important in the GDR as elsewhere. People went fishing, played football, engaged in aerobics, painted, listened to and performed music, and attended literary societies in the GDR as elsewhere. Many had allotments in which they could supplement bought foodstuffs and relax away from political pressures.

While the GDR did regularly canvas the opinions of its citizens and the Stasi wrote voluminous reports on how people felt about issues, there is no guarantee of their accuracy – no more so than the single list of candidates accepted by 99 per cent of voters in elections. Questions and statements for approval in surveys could be loaded or poorly developed. Historian Peter Grieder gives the example of a statement, 'I am proud to be a citizen of our Socialist State', which in 1975 youngsters were asked to agree or disagree with. Only five per cent responded negatively. However, it is unlikely children really understood the statement in all its complexity. Often surveys were vague in what they asked, such as whether respondents supported socialist ideals – they were rarely if ever canvassed on specific issues such as whether they wanted to travel more freely.

Nevertheless there is widespread evidence that people appreciated the social welfare programmes. In 1976 the Institute of Public Opinion Research reported that 75 per cent of 4777 respondents felt **social security** was better in the GDR than FRG. In January 1990, after the demise of the SED, the Institute of Sociology and Social Policy found that of 1500 respondents from varied backgrounds and ages surveyed:

- 58.4 per cent were satisfied with the social security system
- 59.2 per cent with their work
- 61 per cent with childcare
- 60 per cent with housing.

### Criticism

People were more critical of other issues, however. Stasi reports in 1974 show 20 per cent considered the GDR was too close to the USSR and the USSR gained more from the relationship than the GDR. One survey of agricultural workers in 1976 compared their attitudes to the GDR and FRG. While only 36.4 per cent felt their incomes were better than those in the FRG, 80 per cent recognised that social security was better; fewer than half thought anything else was better.

## Key debate

### The 'niche' society

In 1983 a diplomat from the FRG, Günter Gaus, called the GDR a **'niche' society** in which he argued citizens came to terms with the regime by an outward conformity by gaining their satisfaction from their private lives. This idea has more recently been criticised as too simplistic. Since reunification archives have revealed GDR citizens were less conformist than previously supposed, while others have suggested citizens participated in hobbies because they enjoyed them not because they necessarily saw them as an escape from the tentacles of the SED. However, historian Mike Dennis has argued that many GDR citizens saw their quality time with their families as an escape from the regime. Mary Fulbrook, meanwhile, has emphasised the normality of everyday life for most people (see page 356). People just took the realities of life in the GDR for granted and got on with it as best they could. The state, despite what it may have said to the contrary, was satisfied with outward compliance.

It seems overall, however, that tolerance of the regime was shallow. People were busy leading their own lives and saw no alternative than the system under which they lived. Therefore they made the most of it.

## *Eingaben*

*Eingaben* were individual or group petitions to the relevant authorities about concerns or complaints. The authorities took them very seriously as a useful means of accessing current opinion. They could be used to offer useful information to the security forces both about public concerns and individual attitudes. One family in 1983 questioned why their son had been refused an apprenticeship as a sailor. The reply came back that it was because of their contacts with the West and these should be terminated.

Citizens in theory could contact the relevant authorities about anything that concerned them and were guaranteed a reply within four weeks. They were supposed to target their concern at the appropriate level; if they contacted too high an authority, the *Eingaben* would normally just be sent downwards, thus delaying the process. However, if concerns were widespread enough, however apparently petty, they could reach as high as the Politburo. Hence in the late 1970s there was so much concern about the exorbitant cost of real coffee and nastiness of the cheap substitute, *Mischkaffee*, that the Government secretly traded weapons for coffee beans with countries such as Ethiopia and Angola.

*Eingaben* acted as a useful way of allowing citizens to let off steam but the authorities also genuinely saw them as a means of popular participation in the political process. They covered everything: from housing, availability of food, working practices, to the amount of popular music on the radio. Statistically every family in the GDR sent at least one *Eingaben* in the 40 years of the GDR's existence.

Many *Eingaben* resulted in improvements, especially where the complaints were common or came from politically loyal citizens. Hence in 1966 complaints about the shortage of spare parts for motorcycles in Jena led to priorities for their provision in that area, while the vast numbers of complaints about the quality of housing – these comprised 49 per cent of the *Eingaben* sent to the Council of State in 1967 and 44 per cent in 1976 – drove the massive effort to provide better accommodation (see page 384).

## The role of mass organisations

People's lives were controlled to a certain extent through participation in mass organisations which were controlled in turn by the SED. The executives in most organisations were party members. There were organisations for most areas of life, including the Democratic Women's League (DFD) (see page 293), but the largest were The Free German Trade Union Federation (FDGB) and FDJ.

### FDGB

All 16 trade unions were affiliated to the FDGB which represented 97 per cent of the labour force. By the late 1980s its membership stood at 9.6 million. Only farmers, the self-employed and military personnel were excluded. In 1987 the FDGB employed over 16,000 **functionaries**, the vast majority of whom were members of the SED. Its main role was to implement SED policies and ensure workers were compliant. It was committed to fulfilment of the **Five-Year Plans** (see page 337) and offered incentives to workers including honorific titles such as Hero of Labour. Another role was in labour relations; workers had lost the right to strike in 1961 so its weapons of protest were limited. However, the FDGB did conduct opinion polls and reported to the SED on how people felt about issues.

In the 1970s the FDGB became more involved in the implementation of social welfare such as the provision of pensions and **social insurance**. It also organised package holidays and ran 1600 holiday complexes – in 1983, for example, it organised 1.8 million holidays in the GDR and 16,000 abroad – mainly to other Warsaw Pact countries. While the image may have been of enforced jollity and group activities, these nevertheless were cheap, with families paying less than 30 per cent of the cost. However, there were complaints that SED members or particularly compliant workers went to the head of the queue. The FDGB also organised educational activities including political courses for functionaries – the one-year political training course was obligatory for all its employees.

### Free German Youth movement (FDJ)

Youth were clearly important as the adults and functionaries of the future. The FDJ was founded in March 1946 with Erich Honecker as its head. It became the only officially approved youth organisation. Its role was mainly the political indoctrination of the young, although recognising that they wanted more than Marxist-Leninist theory it organised leisure activities such as camping and festivals that were genuinely appreciated. In 1983 over 1 million members attended holiday camps while others did useful community work.

It also arranged activities common to young people throughout the world, such as discos. One state sponsored dance, the 'Lipsi', remained distinctly unpopular however as an alternative to beat music emanating from the West.

Promising athletes and future leaders were often identified through the FDJ whose membership in the 1980s stood at 2.3 million or 75 per cent of 14 to 25 year olds. Children aged 8 to 14 were members of the Ernst Thalmann Pioneers.

Of course, enthusiasm waned as teenagers grew older and it was found that 66 per cent of 18 to 25 year olds left the organisation.

## Conclusion: Repression and control

The GDR was a police state with well-organised institutions of repression which would deal brutally with opposition. The Stasi in particular trusted no one and spied extensively on citizens. While some of its methods may seem farcical, it was no joke to its victims as it operated a vast expanse of prisons and labour camps. The regime tried to engender enthusiasm for it through propaganda involving rallies, parades and the media. It is impossible to judge the effect of these. Extensive censorship attempted to prevent criticism and block out foreign influence. This proved impossible with the ready availability of television from the FRG. It is difficult to judge the reliability of opinions from surveys in a dictatorship but it seems the welfare provisions were genuinely supported. The state also promoted membership of mass organisations run by the SED to develop support for the regime. In the end, however, the leadership may have been satisfied with outward conformity – although with the vast network of informers it would be inaccurate to say they did not pry into people's private lives.

### Work together

Discuss why people seemed generally compliant in the GDR, before preparing for a debate. One of you should take the view that people seemed compliant mainly because of the repression of the Stasi. The other should argue that people were mainly compliant because of control through propaganda and mass organisations. Collect evidence to support the viewpoint you are supporting, then debate the issue.

- Whose case did you find the most convincing and why?
- Now you have heard both points of view, do you think people were mainly compliant through repression or control?

## 3 The SED and the Protestant Churches

Although the SED tried to control the influence of the Protestant Churches and manipulate them to promote support for the regime, they failed to understand them. They failed to understand that Church authorities could not control individual **pastors** or that even the most compliant pastors might place what they perceived of as God's will above state direction.

While there may be different phases in the relationship of the SED with the Protestant Churches, the overarching aim of the SED was to limit their influence and control them. Hence during the early 1950s the Churches were attacked as religious instruction was banned from schools and the youth organisation ***Junge Gemeinde*** was suppressed. Particularly threatening was the introduction of the secular ***Jugendweihe*** which acted as an alternative to **confirmation**.

While relations between the SED and Churches grew closer in the 1960s, the former would not compromise on this issue and the Churches just had to accept it. In 1969 the GDR Churches split from those in the FRG, although FRG funding continued.

The 1970s saw more co-operation between the Churches and the state, particularly in terms of community ventures and support for movements for peace such as protests against the deployment of nuclear weapons. The highlight of Church–State relations was the **Concordat** of 1978, where Honecker allowed the Church more media time and right to build new churches in return for support for the SED. However, when the Churches reached out to those groups excluded from society, they began to gain contact with elements of opposition. As the Churches increasingly became centres of opposition in the 1980s, they were thoroughly infiltrated. The Stasi still distrusted the Church and worked for its downfall.

### Note it down

This section contains just one topic spread over time. Choose the note-making technique which best works in making your notes on the role of the Protestant Churches.

You need to focus on how far the relationship between the Churches and state changed over time and how far the overarching goal of the state was consistent in its attitude to the Churches.

### The Protestant Churches

Christians in the GDR were overwhelmingly Protestant. Roman Catholics accounted for less than 13 per cent of the population in 1946. There was no single Protestant Church but a league of eight different ones, each with different theologies and traditions. This text sometimes refers to Church to encompass all the Churches. While the regime always tried to downplay religion, many citizens of the GDR did have a religious affiliation - 81.6 per cent of the population called themselves Protestants in 1946. While this figure may have fallen during the ensuing years, the Protestant Churches remained important throughout the history of the GDR.

### Relationship between the SED and the Churches

On the surface the relationship between the SED and the Protestant Churches was complex and changing. The Stasi infiltrated the Church and tried to influence appointments of compliant personnel – although one hopes that the former senior Stasi officer who told journalist Anna Funder that as many as 65 per cent of Church leaders were informers was exaggerating. However, the Church played a key role in dissent and was instrumental in the demise of the GDR. The SED never really learned that the Church was diverse and its personnel could not be controlled in the same way that SED **cadres** could. It also failed to understand the power of religious belief where Church members would disobey the state when its doctrines appeared to conflict with those of religious teaching. Allied to this it failed to understand that the Church sometimes acted to enhance its popularity, not because it opposed the regime but because it wanted to convert more people to Christianity – in other words Churches in the GDR had agendas wholly independent of the state, just as they do in other countries.
Mary Fulbrook has identified three key phases in the relationship between the SED, Church and State:

- Antagonism and **rapprochement**, 1945–69
- Co-operation, 1969–78
- Compromise and contention, 1978–89.

While this section follows these periods in discussing the relations between Church, Party and State, it is also important to remember Fulbrook's proviso that despite the different phases and policies, the overall aim of the SED was always the same – to reduce the impact of Christian belief and make the Church into a means of control. While the SED came to realise it could not prevent or obliterate religious belief, it nevertheless, despite its pronouncements to the contrary, saw Christianity as fundamentally opposed to communism and so tried to harness the Church. It did this in two ways:

- By offering concessions in terms of religious belief which was tolerated in all three GDR Constitutions
- By expecting political loyalty to the regime as a result of this toleration, with the veiled threat that dissent could threaten this tolerance.

Fulbrook summarises this relationship in terms of political obedience in return for freedom of spirit – or freedom of religious belief.

## Antagonism and rapprochement, 1945–69

The communists could not openly attack the Church in the immediate post-war period for many reasons:

- The Protestant Churches had 15 million adherents in 1945 and the Roman Catholic Church 1 million out of a population of 17 million.
- The Churches generally had a commendable history of opposition to the Nazis. Although the Protestants were divided and there had been an offshoot Nazi Church, many of its members had been imprisoned and tortured for their opposition.
- In the **concentration camps**, many communist prisoners had got to know and respect their religious fellow-inmates.

However, the authorities did see the Churches potentially as an opposition group and attacked them as being dependent on the West for finance and ideology. Given the uncertainty of the survival of the GDR, Church leaders themselves did not offer compromise with the regime and so the first post-war decade was a period of hostility – the so-called ***Kirchenkampf*** or battle against the Churches.

### Religious education

Communists were determined to exclude the Churches from all but the religious sphere. As early as May 1946 the Law for Democratic German Schools outlawed religious education in schools in the Soviet zone and Church schools were closed. From January 1951 religious children could face discrimination, with over 300 expelled from school in the following few years. The Church youth organisation, *Junge Gemeinde*, was designated a criminal organisation as the only official youth organisation was the SED-controlled FDJ (see page 397).

The year 1953 did see some softening of attitudes in the face of **de-Stalinisation** (see page 342). On 10 June, before the June unrest, the SED admitted it had made mistakes and the expelled children were largely reinstated. In July it acknowledged that the *Junge Gemeinde* should not be viewed as illegal. Although the priority for young people ought to be the FDJ, it recognised that the *Junge Gemeinde* actually had more pleasurable activities and the aim of the FDJ ought to be to make its programmes more appealing so it could compete with it for support.

### *Jugendweihe*

In 1954 the state introduced the *Jugendweihe* as a secular alternative to confirmation. This was usually taken at 14 and marked the rite of passage from childhood to becoming a young adult. In preparing for it candidates were taught an atheistic world view. Although it was voluntary it was made apparent that the state expected most children would participate. Church protests were widespread and unexpected. In November 1957, Bishop Mitzenheim, usually one of the more compliant senior churchmen, gave a sermon to 1500 listeners in which he emphasised that Christians should follow God's commandments where they conflicted with those of the state. However, the *Jugendweihe* remained. While little over 17 per cent of teenagers had taken it in 1954, 90 per cent were doing so by 1969; not to comply was seen as a great disadvantage to education and career.

### Fall in religious participation

The post-war period saw a fall in religious belief and participation throughout the developed world and the GDR was no exception. The new residential areas and suburbs springing up on the edge of cities tended to be without formal religious representation – although informal church groups, such as those which met in the home, might appear. Religious affiliation seemed on the decline, especially among the young – a 1969 survey suggested 43 per cent of children under 14 had no religious belief. Many still did, however, and the state sought to make use of and control it.

### Rapprochement

In 1957 the Ministry of Church Affairs was formed. In 1960 its name was changed to the Secretariat for Church Affairs but its aim was the same: to co-ordinate and direct Church activities in the best interests of the state. In October 1960 Ulbricht announced that 'Christianity and the humanistic goals of socialism were not incompatible', focusing on the (allegedly) common goals of peace but also recognising the importance of the Church in social welfare programmes. In 1967 Church and State celebrated 450 years of the **Reformation**, with the SED highlighting its role as heir to progressive movements in history.

While the Church may have enjoyed a closer relationship with the SED, it was not wholly compliant. It was, for example, instrumental in creating the Construction Force which was created for conscientious objectors who might otherwise refuse conscription (see page 391); 80 per cent of its members were practising Christians. The Church also tried to widen its appeal with youth-based services featuring popular music and dance. SED dismissed their popularity, saying young people were only interested in the music. Nevertheless they were popular.

The 1968 Constitution outlawed all-German groups. As a result, the League of Protestant Churches of the GDR was created, splitting away from the Church in the FRG. However, the split was far from complete. The GDR Churches still received 40 per cent of their budget from the FRG, particularly for the renovation of old buildings. Far from discouraging this, the state welcomed the influx of hard currency into the GDR.

## Co-operation, 1969–78

In 1971 Bishop Schönherr made a key speech in which he said, 'We want to be a Church not alongside, not against, but a Church within socialism.' While the actual meaning of this may be vague, the state took some comfort from it and the 1970s saw co-operation in several ways:

- Community work – the Church ran care homes and community ventures often in collaboration with the state.
- The Church became prominent in the anti-nuclear movement and tended to oppose developments in NATO more vociferously than those in the Warsaw Pact.
- The Church may have taken some role in the gaining of international recognition for the GDR; certainly the fact that it appeared not to be persecuted was a significant factor.
- Toleration of and co-operation with the Churches was in keeping with **Ostpolitik** (see page 365), and the continued involvement of the FRG Churches has already been noted.

Not all Church officials supported co-operation with a communist state. Stasi reports showed that many individual pastors were vehemently anti-communist. On 18 August 1976 pastor Oskar Brüsewitz set himself on fire outside Michaeliskirche in the town of Zeitz to protest against Church–State co-operation. The SED newspaper *Neues Deutschland* branded him a sick psychopath.

Many Churches too had formed programmes to reach out to the homeless, drug addicts and those whose existence a socialist society would prefer not to acknowledge. This could be seen as going beyond the regime. Some historians have seen the beginnings of the role of the Church in opposition in the late 1980s in this period. While on the surface it was a period of co-operation, many issues remained unresolved and more individual Church officials were acting independently to undertake work which may have been Christian but was not sanctioned by the authorities.

## Compromise and contention, 1978–89

In March 1978 Honecker met Church leaders to offer a more formal agreement between Church and State – the Concordat. Honecker agreed the Church could build new centres of worship in the new residential areas and suburbs where they had not hitherto followed the population. Again this was largely funded by welcome infusion of hard currency from the FRG. He allowed the Church more media time and accepted the importation of religious literature from the West – although there were never enough Bibles to meet the growing demand in the 1980s as religion regained adherents.

Honecker was undoubtedly genuine in seeking to normalise relations between Church and State, albeit mainly in favour of the latter. The SED recognised the Church was not going to disappear and so a working relationship had to be affirmed. In addition the SED needed to widen its appeal and support base. If the Church could be incorporated at little cost, then it made sense to do so.

The Churches themselves recognised the need to enjoy a positive relationship with the state. Given their willingness to co-operate, they could not understand why discrimination occurred.

The security forces and in particular the Stasi still distrusted the Church and undoubtedly still aimed in the long term for its demise. In April 1978, a month after Honecker's meeting, Mielke issued a circular to order the subverting, division and paralysis of 'hostile-negative elements' within the Church. The Church was packed with informers – it is estimated that at **synod meetings** 25 per cent of those present could be informers. The Department responsible for Church affairs employed 223 IMs (see page 392) in 1987.

The Church was by no means agreed on its relationship with the state. Some sought accommodation believing they could best moderate its extremes through co-operation and dialogue. Others encouraged and supported opposition groups. There was little intention, however, among influential Church figures (as opposed to individual

**Source E** From Report of the Conference of Protestant Church Leaders, 25 May 1977.

> What 'church in socialism' is must be measured, first and foremost, by whether the individual citizen in the socialist society of the GDR can fully live as a Christian, with his family, and can rest assured that he and his fellow Christians will also be able to do so in the future.
>
> It has been often and strikingly said, most recently by the Chairman of the Council of State, General Secretary Erich Honecker, at the first session of the newly elected People's Parliament: 'Our socialist society offers every citizen, regardless of age and sex, worldview and religious confession, safety and security, a clear perspective, and the chance to fully develop his abilities and talents, his personality. This is something to which we hold fast.'
>
> For us, this sentence seems to express without the shadow of a doubt that the full development of the individual personality should also be guaranteed to the Christian citizen, now and in the future.
>
> Apparently, such clear words have yet to become commonplace enough for their effect to be felt everywhere. In programmatic statements on Communist education, absolutely no room is left for any fundamental viewpoint other than Marxism-Leninism[...]. The problem is precisely the one identified at the Federal Synod in Züssow in 1976: 'The tension between the assurance of freedom of belief and conscience, on the one hand, and the educational goal of [forming] the Communist personality, on the other, requires a fundamental clarification, which must have an impact on the children and young people in our congregations.'

How useful is Source E in highlighting the dilemma facing the Protestant Churches in trying to build a positive relationship with the GDR state?

pastors, members and congregations) to become the centre of opposition to the regime. A more common goal was to embrace opposition groups without compromising the 1978 Concordat. Again this frustrated both the many groups who felt the Churches should be doing more and the state which felt they were not exercising enough control. However, the Church increasingly became the focus of discontent, particularly among individual members, whose role will be discussed in the next chapter (see page 421).

All these factors rendered the relationship between Church and State very complex. Many historians illustrate this by focusing on the moral dilemma of Manfred Stolpe (see box).

## Conclusion: The SED and the Protestant Churches

While the relationship between the SED and the Churches may have changed over time the intention of the SED was always to undermine them. The Party came to understand the usefulness of the Churches, if not their characteristics, and while there were periods of rapprochement they would not give way on fundamental issues – such as the introduction of the *Jugendweihe*. As the 1960s progressed the Churches and the SED began to discover commonalities such as promotion of peace initiatives and community ventures. The apex of Church–State relations was the Concordat of 1978. However, as the 1980s progressed the Churches increasingly came to be associated with opposition to the regime and they were heavily infiltrated by the Stasi.

### Manfred Stolpe, 1936–

Stolpe was a well-respected leading Church figure who became **Minister-President** of Brandenburg after reunification. Unfortunately it subsequently came to light that he may for many years have been a Stasi informer. In the 1980s few people believed that the GDR was about to collapse. It seemed a permanent fixture and so Church leaders, as indeed everyone else, had to find the best strategies that worked for them to promote their own interests while accommodating the regime. Stolpe believed this was through co-operating with the Stasi while working through the influence of the Churches to ameliorate the worst excesses of the regime – in other words co-operation and compromise. This policy of dualism, the belief that collaboration with the regime was in the best interest of the Churches and would enable them best to influence the regime for good, was a commonly held policy.

### Work together

This section lends itself to ideas of change and continuity. The overarching question is how far state attitudes to the Protestant Churches changed over time and how far they remained the same. First of all review your notes and work independently to address this question. Then come together to discuss it.

How far are you in agreement? What can you learn from each other on the issue?

## 4 Western influences on the GDR

The GDR lay on the interface between Western and Eastern Europe. It had never been possible to isolate Western influence. Until the Wall was built, East Berliners could visit the West simply by taking the train. Of course the Wall was built in part to prevent Western influence. However, this was never possible.

No matter how much they tried the SED could not undermine the influence of the FRG. Even when Ostpolitik was developing, the FRG was shown in the media as the enemy – most notoriously in the television programme *The Black Channel* (see page 362). However, most East Germans preferred to watch FRG television and so were often influenced by the Western lifestyles depicted. Increased contact with families and friends in the West led to the availability of more Western goods and hard currency – although those who enjoyed these contacts were often resented by those who did not.

### Note it down

Here you can add to your collection of index cards. This section discusses the impact of Western influences on the GDR. Use your cards to note them and explain their importance. On each card, write the title of the issue:

- Emigration – how far the issue of emigration affected relationships between the GDR and FRG
- Popular music and film – how far these encouraged Western attitudes among people in the GDR
- Western goods – how far the provision of Western goods affected society in the GDR.

On the back, organise your notes in the following way:

- *Definition* – a one- or two-sentence summary of the issue
- *Reason for it* – why it was an issue
- *Impact* – the impact of the issue.

## Emigration and travel

Emigration became a huge issue both for the GDR and FRG and offers an example of how liberalisation can lead to people demanding more. We have seen that the regime allowed those with 'urgent family business to travel to the West' and that the numbers of exit visas issued jumped after the loans of 1983 and 1984 (see page 412). The FRG assured the SED that it had no interest in depopulating the GDR but if its citizens could travel more freely they would be less likely to apply for permanent emigration. The SED appeared to agree and unofficially relaxed the definition of 'urgent family matters' so that 1986 saw as many as 573,000 GDR citizens under retirement age visiting the FRG; the previous year had seen fewer than 200,000. In 1987, 1.2 million made the journey. Added to the number of retired people visiting the West, it could be that up to 20 per cent of the entire population of the GDR visited the FRG at some time in 1987 – and returned. Some 30,000 were given permanent exit visas in 1988, and 48,000 in the first seven months of 1989 before emigration soared into a full-blown crisis (see page 422).

### Problems with emigration and travel

The problem for the FRG was that its welfare resources were coming under pressure from the numbers of emigrants. They also competed for jobs and housing often in the most deprived areas where resources were already stretched. No governing FRG politician wanted emigration to become a political concern. They advised the SED to rationalise their travel and emigration policies. FRG Chancellor Helmut Kohl felt one of the reasons for increasing demand to leave was the uncertainty as to whether the current largely unwritten liberal policies might be rescinded. The SED appeared to assent. In November 1988 they codified the legal conditions by which citizens could apply to leave and also said that public officials must explain their reasons for denying such applications. In January 1989, at a Conference on European Security and Co-operation in Vienna, the GDR signed a document affirming the freedom of every citizen to leave his/her country and return. However, this did not reduce the number of applications to leave. Rather it increased them.

The emigration policies caused resentment within the GDR. Those without contacts in the West increasingly resented those who had them, and the 'secret carriers' (see page 371) were still forbidden to travel at all or have contact with Westerners. This led many to feel that the groups most loyal to the GDR were the ones most penalised.

## Popular music and film

The authorities found it impossible to keep Western influences out of the GDR and young people listened to popular music and went to the cinema in the GDR just as they did elsewhere. The authorities could be inconsistent in their attitudes, and were only partly successful in encouraging GDR versions of popular music, although the GDR film industry was quite well developed and respected.

### Popular music

The GDR was ambivalent in its attitude to pop music which it called 'beat'. Of course ideologically it was seen as decadent. However, with the proximity of the West young people could not be prevented from listening to it. Also leaders of the FDJ realised it could be a useful means of engendering support for the regime among the young. Throughout the GDR leaders had been worried about the lack of engagement of young people due in part to the tediousness of many of the activities and entertainments on offer. They genuinely wanted to improve engagement, to make the message of socialism more appealing – and pop music was not going to go away. If it could be wed to the system, so much the better.

'Germany Meeting' was a massive youth rally of 500,000 participants in Berlin in 1964. Journalists likened it to a giant street party with music, dancing and theatre. A new radio station, DT64, was introduced, playing nothing but pop music at a ratio of 60:40 East German to foreign music.

However, at a Politburo meeting of 11 October 1965, at which Ulbricht was absent, Honecker reversed this toleration and beat music became officially taboo. The city of Leipzig found 44 of its registered 49 beat groups banned. Some 2500 young people protested against this ban; they were met by considerable police brutality and 267 arrests. Some commentators think members of the Stasi and FDJ infiltrated the crowds acting as **agents provocateurs** to provoke the authorities into such retaliation.

'Beat music', which morphed into other forms, notably rock, was circumscribed until the early 1970s, although it survived and was tolerated so long as it remained low profile.

Punk was popular in the GDR and was, as may be expected, completely unacceptable to the SED, so much so that followers of punk were classed as subversives and will be discussed in the section on opposition to the regime.

## Film

In the GDR the cinema was largely seen as the purview of the young and cinema releases tended to reflect this. In 1982 it was estimated that 70 per cent of cinema-goers were young with an average age of 24. Cinema tickets were very cheap at 2 Ostmarks.

Based in the famous Babelsberg studio in East Berlin, the industry was renowned for the quality of its products even if they were censored. By the 1970s the Babelsberg studio was producing about 15 to 20 films per year, three of which were for children and 25 made for television.

In the main, the SED saw films as engendering support for the regime and depicting communist allies sympathetically. In keeping with Marxist-Leninist ideas of capitalist oppression and the evils of **imperialism**, the 1960s saw a series of 'Red Westerns' in which Native Americans were shown heroically. Actor Grojko Mitic, star of the most famous film in this genre, *The Son of the Great Bear*, actually became an honorary Sioux Chief. The 1960s and 1970s saw a series of anti-fascist movies about resistance against the Nazis and the Holocaust, including *Jacob the Liar*, which received international acclaim following its release in 1975. Other notable releases following the liberalisation of the 1970s included *The Legend of Paul and Paula*, which depicted nudity on screen for the first time and was seen by over 3 million viewers in its first year.

**Source F** From 'On Certain Issues in Youth Work and the Emergence of Rowdy Groups', Resolution of the Office of the SED District Leadership, October 13, 1965, PDS-Archiv, District Leadership Leipzig IV A-2/16/464. Reprinted in Christoph Kleßmann and Georg Wagner (eds.), *Das gespaltene Land. Leben in Deutschland 1945–1990* (*The Divided Country. Life in Germany 1945–1990*) (Munich, 1993), pages 471–72.

> The enemy [Western countries] aims to bring about the weakening of our ideology, especially among youth, to foster intemperance and anarchy, in order to pit segments of our youth against their own Workers' and Peasants' State and to incite them to disturb the public peace. They are spreading this agitation through their radio and television stations, especially over Deutschlandfunk, by smuggling indecent and inflammatory literature [into the GDR], but also, quite cunningly, by utilising the non-culture of Western music and dancing, Beatles-ideology and collecting fads, and by encouraging slacking off at work. In West Germany, they depend on these ways of life to poison young people psychologically and to prepare them ideologically for their criminal war plans with all possible means of brutalisation and of stimulation of the basest instincts.
>
> It is our society's duty to combat all influences and manifestations of Western non-culture. Excesses, such as the ever larger recent proliferation of Beatles-groups with American names and almost exclusively Western and indefinable musical repertoires (disguised as original compositions), have nothing in common with progressive life ideals. We support modern and civilised dance music, and we are also not opposed to infectious rhythms, but we decidedly disapprove of those groups that violate all codes of morality and ethics, that perform barefoot and half naked, that contort their bodies and intoxicate our youth with agitating rhythms in order to lead them to excesses.

How useful is Source F to a historian investigating SED attitudes to beat music in the early 1960s?

## Foreign films

American films were often rarities in GDR cinemas not because they were suppressed necessarily but because there were licensing problems. However, they did often appear on television, especially if they appeared critical of the US lifestyle. In 1969 audiences saw *Twelve Angry Men* about a potential miscarriage of justice and *The Man with the Golden Arm* about heroin addiction. *One Flew Over the Cuckoo's Nest* concerning mental illness and its treatment was also widely viewed. British 'kitchen sink' dramas from the early 1960s such as *Saturday Night and Sunday Morning*, which showed the realities of working-class life, were also shown. Journalist Anna McEvoy asserts that Woody Allen films were popular possibly because they suggested Western values led to neuroticism. In an effort to distract television viewers from FRG programmes, French soft porn films were often shown on television on Saturday evenings – although how this was in keeping with the regime's avowal of gender equality was not publicly addressed.

GDR cinema had to reflect the changes of cultural life. When the regime became more liberal in the early 1960s and early 1970s, films risked more. As the regime became more repressive, they were more circumspect.

# Western goods

After the Wall limited personal contact, West Germans regularly sent their GDR friends and relations 'care-packets'. At first these contained essentials such as flour and vegetables, which it was believed were in short supply in the GDR, but later came to include luxuries such as real coffee and chocolate. In the first part of 1962 the East German Post Office impounded 51,000 such packages – and the Stasi in particular were notorious for stealing Christmas presents to give to members of their own families.

East German magazines were not banned from including features on Western lifestyles and readers could follow Western fashions and trends. From 1974, when East Germans were allowed to keep Western currency, Western goods could be purchased in hard currency stores by those who could afford it (see page 388).

While the SED had associated Western ideas with immorality and decadence in the past, by the late 1970s the leadership had softened its position and was no longer concerned with what young people might be wearing. Mary Fulbrook has quoted a 1979 report from the GDR Youth Institute to illustrate the change in attitudes: 'It took the authority of the Party and its General Secretary to make it clear that the length of hair and the tightness of trousers are not sufficient indicators of political attitude and societal involvement.'

# Western media

## Radio

Much of the GDR was subject to Western radio including the US controlled RIAS broadcasting for 24 hours per day. East Germans did not just listen to its high quality news; it featured popular entertainment and satire. As in much of Western and Central Europe, young people inevitably listened to Radio Luxembourg with its non-stop diet of popular music, while later the FRG also aimed transmitters at the GDR. The BBC was respected for the objectivity of its news. By the 1960s many people owned transistor radios so it was almost impossible to prevent people listening.

## Television

Television was the same. By 1961 there were 1 million television sets in the GDR. The FDJ was tasked with finding antennae pointing to the West and ordering their dismantling – even on occasion climbing up ladders themselves. It was, however, a pointless exercise. So many people tuned into Western television, including members of the SED themselves, who justified their actions by saying they needed to know what Western perspectives were so they could be countermanded. One citizen was courageous enough to assert that he would dismantle his western-facing aerial when the SED bigwigs in his village did likewise. It was impossible to jam Western broadcasts and a thriving black market grew up in home-made and less observable antennae.

By 1971, when 85 per cent of GDR families owned a television, it was estimated that 60 to 90 per cent watched Western television programmes. To pretend otherwise was ridiculous. Some Western broadcasters even changed their schedules to ensure their GDR audience could watch popular programmes when returning home from evening shifts – and some SED officials rescheduled meetings to ensure they did not miss episodes of popular serials. The nightly GDR news was sandwiched between FRG bulletins which viewers found more reliable; they even trusted FRG weather forecasts more. Western journalists in the GDR were easily recognised and even approached by citizens and asked to investigate specific issues for future programmes.

In May 1973, Honecker bowed to the inevitable and said that there would be no more attempts to prevent Western viewing. The authorities even made it possible for the residents of Dresden to watch Western television where there had previously been, for topographical reasons, no reception – which is why the region had been called 'the valley of the clueless'.

In the 1980s, therefore, most East Germans had some indication of what life was like in the West and understood that the standard of living in the GDR was generally inferior – although they may not have known by how much.

## Conclusion: Western influences on the GDR

The authorities could not prevent FRG influences although they tried to portray it in the media as the enemy. Young people in the GDR enjoyed popular music and films as elsewhere and these often conveyed Western ideas. The authorities were inconsistent in their attitudes toward the media and popular music was attacked from time to time. Most East Germans had access to Western television and with FRG citizens increasingly able to visit, they brought Western goods and hard currency – which their East German contacts could use in hard currency shops.

### Work together

Read this section again carefully. Working in pairs, divide the content into two. One of you should take the first half, the other take the second. Each of you needs to read your half for a third time. After you have read it put your notes and this book away and explain your 'half' to the other person. Note down any areas that you struggled to explain or where the explanation was unclear. These will serve as reminders for revision.

### Chapter summary

- During the 1970s an informal Social Contract saw improvements in living standards in return for support for the regime.
- Families were placed at the heart of society with widespread welfare provisions to support them.
- Housing was developed but because of the extent of the problems could not meet ambitious targets.
- In education there was tension between the need for conformity and that of producing well-educated adults able to compete in a technological society.
- Vocational education was widespread and compulsory military training was introduced in 1973.
- Women enjoyed equality legally but not in reality; there were few female top managers and they were under-represented in politics.
- The GDR was a police state with extensive forces of repression.
- The Stasi trusted no one and had an extensive system of informers and infiltration.
- It is difficult to accurately judge public opinion but social welfare was appreciated.
- The SED tried to control the Protestant Churches and diminish their influence.
- In 1978 a Concordat normalised relations between Church and State.
- FRG influence grew with widespread contacts between citizens and the availability of FRG television and radio.

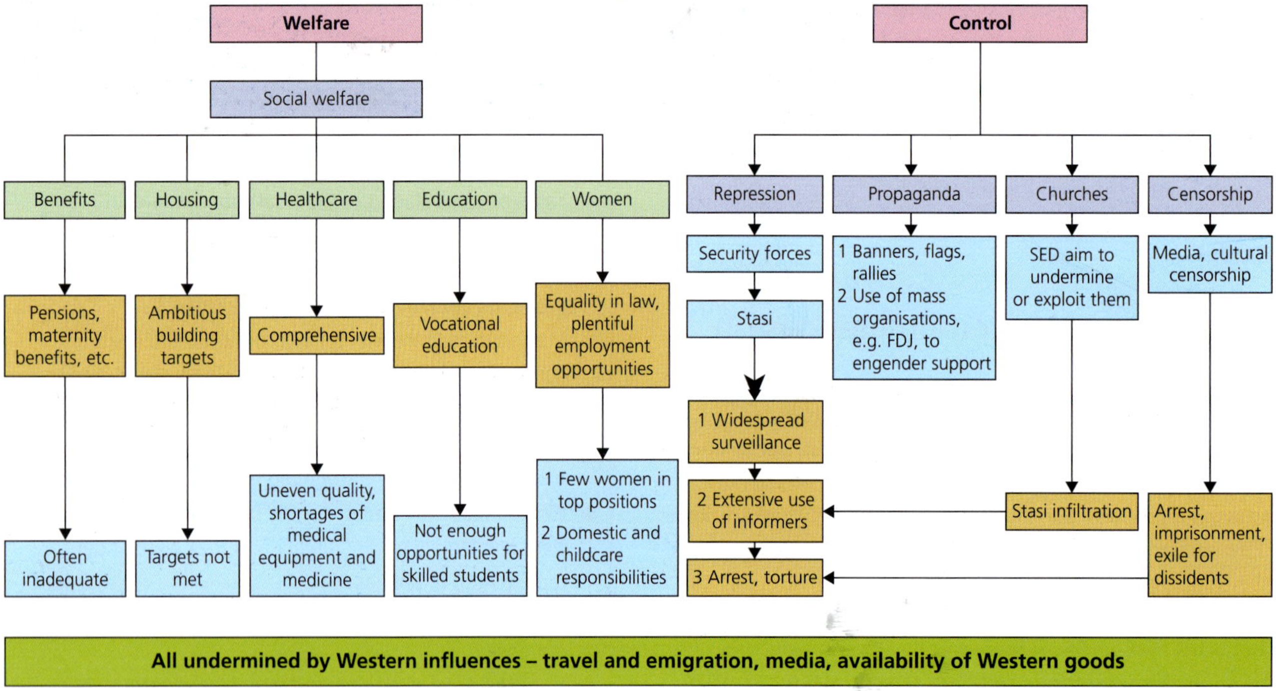


▲ **Summary diagram: Life in East Germany, 1949–85.**

## Recommended reading

D. Childs and R. Popplewell, *The Stasi: The East German Intelligence and Security Service* (Macmillan, 1999). Authoritative account of the workings of the Stasi.

M. Fulbrook, *The People's State: East German Society from Hitler to Honecker* (Yale University Press, 2005). Thorough and engrossing account of everyday life in the GDR.

A. Funder, *Stasiland* (Granta, 2011). Lively account by a popular journalist of the dark side of the GDR; interviews with members of the Stasi and their victims.

A. McElroy, *The Saddled Cow* (Faber and Faber, 1992). Lively journalistic account of life in the GDR.

# Section A: Essay technique

## Contextualising the sources

In order to understand the sources properly, you need to place them in the context in which they were written. Specifically, you need to consider the background or environment in which the source was produced. This may sound obvious, but twentieth-century sources were produced by twentieth-century people, and therefore reflect their experiences, beliefs and prejudices at the time they were written. This means that sources are never stand-alone documents – they should be understood within the context of the values and assumptions of the society that produced them.

In essence, your task when contextualising the sources is to try to understand the world in the same way as the writers of the sources. In short, you should try to see things their way.

Understanding the context is an important part of evaluating the evidence that the sources contain.

Imagine you are answering the following question:

**How far could the historian make use of Sources 1 and 2 (page 408) together to investigate the role of education in the GDR from 1949 to 1990?**

You have read about the role of education in this Key Topic and Key Topic 1 (see page 328). If you wish to remind yourself of this, re-read the relevant sections or your notes. This is important before embarking on an exercise about context.

One way to contextualise the sources is to begin by asking the question: what issue is this source contributing to? The reason for this is that sources are written for specific purposes. In this case they may have been written for propaganda purposes, and intended to boost morale or offer an example to others. Below is an example of an attempt to put Source 1 into context:

**Source 1 From a speech by Margot Honecker, Minister of Education from 1957 to 1990**, at the Eighth Pedagogical Conference on 18 October 1978, found in (ed.) Arthur W. McCardle and A. Bruce Boenau, *East Germany: A New Nation Under* Socialism?, published in 1984. Honecker was explaining the strengths and values of the GDR education system to an audience of education professionals.

> Every school is subordinated to the prevailing ideology. We have never denied this and we admit it with good reason. For in our schools we transmit the ideology of the working classes, an ideology which serves the interests of the people, shows the way to societal liberation, paves the way to a society where man is free of oppression and exploitation and guarantees people a life of happiness, prosperity and peace.
>
> Every mother and father concerned with the welfare of their children can say: What is taught and inculcated in our school is good, because it is an education in respect for human beings and their labour, respect for other people's: it is an education which teaches children to work in word and deed for peace and human happiness.

This article was written by the Education Minister of the GDR for much of its lifetime.

Honecker is attempting to inspire her audience by explaining educational values and how they prepare students for a happy and successful life.

She is assuring her audience that parents can have confidence in the educational values.

She summarises her remarks in a short pithy statement. No one could disagree with these values.

The context for Source 1 helps answer the question in the following ways:

- Honecker is the minister responsible for the delivery of education in the GDR. It is useful to hear her views.
- At an educational conference her role is to inspire educational professionals by outlining the values with which no one could disagree.
- She shows that parents can be reassured of the educational values transmitted to their children.
- However, we should remember that the article acts as propaganda and gives a partial, one-sided view. Its aim is to inspire her audience. It does not, for example, give any detail about how education is delivered or how successful it is. It certainly does not discuss any of the problems in the educational system.

The points on page 407 can be summarised as follows:

Source 1 is useful for showing the views of the minister responsible for education in the GDR from 1957 onwards. She is attempting to inspire educational professionals by outlining the strengths and values of the educational system. She asserts that parents can trust the system to do the best for their children. The extract is, however, very one-sided and does not discuss any of the problems in the educational system.

## Activity: Seeing things their way

Now try contextualising Source 2 on this page.

Re-read the question on page 407 – remind yourself of the specific task you are focusing on.

1 Ask yourself the following questions and annotate a copy of the source with the answers:
   a) What was the purpose of the source?
   b) What attitudes does it display towards education in the GDR?
   c) How does the author imply *Gegenwartskunde* is simply political indoctrination?
   d) What are the limitations of their source as evidence of the role of education in the GDR from 1949 to 1990?
2 Next write a series of bullet points outlining:
   a) the aspects of the source that are useful for answering the question
   b) the aspects of the source that are less useful
   c) a summary of the extent to which the source provides useful evidence concerning the role of education in the GDR from 1949 to 1990.

## Activity: AS-style questions

1 Why is Source 1 (page 407) valuable to the historian for an enquiry into the purposes of education in the GDR?
2 How much weight do you give the evidence of Source 2 for an enquiry into the use of propaganda in education in the GDR in the 1950s?

**Source 2** From Norbert Muhlen, *The Return of Germany* (1953). Here Muhlen, a journalist, is speaking of schools in the GDR. He is a very hostile observer.

> Russian was the only foreign language obligatory in the schools of East Germany. The Russian language teacher 'has to be supported ideologically by all the other teachers', a directive of the Ministry commanded. Another directive excluded from high school any elementary school graduate with bad marks in the Russian language. All other teaching was equally 'politicised': biology, German history, nature (including biology, zoology, chemistry, geography, gymnastics). But the chief subject was Gegenwartskunde – the knowledge of current history, consisting in 1952 altogether of fourteen carefully prepared topics such as the 'The American aggression in Korea'[1], 'Stalin, the leader of the world peace front', 'The Five year Plan as the road to plenty and peace'. This subject was taught twice a week in the high schools of East Germany.

[1] The American aggression in Korea refers to the war of UN forces dominated by the USA against communist North Korea and China, which was going on at the time.

## Work together

Having read Source 2 and completed the activity 'seeing things their way', discuss the following questions with a partner:

1 Did you both agree on:
   a) the reasons the author wrote Source 2
   b) the attitude it displays towards education in the GDR
   c) how the author regards *Gegenwartskunde* as political indoctrination
   d) how the source is limited as evidence of education through the lifetime of the GDR?
2 Did you both agree on:
   a) the aspects of the source that are useful for answering the question
   b) the aspects of the source that are less useful
   c) the overall extent to which the source is useful to the historian investigating the role of education in the GDR from 1949 to 1990?

If you disagreed on the answers to any of these questions try to work out whose answer was better and why.

3 What else would it be useful to know about the source in order to answer the question? Use your discussion to make a three-point list of the ways in which you can use contextual knowledge to improve your essay writing.

# Section B: Essay technique

## Overall judgement

An overall judgement is as important to a Paper 2 Section B essay as it is to essays in Paper 1. You may have already read advice about the characteristics of a good overall judgement (see page 69). Remember, good judgements are supported, and the best judgements consider the relative significance of the key factors you have discussed in your essay.

Now you can practise writing an overall judgement to an essay concerning the relationship between the SED and the Protestant Churches during the period 1949 to 1978.

### Activity

Imagine you are answering the following Section B-style question:

To what extent did the relationship between the SED and the Protestant Churches in the GDR change during the period 1949 to 1978?

1 Read the question and work out what type of question it is.
2 Make a plan that is appropriate to the specific question. Remember it should consist of three or four main points.
3 Add three pieces of detail to support each of your main points. Remember, use the detail that best supports the points you want to make.
4 Write an analytical sentence to conclude each of your main points.
5 Now write a conclusion to the essay.
   - Start by asserting an overall judgement.
   - Support this by weighing the different main points in your plan.
   - Summarise your overall judgement in the final sentence.

### Work together

Having completed a plan in Reactivity, swap it with a partner. Consider the following questions:

1 Did you agree on what type of question you were dealing with? If not, discuss it and work out who was right.
2 Whose plan most clearly focused on the specific type of question?
3 Did you both begin your conclusion with a clear judgement?
4 Did you both weigh up the different key points to support your judgement?
5 Whose overall judgement was better and why?
6 What can you learn from each other's work?

Use these questions to feed back to each other and improve your essay technique.

### Question practice

1 'The Social Contract failed to achieve its goals in the 1970s and 1980s.' How far do you agree with this statement?
2 How accurate is it to say that housing policy was a failure in the GDR? AS
3 How far did women enjoy equality with men in the GDR? AS
4 'The 1978 Concordat was a major turning point in the relationship between the state and the Protestant Churches in the GDR.' How far do you agree with this statement?

# **Key Topic 4** Growing crises and the collapse of communist rule in the GDR, 1985–90

## Overview

The collapse of the GDR took most people by surprise. However, with hindsight its problems seemed unsurmountable. By the 1980s its economy was in deep trouble as a result of a growing national debt. This was caused in turn by growing trade deficits, particularly because of high fuel costs, and withdrawal of Soviet Union subsidies. The GDR negotiated substantial loans from the FRG in 1983 and 1984 and exported oil products. However, living standards fell. To meet domestic fuel demands the Government began to produce cheap lignite coal which was highly pollutant.

The decade saw the growth in protest movements originally shielded by the Protestant Churches. While the Stasi infiltrated most groups, the protests continued, for example about peace and environmental issues. The later 1980s saw a return to repression, and the opening of the borders between Hungary and Austria led to the beginning of a mass exodus. These developments coincided with Mikhail Gorbachev coming to power in the Soviet Union. He spoke of reform through glasnost and perestroika to solve the problems of the USSR and other communist countries. The GDR leadership rejected his advice but he captured the imagination of its citizens and acted as a beacon for reform. More significantly he withdrew Soviet protection. The GDR would have to solve its problems without Soviet help. The resignation of Honecker in October did not stop the momentum and the limited reforms advocated by his successors were too little too late. The protests and emigration continued.

With the emigration reaching crisis proportions, the Berlin Wall came down in November 1989. This acted in part as a catalyst for the collapse of the SED. The demand for reunification grew and politicians were effectively left behind. The USA supported reunification and, while Britain and France were more reluctant, they finally agreed. The Soviet Union did not oppose it and a treaty was signed in September 1990 settling all the post-war issues relating to Germany and its neighbours as a prerequisite to reunification. Reunification formally took place on 3 October 1990. The GDR ceased to exist.

The overarching topic of the growing crises and the collapse of communist rule in the GDR, 1985-90 is covered in four sections:

1. Economic stagnation in the 1980s
2. Gorbachev's influence
3. The events of 1989
4. The end of the GDR 1989-90.

## TIMELINE

| | |
|---|---|
| 1983 March | FRG agrees loans to GDR |
| 1985 March | Gorbachev becomes General Secretary of the Communist Party of the Soviet Union (CPSU) |
| 1987 September | Visit of Erich Honecker to FRG |
| 1989 | Many complaints of falsified election results |
| 1989 September | Hungary opens its borders with Austria |
| 1989 October | Huge demonstrations in Leipzig |
| 1989 October | 40th anniversary celebrations of GDR |
| 1989 October | Resignation of Erich Honecker |
| 1989 November | Collapse of the Berlin Wall |
| 1989 November | Kohl's Ten Points for Reunification |
| 1990 March | First free elections in the GDR |
| 1990 July | GDR accepts the Deutschmark as its currency |
| 1990 September | Four Plus Two Treaty to settle existing post-war disputes and agree borders |
| 1990 October | Germany reunited |

## 1 Economic stagnation in the 1980s

Although the GDR needed to grow to meet the increasing costs of welfare and defence, its economy worsened in the 1980s. Honecker favoured central planning to meet these demands. However, an increasing trade deficit and fuel shortages were causing significant economic problems. The widespread replacement of oil with lignite coal led to environmental concerns and the poor structures of GDR industry were increasingly evident. Massive loans from the FRG bailed out the GDR in 1983 and 1984, and efforts were made to export oil. However, any partial economic recovery was at the expense of living standards and infrastructure.

The economy of the GDR **stagnated**. According to data from the FRG it shrank in 1980, 1982, 1986 and 1987. There were various reasons such as the growth of the national debt, withdrawal of favourable trading conditions with the **Soviet Union** and **COMECON** and the degradation of the infrastructure. We have considered these before in the context of the 1970s (see pages 387–88); they were exacerbated in the 1980s. Honecker, moreover, supported a return to central planning which showed policy-makers were effectively locked into the past and were incapable of addressing new economic realities.

### Note it down

This is another opportunity to add to your themed collections of index cards. In this section there are a series of factors which led to economic stagnation in the 1980s. Follow the pattern of providing a definition for each factor, notes on the reason for it and on its consequences or impact.

Having done this, try to find links between the factors. Write down the factors and draw lines to link them as appropriate. What does this suggest about how the factors are linked together?

### Return to centralised planning

In terms of economic management Erich Honecker preferred a return to centralised direct control which saw the demise of many of the developments under ESS (see page 356). Ultimately the centrally planned economy with less room for local initiative was favoured by the SED because it was preferred by the Soviet Union and produced no threat to central authority through introducing any mechanics of capitalism. It was a case perhaps of ideology outweighing performance. The 1970s had seen thousands of partly privatised ventures being returned fully to state control involving 580,000 employees. By 1972 private enterprise accounted for less than 0.1 per cent of the goods produced in the GDR. However, central planning brought its own problems, not least the increasing gap between theoretical and actual performance. During the 1980s the economy of the GDR went into crisis.

### The growing national debt

The debt owed by the GDR to capitalist countries from whom it was borrowing at high rates of interest rose to astronomical proportions. In 1970 debt to capitalist countries was DM 2.2 billion; by 1980 it was DM 30 billion and by 1989 over DM 46 billion.

Between 1975 and 1985 the **USSR** accounted for 29 to 34 per cent of the GDR foreign trade and Western countries 31 to 36 per cent (including 16 per cent with the FRG). Its socialist partners in COMECON took much of its industrial output, including 85 per cent of its machine production. In return the GDR received 70 per cent of its raw materials from the USSR – so any disruption in this would be significant. Like other COMECON members it imported Western technology financed by credits to be paid later – for example in a year's time. The goal was to modernise and develop economic growth with increased production helping to repay the credits. This did not work – as a result the GDR debt to the West doubled between 1977 and 1981. This was made even worse by the rise in **interest rates** from 5.6 per cent in 1977 to 13.9 per cent in 1981. Its trading deficit with the USSR was 2.3 billion roubles by 1981.

The problem with this amount of debt was that the GDR could never export enough to finance it because of inefficient production techniques and limited demand for its products outside the **Soviet bloc**. While exports did rise by nine per cent over the course of the 1980s, this was to the detriment of the domestic market. Queues for goods grew as shelves were increasingly empty.

### Impact of the USSR

The USSR faced its own significant economic problems in the 1980s. The USSR realised in the 1970s that it could no longer afford to subsidise COMECON members. The Soviet leader Brezhnev gave notice in 1981 that supplies of raw materials would be cut when existing agreements ran out and that the USSR would raise prices to world market levels. This threatened economic collapse for the

GDR which bought 70 per cent of its raw materials from the USSR. In addition it could not earn more through greater exports to the West as it could not compete with the emerging economies of South Asia in the production of manufactured goods.

Brezhnev had complained to Honecker that COMECON members were exploiting the Soviet Union by buying cheap oil from it and often selling the oil on to Western markets at great profit. In 1981 the USSR announced it would reduce oil deliveries. At the same time Poland, faced with its own internal problems, announced it was cutting coal exports. The GDR response was to develop lignite, the cheap brown coal of which it had plentiful supplies. Extraction of lignite rose from 256 million tonnes in 1980 to 312 million tonnes by 1985 – 40 per cent of the world's total. Lignite was inefficient and caused tremendous pollution because of its high sulphur levels.

**Source A** From Harold James, *West Germany's Green Imperialism*, published in the *Sunday Telegraph*, 11 February 1990. James is an expert on Germany. Here he is describing some of the problems the FRG will inherit after reunification.

> In the GDR today, the most immediate and pressing of the multitude of apparently insuperable economic problems is the electricity supply. The brown coal burning plants are spectacularly polluting; while the major nuclear reactor near Greifswald is unsafe and has in the past (in 1976) come close to blowing up. The consequence is that East Germany will need to be dependent on West German electricity.

How useful is Source A for a historian investigating the environmental problems of the GDR?

In weather forecasts heavy cloud became a euphemism for industrial smog. Some obsolete power stations started to operate again because they could use lignite. For many the return to coal away from oil would have been an indicator of economic decline, but the use of lignite suggested economic catastrophe.

Quite simply it was no longer possible for propaganda to suggest that the citizens of the GDR were well off. However, it should be remembered that most citizens had never personally experienced anything different. One woman said that until she visited the West after reunification she had never realised the GDR was so drab and dusty – because she had only ever visited Poland and that was even worse.

## Economic relations with the FRG

By 1982 the GDR was in deep economic crisis. Help came from the FRG with whom it negotiated two massive loans – DM 1 billion in 1983 and DM 950 million in 1984. Historians still debate the motivation. The actual prime mover within the FRG was Franz-Josef Strauss, right-wing **Minister-President** of Bavaria. It may have been that the FRG did not want to see the GDR destabilised at a time of problems elsewhere in Central Europe such as unrest in Poland (see page 372) and an apparent return to **Cold War** with the election of US President Reagan. There seems, too, to have been informal agreements on the dismantling of automatic killing devices on the border, an end to any shoot-to-kill policy and the more generous allocation of exit permits which acted as a softener to the FRG.

The GDR used these loans as security – by depositing them in banks, it made them more creditworthy and by 1984 credit markets were again open to them.

### Koko

There was an alternative economy which did not feature in the official figures. Koko, otherwise known as Commercial Co-ordination, had been created in 1966 within the Ministry of Foreign Trade to bring in **hard currency** outside the normal channels, bypassing COMECON restrictions. It played an important part in bringing in modern technology and had close links with the **Stasi**. From 1972 it was detached from the Ministry of Foreign Trade and was essentially unsupervised by any usual channels such as the banks. It maintained a secret fund of money which could be deployed for covert purposes, such as aid to rebels in Nicaragua, or simply to buy foreign imports where there were domestic shortages – once it spent 2 million **Ostmarks** on foreign apples. Koko eventually controlled hundreds of companies and had hundreds of different bank accounts. It sold weapons illegally to warring factions abroad and art collections confiscated from aristocratic owners, and was responsible for the financial management of the trade in prisoners (see page 368).

## Environmental problems

Much of the industrial areas of the GDR were facing huge environmental problems.

According to UN criteria, one industrial town, Bitterfeld, was no longer fit for human habitation. One journalist reported that after an hour there his face was coated in oily grime. Pollution was caused by pesticide factories, aluminium smelting plants, a dye-making factory, which would have spewed chemicals into the atmosphere, and ten lignite-burning power plants. Children were twice as likely to develop breathing difficulties there as anywhere else in the GDR (itself more likely than most other places in Europe), and had retarded bone growth. Life expectancy in Bitterfeld was five years less for men and eight years less for women than elsewhere in the GDR. Carbon disulphide emissions at ninety times the accepted rate could and did cause serious brain damage. Nearby farm animals were unable to mate.

If Bitterfeld's ecological problems were horrific, they were not much better elsewhere in the GDR. Respiratory problems such as asthma were 20 per cent higher in the industrial south than the more agricultural north; but overall 21 per cent of GDR citizens were subject to excessive pollution which affected their health. Over 50 per cent of forests meanwhile faced ecological damage and water supplies were largely polluted. The excessive use of lignite was a key factor but toxic dust and chemical smogs from chemical plants were also common. In Leipzig, a staggering 91 per cent of the population was exposed to excessive levels of sulphur dioxide, carbon monoxide and heavy metal such as lead pollution. The very cars associated with the GDR, two-stroke engine Trabants, could be seen belching smoke from their exhausts. When Germany was reunited, the FRG had to amend its own pollution laws just to let them on its roads.

▲ A Trabant

## The 1981–85 Five-Year Plan

The 1981–85 **Five-Year Plan** set ambitious targets: to hold down the level of imports while increasing exports, and to speed up scientific and technological advances while at the same time reducing domestic energy consumption. The aim was to invest more in modernisation and improve production. Greater efficiency was the key. The idea was to:

- reduce domestic consumption of energy by 6.1 per cent
- minimise price rises
- expand the volume of consumer retail goods by 20 to 23 per cent.

One main economic problem for the GDR was to maintain sufficient economic growth to finance extensive social welfare and defence programmes. Between 1965 and 1982 the latter rose from 4.4 to 5.8 per cent of **GNP**. Meanwhile in the same period, the increasing scarcity of raw materials meant industrial production rose by only 4 per cent instead of the projected 5.1 per cent. The result was shortages of various goods at various times.

## Statistics in the GDR

One problem with planning was the accuracy of figures. According to the official data, national income rose by 13 per cent between 1971 and 1975 while labour productivity rose by 132 per cent. The reality may have been different, exemplified by the wag who said, 'We pretend to work and you pretend to pay us.' In 1981 the World Bank abandoned using officially produced figures for Eastern European economies because they were so unreliable. Nevertheless the same World Bank classed the GDR as the twelfth most developed economy in the world, on a par with Britain and France.

Whatever the doubts about official figures, there is no doubt that external factors which dated from the 1970s such as huge price rises in raw materials and oil adversely affected the GDR. This was exacerbated in 1975 when the USSR revised its pricing structures and supply of raw materials through COMECON. The GDR faced a doubling of **OPEC** oil prices and reduced deliveries from the USSR. One significant result was the huge growth in GDR foreign debt which worsened during the 1980s.

## Oil exports

Ironically, in a country increasingly reliant for domestic consumption on coal, the GDR modernised its fuel techniques with oil refineries – buying expensive equipment from the West to increase output. Taking advantage of high world price in the early to mid-1980s, it began to export oil products – in fact they constituted 33 per cent of the GDR's export earnings to the West. The cost of this were reductions in domestic investment. Particularly noticeable was the deterioration in road surfaces, as the asphalt needed is largely derived from **crude oil**, which was diverted for export.

Many consumer goods and foodstuffs disappeared from the shelves at this time. It is true that the GDR managed to stabilise its hard currency debt at around 28 million Ostmarks between 1980 and 1986 – but at a cost in domestic living standards and an overreliance on the export of oil at a high price. In 1986, when the world price for crude oil fell, the GDR economy found itself back in serious trouble.

**Source B** From Library of Congress Country Studies East Germany Federal Research Division data up to 1987, written in the late 1980s. Here the authors are discussing GDR economic performance in the 1980s.

> The 1981-85 plan period proved to be a difficult time for the East German economy. The first serious problem was the decision by Western banks in 1981 and 1982 to clamp down on credit for East Germany and the concurrent decision of the Soviet Union to reduce oil deliveries by 10 per cent. The immediate East German response - retrenchment on Western imports and stepped up exports - resulted in domestic bottlenecks and a growth rate of less than 3 per cent. However, by the end of the period the economy had chalked up a respectable overall performance, with an annual average growth rate of 4.5 per cent (the plan target had been 5.1 per cent).

What can you infer from Source B about the economic performance of the GDR in the 1980s?

Overall the problems in the GDR economy had not changed. It was subject to wastage of resources, dependence on expensive raw materials, obsolete equipment, unrealistic targets, untrustworthy data and an unreliable workforce. Economic managers in the State Planning Commission still insisted there must be more investment in modern technology at the expense of social welfare. Honecker refused – the **Social Contract** (see page 383) was still sacrosanct.

## High spending on health and welfare

We have seen that the GDR prided itself on the amount of social welfare it provided for its citizens (see pages 382–86). The problem was that by the 1980s, this was no longer tenable; the country simply could not afford it. Economic experts had long argued whether expensive social welfare provision could be maintained. The State Planning Commission, for example, often pointed out tensions between ambitious social policies and economic performance. The SED, however, would not countenance any reduction for various reasons:

- Members were still convinced that central planning was powerful enough to address economic problems successfully.
- It was still believed that improvements in social welfare would see commensurate improvements in productivity. If people looked at comparisons between the GDR and other Soviet bloc countries, they could find evidence for this. It was estimated that in the 1980s, GDR productivity exceeded that in other COMECON countries by 20 per cent. However in 1985 it was 35 per cent of FRG productivity and the differential was growing.
- Members still believed their own propaganda about the relative strength of the GDR economy. As we have seen, most Western observers disagreed.

Some benefits such as pensions and child benefits increased during the 1980s. Mary Fulbrook has spoken of a whole raft of benefits such as subsidies for transport, housing, basic foodstuffs and children's clothing beyond those normally associated with state provision as 'sacred cows that could not be slaughtered even in the more difficult years of the 1980s when it was increasingly evident even to those without access to the real statistics that the GDR economy was in deep decline'.

## The poor quality of consumer goods

By the 1980s, as consumer expectations rose as a result of becoming more aware of the quality of goods on sale in the West, it became clear that the GDR was lagging further and further behind. We have already mentioned the quality of cars and the long waiting times for delivery of items and services such as telephones considered essential in the West. The quality of other consumer goods such as television sets and refrigerators was often poor also. It was increasingly important to have contacts such as shop assistants who could mysteriously find goods for a price, or experts in DIY – as appliances frequently broke down. This was exacerbated by a general shortage of spare parts so technically adept friends who could improvise with what came to hand were much in demand.

Increasingly, too, people were aware of anomalies in the supposedly egalitarian society. Sixty per cent of GDR public servants had access to a telephone compared with 25 per cent of members of the working class.

## GDR and ICT

Historian Mike Dennis has suggested that what particularly stimulated the crisis in the 1980s was the failure to develop ICT and micro-electronics despite a will on the part of the SED to do so and an injection of 15 billion Ostmarks in the 1985–90 Five-Year Plan. The idea was to catapult the GDR into becoming a world leader in part through the production of a one-megabyte microchip. This alone cost 1 billion Ostmarks but by the time it went into production it was obsolete. A fast moving industry such as ICT well exemplifies how the GDR would get left behind by its competitors. The structure just could not encompass any developments requiring innovation and speed. By the end of the 1980s, Western experts suggested the GDR was five to ten years behind in terms of ICT - hardly then a world leader. There were specific reasons for its laggardness: the isolation of GDR experts from cutting edge research and contact with international colleagues; the stifling bureaucracy; and the dislike of innovation and change.

Honecker, meanwhile, showed how out of touch he was by insisting to a visiting team of FRG microchip experts that progress in the GDR was unstoppable. 'Neither an ox nor an ass will halt **socialism** from its appointed course.' His audience was presumably polite but must have felt he was losing credibility. He presided over a country where in 1989, 72 per cent of telephone technology was over 30 years old, transport links were inadequate and even the roads were suffering because of the shortage of asphalt.

There was always a contradiction between the desire to impose satisfactory standards of living for everyone and individual citizens' desire for personal possessions, with the production of consumer goods often lacking priority. In 1978, for example, the state provided 7 million meals daily for workers in communal canteens to save them buying food to cook at home. Many complained about the standards. The state considered offering a national laundry service to save people having to buy washing machines – which were apparently particularly unreliable in the GDR. However, most people did not want communal feeding or state laundries. They wanted the wherewithal to do these things for themselves and their families.

## Solutions to economic problems

Some USSR economists began to advocate some sort of **confederation** between the GDR and FRG as the only way out of its economic malaise. Soviet leader Mikhail Gorbachev was not in favour of this; he hoped for reform and believed there were talented middle managers who could effect it – a return to the ESS (see page 359). The leaders of the GDR, meanwhile, buried their heads in the sand. Honecker favoured some sort of alliance with other **communist** countries who opposed reform, notably Czechoslovakia and Romania – although in the event neither was to survive much longer than the GDR. He insisted the GDR was among the top ten world economic performers – when he said so in front of Gorbachev at the speeches to mark the GDR's 40th birthday celebrations in 1989, the latter openly snorted with derision.

A confidential memorandum of 1989 from economic experts predicted hard currency debt would soar from 41.5 billion Ostmarks to 52.6 billion by 1995 and felt intervention by the **International Monetary Fund** would be inevitable to keep the country afloat. It felt the only solution would be to cut consumption by 25 to 30 per cent, which would, it acknowledged, destabilise the country and therefore be self-defeating. Cuts in defence were advocated and reductions in wastage. Little happened. Indeed, on 30 October 1989 after the dismissal of Honecker (see page 424), a further confidential memo for the new regime suggested things were even worse. Half of all industrial facilities and machines were obsolete, half of the transport infrastructure was decayed and average productivity was 35 per cent of that of the FRG.

Small wonder that confederation was becoming more commonly suggested – although it was increasingly acknowledged that there would be little point to two German states confederated along capitalist lines because once the socialist economic system was removed, there was no reason for separate development. Interestingly, the new Economic Minister Christa Luft had no idea of the scale of the problem.

## Conclusion: Economic stagnation in the 1980s

The economic problems in the GDR could not be addressed by loans and central planning. They were probably insurmountable and this was becoming more evident as the 1980s progressed. The GDR could not afford its level of welfare spending. The fact that the economy came to rely on lignite, an inefficient and pollutant type of coal, is evidence of the decline. While efforts were made to increase exports by the development of the oil industry, this came at the expense of living standards and infrastructure with the result that there were increasingly consumer shortages and a shoddy look to the country.

### Work together

1 First divide up the factors discussed in this section to explain the economic stagnation of the 1980s. These could include:

- The return to central planning
- The Growing national debt
- Koko
- The Impact of the USSR
- Environmental problems
- Economic relations with the FRG
- The 1981–85 Five-Year Plan
- The high cost of health and welfare.

Using the recommended reading in this book, your class-notes, online research and other independent reading of your own, try to find out more about each of the factors explored here. Share the notes that you have made and make sure that you read them together, explaining any terminology or further details you have discovered.

2 Having done this you should be in a position where you can discuss the following together:

**How far do you agree that the economic problems in the GDR in the 1980s were impossible to solve?**

You need to bring into your discussion all the factors you have researched and developed. Are any factors more important than others in enabling you to come to a judgement?

# 2 Gorbachev's influence

The visit of Erich Honecker to the FRG in 1987 (see page 373) may have marked the high point of SED confidence, but the GDR faced many problems. The appointment of the reformist Gorbachev in the USSR with his twin pillars of **glasnost** and **perestroika** gave hope to dissenters in the GDR but the SED opposed his ideas. More people sought to emigrate and the more the Government accommodated people's demands to travel the more demand there was. The Protestant Churches, protected by the 1978 **Concordat** (see page 400), offered space to protest groups which grew in number even though widely infiltrated by the Stasi. They embraced peace groups, environmental groups and human rights activists. The authorities responded with increasing brutality. However, the problems in the GDR, not least environmental pollution, were becoming evident to all.

### Note it down

Draw a spider diagram, with the spider's body labelled 'How big a problem was this for the GDR?' Label four 'legs' of the spider as follows:

- Impact of Gorbachev's reforms and their influence in the GDR
- Role of the Protestant Churches
- Growth of opposition groups
- Economic and environmental problems.

This will help prepare you for the work together activity on page 421.

## Impact of Gorbachev's reforms

In 1986 Mikhail Gorbachev became ruler of the USSR and found a country on the edge of economic catastrophe. He initiated policies of glasnost (meaning 'open debate') and perestroika (meaning 'reform') to try to address the problems. The aim was not to destroy the communist system but to reform it, to make it workable. This entailed pursuing policies of **détente** with the West to reduce the crippling defence budget and to redirect resources away from the **satellite states** to the USSR itself. Quite simply the USSR could no longer afford to subsidise its satellites or, more importantly perhaps, to prop them up. As the state on the interface of the Cold War, 'Stalin's unloved child', it was assumed that the USSR would always support the GDR. As late as July 1989, at a meeting between the three, Gorbachev informed the FRG Chancellor Helmut Kohl and Erich Honecker that the USSR would not abandon the GDR. What this meant in practice, however, was not made clear.

## Eastern Europe in the 1980s

Communism was threatened throughout the Soviet bloc. By 1987 it was clear that Gorbachev's policies would have major effects: because the problems within communism were so great, his policies were no longer about reform but rather about wholesale change. Gorbachev made a significant speech to the Council of Europe in July 1989 in which he announced that the so-called **Brezhnev Doctrine** was dead – communist countries could no longer rely on the USSR for life support. They had to find their own solutions to their problems. He had already, in July 1988, informed **Warsaw Pact** Defence Ministers that there was no possibility of USSR military intervention in the manner of the invasion of Czechoslovakia in 1968 (see page 366).

In August 1989, Poland elected its first non-communist head of government and multi-party elections were to be held in Hungary in 1990. Both countries had moved towards some degree of capitalism.

## The SED response to Gorbachev's reforms

Both Erich Honecker and Mikhail Gorbachev were communists. However, the latter belonged to a younger generation and had initiated reforms in the Soviet Union to redress what he perceived as the failures of his predecessors – men like Leonid Brezhnev – who Honecker regarded as mentors. When they met at the 11th SED Congress in April 1986, Gorbachev suggested that the GDR might benefit from some economic restructuring. Honecker reposted, 'That young man has been making policy for only a year and already he wants to bite off more than he can chew.'

The SED was unequivocal in its opposition to perestroika and glasnost when, by 1987, it became apparent that they were significant and not merely window dressing. In an

### Mikhail Gorbachev, 1931–

Mikhail Gorbachev was born in March 1931 into a farming family in the southern Russian province of Stavropol Kria. His father was arrested and imprisoned in the purges of the 1930s but Mikhail nevertheless became a loyal communist. He studied law at Moscow State University and worked as a regional Communist Party official. He gained a second degree in agriculture which became his real area of expertise. In 1978 he was called to Moscow to work in the organisation of agriculture where he impressed superiors with his efficiency and modernisation schemes. He was promoted to the **Politburo** of the USSR. In April 1985, at the comparative young age of 54, he became head of the Soviet Union.

Gorbachev had been an **apparatchik**, a loyal and efficient bureaucrat. Little in his background suggested he would become a radical reformer. However, he saw a dire need for change. The USSR was on the brink of economic collapse and could no longer afford to compete in an arms race with the USA. He began his twin pillars of reform at home through glasnost and perestroika. Glasnost involved more openness and dialogue, allowing Russians to discuss the failings of the USSR and how to put them right, while perestroika was a restructuring of the economy. Glasnost certainly stimulated debate but perestroika failed; the economy was beyond repair. However, Gorbachev became hugely popular on the international stage. He wanted an end to the expensive Cold War, and his diplomacy culminated in the 1987 INF treaty which saw an end to the deployment of medium-range missiles.

Gorbachev hoped his communist allies would deploy similar domestic reforms to glasnost and perestroika and made it clear the Soviet Union would not intervene to maintain communist government by force. This stimulated protest throughout the Soviet bloc which saw the demise of communist regimes. The GDR was particularly hostile to reform but when Gorbachev made it clear the Soviet Union would not support its stance, this became a significant reason for its collapse.

Historians debate Gorbachev's intentions and whether it would have been possible to reform **communism** successfully, but his Government saw the demise of it throughout Europe and ultimately, in 1991, the collapse of the Soviet Union itself.

interview published in the West German magazine *Stern* in April 1987, Kurt Hager, responsible for ideology in the GDR, dismissed perestroika as 'redecoration': why should anyone redecorate their house because their neighbour did so? The SED leadership argued that:

- it had undergone economic restructuring in the 1960s
- its economy achieved good growth rates
- its proximity to Western Europe meant it could not allow too much liberalisation.

Given the availability of FRG television, this latter argument was never going to convince anyone.

This is not to suggest that the SED was not afraid that demand for reform might spread. They were well aware of Gorbachev's influence and popularity with the ordinary citizens in the Soviet bloc. The period saw the censorship of Soviet periodicals or their removal from the news-stands, particularly if they published articles critical of the GDR or German communism. Gorbachev's own speeches were subject to censorship and GDR newspapers began to publish articles on alcoholism and food shortages in the Soviet Union. The British communist newspaper *Morning Star* disappeared from the news-stands.

Honecker, meanwhile, began to give speeches asserting GDR sovereignty and independence. It did not need to follow foreign models of Marxist-Leninism.

## Popularity of Gorbachev

Gorbachev was highly popular among many ordinary citizens of the GDR who took heart from his reforms and hoped they would be extended to their country. Although much of the work published about him, and his own speeches and articles, had been banned in the GDR, they supplied a lucrative **black market**. The Central Institute for Youth Research based in Leipzig found in 1988 that 83 per cent of young people questioned supported him. This actually rose to 90 per cent of young SED members, which was particularly worrying for the SED leadership who feared the possibility of a large reformist wing within the Party itself. One teenager said that it was the advent of Gorbachev with an alternative to the type of socialism they were used to that taught them to think. This support came to a head during the 40th anniversary celebrations of the GDR in October 1989 when, in the presence of Honecker and the SED leadership, the crowds began to call out Gorbachev's name, 'Gorby! Gorby!' and 'Gorby! Help Us!'

People in the GDR, particularly the young, latched onto Gorbachev as a new type of communist leader who offered hope. It may not even have been what he actually said so much as what they believed he represented. As people embraced Gorbachev, with his hope for the future, their own regime seemed more ossified and grounded in the past.

Gorbachev had won widespread popularity in the GDR and his reforms in the USSR undoubtedly gave impetus to reformist movements in the GDR. However, they also predated him. The economic and environmental problems we have seen were enough to stimulate protest in themselves. This was particularly so when the leadership seemed increasingly geriatric and out of touch, and prepared to rely on the security forces to maintain their authority rather than listen to what people were saying.

**Source C** From a policy document by Vladimir V. Kuskin entitled 'Gorbachev in East Germany', dated 19 October 1989. Kuskin worked at an organisation called Radio Free Europe Research which monitored developments in Eastern Europe. This section is about Gorbachev's visit to East Berlin on 6 and 7 October 1989 for the 40th anniversary celebrations of the GDR.

> Two Edges. It was clear ... that his presence would have a double edge. On the one hand, he was very probably asked or prevailed upon to go in order to bolster the GDR's fortunes. On the other, Gorbachev could not have been expected to go to the GDR just to endorse East German resistance to change. He also went to speak about the kind of reforms that have become his program, as he had spoken of them during visits to Czechoslovakia and Romania, two other bloc countries saddled with die-hard leaderships.
>
> Gorbachev's pronouncements in East Berlin underlined that his grand scheme of socialist 'renewal' applied to all communist-governed lands, the GDR included. The Soviet and East German leaderships, when agreeing on the visit, presumably concluded that endorsement of Honecker and endorsement of reform could be kept in balance. This was indeed done with the help of two precepts that Moscow and East Berlin hold in common. The one maintains that the GDR's existence, as a strategic outcome of World War II, is non-negotiable; the other disclaims Moscow's right to interfere and makes each communist party responsible for its own country's policy line.

How well does Source C explain Gorbachev's dilemmas with regards to his policy on whether or not to support the Government of the GDR in resisting reform?

## Opposition groups

The late 1970s and 1980s saw the development of opposition groups throughout the GDR. Many recruited heavily from 25 to 40 year olds, 'Ulbricht's children', who had grown up in the GDR during the period of liberalism and **Ostpolitik**. Few sought regime change;

most sought reform in terms of their particular concerns, or at best to improve the quality of life in the GDR. Few members of any opposition groups thought the GDR was about to collapse; it was a permanent fixture which they had to embrace and come to terms with. Many had young children and objected to how they were being indoctrinated from an early age or else feared the society into which they would grow up was no better than the one in which they had themselves been raised. Born in the 1950s and 1960s they had little reason to respect the ageing leaders who had fought the Nazis; they largely saw them as ossified and out of touch. Attitudes hardened after 1987 when the regime grew more repressive (see page 421) and there began to be more focus on democracy as the precursor to reform. The influence of Mikhail Gorbachev and other external factors such as reforms elsewhere in the Soviet bloc had an effect on their growing radicalisation – but it is important to note that most of these groups predated Gorbachev. Indeed groups had demanded reform to varying degrees throughout the period of the GDR's existence.

### The role of the Protestant opposition groups

The 1980s saw a symbiosis between the Protestant Churches and the growing number of opposition groups. Opposition groups were allowed to function as part of Churches because laws restricting freedom of association – groups of more than six unless sanctioned by the SED were technically illegal – excluded Church-run groups. Churches offered opposition groups one of the few places where they could meet. However, the state expected Churches to control the activities of protest and dissident groups. The attitude of Church hierarchies themselves could be ambivalent. When Pastor Rainer Eppelmann and **dissident** Robert Havemann drew up the 'Berlin Appeal' (see page 420), the Church authorities in Brandenburg-Berlin withdrew support saying it was too provocative. Other Church leaders actively campaigned for it.

It should also be remembered that the Churches' leaders lacked control over individual **pastors** so while some actively supported opposition to the regime, others were prepared to give opposition groups space without further involvement and still others opposed them. Often bright but non-conformist young people could find a professional career only in the Churches; many of these were to support and indeed lead opposition groups. As in the 1960s and 1970s, some pastors encouraged young people by vibrant and exciting services – so-called 'blues-masses' which often attracted congregations of 800 or more. These were not necessarily held to subvert the state but rather to convert young people to Christianity – but nevertheless the Stasi saw them very much as subversive.

### Church, State and opposition groups

The relationship between Church, State and opposition groups is then complex, although historian Mary Fulbrook has identified three phases:

- March 1978 to the mid-1980s: Following the Concordat between Church and State (see page 400) it was hoped the Churches would be able to exercise some means of control over opposition groups to channel their dissent into safe avenues or irrelevant discussion. Increasingly, however, the state became frustrated that the Churches were unable to operate such control.
- Mid-1980s to 1987: A transitional period where new modes of dissent were emerging and opposition groups grew ever more frustrated with Church caution. At this time more grass roots groups developed. More people were taking the initiative and forming groups without waiting for a leader from Church leaders or members of the **intelligentsia**. Opposition groups grew more diverse and the Churches less relevant.
- 1987 to 1989: The state became more repressive and opposition groups more organised. The GDR became more politically polarised and unstable.

These phases are complicated by the widespread infiltration of the Stasi, the diverse nature of the Churches and their membership, and the fact that many members of opposition groups were simply using the Churches as a space to meet. However, such was their influence that it is estimated that no Church **synod meetings** of the mid to late 1980s could escape an agenda item on either democratisation or human rights or both.

## Key debate

### The role of the Protestant Churches in the demise of the GDR

Historians agree that the Protestant Churches played a crucial role in the organisation of dissent. German historian Gerhard Rein, writing in 1997, even spoke of a second Protestant **Reformation**, while in Canada, Lee Kuhle, writing in 2008, has shown how the Churches evolved from purely religious and pastoral concerns to providing the umbrella under which activists could operate. Journalist John Simpson has asserted that the contact with dissent actually radicalised many in the Churches themselves. He does, however, remind us, as does Peter Grieder, that the protest groups accepted church space for their meetings but were not necessarily themselves religious. Grieder adds that not all pastors offered refuge and many had been infiltrated by the Stasi. 'Many East Germans who participated in the '***Wende***' did so independently of the Churches.'

## Types of opposition groups

Opposition groups took many different forms.

### Peace groups

Peace groups had grown since the decision taken in April 1978 to introduce compulsory military training into the school curriculum. While this triggered immediate protests from Church groups and many parents, the movement for peace really gathered momentum after the introduction of the annual Dresden Peace Forum in the late 1970s. The 1982 Forum attracted as many as 5000 visitors despite attempts by the SED to prevent travel to Dresden. The Party also banned the 'Swords into Ploughshares' emblem of the peace movement.

Nevertheless the Dresden Forum organised 'Peace Weeks' and 'Peace Workshops' featuring music and entertainment as well as discussion throughout the 1980s. One idea emanating from these discussions was to introduce a 'Community Peace Service' as a further alternative to military conscription involving social welfare activities – leading one member of the Politburo to assert derisively that this was unnecessary because the GDR was itself a 'Community Peace Service'.

In 1982 the influential 'Berlin Appeal' produced by a political dissident Robert Havemann and a Church pastor Rainer Eppelmann:

- proposed a national debate on peace
- opposed the sale of military toys
- promoted the introduction of lessons on 'peace' into the school curriculum
- promoted the withdrawal of all foreign troops from the FRG and GDR.

A Women for Peace Group emerged to campaign against nuclear weapons. It was partly borne out of the decision to introduce female conscription in the event of an emergency; members protested with an **open letter** to Honecker in October 1982 which argued that military service was incompatible with being female and called for a debate on military and nuclear disarmament.

### Greens

Ecological groups were active from the late 1970s when pollution levels were visibly rising. Ecological centres were set up such as the Church Research Centre (KFH) in Wittenberg and, in September 1986, a library devoted to ecological issues was opened in Zionskirche in Berlin. Unfortunately, as part of the general crackdown (see page 421), the library was raided by the Stasi in November 1987, members were arrested and its printing presses confiscated. However, the environmental groups did draw attention to the ecological pollution and its attendant dangers in the GDR and were to form a Green Party during the final months of the GDR.

### Human rights groups

From the mid-1980s Gorbachev's reforms in the USSR stimulated human rights groups in the GDR. The Initiative for Peace and Human Rights (IFM) played a key role in calling for more democracy and freedom to travel, making links with opposition groups elsewhere, such as **Charter 77** in Czechoslovakia, and publishing a journal *Grenzfall*. The IFM was the first protest group wholly independent of the Churches and supporters met in private houses and used their own presses. Membership was informal – anyone deemed to have supported one of its ventures was classed as a member and there was no real structure or hierarchy. Had there been, the IFM would have been an illegal organisation and easier to infiltrate and shut down. Many of those associated with it went on to form **New Forum** (see page 422).

### Determination among protest groups

There were various indicators that protest groups were becoming more determined.

#### Olaf Palme Peace March, October 1987

A march took place to support the idea of world peace. Of course the SED supported this. However, unofficial banners from peace groups appeared side by side with the official ones as members of peace groups joined the march.

#### Rosa Luxemburg–Karl Liebknecht Parade, January 1988

The Rosa Luxemburg–Karl Liebknecht Parade was an annual event to celebrate the lives of the two founders of German communism who had been murdered after the end of the First World War. It was one of the most auspicious dates on the GDR calendar. In 1988 protesters joined the parade, many carrying banners demanding reform and, embarrassingly for the authorities, one of the most prevalent slogans was one of Luxemburg's own: 'Freedom is always the freedom to think differently.' The authorities again reacted with mass arrests and brutality – but this in itself was self-defeating. More and more people realised that change was necessary and were increasingly prepared to demonstrate and join protests.

#### May 1989 elections

In May 1989 citizens groups were formed, usually under the auspices of the Churches, to monitor elections which took place. Despite Stasi intimidation these groups conducted their scrutiny and in many cases reported fraud. The problem was not necessarily in the actual local polling stations where the votes were counted. The votes were then taken to district electoral offices run by the SED for checking. Here the discrepancies occurred. It was discovered that they had in many cases increased the votes in support of the single list, and when individuals protested not a single complaint was upheld.

The Government dismissed the protests as the work of Western agitators. But the damage had been done. Enough people had heard that electoral results in the GDR were unreliable.

## Stasi infiltration and repression

The Stasi infiltrated most groups. Some indeed collapsed because members were too afraid to speak openly. One leading dissident subsequently discovered that her husband was an IM who not only reported on her subversive activities but also their private life. People could be arrested, imprisoned and deported to the FRG. Sometimes infiltrators acted as agents-provocateurs, inciting members to more radical activities prompting extreme reactions from the security forces who had of course been forewarned. Others spread such dissent within the groups that they collapsed with a welter of personal antagonisms or irrelevant, pointless discussions.

The movements, however, seemed unstoppable. In the face of this, for all their power, the Stasi seemed impotent. One example will suffice. About four hundred people met in a Berlin church to draft a letter protesting about the fraudulent May 1989 elections and submit it to the authorities. The Stasi laid on buses to arrest them all, which they did with alarming brutality. One 17-year-old girl was subsequently interrogated all night, alternatively asked to sign a confession that she had been put up to her actions by agents of the FRG and to become an informer. She resisted and was eventually fined 300 Ostmarks. However, when she refused to pay nothing was done. In Leipzig the authorities were ordered to break up the citizens groups monitoring the elections. Members were arrested, beaten up and then allowed to go free – and the electoral scrutiny took place.

It seemed many people were either losing their fear of the Stasi or were so desperate for change that they did not care what might happen to them. The forces of repression were faced with a situation where more and more people were prepared to challenge authority. They might have to countenance mass arrests or even brutal suppression – both of which are hardly characteristic of a regime which claimed mass support. Any loss of confidence on the part of the security forces would inevitably weaken a government relying on them to maintain order.

## The declining authority of the SED

The problems faced by the GDR in the 1980s together with the growing influence of Gorbachev, and ironically the relaxation of control from the Soviet Union, combined to weaken the grip of the SED Government. They tended to react to change by digging in their heels, rejecting reform and responding with greater repression. However, the movement in favour of reform seemed unstoppable. As we shall see many SED functionaries were increasingly losing confidence and looked for leadership which did not appear. Surveys conducted by the Central Institute for Youth Research in Leipzig found an alarming growth of youth dissatisfaction between 1985 and 1989 in areas such as pollution and living standards. The percentage of apprentices surveyed showed that 11 per cent identified with the GDR 'hardly or not at all' in May 1988 and 23 per cent in October 1988. It took courage to be so forthright even in surveys.

# Conclusion: Gorbachev's influence

Problems grew for the GDR throughout the 1980s and the SED increasingly relied on repression. More people wanted to emigrate and those who remained increasingly took part in protest movements which were sheltered by the Protestant Churches. If the SED could have prevented internal threats, however, they could not match the influence of the reformist Mikhail Gorbachev in the USSR. Although the SED rejected his reforms within the GDR, his popularity could not be stopped, and citizens saw him as a hope for the future. Meanwhile, problems were growing, not least the damaging pollution as a result of industrial inefficiencies. More and more people were calling for reform and the authority of the SED Government seemed less certain.

## Work together

Consider the following reasons for protest within the GDR: the role and influence of Mikhail Gorbachev; the role of the Protestant Churches; the growth of opposition groups; economic problems; environmental problems. Working in a group of five, prepare for a debate. Each of you takes one reason. On your own, prepare a case which shows your reason was the most important. Meet together as a group again and deliver your justifications. Afterwards, discuss the following:

1 Whose case was the strongest?
2 Which motives worked well together in explaining why there were such problems within the GDR?
3 How influential was Mikhail Gorbachev in stimulating protest in the GDR?

## 3 The events of 1989

Various external and internal events occurred in autumn 1989 which precipitated the unexpected collapse of the GDR. Hungary opened its borders with Austria, leading to a flood of emigrants. This coincided with the growth of protest movements and demonstrations which the state seemed powerless to stop. While some feared there would be severe repression, Gorbachev reiterated that the Soviet Union would not defend the GDR. As the economic problems mounted, Honecker was overthrown but the problems only grew worse. The new Government opened the Berlin Wall in November 1989 to try to stem the tide of emigration but this in fact had little effect.

### Note it down

This section deals with the events of 1989 which led to the collapse of the Berlin Wall. You should choose your own form of note-making to consider the following:

- The opening of Hungary's borders with Austria and emigration from the GDR
- 40th anniversary celebrations of the GDR and Gorbachev's visit
- The decline of Honecker's influence and his dismissal
- Krenz and the opening of the Berlin Wall.

It is important to note the impact of each issue. Why is each one important in the events of 1989? Which do you think is the most important? Give reasons for your answers.

### Opening of Hungary's borders

In September 1989, Hungary quietly opened its borders with Austria. Historian A. James McAdams has argued the beginning of the end of the GDR could be dated to this one event because it simply made the Berlin Wall superfluous. Thousands of East Germans on holiday in Hungary simply crossed the border. On 10 September Hungary formally declared the border open, thereby abrogating its treaty with the GDR refusing to let East Germans leave its territory without exit visas. In two weeks 30,000 East Germans had crossed into Hungary and thereon to Austria. Others camped out in the West German embassy in Budapest and other communist countries, demanding exit visas. This development took the GDR leadership unawares and they were slow to respond. They could hardly close the border with a fellow Warsaw Pact ally. Clearly, however, the open border between Hungary and Austria made a mockery of the GDR's closed borders with the West.

Following the opening of the border with Austria, the East German authorities banned its citizens from visiting Hungary – but thousands went to Czechoslovakia and Poland instead, setting up camp in the FRG embassies in Prague and Warsaw and demanding exit visas. Honecker finally ordered the GDR's borders closed. His country was now as isolated as Albania or North Korea. This clearly had not been his intention and with the 40th aniversary celebrations coming up, the situation seemed absurd. What was there to celebrate about a country that was isolated from everywhere else in the world?

### The sealed train

Honecker wanted the crisis settled before the 40th anniversary celebrations of the GDR in October. He agreed to let 5500 citizens camped in the embassies leave for the FRG so long as the trains went through the GDR; this would enable the GDR to expel the refugees rather than suggest they were leaving of their own accord.

This propaganda exercise went wrong from the start. Not only did East German citizens try to clamour aboard, but at Dresden the security forces had to physically and brutally try to prevent them from doing so. Similarly, when police climbed aboard to confiscate documents such as GDR identity cards, they found that most had already ripped them up and disposed of them along the track. Worse, the refugees got a hero's welcome on arrival in Hof, the first town across the border in the FRG. All this was recorded on FRG television which East Germans could access. Outside Dresden station where demonstrations continued the police, reluctant to cause carnage, did not suppress them. This, too, was noted elsewhere.

### Protest

Protests spread to almost every city in the GDR. People were protesting about everything – living conditions, pollution, lack of freedom – but not yet demanding regime change as such. Again the authorities failed to realise this. There was little actual organised or co-ordinated leadership behind the protest movements:

- The New Forum, a nationwide political movement, was set up and met in churches demanding democratic reform.
- Supporters of the FRG Green Party became vocal on environmental issues.
- Christians wanted more rights of worship.

But there was no one revolutionary movement.

## Protests in Leipzig

Mass demonstrations took place in Berlin, Dresden and Leipzig – but particularly in the latter where the Nikolaikirche (St Nicholas Church) increasingly became the centre of protest with regular Monday night crowds of 70,000 outside. On Sunday 8 October, Erich Mielke, head of the security forces, gave a red alert effectively authorising forces to shoot to kill. Hospitals were cleared to receive anticipated hordes of wounded.

In the event the protest took place as normal but the security forces did not stop it and certainly did not fire their weapons. Various reasons have been offered:

- Although Honecker had publicly supported the Chinese authorities when they had brutally suppressed similar pro-democracy protests in Tiananmen Square in Peking in June 1989, there was probably little appetite for slaughter among the members of the Politburo. Any regime which killed hundreds of its own citizens could no longer claim legitimacy, let alone popularity – again when supposedly celebrating its 40 years of success.
- USSR troops following Gorbachev's earlier orders remained firmly in barracks.
- The demonstrations themselves were peaceful; 'No Violence!' was a common call. At the huge rally on 9 October eminent supporters such as Kurt Masur, director of the Leipzig Opera, called for restraint and were heeded.
- There was some question about the reliability of the security forces themselves. Mostly these were conscripts, not murderers. If they refused any order to fire, the entire security apparatus would be called into question. If the authorities could only keep control by repression and the agents of such repression refused to be repressive, their authority would collapse. As it was, despite the shoot-to-kill order, the police commander in Leipzig, Gerhard Strassenburg, ordered his troops only to fire in self-defence. They were to fire only if threatened by violence on the part of the protesters as opposed to doing so in an effort to subdue the protests. It may have been that **hardliners** such as Mielke were hoping for provocation to justify state violence, but if so they were thwarted.

## Gorbachev's visit to East Berlin

It has been argued that Honecker did his best to ignore protest and to concentrate on the celebrations to mark the achievements of the GDR. There is no doubt that the anniversary was of supreme personal importance to him. However, the planned festivities on 7 October went awry.

▲ *Nikolaikirche*, Leipzig.

Gorbachev was guest of honour. When he and Honecker presided over a vast torch-lit parade of **FDJ**, many called out his name and 'Gorby! Gorby! Help Us!' These were not disaffected punks or skinheads but supposedly the pride of East German youth. At a later meeting with the Politburo, Gorbachev made a pointed speech about how history leaves reactionary forces behind. One member later said, 'We should have had the *coup d'état* there right in front of his eyes.' He was referring to the overthrow of Honecker. Certain of his colleagues had been plotting this for months. That he had survived is accounted for by their lack of organisation and failure to show initiative. Honecker and before him Ulbricht had effectively been dictators and their acolytes simply were not used to independence of thought. The system was so centralised and so lacking in avenues for dissent that it would take a real crisis to overthrow a leader. As Politburo member Günter Schabowski later wrote, 'One would sooner have committed sodomy than have allowed oneself to be guilty of **factionalism**.' When his colleague Egon Krenz had suggested to Honecker that reform was necessary, Honecker sent him on holiday.

## Honecker's dismissal

Even when Honecker was incapacitated by illness through September 1989, his opponents did not act against him. Indeed they seemed to do nothing in the face of growing opposition groups except leave the Stasi to destroy them. They also blamed the FRG and the West for spreading unrest.

Two events led to Honecker's demise:

- During his visit for the 40th anniversary celebrations, Gorbachev had reiterated that the Soviet Union would not intervene in the internal affairs of the GDR. Ironically when Honecker had been asserting its independence one may have thought this is what he wanted to hear. Not so when it appeared to give carte blanche to dissent by assuring people the Soviet forces in the GDR would remain in their barracks.
- Mass protests took place in Leipzig and elsewhere and the authorities were unable to stop them.

The end for Honecker came quickly, almost without fanfare. He was 77 years old and had been ill for some time. He had already had one cancerous tumour removed but the doctors had missed the one which continued to make him feel unwell and would eventually kill him. At the Politburo meeting of 17 October he was told that he had lost the support of the Party and should resign. Honecker assented but said correctly that his going would not solve the problems.

## Krenz and the opening of the Berlin Wall

Honecker was right; his resignation solved nothing. Demonstrations continued and grew in size. In Leipzig 30,000 marched to call for the resignation of the new leader Egon Krenz. In East Berlin 20,000 did at least listen to the most popular of the SED leaders, Günter Schabowski, but they had no idea – and nor possibly did he – how close the GDR was to bankruptcy (see pages 411–14).

Krenz visited the USSR on 1 November but came away with nothing. He tried to reform the Government by replacing some of the old SED leaders with younger colleagues – noticeably Hans Modrow, the reformist SED leader in Dresden. The changes in government seemed to emphasise just how ineffective the SED had become and Krenz's line seemed to be to offer just enough reform to dampen down protest.

- Krenz hoped the question of emigration would be satisfied by very gradual reform. He offered to liberalise foreign travel. However, even the usually acquiescent ***Volkskammer*** threw out his emigration law of 6 November because it was so vague it said nothing beyond a hint of 30 days travel allowance each year.
- The protests had gathered even more momentum with as many as 750,000 demonstrators on the streets at times.
- The Stasi, meanwhile, began to shred their files.
- Krenz had ordered the reopening of the border with Czechoslovakia on 1 November and the thousands of would-be emigrants began again to travel there. Indeed the Czech authorities threatened to close the border this time; they did not intend to build refugee camps for GDR citizens.

### The opening of the Berlin Wall

On 9 November officials at the Interior Ministry drafted a proposal that East German citizens should be allowed to travel abroad if they had the required passports and visas. Of course this was essentially conceding nothing because passports and visas might not be granted. At an evening press conference Günter Schabowski read out the document which had been handed to him earlier and which he may not have had time to read and digest. The draft suggested that travel restrictions would be ended with immediate effect; there was no mention of needing passports and visas, simply that travel authorisation would be expedited without delay.

This was almost certainly not what the draft actually meant and in the excitement it was forgotten that it said amplification was to be issued on the following day. Journalists pressed Schabowski; did he really mean immediate effect? Schabowski suggested that was the case.

The news spread like wildfire across the world's media and through rumour within the GDR. Ironically perhaps the last people to realise what was going on were the Politburo who were still meeting. Thousands were pressing at the Berlin Wall. Too late did an official announcement on the 10.30 p.m. news remind people that they had to apply for travel permits. The FRG news programmes announced incorrectly that the GDR had opened its borders. Comparatively few in Berlin listened to that either. They were at the Wall applying for visas which they still believed were necessary to get through to the West. At 11.30 p.m. the border guard officer on duty ordered the gates open as a crowd protection measure such was the press of people trying to get through.

They were met by equally excited West Berliners. Thus began, in the words of historian Frederick Taylor, 'the biggest street party in history'.

East Germans trying to cross the Wall in the next few days found it closed again. Not until Sunday 12 November did the respective mayors of West and East Berlin declare it redundant with the opening of new crossing points where people were just waved through.

**Source D** From the testimony of Uwe Nietzold, a student who had been to a poetry reading but wanted to see what was going on. Interviewed by Christopher Hilton in *The Wall: The People's Story* (Sutton Publishing, 2001).

> Friedrichstrasse was totally crowded so we walked to the Invalidenstrasse checkpoint, we stood and looked and we couldn't make up our minds. There were at least 2000 people in the street and we couldn't see the checkpoint! I suppose we were 200 metres away and all we could see were the checkpoint lights. We couldn't see that people were actually crossing. We still didn't believe it was open. We thought they'd keep the border closed. We stood there for about twenty minutes, the time was late and we agreed to go home. We thought it was all a demonstration like so many in the last few days.

Why is Source D useful to a historian studying the opening of the Berlin Wall?

**Source E** The dismantling of the Berlin Wall on 12 November 1989 by citizens of East and West Berlin.

What can you infer from Source E about the opening of the Berlin Wall?

## Effects of the fall of the Berlin Wall

The opening of the Wall did not necessarily mean the end of the GDR. It may have been bankrupt, it may have been haemorrhaging its population, but it still had a functioning government of sorts. The mayor of West Berlin asserted on 10 November that this was not a 'festival of reunification' but 'a festival of seeing each other again'.

Powerful and influential international voices opposed reunification. FRG Chancellor Helmut Kohl still felt at this point that the best solution was wholesale reform so as many people as possible stayed in the GDR. Kohl, like many of his fellow citizens and conscious of the concerns of voters, was worried about the impact of sudden mass immigration on the infrastructure of the FRG.

However, the numbers seeking permanent emigration was rising to unsustainable levels. People increasingly came to realise that the days of the GDR were numbered.

## Conclusion: The events of 1989

Few had anticipated the speedy collapse of the GDR. The triggers were both external and domestic. Once Hungary opened its borders, little could be done to stem the tide of emigration except to seal the GDR off from all its neighbours. The lack of support from the USSR was a deciding factor. Many believed the GDR had only survived this long through their support. The protests at home became too widespread to halt. They precipitated the fall of Honecker. While his successors reopened the Berlin Wall, this did little to halt emigration. The GDR seemed to increasingly be no longer credible.

### Work together

Check each other's notes from this section. From your partner's notes write down in descending order of importance the reasons for the collapse of the Berlin Wall. How far do you agree with your partner's judgements?

If you do not agree with your partner's judgement, revisit your notes to make your own judgements more apparent.

You may wish to revisit each other's notes from Sections 1 and 2 in this chapter to tackle this activity thoroughly.

# 4 The end of the GDR, 1989–90

Politicians seemed unaware of the depth of popular feeling while increasingly moving towards reunification. The SED itself collapsed both at the top and below, where rank and file members lost confidence and direction. It renamed itself the Party of Democratic Socialism (PDS) to fight the first free elections in the GDR in March 1990. FRG parties, anticipating reunification, fought in this election and those parties which favoured the continuation of the GDR fared badly. Not all in the international community welcomed reunification. Britain and France in particular were lukewarm, although the USA offered its support. The FRG itself was unsure until its Chancellor became aware of the level of demand within the GDR. Reunification was prefixed by a series of treaties which settled post-war borders. The road to reunification has not always been easy both in terms of cost and '*Ostalgie*' – nostalgia for certain elements of the GDR, not least its social welfare provision.

### Note it down

Use the 1:2 method (page x) with a slight alteration. You need to make notes on why the GDR ceased to exist. As usual, note down the 'big points', or headings, in the first column. In the second column write the supporting points in note form. This time add a third column. Here note down any concepts, terms, documents or historical figures that you would like to research further. In this section this could include Egon Krenz, Helmut Kohl, the Four Plus Two treaties or *Ostalgie*. When you have completed this section you can then research these points and add the information to this column.

## The collapse of the SED Government

The days following the collapse of the Wall saw a succession of governments in the GDR. Krenz and the older-style SED leaders barely lasted a month while those associated with the excesses of the regime such as Mielke were forced to resign and later faced prosecution.

In a sense the political initiative shifted from the SED to the official government of the GDR – the Council of Ministers in the *Volkskammer*. It will be remembered that this had usually simply rubber-stamped SED directives. Now, however, it grew in importance. Hans Modrow was elected as Minister-President, the formal head of state of the GDR, by the *Volkskammer* on 13 November. Modrow spoke in his inaugural address of why the GDR was still viable and necessary and outlined a series of reforms in education, bureaucracy and how the GDR would grow closer to the FRG and Europe generally. Had such a speech been made five years earlier, people may have listened. As it was, 17,500 GDR citizens applied for exit visas within ten days of the Wall coming down. Modrow, meanwhile, was told of the dire economic situation.

The old-style leadership of the SED collapsed. Mielke and various other former ministers resigned on 13 November. On 8 December the Public Prosecutor charged various former leaders including Honecker, Stolpe and Mielke with corruption and misuse of office. The other parties such as **CDU** East, which had ostensibly been in coalition with the SED since the inception of the GDR (see page 327), ejected their own leaders and left the coalition.

On 4 December Egon Krenz resigned as head of the SED. At an Extraordinary Congress on 9 December, the Party tried to reinvent itself. Moderates and respected figures such as Modrow came to the fore. A Berlin lawyer, Gregor Grys, became Chairman. The position of General Secretary from which Ulbricht, Honecker and (briefly) Krenz had governed the GDR was abolished, as were the offices of Politburo and Central Committee. The revamped party called itself the Socialist Unity Party–Party of Democratic Socialism (SED–PDS). By maintaining the title of SED it hoped to keep access to SED funds.

Many thought it was all window dressing, however. Support fell dramatically and in February 1990 the decision was taken to fight the 18 March election simply as the PDS. The SED had ceased to exist.

### Collapse of the SED

The SED fell apart both from above and below. Grass roots support collapsed. Initially the SED-PDS had adopted a cynical ploy of getting members to publicly disagree with party policy simply to create the illusion of democracy. But few were fooled. Mary Fulbrook has charted desperate letters from party loyalists to Krenz and his successors asking for guidance. Little was forthcoming.

## The final Governments of the GDR

Governments in the GDR, meanwhile, were trying to keep the state afloat. On 17 November, Modrow, whose role as Minister-President became more significant as the SED imploded, offered economic reforms including more autonomy for individual concerns and less central planning. He asserted that the free market would be introduced. He was offering a 'third way' between capitalism and communism, but it seemed few were interested. He also appeared to support the reconstitution of the Ministry of State security, albeit under a new guise – the Office for National Security. In January, meanwhile, the inequities of the communist system came to light through the storming of the Stasi offices and invasion of the SED hierarchy compound at Wandlitz. The former saw the discovery not only of prisons and instruments of repression but of millions of files which showed the extent of state surveillance. Wandlitz was equipped with nice houses, restaurants, swimming pools and entertainment facilities – by no means a super-luxurious resort for millionaires but considerably better than most GDR citizens enjoyed.

Opposition groups, too, tried to preserve the GDR. These centred around the Central Round Table, where political activists from both government organisations and citizens' groups met between December 1989 and March 1990 to discuss the forms and structures of a new democratic GDR. Modrow indeed took eight members into his Government in February to give credibility to his regime.

However, the momentum outside **think-tanks** and government was increasingly for reunification. Surveys of demonstrators in Leipzig found active support for reunification had grown from 39 to 72 per cent between December and February, while active opposition had fallen from 12 to 2 per cent. When Kohl offered monetary union in February, the GDR lost a key responsibility and the FRG Bundesbank effectively controlled its economy.

Modrow decided to bring forward elections to the *Volkskammer* projected for May 1990. They would now take place on the 18 March. There would be elections to municipal and state governments on 6 May and 2 December respectively. These would be the first free elections in the GDR – but they were dominated by political parties from the FRG.

### The elections of March 1990

As demand for reunification gathered apace the political parties in the FRG realised it was vital for them to become involved in GDR politics. Effectively they took over the non-communist parties of the GDR. These were the parties that had been allowed to survive to give the illusion that the GDR was democratic (see page 327).

The Christian Democratic Union (CDU), headed by Chancellor Helmut Kohl in the FRG, absorbed the CDU of the GDR and formed an **electoral coalition** called 'Alliance for Germany' with the German Social Union and the protest group Democratic Awakening. The Social Democratic Party (**SPD**) similarly embraced the GDR SPD.

On 18 March 1990 the first free elections in the GDR took place. The winners were the CDU-dominated alliance with 48 per cent of the popular vote; the SPD gained 21 per cent while the PDS actually gained a respectable 16 per cent. Former citizens' movements such as New Forum gained less than 5 per cent. This may be, as many commentators have argued, because they were not political parties with party organisations, the resources to fight elections effectively or even coherent programmes. However, it might also be because they represented the past; their role was over. Apart from those who sought a return to the past and presumably voted PDS, most people were not interested in groups which spoke of the future of the GDR. It had no future. Historian A. James McAdams has argued that people voted Alliance for Germany because it represented the fastest route to reunification. This was because the CDU was led in the FRG by the Chancellor, who would also be responsible for pushing through reunification.

On 12 April, the CDU leader in East Germany, Lothar de Maizière, became the final leader of the GDR. By this time reunification was inevitable. On 18 May the treaty for currency union was signed and on 1 July all central planning was stopped. Union formally took place through the Unification Treaty of 31 August and the GDR ceased to exist on 3 October.

## The process of reunification

The above short narrative might suggest that reunification was a brief and inevitable process. We can say with hindsight that indeed it was. However, that was not necessarily how it was seen at the time. It is well here to remember the maxim of historian E.W. Maitland that the events of the past one day still lay in the future. Significant groups in the GDR sought to maintain its identity and independence, foreign leaders were ambivalent at best and even the FRG Chancellor thought that reunification would take five to ten years.

### International reactions

The international reaction to German reunification was mixed. Many began to worry about the power and influence of a reunified Germany in the heart of Europe. The USA, however, possibly the country of greatest influence, supported the idea of reunification.

#### Britain

While the British Government under Margaret Thatcher welcomed the demise of communism, it shared with France a concern about a powerful resurgent Germany in the heart of Europe. Its Foreign Minister, Douglas Hurd, even went so far as to say that the Cold War, with a divided Germany, had brought stability to the continent. Prime Minister Margaret Thatcher worried that a united Germany could destabilise Gorbachev's rule in the USSR; he might be blamed for the loss of such an important satellite and hardliners might force his resignation. Thatcher even went to Moscow two months before the fall of the Berlin Wall to assure Mikhail Gorbachev. She said:

> *'We do not want a united Germany ... This would lead to a change to post-war borders, and we cannot allow that because such a development would undermine the stability of the whole international situation and could endanger our security.'*

#### France

France was more prosaic. Both France and the FRG were leading members of the **European Union (EU)**, and the French leader François Mitterand came to believe he could accept reunification if Germany was tied more closely to the EU. He saw greater co-operation and the joint acceptance of a single EU currency as the means by which reunification could be countenanced.

Margaret Thatcher was dubious. On 2 February 1990 she wrote:

> *'The problems will not be overcome by strengthening the EC [predecessor to the EU] ... Germany's ambitions would then become the dominant and active factor.'*

#### The USA

The FRG probably believed if it had the support of the USA it could overcome other opposition. It did. In October 1989 before the collapse of the Berlin Wall the USA had informally let it be known it would support reunification. This was confirmed on 21 November when Secretary of State James Baker reaffirmed US commitment to the process.

#### The Soviet Union

The USSR was less keen on reunification and still hoped that the GDR could reform itself. However, Gorbachev recognised realities. He was facing too many domestic problems and lacked the resources to prevent reunification. There was a crucial meeting with Helmut Kohl on 10 February when Kohl asserted what Gorbachev probably already knew: that the GDR was bankrupt and reunification was the only solution. Gorbachev responded that the German people must decide their own destiny.

However, he intended to drive a hard bargain over support for reunification (see page 430).

## Kohl's attitude to reunification

Chancellor Kohl's support for reunification was surprisingly controlled. Like other leaders he was anxious not to destabilise Europe or antagonise the USSR. In this respect Gorbachev's support must have come as a great relief. The events which energised Kohl were as follows:

- The fall of the Berlin Wall took Kohl by surprise and found him on a state visit to Poland from whence he flew hurriedly back on hearing the news.
- Demands from within the GDR were increasing. The call 'We are one people!' became almost ubiquitous.
- The USSR and USA were supportive (see page 428).
- Kohl was becoming worried about the scale of the exodus and the pressure hundreds of thousands of refugees were placing on the social welfare systems in the FRG. In January 1990 alone over 70,000 left for the FRG.
- In the FRG Parliament or Bundestag on 28 November 1989, Kohl introduced a 'ten-point' plan for a 'confederal' structure or gradual co-operation with the GDR. He hoped to slow down the demand for reunification. Unfortunately this had the opposite effect. In putting any sort of formal co-operation on the agenda, Kohl gave the green light for reunification. People did not listen to what he said; they only heard what they wanted him to say.

By December 1989, Kohl still felt reunification, if it took place at all, would take five to ten years. He favoured a gradual confederation, with aid packages to bring the GDR economy and infrastructures up to FRG standards before any formal union. The rapid collapse of the GDR made him change his mind – although he was flattered by the rapturous reception given him when he visited Dresden on 19 December.

### Reaction within the FRG

While many in the FRG supported reunification, others had concerns, particularly in terms of the cost and problems with acclimatisation of masses of emigrants from the GDR. Some left-wing groups within the FRG also feared the power of a reunified Germany and a possible return to its military past.

**Source F** Germans in the FRG demonstrate against reunification. The banners read: 'Never Again Germany'; 'Against the annexation of the GDR'; 'Against German Nationalism'. From the FRG newspaper *Der Spiegel*, 1990.

How useful is Source F in showing the opposition in the FRG to reunification?

## Reunification

Under pressure from the USA, Britain and France sat down with the USSR and representatives from the two Germanies to thrash out reunification – the so-called Four Plus Two Treaties. This resulted in the Final Settlement, signed in Moscow on 12 September 1990, which allowed reunification to go ahead.

- The borders of Germany were recognised as those of the two existing German states. This pleased Poland which had been worried Germany might want to take back the land it had forcibly ceded to Poland in 1945 (see page 323).
- The four power status in Berlin was ended from midnight on 2 October.
- The united Germany would join **NATO**.
- The Russian army would withdraw its troops from the territory of the former GDR by 1994.

Gorbachev did stipulate that NATO troops could not be stationed within 300 miles of the Polish border but this was ignored. Shortly there would be no USSR to complain.

In return for these concessions the Government of the USSR was awarded $8billion, although it had asked for $20billion.

Reunification formally went ahead on 3 October 1990, less than a year after the fall of the Berlin Wall. By 2003 it had cost the former FRG 1.2 trillion euros. The honeymoon over, both former West Germans and '***Ossis***' had plenty to complain about.

▲ **Figure 1: Europe in 1991 showing a reunified Germany.**

### *Ostalgie*

A survey conducted in 1998 suggested that only ten per cent of respondents living in the territory of the former GDR wanted to see its return. However, this does not mean people did not miss certain aspects of life in the GDR. Indeed within months of reunification there developed the phenomenon known as '*Ostalgie*'.

*Ostalgie* refers to nostalgia for certain elements of life in the GDR. Once the euphoria of reunification had worn off, many former citizens of the GDR were faced with a capitalist system for which they were largely unprepared. While the GDR may have been repressive it nevertheless offered 'cushions', particularly in terms of social welfare, which were now curtailed. The GDR had offered full employment, welfare benefits, cheap housing, free health provision and equality of educational opportunity so long as the student or their family had no background of dissent. With the reunited Germany came unemployment, whereas job security had been guaranteed before, and curtailed welfare benefits. By the early 1990s, unemployment in the former GDR had reached 30 per cent. There was also some resentment at the influx of managers and entrepreneurs from the West. Some '*Ossis*' felt as if they had been colonised.

More subtly perhaps many also felt disorientation and disempowerment. They were faced with a new type of society and did not know how to function effectively in it. Many resented the way the GDR had ended. It had been subsumed into the FRG and nothing of it remained. People were reluctant to criticise the GDR because they believed they would be criticising themselves and 40 years of their lives. Its failures were their failures. In October 2000, one citizen of the former GDR summarised what many must have felt: 'Life in the GDR was not so terrible, because it was a safe life. There was hardly any crime, and I did not have to worry about my future.'

### West Germans

Many West Germans also felt disillusioned with reunification because the East was, to them, so backward. They professed themselves shocked by the apparent squalor and shoddy goods. In the former GDR 33 per cent of the houses still had outdoor toilets, and 60 per cent lacked central heating. The German Government, meanwhile, invested DM 17 billion between 1991 and 1998 to subsidise wages and social services in the former GDR. Historian Tony Judt reported that by 2003 reunification had cost 1.2 trillion euros. This in turn led to slower economic growth throughout the **Eurozone** – so most members of the EU were paying for German reunification.

East Germans were criticised by their Western co-citizens for over-dependency on the state. The provision of work and welfare stifled independence and initiative. The merger of two distinct systems was not easy.

## Conclusion: The end of the GDR, 1989–90

Events both external and domestic conspired to diminish the influence of the SED. While it fought a rearguard action, its powers were inadequate to grasp the range and extent of the problems it faced, from the impact of Gorbachev and his reform agenda both in the USSR and the Soviet bloc to the threatened economic collapse of the GDR itself. The eventual collapse of the GDR in 1989 to 1990 is known as the '*Wende*' or change. This word seems too mild to describe the dramatic events which unfolded and came as such a shock to many.

Reunification may well have been a 'popular revolution' in that it caught politicians by surprise, with the FRG Chancellor anticipating a transition period of at least five years. The movement seemed unstoppable, and FRG politicians effectively hijacked the new political leaders within the GDR to fight the 1990 elections themselves, resulting in victory for the CDU. While foreign reluctance had to be overcome, the support of the USA facilitated this and treaties were signed which solved the existing post-war disputes as a prerequisite to reunification. However, it was not a painless process and some former GDR citizens felt nostalgia for the past.

## Conclusion: The German Democratic Republic, 1949–90

The GDR was a repressive state, although as one commentator has suggested it left behind a mountain of catalogue cards rather than corpses. The Stasi and other security forces were ubiquitous, applied mental and sometimes physical torture and operated a harsh prison regime. Nevertheless the fact that people were so surprised by the extent of their spying and operations suggests they were not a significant factor in the everyday lives of ordinary people.

The leadership of the GDR never felt secure. We have seen that after the 1953 revolt, they never again trusted their citizens. They also knew they were dependent on the USSR for their survival, a fact reinforced by Leonard Brezhnev in his July 1970 discussions with Erich Honecker. The building of the Berlin Wall and quest for international recognition were significant factors in their achieving external security. Even when this was achieved, however, they still lacked confidence. The attempts to gain international prestige and a heightened sense of national identity through sporting achievement based on illegal practices shows this.

While propaganda tried to stimulate a sense of national identity and allegiance, it seems ultimately the most important factor in the survival of the GDR was the unwritten agreement that the citizens should leave the SED to govern in return for the provision of basic standards. Erich Honecker once said that all people need was bread, a dry flat and a job. Unfortunately by the 1980s this was no longer true. The citizens had access to Western television and knowledge of developments elsewhere. Even if the Government had begun to slaughter its citizens it is difficult with hindsight to see how it could have survived in a rapidly changing world. Perhaps Brezhnev had been right: without the Soviet Union there would be no GDR. But with the collapse of communism elsewhere and the development of the information highway it is difficult to see how the GDR could have survived.

## Work together

Imagine you are faced with a Section B exam-style question as follows:

**'Reunification of Germany was dictated by the population rather than the politicians.' How far do you agree with this statement?**

1. Working in pairs, one of you should prepare a response which agrees with the statement and the other one which disagrees with it. Discuss your findings and agree on the information a balanced answer should contain.
2. Each of you should now write out the answer, including a valid judgement at the end based on the evidence you have deployed. Read each other's answers. How similar are they?

## Chapter summary

- By the 1980s the GDR economy could not afford to maintain levels of welfare and defence spending.
- The economy of the GDR was subject to serious weaknesses, for example inefficiencies in planning and production and lack of investment.
- Rising fuel prices in particular caused serious trading deficits.
- To combat fuel shortages the GDR promoted the production of cheap lignite coal which was highly pollutant.
- Improvements in the economy as a result of oil exports came at the cost of falls in living standards and infrastructures.
- Economic relations with the FRG continued to develop, for example with the substantial loans of 1983 and 1984.
- The reformist leader of the Soviet Union, Mikhail Gorbachev, became hugely popular in the GDR but the SED leadership opposed his ideas.
- The Protestant Churches protected more opposition groups.
- While there was widespread infiltration by the Stasi, opposition groups grew, for example peace and environmental groups.
- The later 1980s saw more repression.
- The opening of the border between Hungary and Austria prompted an emigration crisis in the GDR.
- Mass protests grew, for example in Leipzig, demanding reforms and democratisation.
- The Berlin Wall came down in November 1989 and people began to talk of reunification.
- After the collapse of the SED, the demise of the GDR seemed inevitable although its speed took everyone by surprise.
- The GDR ceased to exist and Germany was reunited on 3 October 1990.

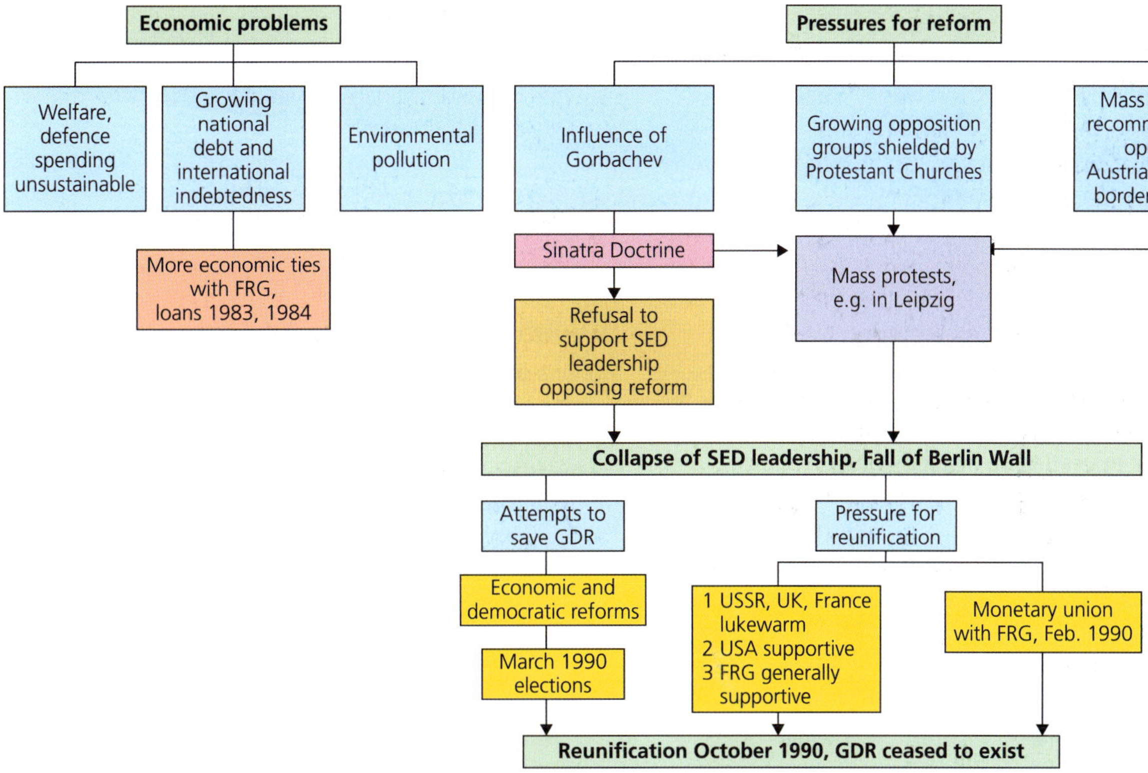


▲ **Summary diagram: Growing crises and the collapse of communist rule in the GDR, 1985–90.**

## Recommended reading

P. Grieder, *The German Democratic Republic* (Palgrave Macmillan, 2012). Succinct analysis with consideration of current interpretations.

C. Hilton, *The Wall: The People's Story* (Sutton Publishing, 2001). Human accounts of life behind the Berlin Wall – and the events which led to its coming down.

A. J. McAdams, *Germany Divided: From the Wall to Reunification* (Princeton University Press, 1993). Readable analysis of Ostpolitik and reunification from the perspective both of the GDR and FRG.

J. Simpson, *The Darkness Crumbles: Dispatches from the Barricades* (Hutchinson, 1992), especially Part III. A masterful commentary as communism collapsed in Eastern Europe.

## Work together

You have reached the end of this book now. This is a good moment to check through your notes and make sure that they are complete. In this final 'work together' activity you will do this with one twist – you will check each other's notes. Together, go through the specification and this book. Create a table. In the first column put the big topic, for example 'Establishing and consolidating communist rule in the GDR'. In the second column put the subsections, for example 'The post-war division of Germany'. Head the third column 'Notes' and the final column 'Revision'. Now swap folders and complete the following tasks for your partner:

- Put the notes in order.
- In the 'notes' column, tick if your partner has a good set of notes on a sub-topic. Leave it blank if they do not have notes or if they are incomplete. You can also use this column to note the type of notes, for example class notes, index cards, independent reading.
- Leave the 'revision' column blank. As your partner revises they can then use this column to tick off the sub-topics as they go.

Now swap your folders again. This should highlight any areas of strength and weakness in your folders.

# Section A: Essay technique

## Evaluating the sources

Evaluating the sources is essential to doing well in the exam. It means working out how far the sources contain evidence that is useful to a historian doing a specific task. There are different levels of evaluation, which are rewarded to different extents.

First, your source evaluation must be relevant to the question:

- Source evaluation that is not clearly linked to the question will be awarded marks in the lower levels.
- Source evaluation which is clearly relevant to the question will be awarded marks in the higher levels.

Secondly, there is the issue of the criteria you use to evaluate the sources see table below.

| | |
|---|---|
| Level 1 | **No criteria** – evaluation is extremely superficial, it does not relate to any criteria. |
| Level 2 | **Questionable criteria** – evaluation is based on a criterion, but the criterion is invalid, simplistic or poorly understood. |
| Level 3 | **Formulaic criteria** – evaluation is based on a discussion of the **nature, origin and purpose** (NOP) of the source. |
| Level 4/5 | **Valid criteria** – at this level responses will use criteria that reflect the kind of source and the kind of specific task that the question focuses on. In this sense the evaluation will be tailored to the question.<br>At Level 4 the criteria will not be applied rigorously.<br>At Level 5 the criteria will be applied rigorously. |

## Evaluating the sources: the criteria

Imagine you are answering the following question:

**How far could the historian make use of Sources 1 and 2 together to investigate the nature of the emigration crisis in the GDR from September to November 1989?**

**Source 1** From *The New York Times*, 10 November, 1989**.**

Mr. Schabowski also said the decision ended the agreement to let East Germans leave through Czechoslovakia and other countries. Some 50,000 East Germans have left through Czechoslovakia, and a 14-mile-long queue of East German cars was reported Thursday at the Schirnding border crossing on the Czech-West German border. Since September, thousands more have left through Hungary and Poland. East German radio announced that the uncontrolled crossings would be ended at 8 A.M. today, after which East Germans would be required to obtain a visa ...

... The extraordinary breach of what had been the most infamous stretch of the Iron Curtain marked the culmination of an extraordinary month that has seen the virtual transformation of East Germany under the dual pressures of unceasing flight and continuing demonstrations. It also marked a breach of a wall that had become the premier symbol of Stalinist oppression and of the divisions of Europe and Germany into hostile camps after World War II.

An Effort to Stem a Tide

The immediate reason for the decision was evidently a recognition by East Germany's embattled authorities that they could not stem the outward tide by opening the door a crack and hoping that rapid liberalization at home would end the urge to flee. They now seemed to hope that an open door would quickly let out those who were determined to leave, and give pause to those who had doubted the sincerity of the Government's pledge of profound change.

**Source 2** Excerpts from the transcript of the Tenth Session of the SED Central Committee, 9 November 1989. Source: SAPMO–BA, tape Y 1/TD 738, transcribed in Hans-Hermann Hertle and Gerd-Rüdiger Stephan (eds.), *Das Ende der SED: Die letzten Tage des Zentralkomitees*, 4th edition (Berlin: Dietz, 1999), pages 303–6. Translated for CWIHP by Howard Sargeant.

**Krenz:** You are aware that there is a problem that wears on us all: the question of exit [from the GDR]. The Czechoslovak comrades are increasingly finding it a burden, as our Hungarian comrades did earlier. And, whatever we do in this situation, it will be a move in the wrong direction. If we close the border to Czechoslovakia then we are basically punishing the upstanding citizens of the GDR, who would not be able to travel, and in this way put pressure on us. Even that would not have led to our gaining control of the situation, since the Permanent Mission of the FRG has already informed us that they have finished with renovations. That means that when they open the building, we will face the same problem again[1].

Decision to change the situation for permanent exit of GDR citizens to the FRG via the SSR[2].

It is decreed:

1. The decree of 30 November 1988 about travel abroad for GDR citizens will no longer be applied until the new travel law comes into force.
2. Starting immediately, the following temporary transition regulation for travel abroad and permanent exits from the GDR are in effect:
   a) Applications for travel abroad by private individuals can now be made without the previously existing requirements (of demonstrating a need to travel or proving familial relationships). The travel authorisations will be issued on short notice.
   b) Grounds for denial will only be applied in particularly exceptional cases.

[...]

   c) Permanent exits are possible via all GDR border crossings to the FRG and (West) Berlin.
   d) The temporary practice of issuing (travel) authorisations through GDR consulates and permanent exit with only a GDR personal identity card via third countries ceases.
3. The attached press release explaining the temporary transition regulation will be issued on 10 November ...: 'As the Press Office of the Ministry of the Interior has announced, the GDR Council of Ministers has decided that the following temporary transition regulation for travel abroad and permanent exit from the GDR will be effective until a corresponding law is put into force by the *Volkskammer*.'

... I said that however way we do this, it will turn out bad. But it is the only solution that saves us from the problems of having to do everything through third countries, which does not further the international prestige of the GDR.

[1] The FRG had been closed for renovations. When it reopened it would be filled again with refugees from the GDR.

[2] Socialist Soviet Republic, in this case Hungary.

## Simplistic source analysis

Having read the sources it is clear that Source 1 is biased against the Government of the GDR. However, this would be a low-level response, because it is not clear why you consider Source 1 biased. Additionally, it is not clear how this statement answers the question.

You could say that Source 1 is unreliable because we do not know whether the author was there to see the Wall opened. However, this is based on questionable criteria: it assumes that only eyewitnesses are useful to historians, which is not true. Additionally, the author of the article is not claiming to be an eyewitness – so the criteria are not appropriate to the source.

Based on this here are two basic tips:

- Avoid simply saying 'Source 1 is biased'. Statements like this are very simplistic and are therefore unlikely to get you a good mark.
- Avoid assuming that the only useful sources are eyewitness accounts.

## Nature, origin and purpose

One way of evaluating the sources is to ask questions about the nature, origin and purpose of the sources:

- Nature: what type of source is this?
- Origin: when and where does the source come from?
- Purpose: why did the author write the source?

This approach is a good place to start. It is also better than making simplistic statements about sources. However, it can lead to formulaic responses, which are unlikely to gain top marks.

## Evaluating sources in their own terms

The best way of evaluating sources is to try to understand them in their own terms. Reading the sources in the context of the time is a good way of evaluating their usefulness. By situating the sources on pages 434–35 in their context, we can argue the following:

- First, **Source 2** comes from a transcript of the actual discussions held by the Politiburo at the time. It shows us how they were thinking. Krenz is worried about losing control of the situation concerning would-be emigrants and also the international reputation of the GDR. By contrast, **Source 1** argues that the fall of the Berlin Wall marks the climax of a series of momentous events and is a recognition that the Government of the GDR had lost control of events. In that sense there is a contrast in the sources in that one shows how the Politburo is trying to regain control of a situation which the newspaper article asserts is lost. Therefore, both sources are useful in the sense that they reflect the differing positions of the Politburo and a journalist trying to analyse the situation.
- Secondly, **Source 2** shows the desperation of the Politburo. Krenz acknowledges that either way it will turn out bad. This then is a damage limitation exercise to prevent the international prestige of the GDR falling even lower. It also emphasises the temporary nature of the decision – until the *Volkskammer* comes up with a permanent law. If the situation had resolved itself the new law could have prevented emigration again. It is this uncertainty that fuelled mass emigration – liberalising policies could be rescinded when circumstances allowed. **Source 1**, however, does suggest that the new emigration policy is a safety valve to rid the country of those who are determined to go while attempting to win the trust of those who remain.
- Thirdly, the sources agree in the pressures facing the Politburo. **Source 2** talks of problems for GDR allies Hungary and Czechoslovakia as a result of the emigration crisis and of international prestige. **Source 1** also shows how bad the GDR looks and adds useful detail such as the 14-mile-long queues to show the extent of the problem.
- Finally, the sources do not give the full picture of emigration from the GDR. Neither mentions any reasons for the level of emigration nor the previous regulations concerning emigration.

**TIPs:**

- Use what you have already learned to help you understand the sources.
- The dates of the sources are often significant. Use what you already know to explore the possible significance of the dates, places and people mentioned in the sources.
- Remember that sources are contributing to a debate. Use your knowledge to situate the sources in the wider debate.

Having read the advice on evaluating the sources, try to evaluate the sources in answer to the question below.

**How far could the historian make use of Sources 3 and 4 together to investigate reactions to the idea of German reunification in 1989 to 1990?**

**Source 3** From an article by Sir Ralf Dahrendorf, 'Germans Lack the Key to Their National Identity', published in the *Independent*, 13 April 1990.

> The German problem of 1990 has to do with money and with identity, both shrouded in dreams and elusions. Perhaps the East Germans will rise up again, once they discover that instead of voting for unity on 18 March they have elected a government bent on recreating their non-existent state and on engaging in endless national and international negotiations. In fact East Germans do not need to rise - they can simply pack up and leave, as 5000 are still doing each week. West Germans on the other hand, seem more worried about the value of the Deutschmark, jobs and housing. Oskar Lafontaine, the Social Democrat candidate for Chancellor in this year's elections, is unlikely to win but he has caught the mood of many with his insistence that social achievements in both the Germanys must not be jeopardised.

**Source 4** From Josef Joffe, 'Germany, Reunification II: This Time No Hobnailed Boots', published in *The New York Times*, 30 September 1990.

> Power in Europe ... is measured not by conquest but by capital surpluses. Not booty or glory define the stakes but questions such as: 'Who determines currency parities?'[1] ... The battle lines are drawn in the balance of payments ledgers and the accounts are settled with dollars and Deutschmarks not blood and iron[2]. The rivalry is about joint welfare not this or that province: both sides lose or win together ...
>
> Still, might not Bonn-Berlin hanker after nuclear weapons and push for revision of eastern borders? What for? The new, more civilised and civilising game of nations offers the largest payoffs to nations such as Germany and Japan. The game has devalued the military chips, delivering power and prestige to those who can back up their bets with investments and loans. Why then should they forego their advantage by changing the rules? In the attempt, they would certainly revive the hostile coalitions that proved their undoing in 1945.

[1] Currency parities – the respective value of currencies.
[2] Blood and iron – reference to German militarism during the nineteenth century.

## Activity: Evaluating the sources

1 Having read the sources on page 436, try to put them in context by answering the following questions:

**a)** What events were taking place in the GDR at the time these sources were written?

**b)** Explain what is meant by the sentence: 'Perhaps the East Germans will rise up again, once they discover that instead of voting for unity on 18 March they have elected a government bent on recreating their non-existent state and on engaging in endless national and international negotiations.'

**c)** What fear relating to a reunified Germany is Source 4 responding to?

2 Now try to evaluate the usefulness of the sources by answering the following questions:

**a)** What does each of the sources argue about reunification of Germany?

**b)** How similar and different are their arguments?

**c)** How far do the sources reflect the full range of debate over the different reactions to reunification in 1989 to 1990?

3 Summarise the extent to which the sources are useful to the historian studying the reactions to reunification in 1989 to 1990. Make sure you deal with the ways in which they are useful and the limits of their usefulness.

## Work together

Having completed Activities 1-3 above, swap them with a partner. Consider the following questions:

1 How far did you agree on the context of the sources?
2 How far did you agree on the usefulness of the sources?
3 If you disagreed on the context or the usefulness, what was helpful in each other's approach?
4 Whose summary of the usefulness of the sources was better and why?

Use this discussion to make a note of three ways that you can improve your Section A technique.

## Activity: AS-style questions

1 Why is Source 3 (page 436) valuable to a historian studying the reasons for German reunification in 1990?

2 How much weight do you give the evidence of Source 4 (page 436) for an enquiry into the possible remilitarisation of a reunited Germany?

## Reaching an overall judgement

Having understood, contextualised and evaluated the sources you should finish your essay with an overall judgement. Reaching a supported overall judgement is an important part of doing well in Section A. Your judgement in Section A is similar to the judgement that you should reach in the other sections of the exam (see pages 68–9). However, in Section A, your judgement should be based on an evaluation of the evidence offered by the sources.

Your judgement should:

- clearly answer the question
- be supported by weighing the evidence of the sources.

In addition to this, the very best essays will distinguish between the levels of certainty of the different aspects of the conclusion.

Imagine you are answering the question on page 436.

Having already read the sources and evaluated them in their context as you did in the activity above, it is possible to reach the overall conclusion below. This is a high-level conclusion as it focuses on the question, reaches a supported judgement and discusses the different levels of certainty of the different claims it makes.

### Work together

Conclusions are made up of a series of claims (a claim is a statement, in this case about the usefulness of the sources for investigating reactions to reunification in Germany between 1989 and 1990).

1. Count the number of claims made in the conclusion below.
2. Do you agree on the number of claims – if not discuss your different views and try to resolve the disagreement.
3. The different claims deal with a series of issues that are not all certain. Did you both spot the same words and phrases?

Use the list and your discussion to make a note of how you could improve your writing.

This focuses directly on the question.

Together the sources are partially useful to a historian studying the different reactions to German reunification between 1989 and 1990. Source 3 looks at problems both in the GDR and the FRG while Source 4 examines wider concerns, in this case the possible resurgence of a military superpower. Source 3 emphasises that at the time of writing, 13 April 1990, the GDR still existed and the electorate had voted for a GDR government not for a reunited Germany. It shows that GDR citizens could still decide to migrate, while those of the FRG were concerned about the cost of reunification and the pressures it may place on the social infrastructure. Source 4 addresses concerns about the remilitarisation of Germany by arguing that it is far more likely to develop its economic power. The sources fail to consider a reunited Germany's foreign relations or indeed international reactions to reunification. There is no mention of reactions to how well the two former states will mesh together. They do not mention how different the GDR and FRG are or the economic problems in the former GDR compared to those in the former FRG. For this reason they are partially useful but more evidence would be necessary to gain a more detailed survey of reactions. Together then the sources could be used to show concerns within the two countries prior to reunification and wider concerns but are partial in covering the complete range of reactions.

The sources are used explicitly and together.

The sources' limitations are acknowledged.

Contextual knowledge is used to explore the limits of the sources' usefulness.

The limits of the sources are summarised.

The uses are also summarised, and a conclusion reached which is supported by the rest of the paragraph.

Imagine you are answering the following question:

**How far could the historian make use of Sources 5 and 6 together to investigate the influence of Mikhail Gorbachev on the demise of the GDR?**

**Source 5** From John Simpson, *The Darkness Crumbles: Dispatches from the Barricades* (Hutchinson, 1992). Simpson is a noted British journalist who reported on the collapse of communism throughout Eastern Europe. Here he is writing about Gorbachev at the 40th anniversary celebrations in the GDR.

If Honecker had ... had no Soviet tanks to back [him], then the only bar to greater freedom was their security police and their army. Gorbachev may have actively undermined [him]; and it was clear he wanted to be rid of [him].

... the guest of honour at the celebrations on 7 October exploded a device of his own. Mikhail Gorbachev allowed it to be known he had warned Erich Honecker that Soviet troops would not be available for use against demonstrations in the GDR. Speculation that he was encouraging the younger and more liberal members of the Politburo to overthrow Honecker grew when he said, 'Life punishes those who hold back.'

**Source 6** Article in the *Los Angeles Times*, 25 October 1989.

'Sinatra Doctrine' at Work in Warsaw Pact, Soviet Says

WASHINGTON – Soviet Foreign Ministry spokesman Gennadi I. Gerasimov today said the Soviet Union has adopted the 'Sinatra Doctrine' in its policy toward Warsaw Pact nations -- they can do things their way. Gerasimov appeared on ABC's 'Good Morning America' to discuss the speech delivered Monday by Soviet Foreign Minister Eduard A. Shevardnadze in which he said that the Soviets now recognise the absolute freedom of choice of all countries, specifically the Warsaw Pact nations.

That marks a huge departure from the past, in which Eastern European countries that strayed too far from communist orthodoxy found Soviet armies on their doorsteps.

'We now have the Frank Sinatra doctrine,' said Gerasimov. 'He has a song, 'I (Did) It My Way.' So every country decides on its own which road to take.'

## Activity: Write your own conclusion

1 Read the question, the sources and the information about the sources above.

2 Put the sources in context:
  **a)** What is the significance of the dates of the sources?
  **b)** What debate or debates are the sources contributing to?
  **c)** How far do the sources agree on the role of Gorbachev?
  **d)** Why did Gorbachev adopt the policies outlined in the sources?

3 Read the question again.

4 Next, write a series of bullet points outlining:
  – the aspects of the sources that are useful for answering the question
  – the aspects of the sources that are less useful
  – a summary of the extent to which the sources provide useful evidence concerning Gorbachev's attitude to the GDR.

5 Now write the conclusion. Remember:
  – You need to weigh the evidence, and therefore you should use words that help you to do that such as 'clearly', 'however' and 'nonetheless'.
  – You should weigh the sources *together*, rather than separately. Make sure you use words and phrases that make it clear that this is what you are doing.
  – You should try to specify how certain you are about your various concluding claims.

## Work together

Having completed your conclusion in the activity above, swap it with a partner. Consider the following questions:

**1** How far did you agree on the context of the sources?
**2** How far did you agree on the usefulness of the sources?
**3** Which conclusion most effectively weighed the evidence of the sources? How was this achieved?
**4** Did both conclusions really consider the sources *together*? How could you improve this aspect of your writing?
**5** Which conclusion most effectively expressed the different degrees of certainty? How was this achieved?
**6** Which conclusion most effectively focused on the question?

Use this discussion to make notes on how you can improve your Section A technique.

# Section B: Essay technique

## Argument, counter-argument and resolution

The highest marks in Section B of the exam are available for sustained analysis. One way of achieving this is to write an essay that develops a clear argument, a counter-argument, and then reaches a resolution. This approach is outlined in the activities that support Paper 1 (see pages 93, 107 and 130–131). This kind of structure is equally applicable to Paper 2 Section B.

### Activity

Imagine you are answering the following question:

**How far was Hungary's decision to open its borders with Austria a turning point in the decision in November 1989 to reopen the Berlin Wall?**

1 Read the question and work out what type of question it is.
2 Make a plan that is appropriate to the specific question. Rather than simply picking four relevant factors, develop an argument, a counter-argument and a resolution to the argument.
3 Add three pieces of detail to support each aspect of your essay. Remember, use the detail that best supports the argument you are creating.
4 Write an introduction that sets out the essential aspects of your argument, counter-argument and resolution.
5 Now write a conclusion to the essay.
   - Start by asserting an overall judgement.
   - Support this by writing an evaluative summary of your argument, counter-argument and resolution.
   - Summarise your overall judgement in the final sentence.

### Work together

Having written your introduction and conclusion in the activity swap them with a partner. Consider the following questions:

1 Did you agree on what type of question you were dealing with? If not, discuss it and work out who was right.
2 Whose plan set out the most compelling overall argument?
3 Which introduction most clearly set out the key claims of your essay?
4 Which conclusion best summarised and evaluated the argument, counter-argument and resolution?
5 What can you learn from each other's work?

Use these questions to feed back to each other and improve your essay technique.

### Question practice

1 How far was the GDR's economic weakness responsible for the collapse of the Communist regine in 1989? AS
2 How accurate is it to say that the living standards of citizens of the GDR improved in the years 1976–1989? AS
3 'The Economy of the GDR was in crisis throughout the 1980s.' How far do you agree with this statement?
4 How far did the Protestant Churches contribute to the protest movements which developed in the 1980s?

# GLOSSARY

## Paper 1: Russia 1917–91: from Lenin to Yeltsin

**1905 Revolution** A series of events during 1905 in Russia which threatened to overthrow the Tsar. The 1905 revolution did not destroy Tsarism, but it did lead to some reforms.

**9+1** An agreement between the Soviet government and nine Republics to create a federation to replace the Soviet Union.

**Absenteeism** Regularly missing work without a good reason.

**All-Russian Congress of Soviets** An organisation representing the whole of Russia. The Congress was elected by Soviets across the whole nation. It met semi-regularly between 1917 and 1922 to decide policy for the whole of Russia. In theory it was the highest law making organisation in the Soviet Union from 1922. However, in reality the leadership of the Communist Party exercised power.

**Anarchists** Political radicals or groups of radicals who wanted the Russian revolution to destroy capitalism and the state. Anarchists were critical of Communists for reintroducing a political police, and for recreating an army after the revolution. The anarchists believed that the Communist government, like all governments, would be repressive.

**Approval rating** An opinion poll in which people pass judgement on a leader.

**Arms race** A competition to develop and produce increasingly deadly weapons. During the Cold War the Arms Race focused on nuclear missiles.

**Authoritarian** A policy, or a style of government that emphasises the importance of strong government control and obedience. Authoritarian governments often have extensive powers with few limits.

**Autonomy** Self-government.

**Black market** The illegal trading of goods and services.

**Bolsheviks** A faction of the Russian Social Democratic Party, led by Lenin. The Bolsheviks led the 1917 Revolution and later called themselves the Communist Party.

**Bourgeoisies** The term used by Karl Marx to describe the middle class.

**Cadre** A group of leaders.

**Capitalism** An economic system based on free trade and the private ownership of property.

**Capri pants** Trousers that were extremely fashionable in the 1950s and 1960s among American women. They tended to by high-waisted and three quarter length, ending mid-calf.

**Central Control Commission** The body within the Communist Party that was responsible for investigating and disciplining Party Members who were accused of corruption.

**Central Powers** A military alliance during the First World War between the German Empire, the Austro-Hungarian Empire and the Ottoman Empire.

**Centralised** A form of organisation in which power is concentrated at the centre. For example, in the Soviet Union, power was centralised in the sense that it was exercised by the leaders of the Communist Party, rather than being dispersed throughout the government or country.

**Cheka** A political police force created by Lenin.

**CIA** Central Intelligence Agency.

**Class enemies** Individuals and groups who were considered to oppose the working class and therefore the Communist Party.

**Class, or social class** Groups of people who have a similar economic and social status, for example the working class and the middle class.

**Coalition government** A government controlled by an alliance of two or more political parties.

**Co-education** Education of female and male students in the same institution.

**Colonies** A territory that is under the control of another state, part of an empire.

**Command economy** An economic system that is centrally directed. Production is organised in accordance with orders issued by the central government.

**Constituent Assembly** An elected body which was supposed to agree a constitution for Russia after the Tsar was deposed. The Assembly met once and was then dissolved by force by Lenin's revolutionary government.

**Constitution of 1918** a document published in 1918 setting out the structure and powers of Lenin's new revolutionary government. Significantly, the Constitution did not reflect the actual nature of Lenin's government which was based on the power of the Communist Party rather than democratically elected Soviets.

**Continuous assessment** A way of judging student work and progress on an on-going basis, rather than through final exams.

**Co-operatives** Businesses that are owned and operated by their workers.

**Corporal punishment** Physical discipline, such as smacking or caning, which inflicts pain as a form of punishment.

**Cosmonaut** A Soviet space traveller.

**Counter-revolutionaries** Individuals and groups who opposed the Communist Party.

**Coup d'état** A violent seizure of power.

**Critique** A well thought through analysis of a policy or point of view.

**Dacha** A holiday house.

**Decrees** Laws usually issued by the central government.

**Despotism** A kind of government in which one person or one groups holds all power.

**Détente** Name given to the process of removal of tensions between the superpowers in the late 1960s and 1970s; features included arms limitations agreements, and state visits.

**English, American and French Revolutions** Russian Communists and Marxists more generally believed that the English, American and French Revolutions had swept away aristocratic governments and created capitalist governments.

**Exit Visas** Documents allowing Soviet citizens to leave the Soviet Union.

**Faction** Groups of people within a political party, who share a common set of beliefs and who are in opposition to the leadership of the party.

**First World War** A global conflict, mainly fought in Europe, between 1914 and 1919. The main participants in the conflict were the French, British and Russian Empires, fighting the Central Powers.

**Flapper style** A fashion similar to that worn by stylish American women in the 1920s.

**Forced confessions** Confessions obtained under interrogation or torture.

**Free love** A social movement that rejected marriage.

**Freedom of assembly** The right to meet with others and organise politically or socially.

**Freedom of expression** The right to speak in public or private, as well as to publish.

**Freedom of religion** The right to believe in or practice whatever religion you chose, or to refrain from religious faith and practice.

**Grain requisitioning** The policy of seizing grain from peasants without payment. Grain requisitioning was often accompanied by violence.

**Gross Domestic Product (GDP)** The total wealth produced by a country in a given period.

**Gulags** Prison labour camps

**Hardliners** A political group reluctant to accept new ideas.

**Helsinki Agreement** An agreement aimed at improving relations between the communist bloc and the West.

**Hyperinflation** An economic situation in which inflation increases dramatically, usually for a sustained period.

**Iconography** Symbolism in which specific images have an accepted meaning

**Idealists** People who believe that governments, organisations and individuals should do what is morally right, regardless of the consequences.

**Imperialism** Either the belief that creating, expanding and defending an empire is beneficial, or policies designed to create, expand and defend an empire.

**Institutions** Organisations that have a social purpose. This can include groups such as churches, schools, government departments and political parties. Social structures such as the family or marriage can also be describe as institutions.

**Internal passports** Documents that allow citizens to travel from one region of a country to another.

**Labour camps** Prison camps built in the late 1920s to house tens of thousands of prisoners. The prisoners were forced to work on big construction projects such as dams or factories. Prison camps were often built in extremely cold parts of Russia. Prisoners were fed barely enough food to survive and, as a result, were effectively worked to death.

**Light industry** Manufacturing that produces consumer goods.

**Mensheviks** A faction of the Russian Social Democratic Party which disagreed with Lenin's interpretation of revolutionary politics. The majority of Mensheviks opposed the October Revolution. The Party continued until the early 1920s when it as finally outlawed by the Communists.

**Monogamous marriage** Marriage with only one person at a time.

**Minister of the Interior** The member of the government responsible for law and order within the Soviet Union.

**Moscow Metro** The underground train network in Moscow.

**Nationalisation** The process by which private property is taken over by the state.

**Nobel Peace Prize** A highly regarded international prize awarded to individuals who have made significant progress in promoting peace.

***Nomenklatura*** Administrators in the Communist Party or the Soviet government.

**Non-conformity** A type of social deviance when a person or group refuse to conform to expected customs, rules, standards or expectations.

**Party theorist** The party leader responsible for analysing the progress of the revolution and explaining it in Marxist terms.

**People's Commissariat of Foreign Affairs** The part of the Communist government that dealt with relations with other countries.

**People's Commissariat of Nationality Affairs** The part of the Communist government that dealt with relations between the different nationalities within the Soviet Union.

**Plateaued** To reach a state in where there is little or no change. In terms of the economy, where the economy stops growing without shrinking.

**Pluralistic** containing a variety of different groups and points of view.

**Politburo** The most senior committee in the Communist Party. For much of the period 1919-1991 the Politburo was effectively the government of the Soviet Union.

**Power vacuum** A political situation in which there is no obvious leader.

**Pragmatic** A person, policy or organisation that makes decisions for practical reasons. Pragmatism is often contrasted with idealism.

**Prefabricated** Ready-made. In terms of architecture, prefabricated buildings contain large sections that are made in factories that can then be assembled quickly during the building process.

**Pretext** A reason that is given which conceals the genuine motive for an action

**Profiteering** Making money through illegal trade.

**Proletariat** A term used by Marxists to describe the class of industrial workers and their families.

**Pronatal** Advocating and advancing childbirth.

**Provisional Government** The government that ruled the Russian Empire on a temporary basis after the fall of the Tsar. The Provisional Government was deposed by Lenin's October Revolution.

**Public sphere** A social realm in which people discuss politics and engage in paid work.

**Rabkrin** The Workers' and Peasants' Inspectorate: a body set up by Lenin to investigate allegations of corruption in the Communist Party. It had the power to discipline and sack members of the Community Party.

**Raw materials** Materials such as oil, coal and iron. These are not finished goods, but are used to create finished goods.

**Red Army** The Soviet Army

**Redistribution** Taking property from one group and giving it to another.

**Rehabilitated** The process by which Communists who were considered criminals by Stalin were pardoned or found not guilty of their alleged crimes after Stalin's death.

**Resolution** A proposal submitted to the Communist Party Congress.

**Russian Federation** The largest nation to emerge from the collapse of the Soviet Union.

**Satellite states** A state that is formally independent, but under heavy influence from another state.

**Sheet steel** Thin, large, flat pieces of steel

**Show Trials** Trials to illustrate an issue where the guilt of the accused is never in doubt.

**Slavs** An ethnic group largely located in central and eastern Europe, the majority ethnic group in Russia.

**Social insurance** Usually government run schemes that provides unemployment benefits and healthcare for working people.

**Social malaise** A situation in which there are widespread social problems, as well as wide spread cynicism, despair and anxiety

**Socialism** An ideology and a political system based on the belief that people should be treated equally. Communists also use the term to refer to a historical period that occurs after capitalism but before communism.

**Sovereign** Possessing supreme power – self governing

**Soviets** Small democratically elected councils which emerged spontaneously after the February Revolution.

**Space Race** An unofficial competition between the US and the Soviet Union to demonstrate their superiority in space travel and exploration. The Space Race was particularly fierce between 1955 and 1972.

**Status quo** The established order.

**Stocks and shares** Forms of private ownership, in which businesses are sold to multiple owners. Parts of the company are known as stocks and shares.

**Tacit** An agreement or understanding that is implied or unstated.

**Tax in kind** A tax in which producers pay the government a proportion of what they make, rather than paying in money.

**Turkic people** An ethnic group living largely in western Asia and eastern Europe.

**United Opposition** A group within the Communist Party lead by Trotsky, Zinoviev and Kamenev that opposed the policies of Stalin and Bukharin.

**Workers' Control** Allows workers to participate in the management of factories.

## Paper 2: Mao's China, 1949–76

**Acupuncture** Ancient Chinese medical practice that uses needles to stimulate pressure points within the body.

**Agrobiologist** A scientist who studies plants and soil conditions in order to increase crop yields.

**Auschwitz** Nazi execution camp built during World War II. Over a million people deemed as racial inferiors by the Nazi State such as Jews and Gypsies were murdered there.

**Autarkic state** A state that is self-sufficient and does not really on help such as trade with other countries.

**Backyard furnaces** Small furnaces that Mao demanded the peasants build during the Great Leap Forward. Mao ordered the peasants to melt down their belongings including cooking utensils and farm tools to make steel. He believed that this would radically increase China's steel production and aid his plan to modernise the economy, but the steel created in the small furnaces was of such poor quality that it was of no use.

**Balanced the budget** The practice of the government not spending more money than it has earned back through trade and taxation.

**Bourgeois feudal classes** A term used by the Communists to denounce opponents as counter-revolutionaries. The Bourgeois were property owners and therefore, a class enemy. Feudal society had a power structure whereby lords demanded services or taxes from peasants in return for permission to work land. Although this feudal society never existed in China, in Mao's eyes its exploitative nature meant that it was like the unequal and outdated type of society in China, and must be destroyed.

**Bourgeoisie** In Marxist thought, the Bourgeoisie are a wealthy class of property owners who are dedicated to retaining the economic power and influence.

**Bureaucratic** A bureaucracy is a very hierarchical system of government administration acting according to set rules. Mao feared that once it came to power, the Communist Party itself would become bureaucratic. Instead of an agent of revolutionary change, it would establish order and rules and act only its own interests, no longer those of the masses of Chinese people. Thus the CCP would become a counter-revolutionary force, an elite just like the one that it had previously fought against.

**Cadres** Dedicated and ideologically committed Communists who were tasked with putting Mao's policies into practice.

**Capitalist** Economic system that advocated free markets and competition for profit between privately owned businesses. Derided as inherently unequal by the Communists because it led to some people earning great wealth whilst others, they believed, were exploited and paid low wages.

**Capitalist roader** A believer in capitalism (see above). Often a convenient label used by the Communists to identify anyone who did not agree with the regime as an opponent.

**Chief of staff** Senior official whose job is to co-ordinate other members of the government in order to put a leaders policies into action.

**Christian missionaries** Christians who travelled to China to spread the message of the Bible.

**Clans** Social organization made up of people with shared ancestors and surnames, sometimes living in the same house. Often members would have very different class and economic situations. The CCP needed to break down the kinship ties and traditionally close loyalties within these clans in order to impose its class based ideology.

**Class-consciousness** According to Marx, before revolution could take place, the people had to acquire a sense that belonged to a social class. Instead of identifying themselves according to racial, regional or ethnic group, they needed to see themselves as suffering the same kind of exploitation as other members of their class. Therefore, a peasant from Canton needed to see that he shared the same plight as one from Hunan. Although they spoke different languages and had very different cultures, they would come to see that they had much in common, namely that they were exploited by their landlords. Once they realized this, they could band together and organize a revolution.

**Common Program for China** Interim Constitution approved by the Chinese People's Political Consultative Conference (CPPCC) in 1949. It set out the structure of the new government and acted as the constitution of China until a permanent constitution was written in 1954.

**Concubines** Women kept as mistresses by married Chinese men. Emperors of China kept thousands of concubines for their sexual pleasure. The practice was banned by the Communists.

**Confucian** The beliefs of the Chinese philosopher, Confucius, who was born in 551 BC. His ideas about ethics, family loyalty and respect for government were hugely influential in China.

**Conscripted** Being forced to join the army, as opposed to volunteering to join. A conscription law was officially introduced in China in 1955, recruiting approximately 800,000 people a year.

**Constitution** Written document that sets out powers of the government and the rights of the people. First introduced in China in 1954.

**Containment** American anti-Communist Cold War policy dedicated to preventing the spread of Communism.

**Co-operative farms** Farms were peasants pooled their labour and resources such as animals, tools and fertiliser.

**Counter-revolutionaries** A label used to identify opponents of the Communist revolution.

**CPPCC Chinese People's Consultative Conference** Meeting organised in 1949 after the Communist's victory in the Civil War. Representatives from a range of parties were invited to discuss the creation of the new Chinese state.

**Cult of personality** An idealized propaganda image created to convince the masses that a leader has near super-human and divine powers. Mao's Cult of Personality, which described Mao as 'The Great Helmsman' who would steer China to a utopian future, reached absurd heights during the Cultural Revolution.

**Cultural Revolution** Period of violent upheaval in China between 1966 and 1976 during which Mao encouraged young people to join Red Guards and attack capitalist and traditional symbols, ideas and beliefs. It led to the purging of any members of the Party not deemed personally loyal enough to Mao. This included very important leaders like Liu Shaoqi and Deng Xiaoping, who Mao damned as not Communist enough.

**Dalai Lama** The religious and political leader of the Tibetan Buddhists. In 1959 the 14th Dalai Lama was forced to flee the Chinese repression of Tibet. He escaped to India.

**Democratic centralism** System of government created by Russian Bolshevik leader Vladimir Lenin, and adopted by the CCP. A synthesis of democracy and central government authority. Elections for representative bodies such as local people's congresses are meant to provide an opportunity for democratic debate and discussion. However, once a decision has been made the central government, all party members must adhere to it.

**Dowry** Payment or gifts given by the family of the bride to the family of the groom when a marriage takes place.

**Emancipation** The awarding of political and economic rights or legal equality to a social group who had previously been exploited or disenfranchised.

**'Evolutionary' historians** These historians debate the nature of the 1949 revolution. Instead of seeing the coming to power of the Communists not as representing a large change in Chinese government, they argue that there was a degree of continuity between who was running China throughout the 1940s and 1950s.

**Fallow** Fallow land is left uncultivated to allow the soil to restore its fertility. Failure to do this risks stripping the soil of its nutrients, greatly reducing the yield of crops growing on it.

**Feudalist** Society based on feudal power structure with a dominant baron or landlord demanding loyalty from poor peasants who paid them in food or taxation in return for rights to live on and work land.

**Feudal-patriarchal ideology** Term used by the Communist Party to discredit alternative ideas as outdated and unfair. Feudal society was unfair because it was based on powerful lords dominating and controlling the peasants whilst a patriarchy is a society is one dominated by men, like pre-revolutionary China.

**Fiefdoms** Personal empires. Before the revolution, warlords ran parts of China as their own personal fiefdoms.

**Filial piety** A concept from Confucian philosophy that argued that all people should be loyal to their fathers, elders and ancestors.

**Forbidden City** The traditional home of the Chinese emperors in Beijing.

**GMD** The Kuomintang (KMT), the official name of the Chinese Nationalist Party who fought against Mao's Communist Party in the Civil War.

**Government bonds** Investment bonds sold by the government to raise revenue. Governments use the sale of bonds to acquire funds for investment, with buyers of bonds promised to eventually receive back a return greater than the initial cost of the bonds.

**Gradualists** Members of the Communist Party who argued that China should take the transition to Communism in a careful and thoughtfully planned out manner.

**Grain requisitioning** The process by which the regime forcibly took food from the peasants to give to the industrial workers in the cities or to sell as exports.

**Great Leap Forward** Misguided policy introduced in 1958 whereby Mao sought to increase agricultural and industrial production at the same time. The people were over-worked and exhausted: crops were left rotting in the fields. Led to the largest man made famine in human history.

**Guerrilla fighting** Form of combat utilized by smaller, less well equipped forces against a larger and better equipped once ones.

**Guerrilla tactics** Guerrilla forces avoid set-piece battles, instead sabotaging enemy equipment or ambushing the enemy and retreating before they can deploy their advanced technology such as air power or artillery.

**Han Chinese** The dominant ethnic group in the People's Republic of China.

**Heavy industry** Large scale factory production such as steel, coal and electric power. China had little heavy industry in 1949 and Mao desperately wanted to change this, believing that industrial production was the key to making China modern.

**Herbalism** The use of plants for medicine. A traditional form of health care.

**Hyperinflation** Out of control inflation whereby the value of the currency falls at such a spectacular rate to render it practically worthless.

**Industrial labourers** Workers in the cities who labored in factories.

**Industrial revolution** The rapid move from an economy based on agricultural production to one dominated by use of machines and large-scale factory production. This took place during the 18th and early 19th century in Europe: China was very slow to adopt advanced manufacturing production techniques and therefore her economy lagged far behind that of its rivals.

**Infanticide** The intentional killing of babies.

**In-migration** Migrants travelling into an area of nation.

**Kindergarten** A pre-school educational facility for young children.

**Kremlin** Fortress in Moscow that housed the government of the USSR.

**Kuomintang** Nationalist enemies of the Communists, led by Chiang Kai-Shek. Fought the Civil War against the Communists before being defeated and fleeing to Taiwan.

**Labour camp** Camp set up to imprison opponents of the regime and force them to undertake harsh physical labour and under go 're-education' to teach them that their opposition to the regime was misguided. In China they provided valuable slave labour for Mao's economic plans.

**Legislature** Institution of government responsible for making laws.

**Lenin** Inspirational Communist leader who led the revolution to seize power in Russia in 1917.

**Liberal arts** Education in the liberal arts includes the learning of literature, philosophy, history and music. Damned by the Communists as irrelevant, they advocated education in more vocational subjects that were economically productive.

**Light industry** Small scale machine based production.

**Mainland** The main landmass of the Peoples Republic of China, not including islands such as Hong Kong.

**Middle schools** School for students of post-elementary school and before high-school age.

**Militia** A military force of non-professional and part-time soldiers. Used by the CCP to keep control of the Communes.

**Ming era** The ruling dynasty of China between 1368 to 1644. Credited with enforcing orderly government control in China.

**Mullahs** Islamic religious leader. In provinces with many Muslims, such as Xinjiang, the Mullahs held important political power and social influence.

**National People's Congress** The law-making parliament of the People's Republic of China.

**Nationalist** Opponents of the Communists during Chinese Civil War.

**Obstructionist bureaucracy** Bureaucrats such as civil servants who deliberately blocked radical policies advocated by Mao in order to protect their own interests such as career advancement or wage differentials.

**Parasitic diseases** Diseases spread by tiny parasites. In China many people were infected by worms through lack of hygiene or clean drinking water. A particular problem was Schistosomiasis, an infection caused by tiny worms that lived inside snails.

**Paris Commune of 1871** Revolutionary working class government that ruled Paris between March and May 1871. An inspiration to radicals in Shanghai who attempted to create a similar kind of workers government in the city during the Cultural Revolution.

**Party Congress** Meeting of members of the CCP in Beijing. Although theoretically important, it does not make major decisions or pass new laws.

**PLA** The People's Liberation Army, the armed forces of the People's Republic of China. It includes the Air force and Navy, as well as the Army. Today it is the biggest army in the world.

**Plants** Industrial plants were large scale factory complexes (does this really need definition?)

**Postpartum** The period immediately after childbirth.

**PRC** The Peoples Republic of China, a Communist state formed in 1949.

**Public Security Bureau** Government controlled police force, answerable to the CCP. Responsible for law enforcement and guaranteeing social order.

**Purge** Removal of opponents of the regime. Could include being humiliated at a Struggle Meeting or imprisoned in the Laogai.

**Qing Last** Dynasty of Imperial China that ruled between 1644 and 1912.

**Radicalism** Belief that Communist principles should be introduced completely, quickly and forcibly, with little account for opposition or for the human cost. Mao believed in radicalism and was opposed by leaders like Liu Shaoqi and Deng Xiaoping, who advocated a more gradual transformation towards Communism.

**Reactionaries** Enemies of the Communists who opposed the revolution and wanted to return to the traditional social and political structures that existed before 1950.

**Rectification campaign** Mass movement to identify and violently remove opponents of Mao from the CCP. Mao used this tactic before he came into power at Yan'an between 1942 and 1944, killing those who he believed were not loyal enough to himself or to his principles. During the 1960s the Cultural Revolution was also in part a Rectification Campaign, with Mao seeking to remove opponents at the very highest levels of the CCP.

**Red Guards** Young people mobilized by Mao into paramilitary groups during the Cultural Revolution. Totally indoctrinated by propaganda, Mao urged them to destroy symbols of old Chinese culture as well as any opponents that were not totally loyal to Mao.

**Red Terror** Wave of violence, torture and murder carried out by the Russian Bolsheviks after they took power in 1917.

**Reunification campaigns** Military campaigns launched after the Communists came to power to seize control of areas of China such as Xinjiang, Tibet and Guangdong.

**Revisionism** Belief that the fundamental principles of Marxism should be altered.

**Revisionists** Believers in revisionism (see above). Used by Communists in a negative way to label opponents as disloyal.

**Revolutionary committee** Form of government supported by Mao during the Cultural Revolution created by an alliance of the people, the PLA and the Party working together.

**'Revolutionary' historians** Scholars who argue that the coming to power of Mao in 1949 marked a clear departure from the past and heralded a massive transformation for the Chinese people.

**Revolutionary martyrs** Committed communist who died fighting against the Japanese or the Nationalists for the cause of the Communist revolution.

**Rightist** Someone who believes in so-called 'right-wing' ideas such as capitalism. Often used as a label in Mao's China to denounce anyone who dared to oppose the regime.

**Right-wingers** Believers in right-wing ideas opposed to Mao, use ideas were very radical, Communist and therefore 'left-wing.'

**Saboteurs** Opponents of the Communists who hoped to sabotage the revolution. During the Civil War this included retreating nationalists who sabotaged industrial machines to avoid it being used by the Communists.

**Separatist** Those who advocated separation of a region, religious or ethnic group from China. Rebels in Xinjiang and Tibet have demanded separation from the PRC.

**Sick Man of Asia** Label given to China by the Western Empires like Great Britain and France before 1949 that denoted its lowly and backward economic and military status.

**Socialist** Political theory that advocates common, shared ownership of resources and co-operative management of the economy.

**Socialist Education Campaign** Personally launched in 1963by Mao, this campaign sought to remove what he believed to be bureaucratic elements from within the CCP. Victims were sent to the countryside to be 're-educated by working amongst the peasants. The campaign was not a success and its failure led to Mao to plan the more radical Cultural Revolution.

**Soviet Union** Shorthand for the USSR, the Union of Soviet Socialist Republics.

**Standing Committee** Group of top Communist leaders who make major policy decisions when the Politburo is not in session.

**Struggle meetings** Meetings in which opponents of the regime were denounced, often by large crowds who shouted abuse at them. The targets were forced to confess their crimes and beg for forgiveness. Often they were beaten, sometimes even killed.

**Subsistence** Agricultural production dedicated to growing enough food to survive, rather than for trade.

**Superpower** A term used to denote a massively powerful nation. After World War II, many nations were economically damaged or militarily weakened. However, two nations, the USSR and the United States became hugely powerful and influential and came to be described as superpowers.

**Trade embargo** A block on trade between nations. Introduced by the United States against China as a result of the Korean War.

**United Nations Security Council** Part of the United Nations organization that was created at the end of World War II to help maintain international co-operation. Dedicated to protecting world peace, the Security Council can pass resolutions to authorize military action.

**Universal education** The principle that all people, regardless of class or gender should be able to access education.

**USSR** The Union of Soviet Socialist Republics, a Communist state created in 1922.

**Utopianism** A belief that perfection or paradise is attainable. Mao's Communist ideas are often described as utopian, meaning that he genuinely believed that true equality of all peoples was possible.

**Vatican** The Vatican City is an independent state with in the city of Rome, Italy. It is the centre of the Roman Catholic Church and is ruled by the head of that church, the Pope.

**Way station** A place used by refugees to stop for rest and food part of the way through a long journey.

**Work teams** Party officials sent by Liu Shaoqi in 1966 into university campuses. Their job was to prevent the radicalism and violence of Red Guards loyal to Mao getting out of hand and attacking the CCP. Liu's support for the work teams was later used by Mao as evidence that Liu was a counter-revolutionary.

## Paper 2: The GDR, 1949–90

**Agents provocateurs** Spies and agents influencing rebellion and unrest.

**Allied Control Council (ACC)** Governing body of the Military Occupation made up of representatives from USA, USSR, Britain and France.

**Anti-Semitic** Anti-Jewish ideas and policies.

**Apparatchik** A bureaucrat who obeys orders.

**Bay of Pigs invasion of Cuba** Attempt by the CIA in April 1961 to launch an invasion of Cuban exiles to topple the communist regime of Fidel Castro.

**Bismarck** Nineteenth-century Prussian statesman instrumental in the unification of Germany.

**Black market** The illegal trading of goods and services.

**Bolsheviks** Russian communists responsible for the 1917 revolutions.

**Border crossers** Name given to those who lived in East Berlin but worked or were educated in the west of the city.

**Brezhnev Doctrine** Policy associated with Russian leader Leonid Brezhnev that the USSR would intervene to protect its interests in any country in the Soviet bloc; formulated to justify the 1968 invasion of Czechoslovakia.

**Cadre** A small group of people trained for a special purpose, in this case to implement communism.

**Capitalist democracy** Political democracy with a capitalist economic system such as the USA and FRG.

**CDU** Christian Democratic Union – conservative political party in the FRG and GDR.

**Charter 77** Policy written by reformers advocating greater democracy in Czechoslovakia.

**Class struggle** The struggle for control between the different classes in society.

**Clients** Customers.

**Cold War** From c1946 to c1987, the USA and the Soviet Union were antagonists in a war that was 'cold' in that neither directly attacked the other. Their enmity was caused by opposing ideologies. The USA believed in a multi-party state with a capitalist economy, while the communist USSR favoured a single-party state and a state-controlled economy.

**Collectivisation** Where farms are gathered into large units to share equipment and resources; usually they work to targets set by the state.

**COMECON** Organisation of communist states for economic co-operation formed in 1949.

**Comintern** Interwar organisation to promote communism throughout the world.

**Communism** The system in which planning and organisation of the economy are under the control of the state so people are rewarded according to their contribution.

**Communist** A person or state that is identified with communism. Communists believe that history moves through a series of stages and that capitalism should be replaced by an economic system in which goods are distributed more equally.

**Concentration camps** Large prison camps.

**Concordat** 1978 Agreement between Church and State.

**Confederation** Two countries joining together for various aspects of government such as a joint currency.

**Confirmation** Rite of passage in Christian belief where someone avows their Christian belief; normally undertaken by teenagers.

**Conscientious objectors** People who oppose war and refuse to join the armed forces.

**Crèches** Nurseries for small children.

**Crude oil** Oil in its natural state before being processed.

**Currency reserves** Money kept by a country for emergency use.

**De facto** Latin term meaning 'in reality'.

**Demarcation** The policy associated with Erich Honecker in the 1970s of minimising contact with the FRG.

**Demilitarisation** Removal of military installations and personnel from a region.

**Denazification** Ridding the country of Nazi ideas and influence.

**De-Stalinisation** The policy of attacking Stalin's ideas associated with Khrushchev's 1956 speech.

**Détente** The process of removal of tensions between the superpowers in the late 1960s and 1970s; features included arms limitations agreements and state visits.

**Dissident** Opponent of a regime.

**DTSB** Organisation controlling sport in the GDR.

**Economies of scale** Making goods in bulk thereby cutting costs of production.

***Eingaben*** Petitions to the authorities.

**Electoral coalition** Different parties who fight together to win elections and may share power if successful in this.

**European Union (EU)** The European alliance for greater ties between members, formerly the European Economic Community (EEC).

**Eurozone** Countries using the Euro as their currency.

**'Evil empire' speech** 1983 speech in which president Reagan of the USA dubbed the Soviet Union 'an evil empire'. It was widely regarded as an important factor in the development of a new Cold War.

**Expropriation** Taking away property or wealth from someone or different groups.

**Factionalism** The splitting of a group into different subgroups who may oppose the majority view.

**FDGB** Free German Trade Unions Federation, a mass organisation associated with the SED.

**FDJ** Free German Youth, a mass organisation.

**Federal republic** Country without a monarchy made up of different states, for example the FRG and USA.

**Five-Year Plan** Plan for economic goals and production targets over a five-year period.

**Frederick the Great** Powerful 18th century Prussian king.

**Functionary** An employee who obeys orders.

**General strike** A strike of the entire national workforce, bringing most of the economy to a halt.

**Gestapo** The secret police in Nazi Germany.

**Glasnost** Gorbachev's policy of openness to discuss the economic ills in the Soviet Union.

**Glass ceiling** An artificial barrier which prevents members of different groups being promoted beyond a certain level.

**GDP** Gross Domestic Product: the total wealth produced by a country in a given period.

**GNP** Gross National Product: an indicator of national wealth which shows the total value of goods and services produced in a country.

**Gulag system** The USSR's system of prison camps.

**Hard currency** Money with a convertible value.

**Hardliner** People who oppose reform.

**Heavy plant machinery** Large-scale machinery such as cranes.

**Hitler Youth** The youth organisation in Nazi Germany.

**Honey traps** Schemes by which people are placed in compromising positions for blackmail purposes.

**Housing census** A census to evaluate housing quality.

**Humanitarian crises** Large-scale catastrophes such as famine or war.

**Imperialism** The acquisition of colonies and empire.

**Industrial plants** Factories.

**Infant mortality rate** The death rate of small children.

**Institutes of Education** Colleges of Education often associated with teacher training.

**Intelligentsia** Intellectuals.

**Interest rates** How much someone pays for borrowing money.

**International city** City belonging to no one country, often administered by the United Nations.

**International Monetary Fund** International fund lending money to countries with economic problems.

**Internationalism** Support for international ideas and co-operation rather than focusing on the national interest.

***Jugendweihe*** Secular ceremony to mark the transition from childhood to adulthood introduced by the SED.

***Junge Gemeinde*** Youth organisation run by the Protestant Churches.

**Kindergarten** School for very young children.

***Kirchenkampf*** Name given to the campaign against the Churches in the early years of the GDR.

**Kremlin** Centre of government of the Soviet Union.

**KVP** The People's Police.

**Labour days** Holidays to celebrate international labour, for example 1 May.

**Labour force** The workforce.

***Länderkammer*** The upper legislative House representing the states, abolished in 1958.

**LPD** Political party which originally supported democracy and opposed state ownership but co-operated with the regime.

**LPG** Large-scale collective farm in the GDR.

**Machine tools** Tools to make goods in factories such as lathes.

**Metropolitan**: title of a senior member of the Russian Orthadox Church.

**Minimum wage** The lowest wage at which an employee can be paid.

**Minister-President** Name given to the Prime Minister or head of government in the GDR (as opposed to the Secretary-General of the SED); also name given to the heads of the states in the FRG.

**Nationalism** The belief that all nations should govern themselves without interference from other nations. It often goes hand in hand with national pride: the feeling that there is something special and admirable about a person's own country.

**Nation-state** A state where people are united by factors such as common language and culture.

**NATO** The North Atlantic Treaty Alliance, a military alliance between North American and Western European countries.

**NCO** Non-commissioned officers.

**New Forum** National movement advocating political reform in the GDR.

**'Niche' society** Theory that citizens outwardly conformed to life in the GDR while placing more importance on their private lives.

**No-man's-land** Area between two opposing forces.

**'Normalisation' thesis** The idea that people accepted life in the GDR because it was all they knew.

**Nuclear family** Basic family unit of parents and children.

**OPEC** Organization of the Petroleum Exporting Countries who determine the supply and cost of oil.

**Open letter** A letter sent to a specific person but intended for public view.

***Ossis*** Name given to former citizens of the GDR.

**Ostmarks** The currency of the GDR.

**Ostpolitik** Policy of closer co-operation between East and West Germany.

**Partisan groups** Resistance fighters against occupying forces.

**Pastors** Protestant clergymen.

**People's Democracy** Communist countries which supposedly operate in the interests of their citizens.

**People's Police (KVP)** The police of the GDR.

***Perestroika*** Gorbachev's reform process in the USSR.

**Personality cult** Media promotion of a particular personality to engender admiration for him/her.

**Plenum** A meeting of political leaders.

**Politburo** The most senior committee in the SED.

**Prague Spring** Period of liberalism in Czechoslovakia ended by the Russian Invasion in August 1968.

**Proportional representation** Where candidates are elected according to the percentage of votes cast for their parties.

**Quotas** Amounts allowed.

**Rapprochement** The resumption of friendly relations between countries.

**Really existing socialism** An emphasis associated with Erich Honecker in the 1970s on what could in reality be achieved rather than utopian ideals for socialism.

**Rectors** Heads of University.

**Reformation** Religious revolution of the sixteenth century which saw the advent of the Protestant Churches.

**Reichstag** The pre-war German Parliament.

**Reparations** Compensation for war damage.

**Republic** A state without a monarch at its head.

**Satellite countries/states (of the USSR)** Countries controlled by the Soviet Union in Eastern and Central Europe such as the GDR and Poland.

**Secretary-General** The leader of the SED and de facto leader of the GDR.

**Show trials** Trials to illustrate an issue where the guilt of the accused is never in doubt.

**Sinecure jobs** Jobs where employees do not have to do very much for their pay, often passed on to the recipient through influential contacts.

**Social Contract** An informal agreement spoken of during the Honecker years whereby the state provided welfare in return for obedience.

**Social Democrat** A member of the SPD.

**Social insurance** National insurance to pay for healthcare and pensions.

**Social security** Benefits to replace or supplement wages.

**Socialism** Term meaning the same as communism in the GDR.

**Socialist realism** Art movement popular in communist countries glorifying the working classes and their struggles against their class enemies.

**Solidarity movement** Trade union movement in Poland largely responsible for the overthrow of communism there in the 1980s.

**Sovereign state** An independent state.

**Soviet bloc** Countries allied to the Soviet Union.

**Soviet Control Commission** Commission responsible for the operation of Soviet policy.

**Soviet Union** In 1922 Russia became known as the Union of Soviet Socialist Republics, USSR or Soviet Union.

**SPD** Social Democratic Party of Germany.

**Sphere of influence** Area of influence such as Soviet control over countries in Central and Eastern Europe.

**Stagnated** Became worse.

**Stakhanovite movement** Movement associated with enhanced worker productivity in the Soviet Union.

**Stasi** The main internal security forces of the GDR.

**State visit** Official visit usually by a head of state.

**Superpower relations** Relations between the USA and USSR.

**Supply and demand** The relationship between the supply of and demand for goods which will help fix their cost, i.e. how much people are prepared to pay for them.

**Synod meetings** Meetings of church organisations.

**Tariffs** Customs duties.

**Think-tank** A panel of experts.

**United Nations** The international organisation responsible for world peace and welfare.

**USSR** In 1922 Russia became known as the Union of Soviet Socialist Republics, USSR or Soviet Union.

**Vocational education** Careers-based education.

***Volkskammer*** The parliament of the GDR.

**Warsaw Pact** The military alliance of the Soviet Union and its communist satellite countries.

***Wende*** German term meaning change, referring specifically to the events in the GDR, 1989–90.

**White collar workers** Office workers.

**Work norms** Expected output levels.

**Zionism** Promotion of the Jewish people, particularly in terms of support for their homeland in Israel.

# ACKNOWLEDGEMENTS

The Publishers would like to thank the following for permission to reproduce copyright material:

Photo credits: **p.2**, **3** © Nikolai Sorokin / Fotolia; **p.5** © Library of Congress Prints and Photographs Division Washington; **p.7** © Illustrated London News; **p.8** © Library of Congress Prints and Photographs Division Washington; **p.19** © Fine Art Images / HIP / TopFoto; **p.24** © RIA Novosti / Alamy; **p.29** *t* © ITAR-TASS Photo Agency / Alamy, *b* © Keystone Pictures USA / Alamy; **p.34** *t* © ITAR-TASS Photo Agency / Alamy, *b* © ITAR-TASS Photo Agency / Alamy; **p.35** © Dmitri Baltermants/The Dmitri Baltermants Collection/Corbis; **p.37** © ITAR-TASS Photo Agency / Alamy; **p.40,41** © Alexander Maximov / Fotolia; **p.47** © ullstein bild/ullstein bild via Getty Images; **p.51** © Fine Art Images / HIP / TopFoto; **p.53** © ITAR-TASS Photo Agency / Alamy; **p.62** Sovfoto / Universal Images Group/REX; **p.70** © Aikon / Fotolia; **p.72** Photo12/UIG via Getty Images; **p.83** © RIA Novosti / Alamy; **p.84** © RIA Novosti / Alamy; **p.85** © RIA Novosti / Alamy; **p.86** © INTERFOTO / Alamy; **p.87** © Heritage Image Partnership Ltd / Alamy; **p.97** © Universal History Archive / Universal Images Group/REX; **p.102** The Collection of Monroe and Aimee Price; **p.103** Courtesy of Roger Bunce; **p.108** © Andrey Lavrov / Fotolia; **p.114** Sovfoto/UIG via Getty Images; p.**117** © Andrey Lavrov / Fotolia; **p.122** © RIA Novosti / Alamy; **p.135** © Heritage Image Partnership Ltd / Alamy; **p.144** © Nikolai Sorokin / Fotolia; **p.149** © ITAR-TASS Photo Agency / Alamy; **p.188** © Allstar Picture Library / Alamy; **p.198, 199** © SeanPavonePhoto/Fotolia; **p.201** © TMAX/Fotolia; **p.202** © Tiberius Gracchus/Fotolia; **p.207** © Photos 12 / Alamy; **p.221**© Mary Evans Picture Library / Alamy; **p.238** © Heritage Image Partnership Ltd / Alamy; **p.243** © Everett Collection Historical / Alamy; **p.244** © Henry Westheim Photography / Alamy; **p.246** Sovfoto/ UIG/Getty Images; **p.260** *t* Keystone/Getty Images, *m* Sovfoto / Getty Images; *bl* © Everett Collection Historical / Alamy *tr* © Photos 12 / Alamy *mr* © INTERFOTO / Alamy *br* Keystone/Getty Images; **p.262** Keystone / Getty Images; **p.265** Peter Gridley/ Getty Images; **p.266** Sovfoto/UIG/Getty Images; **p.267** Keystone / Getty Images; **p.275** *tr* Sovfoto / Getty Images *tr* © Everett Collection Historical / Alamy; *bl* Keystone / Getty Images *br* © INTERFOTO / Alamy; **p.288** © Corbis; **p.291** The Granger Collection, NYC/TopFoto; **p.299** © Everett Collection Historical / Alamy; **p. 307** © Fritz Hoffmann/In Pictures/Corbis; **p.308** © mamahoohooba / Fotolia; **p.309** © age fotostock / Alamy; **p.320, 321** © bimserd / Fotolia; **p.326** © Tiberius Gracchus/Fotolia; **p.334** © Peter Probst / Alamy; **p.344** © ITAR-TASS Photo Agency / Alamy; **p.346** akg-images; **p.347** © Thomas Röske/Fotolia; **p.364** © Bettmann/CORBIS; **p.368** © Peter Probst / Alamy; **p.385** © Holger B; **p.393** © Peter Probst / Alamy; **p.394** © Oliver Woelki/Fotolia; **p.413** © santiago silver / Fotolia; **p. 417** © ITAR-TASS Photo Agency / Alamy; **p.423** © frilled_dragon/Fotolia; **p.425** © Regis Bossu/Sygma/Corbis; **p.429** © dpa picture alliance / Alamy.

## Paper 1 Russia, 1917–91: from Lenin to Yeltsin

Acknowledgements: **p.21** Table 2: The victims of the purges. From D. Evans and J. Jenkins, *Years of Russia, the USSR and the Collapse of Soviet Communism* (Hodder Education, 2008); **p.44** Figure 1 graph: Numbers in the industrial workforce, 1917–22. Data from D. Evans and J. Jenkins, *Years of Russia, the USSR and the Collapse of Soviet Communism*, 2nd edition (Hodder Education, 2008); **p.46** Figure 3: The 'scissors crisis' – industrial and agricultural prices in the Soviet Union, July 1922 to November 1923. From data based on *Biulleten Gosplana 1923* (Gosplan Bulletin 1923), taken from

Mark Harrison, 'Prices in the Politburo, 1927: market equilibrium versus the use of force'. In Paul R. Gregory and Norman Naimark (eds.), *The lost Politburo transcripts: from collective rule to Stalin's dictatorship. Yale-Hoover series on Stalin, Stalinism and the Cold War* (Yale University Press, 2008); **p.56** Figure 6: Cumulative percentage of peasant holdings collectivised in the USSR, 1930–41. Based on M Lynch, *Access to History: Stalin's Russia 1924–53* (Hodder Education, 2008); **p.64** Figure 7: The increase in the availability of consumer goods in the Soviet Union, 1955–66 (ownership per thousand of the population). Data adapted from J.N. Westwood, 'Khrushchev and After', *Purnell's History of the Twentieth Century* (Purnell, 1972); **p.148** Extract 1 From Richard Sakwa, *Soviet Politics in Perspective* (Routledge, 1998); **p.148** Extract 2 From Paul R. Gregory, *The Political Economy of Stalinism* (Cambridge University Press, 2004); **p.152** Extended reading: Interpretation from *The significance of the economic weaknesses of the USSR and the failure of reform* by Martin McCauley; **p.154** Extract 3 From Archie Brown, 'The Gorbachev era', in Ronald Grigor Suny (ed.) *The Cambridge History of Russia* (Cambridge University Press, 2006); **p.154** Extract 4 From Stephen Richards Graubard, *Exit from Communism* (Transaction Publishers, 1998); **p.155** Extract 1 Robert Strayer, *Why Did the Soviet Union Collapse?: Understanding Historical Change* (M.E. Sharpe, 1998); **p.156** Extract 2 Anders Aslund, *Russia's Capitalist Revolution: Why Market Reform Succeeded and Democracy Failed* (Peterson Institute for International Economics, 2007); **p.158** Extract 1 from Jeremy Smith, *The Fall of Soviet Communism, 1986–1991* (Palgrave Macmillan, 2005); **p.158** Extract 2 from Archie Brown, 'The Gorbachev era', in Ronald Grigor Suny (ed.) *The Cambridge History of Russia* (Cambridge University Press, 2006); **p.161** Extract 3 from George W. Breslauer, *Gorbachev and Yeltsin as Leaders* (Cambridge University Press, 2002); **p.161** Extract 4 from David Lane and Cameron Ross, *The Transition from Communism to Capitalism* (Palgrave Macmillan, 1999); **p.163** Extract 5 from Robert Service, *Comrades! A History of world Communism* (Pan Macmillan, 2007); **p.163** Extract 6 from Neil Robinson, *Ideology and Collapse of the Soviet System: A Critical History of Soviet Ideological Discourse* (Edward Elgar Publishing, 1995); **p.165** Extract 1 from George E. Breslauer, *Gorbachev and Yeltsin as Leaders* (Cambridge University Press, 2002); **p.165** Extract 2 From Alec Nove, *An Economic History of the USSR 1917–1991*, (Penguin, 1993); **p.167** Extract 1 from Vladislav M. Zubok, *A Failed Empire: The Soviet Union in the Cold War from Stalin to Gorbachev* (University of North Carolina Press, 2007); **p.167:** Extract 2 from Martin McCauley, *The Rise and Fall of the Soviet Union, Longman History of Russia* (Routledge, 2008); **p.168** Extended Reading: *Gorbachev's reforms and the Soviet collapse* by Richard Sakwa; **p.173:** Map Figure 1: The break-up of the Soviet Empire in the years 1988–91 from Steve Waugh and John Wright, *Peace and War: International Relations 1943–1991* (Hodder Education, 2009); **p.176:** Extract 1 from Ronald Grigor Suny, *The Revenge of the Past: Nationalism, Revolution, and the Collapse of the Soviet Union* (Stanford University Press, 1993); **p.176:** Extract 2 from Anatoly Michailovich Khazanov, *After the USSR: Ethnicity, Nationalism and Politics* (University of Wisconsin Press, 1995); **p.178:** Extract 3 from Peter Kenez, *A History of the Soviet Union from the Beginning to the End* (Cambridge University Press, 2006); **p.178:** Extract 4 from Martin McCauley, *The Rise and Fall of the Soviet Union, Longman History of Russia* (Routledge, 2008); **p.179:** Map Figure 2: The break-up of the Soviet Union into the Commonwealth of Independent States from Steve Waugh and John Wright, *Peace and War: International Relations 1943–1991* (Hodder Education, 2009); **p.180:** Extended reading: Interpretation from *The impact of the nationalist resurgence*, by Robert Hornsby; **p.182:** Extract 1 from Mark R. Beissinger, *Nationalist Mobilization and the Collapse of the Soviet State* (Cambridge University Press, 2002); **p.183**: Extract 2 from Norman M. Naimark, Preface to *The Revenge of the Past* (Stanford University Press, 1993); **p.187:** Extract 1 from Archie Brown, *The Gorbachev Factor* (Oxford University Press, 1997); **p.187** Extract 2 from Peter Kenez, *A History of the Soviet Union from the Beginning to the End* (Cambridge University Press, 1999); **p.191:** Extract 5 from Peter Kenez, *A History of the Soviet Union from the Beginning to the End* (Cambridge University Press, 1999); **p.191** Extract 6 from George W. Breslauer, *Gorbachev and Yeltsin as Leaders* (Cambridge University Press, 2002); **p.192** Extended reading: *Gorbachev, Yeltsin and the fall* *of the Soviet Union* by Christopher Catherwood; **p.194** Extract 1 from Christopher Marsh, *Unparalleled Reforms: China's Rise, Russia's Fall* (Lexington Books, 2005); **p.194** Extract 2 from Dick Combs, *Inside the Soviet Alternative Universe: The Cold War's End and the Soviet Union's Fall Reappraised* (Pennsylvania State University Press, 2008); **p.197:** Extract 1 from Ronald Grigor Suny, *The Revenge of the Past: Nationalism, Revolution, and the Collapse of the Soviet Union* (Stanford University Press, 1993); **p. 197** Extract 2 from Richard Sakwa, *Russian Politics and Society* (Routledge, 2008).

## Paper 2: Mao's China, 1949–76

Acknowledgements: **p.203** Source A from John Melby, *The Mandate of Heaven: Record of a Civil War, China 1945–9* © University of Toronto Press (1968); **p.205** Source B Sidney Rittenberg and Amanda Bennett, *The Man Who Stayed Behind*, (Duke University Press, 2001); **p.206** Source C from John Melby, *The Mandate of Heaven: Record of a Civil War, China 1945–9* © University of Toronto Press (1968); **p.214** Source D On 23 May 1951, Representatives of the PRC and the Dalai Lama signed the Agreement on Measures for the Peaceful Liberation of Tibet, known as the '17-Point Agreement.' Quoted in Linda Benson, *China since 1949* (Pearson, 2002); **p.214** Source E from Dalai Lama, *My Land and My People* (McGraw Hill, 1962), pages 88–89. **p.221** Source G from Zhisui Li, *The Private Life of Chairman Mao* (Arrow Books, 1996); **p.227** Source 1 from Jung Chang's biography of Mao, *Mao: The untold story* (Jonathan Cape, 2005); **p.227** Source 2 from a speech made by Mao in February 1957 entitled 'On the correct handling of contradictions among the People', in Mark Selden (ed.), *The People's Republic of China: A Documentary History of Revolutionary Change* (Monthly Review Press, 1979), pages 232–40; **p.233** Source A from William Hinton, *Fanshen: A Documentary of Revolution in a Chinese Village* (Random House, 1968), pages 137–38; **p.238** Source B Quoted in Jonathan Fenby, *The Penguin History of Modern China: The Fall and Rise of A Great Power, 1850–2009* (Penguin, 2008); **p.239** Source C from the Communist Party newspaper, the *People's Daily*, 'How China Proceeds with the Task of Industrialisation', 23 May 1953, quoted in Mark Selden (ed.), *The People's Republic of China: A Documentary History of Revolutionary Change* (New York: Monthly Review Press, 1979); **p.240** Table 1: The First Five-Year Plan, 1953–57 from Jonathan Spence, *The Search for Modern China* (Norton, 1999), page 516; **p.243** Source D Translation of remarks made by Mao to Chinese students in Moscow, 17 November 1957 from Stuart R. Schram *The Political Thoughts of Chairman Mao* (Frederick A. Praeger, 1969), pages 407–8; **p.245** Table 2: Economic results of the Great Leap Forward from Jonathan Fenby, *The Penguin History of Modern China* (Penguin, 2008); **p.247** Source G Letter from Peng Dehuai to Mao Zedong, 1959, cited in Linda Benson, *China since 1949* (Pearson Education, 2002), pages 101–2; **p.252** Source 1 Zhisui Li, *The Private Life of Chairman Mao* (Arrow Books, 1996); **p.252** Source 2 from Jung Chang, *Wild Swans: Three Daughters of* China (HarperCollins, 1992); **p.254** Source 3 from Wang Yin, 'Women's New Life in Rural People's Communes', China News Service, 1959. Quoted in Mark Selden (ed.), *The People's Republic of China: A Documentary History of Revolutionary Change* (Monthly Review Press, 1980); **p.254** Source 4 from the Panchem Lama's 70,000-Character Petition to Zhou Enlai; **p.255** Source 5 from an article written by Mao for the Party Journal, *Red Flag*, June 1958; **p.256** Source 6 from Tan Man-ni, 'Lushan's Pig-Iron "Sputnik"' an article in the magazine *China Reconstructs*, January 1959; **p.262** Source A The 16 Points: Guidelines for the Great Proletarian Cultural Revolution, quoted in Mark Selden (ed.), *The People's Republic of China: A Documentary History of Revolutionary Change* (Monthly Review Press, 1979), pages 549–56; **p.269** Source E from the autobiography of Rinbur Tulku, a Tibetan monk, reprinted from Warren W. Smith, *China's Tibet: Autonomy or Assimilation* (Rowman and Littlefield, 2008), pages 129–31; **p.274** Source F Lei Feng, quoted in *Mao: A Life*, by Philip Short (Hodder and Stoughton, 1999), page 517; **p.278** Source G from one of Mao's last statements to the Politburo, quoted in Philip Short, *Mao: A Life* (Hodder and Stoughton, 1999), pages 624–25; **p.279**

Source H A poem written on a tribute to honour Zhou Enlai and placed in Tiananmen Square, quoted in Alan Lawrence, *China under Communism* (Routledge, 1998), page 97; **p.283** Source 1 An article from the *People's Daily*, June 1966. The *People's Daily* is an official newspaper of the Chinese Government; **p.284** Source 2 from Han Suyin, *Wind in the Towers: Mao Zedong and the Chinese Revolution, 1949–75* (Jonathan Cape, 1976), pages 291–92; **p.287** Source A Fu Hsuan, *Woman*, third century, quoted in William Hinton, *Fanshen: A Documentary of Revolution in a Chinese Village* (Monthly Review Press, 1966), page 157; **p.289** Source C The Marriage Law of the People's Republic of China (1950), Selected Articles. Quoted in Mark Selden (ed.), *The People's Republic of China: A Documentary History of Revolutionary* (Monthly Review Press, 1979), pages 193–200; **p.298** Source E from J. Horn, *Away With All Pests* (Monthly Review Press, 1969); **p.300** Source G 'Directive on Public Health', June 26, 1965, in *Maurice Messier, Mao's China and After: A History of the People's Republic* (Free Press, 1999), page 271; **p.306** Source H from *The Christian Manifesto*, September 1950, quoted in Richard L. Walker, *China under Communism: The First Five Years* (Yale University Press, 1955), pages 190–91; **p.306** Source I 'How did Imperialism use religion for aggression in China?' from the *People's Daily*, 13 April 1951, quoted in Richard L. Walker, *China under Communism: The First Five Years* (Yale University Press, 1955), pages 190–91; **p.313** Source 1 from *'Women's Life in Rural People's Communes'*, an article by the China News Service, a state-owned news agency, 24 February, 1959; **p.313** Source 2 from an interview with a female Party cadre, quoted in Gail Hershatter, *The Gender of Memory: Rural Women and China's Collective Past* (University of California Press: Berkeley, 2013), page 76; **p.315** Source 3 A party propaganda announcement. Quoted in Warren W. Smith, *China's Tibet?Autonomy or Assimilation* (Rowman & Littlefield Publishers, 2008), page 44; **p.315** Source 4 An extract from a report written by the Panchem Lama, the second most important Buddhist leader in Tibet; **p.317** Source 5 from Dongping Han, *The Unknown Cultural Revolution: Life and Change in a Chinese Village* (Monthly Review Press, 2008); **p.317** Source 6 from Jung Chang, *Wild Swans: Three Daughters of China* (HarperCollins, 1992).

## Paper 2: The German Democratic Republic, 1949–90

Acknowledgements: **p.328** Source A from Wolfgang W.E. Samuel, *German Boy*, (Sceptre, 2002), page 252; **p.328** Table 1: Cost of reparations as a percentage of GNP (Source: J.M. Dennis, *The Rise and Fall of the German Democratic Republic*, 1945–90 (Longman, 2000) page 42; **p.333** Source B Articles 6 and 8 from the 1949 Constitution of the GDR; **p.339** Table 4: Growth of collectives as a result of the forced campaign. From Arthur M. Hanhardt Jnr, *The German Democratic Republic* (1968) (The John Hopkins Press, 1968), page 121; **p.341** Source C verse from *The Solution* by Bertolt Brecht; **p.344** Table 5: Emigration from the GDR to FRG, 1949–61. Source: Matthias Judt, ed., *DDR-Geschichte in Dokumenten (GDR History in Documents)* (Berlin, 1997), pages 545–46; **p.351** Source 1 Extract from Erich Honecker, *From My Life*, (Pergamon Press, 1981); **p.351** Source 2 Extract from Arthur M. Hanhardt Jr, *The German Democratic Republic*, (The Johns Hopkins Press, 1968); **p.357** Source A from an interview with journalist Walter Leonhardt and George Schmidt, quoted in Walter Leonhardt, *This Germany: The Story since the Reich* (Penguin Books, 1964), pages 57–58; **p.358** Table 1: Amount of investment and growth of national income. From M. McCauley, *The German Democratic Republic Since 1945* (London, 1983), pages 107–8; **p.368** Source C from a secret transcript from archives released by the Kremlin after the collapse of the USSR, quoted in Anne McElvoy, The Saddled Cow (Faber and Faber, 1992), page 82; **p.373** Source D from the Joint Communiqué by Erich Honecker and Helmut Kohl (September 8, 1987) translated by Jeremiah Riemer; **p.376** Source 1 Extract from Erich Honecker, *From My Life*, (Pergamon Press, 1981); **p.376** Source 2 Neil Allen, a journalist, *State Aid as Price for Gold*, article in The Times newspaper, Friday 7 November 1971; **p.378** Source 3 Extract from a speech by Walter Ulbricht, First Secretary of the SED, on the 'New Economic System' of the GDR on 16 December 1965, translated by Alison Brown; **p.378** Source 4 Extract from an article by Werner Barm in *Die Welt*, 30 July 1970, translated by Alison Brown; **p.379** Source 5 Extract from Melvin Croan, *East Germany Soviet Connection*, in Washington Paper 36, Centre for Strategic and International Studies, Sage Policy Paper, 1976; **p.380** Source 6 Extract from Oskar Fischer, Foreign Minister of the GDR, 'Cooperation with the Fraternal Socialist States', in (ed.) Arthur W. McCardle and A. Bruce Boenau, *East Germany: A New German Nation under Socialism?* (University Press of America, 1984); **p.390** Source B from Martina Daske, *A Female Engineer Reports*, 1986; **p.394** Source C from a speech by Erich Honecker to members of the Free German Youth (FDJ) movement, June 1984; **p.395** Source D Reiner Oschmann, the Neues Deutschland correspondent in the UK, quoted in Anne McElroy, *The Saddled Cow* (Faber and Faber, 1992), pages 170–171; **p.398** Mary Fulbrook: *Anatomy of a Dictatorship: Inside the GDR 1949–1989* (Oxford University Press, 1995); **p.401** Source E from Report of the Conference of Protestant Church Leaders, 25 May 1977; **p.403** Source F from 'On Certain Issues in Youth Work and the Emergence of Rowdy Groups', Resolution of the Office of the SED District Leadership, October 13, 1965, PDS-Archiv, District Leadership Leipzig IV A-2/16/464; reprinted in Christoph Kleßmann and Georg Wagner, eds., *Das gespaltene Land. Leben in Deutschland 1945–1990 (The Divided Country. Life in Germany 1945–1990)* (C H Beck, 1993), pages 471–72; **p.407** Source 1 Extract from a speech by Margot Honecker, Minister of Education from 1957 to 1990, at the Eighth Pedagogical Conference 18 October 1978, found in Arthur W McCardle and A Bruce Boenau (eds.), *East Germany: A New Nation Under Socialism?*, (University Press of America, 1984); **p.408** Source 2 Extract from Norbert Muhlen, *The Return of Germany: A Tale of Two Countries* (Henry Regnery Company, 1953); **p.412** Source A From *West Germany's Green Imperialism* by Harold James, published in the Sunday Telegraph, 11 February 1990; **p.414** Source B From Library of Congress Country Studies East Germany Federal Research Division data up to 1987, written in the late 1980s; **p.418** Source C From a policy document by Vladimir V. Kuskin entitled 'Gorbachev in East Germany' dated 19 October 1989; **p.425** Source D From the testimony of Uwe Nietzold, a student who had been to a poetry reading but wanted to see what was going on. Interviewed by Christopher Hilton in *The Wall: The People's Story* (Sutton Publishing, 2001); **p.434** Source 1 from The New York Times, 10 November, 1989; **p.435** Source 2 Excerpts from the transcript of the Tenth Session of the SED Central Committee, 9 November 1989. Source: SAPMO–BA, tape Y 1/TD 738, transcribed in Hans-Hermann Hertle and Gerd-Rüdiger Stephan (eds), Das Ende der SED: Die letzten Tage des Zentralkomitees, 4th edition (Berlin: Dietz, 1999), pp. 303–306. Translated for CWIHP by Howard Sargeant; **p.436** Source 3 from an article by Sir Ralf Dahrendorf, 'Germans Lack the Key to Their National Identity', published in the Independent, 13 April 1990. Found in (eds) Harold James and Marla Stone, When the Wall Came Down: Reactions to German Unification (Routledge, 1992); **p.436** Source 4 Extract from Josef Joffe, 'Germany, Reunification 11: This time No Hobnailed Boots', published in the *New York Times*, 30 September 1990, found in (eds) Harold James and Marla Stone, When the Wall Came Down: Reactions to German Unification (Routledge, 1992); **p.439** Source 5 Extract from John Simpson, *The Darkness Crumbles: Dispatches from the Barricades* (Hutchinson,1992); **p.439** Source 6 Article in the *Los Angeles Times*, 25 October 1989.

Every effort has been made to trace all copyright holders, but if any have been inadvertently overlooked the Publishers will be pleased to make the necessary arrangements at the first opportunity.

# ANSWERS

## Answers for Selecting from the Sources on page 255

## Paper 2: Mao's China, 1949–76

1 Women are now engaged in economically productive activity in the countryside.
2 Women have been freed from having to do all the domestic chores like housework.
3 Women now have the free time to be able to attend schools.
4 The Communist Party controls access to food and childcare.
5 The main point of the source is that the standard of living and freedoms of women have been transformed for the better.
6 The motive of the author is to promote the policies of the regime. The author has a political motivation to stress how much better life under the communists is. The source is an example of communist propaganda.
7 It is important to place the source in context: The source was written a year after the start of the Great Leap Forward. The author would seek to counter any rumours that the people in the communes were unhappy with having to undertake so much labour, with the lack of personal freedoms in areas such as diet and childcare. By 1959 some areas of China were already suffering from famine. This source would be seeking to cover up any evidence of this and convince the outside world that communism was working and that Mao's regime had brought great benefits to the people.

## Answers for Selecting from the Sources on page 378

## Paper 2: The German Democratic Republic, 1949–90

1 The New Economic System is the means by which the GDR will build Socialism and advance in terms of technology.
2 It will be deployed to complete the transition from capitalism to socialism.
3 the GDR is a highly developed industrial state which also has a thriving agricultural sector.
4 The GDR has overcome the problems caused by its past and the Second World War.
5 People need to understand the changes the New Economic System will bring.
6 The most important change is to be innovative.
7 People need to learn from innovation and change – only people with the ability to do this will succeed in the New Economic System.

# INDEX